Scot land the Best

PETER IRVINE

Collins

HarperCollins Publishers
77-85 Fulham Palace Road
London W6 8JB

www.collins.co.uk

Collins is a registered trademark of HarperCollins Publishers Ltd.

Text © Pete Irvine 2011
Maps © Collins Bartholomew Ltd 2011
Illustrations © Jilly Sitford
All photographs in the plate section © Peter Irvine except:
p.2 middle © Myrna Schwartinsky/shutterstock.com; p.4 top © TTphoto/shutterstock.com;
p.5 top © Rudolf Kotulán/shutterstock.com; p.6 top © JCElv/shutterstock.com, p.6 middle © Jeff
Banke/shutterstock.com, p.6 bottom © Nicholas Peter Gavin Davies/shutterstock.com;
p.7 bottom left © Bertrand Rieger/Hemis/Corbis; p.8 top © Jean Morrison/shutterstock.com,
p8. bottom © Chris Watt.

Peter Irvine asserts his moral right to be identified as the author of this work

14 13 12

10 9 8 7 6 5 4 3 2 1

First published in Great Britain in 1993 by Mainstream Publishing Company (Edinburgh) Ltd

First published by HarperCollins Publishers in 1997

This edition published in 2011

A catalogue record for this book is available from the British Library.

ISBN-13 978-0-00744244-7

Produced by The Printer's Devil, Glasgow

Printed and bound in Germany by Bercker

Contents

Section 4 *Regional Hotels & Restaurants*

Section 5 *Particular Places to Eat & Stay in Scotland*

Section 6 *Good Food & Drink*

Section 7 *Outdoor Places*

Section 8 *Historical Places*

Section 9 *Strolls, Walks & Hikes*

Introduction

Welcome old friends, new readers, fellow travellers. It's been a long labour of love but here it is, the 11th edition of *Scotland the Best*.

Once again I've been up and down the land. People imagine this to be an enviable way of spending a summer, eating out in all those restaurants, staying in the best hotels, discovering new beaches and so on. Unfortunately there's only me on that trail, speed is of the essence on a fast track as well as an inside track and there's never enough time to stop and savour. It is an odyssey and in this edition some of the sense of that is illustrated in a new photo section: postcards from Scotland, summer 2011.

For new readers please note that this is not a list of options; rather, it's a roll call of the best in a diverse range of what I think a visitor might want know about. This is a book of personal impressions and opinions and while I'm not infallible in these, with each edition I do try to get closer to a definitive version of all the best that Scotland can offer. Everywhere in contention has to be both experienced and compared but I do believe you can identify and ascertain what is the best and over the years it seems many people agree with me. I try to be rigorous in my explorations and deliberations, taking the measure of where Scotland is going, comparing like with like in the categories I've determined and also how our small country measures up in an increasingly competitive world of old and ever-new destinations. Ultimately, *Scotland the Best* is a guide to the good life, not just a good country.

Hotels and restaurants and walks have their own codes. ATMOS is the ineffable something that makes a place affecting to be in, whether it be a ruin or a restaurant and the new code L for LOCATION i.e. location, location, location, points up remarkable settings whether a golf course or the terrace of a bistro overlooking a loch.

This summer the weather was crap – not only Scotland – and it is harder to love Jura with low clouds over the Paps in July and the waves whipping up so the little ferry from Islay can't make it to the quay. But at least we're used to it and the light is invariably splendid. Scotland provides some of the most beautiful and inspirational landscapes and locations in the world as a rash of new major shot-in-Scotland films confirms.

In this edition I've removed some categories that no longer seemed useful and added some to acknowledge, for example, the rise of the afternoon tea, the emergence of 'glamping' and special shops – special because somebody made them so. If there is one thing consistent across all the 11 editions of the book it is that it registers and celebrates the efforts and enterprise of exceptional individuals – the people who help make Scotland the best – many of whom are mentioned in these pages.

Scotland the Best wouldn't be the best if I didn't receive feedback and helpful suggestions from so many people. Please send me your recommendations for new entries to **stb@lumison.co.uk** giving reasons why they should be included and directions if they're hard to find. A bottle of malt and a drum of Tobermory cheddar will be presented at the launch of the next edition to the best three suggestions received by 31 August 2013.

This edition covers not only the Olympic year but also that of the next Commonwealth Games and Ryder Cup, both to be held in Scotland. It's the best of times to be here so come join a winning team – whatever the weather.

Pete Irvine,
Edinburgh, December 2011

How To Use This Book

There are three ways to find things in this book:

1. There's an index at the back.
2. The book can be used by category, e.g. you can look up the best restaurants in the Borders or the best scenic routes in the whole of Scotland. Each entry has an item number in the outside margin. These are in numerical order and allow easy cross-referencing.
3. You can start with the maps and see how individual items are located, how they are grouped together and how much there is that's worth seeing or doing in any particular area. Then just look up the item numbers. If you are travelling around Scotland, I would urge you to use the maps and this method of finding the best of what an area or town has to offer.

Top tip: as a general guide and when searching by using the maps, items numbered below 1490 generally refer to places to eat and stay.

All items have a code which gives (1) the specific item number; (2) the map on which it can be found; and (3) the map co-ordinates. For space reasons, items in Glasgow and Edinburgh are not marked on Maps 1 and 2, although they do have co-ordinates in the margin to give you a rough idea of location. A typical entry is shown below, identifying the various elements that make it up:

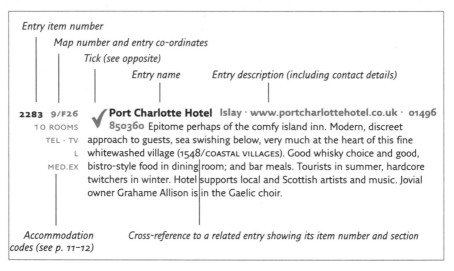

Entry item number

Map number and entry co-ordinates

Tick (see opposite)

Entry name   *Entry description (including contact details)*

2283 9/F26 ✓ **Port Charlotte Hotel** Islay · www.portcharlottehotel.co.uk · 01496
10 ROOMS   850360 Epitome perhaps of the comfy island inn. Modern, discreet
TEL · TV   approach to guests, sea swishing below, very much at the heart of this fine
L   whitewashed village (1548/COASTAL VILLAGES). Good whisky choice and good,
MED.EX   bistro-style food in dining room; and bar meals. Tourists in summer, hardcore
twitchers in winter. Hotel supports local and Scottish artists and music. Jovial
owner Grahame Allison is in the Gaelic choir.

Accommodation   *Cross-reference to a related entry showing its item number and section*
codes (see p. 11–12)

A Note On Categories

Edinburgh and Glasgow, the destinations of most visitors and the nearest cities to more than half of the population, are covered in the substantial Sections 2 and 3. You will probably need a city map to get around, although Maps 1 and 2 should give you the rough layout of the city ce.

For the purposes of maps, and particularly in Section 4 (Regional Hotels & Restaurants), I have used a combination of the subdivision of Scotland based on current standard political regions and on historical ones, eg Argyll, Clyde Valley. Section 4 is meant to give a comprehensive and concise guide to the best of the major Scottish towns in each area. Some recommended hotels and restaurants will be amongst the best in the region (or even amongst the best in Scotland) and have been selected because they are the best there is in the town or the immediate area.

From Sections 5 to 11, the categories are based on activities, interests and geography and are Scotland-wide. Section 12 covers the islands, with a page-by-page guide to the larger ones.

There are some categories like Bed and Breakfasts, Fishing Beats, Antique Shops that haven't been included because at TGP (time of going to press) they are impracticable to assess (there are too many of them, are too small, etc). However, if there are categories that you would like to see in future editions, please let us know at **stb@lumison.co.uk** (see the Introduction).

Ticks For The Best There Is

Although everything listed in the book is notable and remarkable in some way, there are places that are outstanding even in this superlative company. Instead of marking them with a rosette or a star, they have been 'awarded' a tick.

✓ Amongst the very best in Scotland

✓ ✓ Amongst the best (of its type) in the UK

✓ ✓+ A particular commendation for Andrew Fairlie, Martin Wishart and Charlie Lockley, acknowledged as three of the top chefs in Scotland and the UK

✓ ✓ ✓ Amongst the best (of its type) in the world, or simply unique

Listings generally are not in an order of merit although if there is one outstanding item it will always be at the top of the page and this obviously includes anything which has been given a tick. Hotels and restaurants are also grouped according to price and this is why a cross-marked place may appear further down the page (ticks also indicate exceptional value for money).

The Codes

1. The Item Code
At the left-hand margin of every item is a code which will enable you to find it on a map. Thus **2389 9/F26** should be read as follows: **2389** is the item number, listed in simple consecutive order; **9** identifies the particular map at the back of the book; **F26** is the map co-ordinate, to help pinpoint the item's location on the map grid. A co-ordinate such as **xA5** indicates that the item can be reached by leaving the map at grid reference **A5**.

2. The Accommodation & Property Code
Beside each recommended accommodation or property is a series of codes as follows:

16 ROOMS	NO KIDS
MAR-DEC	NO PETS
TEL · TV	DA
NO C/CARDS	GF
LL	HS/NTS
ATMOS	MEDINEXP
☕	

ROOMS indicates the number of bedrooms in total. No differentiation is made as to the type of room. Most hotels will offer twin rooms as singles or put extra beds in doubles if required.
MAR-DEC shows when the accommodation is open. No dates means it is open all year.
TEL · TV refers to the facilities: **TEL** means there are direct-dial phones in the bedrooms while **TV** means there are TVs in the bedrooms.

NO C/CARDS means the establishment does not accept credit cards.

DF denotes a place that welcomes dogs, although often with conditions. Check in advance.

L, LL, LLL indicate places in outstanding locations. **L** is set in a great location; **LL** denotes a special setting; and **LLL** indicates a world-class spot.

ATMOS indicates a place whose special atmosphere is an attraction in itself.

NO KIDS does not necessarily mean children are unwelcome, only that special provisions are not usually made; ask in advance. In other cases, children are welcome, often with special rates.

NO PETS indicates that the hotel does not generally accept pets.

GF denotes a place that has no issue with gay customers and their partners.

HS or **NTS** denotes a place in the care of Historic Scotland or the National Trust for Scotland.

☕ indicates a property with an exceptional tearoom.

CHP/ MED.INX/ MED.EX/ EXP/ LOTS indicates the general cost of the accommodation based on an average twin or double room rate. Many hotels change rates daily depending on occupancy but the broad prices associated with each band are: **CHP** = under £80; **MED.INX** = £80 – 120; **MED.EX** = £120 – 150; **EXP** = £150 – 200; **LOTS** = £200+.

3. The Dining Codes

The price codes marked by eateries refer to the cost of an average dinner per person with a starter, main course and dessert. It excludes wine, coffee and extras. Prices are based on 2011 rates.

Where a hotel is notable also for its restaurant, this is identified by **EAT** on a separate line below the main accommodation description, with details following.

Within the text of an entry, LO means last orders at the kitchen. Some restaurants close earlier if they are quiet and go later on request.

10pm/10.30pm means usually 10pm Mon-Fri, 10.30pm at weekends. It's common, especially for city restaurants, to open later at weekends, particularly in Edinburgh during the Festival (August).

4. The Walk Codes

Beside each of the many walks in the book is a series of codes as follows:

3-10KM   CIRC/ XCIRC   BIKES/ XBIKES/ MTBIKES   1-A-1

3-10KM means the walk(s) described may vary in length between the distances shown.

CIRC means the walk can be circular, while **XCIRC** shows the walk is not circular and you must return more or less the way you came.

BIKES indicates the walk has a path which is suitable for ordinary bikes. **XBIKES** means the walk is not suitable for, or does not permit, cycling. **MTBIKES** means the track is suitable for mountain or all-terrain bikes.

The **1-A-1** Code:

First number (**1**, **2** or **3**) indicates how easy the walk is.

1 the walk is easy.

2 medium difficulty, eg standard hillwalking, not dangerous nor requiring special knowledge or equipment.

3 difficult: care and preparation and a map are needed.

The letters (**A**, **B** or **C**) indicate how easy it is to find the path.

A the route is easy to find. The way is either marked or otherwise obvious.

B the route is not very obvious, but you'll get there.

C you will need a map and preparation or a guide.

The last number (**1**, **2** or **3**) indicates what to wear on your feet.

1 ordinary outdoor shoes, including trainers, are probably okay unless the ground is very wet.

2 you will need walking boots.

3 you will need serious walking or hiking boots.

Apart from designated walks, the 1-A-1 code is employed wherever there is more than a short stroll required to get to somewhere, eg a waterfall or a monument.

High Fives *A Personal Selection*

Edinburgh Hotels

- **The Balmoral**
- **Prestonfield**
- **The Caledonian**
- **Hotel du Vin**
- **The Bonham**

Glasgow Hotels

- **Hotel du Vin**
- **Radisson**
- **The Malmaison**
- **Blythswood Square**
- **Mint Hotel**

Edinburgh Easy Dining

- **The Honours**
- **The Dogs**
- **Urban Angel**
- **The Outsider**
- **Redwood**

Glasgow Easy Dining

- **Stravaigin**
- **Guy's Restaurant & Bar**
- **Cafézique**
- **No. Sixteen**
- **Crabshakk**

Edinburgh European Dining

- **La Garrigue, Jeffrey St (French)**
- **Café Marlayne (French)**
- **L'Escargot Bleu (French)**
- **Hanedan (Turkish)**
- **Nonna's Kitchen (Italian)**

Glasgow European Dining

- **La Parmigiana (Italian)**
- **Battlefield Rest (Italian)**
- **Chardon D'Or (French)**
- **La Vallée Blanche (French)**
- **Konaki (Greek)**

Edinburgh Ethnic Dining

- **Mother India Café (Indian)**
- **Kalpna (Indian)**
- **Mithas (Indian)**
- **Pho Vietnam (Vietnamese)**
- **Dusit (Thai)**

Glasgow Ethnic Dining

- **Mother India (Indian)**
- **Balbir's (Indian)**
- **Asia Style (Chinese)**
- **Rumours (Malaysian)**
- **Persia (Middle Eastern)**

Edinburgh Cafés/Coffee shops

- Falko Konditorei
- Gallery of Modern Art One
- The Broughton Street Deli
- Fruitmarket Café
- Artisan Roast

Glasgow Cafés/Coffee shops

- Café Gandolfi
- Kember & Jones
- Hidden Lane Tearoom
- University Café
- Rio Café

Edinburgh Pubs

- Joseph Pearce's
- Cloisters
- The Canny Man's
- Roseleaf
- The Voodoo Rooms

Glasgow Pubs

- Stravaigin
- Òran Mór
- The Horseshoe
- Bon Accord
- Scotia Bar

Aberdeen Restaurants

- Café 52
- Le Café Bohème
- La Stella
- Silver Darling
- Fusion

Dundee Restaurants

- Jute
- Bon Appétit
- Blue Marlin
- The Playwright
- The Tasting Rooms

Country Hotels

- Monachyle Mhor, near Balquhidder
- Glenfinnan House Hotel
- Lake Hotel, Port of Menteith
- Knockinaam Lodge, Portpatrick
- Gleneagles

Small Town Hotels

- Townhouse, Melrose
- The Barley Bree, Muthill
- Royal Hotel, Comrie
- The Ceilidh Place, Ullapool
- George Hotel, Inveraray

Section 1
Wha's Like Us?

Famously Big Attractions

Among the 'top 10' (paid entry) and the 'top 10' (free) visitor attractions, these are the ones really worth seeing. Find them under their item numbers.

Edinburgh Castle; **Holyrood Palace**; **Edinburgh Zoo**; **The National Museum of Scotland**; **The National Gallery**; **Our Dynamic Earth** 399/403/402/400/407/406/MAIN ATTRACTIONS.
The People's Palace, Glasgow; **The Burrell Collection**; **Kelvingrove**; **The Riverside Museum** 677/675/674/673/MAIN ATTRACTIONS.
The Glasgow Botanic Gardens; **The Gallery of Modern Art** 681/682/OTHER ATTRACTIONS.
The Edinburgh Botanics 410/OTHER ATTRACTIONS.
Culzean Castle; **Stirling Castle**; **Castle of Mey** 1773/1770/1775/BEST CASTLES.
Mount Stuart; **Manderston** 1833/1835/COUNTRY HOUSES.
Skara Brae; **The Callanish Stones** 1812/1814/PREHISTORIC SITES.
Rosslyn Chapel 1864/CHURCHES.

OTHER UNMISSABLES ARE:

1 9/L25 ✓✓✓ **Loch Lomond** Approach via Stirling and A811 to Drymen or from Glasgow, the A82 Dumbarton road to Balloch. Britain's largest inland waterway and a traditional playground, especially for Glaswegians; jet-skis, show-off boats. **Lomond Shores** at Balloch is the heavily retail gateway to the loch (including Jenners) and the **Loch Lomond National Park** which covers a vast area. Orientate and shop here.

The west bank between Balloch and Tarbert is most developed: marinas, cruises, ferry to Inchmurrin Island. Luss is tweeville, like a movie set (it was used in the Scottish TV soap, *High Road*) but has an OK tearoom (The Coach House; 1389/TEAROOMS). The road is more picturesque beyond Tarbert to Ardlui; see 1253/BLOODY GOOD PUBS for the non-tourist/real Scots experience of the **Drover's Inn** at Inverarnan.

The east is more natural, wooded; good lochside and hill walks (1975/MUNROS). The road is winding but picturesque beyond Balmaha towards Ben Lomond. Hire a rowboat at Balmaha to Inchcailloch Island: lovely woodland walks (2026/WALKS).

Cameron House and the Lodge on the Loch are in their different ways excellent hotel options: 482/485/HOTELS OUTSIDE TOWN. Water taxis 01301 702356.

2 7/G19 ✓✓✓ **The Cuillin Mountains** Skye This hugely impressive east range in the south of Skye, often shrouded in cloud or rain, is the romantic heartland of the islands and was 'sold' in 2003 to a combination of public agencies so... it's ours now! The Red Cuillin are smoother and nearer the Portree-Broadford road; the Black Cuillin gather behind and are best approached from **Glen Brittle** (1994/SERIOUS WALKS; 1593/WATERFALLS). This classic, untameable mountain scenery has attracted walkers, climbers and artists for centuries. It still claims lives regularly. For best views apart from Glen Brittle, see 1619/SCENIC ROUTES; 1641/VIEWS. Vast range of walks and scrambles (see also 1656/WILD SWIMMING).

3 7/M18 ✓✓✓ **Loch Ness** Most visits start from Inverness at the north end via the Caledonian Canal. Fort Augustus is at the other end, 56km to the south. Loch Ness is part of the still-navigable Caledonian Canal linking to the west coast at Fort William. Small boats line the shores at certain points; one of the best ways to see the loch is on a cruise from Inverness (**Jacobite Cruises** 01463 233999 1-6 hours, several options). Other cruise operators from Fort Augustus

(01320 366277) and the small, friendly Nessie Hunter from Drumnadrochit (01456 450395). Most tourist traffic uses the main A82 north bank road converging on Drumnadrochit where the Loch Ness Monster industry gobbles up your money. If you must, the official Loch Ness Monster Exhibition is the one to choose. On the A82 you can't miss Urquhart Castle (1808/RUINS). But the two best things about Loch Ness are: the south road (B862) from Fort Augustus back to Inverness (1626/SCENIC ROUTES); and the detour from Drumnadrochit to Cannich to Glen Affric (20-30km) (1577/GLENS; 2001/GLEN & RIVER WALKS; 1589/WATERFALLS). Best bet to drop in, eat (and stay) is the **Loch Ness Inn** at Drumnadrochit, and the top-end eat and stay is Loch Ness Lodge (974/HIGHLAND HOTELS). Best pub grub and stay is **Glenmoriston Arms** (1159/ROADSIDE INNS).

4 10/N25 ✓✓ **Falkirk Wheel** 08700 500 208 · Falkirk Tamfourhill, half-way between Edinburgh and Glasgow, signed from the M9, M80 and locally. The splendid and deliberately dramatic massive boat-lift at the convergence of the (Millennium-funded) reinstated Union and Forth & Clyde canals – the world's first coast-to-coast ship canal (to wander or plooter along). The 35-metre lift is impressive to watch and great to go on. Boats leave the visitor centre every 30 minutes for the 45-minute journey (10am-5.30pm, winter 11am-4pm). Great network of paths to walk and cycle from here.

▮▮▮▮ Favourite Scottish Journeys

5 9/J21 ✓✓ **The West Highland Line** 08457 484950 One of the most picturesque railway journeys in Europe and quite the best way to get to Skye from the south. Travelling from Glasgow to Fort William, you pass the bigger loch (Lomond), the longest (Awe) and the deepest (Morar), and the highest ben (Nevis), the Bonnie Prince Charlie Country (MARY, CHARLIE & BOB, p. 328-9) and much that is close to a railwayman's heart by viaducts (including the Harry Potter one) and tunnels over loch and down dale. It's also possible to make the same journey (from Fort William to Mallaig and/or return) by steam train from mid May to mid Oct (details 01524 737751) on **The Jacobite** – this is generally regarded as one of the great railway journeys of the world (and it is a very busy wee train). There's a museum in the restored station at Glenfinnan with a tearoom and bunk accommodation. Trains for Mallaig leave from Glasgow Queen St, 3 times a day and take about 5 hours.

6 7/H19 ✓ **Glenelg-Kylerhea** www.skyeferry.co.uk · 01599 522273 The shorter of the 2 remaining ferry journeys to Skye and definitely the best way to get there if you're not pushed for time. The drive to Glenelg from the A87 is spectacular (1615/ SCENIC ROUTES) and so is this 5-minute crossing of the deep Narrows of Kylerhea. Easter-Oct every 20 minutes 10am-7pm. The ferry is run by and very much a part of the local community around Glenelg. Cute wee shack to visit before departure. This is a project worth supporting. There's an otter-watch hide at Kylerhea.

7 7/G19 ✓ **Elgol, Isle of Skye** 0871 700 2000 Trips on either the *Bella Jane* (0800 731 3089) or the *Misty Isle* (01471 866288) on Loch Coruisk to see the whales, dolphins, basking sharks and of course the famous view (1641/VIEWS).

8 9/K25 **Wemyss Bay-Rothesay Ferry** www.calmac.co.uk · 01475 650100 The glass-roofed station at Wemyss Bay, the railhead from Glasgow (60km by road on the A78), is redolent of an age-old terminus. The frequent (CalMac) ferry has all

the Scottish traits and treats you can handle, and Rothesay (with its period seaside mansions) appears out of blood-smeared sunsets and rain-sodden mornings alike, a gentle watercolour from summer holidays past. Visit the (Victorian) toilet when you get there and Mount Stuart (1833/HOUSES) on beautiful Bute.

9 9/J22   **Loch Etive Cruises** 01866 822430 From Taynuilt (Oban 20km) through the long narrow waters of one of Scotland's most atmospheric lochs, 2- or 3-hour journeys in a small cruiser with indoor and outdoor seating. The pier is 2km from main Taynuilt crossroads on the A85. Easter-mid Oct. Leaves 10am, 12noon and 2pm (not Sat). Booking not essential. Nice tearoom, Robin's Nest, on the road to the pier (1400/TEAROOMS).
Also **Loch Shiel Cruises** 01687 470322 From near Glenfinnan House Hotel (1180/SCOTTISH HOTELS) on the Road to the Isles, A830 (1628/SCENIC ROUTES). A 1-2-stop cruise on glorious Loch Shiel. Various trips available Easter-Oct.

10 10/L24   **Sailing Loch Katrine** www.lochkatrine.com · 01877 332000/376316 The Legends of the Loch boats sail from May to Oct. The historic steamship *Sir Walter Scott* (he who put it and, at the same time, Scottish tourism on the map) or the smaller cruiser, the afore-invented *Lady of the Lake*. This journey on Loch Katrine is a classic Trossachs experience, especially in the purple-and-golden-tinted autumn. Both do 1-hour or (to the end of the loch) 2-hour cruises. Café/bar and big car park. Cycling a very good idea round here (hire: 01877 376366).

11 9/J21   **Corran Ferry** 01855 841243 Runs from Ardgour on A861 to Nether Lochaber on the A82 across the narrows of Loch Linnhe. A convenient 5-minute crossing which can save time to points south of Mallaig and takes you to the wildernesses of Moidart and Ardnamurchan. A charming and fondly regarded journey in its own right. Runs continuously till 8.50pm in summer, 9.30pm in winter.

12 10/P25   **The *Maid of the Forth* Cruise to Inchcolm Island** 0131 331 4857 The wee boat (though they say it holds 225 people) which leaves every day at different times (phone for details) from Hawes Pier in South Queensferry (15km Central Edinburgh via A90) opposite the Hawes Inn, just under the famous railway bridge (401/MAIN ATTRACTIONS). 45-minute trips under the bridge and on to Inchcolm, an attractive island with walks and an impressive ruined abbey. Much birdlife and also many seals to be seen. 1 hour 30 minutes ashore. Tickets at pier. Mar-Oct.

13 7/M18   **North & West from Inverness** 08457 484950 Two less celebrated (than the West Highland Line above) but mesmerising rail journeys start from Inverness. The journey to Kyle of Lochalsh no longer has an observation car in summer, so get a window seat and take a map; the last section through Glen Carron and around the coast at Loch Carron is especially fine. There are 3 trains a day and it takes 2 hours 30 minutes. Inverness to Wick is a 3 hour 50 minute journey. The section skirting the east coast from Lairg to Helmsdale is full of drama, followed by the transfixing monotony of the Flow Country. 3 trains a day in summer.

14 5/C20   **The Plane to Barra** 01871 890 212 Most of the island plane journeys pass over many smaller islands (eg Glasgow-Tiree, Glasgow-Stornoway, Wick-Orkney) and are fascinating on a clear day, but the daily flight from Glasgow to Barra is doubly special because the island's airport is on Cockleshell Beach in the north (11 km from Castlebay) after a splendid approach. The 12-seater Otter leaves and lands according to the tide. Operated by Flybe; you can go on to Benbecula.

There are many other **Sea and Wildlife Cruises** listed on p. 300–1.

Great Ways To Get Around

15 **By Seaplane** www.lochlomond.seaplanes.com · 01436 675030 See Scotland from the air, landing on land and water in the remoter parts other transport can't reach. From Glasgow Science Centre to Oban and Tobermory and other, mainly west-coast destinations. Routes can be customised. You can reach Loch Lomond in 20 minutes. Operates Mar-Oct.

16 **By VW Campervan** Scoobycampers · www.scoobycampers.com There are others doing vintage campervans now but Scooby were there first. They offer VW microbuses and campervans on a self-drive rental basis to see Scotland at a gentle pace and save on accommodation. All vehicles are classic versions converted with contemporary comforts. Microbuses take 6 people comfortably though not to sleep in (hire their camping equipment). Campervans take 4 – best suited to 2 adults/2 kids. Vehicles have CD radios/DVD players and satnav. 6 options, each with own name. They look cool and you'll find that folk are pleased to see you.

17 **By Classic Car** www.caledonianclassics.co.uk · Caledonian Classic Car Rental · 01259 742476 Choose a fabulous motor and take off round the by-roads, experiencing that old forgotten joy of motoring. Packages are customised, but there's unlimited mileage and free delivery/collection locally for hire of 2 days or more. Short trips come with a complimentary picnic hamper. Cars include Jaguar E-type, Porche 912, MGB Roadster, Austin Healey, Morgan 4/4, Triumph TR6 and Beetle convertible and VW camper. Prices from £140 per day/£1000 per week at TGP. They have their own 4-star B&B in Dollar (a good place to start).

18 **By Motorbike** Scotlandbybike · www.scotlandbybike.com · 07515 851876 Bike your way around Scotland on your own or in private or group guided tours. Scotlandbybike organises a range of tours and packages that combine accommodation, insurance and hire of mainly BMW but also Triumph, Yamaha and Suzuki, including some for smaller riders; or bring your own. Tuition if you want to improve your bike-riding skills *en route*. Tours are from 5 to 10 days; check for rates.

19 **By Kayak** A great way to see parts of Scotland from the sea is by kayak. Bring your own or for instruction, guidance and finding spectacular routes, you couldn't do better than find **Wilderness Scotland** · www.wildernessscotland.com · 0131 625 6635 who operate award-winning adventure holidays from many locations north and west; or **Seafreedom Kayaks** · www.seafreedomkayak.co.uk · 01631 710173 at Connel. The coastline here offers all kinds of sea and loch possibilities including Loch Etive and the island of Seil. Tony Hammoch and his wife Olga can also offer accommodation at their B&B situated on the A85 overlooking the Falls of Connel.

20 **By Traditional Fishing Boat** www.themajesticline.co.uk · The Majestic Line · 0131 623 5012 Unique, all-inclusive holidays on 1 of 2 traditional, wooden, 85-foot fishing boats which have been sensitively converted to a high standard. The Majestic Line operates various itineraries of 3- to 6-night cruises leaving Dunoon and taking in Bute and Arran or departing Oban for Mull and Iona. They also sail the Caledonian Canal and to Skye. 6 ensuite double cabins. Apr-Oct.

21 **Under Sail** Clyde Yachts · www.clydeyachts.com · 01505 503830 West and northwest Scotland offer some of the best sailing in the world. Clyde Yachts is one of the best charters with instructor/guide, operating out of Adrossan.

The Best Annual Events

22
JAN
Up-Helly-Aa 01595 693434 · Lerwick Traditionally on the 24th day after Christmas, but now always the last Tuesday in January. A mid-winter fire festival based on Viking lore where 'the Guizers' haul a galley through the streets of Lerwick and burn it in the park; and the night goes on.

23
JAN
Celtic Connections www.celticconnections.com · 0141 353 8000 · Glasgow A huge, 3-week festival of Celtic music from round the world held in the Royal Concert Hall and other city venues . Concerts, ceilidhs, workshops. Craic.

24
25 JAN
Burns Night The National Bard celebrated with supper. Increasing number of local and family celebrations though no single major event.

25
MID-APR
Glasgow International www.glasgowinternational.org · Glasgow Biennial ('12, '14) festival presenting contemporary visual art in the city's main venues and unusual or found space throughout the city centre; celebrating Glasgow's significance as a source of and platform for important contemporary artists.

26
APR
Melrose Sevens www.melrose7s.com · 0870 608 0404 · Melrose This Border town is completely taken over by the tournament in their small-is-beautiful rugby ground. 7-a-side teams from all over including overseas. Lots of big lads!

27
1 MAY
Beltane Edinburgh The gloriously pagan gathering on the city's Calton Hill to celebrate May Day. Full of light, fire, drumming. Wait for the dawn.

28
MAY
Paps of Jura Fell Race www.jurafellrace.org.uk · 01496 820243 · Jura The amazing hill race up and down the 3 Paps (4 tops in all) on this large, remote island (2229/MAGICAL ISLANDS). About 200 runners take on the 16-mile challenge from the distillery in Craighouse, the village. Winner does it in 3 hours!

29
MAY-JUL
Common Ridings 0870 608 0404 · Border Towns The Border town festivals. Similar formats over different weeks with ride-outs (on horseback to outlying villages, etc), shows, dances and games, culminating on the Friday and Saturday. Total local involvement. Hawick is first, then Selkirk, Peebles/Melrose, Gala, Jedburgh, Kelso and Lauder at the end of July. All authentic and truly local.

30
MAY
Ten Under The Ben 01397 772899 · Fort William A 10-hour mountain-bike endurance event around Ben Nevis. Good fun, though. Run by No Fuss Events (others in the southwest at Kirroughtree and Moray).

31
END MAY
Edinburgh Marathon www.edinburgh-marathon.com The UK's fastest marathon route and perhaps the most picturesque. Also with 5 and 10km, junior events, etc.

32
EARLY JUN
Moonwalk www.walkthewalk.org · Edinburgh · The big pink, hopefully moonlit walk starting at midnight through the streets of Edinburgh in aid of breast-cancer charities. Many, many wimmin (and some guys); euphoric!

33
JUN
RockNess Dores Open-air nedfest in beautiful setting looking over Loch Ness at the tiny village of Dores which is besieged for the weekend. Scotland's second-biggest music festival.

34 **Flower Shows** Edinburgh · 0131 333 0969 · & Ayr Many Scottish towns hold
JUN & flower shows, mainly in autumn, but the big spring show at Gardening Scotland at
EARLY AUG the Royal Highland Centre (Ingliston) is well worth a look. Meanwhile the annual
Ayr show in August is huge! Check local tourist information for details.

35 **Royal Highland Show** 0131 335 6200 · Ingliston Showground, Edinburgh
JUN The premier agricultural show (over 4 days) in Scotland and for the farming world,
the event of the year. Animals, machinery, food, crafts, shopping. 150,000 attend.

36 **Mountain Bike World Cup** 01397 705825 · Fort William Held at Nevis
JUN Range 5K run, around the ski gondola. Awesome course with international competitors over 2 days. Evening events in town. Date varies.

37 **Borders Book Festival** www.bordersbookfestival.org · 0844 357 1060 ·
JUN Melrose The hugely successful and utterly appropriate (to town and times) bookfest held in Harmony Gardens. Intimate, friendly: reads well.

38 **The Caledonian Challenge** 0131 524 0350 · Fort William A very big (80k)
MID JUN walk run by the Scottish Community Foundation, with teams of 4 going through
various check points in Lochaber, using parts of the West Highland Way.

39 **Edinburgh International Film Festival** www.edfilmfest.org.uk · 0131 228
LATE JUN 4051 Various screens and other locations in Edinburgh city centre. One of the
world's oldest film festivals. 10 days of film and movie matters. Changes under
way at TGP; watch that screen.

40 **St Magnus Festival** www.stmagnusfestival.com · 01856 871445 ·
LATE JUN Kirkwall, Orkney Midsummer celebration of the arts has attracted big names
over the years. More highbrow than hoi polloi; the cathedral at its heart. The days
are very long.

41 **Mendelssohn on Mull** www.mullfest.org.uk · 01688 812377 Classical
END JUN music festival in various halls and venues around the island that celebrates the
connection between the composer and this rocky far-flung part of the world. Nice
idea, and a great time to be here (see 2306/MULL).

42 **Scottish Traditional Boat Festival** 01261 842951 · Portsoy Perfect little
EARLY JUL festival in perfect little Moray coast town over a weekend in early July. Old boats in
old and new harbours, an open-air ceilidh and a great atmosphere.

43 **Scottish Game Conservancy Fair** www.scottishfair.com · 01738 554826 ·
JUL Perth Held in the rural and historical setting of Scone Palace, a major Perthshire
day out and gathering for the hunting, shooting, fishing and shopping brigade.

44 **T in the Park** www.tinthepark.com · Balado Airfield near Kinross
JUL Scotland's highly successful pop festival now owned, like almost everything else, by
Live Nation. The T stands for Tennents, the sponsors who are much in evidence.
Not life-changing like Glastonbury, but among the best festivals in the UK.

45 **Hebridean Celtic Festival** www.hebceltfest.com · 01851 621234 ·
MID-JUL Stornoway Folk-rock format festival under canvas on faraway Lewis. Celebrated
16th year in '11 with KT Tunstall and sound others. Music and craic.

46   **The Great Kindrochit Quadrathlon**   www.artemisgreatkindrochit.com ·
MID-JUL   Loch Tay The toughest one-day sporting event – swim 1.6km across the loch, run 24km (including 7 Munros), kayak 11km and cycle 54km. Then slice a melon with a sword. Jings!

47   **Merchant City Festival**   www.merchantcityfestival.com · Glasgow A host
MID-JUL   of free ticketed events bringing life to the city's cultural quarter. Likely to figure significantly in the lead up to Glasgow's hosting of the Commonwealth Games in 2014.

48   **Wickerman Festival**   www.thewickermanfestival.co.uk · near Gatehouse
END JUL   of Fleet Annual music fest for the South West in fields on the A755 between Gatehouse and Kirkcudbright. Under wide skies on a cool coast. They burn a huge effigy at midnight on the Saturday. Audience slow and loose.

49   **Black Isle Show**   www.blackisleshow.info · Muir of Ord Notable agricultural
EARLY AUG   show and countryside gathering for the northeast Highlands. A big family day out.

50   **Art Week**   www.pittenweemartsfestival.co.uk · Pittenweem Remarkable
EARLY AUG   local event where the whole of Pittenweem in Fife becomes a gallery. Over 70 venues show work, including public building and people's houses. The quality is not strained. Other events include fireworks. First full week of August.

51   **Traquair Fair**   www.traquair.co.uk · 01896 830323 · near Innerleithen In
EARLY AUG   the grounds of Traquair House (1836/COUNTRY HOUSES), a mini Glastonbury with music, comedy and crafts. A respite from the Festival up the road in Edinburgh.

52   **Belladrum Tartan Heart Festival**   www.tartanheartfestival.co.uk · 01463
AUG   741366 · near Kiltarlity Off A862 Beauly road west of Inverness. Friendly, 2-day music fest with a loyal local following in terraced grounds. Good for families.

53   **The Edinburgh Festivals: The International Festival**   www.eif.co.uk ·
AUG   0131 473 2000 A major programme of music, drama and dance with the **Virgin Money Fireworks** on the final Sunday. In August Edinburgh hosts the biggest arts festival in the world, including the **International Military Tattoo,** www.edintattoo.co.uk; **The Fringe,** www.edfringe.com with hundreds of events every night; the **Jazz Festival,** www.edinburghjazzfestival.co.uk and (mainly for delegates on a bit of a jolly) the TV festival. This is the best place to be in the world if you're into the arts. And see below.

54   **Edinburgh International Book Festival**   www.edbookfest.co.uk · 0131 718
AUG   5666 · Edinburgh A tented village in Charlotte Sq gardens. Same time as the above but deserving of a separate entry as it is so uniquely good.

55   **The World Pipe Band Championships**   www.theworlds.co.uk · Glasgow
AUG   Unbelievable numbers (3,000-4,000) of pipers from all over the world competing and seriously attuned on Glasgow Green.

56   **Cowal Highland Gathering**   www.cowalgathering.com · 01369 703206 ·
AUG   Dunoon One of many Highland games but this, along with Luss and Loch Lomond Games and Inverness in July, and Braemar (below) are the main events in the calendar that extends from May to September. Expect heavy events (very big lads only), dancing, pipe bands, field and track events and much drinking and chat.

57 **Braemar Gathering** www.braemargathering.org · 01339 755377 ·
EARLY Braemar Another of many Highland games (Aboyne early August, Ballater mid
SEP August on Deeside alone) up north but this is where the royals gather and proba-
bly local laird Billy Connolly and Hollywood A list. Go ogle.

58 **Blas** www.blas-festival.com · 01463 783447 · Highlands Across the
SEP Highlands in a variety of venues. A rapidly expanding celebration of traditional and
Gaelic music with an eclectic line up. It's a long week.

59 **The Ben Nevis Race** www.bennevisrace.co.uk · Fort William The race over
SEP 100 years old up Britain's highest mountain and back. The record is 1 hour 25
minutes which seems amazing. 600 runners though curiously little national, even
local interest. Starts 2pm at Claggan Park off Glen Nevis roundabout.

60 **The Pedal for Scotland Glasgow-to-Edinburgh Bike Ride**
SEP www.pedalforscotland.org Fun, charity fund-raiser and serious annual bike
fest. From Glasgow Green to Victoria Park with a pasta party at the halfway point.
51 miles or 100 miles return (or 9 miles staying in Glasgow).

61 **Wigtown Book Festival** www.wigtownbookfestival.com · Wigtown Small,
SEP–OCT beautiful bookfest in small, quite beautiful booktown in the South West. In mar-
quees in the square with great clubrooms above the shop. Edinburgh goes south.

62 **Loch Ness Marathon** www.lochnessmarathon.com One of the UK's top
EARLY marathons and a festival of running, starting midway along the southeast shore of
OCT the loch and finishing in Inverness. Also 10ks and kids' events.

63 **Tiree Wave Classic** www.tireewaveclassic.com · Isle of Tiree Windsurfing
EARLY heaven of the faraway island (2235/MAGICAL ISLANDS) where beaches offer
OCT challenging wind conditions and islanders offer warm hospitality.

64 **Tour of Mull Rally** www.2300club.org · Isle of Mull The highlight of the
OCT national rally calendar is this raging around Mull weekend. Though drivers enter
from all over the world, the overall winner has often been a local man (well, plenty
time for practice). There's usually a waiting list for accommodation, but the
camping is OK and locals put you up.

65 **Glasgay!** www.glasgay.co.uk · Glasgow Annual, month-long celebration of
OCT–NOV queer culture in different venues in the city centre: film, music, performance, club
nights. It is for everybody.

66 **St Andrew's Night** Increasingly a bigger deal than before, with government-
NOV sponsored events. National holiday, anyone?

67 **Stonehaven Fireball Festival** Stonehaven Celebrated since 1910, a tradi-
31 tional Hogmanay fire festival that probably wouldn't get started nowadays for
DEC 'health and safety' reasons. 40 fireballers throw the fireballs around in the streets
before processing to the harbour and heaving them in. We watch. Arrive early.

68 **Edinburgh's Hogmanay** www.edinburghshogmanay.org · 0131 651 3380 ·
DEC–JAN Edinburgh Everywhere gets booked up but call the tourist information centre for
accommodation. Now the only major Hogmanay in Scotland and one of the
world's major winter festivals, it's launched with a **Torchlight Procession**
through the city centre. The main event is the **Street Party** on 31st. Be part of a
huge, good-natured crowd; it is the Scots at their hospitable best!

69 9/H25   **Knapdale** For a start, hardly anyone knows where Knapdale is – when you get there, it seems like it should be in the Lake District. But it's the north bit of the Kintyre peninsula: the tongues of land bounded by Loch Fyne, the great sealoch to the east and the Sound of Jura in the west. Its location, in the midst of the most serrated of Scotland's coastline, with islands large and small visible from innumerable perspectives, means that from close up and afar it is immensely scenic, possibly the most pleasing place to the eye on the western seaboard.

The area loosely extends from Crinan in the north to Tarbert in the south, both places that are dearly loved, especially by yachties. The **Crinan Hotel** has long been a bastion of good taste, good seafood and unforgettable views over dinner (723/ARGYLL HOTELS). Tayvallich also has its forever fans and now with a summer passenger ferry to Jura (2304/ISLAY & JURA), there's another reason to visit.

But it's the single-track road, the B8024 that follows the coast from Tarbert to Lochgilphead, that skirts and best encapsulates Knapdale (1630/SCENIC ROUTES). Bang in the middle is the excellent **Kilberry Inn** for food and shelter (1277/ GAST-ROPUBS; 1139/ROADSIDE INNS). 3km south towards Tarbert, a sign, To the Coves, takes you 500m to the Kilberry Coves to watch otters and to swim in summer. A new place to eat in the south is **Starfish** at Tarbert (742/ARGYLL RESTAURANTS).

The unique and vital feature of Knapdale is the woodland. Thousands of acres of original, diverse, deciduous woodland – oak, birch, hazel and alder and the wildlife that lives there: owls, red squirrels, eagles and hedgerows and meadows of wild flowers. The Forestry Commission have a leaflet with many walks and cycle routes available locally and at their interpretation centre at Barnluasgan south of Crinan in the heart of the Caledonian Forest Reserve. These are the forests that once clothed Scotland. In Knapdale we rediscover our roots and branches.

70 9/J23   **Loch Awe** Lochs Lomond, Ness and Tay are the big ones in our imaginations and there are many we love to call our own (p. 281–2, The Lochs We Love) but though we may gaze on it on our way to Oban, somehow Loch Awe has gone unloved. I felt so too until one brilliant summer evening in 2009, roof of the car open, I drove over from Inveraray to meet the south Loch Awe road through Caledonian forest of oaks and birch, the loch glittering, Ben Cruachan above, and I realised how resplendent is this mighty body of water that stabs through the heart of Argyll.

A quick evaluation shows how many exceptional places are associated with it: places to stay at Kilchrenan, **Roineabhal**, **Taychreggan** and **Ardanaiseig** located on the water (732/735/ARGYLL HOTELS; 1097/COUNTRY-HOUSE HOTELS). The plethora of woodland walks on **Lochaweside** (2021/WOODLAND WALKS), others in the Forestry Commission pamphlet, *Loch Awe*. Fishing, cycling, picnicking – all that. The spirit of the loch itself seems to seep into the hallowed stones of **St Conan's Kirk**, one of the most atmospheric churches in the land (1865/ CHURCHES) and you sense its power again at **Kilchurn Castle** (1803/RUINS) a short walk from the main A85.

From these perspectives and countless places on the south loch road, it becomes clear that Loch Awe is indeed... awesome.

71 7/H20   **Knoydart** The peninsula in the far west of the mainland, only accessible by boat (from Mallaig) or a long walk (30km) from Kinlochhourn. Often described as the last wilderness in the UK and since 1999 run by the Knoydart Foundation, a part-nership between the local community, local authority, the John Muir Trust and others, it is nevertheless a fascinating and hospitable place offering all kinds of walking and sea-based pursuits and is much visited by photographers. The best accommodation is at **Doune Stone Lodge** (1165/GET AWAY FROM IT ALL), which you mainly get to in their boat. It's 10km from the village, Inverie, and the brilliant pub, **The Old Forge** (1255/BLOODY GOOD PUBS), classed by the Guinness Book of Records as the remotest in Britain (though it's as bustling as many on the mainland); there are also B&Bs (**Seaview** has very contemporary rooms) and a bunkhouse (01687 462163). Eat at the pub or Doune dining room. Many walks start from Inverie (including rare woodland) and there are some serious tops, including the legendary **Larven** (a very long walk in, or shorter by boat). Boat service from Mallaig Pier (3 times a day, 30 mins); there are alternatives. Check www.knoydartfoundation.com

72 10/R27 **The Border Lands** As regular readers will know, I'm a Borders lad; I'm easily drawn back to my roots. My home town Jedburgh doesn't feature a lot in *Scotland the Best* because, if I'm honest (and you know I am), I can't recommend any hotels or restaurants there, though **Jedburgh Abbey** (1905/ABBEYS) and **Mary, Queen of Scots' House** (1918/MARY, CHARLIE & BOB) are well worth visiting. Most visitors trundle past Jedburgh on the A68 as they do with most of the Border towns on the way to or from Edinburgh.

This is a pity! Though its high street seems forlorn, Jedburgh, the first town in Scotland, is picturesque and peaceful. Melrose is much admired and visited and is, in all actuality, the Borders' Food Town (see Borders Hotels & Restaurants, p. 150–3) but there are many villages and towns that invite exploration in the gentle green hills. They include Lilliesleaf, **Bowden** (1877/CHURCHES), Denholm (**Cross Keys**; 1281/GASTROPUBS), Newtown St Boswells and Kelso with its abbey and a couple of good places to eat: **Cobbles** (817/BORDERS RESTAURANTS) and **Under the Sun** (1365/TEAROOMS). I haven't included Hawick in this list though it now has a great deli/café in **Turnbulls** (1446/DELIS) and an intrepid tearoom, **Damascus Drum** (816/BORDERS RESTAURANTS). It's not what you'd call a pretty town and since all the valley communities of the Borders have an issue with the others (and I'm no exception), I find it hard to enthuse about Hawick.

But the best way to appreciate the Borders is to wander in it. There are many hills from which to take in its bucolic serenity: the **Eildons** (1970/HILLS), **Peniel Heugh** and **Smailholm Tower** (1850/1863/MONUMENTS). Other great views are the famous **Scott's View** and my own **Irvine's View** (1644/1636/VIEWS), the best panorama in southern Scotland. The first vista coming into Scotland is worth more than the usual stop you might make at a border (**Carter Bar**; 1654/VIEWS).

All southern Scotland is perhaps a little neglected and we can't go everywhere, but on foot or by bike or just tootling in the car, a trip to the Borders is as soothing an antidote to the city and the stresses of life that you can get for almost nothing.

What The Scots Gave The Modern World...

Scotland's population has only recently topped 5 million and yet we discovered, invented or manufactured for the first time the following quite important things.

The Advertising Film
Anaesthesia
Ante-Natal Clinics
Antiseptics
Artificial Ice
The Alpha Chip
The Arts Festival
The ATM
Bakelite
The Bank of England
The Bicycle
Bovril
The Bowling Green
The Bus
Colour Photographs
The Compass
The Decimal Point
The Documentary
Dolly, the Cloned Sheep
Electric Light
Encyclopaedia Britannica
The Fax Machine
Fingerprinting
The Flushing Toilet
The Fountain Pen
Gardenias
The Gas Mask
Geology
The God Particle
Golf Clubs
The Golf Course
Hallowe'en
Helium
The Hypodermic Syringe
Insulin
Interferon
The Kaleidoscope
Kinetic Energy
The Lawnmower
Life Insurance
The Locomotive

Logarithms
The Mackintosh
Marmalade
The Microwave Oven
Motor Insurance
The Modern Road Surface
Morphine
The MRI Scanner
Neon
The Overdraft
Paraffin
Penicillin
The Photocopier
The Pneumatic Tyre
Postage Stamps
Postcards
Quinine
Radar
The Savings Bank
Sherlock Holmes
Sociology
The Steam Engine
Stocks and Shares
Street Lighting
The Telegraph
The Telephone
Television
Tennis Courts
The Theory of Combustion
The Thermometer
The Thermos Flask
The Threshing Machine
Typhoid Vaccine
Ultrasound
Universal Standard Time
The US Navy
The Vacuum Flask
Video
Wave Power
Whisky
Writing Paper

...and *Auld Lang Syne*

Edinburgh

73 1/D3
168 ROOMS
20 SUITES
TEL · TV
LL
LOTS

✓ ✓ **The Balmoral** www.thebalmoralhotel.com · 0131 556 2414 · **Princes Street** At east end above Waverley Station. Capital landmark, its clock 2 minutes fast (except at Hogmanay); so you might catch your train. The old pile dear to owner Sir Rocco Forte's heart. 4 categories of rooms: internals quieter, all views different; only 'super deluxe' have the castle view. Some top suites. Deluxe feel to the public spaces: the piano-tinkling Palm Court (great afternoon teas 1.30-5.30pm; 1417/TEAS), Calum Innes pics in the foyer. Pool small but beautiful, ESPA and Sundari products in the spa. Few hotels anywhere are so much in the heart of things.
EAT Main restaurant, Number One Princes Street (127/BEST RESTAURANTS), is tops and less formal brasserie, Hadrian's (good power-breakfast venue).
Even the non-pretentious bar, NB, works.

74 1/A4
254 ROOMS
TEL · TV
NO PETS
L
LOTS

✓ **The Caledonian Hilton** www.hilton.co.uk/caledonian · 0131 222 8888 · **Princes Street** An Edinburgh institution at the West End of Princes St: former station hotel built in 1903. Constant refurbishment under the Hilton group continues to reinforce the 5-star status of Edinburgh's other landmark hotel. Good business hotel with all facilities you'd expect though the Hilton brand. 'Living Well' spa would do well to refresh itself. Endearing lack of uniformity in the rooms; castle views at a premium. Main restaurant, The Pompadour, for fine formal dining and afternoon tea in ornate and elegant setting does lack the glamour and gourmet cred of days gone by but Chisholm's on the ground floor is perfectly serviceable. The Cally (whisky) bar is a famous rendezvous with an impressive – 260 and counting – whisky selection. Despite some recent lapse in the luxe, the Cally is a capital experience.

75 1/D2
187 ROOMS
TEL · TV
EXP

✓ **Apex Waterloo Place** www.apexhotels.co.uk · 0845 365 0000 · **23 Waterloo Place** As with all hotels in this Edinburgh-based chain (also in London and Dundee: 885/DUNDEE HOTELS), a central location and a very contemporary look. This, the new flagship (see others, below), opened '09 after a major conversion of the council offices where you used to pay your council tax. Bedrooms may want for a view and public areas (bar and Eliots restaurant) not immediately impressive and the subterranean pool is small, but this is a well-run, modern business hotel with direct access to the back entrance of the station.

76 1/XE1
100 ROOMS
TEL · TV
EXP

✓ **The Malmaison** www.malmaison-edinburgh.com · 0131 468 5000 · **Tower Place, Leith** At the dock gates. This was the first Malmaison all those design-led years ago, wearing reasonably well. All facilities that we who were once smart and young expect. Rooms have that darkish, masculine solidity but well-lit look that has been much adopted elsewhere. Some port views. The brasserie and café-bar have stylish ambience too, and the French brazz menu using local-ish produce is good value. Pity about the flats out front but the waterfront location and outside terrace is pleasant of a summer's evening and there are many bistros and bars over-by. Car parking. It's a good 20 minutes to uptown.

77 1/B5
139 ROOMS
TEL · TV
MED.EX

✓ **The Point** www.point-hotel.co.uk · 0131 221 5555 · **34 Bread Street** This used to be a Co-operative department store and was once mentioned as one of the great designery hotels in the world and on the cover of *Hotel Design*; there's a lot of competition now but the long corridors, cool lighting and well-laid-out rooms (a few with side-lit jacuzzi) still offer a modern, urbane city stopover. Those with castle views are best (with supplement). Café-bar, the Bread St Brasserie, improved of late and the other on-street bar Monboddo is spacious and a good place to rendezvous. Necessary room refurbishments in progress at TGP.

Conference Centre adjacent with great penthouse often used for cool Edinburgh launches and parties (there's a unique view of the city: 450/VIEWS) and they open it as a bar on the last Thursday of the month.

78 1/C4
119/169 ROOMS
TEL · TV
NO PETS
MED.EX

Apex City Hotel & Apex International www.apexhotels.co.uk · 0845 365 0000 Both in the middle of the Grassmarket, the picturesque but rowdy Saturday-night city centre. Modern, *soi-disant* – but close to castle, club life and other bits of essential Edinburgh. More cool to roam from than in, perhaps though the larger International has lots of public space, including a good bar to meet in and Metro restaurant overlooking the street where you can often get a table in the otherwise busy Grassmarket. Here also Heights restaurant on the 5th floor has great view of the castle for breakfast but you can't sit on the terrace. Some castle views (4th-floor rooms at International have balconies). Shared pool and facilities are minimal.

79 1/A4
260 ROOMS
TEL · TV
LOTS

The Sheraton Grand www.sheratonedinburgh.co.uk · 0131 229 9131 · **Festival Square** On Lothian Rd and Conference Sq, this city-centre business hotel won no prizes for architecture when it opened late 1980s between Edinburgh's 2 most recently created squares: Festival Sq (now with BBC screen – to watch the Olympics etc) and Conference Sq behind, a building site at TGP for the expanding Conference Centre. This is a fairly reliable stopover at the heart of the financial district, with excellent service. Many room categories: castle or non-castle views in each. Terrace restaurant (a buffet) is only adequate. **Santini** round the back and kind of far away is better (187/BEST ITALIANS). But the superlative feature of the Sheraton is the health club **One**, routinely identified as one of the best spas in the UK, with great half-outdoor pool (1228/SPAS).

80 1/D4
238 ROOMS
TEL · TV
MED.EX

Radisson BLU SAS www.edinburgh.radissonsas.com · 0131 557 9797 · **80 High Street** Modern but sympathetic building on the Royal Mile, handy for everything (especially during the Festival) and typical Radisson contemporary smart feel. Not great views but Royal Mile rooms are triple-glazed so there's minimal noise. Leisure facilities include tiny, subterranean pool and gym. Itchycoo bar/brasserie and many choices nearby. Adjacent parking handy in a hotel so central (£10.50 at TGP). Not the cheapest option but reliably Radisson!

81 1/B3
249 ROOMS
TEL · TV
EXP

The George www.edinburghgeorgehotel.co.uk · 0131 225 1251 · **George Street** Between Hanover St and St Andrew Sq. Owned by Principal Hotel Group who also have the Grand Central in Glasgow (458/GLASGOW HOTELS) with new extension adding 50 rooms. Robert Adam-designed and dating back to the late 18th century, this is a classy joint. Views of the Forth (or the castle) only from the deluxe rooms in the older part. It's all a bit pricey, but you pay for the location and the Georgian niceties. Busy on-street bar. Good Festival and Hogmanay hotel close to the heart of things (taken over by luvvies during TV Festival). The George has successfully shrugged off its staid, traditional image, fitting in to George St's more progressive, more opportunistic present.
EAT Impressive brasserie restaurant **Tempus**: chandeliered and banquetted, one of the most impressive dining rooms in town; food less remarkable. LO 9.45pm.

82 1/F2
94 ROOMS
13 SUITES
TEL · TV
NO PETS
MED.EX

Royal Terrace www.primahotels.co.uk/royal-terrace.html · 0131 557 3222 · **18 Royal Terrace** Discreet multi-townhouse hotel along elegant terrace backing on to Calton Hill. Multi-level terraced garden out back. Deceptively large number of rooms, many with great views. Townhouse décor is a tad on the Baroque side, making this fabulous for some, merely a good business bet for others. Bar/restaurant not so notable among the natives but we love the garden in summer.

The Best Individual & Boutique Hotels

83 1/XE5
24 ROOMS
TEL · TV
NO KIDS
ATMOS
LOTS

✓ ✓ ✓ **Prestonfield** www.prestonfield.com · 0131 668 3346 · off **Priestfield Road** 3km south of city centre. I admit that the last 3 editions of *StB* have been launched at Prestonfield and I like many others have enjoyed the lavish hospitalities of owner James Thomson but Prestonfield gets 3 ticks because there's simply nothing like it anywhere else in the world. The Heilan' cattle in the 14-acre grounds tell you this isn't your average urban bed for the night. A romantic, almost other-worldly 17th-century building with period features still intact. In 2003 James, Edinburgh's most notable restauranteur of The Tower (133/BEST RESTAURANTS) and The Witchery (134/BEST RESTAURANTS), turned this old bastion of Edinburgh sensibilities into Scotland's most sumptuous hotel. The architecture and the detail is exceptional and romantic. All rooms are highly individualistic with hand-picked antiques and artefacts, flat screens and the usual technologies. Prestonfield probably hosts more awards dinners and accommodates more celebrity guests than anywhere else in town, and it itself wins more awards, especially as a 'romantic' or 'individual' hotel. In summer the nightly Scottish cabaret (in the stable block) is hugely popular.
EAT House restaurant Rhubarb: a memorable experience (135/BEST RESTAURANTS).

84 1/D5
47 ROOMS
TEL · TV
NO PETS
MED.EX

✓ ✓ **Hotel du Vin** www.hotelduvin.com · 0131 247 4900 · 11 Bristo **Place** One of the latest in the expanding chain of hotels (464/GLASGOW HOTELS) created by imaginative and sympatico conversion of city-centre, often historic buildings – in this case, the Lunatic Asylum and Infirmary where Robert Fergusson, one of Scotland's iconic poets and revered by Robert Burns, died in 1774. So this place was old! The hotel however, enclosing a courtyard (with 'cigar bothy') and making maximum use of the up-and-down labyrinthine space, is comfortable and modern. Rooms in 4 categories are all different but have the same look. Monsoon showers in all but standard rooms. All, including suites, are well priced. Bar (24 hours for guests), a whisky snug (250 to try) and a very bistro bistro (154/BISTROS). As with other H du V, there's much to-do about wine. In busy quarter near university and museum; great for the Festival if you can get in.

85 1/C4
8 SUITES
TEL · TV
LOTS

✓ ✓ **The Witchery by the Castle** www.thewitchery.com · 0131 225 5613 · **Castlehill** James Thomson's (Prestonfield, above) much-celebrated and -awarded suites at the top of the Royal Mile. The Inner Sanctum and the Old Rectory are now joined by 6 other, all highly individual, indulgent, theatrical and gorgeous, and consolidated into a uniquely Edinburgh experience around his restaurant and first venture, The Witchery (134/BEST RESTAURANTS). At the heart of the Old Town, here at its most atmospheric. Join a guest list that stretches from Vivienne Westwood (naturally) through Jack Nicholson to Dannii Minogue. You are in good company but you will not be disturbed. You may not want to go out! Routinely regarded as among the most romantic and sexiest suites in the world. Check the website to find out why (but this is one place you won't find much reviewed on TripAdvisor).

86 1/XA3
42 ROOMS
TEL · TV
NO KIDS · GF
EXP

✓ ✓ **The Bonham** www.thebonham.com · 0131 226 6050 · **35 Drumsheugh Gardens** Discreet townhouse in quiet West End crescent. Cosmopolitan service and ambience a stroll from Princes St. Much favoured by visiting celebs and writers at the Book Festival. The remaining Edinburgh hotel in the estimable Townhouse collection (Blythswood Square; 465/GLASGOW HOTELS). Rooms are stylish and individual (with some bold colour schemes) - they created The Howard and Channings, below. Great views out back over Dean Village and New Town from floors 2 and up. One room for doggies. No bar.

EAT Elegant dining in calm, spacious restaurant (especially the end table by back window). Chef Michel Bouyer forges a foody Auld Alliance of top Scottish ingredients and French flair. No-nonsense, simple 4/5 choices described in plain English. Popular 'boozy snoozy' lunch at weekends. 4 people, 2 bottles of wine for £88. Daily Market Menu (£20 for 3 courses at TGP) one of the best foody deals in town.

87 1/C2
33 ROOMS
TEL · TV
NO PETS
EXP

✓✓ **Tigerlily** www.tigerlilyedinburgh.co.uk · 0131 225 5005 · **125 George Street** Edinburgh's designtastic hotel on style boulevard by Montpellier Group who have Rick's nearby which has cheaper rooms (99/INDIVID-UAL HOTELS). This surprisingly large hotel sits atop the never-other-than-rammed Tigerlily bar and restaurant. Rooms uniquely different but in the contemporary/calm house style. Various categories up to the Georgian Suites. Most have walk-in showers; all have cool touches. Probably the most fashionista in town but you pay to be this close to the pulse. Downstairs in the basement is the nightclub Lulu: guests have complementary admission.
EAT Fair to say food ain't the main event – the people are – but it's fun and fast and probably better than it has to be. Big room, big atmosphere, some quiet corners and a great little smoking terrace. Excellent service!

88 1/D3
69 ROOMS
TEL · TV
NO PETS
ATMOS
EXP

✓ **The Scotsman** www.thescotsmanhotel.co.uk · 0131 556 5565 · **North Bridge** Deluxe boutique hotel (Eton Hotels group) in landmark building (the old offices of *The Scotsman* newspaper group) converted into chic, highly individual accommodation with impressive original features – stained glass, panelling and newspaper nostalgia (rooms are studys, editors' rooms, etc) and some modern touches, eg privacy locker in all rooms. Labyrinthine lay-out (stairs and firedoors everywhere) and slow lifts apart, this is the convenient hotel in mid-town, if feeling slightly in need of TLC now with dining confined to the nevertheless buzzy North Bridge brasserie. Spa below has a beautiful, low-lit, steel pool, gym and treatments.

89 1/C4
136 ROOMS
TEL · TV
EXP

✓ **Hotel Missoni** www.hotelmissoni.com · 0131 240 1666 · **1 George IV Bridge** Converted from an old eyesore council building and opened summer '09, this is the first Missoni hotel in the UK, the design statement made from the start: all Italian retro and moderno, and either you like that stuff or you don't. From the jaggedy-kilted doorman to the enormous rooms, 'The Look' is everywhere: 'Missoni', 'Maggiori' and the 5th-floor suites, categories determined by size and view. All have complementary mini-bar. It's on a busy corner of the Royal Mile with its tourist tide, but rooms are quiet. Cucina is rather better than Pizza Express slotted into the same building (in fact it's very good) and Ondine adjacent (207/SEAFOOD RESTAURANTS) complete a strong choice for dining. The bar, perhaps a little too cool for its own good, always feels like it landed from Glasgow.
EAT Great Italian food and smart dining at a price. 179/ITALIAN RESTAURANTS.

90 1/D4
75 ROOMS
TEL · TV
NO PETS
MED.EX

✓ **Fraser Suites** www.fraserhospitality.com · 0131 221 7200 · **12-26 St Giles Street** More or less on the Royal Mile in the middle near the cathedral. The international chain (mainly in Asia) of Aparthotels, a slightly misleading name because this is in every sense a hotel (some rooms have basic, others proper kitchen facilities). From 'classic' rooms to apartments, all done to a high contemporary standard. Some great views over Princes St. Bistro. Not on everyone's radar, this is a classy, very central option and not overpriced.

91 1/E2
65 ROOMS
TEL · TV
NO PETS
EXP

✓ **The Glasshouse** www.e-travelguide.info/glasshouse · 0131 525 8200 · **2 Greenside Place** Between Playhouse Theatre and the Omnicentre. It's built above the multiplex (rooms on 2 floors) and the restaurants in the mall below. Surprisingly large and labyrinthine. Part of Eton Hotels, as The Scotsman (88/INDIVIDUAL HOTELS). Main feature is the extensive lawned garden on the roof on to which most rooms look out – patios have reasonable privacy. Great views to Calton Hill and perspective on the city. No restaurant (breakfast in room or The Observatory); honesty bar. The Mall below is a disappointment; the restaurants all High St staples but guests can use Virgin Active health facilities and spa (including 25m pool); £10 per 24 hours.

92 1/XA3
29 ROOMS
TEL · TV
NO PETS
EXP

✓ **Edinburgh Residence** www.theedinburghresidence.com · 0131 226 3380 · **7 Rothesay Terrace** Your home in the city on an extravagant scale. 3 Victorian townhouses have been joined into an elegant apartment hotel once owned by the outstanding Townhouse Group along with The Howard and The Bonham (above). The Residence now has a restaurant for lunch and dinner though breakfast is set out in your room and there is 24-hour and concièrge room service. A discreet and distinctive stopover in 3 different levels of suite. Big bathrooms, views of Dean Village. Drawing room if you're feeling lonely in this quiet West End retreat; nightlife and shops are a stroll away.

93 1/C1
18 ROOMS
TEL · TV
NO PETS
NO KIDS
LOTS

✓ **The Howard** www.thehoward.com · 0131 315 2220 · **34 Great King Street** In the heart of the Georgian New Town, 3 townhouses in a splendid street imbued with quiet elegance though only 5 minutes from Princes Street. No bar but restful drawing room. 15 spacious individual rooms, sympatico with architecture and 3 suites downstairs with own entrances for discreet liaisons or just convenience and own drawing room for entertaining. 24-hour room service. Athol restaurant for breakfast or dinner; and a delightful afternoon tea. Cute garden. No leisure facilities. A very Edinburgh accommodation under different ownership now from its creators. We can see if it keeps its cachet!

94 1/E4
78 ROOMS
TEL · TV
NO PETS
MED.INX

✓ **10 Hill Place** 0131 662 2080 Address as title on surprising little square on Southside near the university, only 100m from busy Nicolson St. Unlikely and surprising departure for the Royal College of Surgeons (412/OTHER ATTRACTIONS) who occupy the nearby imposing neoclassical building complex which fronts onto Nicolson St, and who built this unfussy, utilitarian, very modern hotel that's probably the best-value boutique hotel in town. Masculine, clean elegance in uniform design in 3 categories of rooms depending on size and view (some of Arthur's Seat). Small restaurant and bar. No leisure facilities; limited parking.

95 1/XA3
41 ROOMS
TEL · TV
NO PETS
MED.EX

Channings www.townhousecompany.com · 0131 315 2226 · **South Learmonth Gardens** Parallel to Queensferry Rd after Dean Bridge. Tasteful alternative to big-chain hospitality. 5 period townhouses joined to form a quietly elegant West End hotel. Efficient and individual service including 24-hour room service. Great views from top-floor rooms. Top Rooms: The Shackleton Suites – 5 on the top floor with great views and fabulous bathrooms. The polar explorer once lived here and pictures of his expedition adorn the walls. Restaurant and bar downstairs. No leisure facilities (there's a relationship with Westwood's Gym, some distance away). Still a discerning and discreet corner of the West End.

96 1/A3
12 ROOMS
TEL · TV
NO PETS
NO KIDS
MED.EX

The Rutland Hotel www.therutlandhotel.com · 0131 229 3402 ·
1 Rutland Street Corner at the West End of Princes St. Opposite (in every respect) to the staid old Cally (the landmark Caledonian Hotel; 74/MAJOR HOTELS). This brash and boldly Baroque arriviste is designed from top to (probably black) painted toe and if you like shiny modern chic, this is for you. Rooms individual but all on-message, some views; no lift. Buzzy street-level bar.
EAT Wrap-around first-floor restaurant with great city perspective and seriously sourced Scottish-centric menu which has won plaudits and is busy for lunch and dinner.

97 1/B3
18 ROOMS
TEL · TV
NO PETS
NO KIDS
MED.EX

Le Monde www.lemondehotel.co.uk · 0131 270 3900 · 16 George Street Central boutique hotel on Edinburgh's emerging designer-dressed street. Part of megabar/restaurant all themed on the world on our doorstep. Individual rooms are named after foreign cities and designed accordingly: Havana, Rome, Miami – Dublin one of the quieter ones. Serious attention to detail and very rock 'n' roll. All a tad OTT (the bar not the coolest in town) but the theme does work and beds/bathrooms/facilities would suit young professionals thrusting.

98 1/A3
31 ROOMS
TEL · TV
NO PETS
NO KIDS
MED.INX

The Hudson Hotel 0131 247 7000 · 9-11 Hope Street Near corner of Charlotte Sq. Paying passing homage to North America or more specifically NYC, this very urban boutique-style bedbox is good value with often good walk-in rates. Café-bar on street level has never attracted the crowds of nearby George St but is a convenient rendezvous. Busy night club and handy pick-up joint in basement open till 3am Fri/Sat but noise does not intrude on higher floors.

99 1/B2
10 ROOMS
TEL · TV
NO PETS
NO KIDS
MED.EX

Rick's www.ricksedinburgh.co.uk · 0131 622 7800 · 55 Frederick Street Very city centre hotel and bar/restaurant in a downtown location a stone's throw from George St. By same people who have indigo (yard), a buzzing bistro in the West End and their other stylee hotel, Tigerlily (87/BEST HOTELS). Restaurant (166/GASTROPUBS) has (loud) contemporary dining. Rooms through the bar and upstairs are surprisingly quiet. Modern, urban feel as standard. Book well in advance. Don't let the rooms above the bar thing put you off but get as high as you can! Well, you know what I mean!

Excellent Lodgings

100 1/B2
5 ROOMS
TV
NO PETS
LOTS

One Royal Circus www.oneroyalcircus.com · 0131 625 6669 · House mobile 07771 930816 Address as is in the heart of the New Town at the corner of elegant Circus Place. Mike Gordon's exclusive and sumptuous townhouse is the classiest B&B in town. The guestbook is a rollcall of famous folk. Bookable by the day (weekends 2-day minimum). Reserve by email.

101 1/E2
4 ROOMS
TEL · TV
NO PETS
EXP

21212 www.21212restaurant.co.uk · 0845 22 21212 · 3 Royal Terrace Mainly a restaurant, all lavish and urban and Michelin-starred. 4 rooms up the Georgian staircase (no lift), comfortable and sexy with views to the cruisy gardens opposite and lush, leafy Calton Hill at the back. No leisure facilities to work off your gorgeous dinner (130/FINE DINING) but the bedrooms are made for activities not provided for in a gym.

102 1/XE5
9 ROOMS
TEL · TV
NO PETS · GF
MED.INX

23 Mayfield www.mayfield.co.uk · 0131 667 5806 · 23 Mayfield Gardens On one of the long roads south from the city centre, lined with indifferent hotels, 23 'a boutique guest house stands out'; in fact they were Guest House of the Year 2011 for the AA. Patrons Ross and Kathleen Birnie have aimed for the top, from the underfloor heating, the Indonesian furniture, Roth sound systems in all rooms to their TripAdvisor-celebrated gourmet breakfast with its prodigious choice. They have mountain bikes and are on the absolutely right track.

103 1/XF5
7 ROOMS
TEL · TV
NO PETS · GF
MED.INX

94DR www.94dr.com · 0131 662 9265 · 94 Dalkeith Road As 23 Mayfield (above), this boutique guest house is one of many on a main road south. Once again, this is more than a cut above the rest. Paul Lightfoot and John MacEwan (and the dug) have created a very calm and contemporary home from home here, with great, no-frills attention to detail and an eye to design in everything. Great breakfast, I'm told. Five-star friendly! Some parking.

104 1/XF1
4 ROOMS
NO PETS
CHP

Six Brunton Place www.sixbruntonplace.com · 0131 662 0042 Address as is; actually on London Rd, the busy artery heading east from town, eventually to London. Sue Thompson's tasteful townhouse (once the home of the guy who started the city's famous One o' Clock Gun) is consistently at the top of B&B lists for its spacious, calm interiors, walls filled with pleasing art, bathrooms with very mod cons and the considerate attention of its owner. A bit of a walk to the town centre but calm respite when you get home. The garden room is superb.

105 1/B4
2 ROOMS
TV
CHP

2b Cambridge Street 0131 478 0005 Address as is, near the Usher Hall, Traverse Theatre and the West End. Only 2 rooms, so you'll be lucky, but Erlend and Helene Clouston's very individual and beautiful B&B clearly deserves a mention here. A calm in any storm: zen-like garden, tea by the fire, particular hospitality. Media bods and creatives feel comfortable here.

106 1/XE5
8 ROOMS
TEL · TV
NO PETS · GF
MED.INX

Southside www.southsideguesthouse.co.uk · 0131 668 4422 · 8 Newington Road On main street in Southside where indifferent hotels and guesthouses stretch halfway to Dalkeith, this a surprisingly civilised haven. Attention to decor and detail and excellent breakfast. Nice prints, rugs, books and DVDs. Some traffic noise, but upstairs rooms double-glazed. There are 2 4-poster rooms. Parking nearby.

107 1/XE1
5 ROOMS · TV
GF
CHP

Ardmor House www.ardmorhouse.com · 0131 554 4944 · 74 Pilrig Street Off (and halfway down) Leith Walk with lots of other B&Bs but this the top spot. Individual, contemporary and relaxed. Nice touches like homemade oatcakes and Artisan Roast coffee (275/COFFEE SHOPS). Proprietors also have lovely New Town apartments for short lets. They provide you with their own Best of Edinburgh guide somewhat following mine I think (chaps!).

108 1/D2 — **Queens Guest House** www.queensgh.com · 0131 556 8261 · 43 Queen
13 ROOMS — **Street** Very central – in fact, in the middle of busy, arterial Queen St between
TV — Frederick and Castle Sts. Well appointed, good value and handy for all things mid-
CHP — town. Access as a guest to gorgeous Queen St Gardens is a real plus.

109 1/C1 — **Bouverie B&B** www.edinburghbedandbreakfast.co.uk · 0131 556 5080 ·
4 ROOMS — **9b Scotland Street** Demonstrating the power of a good url, this basement B&B
CHP — in the heart of the New Town (Scotland St no less, as elevated by Alexander McCall
Smith with his series about No. 10) is busy all year but also because Archie and
Cassie Bouverie preside over a comfy, very informal household and you become
part of it. Double basement so some rooms are well subterranean and half not
ensuite. Nice garden.

The Best Economy Hotels

110 1/D4 — ✓ **Ibis** www.ibishotel.com · 0131 240 7000 · **Hunter Square** First in
99 ROOMS — Scotland of the Euro budget chain (one other in Glasgow, 476/TRAVEL
TEL · TV — LODGES). Dead central behind the Tron. Serviceable and efficient. For tourists doing
CHP — the sights, this is the best bedbox for location but it's crowded and a bit crazy outside (stag party central). Rates vary hugely.

111 1/XE5 — **Borough Hotel** www.theboroughhotel.com · 0131 668 2255 · **42 Cause-**
11 ROOMS — **wayside** Their claim to be a small luxury hotel is pushing it a little, though for the
TEL · TV — price and compared with even top-end guest houses in this town, this designery
NO PETS — (by Ben Kelly, of the legendary Hacienda) box of rooms above the bar/restaurant is
NO KIDS — a bit of a deal. On the Southside near the Meadows so downwind of 'the action'
CHP — but the bar itself has sports, quiz and poker nights and a good sound track.
Restaurant better than any other option on this page by far (LO 9.30pm, bar 1am).

112 1/E2 — **Holiday Inn Express** www.hieedinburgh.co.uk · 0131 558 2300/0800
160 ROOMS — 434040 · **16 Picardy Place & 300 Cowgate** ·0131 524 8400 The first is a not
TEL · TV — unpleasant conversion of several New Town houses in an exceptionally convenient
NO PETS — location opposite the Playhouse Theatre. Rooms all same standard (twin or
MED.INX — double). Bar, no restaurant but area awash with options. This is a very clever
Holiday Inn. The Cowgate location, close to night-time action (including stag
nights), is not bad and there are 2 others in town.

113 1/C5 — **Novotel Edinburgh Centre** www.novotel.com · 0131 656 3500 ·
180 ROOMS — **80 Lauriston Place** New-build near Tollcross and the university. No charm but
TEL · TV — functional and reasonably modern. Small pool, bar and contemporary-like brasserie.
NO PETS — Good beds and facilities. But Premier Travel Inn adjacent is half the price (see
MED.INX — below). There's another Novotel at Edinburgh Park near the airport.

114 1/C5 — **Premier Travel Inn Chain** www.premiertravelinn.co.uk 7 (and counting) in
1/XA4 — Edinburgh area. All much of a less-ness. Most handy for Old Town is at 82
1/XE1 — Lauriston Place (0870 990 6610) near university. 1 Morrison Link (0870 238 3319)
CHP — is near Haymarket Station. The best one in Newhaven/Leith (taxi/bus away from
town) (08701 977 093) is near the bars and restaurants of Leith with Loch Fyne
(215/SEAFOOD) adjacent and David Lloyd health club (helpfully not available to
guests). 30 rooms have surprising sea and sunset views. Other Inns are suburban.

The Best Hostels

115 1/XE1
71 ROOMS
24 HOURS
CHP

✔ ✔ **SY Edinburgh Central** www.syha.org.uk · 0131 524 2090 · **9 Haddington Place** Central it is in a good part of town though perhaps unobvious to casual visitors, ie it's not in the Old Town area. Haddington Pl is part of Leith Walk (corner of Annandale St) near theatres/bars/restaurants and gay quarter and on way to Leith. Converted from office block with café, internet and every hostel facility. Clean, efficient; rooms from singles to family 4-8 beds. Run by the Scottish Youth Hostels Association.

116 1/E4
624 BEDS
24 HOURS
CHP

✔ ✔ **Smartcity Hostels** 0870 892 3000 · **50 Blackfriars Street** Building is enormous and also opens on to Cowgate. £10 million made this place as hotel-like as you get without completely losing the hostel vibe. Self-service restaurant, extensive bar, facilities including roof terrace (with heaters and sometimes BBQ), self-catering kitchens and lots of cool things like mobile-phone-charging boxes, snooker tables and internet zones; and hordes of staying-up/out-late people. Massive number of rooms round the interior courtyard, varying from 2-12 occupancy. Students stay here in term time. Good location and well smart.

117 1/C4
24 HOURS
CHP

✔ **Royal Mile Backpackers** www.royalmilebackpackers.com · 0131 557 6120 · **105 High Street** On the Royal Mile, near the Cowgate with its late-night bars. Ideal central cheap 24-hour crash-out dormitory accommodation with all the facilities itinerant youth on a budget might look for. The original hostel in the group, The **High Street Hostel**, 8 Blackfriars St (0131 557 3984) is just across the street, and The **Castle Rock**, 15 Johnston Terrace (0131 225 9666) at the top of the Royal Mile in the old Council Environmental Health HQ is huge (190 beds in various dorms; 'private' rooms book up fast) and some great views across the Grassmarket or to the castle which is just over there. Same folk also have hostels in Fort William, Inverness, Oban, Pitlochry and Skye, and Mac Backpacker tours so expect to be sold a trip to the Highlands.

118 1/XB3
CHP

✔ **Argyle Backpackers Hotel** www.sol.co.uk/a/argyle · 0131 667 9991 · **14 Argyle Place** Quiet area though in Marchmont there are great bars eg the Earl of Marchmont (393/COOL BARS) and interesting shops nearby. 1km to centre across the Meadows (not advised for women at night). This is a bit like living in a student flat and there are tenements full of them all around. But it's homely with 2 kitchens, internet, lounge, conservatory and garden. Own key. They have mountain bikes.

119 1/D3
160 BEDS
NO PETS
CHP

✔ **St Christopher Inn** www.st-christophers.co.uk · 0207 407 1856 · **9-13 Market Street** Couldn't be handier for the station or city centre. This (with branches in London and other Euro cultural cities) a hostel rather than hotel with bunk rooms though there are single and double rooms. As always, price depends on number sharing. Belushi's café-bar on ground floor open till 1am (food 10.30pm). A very central option, better than most other hostels (facilities are ensuite) but not so cheap.

120 1/C4
196 BEDS
CHP

Art Roch Hostel www.artrochhostel.com · 0131 228 9981 · **2 West Port** At the corner of the Grassmarket. A recent conversion of an old, characterful building below the Art College on the Grassmarket where many stags and also hen parties run. Some private (2) rooms and dorms up to 18/24. Mix 'n' match furniture café/lounge where you can mix 'n' match too 24/7.

The Best Hotels Outside Town

✓ ✓ **Greywalls** www.greywalls.co.uk · 01620 842144 · Gullane In splendid gardens 36km east of Edinburgh, this is the country-house hotel in the region, a mecca for golfers and foodies. Report: 818/LOTHIAN HOTELS.
EAT An Albert Roux suite of dining rooms. Bar meals too; and afternoon tea.

121 10/P25
16 ROOMS
TEL · TV
NO PETS
EXP

✓ ✓ **Champany Inn** www.champany.com · 01506 834532 · near Linlithgow On A904, 3km Linlithgow on road to Forth Road Bridge and South Queensferry. Exemplary restaurant with rooms, some overlooking the garden. Legendary steaks and seafood; ambience and service. Breakfast in cosy dining kitchen is excellent (nice bacon, of course!). Extraordinary wine list and cellar shop for take home (daily 12-10pm). But veggies best not to venture here.
EAT Superb. 257/BURGERS & STEAKS.

122 10/P25
132 ROOMS
TEL · TV
NO PETS
MED.EX

✓ ✓ **Dakota** www.dakotahotels.co.uk · 0870 423 4293 · South Queensferry From the people who brought us the Malmaisons and before that, 1 Devonshire Gardens (now Hotel du Vin; 464/GLASGOW HOTELS), a bold concept, from the black metropolis-block design statement to the paean-to-travel theme inside. On the edge of South Queensferry but on main carriageway north from Edinburgh by the Forth Road Bridge. It's all quite brilliant, a designer (Amanda Rosa) world away from anonymous others of the ilk. Rooms are calm and whisper 'understated chic'. The Grill restaurant a destination in itself (guests should book when they make a room reservation). Mr McCulloch's vision and restless energy: unceasing! See also 483/HOTELS OUTSIDE GLASGOW.
EAT Brasserie-type daily-changing menu in setting reminiscent of a Malmaison. Seafood, including 3 varieties of oyster. A destination restaurant.

123 10/P25
83 ROOMS
TEL · TV
NO PETS
MED.EX

✓ ✓ **Norton House** www.handpickedhotels.co.uk · 0131 333 1275 · Ingliston Off A8 near the airport, 10km west of city centre. Victorian country house in 55 acres of greenery, surprisingly woody and pastoral so close to city. Highly regarded Hand-Picked Hotel group. 'Executive' rooms have countryside views. Labyrinthine layout with good conference/function facilities. Brasserie and small internal restaurant. Good contemporary (the bedrooms) and traditional (public rooms) mix. Some rooms quite swish. Gorgeous new spa with pool etc.

124 10/Q25
83 ROOMS
TEL · TV
MED.INX

✓ **Carberry Tower** Musselburgh · www.carberrytower.com · 0131 665 3135 Set in extensive, well-kept grounds 3km south of Musselburgh and less than 30 minutes from the city centre, this is a historic house (parts date back to the 15th century) in fabulous grounds of 35 acres notable for their splendid diversity of trees (including an avenue of redwoods). Big range also of accommodation in the house (with good suites), an annexe and lodges. Stained glass and turret rooms and a chapel over-by, this is a good-value, not-on-everybody's-radar retreat from the city.

125 10/P25
18 ROOMS
TEL · TV
NO PETS
MED.INX

✓ **Orocco Pier** www.oroccopier.co.uk · 0131 331 1298 · Main Street, South Queensferry A buzzy restaurant and boutique-style hotel, in often tourist-thronged South Q with great views of the Forth and the bridge (401/MAIN ATTRACTIONS). From Edinburgh take first turnoff from dual carriageway. Formerly the Queensferry Arms, but a substantial makeover has created a cool bistro and contemporary rooms above and beside (not all have views). Food in bar, restaurant or terrace (LO 10pm). Event programme and they do conferences, weddings, etc. Parking tricky, but a great outside-town option.
EAT Pub/bistro/restaurant options; and the bridge.

The Best Fine-Dining Restaurants

126 1/XE1
>£35

✓ ✓+ **Martin Wishart** www.martin-wishart.co.uk · 0131 553 3557 · 54 The Shore Discreet waterside frontage for what in my view is still Edinburgh's most notable fine-dining restaurant and the standard by which others in Edinburgh and Glasgow can be judged. Room designed on simple lines; uncomplicated menu and wine list (though not a lot in lower price ranges). Michelin-star chef Martin; reputation precedes and raises expectations, but preparation, cooking and presentation are demonstrably a cut above the rest. Great vegetarian menu. Unobtrusive service. A la carte and tasting menus reliably superb. Martin has a cook school round the corner, is executive chef at Cameron House, Loch Lomond (482/HOTELS OUTSIDE GLASGOW) and in summer 2011 opened The Honours, an uptown brasserie (136/BISTROS). I rarely give 2 ticks-plus but this is a restaurant most definitely in the UK forefront. Lunch Tue-Fri, Dinner Tue-Sat. LO 9.30pm.

127 1/D3
>£35

✓ ✓ **Number One Princes Street** www.thebalmoralhotel.com · 0131 556 2414 Though not many Edinburgers venture for a night on the town below stairs at the Balmoral, the landmark hotel they pass every day on Princes St, they're missing one of the best dining experiences in foodtown. Subterranean opulence with only opaque light from the windows on Waverley Steps. The calm, cosmopolitan ambience perfectly complements Craig Sandle's confident cuisine. Michelin starred since 2003. A la carte and tasting menus with vegetarian option, from canapés to petits fours with many mmm... moments. Attentive, not too fussing-over-you staff: knowledgeable sommelier and 'cheesellier' can talk you through the impressive list (especially French) and board (also especially French). 7 days. Dinner only LO 9.45pm. **Hadrian's Brasserie,** a lounge at street level (grills and light choices among the mains), complements well. Lunch; LO 9.30pm.

128 1/B4
>£35

✓ ✓ **Castle Terrace** 0131 229 1222 · 33 Castle Terrace Near the Usher Hall, Lyceum and Traverse Theatre. New in 2010, chef-patron Dominic Jack's smart city restaurant quickly established itself on the foody map in a location which had perhaps never quite worked. The fact that it did is due to the flair of the chef under the aegis of Tom Kitchin and eponymous Michelin-starred restaurant in Leith (see below), the no-nonsense approach and the very good dinner there is to be had here (and excellent-value lunches). Room fresh and modern, like the food. Michelin star 2012.

129 1/XE1
>£35

✓ ✓ **The Kitchin** www.thekitchin.com · 0131 555 1755 · 78 Commercial Quay, Leith In the row of restaurants in front of the Scottish government offices, Tom Kitchin's brilliant, busy kitchen looks out on the calm, urbane restaurant which has received much attention and many awards since it opened in '06, including an early Michelin star. Though Tom is a TV chef fixture on the foodfest circuit, he seems omnipresent in the kitchen keeping an eye on us as well as what we eat. Good-value lunch menu (set and à la carte), tasting (6-course) and 'celebration of the season' menus in the evening; so lots of choice but all driven by impeccable and serious sourcing of local and market ingredients. He calls it *From Nature to Plate* (also his cookbook title). Not a large room, you do get lots of attention. Wine list as you would expect, superb and the sommelier will guide you through it (many suggestions already on the menu). In UK terms this is great value at this standard. Lunch and dinner. LO 10pm. Closed Sun/Mon.

130 1/E2
>£35

✓ **21212** www.21212restaurant.co.uk · 0845 22 21212 · 3 Royal Terrace Paul and Katie Kitching's beautiful Michelin-starred restaurant in an elegant townhouse backing on to Calton Hill. Name describes the appealing and very workable format of 2 choices for starters, mains and puds with a soupçon of soup (no choice) and a cheese plate in between (the cheese rarely Scottish, all in tip-top condition). Food is playful and innovative, mixing surprise ingredients prepared by a small army of chefs in the shiny kitchen at the end of the sexily attired dining room. Good-value wine list. This Michelin in the right hands. 181/INDIVIDUAL HOTELS.

131 1/XE1
>£35

✓ **Plumed Horse** 0131 554 5556 · 50 Henderson Street In a backstreet location between Great Junction St and The Shore, this is nevertheless on a corner of the Michelin-starred-restaurant triangle of Leith and a destination for the inspired, understated cookery of the inimitable Tony Borthwick. Straight-talking in every sense, the room, the menu and the man himself are without the flourishes that can add an unwelcome faux brilliance to many a Michelin star. So, expect unfussy service, easy-to-tackle à la carte and tasting menus and some of the best-value fine-dining (and wine list including many halves) in this town. Lunch and LO 9pm. Tue-Sat.

132 1/D2
>£35

✓ **Mark Greenaway** www.12picardyplace.com · 0131 557 0952 · 12 Picardy Place Near the Playhouse Theatre. A room in a townhouse hosts a new restaurant and kid on the block that received unanimous plaudits from food critics when it opened 2011. Mark Greenaway the chef/patron in question presents a straightforward à la carte menu and great-value wine list with great appeal and aplomb; at TGP awards and rewards await. Tue-Sat, lunch and dinner.

133 1/D4
>£35

✓ **The Tower** www.tower-restaurant.co.uk · 0131 225 3003 · Chambers Street At George IV Bridge above the Museum of Scotland. Restaurant supremo James Thomson's celebrated and celebrity-strewn restaurant atop the distinctive tower on the corner of the sandstone museum building benefits from the much-admired grand design and detail of Gordon Benson's architectural vision. The long, narrow room with terrace tables and banquettes is a sophisticated urban setting, looking over Edinburgh rooftops to the castle. Kitchens far below in 'Prehistoric Scotland', but food everything one would expect – Scottish slant on modern British, eg a classic Waldorf salad – and the menu simple and to the point. Almost faultless efficiency. There's also Tea at the Tower with all the niceties (and champagne if you wish), 3-5pm. Lunch and dinner LO 11pm. 7 days.

134 1/C4
ATMOS
>£35

✓ **The Witchery** www.thewitchery.com · 0131 225 5613 · Castlehill At the top of the Royal Mile where the tourists throng, maybe unaware that this is the city's most stylishly atmospheric restaurant with more awards than famous names in the guest book (and there are a lot). In 2 salons, the upper more 'witchery' and the 'secret garden' downstairs, a converted school playground, James Thomson has created a more spacious ambience for the (same) elegant Scottish menu. Locals on a treat, many regulars and visiting celebs pack this place out, and although they efficiently turn round the tables, you should book. The Witchery by the Castle hotel encapsulates this remarkable and indulgent ambience (85/INDIVIDUAL HOTELS). The wine list is exceptional, the atmosphere *sans pareil*. Lunch and dinner. LO a very civilised 11.30pm. The theatre supper menu (5.30-6.30pm) at £15 is sensibly repeated from 10.30-11.30pm. See 300/LATE-NIGHT RESTAURANTS.

135 1/XE5
ATMOS
>£35

✓ **Rhubarb @ Prestonfield** www.prestonfield.com · 0131 668 3346 A little out of town but the restaurant of fabulous Prestonfield (83/INDIVIDUAL HOTELS) makes 3 in a row of great restaurants for James Thomson (see above). And as above it's the whole dining experience rather than Michelin-minded menus that drives their success. Rhubarb is the most gorgeously decadent in opulent Regency rooms at the heart of the hotel; the public rooms adjacent for before and après are superb, especially the upstairs drawing rooms. An evening of rich romance awaits. And you get your (rhubarb) desserts.

The Best Bistros & Brasseries

136 1/B2
£25-35

✓ ✓ **The Honours** www.martin-wishart.co.uk · 0131 225 2515 · 58a Castle Street There was much anticipation when following the runaway success of the restaurant in Leith (126/FINE DINING) and then Loch Lomond (488/OUTSIDE GLASGOW), Martin Wishart opened this brasserie summer '11 on the site of Edinburgh's long-ago top Italian restaurant and others which didn't last. The completely remodelled, loudly contemporary space was full from the start which led to much muttering about the service among the muttering classes. Nevertheless the classic, brazz menu (both in content and presentation) with grill section, Cornish oysters (because they were the best in focus tasting), a prix-fixe lunch and dinner (Tue-Fri) and the wicked ice-cream sundaes from a strong team headed by Paul Tumburrini meant we had to cajole and queue for a table. And we still do. Long lunch and LO 10.30pm, Sun till 4.30. Closed Mon.

137 1/D2
£25-35
L

✓ ✓ **Forth Floor, Harvey Nichols** www.harveynichols.com · 0131 524 8350 · St Andrews Square On the fourth, the foody floor: the Deli, Yo Sushi and the Chocolate Lounge with champagne and cake on the conveyor. Brasserie and more expensive (but similar) Modern British comfort-food menus either side of the bar. Estimable chef Stuart Muir with HN since it opened. Nice just to come for cocktails and the view! Lunch 7 days, dinner Tue-Sat LO 10.30pm.

138 1/C2
ATMOS
£15-25

✓ ✓ **The Dogs** www.thedogsonline.co.uk · 0131 220 1208 · 110 Hanover Street Upstairs on busy Hanover St, the first of the Dog pack of brusquely charming, incredibly thin and inspired patron Dave Ramsden. Lofty, busy main and smaller back room always rammed (and you are rammed). Old-fashioned, simple, robust food at giveaway prices. Fidget Pie, Stargazy Pie, Devilled Ox Liver and Lardy Chips but good vegetarian too. Great deal on wine. It works! 7 days lunch and LO 10pm (bar 11pm). We loved it a lot so then came **Amore Dogs** downstairs (181/ITALIAN RESTAURANTS), then the others.

139 1/C2
£15-25

✓ ✓ **Urban Angel** www.urban-angel.co.uk · 0131 225 6215 · 121 Hanover Street & 0131 556 6323 · 1 Forth Street In a basement near Queen St and the East Village version. Gilli Macpherson's understated but well judged café-restaurants are perfectly of their time and place. Contemporary, relaxed, great value and, not surprisingly, busy and buzzing. Organic where sensible, Fair-trade and free-range; conscientiously sourced. Food is wholesome British but with a light touch and a great pastry chef, Hubert Lamort, supplying both places. Takeaway counter and great Sunday brunch rendezvous (307/SUNDAY BREAKFAST). 7 days breakfast, lunch and dinner. LO 9.45pm (Sun 5pm).

140 1/D4
ATMOS
£15-25

✓ ✓ **The Outsider** 0131 226 3131 · 15 George IV Bridge The downtown dining room of The Apartment (below). I'm not going to say a thing about its notoriously rude owner Malcolm Innes 'cos he's always gadding about somewhere else and the staff here are gorgeous and super-helpful. Minimalist design with surprising view of the castle; and art! Innovative menu contrasts – the signature beetroot coleslaw in pitta bread is a must! Big helpings, pretty people. We go here a lot. 7 days, lunch and LO 10.30pm.

141 1/B3
£25-35
>£35

✓ **Oloroso** www.oloroso.co.uk · 0131 226 7614 · 33 Castle Street Unassuming entrance and lift to this rooftop restaurant renowned for its terrace with views of the castle, the New Town and Fife. Bar snacks are a great deal – can't go wrong with 'curry of the day'. Chef/prop Tony Singh excels especially with the meatier dishes and in the main dining room, light and spacious and spilling on to the terrace, steaks are rightly popular though there are many imaginative dishes with fish. It's still a fashionable, foody room at the top. Some Indo interest. Excellent for evening cocktails and a top private dining space. Lunch and dinner LO 10pm. 7 days. Bar till 1am.

142 1/XA4
£15-25

✓ **First Coast** www.first-coast.co.uk · 0131 313 4404 · **99 Dalry Road** Named after a place in the far north where chef/patron Hector McRae used to go on his holidays, this cool urban restaurant is also on the edge of the visited world – well, Dalry Rd. Superb value and full of integrity. Straight-talking menu with no bamboozling choices and they make everything including bread. First Coast would grace any neighbourhood. Mon-Sat lunch and LO 10.30pm.

143 1/E4
£15-25

✓ **Spoon** www.spooncafebistro.co.uk · 0131 557 4567 · **6a Nicolson Street** Upstairs opposite the Festival Theatre whose audiences it conveniently and ably serves. *The List Food Guide* calls it 'quirky', like a loft apartment, and it is: individualist and spacious with interesting furniture and lighting. After some josh with management and on further consideration, yes the lighting works; in fact, it all works. Food similarly retro, no pretence and good value. A reliable redoubt on the unlovely Bridges/Nicolson St rat run. 10am-10pm. Closed Sun.

144 1/B2
£15-25

✓ **Iris** www.irisedinburgh.co.uk · 0131 220 2111 · **47 Thistle Street** In a street of many bistros, those that know head for Iris. Not immediately obvious perhaps, but expect elegant, modern rooms, well judged, light and Modern British menu and excellent service. Sun 'Brekkies'. 7 days lunch and LO 10pm.

145 1/XE5
£15-25

✓ **Home Bistro** 0131 667 7010 · **41 West Nicolson Street** I once described it at 'comfort food heaven' and they put it in the window so I can't (or shan't) demur. Tiny living-room bistro on Southside near the university. Rowland Thomson and chef Richard Logan's formula of simple, reassuring modern and traditional British – well, Scottish – grub. Home-made everything from bread to bread-and-butter pudding. Lovely kipper pâté, scrummy cottage pie! Great value and precious simplicity. Lunch and dinner Wed-Sat.

146 1/A1
£15-25

✓ **Redwood** www.redwood-restaurant.co.uk · 0131 225 8342 · **33 St Stephen Street** Much-loved, basement bistro in the middle of once 'trendy' St Stephen St at the heart of Stockbridge. Annette Spraghe's take on Californian cuisine means lovely, light food with lots going on the plate. Simple (ie 3/4 starters, mains, puds from a tiny kitchen) seasonal menu, great salads; a vegetarian choice. A wee gem and we do mean 'wee', so best book. Dinner Wed-Sat. LO 9.30pm.

147 1/XB5
£15-25

✓ **The Apartment** 0131 228 6456 · **7 Barclay Place** The first of Malcolm Innes's hugely popular contemporary eating-out experiences (see also The Outsider, above) is a Bruntsfield food destination and fixture but it stays fresh, and well... we always go there too (especially if we're at the Cameo or the King's Theatre): a civilised supper guaranteed. 7 days dinner; LO 11pm. Sat/Sun from 12noon.

148 1/XE1
ATMOS
£25-35

✓ **The Vintners Rooms** www.thevintnersrooms.com · 0131 554 6767 · **The Vaults, 87 Giles Street** Off a courtyard in a Leith backstreet, this long-established bar/restaurant in the vaults (the oldest building in Scotland continuously in use for the same purpose, ie since the 15th century) offers one of the most atmospheric dinners in town. As you would expect, a fantastic wine list (especially Barolos and Tuscans) but ubiquitous maître d' Silvio Praino has also assembled a staggering (1500 and counting) collection of whiskies, all available by the glass. Food in bar (also at lunch) and more formally in the 18th-century dining room lit by candlelight. Lunch and LO 9.45pm. Bar 11/12midnight. Closed Sun/Mon.

149 1/B5
£15-25
✓ **Bia Bistrot** 0131 452 8453 · 19 Colinton Road In a small strip of shops at the beginning of Colinton Rd near Holy Corner, a spot that has seen many caffs come and go. This, the Irish (Roisin) and French (Matthias) Llorentes's combination of Bia (Irish for food) and Bistrot (the authentic French bistro) works well. The room ain't decor-tastic but it's unpretentious and so is the straight-talking, carefully sourced menu. These guys are cooking for Scotland and we love it the more because it's great value. Wines by the estimable Villeneuve, ice cream by La Cerise which is next door to my office in Leith so gets a mention here. BB won *The List* Newcomer of the Year award 2011. Tue-Sat lunch and LO 10pm.

150 1/XB5
£25-35
✓ **Sweet Melinda's** www.sweetmelindas.co.uk · 0131 229 7953 · 11 Roseneath Street This entry has not changed since the last edition: reassuringly, it's still correct. Owner-chef Kevin O'Connor's living-room restaurant in deepest Marchmont catering for the neighbourhood (not short of a bob) clientele but loved across the city. Mainly fish (from estimable Eddie's over the road), but 1 meat and 1 vegetarian. Everything made from scratch. Great touches, good wines and fizz. Lunch (not Mon) and LO 10pm. Closed Sun. BYO Tue £3.

151 1/E3
£25-35
✓ **Wedgwood** www.wedgwoodtherestaurant.co.uk · 0131 558 8737 · 267 Canongate Just below St Mary's St. The compact, all-present-and-correct Old Town bistro of Paul Wedgwood. Creative, Modern Scottish cookery with a big, loyal following and excellent lunch deals. 7 days lunch and dinner, LO 10pm.

152 1/D4
>£35
✓ **Angels With Bagpipes** www.angelswithbagpipes.co.uk · 0131 220 1111 343 High Street In the Royal Mile opposite the cathedral from which the slightly daft name derives – somewhere inside there's a wooden angel cradling the said bagpipe. No matter, Marina Crolla's stylish, contemporary bistro is no' daft at all. Space stretched but there's plenty of it when you count the great Old Town patio downstairs. Paul Whitecross's Modern British menus with Italian pitch and Scottish produce. Way better (but a tad more pricey) than most on the Mile.

153 1/E3
£15-25
Monteith's www.monteithsbar.co.uk · 0131 557 0330 · 57 High Street Down a fairy-lit close at the tartan-clad centre of the Royal Mile, a cool, woody and clubby bar/restaurant (it's like a library) with great food, drinkies (including cocktails) and smart, sexy service. The gastropub-style menu is quite meaty. Lunch goes through to 5pm then à la carte. 7 days 12noon-LO 10/10.30pm. Bar 1am.

154 1/D5
£25-35
Bistro du Vin www.hotelduvin.com · 0131 247 4900 · 11 Bristo Place Restaurant of the Hotel du Vin (84/BOUTIQUE HOTELS), entered through the sprawling and tightly fitting courtyard and reception. Though a chain, there's nothing uniform in sight or on the menu which offers classic French bistro fare. Somehow neither the room nor the food have quite lived up to expectation but the all-round experience is agréable and the wine list, with impressive sommellier support, is excellent. 7 days lunch and LO 10.30pm.

155 1/A1
£15-25
Stockbridge Restaurant 0131 226 6766 · 54 St Stephen Street Basement on boho-chic street and one of the New Town's reliable bistros, with carefully sourced ingredients served in classic Modern British dishes. Linen tablecloths, intimate lighting; good à deux. Often 'offers', eg BYOB on Sun. Dinner Tue-Sun.

156 1/E5
£15-25
Pink Olive www.ilovepinkolive.co.uk · 0131 662 4493 · 55-57 West Nicolson Street Corner of West Nicolson St and the university whence comes much of the clientele. Airy, clean lines, bistro candlelit at night. Simple, not fussed and Steven Todd's scrumptious Modern Scottish food with good vegetarian choice. Yum! ice cream! Lunch and LO 9.30/10.30. Sun 10.30-4pm. Closed Mon.

Gastropubs

157 1/XB5 ✓ **The Canny Man's** 0131 447 1484 · 237 **Morningside Road** Aka The
ATMOS Volunteer Arms on the A702 via Tollcross, 7km from centre. Idiosyncratic
£15-25 renowned eaterie with a certain hauteur and a labyrinth of atmospheric rooms; a
true, original gastropub. Carries a complement of malts as long as your arm and a
serious wine list. Smorrebrod (soup, some seafood) lunches (12noon-3pm) and
evenings (6.30-9.30pm). There's a complementary buffet 5-6.30pm. No loonies or
undesirables welcome nor mobile phones, cameras or backpackers, so they have
their rules but this is a very civilised pub of good taste with a lovely patio/garden.
Till 11pm Sun-Thu, 1am Fri, 12midnight Sat. 357/REAL-ALE PUBS. No credit cards.

158 1/D1 ✓ **The Magnum** 0131 557 4366 · 1 **Albany Street** Since Chris Graham took
£15-25 over this corner pub in the east New Town, it's become a damned good gastropub. It's in my 'hood so it's a personal favourite. Bar and raised dining area. Bar
menu available in both has the pub staples (excellent tempura fish 'n' chips) and à
la carte. Simple, casual dining and great staff. 7 days lunch and LO 10.30pm; bar till
11.30pm (12.30am weekends).

159 1/XE1 ✓ **The Shore** www.theshore.biz · 0131 553 5080 · 3 **The Shore, Leith**
ATMOS Long established as a gastropub; an *StB* favourite. This is where I went with
£15-25 the people from Collins to seal the deal on this book. Run by people from Fishers
next door (208/BEST SEAFOOD) with a similar sympatico ambience but more pubby,
less fishy. Real fire and large windows looking out to the quayside, strewn with
bods on summer nights coz when it's sunny we head to The Shore (not of course
in rainy '11). Modern British menu in cosy-in-winter, woody bar (selective live music
Tue-Thu, Sun) or quieter restaurant. 7 days lunch and LO 10pm, bar till 12midnight.

160 1/XE1 ✓ **King's Wark** 0131 554 9260 · 36 **The Shore** On the corner of Bernard St.
£15-25 Woody, candlelit, stone-walled and comfortable – a classic gastropub, the
emphasis on the food. Bar and bistro dining room. Pub-food classics and more
adventurous evening menu. Though traditional and dark rather than pale, light and
modern, this has long been one of the best bets in Leith. It has been Scottish
Gastropub of the Year. Scottish slant on the big menu from a small kitchen, with
excellent fish including their famous beer-batter and chips. Lunch and LO 9.45pm.
Bar open to 11pm, 12midnight Fri-Sat.

161 1/XA5 ✓ **Caley Sample Room** www.thecaleysampleroom.co.uk · 0131 337 7204 ·
£15-25 58 **Angle Park Terrace** The CSR sells all the expected Caledonian real ales
from nearby brewery and a couple of guests besides. Run by the people who have
the Cambridge Bar (below) and Wannaburger (261/BURGERS) so great burgers and
steaks but eclectic and full menu with daily specials. Nice, woody ambience.
Loadsa wine by the glass. Out-of-the-way location but this is *the* west-of-the-city
destination for great pub grub. A little live music! 7 days LO 9pm, 10pm Fri/Sat. Bar
much later.

162 1/XE1 ✓ **The Ship on the Shore** 0131 555 0409 · 24 **The Shore** And midway
£15-25 between The Shore and The Wark (above), also with a reputation as a great
quayside bistro/gastropub, especially for seafood. Good ingredient sourcing and
wine list (top by-the-glass selection, including fizz). Excellent fruits de mer, fish 'n'
chips (Hoegaarden batter) and a buzzy ambience to enjoy them. Erick Becquemont
a consummate maître d'. 7 days 12noon-10pm. Bar 11pm.

163 1/XC1 ✓ **The Orchard** www.theorchardbar.co.uk · 0131 550 0850 · 1 Howard
<£15 **Place** At Inverleith Row near the Botanics. Light, airy and as you'd expect, pubby. Light touch in the kitchen too from chef James Fletcher. Seasonal, well-thought-out and monthly changing menu. Sourced from all the right suppliers (Cockburns, Armstrongs, Fletchers, Ramsays). If this place was further uptown you'd fight for a table, which means you can relax! 7 days, 12noon to 8.30pm.

164 1/XB5 **The New Bell** www.thenewbell.com · 0131 668 2868 · 233 Causewayside
£15-25 Way down Causewayside in the Southside, the New Bell is now part of the rejuvenated Old Bell; you may walk through the pub and upstairs. Recent refurbishment not revisited at TGP but we expect a woody, warm, pubby atmosphere. Food and very decent vino well-priced; quality and smart delivery. 7 days lunch and LO 10pm.

165 1/XB5 **Montpeliers** www.montpeliersedinburgh.co.uk · 0131 229 3115 ·
£15-25 **159 Bruntsfield Place** They call it Montpeliers of Bruntsfield and it is almost an institution south of the Meadows. Same ownership as Rick's (below) and similar buzz and noise levels, but more accent on food. From breakfast menu to late supper, they've thought of everything. All the contemporary faves. Sunday roasts. Gets very busy. 7 days 10am-10pm. LO 10pm. Bar till 1am.

166 1/B2 **Rick's** www.ricksedinburgh.co.uk · 0131 622 7800 · 55a Frederick Street
£15-25 Basement bar/restaurant along with Rick's Hotel (99/INDIVIDUAL HOTELS) by same people as Montpeliers (above) and Tigerlily (87/INDIVIDUAL HOTELS). Drinking is the main activity here but they do have a variable, ie highs and lows, restaurant menu. Later on maybe too noisy to enjoy food, so choose time and table carefully. Inner courtyard best for dining. Up-for-it crowd enjoy champagne, cocktails and shouting. 7 days all day. LO 10pm (11pm weekends). Bar 1am. Also open for breakfast from 8am.

167 1/XE1 **A Room In Leith** www.aroomin.co.uk · 0131 554 7427 · 1c Dock Place
ATMOS Here-for-decades wine bar in this foody corner of the waterfront spilling over the
£15-25 quayside renamed Teuchter's Landing. The conservatory overlooks the backwater dock. Scottish-slanted bistro menu (Loch Creran oysters, Shetland mussels) with half- or full-pint 'Mug' menu to eat in or out (cullen skink, mac cheese and other comfort favourites). Excellent wine and malt selection. 7 days all day. LO 9.30/10pm. Bar 12midnight/1am.

168 1/D3
£25-35
✓ ✓ **La Garrigue** www.lagarrigue.co.uk · 0131 557 3032 · 31 Jeffrey Street & **La Garrigue in the New Town** 0131 558 1608 · 14 Eyre Place & **La Garrigue in Leith** 0131 553 5933 · 88 Commercial Street The original is an airy yet intimate restaurant near Royal Mile. Chef/proprietor Jean Michel Gauffre brings warm Languedoc to your plate. Expect cassoulets, croustillant. Terroir with a sure touch. Veggies may flounder between the leggy langoustines and les lapins but meat eaters and Francophiles are très content here. The newest outpost (and it is quite far down in the New Town) replaces Jean Michel's bold attempt to open a French-leaning vegetarian restaurant. Here, herbivores may be happier than uptown but the menu is fastidiously and fabulously French too and Jean Michel seems somehow to be in two places at once. Then there was Leith, standard bistro fare, perhaps a league too far! Mon-Sat lunch and LO 9pm. Closed Sun. New Town, lunch and LO 9pm, 7 days.

169 1/B2
£15-25
✓ ✓ **Café Marlayne** 0131 226 2230 · 76 Thistle Street The first in the triumvirate of excellent and authentic French eateries within 100m of another (Café St Honoré, La P'tite Folie; below), this is a well-worn gem (a wee gem). Personal, intimate and very, very French. Food reliably fab (though not great for veggies). This really is like a place you find in rural France on your hols; you would say 'charmant'! Lunch and LO 10pm.

170 1/D1
£15-25
✓ ✓ **L'Escargot Bleu** www.lescargotbleu.co.uk · 0131 557 1600 · 56 Broughton Street In a strong French field in this city, another authentic Auld Alliance bistro (and downstairs L'Epicerie; 327/DELIS) – this one en famille (the busy Berkmillers) with L'Escargot Blanc in Queensferry St. Very French atmosphere and menu so expect tartare to mean tartare and snails to be escargots. Well-sourced ingredients mainly Ecossaise. Great cheese selection. Michelin Bib and always busy. Mon-Sat, lunch and LO 10pm.

171 1/E1
£15-25
✓ **The New Café Marlayne** 0131 558 8244 · 13 Antigua Street, Leith Walk Surprisingly large eastern extension of the mini bistro above, very welcome in the strip of restaurants opposite the Playhouse Theatre. Cavernous back room means you can usually get a table when the musical punters ram this row. Few are aware that this is the best value and the most authentic; but you are! Islay Fraser, Madame Marlayne herself, in the kitchen. Out-front caff during the day has good home baking! 7 days 9am-10pm.

172 1/B2
ATMOS
£25-35
✓ **Café Saint Honoré** www.cafesthonore.com · 0131 226 2211 · 34 Thistle Street Lane Between Frederick and Hanover Sts down a lane, a classic bistro with classics on the menu. Oozes atmosphere and good food. Linen tablecloths, tiles and mirrors; at night in candlelight, it twinkles. Scottish sourcing and a daily-changing menu; part of the slow-food movement. Meat dishes are especially good; minimal vegetarian choice. Lunch Mon-Sat, LO 10pm.

173 1/C4
£15-25
✓ **Petit Paris** www.petitparis-restaurant.co.uk · 0131 226 2442 · 40 Grassmarket On busy north side of street below the castle; teems on weekend nights – get an outside table and watch. The terrace spreads across to the central reservation in summer: this could be Montmartre apart from the general inebriation and bad behaviour. Good atmosphere and value with très typical menu. BYOB (not weekends); corkage £3.50. 7 days lunch and LO 10pm.

174 1/B2
£15-25
✓ **La P'tite Folie** www.laptitefolie.co.uk · 0131 225 7983 · **61 Frederick Street & Randolph Place** Best word for it: 'unpretentious'; maybe 'ambiente'. Mismatched furniture, inexpensive French *plat du jour*. Relaxed dining in single New Town room or the two-floor Tudoresque 'maison' in West End cul de sac. Both great value. LO 10pm (10.45pm weekends). Both closed Sun. In Randolph Pl, **La Di-Vin** adjacent is a large, lofty wine bar and a surprise find behind the bistro. Great wine list and atmosphere (and bar food). Lunch and bar 12/1am.

175 1/XD1
£15-25
✓ **Chez Pierre** www.pierrelevicky.co.uk · 0131 556 0006 · **18 Eyre Place** The irrepressible Pierre Levicky bounced back here from self-imposed exile in France after his famously cheap Pierre Victoire chain went belly-up. Once again with a winning formula of great-value, authentic French country cooking, this place is invariably très occupé. It's the deal as well as the feel that packs them in with sometimes, all-you-can-eat dinner for 10 quid. 7 days lunch and LO 10pm.

176 1/A3
£15-25
✓ **L'Escargot Blanc** 0131 226 1890 · **Queensferry Street at Alva Street** Upstairs bistro once associated with Petit Paris above, but now very much to do and à deux with L'Escargot below. Popular with a loyal following who like the authentic, lively atmosphere and the inexpensive food and fine wines. Raclette suppers on Tue. Lunch and LO 10/10.30pm. Closed Sun.

177 1/C4
£15-25
✓ **Maison Bleue** www.maisonbleuerestaurant.com · 0131 226 1900 · **36 Victoria Street** For 15 years now (you locals may have missed but go see) a cosy, very Edinburgh café-bistro: convivial, grazing all the right notes. French and tapas/mezze approach, building a meal from smallish dishes they call bouchées. The point is, the food here is way good! 7 days 12noon to LO 9.30/10pm.

✓ ✓+ **Restaurant Martin Wishart** 54 **The Shore** French influence on finest dining. Report: 126/BEST RESTAURANTS.

▰▰▰▰ The Best Italian Restaurants

178 1/XB5
£25-35
✓ **Nonna's Kitchen** www.nonnaskitchen.co.uk · 0131 466 6767 · 45 **Morningside Road** Serving the affluent denizens of Morningside/Bruntsfield but way too good to be just for them, Nonna's combines friendliness and flair to a degree that repeat custom alone means you probably have to book most evenings. The Stornaivolo family – Mimmo in the kitchen, Gino out front and mama Carmela presiding with Jimmy their trusty lieutenant (who never falters in reading the prodigious list of daily, mainly seafood specials) all work damned hard to make this the primo easygoing Italian place in town. Pasta/pizza, long à la carte and specials. You could come here for a month and not have the same thing twice. Those lucky Morningsiders: well, to those that have... Lunch and LO 10pm. Closed Mon.

179 1/C4
>£35
✓ **La Cucina @ Hotel Missoni** 0131 240 1666 · 1 **George IV Bridge** At the Royal Mile. The upstairs Italian kitchen of the first Missoni hotel (89/INDIVIDUAL HOTELS) where fashion, ie that zig-zag brand, comes first. But the food here Locatelli-style is excellent and not at all fancified. Ambience relaxed, chic and sexy, like the trousers and the kilts. Smart, solicitous service; good sommelier dispensing a serious Italian wine list. Cheap it ain't. Breakfast, lunch and dinner LO 10/11pm.

180 1/D1
£15-25
✓ **Locando de Gusti** 0131 558 9581 · 7 **East London Street** On the roundabout at the bottom of Broughton St. The former (but pretty much the same approach and menu) Bella Mbriana continues its homage to Napoli in this

modern Italian eaterie. Good reviews and plaudits largely down to the once-large Rosario Sartore with a good team out front and in the visible, busy little kitchen. Good seafood. Nice table in the wine cellar downstairs. Lunch and LO 10.30pm. Closed Sun/Mon

181 1/C2 ✓ **Amore Dogs** www.amoredogs.co.uk · 0131 220 5155 · **104 Hanover** £15-25 **Street** Named after the hugely successful bistro upstairs (138/BISTROS), itself named after the 'dog' of amusingly eccentric proprietor Dave Ramsden, this Italian version is also to love. It's got all the staples of a British tratt (pizzas, pastas, tiramisu) and though some have referred to the cuisine as 'a dog's dinner', the light Med menu is easy to take and to like, especially on the wallet. Hallmark buzzing atmosphere in the main room and mezzanine. 7 days 12noon-LO 10pm. Down below and ideal for an aperitif or digestif is **Underdogs**, a laid-back bar with slouchy seats and Dave's trademark chutzpah. 5pm-11/12pm. Closed Sun.

182 1/XA4 ✓ **La Bruschetta** www.labruschetta.co.uk · 0131 467 7464 · **13 Clifton** £15-25 **Terrace** Extension of Shandwick Pl opposite Haymarket Station (regulars come by train!). Giovanni Cariello's Italian kitchen and tiny dining room in the West End. A modest ristorante with form and a following; so book. The space does not cramp their old-school style nor the excellent service. Lunch and LO 10.30pm. Closed Sun/Mon.

183 1/E1 ✓ **Valvona & Crolla** www.valvonacrolla.co.uk · 0131 556 6066 · **19 Elm** £25-35 **Row** First caff of the empire which spread to Multrees Walk (see below) and to London, this one discreetly buzzing away at the back of the legendary deli (324/DELIS). An Alexander McCall Smith kind of café much favoured by ladies who lunch. First-class ingredients and great Italian domestic cooking. Own bakery. One of the best and healthiest breakfasts in town (till 11.15am), fabuloso lunch and afternoon tea (from 3pm). Can BYOB from shop (£3 corkage). Mon-Sat 8am-5pm, Sun 10.30am-4.30pm. VC also do Jenners' food hall.

184 1/B3 ✓ **Centotre** www.centotre.com · 0131 225 1550 · **103 George Street**
ATMOS Fabulous conversion by Victor and Carina Contini of a lofty, pillared Georgian £15-25 room towards the west end of Edinburgh's better boulevard into the classiest restaurant on the street and the most stylish Italian joint in town. Passion for food and good service always evident; and they are ubiquitous (though they also run the Scottish Restaurant in Princes St Gardens; 228/BEST SCOTTISH RESTAURANTS). Bar and central pizza oven, unexpected combos in a straightforward, oft-changing menu. Great people-watching strip of tables on the street. 7.30am till LO 10pm (11pm Fri/Sat), 11am-9pm Sun. Bar open later.

185 1/D2 ✓ **Vin Caffe** www.valvonacrolla.co.uk · 0131 557 0088 · **Multrees Walk** £15-25 The downtown smart eaterie of the Valvona & Crolla dynasty (see above) in the posh-shop passage beside Harvey Nix. Café counter downstairs, restaurant above. Interesting pastas, pizzas and proper principalis. It's always busy downstairs for authentic espresso and fast snacks. Upstairs has black-and-white classic movies projected, Friday night jazz and the occasional tea dances. A dolce vita kind of place. 7 days 8am-9.15/10.15pm, Sun 11am-5pm.

186 1/XE1 ✓ **La Favorita** www.la-favorita.com · 0131 554 2430 · **325 Leith Walk** £15-25 Tony Crolla's (of Vittoria; 188/TRATTS) upmarket pizzeria halfway down the Walk where the trams may come one day. From the twin, specially imported, wood-fired ovens, Tony was determined to produce 'the best pizza in Scotland' and in '09 he did win Best in the UK (is there a food mafia? 193/PIZZAS)! Gluten-free available and a menu of fancy pastas. Family-friendly, especially on Sunday. This is many folks' favorita and good to go from the takeaway next door (it's our office favourite, too). 7 days 12noon–11pm.

187 1/A4
£15-35
Santini www.santiniedinburgh.co.uk · 0131 221 7788 · **Conference Square** Back (well, way back) of the Sheraton (of which it's a part, below their excellent One Spa). Business-like Italian restaurant and bistro. Waiters and ingredients Italia. Casual dining looking out on a people-less piazza (where the annex of the Conference Centre will arise 2012). A quietly good bet and surprisingly good value. Lunch and dinner LO 10.30pm. Closed Sun.

▮▮▮ The Trusty Tratts

188 1/E1
1/D4
£15-25
✓ ✓ **Vittoria** www.vittoriarestaurant.com · 0131 556 6171 · **Brunswick Street** The original on the corner of Leith Walk, also at 19 **George IV Bridge** (0131 225 1740) and the new caff by the Playhouse. For aeons Tony Crolla has provided one of the best, least pretentious Scottish-Italian café-restaurants in town. Uptown branch near the university equally full-on: smartened up with recent refurbishment and chic Divino Enoteca downstairs (365/BAR FOOD). Despite expanding in waistline (perhaps) and empire (certainly), Tony knows how to work the zeitgeist! Full Italian menu with classic and contemporary pastas. In Leith the outside tables on an interesting corner are always packed when the sun's out. Nice for kids (266/KID-FRIENDLY) and for breakfast (porridge, omelettes). Pizzeria/ristorante further down the Walk (La Favorita 193/ITALIAN RESTAURANTS) is another fave. All. 7 days. 10am–10/11pm.

189 1/XA4
£15-25
✓ **La Partenhope** 0131 347 8880 · **96 Dalry Road** A corner and cucina of Naples halfway up Dalry Rd (about 200m from Haymarket) where chef Paolo Tersigni presides over what has long been one of the most loved tratts in town. Menu changes weekly with daily specials from market produce. Fish specials are tops. Even the most basic aglio e olio shows how it should be done. This place fills up fast – book weekends. Lunch Tue-Sat, dinner LO 10.45pm. Closed Sun/Mon.

190 1/A3
£15-25
✓ **Bar Roma** www.bar-roma.co.uk · 0131 226 2977 · **39 Queensferry Street** A long-standing fave Italian. Inside it's massive and always bustling (this includes the menu) with Italian rudeboy waiters as the floor show. We love their chat; they love their football. 7 days, all day. LO 11pm (later weekends).

191 1/D2
£15-25
✓ **Giuliano's** www.giulianos.co.uk · 0131 556 6590 · **18 Union Place** Top of Leith Walk opposite Playhouse Theatre. Giuli's also has the Al Fresco restaurant down the street after the takeaway counter but it's the original that rocks and it feeds the Playhouse opposite. I've said it (many times) before: it's just pasta and pizza but it's what we like. Surprisingly good wine list, staff that have been here forever. The din is loud and it's always somebody's birthday. Lunch and LO 2am daily. **Giuliano's on The Shore** (0131 554 5272) on the corner of the bridge in Leith Central has recently had a makeover but it's the same, reliable tratt menu. Especially good for kids (267/KID-FRIENDLY). Also 7 days, LO 10.30/11pm.

192 1/C2
£15-25
La Lanterna 0131 226 3090 · **83 Hanover Street** One of several tratts sub street level in this block, all family-owned. But this gets our vote. For well over 20 years the Zainos have produced a straight-down-the-line Italian menu from their open kitchen at the back of their long, low, no-frills restaurant. Most of their customers are regulars and wouldn't go anywhere else. Well chosen wines. Lunch and LO 10pm. Closed Sun/Mon. It's a family affair!

The Best Pizza

193 1/XE1 ✓ **La Favorita** www.la-favorita.com · 0131 554 2430 · **325 Leith Walk**
£25-35 They say it's 'the best' and then the rest of the UK agreed: Tony got the 'award' and the reward for dedication and doing it right. Huge variety, great mozza; takeaway and home delivery and now on the road at festivals. This pizza has travelled (often to our office)! Report: 186/ITALIAN RESTAURANTS.

194 1/XE1 ✓ **Origano** 0131 554 6539 · **277 Leith Walk** Down the Walk and down from
<£15 Favorita (above), a sweet little caff where the pizzas, some say, are better. Certainly it's what to order here but there's other home-made Med food on the menu. Few tables, intimate and friendly.

195 1/B1 **Anima** 0131 558 2918 · **11 Henderson Row** The takeaway pizza section of the
<£15 estimable fish 'n' chip shop L'Alba D'Oro next door (217/FISH & CHIPS). Definitely a slice above the rest. 3 sizes (including individual 7-inch) and infinite toppings to go. Not thin but crispy and crunchy. Also pasta, great wine to go, olive oils, Luca's ice cream and fresh OJ. This is no ordinary takeaway (see 316/TAKEAWAY)! 7 days lunch (not Sun) and LO 11pm.

196 1/C4 **Mamma's** www.mammaspizza.co.uk · 0131 225 6464 · **30 Grassmarket**
<£15 Busy, inexpensive American-style pizza. Some alternatives, eg nachos, but you come to mix 'n' match – haggis, calamari and BBQ sauce and 40 other toppings piled deep with quite chunky crust. Good bottled beer selection. Outside tables on revamped Grassmarket. Stag and hen parties are not welcomed here (hurrah!). 7 days till 10.30/11pm weekends.

197 1/XF2 **Caprice 2 Go** 0131 665 2991 · **198 High Street, Musselburgh** Near the
£15-25 bridge. The number is for their takeaway joint round the corner which delivers to this eastern suburb of the city and other nearby East Lothian towns. The adjacent restaurant serves the same wood-fired pizza and the usual Italian fare. Ask them to crisp it but pizza here still lighter than most. 7 days lunch and till 11pm.

198 1/XB5 **Nonna's Kitchen** www.nonnaskitchen.co.uk · 0131 466 6767 · **45**
£15-25 **Morningside Road** Like everything else here (178/ITALIAN RESTAURANTS), the pizzas are just so. Hard to choose though amongst a menu of myriad good things. Lunch and LO 10pm. Closed Mon.

The Best Mediterranean Food

199 1/XE5
£15-25

✓ ✓ **Hanedan** 0131 667 4242 · 42 West Preston Street Small, friendly, Southside neighbourhood Turkish restaurant. Chef/owner Gursel Bahar a considerate, enthusiastic host. Hot and cold meze to share and shish/kofte/musakka (sic) menu. Daily fish (those charcoal-grilled sardines!) and good vegetarian. Short pud and wine lists complement well. Lunch and LO 10pm. Closed Mon.

200 1/C2
£15-25

✓ **Nargile** www.nargile.co.uk · 0131 225 5755 · 73 Hanover Street Not so much Mediterranean, most definitely Turkish. This is where to go to mess with the meze. Huge choice of all east-of-the-Med fares from houmous to shashlik with lots for veggies and better choice of fish dishes than before. Kuskus and chips! Tables cramped but this is a night out with the mate(s) kind of place. Buzbag as expected and fair selection of other Turkish and non-Turkish wines. 12noon-10pm. Closed Sun.

201 1/A1
£15-25

✓ **Rafael's** 0131 332 1469 · 2 Deanhaugh Street Secret subterranean Spanish restaurant in corner of Stockbridge by the bridge: a Stockbridge living room! Daily menu as it comes from Rafael Torrubia's tiny kitchen. Simple operation with honest and often sublime homemade food; great fish. A bit of a let down for veggies but great puds. Dinner only Tue-Sat. LO 9.45pm.

202 1/XE1
& C2
<£15

✓ **Tapa** www.tapaedinburgh.co.uk · 0131 476 6776 · 19 Shore Place & 97 Hanover Street · 0131 623 1934 Great value, reasonably authentic tapas: chef's selection, 7 small tapas for £10 (till 5.30pm) and great (as we do) for an office outing (Shore Pl is tucked behind The Shore in Leith). Better and more satisfying by far than High St tapas chains. Good vino and more Spanish beers than you knew existed. 7 days 12-10pm.

203 1/A5
<£15

✓ **Papoli** www.papoli.co.uk · 0131 477 7047 · 244 Morrison Street Up from Haymarket Station. Modest (8 tables) and homely Mediterranean/Italian café/bistro run by the Persian (well, Iranian) Parvis family. Mainly Italian staples but imaginative as well as wholesome. Main thing is the incredibly good value – pastas, pizzas and wine all less than a tenner. Set menu and à la carte. Lunch and LO 10pm. Closed Sun.

204 1/D3
£15-25

Igg's 0131 557 8184 · 15 Jeffrey Street Since 1989 – that's nearly 25 years, everybody – this has been a corner of Spain in Scotland near the Royal Mile, a grown-up restaurant for business affairs or just, affairs. Igg is still aqui y ahora. The warm south is reflected in the excellent and decent-value wine list which he will enthusiastically explain. Food from well-sourced Scottish ingredients, especially fish, but with Iberico meats. Some tapas; but see Barioja below. Good biz-lunch spot. Lunch and LO 10.30pm. Closed Sun.

205 1/D3
£15-25

Barioja 0131 557 3622 · 19 Jeffrey Street Next to Igg's (see above), and joined down below. The first tapas place in Edinburgh, in what has become a vast, predictable plain for grazing. Small tables but an open, light room. Fairly típico tapas menu: pan con tomate, gambas pil-pil, patatas bravas, but not the sideboard- or counter-full we love in Spain – it's The Rules! 11am-11pm (Sun 12noon-10pm).

206 1/E4
ATMOS
£15-25

Empires 0131 466 0100 · 24 St Mary's Street Cosy, charming, chaotic, this tiny up-and-down restaurant is always an experience – pure Turkish delight. Full of ceramics, rugs and all kinds of people. Usual and unusual meze; great coffee. Good for vegetarians. Service a bit mad but great atmosphere. Only 3 small tables and 3 big ones to gather round. 7 days 12noon-10pm. Winter closed Mon. BYOB (£3).

The Best Seafood Restaurants

207 1/C4
√ √ **Ondine** 0131 226 1888 · George IV Bridge By the Missoni Hotel.
≥£33
Shiny, glass-encased, discreet destination upstairs and just off the Royal
Mile. Since opening in 2009, chef/patron Roy Brett, who was with Rick Stein in
Padstow, has worked hard to make this the city's big fish boat in the marina.
Impeccable sourcing, sure hands in the kitchen and a strong signature on the oys-
ter rarebit! 1 or 2 meat options, little vegetarian. More casual crustaceans at the
bar. 7 days lunch and LO 10pm.

208 1/XE1
£15-25
√ **Fishers** www.fishersbistros.co.uk · 0131 554 5666 · Corner of The
Shore & Tower Street, Leith Original location (see below), definitely the
bistro-best. At the foot of an 18th-century tower opposite Malmaison Hotel and
right on the quay (though no boats come by). Seafood cooking with flair and commitment from small kitchen in boat-like surroundings; traditional Scots dishes
(Finnan haddies) get an imaginative twist and their fish features are all faves. Some
stools around bar and tables outside in summer (can be a windy corner). Often, all
are packed, so best book. 7 days. 12noon-10pm.

209 1/E1
£15-25
√ **Café Fish** www.cafefish.net · 0131 225 4431 · 15 North West Circus
Place After establishing a great reputation for integrity seafood in Leith but
no passing trade, Richard Muir moved uptown to Stockbridge summer '11 and
quickly filled his contemporary café-bar with lovers of simple, good seafood.
Impeccable sourcing and a room (after several previous occupants) that feels like
it's meant to be here. Can eat at the bar. 7 days 12noon-9.30pm.

210 1/C2
>£35
√ **Fishers In The City** www.fishersbistros.co.uk · 0131 225 5109 ·
58 Thistle Street Uptown version of Leith eaterie (above); this place works
on all its levels (we're talking mezzanine). Fisher fan staples ('features') all here –
the fishcakes, soup and blackboard specials; Leith menu but with an uptown edge.
Excellent wine list and great service. Some vegetarian and meat (steaks a special).
There's a Hot Shellfish Platter at £80 for two (24 hours' notice). 7 days. LO 10.30pm.

211 1/C3
£15-25
√ **Seadogs** www.seadogsonline.co.uk · 0131 225 8028 · 43 Rose Street
Unlikely, very midtown location on a street crawling with drinkers and shop-
pers who probably couldn't care that this is one of the best food-wise and value-
wise seafood caffs (and it is caff-like) in the city. It follows the other Dogs
(181/ITALIAN, 138/BISTROS), both nearby and the creation – and we do mean creation – of Dave Ramsden, patron and perpetual-motion machine. Jamie Ross, the
estimable chef, turns out properly sourced and served seafood of course, but
there's a fair selection of vegetarian and Dogs-type meaty options. And this Dog,
as the others, is well trained and easy to live with.

212 1/D4
£15-25
√ **Creelers** www.creelers.co.uk · 0131 220 4447 · 3 Hunter Square Tim
and Fran James's corner of Arran in the city behind the Tron Church is a short
cast from the Royal Mile (tables alfresco in summer). West-coast supplies direct
from their own boat and Arran (eg hand-dived scallops) where they have another
restaurant (2303/ARRAN) and smokery. They also do the Edinburgh Farmers'
Market. Couple of meat and a token vegetarian dish but this is a straight-up and
very decent seafood caff. Lunch and LO 10.30/11pm.

213 1/D2
ATMOS
£15-25
√ **Café Royal Oyster Bar** www.thespiritgroup.com · 0131 556 1884 ·
17 West Register Street On the corner between St Andrews Sq and Burger
King at the east end of Princes St. Long-standing – and we do mean 'long': a classic Victorian oyster bar. Decor is unchanged so the marble, dark wood, tiles and

glass partition are all major reasons for coming here. Food has been up and down over the years and this is a Punch Tavern, but keep it simple from the classic seafood menu and you won't go wrong. The Oyster Bar is back and winning awards again! 7 days lunch and LO 9.30pm. The bar through the partition is more fish 'n' chips but it's also a classic (336/UNIQUE BARS); food here till 10pm.

214 1/B3 **The Mussel Inn** www.mussel-inn.com · 0131 225 5979 · **61 Rose Street**
£15-25 Popular, populist. In the heart of the city centre where food with integrity is hard to find, a great little seafood bistro specialising in mussels and scallops (kings and queens) which the proprietors rear/find themselves. Also catch of the day, some non-fish options and home-made puds. Mon-Thu offer of half kilo of mussels, chips or salad quickie for £7.50. This formula could travel but the owners have wisely decided not to travel far – they're also in Glasgow (580/SEAFOOD RESTAURANTS). Lunch and dinner. LO 10pm (all-day menu Fri/Sat).

215 1/XE1 **The Loch Fyne Restaurant** www.lochfyne.com · 0131 559 3900 ·
£15-25 **Newhaven** Large, lofty seafood canteen in excellent location on the harbour though somewhat removed from Leith, the restaurant quarter. Outside tables have sunset potential. Exemplary outpost of the UK chain, this at least a bit nearer to the original and its oysters (1327/SEAFOOD RESTAURANTS). Great room and very on the waterfront, but not cheap, mes amis, and a little patchy on delivery. Stick to fish and a crisp white and you'll be... fyne. 7 days all day and LO 10pm.

The Best Fish & Chips

216 1/XE1 ✓ **The Tailend Restaurant & Fish Bar** 0131 555 3577 · 14 Albert Place
On the right-hand side of Leith Walk going down. Thankfully reopened from their chip-shop fire in 2011. Unpretentious caff where you can often get a table (only 10) though the menu, from starters to simple-choice puds, is all good stuff. Menu of fish du jour, battered, grilled and with a variety of sauces. Caff and counter cook to order, so fresh as it comes. A drop-in favourite! They're also in St Andrews (852/ST ANDREWS). They do lard it! 7 days 11.30am-10pm.

217 1/B1 ✓ **L'Alba D'Oro** Henderson Row Near corner with Dundas St. Large selection of deep-fried goodies, including many vegetarian savouries. Since 1975 Filippo Crolla's chipper has been way above the ordinary – as several plaques on the wall attest (including *StB!*); the pasta/pizza counter Anima next door is also a winner (195/PIZZAS, 316/TAKEAWAY). Surprising and notable wine selection (including fine wines and champagne), olive oils, Luca's ice cream. Vegetable oil used, though like everywhere else they do fry some meaty things in it. Open 5pm-11pm (12midnight weekends); pizza 10pm (11pm weekends).

218 1/E2 ✓ **The Deep Sea** Leith Walk Opposite Playhouse Theatre. Open late and often has queues but these are quickly dispatched. The haddock has to be of a certain size and is famously fresh (via Something Fishy in Broughton St nearby). Traditional menu and the deep-fried Mars Bar. Now there's also kebabs but stick to one of the most reliable fish suppers in town and feed your impending hangover (there's a pharmacy of pills alongside the Irn Bru). Open till 2am-ish (3am Fri-Sat).

219 1/E1 ✓ **The Montgomery** Montgomery Street Just off Leith Walk and midway between the Tailend and the Deep Sea, some swear this place is the chipper to choose. Sit in the friendly, very traditional caff adjacent or take away. Closed Sun.

220 1/D2 **Caffe Piccante** Broughton Street Takeaway and café with tables on the black 'n' white tiles. Near the Playhouse Theatre, this is the clubbers' chippy (occasional DJs) with unhealthy lads purveying delicious unhealthy food to the flotsam of the Pink Triangle and club world. Including deep fried Mars Bars (you'd need to be well out of it). You can sit in. Open till 2am (3am weekends).

████████ The Best Vegetarian Restaurants

221 1/E5
£15-25 ✓✓ **David Bann's** www.davidbann.com · 0131 556 5888 · St Mary's Street Bottom of the street off Royal Mile – a bit off the beaten track, but always a busy restaurant and not only with non-meaters, because this is one of the best restaurants in the city and, for vegetarian food, in the UK: mood lighting, non-moody staff and no dodgy stodge. A creative take on round-the-world dishes, changing seasonally. Light meal selection; lovely tartlets and 'parcels'. Ooh, and nice chips! Not a huge vegan selection and no ostentatious 'organics' (there are vegetarian wines), just honest-to-goodness good. 7 days. Lunch and LO 10pm.

222 1/E5
£15-25 ✓✓ **Kalpna** www.kalpnarestaurant.com · 0131 667 9890 · 2-3 St Patrick Square They say 'you do not have to eat meat to be strong and wise' and they are of course right. Maxim taken seriously in this lovely Indian restaurant on the Southside for over 25 years, one of the best vegetarian menus in the UK; ever-dependable, vegetarian or not. Thali gives a good overview. The butter masala is the definitive dosa. Lovely, light and long may it prevail. Mon-Sat lunch (buffet £7) and LO 10.30pm. Open Sun in summer. Report: 234/INDIAN RESTAURANTS.

223 1/C2
ATMOS
<£15 ✓✓ **Henderson's** www.hendersonsofedinburgh.co.uk · 0131 225 2131 · 94 Hanover Street Edinburgh's original and trail-blazing basement vegetarian self-serve café-cum-wine bar. A national treasure! Canteen seating to the left, candles and nightly live music down a few stairs to the right (pine interior is retro-perfect). Happy wee wine list and organic real ales. Those salads, hot main dishes and famous puds will go on forever. 8am-9.30pm. Closed Sun.
Farm Shop upstairs with a deli and takeaway and, round the corner in Thistle St, the cosier **Henderson's Bistro** with waiter service (open 7 days, LO 8.30pm, 9.30pm weekends). The Bistro is now full vegetarian: quiche, crêpes, nutburgers. See also **Henderson's @ St John's**, below. And remember: Henderson's (organic) oatcakes are the best.

224 1/D5
& E5
ATMOS
<£15 ✓ **Mosque Kitchen** 0131 667 4035 · 33 Nicolson Square & 3 Bristo Place They started off as a kitchen behind the mosque – an open-air canteen where you ordered your curry in the kitchen – and have spread their hugely successful formula to this prominent corner site by Nicolson Sq and, in late 2011, to the former, funky Forest Café. Excellent pots of vegetarian curries and the stuff to go with. You order and before you know it, it's there. Real fast food! A no-alcohol zone. Times to be confirmed. 11.30am-11pm. Closed Friday 12.50-1.50pm for prayers.

225 1/E5
<£15 ✓ **Ann Purna** 0131 662 1807 · 45 St Patrick Square Excellent vegetarian restaurant near Edinburgh University with genuine Gujarati cuisine. Good atmosphere – old customers are greeted like friends by Mr and Mrs Pandya. Top thalies. Indian beer, some suitable wines. 7 days, lunch and LO 10.30pm. See also: 238/INDIAN RESTAURANTS.

226 1/XE5
<£15

✓ **Engine Shed Café** www.engineshed.org.uk · 0131 662 0040 ·
19 St Leonard's Lane Hidden away off St Leonard's St, this is a lunch-oriented vegetarian café where much of the work is done by adults with learning difficulties on training placements. It's worth supporting and it's light, airy and a good place to hang out. Simple, decent food and great bread – baked on premises, for sale separately and found across town. Nice stopping-off point after a tramp over Arthur's Seat. 10am-3.30pm. Closed Sun.

227 1/A3
<£15

Henderson's @ St John's 0131 229 0212 · **Princes Street** At Lothian Rd underneath St John's Church at the corner. Very central and PC self-service coffee shop in church vaults run by the kings of vegetarian food, the Hendersons (see above). Bakes etc from the family bakery, salads and 2/3 hot dishes (usually gone by 2.30pm) change daily. Some seats outside in summer (in the graveyard!) and market stalls during the Festival. A respite from the fast-food frenzy of Princes St. Open 10am-4pm (later in Festival). Closed Sun.

✓ ✓+ **Restaurant Martin Wishart** 0131 553 3557 · **54 The Shore**
Not of course a vegetarian restaurant, but does have a vegetarian menu. Food, ingredients and presentation are taken seriously here, so this is where to go for *the best* vegetarian food in Scotland. Report: 123/BEST RESTAURANTS.

▬▬ The Best Scottish Restaurants

228 1/C3
L
£15-25

✓ **The Scottish Restaurant** www.thescottishcafeandrestaurant.com ·
0131 226 6524 · **The Mound** Below and very much part of the National Gallery. Victor and Carina (of Cenotre, 184/ITALIAN RESTAURANTS) have cast their magic dining dust over the never-quite-worked gallery café and now this comfort zone of great Scottish cooking is a destination in itself. You enter from Princes St Gardens which the windows overlook (watch the ice rink in winter) and you walk past their cute herb garden. Cullen skink, mac cheese, Victoria sponge: your faves are all here! 8am-6pm (7pm Thu). Sun from 10am (306/SUNDAY BREAKFAST).

229 1/D3
£25-35

✓ **Dubh Prais** www.dubhpraisrestaurant.com · 0131 557 5732 ·
123b High Street Slap bang (but downstairs) on the Royal Mile opposite the Radisson. Only 24 covers and a miniature galley kitchen from which proprietor/ chef James McWilliams and his team have produced a remarkably reliable and à la carte menu and specials all simply put: 'Melrose lamb', 'Roast salmon'. The Atholl brose is as good as it gets. Here for almost 25 years – a very regular clientele and lucked-out tourists in this outpost of culinary integrity on the High St. Closed Sun/Mon. Dinner only LO 10pm. Pronounced Du Prash.

230 1/C4
ATMOS
£25-35

✓ **The Grain Store** www.grainstore-restaurant.co.uk · 0131 225 7635 ·
30 Victoria Street Long-established, revered bistro in interesting street near Royal Mile. Regulars and discerning tourists climb the stairs for a great-value graz-ing lunch menu or innovative à la carte at night. A laid-back first-floor eaterie in a welcoming stone-walled labyrinth. Good for groups. Perhaps more Modern British than simply Scottish. Chef/proprietor Carlo Coxon here 20 years; the team work damned hard to deliver quality. Hunting/shooting/fishing ingredients like roe deer, woodcock along with your usual oysters. 7 days lunch and LO 10pm (11pm Fri/Sat).

231 1/B2
£15-25

A Room In The Town www.aroomin.co.uk · 0131 225 8204 · **18 Howe Street** Corner of Jamaica St. The 'room' is in the New Town for these lads (Peter Knight and John Tindal) originally from the Highlands and reflects something of that legendary hospitality. So good value, friendly service; you can BYOB (£3 corkage at all their branches). Mainly Scottish menu with twists. Expect haggis, game, salmon. A vast range of Scottish beers and malts.

A Room In The West End (0131 226 1036) in William St with upstairs bar **Teuchters** (Scots word for northern, rural folk with no manners: these guys love to be outsiders). The bar dispenses their signature Pies and Pots of Scottish comfort food. Staples as in **A Room In Leith** (167/GASTROPUBS). Restaurant downstairs has similar to their In Town menu. 7 days lunch and LO 10pm. Bar, lunch and supper Sun-Thu. Oh, and Teuchters has a brilliant whisky section.

√ **The Witchery** 0131 225 5613 Top restaurant that really couldn't be anywhere else but Scotland. Report: 134/BEST RESTAURANTS.

The Best Mexican Restaurant

232 1/D3
£15-25

√ **Viva Mexico** www.viva-mexico.co.uk · 0131 226 5145 · Anchor Close, Cockburn Street Since 1984 the pre-eminent and (only decent) Mexican bistro in town. Judy Gonzalez's menu still innovates, although all the expected dishes are here. Genuine originals, famously good calamares and fajitas; lovely salad sides. Lots of seafood. Reliable venue for those times when nothing else fits the mood but proper fajitas and limey lager. 2 floors; nice atmosphere even downstairs. Lunch (not Sun) and LO 10.30pm (Sun 10pm).

The Best Japanese Restaurant

233 1/E5
£15-25

√ **Bonsai** www.bonsaibarbistro.co.uk · 0131 668 3847 · 46 West Richmond Street On discreet street on Southside, a Jap café/bistro (actually feels like a Japanese pub) where Andrew and Noriko Ramage show a deft hand in the kitchen. Unlike the sushi crop that has sprung up in Edinburgh (and everywhere), this is at least Japanese owned, so the freshly made sushi/yakitori and teppanyaki are the real McCoy. No conveyor belt in sight, just superb value in downbeat neighbourhood café setting. A la carte and specials and delicious puds, all home made. 7 days 12noon-10pm (not Sun lunch). Can BYOB (£5). Still no better taste of Tokyo in this town.

The Best Indian Restaurants

234 1/E5
£15-25

√√ **Kalpna** www.kalpnarestaurant.com · 0131 667 9890 · St Patrick Square The original Edinburgh Indian veggie restaurant, still very much the business. Favourites remain on the Gujarati menu and the thalis are famous but also unique dishes and dosas to die for. Report 222/VEGETARIAN RESTAURANTS.

235 1/E4
£15-25

√√ **Mother India Café** 0131 524 9801 · 3 Infirmary Street Off South Bridge. That rare thing: a restaurant successfully transferred from Glasgow (543/GLASGOW INDIAN RESTAURANTS), this the eastern outpost in Monir Mohammed's growing empire. Has all the things that made it work in Glasgow's West End: neighbourhood feel, great value, small tapas-like dishes to share (40 to choose from), some specials; great service. We always go back to Mum. 7 days lunch and LO 10.15pm. Sat & Sun 12noon onwards.

236 1/XE1
>35

✓ **Mithas** www.mithas.co.uk · 0131 554 0008 · **7 Dock Place** Corner of Commercial Quay, Leith's restaurant row. First (and we do mean first, ie 60 years ago), there was Kushi's (see below); and now in Edinburgh's centre of top-end dining, an Indian restaurant that sets its heights high. Beautifully presented and smartly served, the light, innovative food comes to share; look no further than their kebabs, unlike any other. Tasting menu and the tastes are subtle, complex and quite the spice of life. Discreetly lit chambers, spacious and shiny. You're in the New India. No alcohol but BYO including through a glass door from the adjacent bar though not part of the restaurant. Lunch and dinner. Closed Mon.

237 1/E5
<£15

✓ **Khushi's Diner** www.khushisdiner.com · 0131 667 4871 · **32b West Nicolson Street** Go downstairs on busy-with-restaurants, off-campus street to a big and usually busy restaurant, the home of Edinburgh's legendary Khushi's, started so long ago nearby in Drummond St. Sons of Khushi, Islam and Riaz moved here '09 after a huge fire destroyed their pride and joy in Victoria St; their loyal clientele followed and now they're everywhere (Dunfermline, Dundee and expanding in Edinburgh at TGP). The room is fresh and contemporary and the Punjabi-driven menu is full of the usual and the unusual flavas. Fast service. No alcohol but BYO is free. 7 days, no Sun lunch.

238 1/E5
<£15

✓ **Ann Purna** 0131 662 1807 · **45 St Patrick Square** Friendly and family-run Gujarati veggie restaurant with seriously good-value business lunch, harmonious food at all times. Proper pooris, thalies. See 225/VEGETARIAN RESTAURANTS.

239 1/D5
<£15

✓ **Kebab Mahal** www.kebab-mahal.co.uk · 0131 667 5214 · **7 Nicolson Square** Near Edinburgh University and Festival Theatre. Since 1979 Zahid Khan's slightly misnamed Indian diner (kebabs figure only slightly on a mainly curry menu) has been a word-of-mouth winner. As a no-frills Indo-Pakistani halal café it attracts Asian families as well as students and others who know. Great takeaway selection of pakoras, samosas, etc. One of Edinburgh's most cosmopolitan restaurants. And it's open late! 7 days 12noon-12midnight (2am Fri/Sat). Prayers on Fri (1-2pm). A no-alcohol zone.

240 1/D4
£15-25

Saffrani 0131 667 1597 · **11 South College Street** Off South Bridge and behind the Old Quad of the university. Small, tucked-away, personally run Indian bistro. No prizes for decor or atmosphere but conscientious, delicious and quite the real thing. North Indian menu and good for seafood. 7 days lunch and LO 11pm.

241 1/D2
£15-25

9 Cellars www.9cellars.co.uk · 0131 557 9899 · **3 York Place** This small basement restaurant tucked away on busy York Pl is an Indian food lover's secret. Chef P.C. Thakur from Shimla ensures that this is one of the most authentic and unpretentious Indian meals in midtown. 7 days lunch and LO 10.30pm.

242 1/XA4
£15-25

Indian Cavalry Club www.indiancavalryclub.co.uk · 0131 228 3282 · **22 Coates Crescent** Off the main Glasgow road between Haymarket and Princes St. More upmarket than most on this page: with smart waiters and linen cloths, the CC has always attracted the West End suits, especially at lunchtime. Good buzz here and food always pukka, served in small copper tureens: confident Indian cooking. Good vegetarian. An unlikely carry-out place, but they do, and it's one of the best to your door. Lunch and LO till 10.45pm.

In Delhi Nicolson Street Chai shop. Report: 292/CAFÉS.

Punjab'n De Rasoi Leith Walk Report: 295/CAFÉS.

The Best Thai Restaurants

243 1/C2
£25-35
✓✓ **Dusit** www.dusit.co.uk · 0131 220 6846 · 49 Thistle Street In the continuing proliferation of Thai restaurants in Edinburgh, this one still gets the gold orchid. Elegant interior, excellent service and food that's good in any language but just happens to be exquisite Thai cuisine. Tantalising combinations with atypical Scottish ingredients; strong signature dishes. Decent wine list. Lunch and LO 10.30pm.

244 1/XB5
£ 15-25
✓ **Leven's** 0131 229 8988 · 30 Leven Street Near the Cameo Cinema (and best nearby food). Almost gave this contemporary Thai restaurant 2 ticks coz it's so different to the others below and it always has so many dishes I like. Owned by the same people who have Thai Lemongrass (and many others) but here Bangkok chef Nat Kowitwattana does something new with the cuisine so you'll find sautéed potatoes, not rice with your monkfish and lemongrass. You can construct your own curry and the vegetarian version is exquisite. The fusion does work for once; great service. 7 days lunch and LO 10.30pm. Sat/Sun all day.

245 1/XA5
<£15
✓ **Pho Vietnam** www.vietnamhousescotland.com · 0131 228 3383 · 3 Grove Street This tiny (6 tables) Vietnamese café is a long way from its 'parent' in Saigon but is delightful in every way from proprietor Jodie-Nguyen, and its pictured menu featuring phos (pronounced Fuh) rice-noodle soups through its single sticky rice-cake dessert to a small bill at the end. Go west for this corner of the East. Can BYOB (£1). Mon-Fri lunch, Mon-Sat 5-10pm. Closed Sun.

246 1/XB5
£15-25
✓ **Thai Lemongrass** 0131 229 2225 · 40 Bruntsfield Place Smart but intimate, not too tiddlythai eatery by the people who have the estimable Jasmine (253/BEST CHINESE) and a few other Thais to boot. This one has a nice, solid, woody ambience, charming waitresses (Thai and Chinese) and food that's well good enough for Euro/Thai afficionados. Can BYOB (hefty £6 corkage) though has good wine list. Lunch Fri-Sun. Dinner 7 days, LO 11pm.

247 1/XE1
£15-25
✓ **Port of Siam** www.portofsiam.com · 0131 467 8628 · 3 Pier Place Small, contemporary Thai café at Newhaven harbour on the main road. Thai chef Phaitoon and Australian Padley Stuart's eclectic and rather mouth-watering take on modern Thai fusion food. Small, possibly cramped; always busy so must book despite far-from-uptown location (though there are plans to open city cente at TGP). Lunch Thu-Sun, Dinner LO 9.30pm. Closed Mon.

248 1/F1
£15-25
Phuket Pavilion 0131 556 4323 · 8 Union Street Near the Playhouse Theatre and Omni Cinemaplex. When other restaurants in this busy area are full, you can often get a table at Bill Parkinson's roomy, unpretentious Thai place that never lets you down. Decor nothing to write home from Phuket about but friendly Thai staff and just the right sprinkle of holy basil. 7 days. LO 10.30pm.

249 1/B2
£15-25
Ruan Siam 0131 226 3675 · 48 Howe Street A discreet basement on the corner of SE Circus Pl. Since 2002, those that know go here for authentic Thai cooking using authentic Scottish produce (from all the right suppliers), even including Luca's ice cream and top wine list. Lunch Mon-Sat and dinner 7 days. LO 10.30pm.

250 1/XB5
£15-25
Passorn www.passornthai.com · 0131 229 1537 · 23 Brougham Place, Tollcross Open for over a year but just discovered this unpretentious, innovative Thai bistro on the night I finished this book (in effect, its last entry!). Cindy Sirapassorn's enthusiasm and creativity evident in every mouthful. Lunch and LO 11pm. Closed Sun and Mon lunch.

The Best Chinese Restaurants

251 1/B1
£25-35

✓ **Kweilin** www.kweilin.co.uk · 0131 557 1875 · **19 Dundas Street** Though recent new owners, after 25 years this is still the New Town choice for imaginative Cantonese cooking (and other regions). Very good seafood and genuine dim sum in pleasant though somewhat uninspired setting. Excellent wine list. No kids allowed in the evening, so somewhere for grown-ups to eat their quail and especially good seafood in peace. You may have to book. LO 10.45pm (11.30pm Fri/Sat). Closed Mon and Sun lunch.

252 1/XA5
ATMOS
<£15

✓ **Chop Chop** 0131 221 1155 · **248 Morrison Street & Commercial Quay** · 0131 553 1818 The first near Haymarket Station, the other on Leith's restaurant row. Authenticity and simplicity are the watchwords in Madame Wang's Chinese diners, the original stripped down and bright, the newer Leith version (in posher company) smarter but no less brisk. Company makes dumplings wholesale and supplies Sainsbury's so they're de rigeur here; there's a vast selection. As with everything else. All comes in small dishes when ready. It's a sharing, daring, dumpling experience; full of people on the go like China. Note though that much as we love it, there are very few Chinese people in the room. Lunch Tue-Fri, dinner Tue-Sun. LO 10pm.

253 1/B4
£15-25

✓ **Jasmine** 0131 229 5757 · **32 Grindlay Street** Opposite Lyceum Theatre. Very Chinesey restaurant with big following and the only Chinese restaurant of the Chinese owners of an expanding Thai chain (Thai Lemongrass, above, and the one next door in Grindlay St). Pre- and post-theatre menus and good service to match (though it can be brusque). Seafood a speciality (Cantonese style). May need to book or queue in tiny doorway. Some memorable dishes await. Mon-Fri lunch. Dinner 7 days, LO 11.30pm.

254 1/XB1
£15-25

Loon Fung 0131 556 1781 · **2 Warriston Place, Canonmills** This place has been a destination diner since 1972. Famous lemon chicken and crispy duck signature dishes in a traditional neighbourhood restaurant specialising in Cantonese food. Good dim sum. Mon-Thu 12noon-11pm, weekends 2pm-12midnight.

255 1/XE1
ATMOS
<£15

The Golden Bridge 0131 467 5441 · **16 Henderson Street** Backstreet Leith; easy to miss. This back-to-basics diner makes up for the 70s decor (including wax tablecloths and plastic ivy) with excellent authentic Chinese soulfood and charming service from Sue Ma, the fastidious owner. Loyal and avid following, no longer a well-kept secret. Evenings only, LO 10.30/11.30pm. No licence; BYO (£1.50). No credit cards. Closed Mon.

256 1/XF5
£15-25

Karen Wong's 0131 622 0777 · **107 St Leonard's Street** Two front rooms on the Southside; Ms Wong is always there to welcome you, smile and advise in her charming Sino-Southside accent. Mr Wong in the kitchen turning out the usual and the unusual in a dizzying array of dishes. Daily 4-11pm. Closed Tue. Takeaway.

The Best Burgers & Steaks

257 10/P25
NTI188
£25-35
>£35

✓ ✓ **Champany's** www.champany.com · 01506 834532 On A904, Linlithgow to South Queensferry road (3km Linlithgow) near M9 at junction 3. Accolade-laden restaurant (and 'Chop and Ale House') different from others below because it's out of town (and out of some pockets). Superbly surf 'n' turf. Live lobsters. The best Aberdeen Angus beef hung 3 weeks and butchered on premises. Good service, huge helpings (Americans may feel at home). Top wine list (and wine cellar shop). Chop House also has great home-made sausages. 7 days, from noon onwards at weekends; lunch and LO 10pm. Restaurant lunch (not Sat) and LO 10pm. Closed Sun. Hotel rooms adjacent (121/HOTELS OUTSIDE TOWN).

258 1/A1
£15-25

✓ **Bell's Diner** 0131 225 8116 · 7 St Stephen Street Edinburgh's small but celebrated burger joint, the antithesis of the posh nosh. No seasonal/locally sourced/slow food or organic nonsense here. Nothing has changed in over 30 years except the annual paint job and (with an unusually low turnover) the gorgeous staff. Some people go to Bill Allen's Bell's *every* week in life and why? For perfect burgers, steaks, shakes and coincidentally, the best veggie (nut) burger in town. Bill's pushing on now but even if he can't, Bell's Diner runs and runs. Sun-Fri 6-10.30pm, Sat 12noon-10.30pm.

259 1/D3
£15-25

✓ **Buffalo Grill** www.buffalogrill.co.uk · 0131 667 7427 · 12-14 Chapel Street & 0131 332 3846 · 1 Raeburn Place Opposite Appleton Tower on the university campus and on a Stockbridge corner. Over 25 years in burgerland, this diner trades on its reputation for steaks and such-like (Scotch beef natch) but there's a lot more going on (prawn and palm salad!) and some concessions to veggies. And they still do corn on the cob like burger joints used to. Both great spots for easy-going nights out with chums; not large, so book. BYOB at Chapel St (corkage only £1). Lunch Mon-Fri, LO 10pm.

260 1/D1
1/XE1
£15-25

Smoke Stack www.smokestack.org.uk · 0131 556 6032 · 53-55 Broughton Street Presenting itself as more of a steakhouse of late, the Smoke Stack is an East Village staple and with its proposed (at TGP) opened-up frontage, will have a sharper, more welcoming look. Friendly service. Carnivores will come here forever. Lunch Mon-Sat, dinner 7 days, LO 10.30pm.

261 1/D4
1/A3
£15-25

Wannaburger www.wannaburger.com · Queensferry Street · 0131 220 0036 A large West End window-watching room, emphatically a (gastro) burger joint with no starters and limited desserts (though Mackie's ice cream and milkshakes). Towering burgers in huge variety (and vegetarian versions) and top toppings. Great for breakfast from 8am (Sun 10am). Same people have the Caley Sample Room (161/GASTROPUBS) Cambridge Bar. You may wanna take the kids here too and there's BYO (£2). 7 days all day, LO 9.30pm.

262 1/XE1
<£15

Diner 7 0131 553 0624 · 7 Commercial Street Along from the bridge at the shore in Leith. Sliver of local diner/restaurant on a busy road. Burgers, steaks and some more adventurous dishes with fish and vegetarian all at cheapo prices make this a popular, casual and local diner. 7 days 4pm-10pm (Sun from 11am).

263 1/XB5
£15-25
✓ **Luca's** www.s-luca.co.uk · 0131 446 0233 · 16 Morningside Road The ice-cream kings (1432/ICE CREAM) from Musselburgh brought this modern ice creamerie and café to Holy Corner where kids with dads will enjoy their spag and their sundae Sundays. Big cups of capp. Crowded and clamouring upstairs especially on weekends. Daytime snacks and family evening meals. Food not fab but the gorgeous ice cream at all times. BYOB. 9am-10pm. 7 days.

264 1/XF2
<£15
✓ **Reds** 0131 669 5558 · 254 High Street, Portobello In main street, along from the shops, a purposefully kid-friendly café (Derek and Louise have 4 kids themselves). A camera projects the rear playing/climbing area to a plasma screen in front. Kids get their portions from the adult menu freshly and conscientiously prepared, so a no-nugget zone. 10am-3pm and Fri-Sun 8pm.

265 1/E1
✓ **Joseph Pearce's** www.bodabar.com · 0131 556 4140 · 23 Elm Row Leith Walk below London St. Because they've thought of everything that a vibrant and vital pub should (341/UNIQUE PUBS), they've also thought about the kids of their living-the-life clients. Bar but also a delightfully informal café-restaurant. Kids are made welcome till 5pm. And kept amused!

266 1/E1
✓ **Vittoria** www.vittoriarestaurant.com · 0131 556 6171 · Corner of Brunswick Street & Leith Walk Excellent Italian all-rounder that can seat 200 people including outside on the pavement on a people-watching corner. Kids eat for £1 which is donated to a kids' charity. And they get a balloon and crayons and stuff. Now that's friendly. Report: 188/ TRUSTY TRATTS.

267 1/XE1
£15-25
✓ **Giuliano's on the Shore** www.giulianos.co.uk · 0131 554 5272 · 1 Commercial Street By the bridge, the Leith version of Giuli's (191/TRUSTY TRATTS) has all the traditional Italian trappings especially through the back (with a more contemporary feeling front-end; same food throughout). Cheerful pizza/pasta and waiters. Kids can make their own pizzas. For grown-ups nice antipasto, fish specials and a decent wine list. Always a birthday party happening at weekends. Luca's ice-cream (see above). 12noon-10.15/10.45pm. 7 days.

268 1/E3
✓ **The Scottish Storytelling Centre** 0131 556 9579 · 43 High Street The Royal Mile adjacent John Knox's House. The café that's part of this uniquely special place to take kids and grown-ups, well... to hear stories. Exhibitions and shop. Kids can sit or otherwise run free in the open and light court by the café and the food, by the same people who do The Fruitmarket Gallery (279/COFFEE SHOPS), is excellent. 10am-5pm (hot food 12-4pm). Closed Sun.

269 1/XA5
✓ **Cuthberts Coffee & Sandwich Bar** www.cuthbertscoffee.co.uk · 0131 228 1070 · 94A Fountainbridge Next door to Loudons (284/COFFEE SHOPS) in this West End extension. Similar offering though more meals here and a focus on film (sic) and kids. Kids' menu is a home-made version of what they like, eg '100% chicken nuggets', 'lunch on a stick'. At weekends, classic kids' movies are projected above. A friendly place. 7 days 8am-5pm.

Wannaburger 0131 220 0036 · 7 Queensferry Street For report, see 261/ BEST BURGERS above. It is exactly that and it's roomy and welcoming to families.

OUTSIDE TOWN

270 10/Q26
£15-25
Cramond Brig www.cramondbrig.com · 0131 339 4350 · Cramond At the River Almond as you hit Edinburgh on the dual carriageway from the Forth Road Bridge. Outside there's a play area by the old brig itself and a river walk. Kids' menu and half portions available from the à la carte. Lunch and LO 9pm, 7 days. Weekends 12noon onwards. At the other end of the Almond river walk at Cramond itself, **The Cramond Inn** (0131 336 2035) has a very decent pub-grub menu (famously good chips) and is family-friendly and laid-back. Outside is the prom and the island (427/WALKS IN THE CITY).

271 10/R25
£15-25
Goblin Ha' www.goblinha.com · 01620 810244 · Gifford 35km from town in neat East Lothian village. One of two hotels, this has the pub grub cornered. Lunch and supper (6-9pm, 9.30pm Fri-Sat). The garden, busy in summer, is nice for kids and there's pizza.

272 10/P25
£15-25
Bridge Inn www.bridgeinn.com · 0131 333 1320· Ratho 16km west of centre via A71, turning right opposite Dalmahoy Golf Club. Recent new owners and haven't been since. Refurbished and rethought but still a thrill for kids; occasional canal cruises (must book). Proper food for kids and grown-ups. Restaurant lunch daily and LO 9pm Mon-Sat. Bar till 11pm, 12midnight Fri-Sat.

The Best Tearooms & Coffee Shops

273 1/XB5
ATMOS
✓✓ **Loopy Lorna's Teahouse** www.loopylornas.com · 0131 447 9217 · **370 Morningside Road** At the Churchill Theatre. LL's original home further down on the corner of Maxwell St closed unexpectedly just as *StB* was going to press, but still if you're into teacakes or top snacks LL's is the real deal and this church-hall atmos is curiously just right. Mad selection of tea and big cakes plus lunch dishes, savoury tarts, etc. High level of chat and tea-pot envy and very silly tea cosies among some cool crockery. 7 days 9am-5pm.

274 1/XB5
ATMOS
✓✓ **Falko Konditorei** www.falko.co.uk · 0131 656 0763 · **185 Bruntsfield Place** At the other (town) end of Morningside to LL's above, another exquisite teashop – some would say the Morningside matrons are too well served but Falko (who are also in Gullane; 1369/TEASHOPS) is baking at its best (from the 'Meisterhand'). Well known for their artisan bread (at the Farmers Market), the tortes are practically irresistible (to me, anyway). Great tea list; soup at lunchtime. Daytime only from 8.45am. Closed Mon/Tue

275 1/D1
✓✓ **Artisan Roast** no phone · 57 Broughton Street A great addition to Broughton St society and possibly the best coffee in town. An odd system – the guy stands by the machine and there's no counter. Most of the very laid-back seating is in the backroom, like someone's pad. 2 blends: the earthy Janszoon and the lighter Primavera have different proportions of Brazilian and Sumatran beans. No paninis in sight, though there is cake. 8am-7.30pm Mon-Fri, 9am-6.30pm Sat, 10am-6.30pm Sun. See also 589/GLASGOW COFFEE SHOPS.

276 1/XA3
✓ **Gallery (of Modern Art) Café** www.nationalgalleries.org · Belford Road Unbeatable on a fine day when you can sit out on the patio on the lawn, with sculptures around, have some wine and a plate of Scottish cheese and oatcakes. Hot dishes are good – always 2 soups, meat/fish and vegetarian baked potatoes. Cakes and stuff! 7 days 10am-4.30pm (413/OTHER ATTRACTIONS). Lunch

dishes usually gone by 2.30pm. **Café Newton** at GOMA 2 (414/OTHER ATTRAC-TIONS) across the main road and the gardens is a smaller, more interior café by the same people (Heritage Portfolio here much less corporate catering than you might expect). Soup, sandwiches and 2 hot lunch dishes. Same hours as GOMA 1. Paolozzi's *Vulcan* towers above.

277 1/XE1
& C3
✓ **Porto And Fi** www.portofi.com · 0131 551 1900 · **47 Newhaven Main Street & 9 North Bank Street** · 0131 225 9494 The original on the corner of Craighall Rd, Trinity, set back from the busy shoreline road. Light, just right room where Fi's home cooking and baking hits the spot for the ladies (and others) who lunch. The newer central branch is on The Mound near the Royal Mile and in summer is stuffed with tourists like you. Orkney ice cream, Black Isle ales. 7 days. Newhaven 8am-8pm (Sun 10-6pm); Mound 10am-10pm.

278 1/XE1
✓ **Mimi's** www.mimisbakehouse.com · 0131 555 5908· **63 The Shore** They call it a bakehouse and they do with a big selection of home-baked goodies out of their small kitchen, not least their signature cakes. Open breakfast till teatime, and though the meals are perhaps less successful than the bakes, at last foody Leith has a cupcake to call its own. 7 days 9am-5pm (6pm weekends).

279 1/D3
✓ **Fruitmarket Café** www.fruitmarket.co.uk · 0131 226 1843 · **45 Market Street** Attached to the Fruitmarket Gallery, a cool, spacious place for coffee, pastries or a light lunch. Big salads, home cookin', deli-plates and 2/3 daily specials. Pastries by Fisher and Donaldson. All presided over and assembled by Mhairi and Roy (1461/FARM SHOPS) who also have the self-service coffee shop in the crypt of **St Giles' Cathedral** (416/ATTRACTIONS), the Storytelling Centre (268/KIDS) – a similar set-up without the big windows – and the City Art Centre. Both attract a mix of tourists and Edinburgers who meet and know that this is where to eat. The art world and the rest of the world go by. Fruitmarket: Mon-Sat 11.30am-4pm, Sun 12noon-4.30pm. Open till 5.30pm for coffee and cakes. St Giles 9am-4pm, Sun 12.30-4pm.

280 1/XD5
✓ **Peter's Yard** www.petersyard.com · 0131 228 5876 · **Quartermile** Actually located on Middle Meadow Walk, the pedestrian path through the Meadows, part of the new- (and old-) build Quartermile project that was once the Edinburgh Royal Infirmary. Light, airy bakery/deli/café that feels not like Edinburgh. Soup, salads, artisan bread and non-cream-laden cakes: big on baking. It gets very busy and the ordering system is a bit annoying but... you wait! Nice, outside, people-watching patio. 7am-6pm (from 9am Sat/Sun). A newer, less frentic PY is behind within the Project from 11am.

281 1/C2
✓ **G&T (Glass & Thompson)** 0131 557 0909 · **2 Dundas Street** Definitive New Town coffee shop and deli with food attitude. Many 'ladies who latte', a phrase coined by Alexander McCall Smith whom you'd expect to see with a notepad in a corner seat. Great antipasti, soups, salads, sandwiches to go; David Milanese's very fine cakes and Au Gourmand artisan breads. 8.30am-5.30pm, Sun 10.30am-4.15pm. See 317/TAKEAWAYS.

282 1/F3
✓ **Clarinda's** 0131 557 1888 · **69 Canongate** Near the bottom of the Royal Mile near Holyrood Palace and the parliament building. Small but with total tearoom integrity. Hot dishes and snacks worth the sit-down stop on the tourist trail and some of the best home baking in town. Inexpensive; run by good Edinburgh folk (Marion Thomson and team) who work that tiny kitchen. Takeaways possible. Outside tables overlook the garden. 7 days 8.30am-4.45pm (from 9.30am Sun). For over 25 years, the best apple pie in town. Believe it!

283 1/XB1   **Circle Coffee Shop** 0131 624 4666 · Canonmills Near the clock. Cute deli/ takeaway counter; lovely café in the back. Hot meals, salads, soups, frittatas made to order. Nice place to read the papers or linger after Sunday breakfast and eggs Benedict! A very New Town rendezvous. 7 days 0.30am 4.30pm. Sun 9am 4pm.

284 1/XA5   **Loudons** www.loudons-cafe.co.uk · 0131 228 9774 · 94b Fountainbridge In a new development on the right going west, 200m from Lothian Road. A large, ambitious, contemporary caff operation – they say: a café and bakery, and certainly the afternoon is full of tempting cakes. Otherwise, sandwiches, soups and quiches. Good presentation: Loudon is a fan of London's Leon. May be a brave location (though the kinda-similar St Cuthberts is also there; 269/KIDS), but you gotta wish the boy well. 8am-6pm Mon-Sat, from 9am Sun.

285 1/XD5   **Toast** 0131 446 9873 · 146 Marchmont Road Converted bank and popular hangout on the Marchmont fringes. Brill brunch spot with home-made just about everything. Famously good for breakfast but damned good home cooking in evenings, too. Yum! ice cream. 7 days 10am-9.30pm (Sun till 5pm).

286 1/D4   **The Elephant House** www.elephant-house.co.uk · 0131 220 5355 · 21 George IV Bridge Near libraries and Edinburgh University, a rather self-conscious but elephantine, ie large, and well-run coffee shop with light snacks and big choice. J.K. Rowling (1936/LITERARY PLACES) once sat here: they say 'the birth-place of Harry Potter' and they make rather a lot of their literary connections. Counter during day, waitress service evenings. Cakes/pastries are bought in but can be taken out. View of graveyard and castle to dream away a student life in Edinburgh. 7 days 8am-11pm (7pm in winter).

287 1/XB1   **Botanic Gardens** www.rbge.org.uk There are 3 coffee-shop options in these famous and fabulous gardens (410/ATTRACTIONS). Firstly, the small snack-bar café at the Inverleith Road entrance. Then The Terrace by 'The House' (where there are regular exhibitions; enter by Arboretum Place): this self-service food operation is better than it was but the outside tables and view of the city are why we come here. And the cheeky, not-red squirrels. And there's the new Gateway Restaurant atop the shop in the landmark John Muir Gateway on Arboretum Place. Waited service for breakfast, lunch and afternoon tea from 3pm. All 10am-15 minutes before the gardens close (times vary).

The Best Caffs

Also see Best Takeaway Places, p. 67.

288 1/XB5 ✓ **Zulu Lounge** www.thezululounge.com · 0131 466 8337 · **366 Morningside Road** Way at the end of Morningside Rd. Tiny, tucked-away South African tea shack run by brother-and-sister team Chris and Kim Wedge. Soups, sandwiches, great home-made muffins. Miele bread and biltong and their signature espresso made from red Rooibos tea. What Kim produces from that miniscule kitchen is kinda miraculous. 8am-6pm. Sun 8.30am-5pm.

289 1/D1 ✓ **The Broughton Street Deli** 0131 558 7111 · **7 Barony Street** Just around the corner from Broughton St itself. Takeaway counter and some deli items (serve-yourself olive oil), but much frequented as a caff. Soups, tarts, hot dishes and imaginative salads. Great home baking. My local lunchbox. Open for early supper till 7pm/8pm. BYO.

290 1/E4 ✓ **The Edinburgh Larder** 0131 556 6922 ·**15 Blackfriars Street** Off the middle part of the Royal Mile. Deli, caff and takeaway food stop (and gallery space). Certainly more than a soup 'n' sandwich place, with home-made specials and a foodie approach. A wee Scottish gem, probably missed by the tourists around here who are looking for one. 8am-5pm. Sun from 9am .

291 1/E1 ✓ **Café Renroc** 0131 556 0432 · **91 Montgomery Street** Billy and Jane Ross's neighbourhood cool caff on the corner ('renroc' backwards) with out-side tables and more downstairs beside the Nevo health suites (acupuncture, mas-sage and other treatments). A popular hangout. Breakfasts, ciabattas, stromboli, nice coffee, fresh OJ. 7 days 10am-6pm (till 10pm Fri/Sat).

292 1/E5 ✓ **In Delhi** **Nicolson Street** Near Nicolson Sq and university. A mini maha-rajah's tent on the Southside, homage to Bollywood (movies on TV) and sweet memories of India. Chai and Pekoe teas (including Masala tea), soups and a bit of curry and daal. Chilled vibe, nice people. A no-alcohol zone. 7 days 10am-10pm.

293 1/XB5 ✓ **Luca's** www.s-luca.co.uk · 0131 446 0233 · **16 Morningside Road** In-town version of legendary ice-cream parlour in Musselburgh (1432/ICE CREAM). Ice cream and snacks downstairs, more family food parlour up. Cheap and cheerful. Great for kids. 7 days. 266/KIDS.

294 1/A1 ✓ **Sprio** 0131 226 7533 · **37 St Stephen Street** Tiny, authentic Italian coffee shop – a splash of Milano style in old St Stephen St. Few tables but you can take away. Paninis, piadines (northern Italian unleavened bread), cured meats, cakes and the *best* espresso – and the home-made lemonade. 7 days. Mon-Sat 8.30am-5pm, Sun 10.30am-5pm.

295 1/XE1 ✓ **Punjab'n De Rasoi** **122 Leith Walk** Almost at the foot of the Walk, a real taste of Punjab in a simple caff run by (and 'empowering') Punjabi women. Snacks (pakoras, samosas), daals and curries. Inexpensive thali and genuine sweet desserts. The real deal and great value. Wed-Sat, 11am-8pm.

296 1/D1 **Blue Moon Café** www.bluemooncafe.co.uk · 0131 557 0911 · **1 Barony Street** Longest-established gay café in Scotland (1067/GAY EDINBURGH). Straight-friendly and a good place to hang out from breakfast to late. All-day breakfast. Nachos-and-burgers kind of menu. 7 days 10am-10pm. Food till 10pm, bar till 11pm. There's a Hamburger Heaven attached (enter from Broughton St).

297 1/XE1   **Drill Hall Arts Café** www.outoftheblue.org.uk · 0131 555 7100 ·
34 Dalmeny Street Off Leith Walk. A drill hall right enough, turned into a vibrant
and vital arts centre and neighbourhood social hub by Out of the Blue.
Collectivism and community arts very much alive here; it buzzes, especially on
Saturdays at the Food Market. Studios, dance classes, workshops, music at the
heart of this eco/Fair-trade/creative food kitchen. Soups, sandwiches; big for
brunch. 10-5pm. Closed Sun. The beating heart of Leith.

298 1/D5   **Monster Mash** 0131 225 7069 · 4 Forrest Road Near the university. Comfort-
food café capitalising on the mash comeback with properly sourced big sausages
and gravy, shepherd's pie, steak pie, etc. Puds similarly retro. Nicely Scottish and
not a chain restaurant. Good for little as well as us big kids. 7 days 8am-10pm (Sat
9am, Sun 10am).

299 1/D4   **Always Sunday** www.alwayssunday.co.uk · 0131 622 0667 · 170 High
Street A café on the Royal Mile near the cathedral and better than most. They
care! Home cooking and baking. Deli-style counter offering 'healthy' breakfasts
through lunch to afternoon 'treats'. 2 hot specials and soups. 7 days 8am-6pm
(Sat/Sun from 9am).

▮▮▮▮ The Best Late-Night Restaurants

300 1/C4   ✓ **The Witchery** www.thewitchery.com · 0131 225 5613 · Castlehill Top
ATMOS   of Royal Mile near the castle. Excellent value menu post- (and pre-) theatre
£25-35   menu from one of the city's best restaurants which means there's somewhere
good to go late that's civilised. 2 courses only £15 at TGP. Worth it for the atmosphere alone. (134/BEST RESTAURANTS). 7 days, lunch and **LO 11.30pm**.

301 1/D5   ✓ **Negociants** 0131 225 6313 · 45 Lothian Street Near the university, a
£15-25   long-established all-day and late-night hangout. Chairs outside in summer.
Food of the popular variety ain't the strongest point but it is as good as it gets this
late. Good mix of people. DJs in Medina downstairs at weekends. **Till 11.30pm &**
2am Fri-Sat. Club 10pm-3am.

302 1/E2   ✓ **Giuliano's** www.giulianos.co.uk · 0131 556 6590 · 18 Union Place Leith
£15-25   Walk opposite Playhouse. Buzzing Italian tratt day and night. Report 191/
TRUSTY TRATTS. **Till 2am (2.30am weekends).**

303 1/D5   **Favorit** 0131 220 6880 · 20 Teviot Place New York diner-type café/restaurant
£25-35   – salads, pasta, wraps, Ben & Jerry's. Food not so favourite but this is a useful
nightowl/nighthawk spot. **7 days till midnight, Fri/Sat 2.30am.**

304 1/A3   **Bar Roma** www.bar-roma.co.uk · 0131 226 2977 · 39a Queensferry Street
£15-25   An Edinburgh institution, buzzing day and night. The old standbys snappily served
and lots of late-night Italian jive. The best wine list you'll find in West End after ordinary hours (see 190/TRUSTY TRATTS). **12noon-11pm Sun-Thu; midnight Fri-Sat.**

305 1/C4   **Mamma's** www.mammaspizza.co.uk · 0131 225 6464 · 30 Grassmarket
£15-25   Open **till 11pm always & 12midnight** if you're lucky. Report: 196/PIZZAS.

Good Places For Sunday Breakfast

306 1/C3 ✓ **The Scottish Restaurant** www.thescottishcafeandrestaurant.com · 0131 226 6524 · The Mound Below the National Gallery; enter via Princes St Gardens. The definitive Scottish breakfast of course, but many variations. Great location for easing into Sunday, and upstairs there's very good art. 8am-6pm (7pm Thu). **From 9am.** See 228/SCOTTISH RESTAURANTS.

307 1/C2 ✓ **Urban Angel** www.urban-angel.co.uk · 0131 225 6215 · 121 Hanover Street & 1 Forth Street · 0131 556 6323 Convivial, contemporary breakfast from eggs Benedict to honey and waffles. Freshly made croissants and the potato scones (139/BISTROS)! Saturday night a distant memory. **From 9am Forth St, 10am Hanover St.**

308 1/B2 ✓ **Rick's** www.ricksedinburgh.co.uk · 0131 622 7800 · 55a Frederick Street The buzzing café-bar (394/COOL BARS) with rooms (96/INDIVIDUAL HOTELS) opens early as well as late; an excellent spot for laid-back or power breakfast brunch 7 days, including unusually early start on Sundays. Eclectic, contemporary menu. **Open 7 days from 8am.**

309 1/D4 **City Café** 131 220 0125 · Blair Street It's been here a long time but it keeps on (as they used to say) truckin'. BIG for breakfast (carnivore or veggie), few places in the city beat it for content or American-diner atmosphere. Slow to get going; most of the clientele have been up very late, but it does! **From 10am.**

310 1/XE1 **King's Wark** 0131 554 9260 · 36 The Shore On busy corner for traffic, but calm and comforting inside. Dining room or bar. No early start (**11am**), but a civilised brunch on the waterfront.

311 1/D5 **Negociants** 0131 225 6313 · 45 Lothian Street Negociants so good late (see 301/LATE-NIGHT RESTAURANTS) is also good early (the next day). Very good breakfast in or (in summer) out till 3pm. **From 10am.**

312 1/D4 **Elephant House** www.elephant-house.co.uk · 0131 220 5355 · 21 George IV Bridge Another (this time extensive) coffee-house near the university that's open early for caffeine and sustenance. 286/COFFEE SHOPS. **From 8am.**

313 1/D1 **The Broughton Street Breakfast** There's lots of choice in the main street of Edinburgh's East Village. From the top down: Lovely-looking **Treacle** kicks in from **10am** with upmarket gastropub choices. **Artisan Roast** has the best coffee: from **10am. The Basement** also does Tex-Mex brex from **12noon** and regulars attest to its ability to hit the spot. Further down on the corner with people-watching windows is **The Barony** with breakfast and papers from **12.30-3.30pm** (great live music Sun evenings); **The New Town Deli** on the corner of Barony St is neither a deli nor a café but has a few seats, the papers and is open from **9am** (till 4pm). The **NTD** is also at **23 Henderson Row**; 321/TAKEAWAYS. And special mention for:

314 1/D1 **The Olive Branch** www.theolivebranchscotland.co.uk · 0131 557 8589 · Corner of Broughton Street & Broughton Place The definitive **Broughton St Breakfast**: big windows, outside tables. Med menu and breakfast fry-ups. This place is routinely packed. On Sundays you pray for a table. **From 10am.**

The Best Takeaway Places

315 1/B2 ✓ **Appetite @ Rowland's** www.appetitedirect.com · 0131 225 3711 · 42 Howe Street Great home-made food for takeaway, parties or just for your own supper/picnic, etc. Nearest thing in Edinburgh to a traiteur. Daily soups/curry/quiche/pizza and specials. Good vegetarian and salads (hot food till 4.30pm). Artisan Roast coffee. Best in the Stockbridge quarter; just possibly the best in town. Mon-Fri 8.30am-6pm.

316 1/B1 ✓ **Anima** 0131 558 2918 · 11 Henderson Row Adjacent and part of L'Alba D'Oro (217/FISH & CHIPS). Smart, busy Italian hot 'n' cold takeaway. 'Italian soul food' includes great pizza, freshly prepared pastas made to order. Excellent wine selection, some desserts. A welcome expansion from chips – our soul food – to theirs. 7 days. Lunch and 5pm-10pm LO (11pm weekends). Closed Sun lunch.

317 1/C2 ✓ **G&T (Glass & Thompson)** 0131 557 0909 · 2 Dundas Street Deli and coffee shop offering takeaway sandwiches/rolls in infinite formats using their drool-making selection of quality ingredients. Very fine cakes. Take to office, dinner party or gardens. Sit-in area and small terrace with New Townies and their chat. Mon-Sat 8am-5.45pm, Sun 10.30am-4.15pm. Report: 281/BEST TEAROOMS.

318 1/E5 **Kebab Mahal** 0131 667 5214 · 7 Nicolson Square For 30 years this unassuming but cosmopolitan Indian diner and takeaway has occupied a fond place on the edge of the university quarter for snacks, curries, babas, kulfi and lassis. Open late. 12noon-12midnight, till 2am Fri/Sat.

319 1/XF1 **The Manna House** 0131 652 2349 · 22 Easter Road Unlikely spot for relatively genuine French pâtisserie. Cakes to covet, artisan bread and baps; some tables and a quiche/salad/sandwich menu. Bakery through back. 8am-6pm. Closed Sun.

320 1/XE1 **Embo** 0131 652 3880 · 29 Haddington Place Halfway down Leith Walk and a reason for going that far. Mike Marshall's neighbourhood hangout and takeaway is just better than the rest. Bespoke sandwiches, wraps, etc. Excellent coffee and smoothies. Few seats in and a couple of tables outside the door. Nice cakes. Local sourcing. This place is good to know. Mon-Fri 8am-4pm, from 9am Sat. Closed Sun.

321 1/D1 **The New Town Deli** 0131 558 3837 · 42 Broughton Street This misleadingly named soup 'n' sandwich place on a corner of the East Village is by no stretch a deli. Open all day till 3/4pm for sandwiches, rolls and focaccia. Big window for people-watching. Non New Town branches at **23 Henderson Row** and **Bernard St, Leith** (another busy shop on the corner). Henderson Row branch the best for real breakfast and newspaper reading, especially on Sundays (outside tables).

322 1/XB1 **Eastern Spices** 0131 558 3609 · 6 Howard Street In Canonmills along from their original home by the clock. It varies a bit but when they're on spice, they're hard to beat. Also home delivery in a 5-mile radius. Vast Indian menu from pakora to pasanda and meals for one. 5-11.30pm. 7 days.

323 1/XA4 **Herbie** 0131 226 6366 · 7 William Street Related to Herbie, the deli and cheeserie in Stockbridge, this is an immensely popular lunchtime fuel stop. Many soups, daily quiche, sandwich central. Always a line, but they're quick! 7 days 7am-4.15pm, Sat from 9am, Sun from 10am.

The Best Delis

324 1/E1
ATMOS
✓ ✓ ✓ **Valvona & Crolla** www.valvonacrolla.com · 19 Elm Row
Near top of Leith Walk. Since 1934 an Edinburgh institution, the perfect provisioner for the good things in life. Full of smells, genial, knowledgeable staff and a floor-to-ceiling range of cheese, meats, oils, wines and artisan bread. Superlative fresh produce, irresistible cheese counter, on-premises bakery, great café/ bar (183/ITALIAN RESTAURANTS). Demos, tastings and a Fringe venue – it's a national treasure. Mon-Thu 8.30am-6pm, Fri/Sat 8am-6.30pm, Sun 10.30am-4pm.

325 1/C4
✓ ✓ **I.J. Mellis** www.mellischeese.co.uk · Victoria Street, Morningside Road & Baker's Place, Stockbridge   Started out as the cheese guy, now more of a very select deli for food that's good and 'slow'. Coffees, hams, sausages, olives and seasonal stuff like apples and mushrooms (branches vary); smells mingle. Branches also in Glasgow (636/GLASGOW DELIS) and St Andrews (1441/DELIS). Times vary. See also 1468/CHEESES. He's still the cheese guy.

326 1/XD5
✓ ✓ **Earthy** 33 Ratcliffe Terrace   Tucked-away kitchen, garden and lifestyle emporium on Southside via Causewayside. An ambitious 2-floor shop and café (that feels like a market) with plants outside. Kind of co-op of like-minded gardeners and growers passionate about food, so all suppliers are hand-picked along with most of the fruit and veg (source countries noted). Related to Phantassie, the organic farm in East Lothian. Local, Fair-trade and seasonal are the watchwords here. Superb range of everything (even the oatcakes). Initially not easy to find, but you will do. 10am-7pm (6pm Sun). Café 10am-5pm.

327 1/D1
✓ **L'Epicerie** 56 Broughton Street   Below and part of L'Escargot Bleu and Blanc (176/FRENCH RESTAURANTS). As the restaurant, this is the real deal. Artisan cheese, Oliveology oils, strings of garlic and shallots and the best macarons. Living round the corner, I'm so glad they're here! 10am-7.30pm. Closed Sun.

328 1/A1
✓ **Herbie** 1 North West Circus Place, 66 Raeburn Place   Notable originally for cheese (that Brie!) and other cold-counter irresistibles (1469/CHEESES). There's always a queue in their packed-from-floor-to-ceiling emporium of good things. Nice home-made bread and scrumptious munchies. They're related to the takeaway in William St (323/TAKEAWAY). 9am-7pm; Sat till 6pm. Closed Sun.

329 1/D1
✓ **Broughton Delicatessen** 7 Barony Street   2 doors from Broughton St corner but busy through reputation and loyal clientele. Some tables. Mainly a coffee shop but with a selection of good products: salads, quiche, hot dishes and home-made cakes to stay or to go. 9am-7pm (Sat 5pm), Sun 11am-5pm.

330 1/XD5
✓ **Victor Hugo** www.victorhugodeli.com · 0131 667 1827 · 26 Melville Terrace   On the road parallel to the main road through the Meadows and overlooking the parkland. Here since 1940 and recently with mixed fortunes but now under Alan Thomson firmly back on track, especially for snacking; with tables in and out. Selectivity in olives, cheeses, cooked meats; traiteur-type meals to eat in or takeaway. 7 days 8am-8pm, Sat 9am-6pm, Sun 10am-5pm.

331 1/XB5
& XA1
✓ **Henri's Fine Foods & Wine** www.henrisofedinburgh.co.uk · 376 Morningside Road · 0131 447 8877 & Raeburn Place · 0131 332 8963
Specialising in French cheese (they supply many top restaurants) and wine. 7 days.

332 1/C2
✓ **G&T (Glass & Thompson)** 2 Dundas Street   Exemplary, contemporary provisioner. Med-style goodies to eat or take away. Report: 281/TEAROOMS.

Unique Edinburgh Pubs

333 1/XE1
ATMOS
DA
✓ **Port o' Leith** 58 Constitution Street The legendary Leith bar on the busy road to what used to be the docks is perhaps not what it once was when Mary Moriarty was Madame, but some aura still remains. Still a port in the storm for a' sorts. Till 1am.

334 1/XB5
ATMOS
✓ **Bennet's** Leven Street By King's Theatre. Stand at the back and don't watch the sports, watch light stream through the stained glass like it always did. Same era as Café Royal and similar ambience, mirrors and tiles. Decent food at lunch and early evening (370/PUB FOOD). Till 12.30am Mon-Fri, 1am Sat, 11pm Sun.

335 1/D5
ATMOS
✓ **Sandy Bells** 0131 225 2751 · Forrest Road Near the university and Greyfriars Kirk; it seems like it's been there as long. Mainly known as a folky/traditional music haven (live 7 nights), it reeks (and we do mean reeks) of atmosphere. Should be given a dispensation from the smoking ban. Long may it... 7 days till 1am (Sun 11pm).

336 1/D2
ATMOS
✓ **Café Royal** West Register Street Behind Burger King at the east end of Princes Street, one of Edinburgh's longest-celebrated pubs. Unrelated to the London version, though there is a similar Victorian/Baroque elegance. Through the partition is the Oyster Bar (with perfect atmosphere for oysters and all; 213/ SEAFOOD RESTAURANTS). Central counter and often standing room only. Open to 11pm (later at weekends). Bar food till 9.45pm.

337 1/D1
Barony Bar 81 Broughton Street East Village venue with a mixed clientele and always a good vibe. Belgian and guest beers. Newspapers to browse over a Sunday-afternoon breakfast. Bert's band and others on Sunday afternoons/ evenings one of the best pub-music nights in town. Till 12midnight Mon-Thu, 12.30am Fri-Sat, 11pm Sun.

338 1/D1
The Basement www.thebasement.org.uk · 109 Broughton Street New ownership since the last edition for this much-imitated but still crucial, chunky, happening sort of, er, basement with perennially popular Mex-style food served by smiley staff in Hawaiian shirts. At night, the punters are well up for it – late, loud and still alive. Till 1am daily.

339 1/B2
ATMOS
Kay's Bar 39 Jamaica Street The New Town – including Jamaica St – sometimes gives the impression that it's populated by people who were around in the late 18th century. It's an Edinburgh thing (mainly male). They care for the beer (361/REAL-ALE PUBS) and do nice grub at lunchtime (anything that goes with HP Sauce). Until 11.45pm (11pm Sun).

340 1/A3
Mather's 1 Queensferry Street Edinburgh's West End has a complement of 'smart' bars that cater for people with ties and no (domestic) ties. The alternative is here – a stand-up space for old-fashioned pubbery, slack coiffure and idle talk (353/UNSPOILT PUBS). Wimmin rarely venture. Till 12midnight Mon-Thu, 1am Fri-Sat, 11pm Sun.

341 1/E1
Sofi/Boda/Joseph Pearce/Victoria Leith 4 pubs all in the Leith area where Anna and Mike Christopherson have built a very particular little empire that could only happen in Edinburgh. All have been transformed from old, defunct pubs and are fresh, quirky, laid-back, mix 'n' match and full of individual touches. Sofi is the smallest, in a Leith backstreet (Henderson St); JP the largest on a busy corner (Elm

Row) at the top of Leith Walk (with good pub-grub menu and outside tables, Scrabble nights, 'language café', a jogging club – you get the picture?); the others are on corners on The Walk. All till 12midnight/1am.

342 1/XE1 **Robbie's** Leith Walk On the corner with Iona St. Some bars on Leith Walk are downright scary and there are many new, fluffier ones of late but Robbie's stays real. Good range of beer, TV will have the football on (or not) and there are 4 screens so there's no escape. Magi-mix of Trainspotters, locals and the odd dodgy character (350/'UNSPOILT' PUBS). Till 12midnight Mon-Sat, 11pm Sun.

343 1/D4 **City Café** 0131 220 0127 · 19 Blair Street 20 years on, the retro Americana chic has aged gracefully and has recently been leathered up with more banquettes. All-day diner food, decent coffee. A hip Edinburgh bar that has stood the test of mind-altering time. DJs weekends; and see 309/SUNDAY BREAKFAST. 10am-1am daily (food till 10pm).

344 1/A3 **Ghillie Dhu** www.ghillie-dhu.co.uk · 0131 222 9930 · 2 Rutland Place Opposite the Caledonian Hotel. Recent conversion of a lofty church space into a Scottish-themed food and music experience by the very experienced GI group. It was a 'mess' during both world wars and there is something canteen-like about the snacks and 'Scottish fayre' served by kilty waiters. The main interest is the upstairs live-music space (Sat) and the Friday night ceilidh, a backpacker must! Till 3am, food till 10pm.

345 1/XE5 **Sheep Heid** www.sheepheid.co.uk · 0131 656 6951 · Causeway, ATMOS Duddingston 18th-century inn 6km from centre behind Arthur's Seat and reached most easily through the Queen's Park. Village and nearby wildfowl loch should be strolled around if you have time. So-so but can be al fresco; comfy upstairs room. Atmosphere and history is why we come. Lunch and 6.30-8pm, LO 7.45pm. Bar till 11pm/12midnight. Book weekends.

346 1/C2 **The Dome** www.thedomeedinburgh.com · 0131 624 8624 · 14 George Street Edinburgh's first megabar in truly impressive former bank and grandiose in a way that only a converted temple to Mammon could be. The main part sits 15m under an elegant domed roof with an island bar and raised platform at back (The Grill) for determined diners. Big chandeliers, big, big flower arrangements: you come for the surroundings more than the victuals, perhaps. Adjacent and separate Club Room is more intimate, more clubby, better for a blether. 'Garden' patio bar at back (in good weather) – enter via Rose Street. Final bit, downstairs: Why Not? – a nightclub for over-25s still lookin' for lurvv (Fri/Sat). Main bar Sun-Thu till 11.30pm, Fri-Sat till 1am. Food till 10pm.

347 1/D3 **The Doric** www.the-doric.com · 0131 225 1084 · 15 Market Street Long-serving and mixed fortunes as a bistro, ie the food, but the upstairs wine bar is Edinburgh in a nutshell. The window tables looking over the town to the Balmoral offer one of the defining views of the city. Bar also on street level.

The Best Old 'Unspoilt' Pubs

Of course it's not necessarily the case that when a pub's done up, it's spoiled, or that all old pubs are worth preserving, but some have resisted change and that's part of their appeal. Money and effort are often spent to 'oldify' bars and contrive an atmosphere. The following places don't have to try.

348 1/XA4 ✓ **The Diggers** 1 Angle Park Terrace (Officially the Athletic Arms.) Jambo pub *par excellence*, stowed with the Tynecastle faithful before and after games. Still keeps a great pint of locally brewed 80/-. The food is basic, ie pies at lunchtime (from local baker's, Morrison's). Till 11pm/12midnight Mon-Sat, 11pm Sun.

349 1/D4 ✓ **The Royal Oak** www.royal-oak-folk.com · Infirmary Street Tiny
ATMOS upstairs and not much bigger down. During the day, pensioners sip their pints (couple of real ales), downstairs 'lounge' from 9pm. Has surprisingly survived the smoking ban. Mainly known as a folk-music stronghold (live music every night for 50 years!) and home of The Wee Folk Club, they definitely don't make 'em like this any more. Gold-carat pubness.

350 1/XA4 ✓ **Roseburn Bar** 1 Roseburn Terrace On main Glasgow road out west from Haymarket and one of the nearest pubs to Murrayfield Stadium. Wood and grandeur and red leather; bonny wee snug. Fine pint of McEwan's and wall-to-wall rugby, of course. Heaving and heaven before internationals. Till 11pm (12midnight weekends).

351 1/XE1 **Robbie's** Leith Walk On the corner of Iona St. Real ales and new lagers in a neighbourhood howff that takes all sorts. More rough than smooth of course, but with the footy on the box, a pint and a packet of Hula Hoops – this is a bar to save or savour life. Till 12midnight Mon-Sat, 11pm Sun. Report: 342/UNIQUE EDINBURGH PUBS.

352 1/B3 **Oxford Bar** www.oxfordbar.com · 8 Young Street Downhill from George St. No time machine needed – just step in the door and find one of Edinburgh's most celebrated non-reconstructed bars. Inspector Rebus wuz here. Be prepared to be scrutinised when you come in. Some real ales but they're as beside the point as the pies. Till 1am (12midnight Sun).

353 1/A3 **Mather's** 1 Queensferry Street Not only a reasonable real-ale pub but almost worth visiting just to look at the ornate fixtures and fittings – frieze and bar especially. Unreconstructed in every sense since 1903. Pies all day. Till 12midnight Mon-Thu, 1am Fri-Sat, 11pm Sun. Report: 340/UNIQUE PUBS. There's another, unrelated, **Mather's** in Broughton St which is managing to keep its head in the city's grooviest street by remaining pub-like and unpretentious. Football on the telly.

The Best Real-Ale Pubs

354 1/C1 ✓ **The Cumberland Bar** www.cumberlandbar.co.uk · Cumberland
DA Street Corner of Dundonald St. After work this New Town bar attracts its share of suits, but later the locals (and droves of posh students) claim it. CAMRA (Campaign for Real Ale) supporters seek it out too. Average of 8 real ales on tap. Nicely appointed, decent pub lunches, Monday quiz, unexpected beer garden (12noon-evening Sat/Sun; 380/DRINK OUTDOORS). 7 days till 1am.

355 1/C4 ✓ **The Bow Bar** 80 West Bow Halfway down Victoria St. They know how to
DA treat drink in this excellent wee bar. Huge selection of ales (usually 5 guests)
and whiskies – no cocktails! One of the few places in the Grassmarket area an
over-25-year-old might not feel out of place. Pie 'n' pint at lunch. Till 11.30pm
Mon-Sat, 11pm Sun.

356 1/B5 ✓ **Cloisters** 26 Brougham Street, Tollcross This is a drinker's paradise: 10
ales on tap, 70 whiskies with 35ml measures and many wines by the glass in
this simple and unfussy bar with wooden floors and laid-back approach. Same
owners as the Bow Bar (above). Good pub grub; times vary and not Mon or Fri. Bar
closes 12midnight (12.30am Fri-Sat). Both pubby and clubby; girls go too! The
same people own the **Stockbridge Tap** on the corner of busy Raeburn Pl (no. 2).
6 ales, food till 8pm. Good neighbourhood spot.

357 1/XB5 ✓ **The Canny Man's** 237 Morningside Road Officially the Volunteer Arms
but everybody calls it the Canny Man's. Smorrebrod at lunch and evenings
(157/GASTROPUBS), a wide range of real ales and myriad malts. Casual visitors may
feel management have too much attitude – there's a list of dos and don'ts on the
door – but this much-loved family fiefdom is one of the city's most convivial pubs.

358 1/D2 ✓ **The Guildford Arms** www.guildfordarms.com · 1 West Register Street
Behind Burger King at east end of Princes St on same block as the Café Royal
(336/UNIQUE PUBS). Forever in the same family. Lofty, ornate Victorian hostelry
with loadsa good ales, typically 7 Scottish, 3 English (and 16 wines by the glass).
There are some you won't find anywhere else in the city. Pub grub available on
'gallery' floor as well as bar. Big wallpaper and carpet (don't drink too much). Sun-
Wed till 11pm, Thu-Sat till 12midnight.

359 1/B5 ✓ **Blue Blazer** 2 Spittal Street Opposite Point Hotel (76/HOTELS). No frills,
no pretensions, just wooden fixtures and fittings and toasties to snack in this
fine howff that carries a huge range of real ales. Regularly a CAMRA pub of the
year with 8 ales on tap. Extraordinary rum and gin list and then the malts. Much
more soul than its competitors nearby. 7 days till 1am.

360 1/XA4 **Bert's** 29 William Street Rare ales as well as house IPA and 80/-, suits as well
as casual crowd in this faux Edwardian bar. Decent pies for carnivores or veggies
alike all day, with other good pub-grub lunch till 10pm. Good range of up to 8
guest ales. Till 11pm Sun-Thu, 12midnight Fri-Sat.

361 1/B2 **Kay's Bar** 39 Jamaica Street Off India St in the New Town. Go on an afternoon
when gentlemen of a certain age talk politics, history and rugby over pints of
porter. The knowledgeable barman patiently serves. All red and black and vaguely
distinguished with a tiny snug: the Library. Comfort food simmers in the window
(lunch only). Till 12midnight (11pm Sun). (339/UNIQUE PUBS.)

362 1/XB1 **Starbank Inn** www.starbankinn.co.uk · 64 Laverockbank Road, Newhaven
A Belhaven house on the seafront road west of Newhaven Harbour. 8 different ales
on offer. Great place to sit with pint in hand and watch the sun sink over the Forth.
The food is fine (till 9pm). Bar till 11pm Sun-Wed, 12midnight Thu-Sat.

363 1/D1 **Cask & Barrel** 115 Broughton Street & 24 West Preston Street Wall-to-
wall distressed wood, great selection of real ales (8) and a couldn't-care-less crowd
at the foot of gay and groovy Broughton St. Here they prefer a good pint and the
football. Till 12.30am Sun-Wed, 1am Thu-Sat. Outside tables on a windy corner.
New Southside version has the ales, the TV and the space same as.

Bars With Good Food

Also see Gastropubs, p. 43. These below are not so high-falutin' foodwise but nevertheless are worth going to for food as well as drink.

364 1/XE1 ✓ **Roseleaf** www.roseleaf.co.uk · 0131 476 5268 · 24 Sandport Place
Corner of Quayside between The Shore and busy Commercial St. They see themselves as a 'cosy wee hidden treasure' and they're not wrong. Food definitely the thing here with absolutely everything home-made, including an afternoon tea on a tier (preorder). Small it is and perfectly formed. Weekends you'd better book. 7 days 11am-10pm. Bar 11/12pm.

365 1/D4 ✓ **Divino Enoteca** www.divinoedinburgh.com · 0131 225 1770 ·
5 Merchant Street This is the downstairs of Vittoria (188/TRATTS), the wine and food bar of maestro Tony Crolla. You can enter through the restaurant from George IV Bridge but you usually enter at ground level off the Cowgate. Atmosphere of dark materials and fairy-lit garden, designed to make you love Italian wine. Small plate/grazing menu and more substantial dishes. The fancy machinery keeps the wines pristine. 3pm-12midnight, Saturday 12noon-1am.

366 1/XE1 **The Compass** 0131 554 1979 · 44 Queen Charlotte Street Corner of Constitution St opposite Leith Police Station. This 'bar & grill' is a popular Leith haunt, maybe missed by uptown grazers. Stone and woody look with mix-match furniture; food better and more ambitious than you might first think, and all home-made. Staple fare. Bar kicks in later. 7 days, 10am-10pm.

367 1/A3 **Cambridge Bar** www.thecambridgebar.co.uk · 0131 226 2120 ·
£15-22 20 Young Street On the west extension of Thistle St. Discreet doorway to Edinburgh institution. Sporty in a rugger kind of way and more recently notable for its gastroburgers, probably among the best in town. Huge and huge choice including vegetarian (bean burgers); Mackie's estimable ice-cream to follow. Sadly only a handful of tables but same folk (and same menu) have Wannaburger (261/BURGERS). Food 12noon-8.45pm. Bar 11pm/12midnight and 1am Fri/Sat.

368 1/XF1 **The Espy** www.the-espy.com · 0131 669 0082 · 62 Bath Street, Portobello At the end of the said Esplanade. The place for pub grub in Porty (the Portobello seaside suburb) with slouchy couches in the lounge area and a fair few tables (including in the window, with a view of the espy, the surprising beach and the sea), usually full. Food all fresh and cooked to order; good burgers. Occasional live music. Some tables outside. 7 days 12noon-9.30pm. Bar 1am.

369 1/XE1 **Guilty Lily** 0131 554 5824 · 284 Bonnington Road The back road to Leith. A moribund pub taken over by the same people who have the Espy (above) and transformed with great pub food into a destination. Simple menu (lotsa burgers) but all freshly and conscientiously done, from daily meze to crumbles. Book weekends. 11am-9pm (later weekends). Bar 12midnight/1am.

370 1/XB5 **Bennet's** 0131 229 5143 · 8 Leven Street Next to the King's Theatre. An
ATMOS Edinburgh standby, listed for several reasons (334/UNIQUE PUBS), not least its honest-to-goodness (and cheap) pub lunch. A la carte (stovies, steak pie, etc.) and daily specials under the enormous mirrors. Lunch and till 8.30pm (not Sun).

371 1/C3 **The Abbotsford** www.theabbotsford.com · 0131 225 5276 · 3 Rose Street
A doughty remnant of Rose St drinking days of yore, and still the best pub lunch near Princes St. Fancier than it used to be but still grills and bread-and-butter

pudding. Huge portions. Restaurant upstairs more cuisine. Lunch and LO 9.45pm. Bar till 11pm/12midnight. Closed Sun.

372 1/B2   **Iglu** 0131 476 5333 · **2b Jamaica Street** Tiny upstairs bistro and cosy down-
    ECO stairs bar in a New Town corner near Stockbridge. Organic approach to ingredients. Scottish/local and quite meaty menu. You fit in tight but Iglu attracts a sympatico crowd. Book at weekends. Lunch Fri-Sun, dinner 7 days. LO 10pm, bar 1am.

373 1/B2   **Bon Vivant** www.bonvivantedinburgh.co.uk · 0131 225 3275 · **55 Thistle Street** In a street of many food options, this may get overlooked but it is a good hangout: candlelit atmosphere, DJs and a great selection of wine or champagne by the glass. Bite-size grazings and mains creatively put. 12noon-10pm. Bar till 1am.

The Best Places To Drink Outdoors

374 1/C4   **The (Café) Hub** www.thehub-edinburgh.com · 0131 473 2067 · **Castlehill** The café-bar of the International Festival Centre much improved for food and with a great enclosed terrace for people-watching. Brollies and heaters extend the possibilities. Ok for kids. 7 days 9.30am-10pm (till 6.30pm Sun).

375 1/XE1   **The Shore** www.theshore.biz · 0131 553 5080 · **3 The Shore, Leith** Excellent place to eat (159/GASTROPUBS), some tables just outside the door, but it's fine to wander over to the quayside and sit with your legs over the edge. Do try not to fall in. From 11am daily.

376 1/XE1   **Malmaison** 0131 468 5000 · **Tower Place, Leith** Just along from The Shore (above), this hotel (part of the chain) has more proper seating; a terrace. If you can ignore the nearby flats, it's a great Leith vantage point.

377 1/XE1   **Teuchter's Landing** www.aroomin.co.uk · 0131 554 7427 · **1c Dock Place** Another very good Leith eaterie (167/GASTROPUBS) but with waterside tables and spread over adjacent pontoons. Mugs of prawns, stovies, etc in half- or full-pint portions. Great wine list – 20 by the glass. From 12noon Mon-Sat, 12.30pm Sun.

378 1/D5   **Pear Tree** 0131 667 7533 · **38 West Nicholson Street** Adjacent to parts of Edinburgh University so real student style with big beer garden. Serried ranks of tables and refectory-style food not to everybody's taste. Stage for occasional live music, and BBQ. Good malt list. From 12noon Mon-Sat, 12.30pm Sun.

379 1/D2   **The Outhouse** 0131 557 6668 · **12a Broughton Street Lane** Large enclosed patio out back, home to summer Sunday afternoon barbecues once a month. No view except of other people.

380 1/B1   **The Cumberland Bar** 0131 558 3134 · **Cumberland Street** Some tables by the door slightly raised above street level but more space in the beer garden below. Packed on summer evenings (till 10pm). Report: 354/REAL ALE.

381 1/E4   **The Pleasance** www.pleasance.co.uk · **The Pleasance & George Square Gardens** Both open during the Festival only, these are major Fringe venues, one a large, open courtyard and the other in the heart of the university and the new south-centred Fringe. If you're here, you're on the Fringe, so to speak.

382 1/A5   **Cargo** 0131 659 7880 · 129 Fountainbridge At the so-called 'Edinburgh Quay'. Lofty emporium pub; food is eaten. Mainly distinguished by outdoor seating (in ranks of tables) on the basin of the Caledonian Canal – a surprising waterside spot in the city centre, it ain't Camden Lock.

383 1/D2   **The Street** 0131 556 4272 · Picardy Place at Broughton Street Great people-watching potential on busy corner. Gay in and out. See 392/COOL BARS.

General locations: Greenside Place (**Theatre Royal** and **Café Habana**), bars in **The Grassmarket**, and **Negociants** and **Assembly** on Lothian Street. All rise (or sit down) to pavement café culture when the sun's out.

Cool Bars

Depends what you mean by 'cool': the ultra-contemporary, style-bar ethos of Voodoo Rooms or Rick's and the funkier, not-trying-so-hard ambience of 99 Hanover and Nobles. It may depend on whether you prefer looks or feels.

384 1/C2 ✓ ✓ **Bramble** 0131 226 6343 · Queen Street At Hanover St. A discreet, hidden-away corner basement; cool and comfy and big on cocktails. Discerning drinkers' haven so great voddies, whiskies and over 60 gins. Nice Gen X (and Y and Z) people in the mix and non-compromising soundtrack rather than fluffy lounge music. DJs Fri/Sat. Evenings only; till 1am.

385 1/XD2 ✓ ✓ **The Voodoo Rooms** www.thevoodoorooms.com · 0131 556 7060 · West Register Street Between St Andrew's Sq and the east end of Princes St. Opulent Victorian rooms above the Café Royal (336/UNIQUE PUBS, 213/SEAFOOD RESTAURANTS) transformed into a very contemporary, very happening group of salons for drinking, eating, carousing. Major Edinburgh live-music venue for interesting new bands. Food (till 9.45pm). Bars 1am.

386 1/B4 ✓ ✓ **Dragonfly** www.dragonflycocktailbar.com · 0131 228 4543 · West Port On the western extension of the Grassmarket. Discreet frontage but you enter a more beautiful, more stylish world where alcohol is treated like food in a fine-dining restaurant and cocktails are king. Lofty room with mezzanine. Not too many distractions from the aesthetic. No food but pizzas are delivered from Mammas nearby (196/PIZZA). 7 days till 1am.

387 1/C2 ✓ **Tigerlily** 0131 225 5005 · 125 George Street Some will revel in it, others go 'yuck' to this style-blinding bar/restaurant/hotel. Front lounge, quite pink and girlie, opens into a vast, always-buzzing bar/restaurant (87/HOTELS). Every design feature of these times with great attention to detail. A destination for the smart and ambitious and those with nice hair and teeth. 7 days till 1am.

388 1/C3 ✓ **99 Hanover Street** 0131 225 8200 Address as is. Unlikely up-the-town location but a civilised, draped and candlelit world with chabby-chic, pick 'n' mix furniture, crap pictures, cool clientele and excellent music. It rocks. Food for lunch and 5-9pm. DJs Thu-Sat. Till 1am.

389 1/D4 ✓ **The Jazz Bar** 0131 220 4298 · Chambers Street Down long stairs to Bill Kyle's jazz cellar, this is not an obvious cool bar unless you like good music and then it's very cool. No live band tokenism: funk, hip-hop, ambient... and jazz. Great ambience, interesting people. Mostly free but occasional name-band nights. An Edinburgh treasure chest. 7 days 5pm-3am, Sat from 2.30pm. A groove!

390 1/D4 **Brewdog** www.brewdog.com · 01346 519009 · **143 Cowgate** Proclaiming the 'craft-beer revolution', the heavy-duty beer brand from Fraserburgh arrived in grungy Cowgate in 2011. Also in Aberdeen and Glasgow (669/COOL BARS), this glass/ brick/steel NYC kind of bar is a long way from real-ale watering holes elsewhere. Up to 9 of their own quirky-named beers on tap and bespoke bottlings from across the world. In a hard- and binge-drinking street this high-gravity hostelry is surprisingly civilised. These guys are on a roll; expect more Brewdogs near you. Till 1am.

391 1/D4 **Villager** www.villager-e.com · 0131 226 2781 · **50 George IV Bridge** Near university and National Library, a funked-up, laid-back place to hang out. Wall art by Elph. DJs (Fri/Sat). More foody of late (till 9.30pm) but mainly the right faces in a photo from the early days of the 21st century. Bar till 1am.

392 1/D2 **The Street** 0131 556 4272 · **2 Picardy Place** Corner glass box at the top of Broughton Street at central crossroads in the Pink Triangle; gay friendly. Great people-watching spot (outside tables) and pre-club venue. DJs weekends. Madame (Trendy) Wendy and gals manage the groove. 7 days till 1am.

393 1/C5 **Earl of Marchmont** 0131 667 1398 · **22 Marchmont Crescent** Corner with Roseneath St in the heart of studentmont, though this attracts a very mixed crowd including women with kids. Definitive bar of the area by the people who have cool caff Renroc (291/CAFFS). Pub grub till 9pm, nice wines, outside tables, DJs on Sat only. Plus good vibe; it works. 7 days till 1am (Sun 12midnight).

394 1/B2 **Rick's** www.ricksedinburgh.co.uk · 0131 622 7800 · **55a Frederick Street** New Town café-bar-restaurant with rooms (99/BOUTIQUE HOTELS). Same people have Tigerlily (above and 87/HOTELS), **Lulu** and the **Opal Lounge**, both nightclubs on George St. Rick's is more laid back and opens nicely to the outdoors. Food till 10pm. Smart service; they do know how to make cocktails. Rocks from 10pm on.

395 1/E4 **Brass Monkey** 0131 556 1961 · **14 Drummond Street** Student, Gen X and funky Southside pub with backroom Bedouin boudoir full of cushions to lounge and big screen (movies at 3pm daily); can hire for private functions. 7 days. LO 12.45am. There's a newer BM (at **362 Leith Walk**): with another nice vibe, it's always busy; the original methinks is the funkier version.

396 1/XE1 **Nobles** 0131 629 7215 · **44 Constitution Street** Heart-of-Leith pub which has become, well, much cooler since Faye and Niall took over. Food, quiz nights, cupcakes and lotsa live stuff keep it lively; a good place to hang. Food 12noon-9pm.

397 1/XE1 **The Village** **16 South Fort Street** Near the east end of Ferry Rd, and Leith. This neighbourhood bar has been a quietly happening place for years and somehow I missed it till recently. Known for its eclectic live-music programme (Leith Folk Club meet here), it's one of those places that feels just right. 12noon-1am.

398 1/XE1 **The Tourmalet** **Iona & Buchanan Streets, Leith** Named after a mountain in the Pyrenées, a stage in the Tour de France cycle race, this neighbourhood pub is something to do with cycling, fish tanks and train sets but mainly about the quirks and passions of owner Murray McKean. 4pm-12midnight.

The Main Attractions

399 1/B4
HS
ADMISSION
✓ ✓ ✓ **Edinburgh Castle** www.edinburghcastle.gov.uk · 0131 225 9846 Go to Princes St and look up! Extremely busy all year round and yet the city's must-see main attraction does not disappoint. St Margaret's 12th-century chapel is simple and beautiful; the rolling history lesson that leads up to the display of Scotland's crown jewels is fascinating; the Stone of Destiny is a big deal to the Scots (though others may not see why). And, ultimately, the Scottish National War Memorial is one of the most genuinely affecting places in the country – a simple, dignified testament to shared pain and loss. The Esplanade is a major concert venue just before the International Tattoo in July, the single major event of the Festival in August, with much-needed new seating in 2011. Last ticket 45 minutes before closing. Apr-Sep 9.30am-6pm, Oct-Mar 9.30am-5pm.

400 1/B4
FREE
✓ ✓ ✓ **The National Museum of Scotland** www.nms.ac.uk · 0300 123 6789 · **Chambers Street** After an almost £50million refit, the fully integrated and effectively re-invented NMS opened to huge acclaim in summer 2011. New basement entrance (and restaurant), restored-to-former-Victorian-grandeur atrium, thousands of obects not seen before in state-of-the-art displays and interactivity, along with the adjacent Museum of Scotland (opened in 1999), make this a uniquely special homage and celebration of the ingenuity, industry and influence of a small country that changed the world. Not to forget the big animals and all that went before! With the Riverside Museum in Glasgow, Scotland has 2 paeans to its proud past that are in themselves everything to be proud of. 7 days 10am-5pm. A roof terrace reveals the city skyline. The independently run Tower Restaurant is rather good (133/FINE DINING).

401 10/P25
✓ ✓ ✓ **The Forth Bridge** www.forthbridges.org.uk · **South Queensferry** 20km west of Edinburgh via A90. First turning for South Queensferry from dual carriageway; don't confuse with signs for road bridge. Or train from Waverley to Dalmeny, and walk 1km. Knocking on now and seeming to be permanently under shrouds, the bridge was 100 in 1990. The less lovely Road Bridge will soon be followed by another but there's no cash or perhaps vision to appropriately reflect or match the original this century. An international symbol of Scotland, it should be seen, but go to the north side: South Queensferry's very crowded and a bit tacky though improving these days (shame on Tesco for spoiling the view from the road bridge approach and well done the Dakota for dramatising it; 122/HOTELS OUTSIDE TOWN). There is also a good hotel restaurant in South Queensferry (125/HOTELS OUTSIDE TOWN) with views of the bridge.

402 1/XA4
ADMISSION
✓ ✓ ✓ **Edinburgh Zoo** www.edinburghzoo.org.uk · 0131 334 9171 · **Corstorphine Road** 4km west of Princes St; buses from Princes St Gardens side. Opened in 1909, this is no ordinary zoo. Apart from being fun and educational and all that, its conservation work and serious zoology is highly respected (hence the imminent arrival at TGP of the giant pandas). Penguins parade at 2.15pm daily in summer months and there are many other old friends and favourites as well as new ones: the Sumatran tigers, the only UK koalas and the beavers – there are many animals here to love and cherish. And you will not be able to miss the pandas! Open all year 7 days, Apr-Sep 9am-6pm, Nov-Feb 9am-4.30pm, Mar and Oct 9am-5pm. (1677/KIDS)

403 1/XF3
HS
▢
ADMISSION
✓ ✓ **Palace of Holyroodhouse** www.royalcollection.org.uk · 0131 556 5100 Foot of the Royal Mile, the Queen's North British timeshare – she's here for a wee while late June/early July. Large parts of the palace are dull (Duke of Hamilton's loo, Queen's wardrobes) and only a dozen or so rooms are open, most

dating from the 17th century with a couple from the earlier 16th. Lovely cornices abound. Anomalous Stuart features, adjacent 12th-century abbey ruins quite interesting. Courtyard and conservatory café one of the nicest in town. Apr-Oct: 9.30am-5pm (last ticket) daily. Nov-Mar: 9.30am-3.30pm (last ticket) daily. Also...
The Queen's Gallery 0131 556 5100 Visually appealing addition opposite the Parliament building with separate entrance. By architect Ben Tindall (who also did The Hub at the top of the Royal Mile, though this is better). Beautiful, contemporary setting for changing exhibits from Royal Collection every 6 months which include art, ceramics, tapestries, etc. Shop stuffed with monarchist mementoes. 10am-4pm (last entry). Aug-Sep from 9.30am.

404 1/C4
1/D4
1/D3
1/E3
1/F3

✓✓ **The Royal Mile** www.edinburgh-royalmile.com The High Street, the medieval main thoroughfare of the capital follows the trail from the volcanic crag of Castle Rock and connects the castle and palace (above). Heaving during the Festival but if on a winter's night you chance by with a frost settling on the cobbles and no one is around, it's magical. Always interesting with its wynds and closes (Dunbar's Close, Whitehorse Close, the secret garden opposite Huntly House), but lots of disgraceful, made-in-China tartan shops too. Central block closed to traffic and during the Festival Fringe it's the best street-performance space in UK. See the Mile on a walking tour: there are several especially at night (ghost/ghouls/witches, etc.). Mercat Tours (0131 225 5445), Cadies and Witchery Tours (0131 225 6745) and City of the Dead (0131 225 9044) are pretty good.
The Real Mary King's Close 0845 070 6244 Part of a medieval street under the Royal Mile. Tours daily 10am (9am in Aug)-9pm (last tour), till 5pm Nov-Mar (9pm Fri/Sat). Enter by Warriston's Close near City Chambers. **Scottish Poetry Library** is in Crichton's Close on right between St Mary's St and the parliament. Great collections, lovely contemplative space. Endorses Edinburgh's status as City of Literature. Tue-Fri 10am-5pm (Thu till 8pm), Sat 10am-4pm. Closed Sun/Mon.

405 1/F3
ADMISSION

✓✓ **The Scottish Parliament** www.scottish.parliament.uk · Royal Mile · 0131 348 5200 Adjacent Holyroodhouse (above) and Our Dynamic Earth (below). Designed by Catalan architect Enric Morales who died long before it opened, this building was mired in controversy since first First Minister Donald Dewar laid the first stone. We're getting over it now though it is still is loved and hated in equal measure. However it's used publically a lot and in my view it should not be missed – it is the finest modern building in the city (it won the 2005 Stirling Prize, the UK's premier architectural award). Tour (including a visit to the Debating Chamber) times vary; book in advance.

406 1/F3
ADMISSION

✓✓ **Our Dynamic Earth** www.dynamicearth.co.uk · 0131 550 7800 · Holyrood Road Edinburgh's Dome, an interactive museum/visitor attraction, made with Millennium money and a huge success when it opened summer '99 though perhaps a little less dynamic than it was. For kids really! Now within the orbit and campus of the parliament building. Salisbury Crags rise above. Vast restaurant, and outside an amphitheatre. Apr-Oct 10am-5.30pm daily. Jul/Aug 10am-6pm. Nov-Mar 10am-5.30pm, Wed-Sun. Last admission 1 hour 30 minutes before closing.

407 1/C3
FREE

✓✓ **National Gallery of Scotland** www.nationalgalleries.org · 0131 624 6200 · The Mound Neoclassical buildings housing a superb Old Masters collection in a series of hushed salons. Many are world famous but you don't emerge goggle-eyed as from the National in London – more quietly elevated. The building in front, the **Royal Scottish Academy**, often has blockbuster exhibitions. Daily 10am-5pm, Thu 7pm. Extended hours during Festival. Serviceable caff.

408 1/XE1
ADMISSION

✓ ✓ **Royal Yacht** *Britannia* www.royalyachtbritannia.co.uk · **0131 555 5566** · **Ocean Drive, Leith** In the docks, enter by Commercial St at end of Great Junction St. Berthed outside Conran's shopping mall, the Ocean Terminal Done with ruling the waves, the royal yacht has found a permanent home as a tourist attraction (and prestigious corporate night out). Check out the new Royal Deck tearoom. Close up, the Art Deco lines are surprisingly attractive, while the interior was one of the sets for our best-ever soap opera. Apr-Oct 10am-4pm; Jul-Sep 9.30am-4.30pm; Jan-Mar & Nov-Dec 10am-3.30pm. Booking advised in Aug.

409 10/Q26
ATMOS
ADMISSION

✓ ✓ ✓ **Rosslyn Chapel, Roslin** www.rosslynchapel.org.uk · **0131 440 2159** The ancient chapel 12km south of city, made famous recently by the world bestseller, *The Da Vinci Code*. The huge conservation and site-improvement project almost complete at TGP. 9.30am-5.30pm. Sun 12noon-4.15pm Report: 1864/CHURCHES.

▇▇▇ The Other Attractions

410 1/XB1
▢
ADMISSION
FOR
GLASSHOUSES;
OTHERWISE
FREE

✓ ✓ ✓ **Royal Botanic Garden** www.rbge.org.uk · **0131 552 7171** · **Inverleith Row** 3km Princes Street. Enter from Inverleith Row or the landmark John Muir gateway in Arboretum Place. 70 acres of ornamental gardens, trees and walkways; a joy in every season. Tropical plant houses, landscaped rock and heath garden and space just to wander. Chinese Garden coming on nicely, precocious squirrels everywhere. The Botanics have talks, guided tours, events (info 0131 248 2968). They also look after other important outstanding gardens in Scotland. Gallery with occasional exhibitions and 3 separate cafés, one with an outdoor terrace for afternoon teas (287/BEST TEAROOMS), and views. Total integrity and the natural high. Houses the National Biodiversity Interpretation Centre and Garden. Open 7 days Nov-Jan 10am-4pm, Feb-Oct 10-6pm.

411 1/C2
ATMOS
▢
FREE

✓ ✓ **Scottish National Portrait Gallery** www.nationalgalleries.org · **0131 624 6200** · **1 Queen Street** Sir Robert Rowand Anderson's fabulous, custom-built neo-Gothic pile holds paintings and photos of the good, great and merely famous. Alex Ferguson hangs out next to Queen Mum and Nasmyth's familiar Burns pic is here. Good venue for photo exhibitions, beautiful atrium with star-flecked ceiling and frieze of (mainly) men in Scottish history from a Stone Age chief to Carlyle. After a lengthy mega internal revamp, NPG is reopening on the day this book comes out!

412 1/E4
ADMISSION

✓ ✓ **Surgeons' Hall Museum** www.museum.rcsed.ac.uk · **0131 527 1649** · **Nicolson Street** Housed in the landmark Playfair building (1832), this museum is the real deal, integrity writ large and full of fascinating stuff. For over 500 years the Royal College of Surgeons has set and tested the standards of their craft and this museum records the growth of scientific medicine and Edinburgh's extraordinary contribution to it. Changing exhibitions but wonder and wince through the Pathology Museum and get your teeth into the Dentistry Collection, both the finest in the UK. Mon-Fri 12-4pm. 12-4pm Sat/Sun Apr-Oct.

413 1/XA3
▢
FREE

✓ **Scottish National Gallery of Modern Art One** **0131 624 6200** · **Belford Road** · www.nationalgalleries.org Between Queensferry Rd and Dean Village (nice to walk through). Best to start from Palmerston Pl and keep left; or see below (GOMA 2). Former school with permanent collection from Impressionism to Emin; the Scottish painters alongside and a growing collection of the conceptual art in which Scotland is notably strong (see the Douglas Gordon on the staircase and see if you can find my name – I couldn't!). All in all, an intimate space where you can fall in love (with paintings or each other). Around 3 major temporary exhibitions annually. Excellent café (278/BEST TEAROOMS). Charles Jencks art in the landscape piece outside is stunning. 10am-5pm. Extended hours during Festival.

414 1/XA3 ✓ **Scottish National Gallery of Modern Art Two** 0131 624 6200 ·
☞ **Belford Road** · **www.nationalgalleries.org** Across the road from GOMA
FREE (above). Formerly the Dean Gallery. In spacious grounds, a mansion of intimate spaces. Cool coffee shop, gardens to wander. Superb 20th-century collection; many surreal moments. Great way to approach both galleries is by Water of Leith walkway (425/WALKS IN THE CITY). No miracles here but there is magic. 10am-5pm.

415 1/E3 **Museum of Childhood** **www.museumofchildhood.org.uk** · 0131 529 4142 ·
FREE **42 High Street** Local-authority-run shrine to the dreamstuff of tender days where you'll find everything from tin soldiers to Lady Penelope on video. Full of adults saying, 'I had one of them!' Child-size mannequins in upper gallery can be very spooky if you're up there alone. Mon-Sat 10am-5pm. Sun 12-5pm.

416 1/D4 **St Giles' Cathedral** **www.stgilescathedral.org.uk** · 0131 225 9442 · **Royal**
☞ **Mile** Not really a cathedral any more, though it was once: the High Kirk of
FREE Edinburgh, Church of Scotland central since the 16th century and heart of the city since the 9th. The building is mainly medieval with Norman fragments encased in a Georgian exterior. Lorimer's oddly ornate chapel and the 'big organ' are impressive. Simple, austere design and bronze of John Knox set the tone historically. Holy Communion daily; other regular services. Atmospheric coffee shop in the crypt by Mhairi and Roy (279/COFFEE SHOPS). Mon-Fri 9am-7pm (till 5pm in winter), Sat 9am-5pm, Sun 1-5pm.

417 1/A3 **The Georgian House** **www.nts.org.uk** · 0131 225 2160 · **7 Charlotte Square**
NTS Built in the 1790s, Robert Adam's masterpiece of urban architecture is full of
ADMISSION period furniture and fittings. Not many rooms, but the dining room and kitchen are drop-dead gorgeous – you want to eat and cook there. Delightful ladies from the National Trust for Scotland answer your queries. Apr-Oct 10am-5pm (1 Jul-31 August 10am-6pm), Mar 11am-4pm, Nov 11am-3pm. Closed Dec-Feb.

418 10/P25 **Lauriston Castle** **www.edinburghmuseums.org.uk** · 0131 336 2060 ·
ADMISSION **Cramond Road South** 9km west of centre by A90, turn right for Cramond. Elegant architecture and gracious living. Largely Jacobean tower house set in tranquil grounds overlooking the Forth. The liveability of the house and preoccupations of the Reid family make you wish you could poke around but exquisite decorative pieces and furniture mean it's guided tours only. Continue to Cramond for the air (427/WALKS IN THE CITY). Apr-Oct 2pm. Closed Fri. Nov-Mar 2pm weekends only.

Arthur's Seat Report: 426/WALKS IN THE CITY.
The Pentlands Report: 429/WALKS OUTSIDE THE CITY.
The Scott Monument/Calton Hill Report: 452/448/BEST VIEWS.
Newhailes House Report: 1837/COUNTRY HOUSES.
Dr Neil's (Secret) Garden Report: 1506/GARDENS.

The Best Small Galleries

419 1/XF2 ✓✓ **Ingleby Gallery** www.inglebygallery.com · 0131 556 4441 · 6 Calton Road Light exhibition rooms behind Waverley Station for this important contemporary gallery. Shows work by significant UK artists and the Scots, eg Callum Innes and Alison Watt with a refreshing and innovative approach to the constantly changing exhibition programme.

420 1/D3 ✓✓ **The Fruitmarket Gallery** www.fruitmarket.co.uk · 0131 225 2383 · Market Street Behind Waverley Station and opposite City Art Centre. A 2-floor, warehousey gallery showing international work, retrospectives, installations; this is the city's most contemporary art space. Excellent bookshop. Always interesting. Café (279/BEST TEAROOMS) highly recommended for meeting and eating and watching the world and the art world go by.

421 1/C2 ✓ **Open Eye Gallery** www.openeyegallery.co.uk · 0131 557 1020 & **i2** 0131 558 9872 · both at 34 Abercromby Place. Excellent 2 galleries in residential part of New Town. Always worth checking out for accessible contemporary painting and ceramics. Almost too accessible (take a cheque book) – Tom Wilson will know what you want (and probably sell it to you).

422 1/E1 ✓ **The Printmakers' Workshop & Gallery** 0131 557 2479 · 23 Union Street · www.edinburgh-printmakers.co.uk Off Leith Walk near London Rd roundabout. Workshops that you can look over. Exhibitions of work by contemporary printmakers and shop where prints from many of the notable names in Scotland are on sale at reasonable prices. A local treasure.

423 1/D3 **The Collective Gallery** www.collectivegallery.net · 0131 220 1260 · 22 Cockburn Street Installations of Scottish and other young contemporary trailblazers. Members' work won't break the bank.

424 1/C2 **The Scottish Gallery** www.scottish-gallery.co.uk · 0131 558 1200 · 16 Dundas Street Guy Peploe's influential New Town gallery. Where to go to buy something painted, sculpted, thrown or crafted by up-and-comers or established names – everything from affordable jewellery to original Joan Eardleys. Or just look.

The Best Walks In The City

See p. 12 for walk codes.

425 1/XA2
1/A2
1/A1
1/XA1
1-15KM
XCIRC
BIKES
1-A-1

✓ ✓ **Water of Leith** www.waterofleith.org.uk The indefatigable wee river that runs from the Pentlands through the city and into the docks at Leith can be walked for most of its length. The longest section is from Balerno 12km outside the city, through Colinton Dell to the Dell Inn car park on Lanark Road (4km from city centre). The dell itself is a popular glen walk (1-2km). All in all a superb urban walk. The Water of Leith visitor centre is worth a look. (0131 455 7367). Open 7 days 10am-4pm all year round.
STARTS (A) A70 to Currie, Juniper Green, Balerno; park by the high school. (B) Dean Village to Stockbridge: enter through a marked gate opposite the hotel on Belford Road (combine with a visit to the art galleries) (413/414/ATTRACTIONS). (C) Warriston, past the spooky old graveyard to The Shore in Leith (plenty of pubs to repair to). Enter by going to the end of the cul-de-sac at Warriston Crescent in Canonmills; climb up the bank and turn left. Most of the Walkway (A, B and C) is cinder track and good for cycling.

426 1/XF3
1-8KM
CIRC
MTBIKES
(RESTRICTED
ACCESS)
2-B-2

✓ ✓ **Arthur's Seat** Of many walks, a good circular one taking in the wilder bits, the lochs and great views (449/BEST VIEWS) starts from St Margaret's Loch at the far end of the park from Holyrood Palace. Leaving the car park, skirt the loch and head for the ruined chapel. After 250m in a dry valley, the buttress of the main summit rears above you on the right. Keeping it to the right, ascend over a saddle joining the main route from Dunsapie Loch which appears below on the left. Crow Hill is the other peak crowned by a triangular cairn – both can be slippery when wet. From Arthur's Seat head for and traverse the long steep incline of Salisbury Crags. Paths parallel to the edge lead back to the chapel. Just cross the road by the Palace and head up. No mountain bikes. For info on the Ranger service and special events through the year, call 0131 652 8150. Arthur's Seat the centre-piece of the Olympic Speed of Light project Aug 2012.
PARK There are car parks beside the loch and in front of the palace (paths start here too, across the road).
START Enter park at palace by the parliament. Cross the main road or follow it and find your path, eg via the ruined chapel.

427 1/XA1
1/3/8KM
XCIRC
BIKES
1-A-1

Cramond The charming village (though not so the suburb) on the Forth at the mouth of the Almond with a variety of great walks. (A) To the right along the prom; the traditional seaside stroll. (B) Across the causeway at low tide to Cramond Island (1km). Best to follow the tide out; this allows 4 hours (tides are posted). People have been known to stay the night in summer, but this is discouraged. (C) Past the boathouse, up the River Almond Heritage Trail which goes eventually to the Cramond Brig Hotel on the A90 and thence to the old airport (3-8km). Though it goes through suburbs and seems to be on the flight path of the London shuttle, the Almond is a real river with a charm and ecosystem of its own. **The Cramond Gallery Bistro** (0131 312 6555) on the riverside is not a bad wee caff – great cakes await your return. 7 days. **Cramond Inn** is another great place to recharge with decent pub grub.
START Leave centre by Queensferry Rd (A90), then right following signs for Cramond. Cramond Rd North leads to Cramond Glebe Rd; go to end.
PARK Large car park off Cramond Glebe Rd to right. Walk 100m to the sea.

428 1/XA4
1-7KM
CIRC
~~LIMITED~~
1-A-1

Corstorphine Hill www.corstorphinehill.org.uk West of centre, a knobbly, hilly area of birch, beech and oak, criss-crossed by trails. A perfect place for the contemplation of life's little mysteries and mistakes. Or walking the dog. It has a *radio mast*, a ruined tower, a boundary with the wild plains of Africa (at the zoo) and a vast redundant nuclear shelter that nobody's supposed to know about. See how many you can spot. If it had a tearoom in an old pavilion, it would be perfect. **START** Leave centre by Queensferry Rd and 8km out turn left at lights, signed Clermiston. The hill is on your left for the next 2km. **PARK** Park where safe, on or near this road (Clermiston Rd).

Easy Walks Outside The City

429 10/P26
1-20KM
CAN BE CIRC
MTBIKES
2-B-2

✓ **The Pentlands** www.pentlandhills.org · 01968 677879 or 0131 445 3383 A serious range of hills rising to almost 600m, remote in parts and offering some fine walking. There are many paths up the various tops and round the lochs and reservoirs. (A) A good start in town is made by going off the bypass at Colinton, follow signs for Colinton Village, then the left fork up Woodhall Road. Go left (signed Pentland Hills Regional Park). Drive/walk as far as you can (2km) and park by the gate leading to the hill proper where there is a map showing routes. The path to Glencorse is one of the classic Pentland walks. (B) Most walks start from signposted gateways on the A702 Biggar Road. There are starts at Boghall (5km after Hillend ski slope); on the long straight stretch before Silverburn (a 10km path to Balerno); from Habbie's Howe about 18km from town; and from the village of Carlops, 22km from town. (C) The most popular start is probably from the visitor centre behind the Flotterstone Inn, also on the A702, 14km from town (decent pub lunch and 6-10pm, all day weekends); trailboard and ranger service. The remoter tops around Loganlea Reservoir are worth the extra mile.

430 10/Q25
1-4KM
CAN BE CIRC
XBIKES
1-A-1

Hermitage of Braid www.fohb.org Strictly speaking, still in town, but a real sense of being in a country glen and from the windy tops of the Braid Hills there are some marvellous views back over the city. Main track along the burn is easy to follow and you eventually come to Hermitage House info centre; any paths ascending to the right take you to the ridge of Blackford Hill. In snowy winters there's a great sledging place over the first bridge up to the left across the main road. **START** Blackford Glen Road. Go south on Mayfield to main T-junction with Liberton Road, turn right (signed Penicuik) then hard right. Ranger: 0131 447 7145.

431 10/Q26
1-8KM
XCIRC
BIKES
1-A-1

Roslin Glen www.midlothian.gov.uk Spiritual, historical, enchanting and famous (thanks to *The Da Vinci Code*) with the chapel (1864/CHURCHES), a ruined castle and woodland walks along the River Esk, though the map at the new visitor centre isn't that helpful and there's no waymarking. **START** A701 from Mayfield, Newington or bypass: turnoff Penicuik, A702 then left at Gowkley roundabout and other signed roads). Park near chapel 500m from Main St/Manse Rd corner, or follow B7003 to Rosewell (also marked Rosslynlee Hospital) and 1km from village the main car park is to the left.

432 10/P25
2-8KM
XCIRC
BIKES
1-A-1

Almondell www.beecraigs.com · 01506 882254 A country park west of city (18km) near Livingston. A deep, peaceful woody cleft with easy paths and riverine meadows. Fine for kids, lovers and dog walkers. Visitor centre with teashop. Trails marked. Event programme. **START** From Edinburgh by A71 via Sighthill. After Wilkieston, turn right for Camps (B7015); follow signs. Or A89 to Broxburn; follow signs from Broxburn.

433 10/N25 **Beecraigs & Cockleroy Hill** www.beecraigs.com Another country park
2-8KM south of Linlithgow with trails and clearings in mixed woods, a deer farm and a
CIRC fishing loch. Great adventure playground for kids. Best is the climb and extra-
MTBIKES ordinary view from Cockleroy Hill, far better than you'd expect for the effort – from
1-A-1 Ben Lomond to the Bass Rock; and the gunge of Grangemouth in the sky to the
east. 01506 844516 for park and visitor centre opening times. The hill never closes.
START M9o to Linlithgow (26km), through town and left on Preston Rd. Go on
4km, park is signed, but for hill you don't need to take the left turn. The hill, and
nearest car park to it, are on the right.

434 10/Q26 **Borthwick & Crichton Castles** www.borthwickcastle.com Takes in 2
7KM impressive castles, the first a posh hotel, the other an imposing ruin on a ridge
XCIRC overlooking the Tyne. Walk through dramatic Border country steeped in lore. From
XBIKES Borthwick follow the old railway line. From Crichton, start behind the ruined
1-B-2 chapel. In summer vegetation can be high and may defeat you.
START From Borthwick: A7 south for 16km, past Gorebridge, left at North
Middleton; signed. From Crichton: A68 almost to Pathhead, signed then 3km past
church. Park and walk 250m.

Woodland Walks Near Edinburgh

435 10/P27 ✓ **Dawyck Gardens** www.rbge.org.uk · 01721 760254 · Near Stobo 10km
ADMISSION west of Peebles on B712 Moffat road. Outstation of the Edinburgh Botanics.
Tree planting here goes back 300 years. Sloping grounds around the Scrape Burn
which trickles into the Tweed. Landscaped woody pathways for meditative walks.
Famous for shrubs, fungi and blue Himalayan poppies. Visitor centre, café, studio
and shop. Last entry 1 hour before gardens close. Apr-Sep 10am-6pm, Mar and Oct
10am-5pm, Nov and Feb 10am-4pm. 7 days. Closed Dec-Jan.

436 10/Q25 ✓ **Dalkeith Country Park** www.dalkeithcountryestate.com · Dalkeith
ADMISSION 15km SE by A68. The wooded policies of Dalkeith House; enter at end of Main
St. Along the river banks and under these stately deciduous trees, carpets of blue-
bells, daffs and snowdrops, primroses and wild garlic according to season. Most
extensive preserved ancient oak forest in southern Scotland. Excellent adventure
playground. Rangers 0131 654 1666. Open 7 days 10am-5.30pm.

437 10/R26 ✓ **The Yester Estate** Gifford Large estate around the impressive big house
in which there are some beautiful woodland walks. Hard to find (and I won't
tell you how) is the legendary **Goblin Ha'**, the bad-fairy place (the hotel in the village takes its name; 1305/GASTROPUBS). Access directly from the village unwelcome of late (it's now a shooting estate and probably unwise to walk Nov-Feb).
3km along the B6365 road, foot of steep tree-lined hill, on bend. Park by house
and go through marked gate. 3km through to village, it's 2km to Goblin Ha' itself.

438 10/R26 **Humbie Woods** 25km SE by A68 turnoff at Fala; signed for church. Beech woods
past car park. Churchyard a reassuring place to be buried; if you're set on cremation, come and think of this earth. Follow path from churchyard wall past cottage.

439 10/P25 **Cammo Estate** On north edge of the city via road to Forth Bridge. After Barnton
roundabout, left on Cammo Rd, past the gatehouse (and visitor centre) to the car
park. A lungful of fields and woods close to home.

440 10/R25 **Smeaton Nursery Gardens** www.smeatonnurserygardens.co.uk · 01620
860501 · East Linton 2km from village on North Berwick road (signed Smeaton).

Up a drive in an old estate is this early-19th-century walled garden. An additional pleasure is the Lake Walk halfway down the drive through a small gate in the woods. A 1km stroll round a secret finger lake in magnificent woodland. Garden Centre hours Mon-Sat 9.30am-4.30pm, Sun from 10.30am; phone for winter hours. Tearoom pleasant 10.30am-4pm Mon-Sun (2227/GARDEN CENTRES). (Lake walk 10am-dusk, not on their website.)

441 10/Q26 Vogrie Country Park www.midlothian.gov.uk · Near Gorebridge 25km south by A7 then B6372 6km from Gorebridge. Small country park well organised for 'recreational pursuits'. 9-hole golf course, tearoom and country-ranger staff. 01875 821990 for events and opening times. Busy on Sundays, but a spacious corral of countryside on the very edge of town. Open 7.30am-sunset.

442 10/Q27 Cardrona Forest/Glentress www.7stanes.gov.uk · Near Peebles 40km south to Peebles, 8km east on B7062 and similar distance on A72. Cardrona on same road as Kailzie Garden. Tearoom (Apr-Oct). Forestry Commission woodlands so mostly regimented firs, but Scots pine and deciduous trees up the burn. Glentress (on A72 to Innerleithen) has become a major destination for mountain bikers, but tracks also to walk. Consult at the new visitor centre.

The Best Beaches

443 10/R25 ✓ Seacliff The best: least crowded/littered; perfect for picnics, beachcombing and rock-pool gazing. Old harbour good for swimming. 50km from Edinburgh off the A198 out of North Berwick, 3km after Tantallon Castle (1806/RUINS). At a bend in the road and a farm (Auldhame) is an unsigned road to the left. 2km on there's a barrier, costing £2 (2 x £1 coins) for cars. Car park 1km then walk. From A1, take East Linton turnoff, go past Whitekirk towards North Berwick.

444 10/Q25 ✓ Tyninghame Beach & St Baldred's Cradle Also off A198: going towards North Berwick from the A1, it's the first (unmarked) turning on the right after Tyninghame village. 1km then park, walk to left through gate 1km, past log cabin on clifftop which you can hire for parties (like I have); great wild camping and the beach magnificent. Nice caff in Tyninghame village. And nearer North Berwick beyond the Glen Golf Club off the A198 to Tantallon is gorgeous little **Canty Bay**.

445 10/Q25 Portobello Edinburgh's town beach, 8km from centre by London Rd. When sunny chips, lager, bad ice cream and hordes of people, like Bondi, minus the surf. When miserable – soulful dog-walkers and the echo of summers past. Arcades, mini-funfair, long prom and pool. The **Espy** is great for a seaside drink and especially food (368/BARS WITH GOOD FOOD).

446 10/R25 Yellowcraigs Another East Lothian splendour 35km from town. A1 or bypass, then A198 coast road. Left outside Dirleton for 2km, park and walk 100m across links to fairly clean strand and sea. Gets busy, but big enough to share. Hardly anyone swims, but you can. Many a barbie has braved the indifferent breeze, but on summer evenings, the sea slips ashore like liquid gold. See also 1680/KIDS PLACES. Scenic. **Gullane Bents**, a sweep of beach, is nearby and reached from village main street. Connects westwards with **Aberlady Reserve**.

447 10/P25 Silver Sands Aberdour Over Forth Bridge on edge of charming Fife village (1551/COASTAL VILLAGES). Train from Edinburgh (nice station). Also cliff walk.

The Best Views Of The City

448 1/E2 ✓✓ **Calton Hill** Great view of the city easily gained by walking up from east end of Princes Street by Waterloo Place to the end of the buildings and then up stairs on the left. The City Observatory and Greek-style folly lend an elegant backdrop to a panorama (unfolding as you walk round) where the view up Princes St and the sweep of the Forth estuary are particularly fine. At night the city twinkles. Popular cruising area for gays; take care if you do. Home of the Hogmanay Festival Son et Lumière (30 Dec) and the Beltane Festival (30 Apr). 68/27/EVENTS.

449 1/XF3 ✓✓ **Arthur's Seat** East of city centre. Best approach through Holyrood Park from the foot of Canongate by Holyrood Palace. The igneous core of an extinct volcano with the precipitous sill of Salisbury Crags presiding over the city and offering fine views for the fit. Top is 251m; on a clear day you can see 100km. Surprisingly wild considering proximity to city. Report: 426/WALKS IN THE CITY.

450 1/B5 **Penthouse of the Point Hotel** www.pointhoteledinburgh.co.uk · 0131 221 5555 · 34 Bread Street Unadvertised spot but the penthouse function space of the cool, design-driven Point Hotel (77/MAJOR HOTELS) offers a unique perspective of the city. They may allow you up if there's nothing booked in but it opens as a public bar on the last Thursday of the month.

451 1/D4 **The National Museum of Scotland Terrace** www.nms.ac.uk · 0131 247 4422 · Chambers Street 6th floor of the fabulous recreated museum (400/ATTRACTIONS) has a beautiful terrace planted all round and offering revealing city-skyline views and a great castle perspective. Andy Goldsworthy sculptures.

452 1/C3 ADMISSION **Scott Monument** www.edinburghmuseums.org.uk · 0131 529 4068 · Princes Street Design inspiration for Thunderbird 3. This 1844 Gothic memorial to one of Scotland's best-kent literary sons (1934/LITERARY PLACES) rises 61.5m above the main drag and provides scope for the vertiginous to come to terms with their affliction. 287 steps mean it's no cakewalk; narrow stairwells weed out claustrophobics too. 4 landings to catch the breath and view. Those who make it to the top are rewarded with fine views. Underneath, a statue of the mournful Sir Walter gazes across at Jenners. Apr-Sep, Mon-Sat 10am-7pm, Sun 10am-6pm; Oct-Mar, Mon-Sat 9am-4pm, Sun 10am-6pm. (Last entry 30 minutes before closing.)

453 1/C4 ADMISSION **Camera Obscura & World of Illusions** www.camera-obscura.co.uk · 0131 226 3709 · Castlehill At very top of the Royal Mile near the castle entrance, a tourist attraction that, surprisingly, has been there for over a century. You ascend through a shop, photography exhibitions and interactive gallery to the viewing area where a continuous stream of small groups are shown the effect of the giant revolving periscope thingie. An Alice in Wonderland room, a revolving tunnel of light, hall of mirrors: plenty to distort your view of reality! Apr-Oct 9.30am-6pm; later in high season. Nov-Mar 10am-5pm. 7 days.

454 10/R25 BOTH 1-A-1 **North Berwick Law** www.eastlothian.gov.uk The conical volcanic hill, a 170m-high beacon in the East Lothian landscape easily reached from downtown North Berwick. **Traprain Law** nearby (signed from the A1 south of Haddington) is higher, more frequented by rock climbers but has major prehistoric hill-fort citadel of the Goddodin and a definite aura. Both are good family climbs. Allow 2-3 hours.

The Pentlands/Hermitage Report: 429/430/WALKS OUTSIDE CITY.
Edinburgh Castle Ramparts Report: 399/ATTRACTIONS.
Oloroso Terrace Report: 141/BEST RESTAURANTS.

Glasgow

The Major Hotels

455 2/C2
247 ROOMS
TEL · TV
NO PETS
EXP

✓ ✓ **Radisson SAS** www.glasgow.radissonsas.com · **0141 204 3333** · **301 Argyle Street** Probably the best of the big city-centre hotels, which is why there's nearly always a do on upstairs on the mezzanine – awards ceremonies, etc. Frontage makes major modernist statement, lifts the coolest in town. Leaning to minimalism but rooms have all you need, though no great views; some face the internal 'garden'. All in all a sexy urban bed for the night. Good rendezvous bar in large, open foyer. Collage, the only restaurant, is curiously small. Fitness facilities c/o LA Leisure Club in basement include a pool. No parking.

456 2/B2
72 ROOMS
TEL · TV
NO PETS
MED.EX

✓ **The Malmaison** www.malmaison-glasgow.com · **0141 572 1000** · **278 West George Street** Sister hotel of the ones in Edinburgh, Aberdeen and elsewhere. This chain of good design hotels has all the must-have features – well-proportioned rooms (though mostly small, the 4 duplex suites are great spaces), with DVDs, cable, etc. – though the central location affords no great views. However this is reliable, stylish and discreet. Contemporary and very competitively priced French menu sits well in the woody clubbiness of The Brasserie downstairs; central Scotland sourcing (535/FRENCH RESTAURANTS).

457 2/XA4
166 ROOMS
TEL · TV
NO PETS
NO KIDS
MED.INX

✓ **Mint Hotel** www.minthotel.com · **0141 240 1002** · **Finnieston Quay** Modern block by the big crane near the SECC makes most of its Clydeside location with deck and views; rooms here are a cut above the usual though not large. Uniformity throughout but thought out. Formerly the City Inn, the City Café bar/restaurant on the ground floor extends outside over the walkway to a riverside terrace under the purple-lit-at-night Clyde Arc ('Squinty') Bridge: it's a good spot! Imax TV and computer facilities in all rooms, gym facilities nearby. Part of small UK chain, price and particularity elevate from the economy travel lodge to the designer (though not quite boutique) hotel. The river's the thing.

458 2/C3
200+ ROOMS
TEL · TV
NO PETS
L
MED.INX

✓ **Grand Central** www.thegrandcentral-hotel.co.uk · **0141 240 3720** · **99 Gordon Street** Beside and very much on Central Station. In new hands (Principal Hayley who have The George in Edinburgh) finally and extensively (£20million) refurbished in 2010, restoring its position as an iconic hotel and gathering place (there are many function suites) for the city. The famously long corridors still go on forever but rooms are all that they should be (at this price). Champagne bar is very Glasgow and it does get drunk, Tempus so-so for food, the Deli a caff on the go. Out there the station and the full-on Saturday night. Parking a pain but you would arrive by train, wouldn't you?

459 2/C2
63 ROOMS
TEL · TV
NO PETS
MED.INX

✓ **Abode Glasgow** www.abodehotels.co.uk/glasgow · **0141 572 6000** · **129 Bath Street** Smart, contemporary townhouse hotel, formerly The Arthouse, with wide, tiled stairwell and funky lift to 3 floors of individual rooms (so size, views and noise levels vary a lot). Fab gold embossed wallpaper in the hallways, notable stained glass and some ok art. Grill downstairs has Modern British dishes and Bar MC open till 3am for guests.

460 2/D2
100 ROOMS
TEL · TV
NO PETS
MED.INX

Park Inn www.glasgow.parkinn.co.uk · **0141 333 1500** · **Port Dundas Place** Near the Concert Hall. Modern high-rise hotel with millennium-period designs a little tired now. Glass tiles in internal bathroom wall and sunken beds won't suit everybody. Satellite TV/DVD and Playstations. Restaurant so-so and no leisure facilities to speak of. Innovative late-checkout facility on Sundays (you pay by the hour after 12noon). Parking 200m and drop-off a bit tricky, but handily close to Queen St Station and the Concert Hall.

461 2/D3 **The Millennium Hotel** www.millenniumhotels.com · 0141 332 6711 ·
117 ROOMS **50 George Square** International Group hotel situated on the square which is the
TEL · TV municipal heart of the city and next to Queen St Station (trains to Edinburgh and
FIELD.EX points north), Glasgow will be going on all about you and there's a conservatory
terrace, serving breakfast and afternoon tea, from which to watch. Bedrooms vary;
refurbishments usually in progress but first floor front are best. No parking or
leisure facilities.

462 2/B3 **Glasgow Hilton** www.hilton.co.uk/glasgow · 0141 204 5555 ·
319 ROOMS **1 William Street** Approach from the M8 slip road or from city centre via a less
TEL · TV straightforward route. It has a forbidding Fritz Lang/Metropolis appearance and the
EXP entrance via the underground car park is grim. Though this hotel could be in any
city anywhere with motorways scything around it, it's probably the most metropol-
itan hotel in Scotland. Dated now, its huge atrium, bars, 2 restaurants and 20
floors of rooms (3 are 'Executive') makes it good for business, less so for happy
hols. Views from some rooms to the north are stunning. Leisure facilities include
pool. Both restaurants are interior; you'd eat here because you couldn't be both-
ered going into town. Cameron's the finer dining, Minsky's a popular buffet.
The other Hilton, the **Grosvenor** (0141 339 8811) on Gt Western Rd at Byres Rd (96
rooms) has no more charm but is opposite the lovely Botanic Gardens
(681/ATTRACTIONS) and close to many bars and restaurants.

463 2/XA4 **Crown Plaza** www.qmh-hotels.com · 0870 448 1691 · Congress Road
283 ROOMS Beside the SECC on the Clyde, this towering, glass monument to the 1980s is
TEL · TV another urban edifice which serves its business bedbox purpose but it wouldn't cut
EXP it in many of the world's emerging cities. The Science Centre and Tower gleam and
twinkle on the opposite bank near the new BBC HQ; there's a footbridge across.
Some good river views from the 16 floors (pay the premium for the corner suites!).
The One Restaurant in the lobby has a carvery and some ringside seating for river-
gazing. Somewhat removed from city centre (about 3km; you wouldn't want to
walk), it's especially handy for the SECC and the Armadillo concerts, conferences,
etc.

▰▰▰▰▰ The Best Individual & Boutique Hotels

464 2/C2 ✓✓ **Hotel du Vin** www.hotelduvin.com · 0141 339 2001 · 1 Devonshire
49 ROOMS **Gardens, off Great Western Road** Long Glasgow's landmark smart
TEL · TV hotel (as One Devonshire Gardens, the first boutique hotel in the UK), now part of
ATMOS the small but beautiful Hotel/Bistro du Vin chain. Unquestionably the hotel offer-
LOTS ing the most individual experience and the smartest, most solicitous service in
town. Five townhouses, the whole of a West End terrace integrated into an elegant
and sumptuous retreat but a world away from Glasgow's wilder West End (centred
on Byres Rd). Even parking is easy. House 1 has the bistro, bar, etc, House 5 the
function rooms, but each retains character with fabulous stained glass, staircases
and own doors to the street (though enter by reception in House 3). Cosy sitting
rooms everywhere. Rooms large, as are beds, bathrooms, drapes, etc. Great bar
(especially late) with malt list and as you'd expect, well chosen wines. No spa,
pool, but there is a small gym. Long after its original conception, this is still an
enduring oasis of style.
EAT Chic dining in elegant salons with fastidious service and excellent wine list.

465 2/E4
100 ROOMS
TEL · TV
EXP

✓ ✓ **Blythswood Square** www.blythswoodsquare.com · 0141 208 2458 · **11 Blythswood Square** Address as is along one side of a serene square (one of Glasgow's dear green places) in the city centre. A huge and sympathetic conversion of the historic building that was home to the RAC Club; the motoring theme is everywhere. When I launched the last edition of *StB* here in 2009 just after it had (partially) opened, proprietor Peter Taylor said in a speech that this immense project had been a very long haul and he hoped (since he was known for his Edinburgh hotels, though now they own only The Bonham – 86/HOTELS) that Glasgow would take his impassioned enterprise to its heart. Well, they have! The restaurant buzzes, the upstairs salon bar is a civilised rendezvous for cocktails and afternoon tea and the seductive, state-of-the-art, chilled-out spa is almost too busy to keep its calm (1231/SPAS). Original classic features (that lobby floor) and contemporary furnishings (acres of marble in the rooms and Harris tweed big lamps) throughout. Rooms, all in house style, vary in size and amount of light – larger in the original section while others round an internal courtyard can be dark but are quiet. All in all, a great addition to the city.
EAT Restaurant/brasserie menu reflects classic and contemporary theme. Always busy, it's the most buzzing of hotel dining in town.

466 2/D2
198 ROOMS
TEL
NO PETS
NO KIDS
CHP

✓ **Citizen M** www.citizenm.com · 0141 404 9485 · 60 Renfrew Street Between the Theatre Royal and the Pavilion Theatre – not that most of the clientele would be seen dead there. Your heart may sink when you walk in off the street (parking a long way off) and they proclaim in the downstairs foyer that they're the 'Trendiest Hotel in the World', according to TripAdvisor, but this is in fact a very superior bed- (or identical pod) box, very-good-value boutique hotel. Part of an international chain, it's spot-on for Glasgow. Rooms solid, sexy and for once not just ergonomic but well designed. No restaurant but café/bar (till 3am) and 24-hour tuck shop. Online check in, EasyJet-style, iPod stations, electric black-out, great showers. Ubiquitous exhortations to 'Get Together' and total brand immersion a bit gagging, but this is way ahead of Ibis/Yotel and a host of urban-chic arrivistes.

467 2/A1
5 ROOMS
TV
NO PETS
CHP

✓ **15 Woodside** www.15glasgow.com · 0141 332 1263 Address as is. Elegant and superbly appointed townhouse in a quiet street overlooking a private garden at the western end of Sauchiehall St beyond Charing Cross and the M8. Contemporary Farrow & Ball-kind of decor; the rooms are large so you probably don't even need to use the guest lounge. Good for exclusive-use houseparties. Laura and Shane McKenzie your discreetly solicious hosts: Tunnock's teacakes and flowers! A very superior B&B in a city where good ones are few and far between.

468 2/C3
95 ROOMS
TEL · TV
NO PETS
MED.INX

✓ **Hotel Indigo** www.hotelindigo.com · 0871 423 4876 · 75 Waterloo Street The third to open in the UK of Intercontinental Hotel inexpensive boutique chain (in Edinburgh '13). Sympathetic conversion of historic building in Glasgow's downtown financial district. The city referenced throughout: portraits of well-kent 'weegies' in bar, themed floors (theatre, Clyde, etc). Uniform but high design values. Well-priced and often booked weekends. Limelight Bar and Grill.

469 2/E3
18 ROOMS
TEL · TV
NO PETS
CHP

✓ **The Brunswick Hotel** www.brunswickhotel.co.uk · 0141 552 0001 · 104-108 Brunswick Street Contemporary, minimalist hotel that emerged back in the 90s as part of the new Merchant City. Time, perhaps, for titivation but rooms make use of tight space and are good value. Bold colours. Good base for nocturnal forays into pub- and clubland. Restaurant till 10pm, breakfast pleasant, especially Sundays. Penthouse suite often used for parties. No parking.

470 2/C3
51 ROOMS
TV
CHP

✓ **Artto Hotel** www.arttohotel.com · 0141 248 2480 · 37 Hope Street
Surprising, boutique-ish hotel very centrally situated behind Central Station on busy-with-buses Hope St, though its rooms are double-glazed and quiet. Facilities basic but this place is amazing value. Restaurant adjacent – Bombay Blue, which features an Indian buffet, though breakfast here is continental.

471 2/C2
103 ROOMS
TEL · TV
MED.INX

Marks Hotel www.markshotels.com · 0141 353 0800 · 110 Bath Street
In the downtown section of Bath St but near the style bars and designer restaurants, a bedblock with a little more taste and character than most. Contemporary, of course, with big wallpaper and free WiFi; small supplement for the city views from the fourth floor up (of 8). Restaurant on Bath St itself: One Ten bar and grill. Very central location though parking not so close.

472 2/B2
6 ROOMS
TEL · TV
NO PETS
NO KIDS
MED.INX

St Jude's www.saintjudes.com · 0141 352 0220 · 190 Bath Street Glasgow's first small boutique hotel began as a northern Groucho Club. Some changes of ownership later, St Jude's remains a designery destination in Bath St of many bars (including their own – The Saint, known for its cocktails and with a restaurant through the back). Rooms are all upstairs (no lift) with big wallpaper, plasmas, etc. Bathrooms retain their '90s chic. Penthouse suite if you want to impress.

473 2/D1
8 ROOMS
TEL · TV
NO PETS
CHP

The Pipers' Tryst Hotel www.thepipingcentre.co.uk · 0141 353 5551 · **McPhater Street** Opposite the top of Hope St and visible from dual carriageway near *The Herald* HQ at Cowcaddens. Circuitous route to the street by car. Hotel upstairs from café-bar of the adjacent piping centre and whole complex a nice conversion of an old church and manse. Centre has courses, conferences and a museum, so staying here is to get close to Highland culture. Small restaurant.

474 2/XF3
7 ROOMS
TEL · TV
£75-90

Cathedral House www.cathedralhousehotel.org · 0141 552 3519 · **Cathedral Square** Opposite Glasgow Cathedral. Rooms above the bar; their main appeal is the outlook to the edifice, ie cathedral and Necropolis (1887/GRAVEYARDS). Functional and friendly though needs TLC. A walk to the Merchant City.

475 2/F3
6 ROOMS
TEL · NO PETS
NO KIDS
CHP

Babbity Bowster 0141 552 5055 · **16-18 Blackfriars Street** This 18th-century townhouse was pivotal in the redevelopment of the Merchant City and famous for its bar (655/REAL-ALE PUBS, 540/SCOTTISH RESTAURANTS), where you get breakfast, and beer garden. Schottische restaurant upstairs; rooms are above with basic facilities. No TV but nice books. A very Glasgow hostelry and popular, so book ahead.

Travel Lodges

476 2/E2
2/B2
278,239
ROOMS
TEL · TV
NO PETS
CHP

Premier Travel Inns www.premiertravelinn.co.uk Of 4 in the city centre, the most convenient is probably east on a Merchant City corner at **187 George Street** (0870 238 3320) and west at **10 Elmbank Gardens** (0870 990 6312) above Charing Cross Station. The latter once an office block, now a vast city-centre budget hotel with no frills or pretence, but a cheap, adequate room for the night. Functionality, anonymity and urban melancholy may suit lonesome travellers or the families/mates packed into a room. George St in area of many restaurants, Charing Cross opposite the excellent Baby Grand (612/LATE-NIGHT RESTAURANTS).

477 2/B2
139,141
ROOMS
TEL · TV
MED.INX

Novotel www.novotel.com · 0141 222 2775 · **181 Pitt Street** Branch of the French bedbox empire in quiet corner near the west end of Sauchiehall St. Nothing much to distinguish, but brasserie/restaurant is bright enough and Novotel beds are very good. Small bathrooms. The 2-star **Ibis** (0141 225 6000) is adjacent (as opposed to Novotel's 3). If it's merely a bed for the night you want, it's cheaper, though sometimes not by much, and hard to see what difference a star makes. They're both pretty soulless but parent chain Accor do accord better than UK rivals.

478 2/D2
113, 119 RMS
TEL · TV
MED.INX

Holiday Inn, City Centre www.higlasgow.com · 0141 352 8300 · **161 West Nile Street** Another block off the old block. In the city centre near Concert Hall. Gym but no pool; restaurant but not great shakes. Holiday Inn Express adjacent is better value (25% less). Room rates vary. A lot of shopping goes on around you.

479 2/D5
128 ROOMS
CHP

Express by Holiday Inn www.hiexpressglasgow.co.uk · 0141 548 5000 · **Corner of Stockwell & Clyde Streets** Functional bed-box that's not a bad deal, when all you do is sleep here. Sadly, only 5 rooms on the river (pot-luck apples!). Near Merchant City so lots of restaurants, nightlife and other distractions; midway between 2 of Glasgow's oldest bars, the Scotia and Victoria (642/646/UNIQUE PUBS). Another Express by Holiday Inn, City Centre (above), but this one is best.

The Best Hostels

SYHA is the Scottish Youth Hostel Association. Phone 01786 451181 for details, contact any YHA hostel or visit their website: www.syha.org.uk

480 2/XA1
150 BEDS

✓ **SY Hostel** www.syha.org.uk · 0870 004 1119 · **8 Park Terrace** Oddly quiet and up-market location in an elegant terrace in posh West End near the university and Kelvingrove Park. This building was converted in 1992 from the Beacons Hotel, which was where rock 'n' roll bands used to stay in the 1980s. Dorms for 4-6 (some larger) and the public rooms are common rooms with TV, games, etc. Coffee shop and breakfast room in the basement (12noon-8pm).

481 2/C4
365 BEDS

Euro Hostel Glasgow www.euro-hostels.co.uk · 0141 222 2828 · **318 Clyde Street** A very central (2 minutes Central Station) independent hostel block at the bottom of Union/Renfield St and almost overlooking the river. Mix of single, twin or dorm accommodation, but all ensuite and clean. Breakfast included in price. Kitchen and laundry. Games and TV room. The ground-floor bar, **Osmosis** (they see themselves as a hot pre-, even après-club/gig bar), is open to the public. A good all-round spot, especially if you're with a bunch of mates.

The Best Hotels Outside Town

482 9/L25
ɑ ̯ ⌷ ⵏ ⌷ ⵏ ̯ ⵏ ̯ ⵏ
TEL · TV
NO PETS
LOTS

✔ ✔ **De Vere Cameron House Hotel** www.devere.co.uk · 01780
/55505 · Loch Lomond A82 via West End or Erskine Bridge and M8. 45km from centre. De Vere de luxe hotel complex with excellent leisure facilities in 100 acres of open grounds on the loch's bonny banks (and the new Carrick golf course and spa 5km along the lochside). Interiors plush, sombre, urbane; you swish. Sports include 9-hole golf by the hotel ('the wee demon' – no booking) as well as the 18-hole Carrick, 2 pools (1 with chutes for kids), tennis, snooker and lots to do on the loch including windsurfing and cruising (and you can arrive by sea-plane). Casual dining at poolside or the Cameron Grill (some mixed reviews and not great for vegetarians – the meat is visibly well-hung) and notably **Martin Wishart**, the western outpost of Scotland's best urban restaurant (126/EDINBURGH FINE DINING). Excellent whisky bar pre- and après. The Spa with a huge range of treatments and pamperings has outdoor deck and pool, bar/restaurant. All this ain't cheap, but as they say, 'this is the life': they're not wrong.
EAT 4 restaurants to choose from including Michelin-star-chef Martin Wishart's make this the best dining-out prospect west of the city.

483 10/M26
92 ROOMS
TEL · TV
NO PETS
MED.INX

✔ ✔ **Dakota** www.dakotahotels.co.uk · 0870 220 8281 · EuroCentral 24km from centre on the M8. Like the South Queensferry version (122/HOTELS OUTSIDE EDINBURGH) this is a chip off the new (black granite, smoked glass) block and similarly situated overlooking the highway, in the spot of regenerating Lanarkshire they call EuroCentral. Behind the severe exterior is a design-driven roadhouse that is a paean to travel and elegantly rises to meet the requirements of modern travellers. You come off the thrashing M8 into an oasis of subdued colour, wood and brick – a perfect antidote. Another hotel hit for the McCulloch/Rosa team. 4th floor rooms have the larger windows, 'Executive' have bigger everything.
EAT The Grill is superb: way the best motorway caff in the UK?

484 9/L25
53 ROOMS
TEL · TV
NO PETS
EXP

✔ ✔ **Mar Hall** www.marhall.com · 0141 812 9999 · Earl of Mar Estate, Bishopton M8 junction 28A/29, A726 then A8 into Bishopton. 5-star luxury a very convenient 10 minutes from the airport and 25 minutes from central Glasgow. Impressive conversion of imposing, *très elegant* baronial house with grand though slightly gloomy public spaces including the central grand hall where you congregate and rooms that vary (some huge) but all with 5-star niceties. (Aveda) spa/leisure club adjacent with 15m pool, gym and fitness programme: it's a lift and a wee walk away. The Cristal, with long windows on to the gardens, is the fine-dining restaurant under Leon Quate; casual lunches and suppers in the hall! Opulent though it is, Mar Hall is very much part of the local Erskine community. And there's the 18-hole golf course. It all overlooks the Clyde and it's become the new rock 'n' roll stopover for the city (Take That take that).

485 9/L24
47 ROOMS
TEL · TV
EXP

✔ **The Lodge on Loch Lomond** www.lochlomondlodge.co.uk · 01436 860201 Edge of Luss on A82 north from Balloch; 40 minutes to Glasgow's West End. In a linear arrangement that makes the most of a great lochside setting. This hotel, ignored by the posher guides, is an excellent prospect. Wood-lined rooms (the Corbetts) overlook the bonny banks with balconies and saunas, then there's the Grahams and in the adjacent, newer, higher block, the Munros - it's a Scottish hill thing. Colquhoun's restaurant has the view and the terrace and is surprisingly good; book at weekends. Rooms in Munro block, back from lochside, are more corporate. Spa, nice pool, weddings; and once, Bill Clinton.

Eglinton Arms Hotel 01355 302631· Eaglesham Surprisingly close, great value in a quiet village near a fast track (M77) to town. Report: 1148/BEST INNS.

The Best Fine-Dining Restaurants

486 2/XA1
£25-35
ATMOS
✔ ✔ **Ubiquitous Chip** www.ubiquitouschip.co.uk · 0141 334 5007 · 12 Ashton Lane The pioneering creation of Ronnie Clydesdale who passed away in 2010, now in the hands of son and chef Colin and his wife Carol, moves onwards and upwards. Some say it's better than ever. Certainly its signature smart and friendly service and unpretentious fine dining with conscientiously sourced ingredients is much in evidence. More than 40 years on, The Chip remains the destination restaurant in the West End. It is handily open later than most. Daily lunch and 6.30-11pm.

487 2/XA1
£25-35
✔ ✔ **Bistro du Vin** 0141 339 2001 · 1 Devonshire Gardens, off Great Western Road Glasgow's oldest and, well, best boutique hotel (464/BEST HOTELS) has, since it opened, had one of the city's classiest fine-dining salons. The dining rooms in house 5 in this elegant row are comfortable to be in rather than fawning and formal, happy rather than hushed: like dining in your club. Recently installed chef Darin Campbell is at the top of his form. Presentation and service exemplary. Menu changing at TGP but à la carte and grill. It's not expensive at this level. Cosy bar for pre/après and if you don't want the whole number there's a great bar menu (11am-11pm) where you get the kitchen's accomplishments for gastropub prices. All-round top spot in the West End. 7 days lunch and dinner (closed Sun lunch). LO 9.30pm.

488 9/L25
>£35
✔ ✔ **Martin Wishart at Loch Lomond** www.devere.co.uk · 01389 755565 · Loch Lomond This not-in-Glasgow restaurant is probably the best restaurant in Glasgow. Michelin-starred Martin Wishart (of the watery logo) here on the lochside at Cameron House (482/HOTELS OUTSIDE TOWN) from the water (of Leith) side location in Edinburgh (126/EDINBURGH FINE DINING). Though the man himself is only here 2 weekends a month, the kitchen under long-serving chef Canadian Stewart Boyles, produces its 6-course tasting menu complete with vegetarian version (and à la carte) with expected purpose and panache. Fans of Martin, of which I am one, will love this simply stylish room by the loch. Michelin starred 2012. 7 days dinner and Sun lunch. The hotel also has the Cameron Grill which does what it says on the tin.

489 2/C2
£25-35
✔ **Le Chardon D'Or** www.brianmaule.com · 0141 248 3801 · 176 West Regent Street Brian Maule's (formerly head chef at the Roux brothers' famed Le Gavroche) mid-town eaterie. Golden Thistle in French with contemporary spin on Auld Alliance as far as the food's concerned: impeccable ingredients, French influence in the prep. A delightfully simple, unpretentious menu and a tranquil room in one of Glasgow's temples to culinary excellence. Every year when Glasgow is passed over for Michelin-starred restaurants, the papers speculate which chef should be a contender. Invariably Brian's name comes up. Well, this ain't really Michelin territory, it's too honest and unfussy and it's all the better for that: great value, great food! This too in an exemplary wine list with possibly the best organic list in Scotland (available in all, easy-to-understand grape-type categories). Michelin Schmichelin! Lunch Mon-Fri, LO 9.30pm. Closed Sun.

490 2/A3
ATMOS
>£35
✔ **Two Fat Ladies At The Buttery** www.twofatladiesrestaurant.com · 0141 221 8188 · 652 Argyle Street The quite-hard-to-find or even hard-to-explain-how-to-find extension of Argyle St west of the M8: satnav or phone. Under Ryan James and his team the Buttery, aeons ago *the* best restaurant in Glasgow, came back, and with fastidious attention and ever-changing detail determinedly remains among Glasgow's finest. Mahogany-dark, discreetly sumptuous surroundings, gorgeous period tablewear, slick service in a calm backwater of enticing

excellence. Chef's table in a glass box in the kitchen where Stephen Johnson leads a well-oiled (maybe olive oil) team. Lotta fish, good vegetarian. Didn't eat here recently – in a way, don't have to – it clearly works and continues to win awards. **Shandon Belles**, the Ladies' thinner sister is downstairs. This bistro version is cosier and less costly. Indeed, not just less; the Belles packs 'em in with 2-courses-for-£11 and 3-for-£13 menus. And some careful attention to detail (the side-plates!); the wine! Both 7 days lunch and dinner LO 10/11pm. Sun 12noon-9pm.

£15-25

491 2/D3
ATMOS
>£35

✓ **Rogano** www.roganoglasgow.com · 0141 248 4055 · **11 Exchange Place** Between Buchanan and Queen Sts. A Glasgow institution since the 1930s. Decor replicating a Cunard ship, the *Queen Mary*, is the major attraction. A flagship restaurant for the city, the kitchen under long-serving Andy Cummings serves contemporary surf (those oysters) and turf (that steak) brasserie style menu of reassuringly high quality. Spacious and perennially fashionable, the buzzing old-style glamour still holds. Downstairs Café Rogano is the cheaper alternative. Outdoor heated 'terrace' with 'hedges' is pure dead Glasgow. Restaurant lunch and 6pm-10.30pm. Café Rogano 12noon-11pm (Sun until 10pm).

███████ # The Best Bistros & Brasseries

See also Best Scottish Restaurants, p. 102.

492 2/XA1
ATMOS
£15-35

✓✓ **Stravaigin** www.stravaigin.com · 0141 334 2665 · **28-30 Gibson Street** This indispensable bar/restaurant along with Stravaigin 2, below, and the Ubiquitous Chip (486/FINE DINING) comprise the feel-good and foody emporia of Colin and Carol Clydesdale. The original restaurant downstairs and food served in both bar areas (no apologies for flagging it up also in 512/GASTROPUBS). In standards, the Stravaigins set a high bar. Mixes cuisines, especially Asian and Pacific Rim: the mantra of 'think global, eat local'. Excellent, affordable food without the formalities and open later than most. All areas can be cramped but it buzzes brilliantly. 7 days 11am-11pm; bar till 12midnight. Also **Stravaigin 2** which is different but awfy good, too (below).

493 2/XA1
ATMOS
£15-25

✓✓ **Cafezique** 0141 339 7180 · **66 Hyndland Street** The original location for Mhairi Taylor's landmark deli (which moved 2 doors up: 633/DELIS) is now possibly the definitive West End grazing spot and hugely popular (book at weekends). Convivial is the word and though cramped, the ground floor and mezzanine buzz along nicely day and night. Light, easy food with top ingredients, Mediterranean with apple crumble. 'Tiny things', 'wee things', 'big things' – they're all good things. From brilliant (all-day) breakfast to civilised last orders at 10.30pm, you can only wish you had a café like this (and the deli) in your neighbourhood. But then it's probably a Hyndland thing! Perfect pitch! 7 days 8am-10.30pm.

494 2/E4
ATMOS
£15-25

✓✓ **Guy's Restaurant & Bar** www.guysrestaurant.co.uk · 0141 552 1114 · **24 Candleriggs** This intimate and busy Merchant City restaurant does 'real food' really well and is unquestionably one of the best restaurants in the quarter. The menu is long and diverse and never disappoints. In a welcoming old-style room, the eponymous Guy and family serve you Scottish staples like mince 'n' tatties and prawn cocktail (and sushi) and particularly good pasta. Absolutely everything home made. Wines vary from good house to Crystal Rosé at £600 a bottle. Live but sympatico music Thu-Sat and Sun afternoons. 12noon-10.30/11.30pm. Closed Mon. Good for late suppers. Guy is the guy!

495 2/XA1 ✓ **No. Sixteen** www.number16.co.uk · **0141 339 2544** · **16 Byres Road**
£25-35   The well-loved No. 16 (some say 2 ticks due) at the unfashionable, Partick end of Byres Rd. Small upstairs and ground-floor bistro one of the most consistently good spots for unpretentious, inexpensive contemporary food. I'm a fussy guy but recently I found I wanted everything on the menu. Irresistible, indispensable! Cramped perhaps, but calm. 7 days, lunch and LO 10pm.

496 2/XA1 ✓ **Stravaigin 2** www.stravaigin.5pm.co.uk · **0141 334 7165** · **8 Ruthven**
£15-25   **Lane** Just off Byres Rd through vennel opposite underground station. Off-shoot of **Stravaigin** (above), one of Glasgow's finest. Similar eclectic, often inspirational food. I had the best curry here recently that I'd had in a while. They also think global and cook local and that does sum it up. Upper room brighter; both buzz. Attentive, friendly service is their signature dish. 7 days 11am/12noon-11pm.

497 2/XC5 ✓ **Cookie** www.cookiescotland.com · **0141 423 1411** · **72 Nithsdale Road**
£15-25   A cookie kind of neighbourhood eatery, café, bakery, off licence (well-selected wine list) that's easy to miss, deep in the South Side. It is worth the schlepp across town. Comfy surroundings, comfy home-made everything. All day from breakfast through lunch and afternoon tea till supper (book). LO 10/10.30pm. Closed Mon.

498 2/XA1 ✓ **The Left Bank** www.theleftbank.co.uk · **0141 339 5969** · **33 Gibson**
£15-25   **Street** Laid-back, stylish, all-round eaterie, a West End feature near the university. Together with Stravaigin (above) which is opposite, they make Gibson St the destination for casual dining. From healthy, imaginative breakfast (that granola!) to great-value, prix-fixe menus (12noon-7pm), this is a grown-up Glasgow place to hang and graze with friends. Good vegetarian food. 7 days 9am-10pm.

499 2/XA5 ✓ **Ian Brown Food & Drink** www.ianbrownrestaurant.co.uk · **0141 638**
£15-25   **8422** · **55 Eastwoodmains Road** A neighbourhood restaurant (albeit an affluent one): it's a long way from town on the South Side. Over 20 years head chef of the Ubiquitous Chip and Ronnie Clydesdale's right-hand man so expectations were high when he and the missus opened in this modest room in '10. Unpretentious, excellent-value, confident cooking ensured packed houses ever since. He's on the windae, visible in the kitchen and talks round the tables: you can see, he cares.

500 2/XA2 ✓ **Fanny Trollopes** www.fannytrollopes.co.uk · **0141 564 6464** ·
£15-25   **1066 Argyle Street** Discreet presence on this unlovely boulevard and a narrow room, but Fanny's has always been a dining destination (and Glasgow's 'no. 1 restaurant', according to a very large number of reviews on TripAdvisor, ie unlikely to be rigged, at TGP). Unpretentious, great value and flair in the kitchen from chef/patron Gary Bayless is why this is a Glasgow fave night out and you should book! Franco-Scottish, ie Celtic menu with lovely puds. Can BYO £4. No credit cards. Sat lunch and LO 9.30/10pm. Closed Mon.

501 2/XA3 ✓ **Pelican Café** www.thepelicancafe.co.uk · **0844 573 0670** · **1377 Argyle**
£15-25   **Street** Directly across the street from the edifice of Kelvingrove Art Gallery. Well-situated and well-run bistro (same folk have Deli 1901 on the South Side; 639/DELIS): small plates and delish salads, big burger and steak choice; some vegetarian. Suppliers are listed. Particularly good wine list; they line the walls so there's a vinoteca feel to the room. People like it here! 12noon-10pm, Sun till 9pm.

502 2/XA1 ✓ **Velvet Elvis** www.velvet-elvis.com · **0141 334 6677** · **566 Dumbarton**
ATMOS   **Road** & **Criterion Café** www.criterioncafe.com · **0141 334 1964** · **568**
<£15   **Dumbarton Road** With Pintxo (567/SPANISH RESTAURANTS) next door, these sympatico bar/restaurants were the loving creation of Allen Mawn who died in 2011.

He put Partick on the culinary map and so it remains. Elvis is a treasure trove of cool things and found objects from the golden age of music. Menus come in old LP covers and the jukebox (4 plays £1) is filled with classics. The Criterion (a saloon and cocktail bar) pays similar nostalgic respect to Penguin Books. Both (under Allen's partner, Lindsay Hendry) have a similar comfort, gastropub kind of menu. It's the ambience he made so good! 7 days 12noon-9/10pm.

503 2/XF3
£15-25
✓ **Tibo** www.cafetibo.com · 0141 550 2050 · 443 Duke Street, Dennistoun Neighbourhood cool caff/bistro. Kinda funky and kinda rustic-in-the-city. Full-on menu but can graze and great for breakfast. It's an East End thing! 7 days 10am-10pm (9.45pm Fri/Sat).

504 2/D3
£25-35
✓ **The Urban Bar & Brasserie** www.urbanbrasserie.co.uk · 0141 248 5636 · 23 St Vincent Place Very central (off George Sq), urban as they say – a very Glasgow restaurant. Great brasserie atmosphere; it just works as you might expect from proprietor Alan Tomkins (Gamba, 576/SEAFOOD). Clubby atmosphere in different seating areas; outside terrace for people-watching. Bar and congenial à la carte and lunch menu (many ladies do). Lunch and LO 10pm; 10.30pm Fri/Sat.

505 2/XA5
£15-25
✓ **Art Lover's Café** www.houseforanartlover.co.uk · 0141 353 4779 · 10 Dumbreck Road, Bellahouston Park Near the artificial ski slope and the walled garden, on the ground floor of House for an Art Lover, a building based on drawings left by Mackintosh. Bright room, crisp presentation and a counterpoint to wrought iron, purply, swirly Mockintosh caffs elsewhere. This is unfussy and elegant. Soup 'n' sandwiches and à la carte all beautifully presented; a serious and aesthetically pleasing lunch spot. 7 days from 10am. LO 4pm.

506 2/XA1
£25-35
✓ **Wee Lochan** 0141 338 6606 · 340 Crow Road A reworking of An Lochan, the previous restaurant here, by the chef/proprietors of No. Sixteen (495/BISTROS), Rupert and Aisla Staniforth. Less fishy than before but as a neighbourhood café or short diversion from the West End food belt, this wee lochan is worth diving into. A Mod Brit menu, affable staff. Doubtless, reputation of the 16 will pack us in at 340.

507 2/C2
£15-25
Red Onion www.red-onion.co.uk · 0141 221 6000 · 247 West Campbell Street John Quigley's good-value, feels-just-right room and eclectic menu featuring all the things we like from sound, safe choices to food with more flourish and Quigley flair. Though not so multi-layered, the Onion is informal, accessible and easy to drop in at any time. 7 days 12noon-10.30/11pm.

508 2/D3
£15-25
The Restaurant Bar & Grill www.therestaurantbarandgrill.co.uk · 0141 225 5620 · Princes Square, Buchanan Street Upstairs in this long-established but no longer exclusively upmarket mall on Glasgow's principal shopping street, one of many restaurants and the best bet (though Fifi & Ally is a great caff; 591/TEAROOMS). Huge number of tables but often busy, attesting to appeal. Contemporary British menu with Scottish sourcing. 7 days 10am-11pm, Sun 12noon-6pm.

509 2/XA5
£15-25
The Giffnock Ivy 0141 620 1003 · 219 Fenwick Road, Giffnock Set on this long road out of town (to Kilmarnock). Glasgow's South Side and not London's West End – the joke may or may not be lost. Great bistro atmosphere in small, busy room; white linen adds a refined touch. Modest menu with blackboard specials and a lot of steak going on. 7 days, lunch and LO 9.30pm. Closed Mon.

510 2/XA1
£15-25
Sisters Jordanhill www.thesisters.co.uk · 0141 434 1179 · 1a Ashwood Gardens, off Crow Road Out of the way and a little out of the ordinary, a great

Scottish eaterie by sisters Pauline and Jacqueline O'Donnell. Great atmosphere, home cooking from fine ingredients. Loyal clientele. Phone for directions if you've never been beyond the bright lights of Byres Rd. Tue-Sun lunch; dinner. LO 9.30pm.

511 2/XA1 **Sisters Kelvingrove** www.thesisters.co.uk · 0141 564 1157 · **36 Kelvingrove**
£15-25 **Street** From the same sisters as above though here on a busy West End corner in a (not large) light, easy-going room. Seasonal menu with Scottish-sourced ingredients and the signature puff-candy ice cream. Decent value for this standard of conscientious cookery. Lunch and LO 9/9.30pm (Sun 8pm). Closed Mon.

✓ ✓**Café Gandolfi** Now and forever. See 586/BEST TEAROOMS.

✓ ✓**City Merchant** A Merchant City must. See 536/SCOTTISH RESTAURANTS.

✓**Firebird** Well-loved West End corner bistro. See: 529/BEST PIZZA.

Gastropubs

512 2/XA1 ✓ ✓**Stravaigin** www.stravaigin.5pm.co.uk · 0141 334 2665 · **28-30**
ATMOS **Gibson Street** Excellent pub food upstairs in doubled-up rooms from
£15-25 one of the best restaurants in town. Doors open on to sunny Gibson St and mezzanine gallery above. Often packed, but inspirational grub; no pretence. These must be the busiest, most exercised waiters in town Nice wines to go with. 7 days all day and LO 10pm. Report: 492/BEST RESTAURANTS.

513 2/E4 ✓ ✓**Bar Gandolfi** www.cafegandolfi.com · 0141 552 6813 · **64 Albion**
<£15 **Street** Above Merchant City landmark Café Gandolfi (586/TEAROOMS) in a light, airy upstairs garret with a congenial atmosphere and classy comfort food served till 10pm. Bar 11.45pm. Good veggie choice. Great rendezvous spot. 7 days.

514 2/XA1 ✓ ✓**The Bar @ Hotel du Vin** 0141 339 2001 · **1 Devonshire Gardens**
£15-25 Alongside Great Western Rd. Not really a gastropub nor even a pub but mentioned here because one of the best restaurants in town – Bistro du Vin (487/FINE-DINING RESTAURANTS) – has an adjacent cosy lounge with a simple bar menu done typically and stylishly well. Burgers et al and no dinner frills. LO 11pm.

515 2/C4 ✓**MacSorley's** 0141 248 8581 · **42 Jamaica Street** From the makers of the
£15-25 legendary Sub Club, a re-invigoration of a great old Glasgow pub (from 1899) with mahogany bar and old-world style and atmosphere intact. Celebrating music and food: live bands and Sam Carswell's seasonal, Scottish-centric menu; tables up top on the mezzanine. Some quite fancy cooking, artisan cheeses – a contemporary menu amidst the old wood and the old rock 'n' roll. 7 days, lunch and LO 8pm.

516 2/XA1 **Òran Mór** www.oran-mor.co.uk · 0141 357 6200 · **731 Great Western Road**
ATMOS Converted church at Byres Rd corner. Reverence due for the scale of ambition and
£15-25 unflagging commitment, a paean to all things Scottish Contemporary. Every cloister and chapel has been turned into a den for drinking and while there's a bar menu throughout, the John Muir Conservatory to one side has a very light and less full-on ambience conducive to their gastropub grub. Think mince 'n' tatties with chive dumplings. The brasserie through by gets kinda mixed reviews. Lunch and LO 9pm.

✓**Babbity Bowsters** Report: 540/SCOTTISH RESTAURANTS.

The Best Italian Restaurants

517 2/XA1
£25-35

✓**La Parmigiana** www.laparmigiana.co.uk · 0141 334 0686 · 117 Great Western Road Long-established, top ristorante near Kelvin Bridge by the Giovanazzi brothers (Sandro here) who also have Paperino's (526/TRATTS). They're always mentioned (though not starred) in Michelin. No great surprises on the menu but reliably fine. Traditional, solicitous service, authentic ingredients and contemporary Italian cooking meld into a seamless performance. Carefully chosen wine list. La P is still the best! Mon-Sat lunch and 6-10pm. Sun till 6pm.

518 2/E3
£15-25

✓**Jamie's Italian** www.jamiesitalian.com · 0141 404 2690 · 1 George Square We'd have to allow that the Oliver boy done good and nowhere is this more obvious than here where Glasgow takes his formulaic restaurant totally to heart. In one of the city's impressive Grade A-listed buildings; part of the former Post Office so appropriately you queue for a table (or just wait downstairs in the bar). In the cavernous, loud canteen you know what you're gonna get and you do. Let's just consume! 12noon-11pm (10.30 Sun).

519 2/D2
2/C2
ATMOS
£15-35

✓**Fratelli Sarti** www.sarti.co.uk · 0141 248 2228 · 133 Wellington Street & 0141 204 0440 (best number for bookings) 121 Bath Street Glasgow's famed *emporio d'Italia* combining a deli/wine shop in Wellington St, wine shop in Bath St and bistro in each. Great, bustling atmosphere. Eating upstairs in deli has more atmosphere. Good pizza, specials change every day, *dolci* and *gelati* in super-calorific abundance. 7 days 8am-10/11pm (Sun from 12noon) (532/PIZZA). The **Sarti** restaurant at **43 Renfield St** (corner of West George St; 0141 572 7000) is more like dining; an elegant room with exceptional marble tiling and wine list. Same menu as others, but more ristorante specials. 7 days 8am-10.30pm (Sat from 10am, Sun from 12noon). The Club Amici is a good idea (meets include Italian lessons, wine tasting and jazz evenings) if you live in Glasgow and love Italy!

520 2/F3
£15-25

✓**The Italian Caffe** www.theitaliancaffe.co.uk · 0141 552 3186 · 92 Albion Street Modelled on a traditional enoteca (a wine bar with small, tapas-like plates of food), it's too sophisticated to see itself as a mere tratt. Well located and usually packed. Some flair and attention in the kitchen, a lotta risotto and cute pizzas, fritattas. Good wine selection. 7 days lunch and LO 10/10.30pm.

521 2/XA5
ATMOS
£15-25

La Fiorentina/Little Tuscany www.la-fiorentina.com · 0141 420 1585 · 2 Paisley Road West Not far from river and motorway over Kingston Bridge, but approach from Eglinton St (A77 Kilmarnock Rd). It's at the Y-junction with Govan Rd. Fiorentina has absorbed traditional tratt Little Tuscany from next door which is only open when they're very busy. Fabulous, old-style room and service, always buzzing. Usually seafood specials; lighter Tuscan menu. As Italian as you want it to be; enormous menu and wine list. Mon-Sat lunch and LO 10.30pm. Closed Sun.

522 2/D3
£25-35

✓**Barolo** www.barologrill.co.uk · 0141 221 0971 · 92 Mitchell Street From the decades-old pure Glasgow L'Ariosto, an arriviste in the brash style of an arriviste and an instant success 2011 on this developing street near Central Station. Part of the Di Maggio group (607/KIDS), there's a similar big-scale pasta/pizza operation in Edinburgh (Amarone). Here in the heartland it seems to work better, the banquettes always abrim, the calorific carbs hitting the spot. Some barolos on the wine list possibly outwith the price range of most of the happy punters. 7 days 12noon-10pm (from 10.30am Fri/Sat).

The Trusty Tratts

523 2/XB5
£15-25
✓ **Battlefield Rest** www.battlefieldrest.co.uk · 0141 636 6955 · 55 Battle-field Road On South Side opposite the old Victoria Infirmary in a landmark pavilion building, a former tram station. Their PAPA (industry) awards – best Italian Restaurant and Best Pizza UK 2010 are proudly displayed. Mario Giannasi at the helm. Family-run, lovingly home-made, great Italian atmosphere. Small, with good daylight, this place unquestionably is still one of the most convivial places to eat on the South Side. You should book! All-day menu 10am-10pm. Closed Sun.

524 2/XA5
£15-25
✓ **Bella Napoli** 0141 632 4222 · 83 Kilmarnock Road Fabulously full-on family tratt on main road through the South Side, a restaurant that's a' things to a' body (ie universal appeal). Big hams in the cold counter may amuse the kids. Bright presence on the street, inside the space goes on forever. Linen tablecloths in the back section; it all goes like a Glasgow fair. 7 days 9am onwards. LO 10.30pm.

525 2/XA5
£15-25
Roma Mia www.romamiaglasgow.co.uk · 0141 423 6694 · 164 Darnley Street Near the Tramway on the South Side and the best option pre/post theatre. Family-friendly tratt, members of Ciao Italia (denoting a real Italian restaurant). Out of the way, but this could be a backstreet of Rome, not just Glasgow. Those in the know go! Closed Mon. LO 10pm.

526 2/B1
WE
£15-25
Paperino's www.paperinosglasgow.com · 0141 332 3800 · 283 Sauchiehall Street & 227 Byres Road · 0141 334 3811 & 78 St Vincent Street · 0141 248 7878 3 smart Italians that are simply better than the rest; down to the Giovanazzi brothers who also own La Parmigiana (517/ITALIAN RESTAURANTS) and The Big Blue (610/KIDS). Perfect pasta, good service. Byres Rd is vast but often packed. Attests to endless attraction of regular UK Italian food done well. 7 days. LO 10/10.30pm.

527 2/XA5
<£15
Buongiorno 0141 649 1029 · 1012 Pollokshaws Road Near Shawlands Cross. Ronaldo follows parents' footsteps and recipe book. Pasta/pizza straight-up. Some home-made desserts. Conveniently there are 3 good tratts within 100m of each other near these corners: **Di Maggio's**, the **Brooklyn** (601/CAFÉS) and this small-ish Buongiorno. All are often full, so it's good to have the choice. Takeaway menu. 7 days, lunch and LO 9.30pm.

528 2/XA1
£15-22
Partners Italian Bistro www.theitalianbistro.co.uk · 0141 339 5575 · 1051 Great Western Road Out west beyond luvvyland next to Gartnavel Hospital. There's been eating out here for years but these Partners have settled for a well-worked-out Italian diner in nice surroundings to go with their Tapela in town and Tattie Mac's near the university (542/SCOTTISH). Friendly but... in Glasgow, this means friendly, with no buts. 7 days. 10am-10pm, later at weekends.

✓ **The Big Blue** Report: 531/PIZZA.

The Best Pizza

529 2/XA1 ✓ **Firebird** www.firebirdglasgow.com · 0141 334 0594 · 1321 Argyle
£15-25 **Street** Big-windowed, spacious bistro at the far west end of Argyle St. Mixed modern menu and everything covered but notable for their light, imaginative pizzas and pastas. Firebird is a perennially popular hangout and still a key spirit-of-Glasgow spot. 12noon-10/10.30pm (bar 12midnight/1am).

530 2/E3 ✓ **The Brunswick (Hotel Bar/Café)** www.brunswickhotel.co.uk · 0141
£15-25 552 0001 · 104 Brunswick Street The not-large, usually bustling bar and restaurant of this hip-ish hotel in the Merchant City (469/BOUTIQUE HOTELS, 668/
· COOL BARS) has a big reputation for its brutti bread, a delicious, thin pizza – the star on a grazing/sharing menu turned out from a gantry kitchen. 7 days till 10pm.

531 2/XA1 **The Big Blue** 0141 357 1038 · 445 Great Western Road On corner of Kelvin
£15-25 Bridge and with terrace overlooking the river. Bar and restaurant together so noise can obliterate meal and conversation later on. Lots of other dishes and morsels including spot-on pasta, but the big thin pizzas here are good – that's a well-known fact. 7 days lunch and LO 9.45pm (weekends 10.30pm).

532 2/C2 **Fratelli Sarti** www.sarti.co.uk · 0141 248 2228 · 133 Wellington Street,
2/D2 121 Bath Street & 404 Sauchiehall Street Excellent, thin-crust pie, buffalo
£15-25 mozzarella and freshly made *pomodoro*. 7 days, hours vary. It's the ingredients that count here, the pizza dough a bit on the chunky side. 519/ITALIAN RESTAURANTS.

533 2/C3 **Bier Halles** www.republicbierhalle.com · 0141 204 0706 · Gordon Street &
& B2 323 Sauchiehall St The first near Buchanan St and Central Station, the other the
<£15 Bier Halle Hippo Lounge. Notable of course for their mind-boggling and presum-ably mind-altering selection of beers from all over the world, they also do a great pizza. It's a fact! 12noon-12midnight; pizza till 10pm (there are other things on the menu).

The Best French Restaurants

✓✓ **Le Chardon D'Or** www.brianmaule.com · 0141 248 3801 ·
176 West Regent Street Glasgow's finest. Report: 489/FINE DINING.

534 2/XA1 ✓ **La Vallée Blanche** www.lavalleeblanche.com · 0141 334 3333 ·
ATMOS 360 Byres Road Upstairs and small street presence. Straight-up brasserie-
£25-35 type menu using seasonal produce in a room that's woody and cosy at night and light during the day (prix-fixe lunch a great deal). Veal and rabbit with Peterhead halibut; not so much vegetarian choice (they stick to being French). Welcoming and fastidious service. Lunch and LO 9.45pm. Closed Mon.

535 2/B2 ✓ **Malmaison** www.malmaison-glasgow.com · 0141 572 1001 · 278 West
£25-35 George Street The brasserie in the basement of the hotel (456/MAJOR HOTELS) with the same setup as Edinburgh and elsewhere and a very similar menu – based on the classic Parisian brasseries of Montparnasse. Excellent brasserie ambience in woody if dark salon. Seating layout and busy waiters mean lots of buzz. Scottish ingredients with suppliers described. Food here is surprisingly (per-haps) well priced. 7 days, breakfast, lunch and LO 10.30pm.

The Best Scottish Restaurants

536 2/E3
£25-35
✓ ✓ **City Merchant** www.citymerchant.co.uk · 0141 553 1577 · **97 Candleriggs** Here long before the Merchant City and still one of the first restaurants in the district. The Matteos have now passed it on to 'friends of the family' so one Tony has been replaced by another but nothing has changed including its enduring appeal and high standards. Seafood, game, steaks, focussing on quality Scottish produce with Italian flair. Lovely oysters; top fish platter. Daily and à la carte menus in warm bistro atmosphere. Good biz restaurant or intimate rendezvous. Lunch and dinner LO 10.30pm (Sun 9pm).

537 2/XA1
£15-25
✓ **Roastit Bubbly Jocks** 0141 339 3355 · **450 Dumbarton Road** Far up in the West End but we do beat our way to this Partick dining room where Mo Abdulla runs a seriously good kitchen at unbelievably good value to us, the well-fed customers. Which is why they don't take credit cards and you'll have to book at weekends. It's very Scottish, by the way! Lunch (weekends only). LO 9.30pm. Can BYOB (£5).

538 2/F3
£15-25
✓ **Arisaig** www.arisaigrestaurant.co.uk · 0141 553 1010 · **1 Merchant Square** On one side of this somewhat tacky indoor square/mall and one among many, Arisaig is probably better than it needs to be. Downstairs brasserie, upstairs (Thu-Sat only) more formal dining in surprisingly spacious mezzanine terrace. Well-sourced Scottish and good value produce from land and sea. Smart and convivial. 7 days 11am-9.30/10.30pm.

539 2/XA1
£25-35
✓ **Cail Bruich West** www.cailbruich.co.uk · 0141 334 6265 · **725 Great Western Road** The bit of Great Western Rd near the end of Byres Rd. The name means 'eat well' and you do in this small bistro with a nice, light ambience. Scottish take and all produce seasonal and properly sourced: 28-days-hung Scotch beef, triple-cooked chips; their broccoli would be sprouting! Good-value lunch. Lunch and LO 9.30pm (Sun 8pm). Closed Mon.

540 2/F3
<£15
✓ **Babbity Bowster** 0141 552 5055 · **16 Blackfriars Street** Listed as a pub for real ale and as a hotel (there are rooms upstairs), their all home-made food is mentioned mainly for its authentic Scottishness (haggis and stovies) and all-day availability. It's pleasant to eat outside on the patio/garden in summer. The restaurant upstairs, **Schottische**, is open for dinner (Thu-Sat). Report: 655/REAL-ALE PUBS, 475/INDIVIDUAL HOTELS.

541 2/D3
ATMOS
<£15
✓ **The Horseshoe** 0141 204 4056 · **17 Drury Street** A classic pub to be recommended for all kinds of reasons, and on this page because it's the epitome of the Scottish pub 'bar lunch'. And it is a particularly good deal upstairs in the lounge with 3 courses for £4.25 at TGP: old favourites on the menu like mushy peas, macaroni cheese, jelly and fruit. High tea till 7.45pm (not Sun) then – the karaoke. Pub open daily till 12midnight. Report: 643/UNIQUE GLASGOW PUBS.

542 2/XA1
£15-25
✓ **Tattie Mac's** www.tattiemacs.co.uk · 0141 337 2282 · **61 Otago Street** Decidedly neighbourhood bistro in a quiet wee street near the university, well known to West Enders (it's off Gibson St). This place has been all over the place over the years but now under the capable hands of The Partners (528/TRUSTY TRATTS), its future as a good contemporary bistro with Scottish context and Glasgow feel is more likely to be secure. Breakfast through to supper. Some outside tables. 7 days 10am-10pm.

Òran Mór 516/GASTROPUBS, 641/UNIQUE PUBS.

The Best Indian Restaurants

343 2/XA1
ATMOS
£15-25
✓ ✓ **Mother India** www.motherindiaglasgow.co.uk · 0141 221 1663 ·
28 Westminster Terrace Monir Mohammed's mothership restaurant
just gets better. Recent refreshings now offer different dining experiences on each
of 3 floors though the straightforward, not-absurdly-long menu with old and new
favourites is the same in each. Ground floor more clubby with panelling and leather
benches, the larger upstairs room intimate, candlelit, and downstairs a more contemporary ambience. It's all stylish, solid and quite the best Indian restaurant in
town (Mother's also in Edinburgh; 235/EDINBURGH INDIAN RESTAURANTS). House
wine and Kingfisher beer but for 2 quid corkage you can BYOB. Best book. Lots of
vegetarian choice. 7 days, lunch (not Sun-Tue) and LO 10.30/11pm. Takeaway too.

544 2/XA1
<£15
✓ **Mother India Café** www.motherindiaglasgow.co.uk · 0141 339 9145 ·
1355 Argyle Street Opposite Kelvingrove Museum and Art Gallery
(674/ATTRACTIONS). Rudely healthy progeny of Mother (above) and cousins to Wee
Currys (below); a distinctive twist here ensures another packed house at all times.
Menu made up of 40 thali or tapas-like dishes (4/5 for a party of 2), so just as we
always did, we get tastes of each other's choices – only it's cheaper! Fastidious
waiters (do turn round the tables). Miraculous tiny kitchen. Can't book; you may
wait! Lunch and LO 10/10.30pm.

545 2/XA1
£15-25
✓ **Dining In With Mother India** www.motherindiaglasgow.co.uk · 0141
334 3815 · 1347 Argyle Street Right next door to Mother India Café. OMG
Monir is reproducing like India. And every one's a winner. Somewhere between
Mother herself and the tapas-driven caff is this more laid-back place also known as
The Den with hot (ie temperature) and cold dishes. You can dine in here or take it
home. The usual signature irresistible curries and breads. 12noon-10pm. Nobody
would suggest sticking a sock on it!

546 2/C1
2/XA1
<£15
✓ **The Wee Curry Shop** www.weecurryshopglasgow.co.uk · 0141 353
0777 · 7 Buccleuch Street & Ashton Lane · 0141 357 5280 & 41 Byres
Road · 0141 339 1339 Tiny outposts of Mother India above, 3 neighbourhood
home-style-cooking curry shops, just as they say. Cheap, always cheerful.
Stripped-down menu in small, if not micro rooms. Buccleuch St 8 tables; Ashton
Lane the biggest with 2 sittings (7 & 9pm) at weekends. House red and white and
Kingfisher but can BYOB (wine only; £3.50). Lunch and LO 10.30pm. Closed Sun
lunch except Byres Rd. No credit cards.

547 2/XA1
£15-25
✓ **Balbir's** www.balbirsrestaurants.co.uk · 0141 439 7711 · 7 Church
Street At the bottom end of Byres Rd the grandee Glasgow proprietor Balbir
Singh Sumal presides in a cavernous, chandelier-chic, routinely packed restaurant.
Both regular and innovative dishes from the Subcontinent that Glasgow has taken
to its heart (though low-cholesterol rapeseed oil is used instead of ghee) and
stomach. Closed lunch. LO 10.30/11pm. Balbir also has the more contemporary (although menus are indistinguishable) **Saffron Lounge** at 61 Kilmarnock Road (0141
632 8564) and **Tiffin Rooms** at 573 Sauchiehall St (0141 221 3696) west of the M8.

548 2/XA2
£15-25
Shish Mahal www.shishmahal.co.uk · 0141 339 8256 · 68 Park Road First-
generation Indian restaurant that still, after (unbelievably) almost 50 years,
remains one of the city's faves. Modernised some years back but not compromised
and still feels like it's been here forever. Menu of epic size. Many different influences in the cooking, and total commitment to the Glasgow curry (and chips). The
Shish Mahal's great claim to fame is that it actually invented chicken tikka masala,
the UK's favourite curry. 7 days till 11/11.30pm.

549 2/XA1
ATMOS
<£15
Banana Leaf www.thebananaleaf.co.uk · 0141 334 4445 · 76 Old Dumbarton Road Across Argyle St from Kelvingrove Art Gallery, up Regent Moray St, turn left. Discreet doorway into 2 tiny south Indian living rooms in a Glasgow tenement. Some chicken and lamb dishes but mostly vegetarian and loadsa dosas. Disarmingly real, cheap as chapatis; even the slightly chaotic service and mad kitchen is reminiscent of downtown Cochin. The takeaway operation can be a bit irritatingly offhand. 7 days 11.30am-11pm. Sun 10am-11pm.

550 2/E3
£15-25
Dakhin www.dakhin.com · 0141 553 2585 · 89 Candleriggs Upstairs, out of sight and a good find for lovers of Indian food. Same owners as The Dhabba (below) but menu is a subcontinent away (ie south as opposed to north India). Lighter and saucier with coconut, ginger and chilli and light-as-a-feather dosas make essential difference to the tandoori/tikka-driven menus of most other restaurants in this category. Signature dish: must-have paper dosa. 7 days. Lunch and LO 10/10.30pm.

551 2/XA1
£15-25
Ashoka Ashton Lane www.harlequinrestaurants.com · 0141 357 5904 · 19 Ashton Lane & Ashoka West End · 0141 339 0936 · 1284 Argyle Street Part of the Harlequin Restaurants chain, they have always been good, simple and dependable places to go for curry but have kept up with the times. Argyle St is *the* original. Nothing surprising about the menus, just sound Punjabi via Glasgow fare. Good takeaway service (0800 195 3195). Lunch and LO 11.30pm (West End evenings only at weekends). Open till 12midnight.

552 2/E4
£15-25
The Dhabba www.thedhabba.com · 0141 553 1249 · 44 Candleriggs Mid-Merchant City curry house serving north Indian cuisine in big-window diner. Complemented by sister restaurant Dakhin (above) and often busy, the Dhabba is overall a decent and popular Merchant City choice. 7 days 12noon-10.30pm.

553 2/XB5
£15-25
Ali Shan www.alishantandoori.co.uk · 0141 632 5294 · 250 Battlefield Road South Siders and many from further afield swear by this Indo-Pak restaurant that's especially good for veggie and other diets. It's been here for 20 years and it shows but honesty and integrity are in their mix of spices on a very long menu. 7 days from 5pm, LO 11pm (12midnight or later weekends).

The Best Far-Eastern Restaurants

THAI

554 2/D2
£25-35
✓ **Thai Lemongrass** 0141 331 1315 · 24 Renfrew Street Noticing perhaps that Glasgow has far fewer good Thai restaurants than Edinburgh (see p. 57), TL opened up here, near the Concert Hall and opposite Cineworld; it is one of the best in town. Contemporary (those banquettes) while still cosy. Good service and presentation of the now-ubiquitous Thai faves. 7 days lunch and LO 11pm.

555 2/XA2
£25-35
Thai Siam www.thaisiamglasgow.com · 0141 229 1191 · 1191 Argyle Street Traditional, low-lit atmosphere but a discerning clientele forgive the decor and get their heads down into fragrant curries et al. All-Thai staff maintain authenticity. What it lacks in style up front it makes up for in the kitchen. Lunch and LO 11pm. Closed Sun lunch.

CHINESE

556 2/XA1
<£15
✓ **Asia Style** 0141 332 8828 · 185 St George's Road Near Charing Cross. Discreet, authentic and exceptionally good value, this makes for an excellent late-night rendezvous though they make no compromises to a Scottish/Chinese

palate. Bright canteen with banter to match. Traditional Chinese without MSG. Malaysian dishes and a reputation for shellfish. Think old Singapore! 7 days, dinner only from 5.30pm. LO 2.30am. Cash only.

557 2/D1 ✓ **Dragon-i** www.dragon-i.co.uk · 0141 332 7728 · 311 Hope Street
£25-35   Refreshingly contemporary Chinese-pan-Asian opposite Theatre Royal. Thai/Malaysia and rice/noodle/tempura dishes with sound non-MSG, often unlikely Scottish ingredients make for fusion at its best. Proper puds. Chilled-out room and creative Chinese cuisine. Lunch Mon-Fri, dinner 7 days LO 12midnight (11pm Sun).

558 2/C2 ✓ **Amber Regent** www.amberregent.com · 0141 331 1655 · 50 West
£25-35   Regent Street Elegant Cantonese restaurant that prides itself on courteous service and the quality of its cuisine, especially seafood. Chung family here almost 25 years. The menu is traditional as is the atmosphere. Influences from Mongolia to Malaysia. Creditable wine list, quite romantic at night and a good business-lunch spot. The only Glasgow Chinese restaurant regularly featured in both AA and Michelin. Lunch, LO 10.30pm. Sat 12noon-11.30pm. Closed Sun.

559 2/XA1 ✓ **Chow** 0141 334 9818 · 98 Byres Road Away from other Chinese restau-
£15-25   rants clustered downtown, this is the contemporary, smarter and buzzy West End version. Broad menu imaginative and different. Good vegetarian choice. Can be a tight squeeze down or up. Takeaway and delivery. Good value, especially lunch. 7 days lunch and dinner (Sun from 4.30pm). LO 11.30pm.

560 2/C4 ✓ **Ho Wong** www.ho-wong.com · 0141 221 3550 · 82 York Street
£25-35   Inconspicuous location for a discreet, urbane Pekinese/Cantonese restaurant which relies on its reputation and makes few compromises. Calm, quite chic room with mainly up-market clientele; an ambience you either love (a lot) or hate. Good champagne list. Reassuringly expensive. Notable for seafood and duck. Lunch (not Sun) and LO 11/11.30pm.

561 2/B1 **Glasgow Noodle Bar** 0141 333 1883 · 482 Sauchiehall Street Authentic,
<£15   stripped-back Chinese-style noodle bar, 100m from Charing Cross. A fast-food joint with genuine, made-on-the-spot – in the wok – food late into the AM. Not the smartest diner hereabouts but quite groovy in a clubzone way. 7 days, 12noon-4am. 614/LATE-NIGHT RESTAURANTS.

562 2/B2 **Wok To Walk** www.woktowalk.com · 304 Sauchiehall Street Glasgow
<£15   station of international Asian fast-food chain, like Wagamama below, formulaic to the last grain of rice or noodle, but fun. Wok in the windae, choose ingredients and 8 sauces from Shanghai to Bali. All day till 1am and 4am Thu-Sat.

JAPANESE

563 2/D2 **Wagamama** www.wagamama.com · 0141 229 1468 · 97 West George
£15-25   Street Wagamama brand and formula here in midtown near the stations (also in Silverburn shopping mall). We don't do chains in StB but if you like fast Asian food that's good for you, you'll be a fan of their big canteen tables and 'healthy' Japanese-based food made to order and brought when ready. Seems to work universally though the novelty does wear off. 7 days 12noon-11pm (Sun 12.30-10pm).

564 2/D3 **Ichiban** www.ichiban.co.uk · 0141 204 4200 · 50 Queen Street &
WE   184 Dumbarton Road, Partick Noodle bar based loosely on the Wagamama
£15-25   formula. Fundamental food, egalitarian presentation, some technology. Ramen, udon, soba noodle dishes; also chow meins, tempuras and other Japanese snacks. Long tables, eat-as-it-comes 'methodology'. Light, calm, modern. Midday to LO

10pm (weekends 11pm), Sun 1-10pm. The Partick Ichiban which is near Byres Rd is possibly better of the 2; a healthy option in both quarters.

FUSION

565 2/E3 **✓Rumours** www.rumourskopitiam.co.uk · 0141 353 0678 · **21 Bath**
£15-25 **Street** From an elevated first-floor position at the corner of West Nile and Bath Sts, this Malaysian caff (or kopitiam) eschews the style dictates of the restaurant/bar culture further along Bath St and is the better for it. Odd name but the word on the street is that this is the real deal: fusion/Malaysian cooking that is fresh and authentic and a long, unusual, non-alcoholic drinks list (though also Tiger, Singha and wine). 7 days 12noon-10pm.

566 2/XA4 **Yen** www.yenrotunda.com · 0141 847 0110 · **28 Tunnel Street** In the
£15-25 Rotunda near the SECC so often busy with pre- or après-concert audiences.
£25-35 Upstairs café by the people who brought us the Amber Regent (above) has Cantonese/Japanese/Thai noodle vibe, ground floor has more expensive, more full-on teppanyaki restaurant with 8-course menus prepared as you sit round the searing hobs. 7 days, lunch and LO 10.30pm (closed Sun lunch).

Other Ethnic Restaurants

SPANISH

567 2/XA1 **✓Pintxo** 0141 334 8886 · **562 Dumbarton Road** Part of the Partick triumvi-
<£15 rate which includes Velvet Elvis (502/BISTROS) and the Criterion, this with the most distinctive cuisine, viz. tapas. Though the name is Basque, the menu has highlights from all over as well as wines. Hard to know what to choose sometimes but this is food to share. 7 days. 5pm-10pm, Sat 1pm-10pm.

568 2/XA1 **Café Andaluz** www.cafeandaluz.com · 0141 339 1111 · **2 Cresswell Lane, off**
2/D3 **Byres Road & St Vincent Place** · 0141 222 2255 The original is a basement on
£15-25 corner of Cresswell (the less heaving of the Byres Rd lanes) where folks gather of an evening (outside benches are cool). Nice atmosphere encased in ceramica with a wide choice of passable tapas and mains (also vegetarian). Owned by Di Maggio (Italian) chain. St Vincent Pl also busy but through location perhaps rather than as a destination. 7 days LO 10/10.30pm. Edinburgh Andaluz is possibly best of the 3.

569 2/XB5 **Tinto Tapas Bar** 0141 636 6838 · **138 Battlefield Road** On the South Side
<£15 near the Victoria Infirmary. Sliver of a restaurant serving tapas and specials all day with good, inexpensive wine selection. 7 days 10.30am-9.45pm (10.30pm Fri-Sun).

GREEK

570 2/XA1 **Konaki** www.konakitaverna.co.uk · 0141 342 4010 · **920 Sauchiehall Street**
ATMOS Far end of Sauchiehall St beyond the M8. Giorgios and Dimitri's mutual love affair
<£15 with Glasgow and Crete. A down-to-earth taverna/deli that's great value and good fun. Oregano and olive oil shipped over from their home village. All Greek faves are here, from mezze to honeyed puds and much melt-in-the-mouth meat between. Deli in front, surprisingly big room through the back. A Greek treat and not so expensive. 7 days, lunch and dinner (not Sun lunch). LO 11pm.

571 2/E3 **Elia** www.eliagreekrestaurant.com · 0141 221 9988 · **24 George Square**
£15-25 Slap bang on the city's landmark square (Queen St side), a surprising location for an authentic Greek family-run bistro (cf Jamie Oliver's mainstream operation over-by). Menu in Greek and English, Mythos and Keo beers and good Boutari. Some Italian and Spanish dishes but mainly the real Greek. 7 days. 12noon-10pm.

TURKISH

572 2/B1 **Alla Turca** www.allaturca.co.uk · 0141 332 5300 · **192 Pitt Street** Tucked
<£15 away a bit between Bath St and Sauchiehall St and handy for the King's Theatre
Bigger than you first think, a contemporary room with cool lighting. Lotsa mezes in
a big menu where fresh ingredients and slow-cooked dishes come as standard.
Good vegetarian choice. And kebabs! Soulful, atmospheric live music may accom-
pany your supper. Lunch and LO 10/11pm (all day Sat).

573 2/C3 **Anatolia** www.anatoliachargrill.co.uk · 0141 221 8777 · **140 St Vincent**
£15-25 **Street** Midtown corner location for this unexpectedly big, assuredly Turkish
restaurant that has gathered good reviews since opening late 2010. Nice flatbreads
and olive appetiser then a long menu to choose from, much from the charcoal
grill; mostly chicken and lamb, of course. Thin Turkish pizzas are a steal at £4.
7 days 12noon-10/11pm.

IRANIAN/PERSIAN

574 2/XA1 ✓**Persia** www.persiaglasgow.com · 0141 237 4471 · **665 Great Western**
£15-25 **Road** Near Byres Rd. Recent welcome addition to West End dining and life. It
is Persian even though that more exotic country technically doesn't exist any
more. Lovely, light bread from the tandoor then a long, tantalising set of choices –
lamb, chicken, seafood and a strong vegetarian list. Many rices. More herbs than
spices. 7 days 12noon-10/11pm.

NORTH AFRICAN

575 2/XA2 **Mzouda** 0141 221 3910 · **141 Elderslie Street** Behind the Mitchell Theatre, a
£15-25 small, airy eaterie named after a faraway village in the Atlas Mountains. Mix of
Catalan and Moroccan 'country' cuisine. Menu somewhere between Berber and
Basque is a refreshing change. Signature dish: Djas Harissa is... hot. Tapas at
lunch. Lunch (not Fri or Sun) and LO 9/10pm.

The Best Seafood & Fish

576 2/C2
£25-35

✓ ✓ **Gamba** www.gamba.co.uk · 0141 572 0899 · 225a West George Street In basement at corner of West Campbell St, a seafood bistro which for a long time now has been one of the best restaurants in the city. Lowlight, understated – a grown-up kind of ambience. A great maître d' and the service to follow. Then there's the food! You just want to eat everything. Somehow chef/proprietor Derek Marshall can't put a finger wrong. His signature fish soup with prawn dumplings is always there but menu changes around every 8 weeks. One meat, one vegetarian choice and the Market Menu brilliant value. Exemplary wine list includes halves. Gamba unlike many, open on Monday. They take the sustainable fishing code seriously like we should. Lunch and LO 10.30pm (closed Sun).

577 2/E4
£25-35

✓ ✓ **Gandolfi Fish** www.cafegandolfi.com · 0141 552 9475 · 84 Albion Street Adjacent the much-loved caff and bar, the big-windowed bistro has a good location, stylish look, good proprietorship (Seumas MacInnes) and a direct link to the West Coast and Hebridean fishing grounds (especially Barra where Seumas is from) and fish supplier Jonathan Boyd. Everything authentic here except the topiary. Lunch and LO 10.30pm (Sun till 9pm). Closed Mon.

578 2/A3
2/C2
ATMOS
£25-35

✓ ✓ **Two Fat Ladies** www.twofatladiesrestaurant.com · 0141 339 1944 · 88 Dumbarton Road & 118 Blythswood Square · 0141 847 0088 The landmark West End restaurant and its city extension. Everything selectively sourced; both tiny kitchens produce delicious dishes with a light touch for packed-in discerning diners. Splendid puds. Similar, though not the same menus. West End 7 days; dinner only LO 10/10.30pm. Blythswood 7 days; lunch (not Sun) and LO 10.30pm. More Ladies also at the brilliant Buttery: 490/FINE DINING.

579 2/XA2
ATMOS
£15-25

✓ ✓ **Crabshakk** www.crabshakk.com · 0141 334 6127 · 1114 Argyle Street Ask any foodie where they recommend to eat out in Glasgow – Crabshakk always in the list. John Macleod's tiny, 3-floor caffshakk has been packed since it opened '09. Champagne and oysters to fab fish 'n' chips, but most notably the meat of shell and claw in a drop-in, grab-a-seat kind of atmosphere. Do wonder myself whether Crabshakk is now a tad overrated but you're always best to book. 11am-10pm (Sun 12noon-6pm). Bar till 12midnight. Closed Mon.

580 2/C2
£15-25

✓ **Mussel Inn** www.mussel-inn.com · 0141 572 1405 · 157 Hope Street Downtown location for light, bright bistro (big windows) where seafood is serious, but fun. From cold waters up north. Mussels, scallops, oysters, catch-of-the-day-type blackboard specials; vegetarian options. Mussels in variant concoctions; kilo pots are the thing, of course. As in Edinburgh (214/SEAFOOD), this formula is sound; the owners are to be commended for keeping it real. 7 days. Lunch and LO 10pm (not Sun lunch).

✓ **An Lochan** Report: 506/BISTROS.

Rogano Report: 491/BEST RESTAURANTS.

The Best Vegetarian Restaurants

581 2/C3
ATMOS
<£15

✓ **Stereo** www.stereocafebar.com · 0141 222 2254 · 20 Renfield Lane
Unobtrusive in this lane off Renfield St near Central Station, Stereo neverthe-less happily occupies a notable building, the former *Daily Record* printing works designed by Charles Rennie Mackintosh (720/MACKINTOSH) and built in 1900. Sits above street level with a music venue downstairs and is crowded weekends. Menu is all vegetarian and basically organic. Much to graze; daily specials. Hand-made and more delicious than the somewhat grungy surroundings may suggest. 7 days 11am-8pm. Bar till 12midnight.

582 2/E4
<£15

✓ **Mono** 0141 553 2400 · Kings Court In odd no-man's land between the Merchant City and East End behind Parnie St, a cool hangout in a forlorn mall. An alternative world! PC in a 'people's collective' kind of way; the antithesis of Glasgow's manufactured style. Great space with art, music (and a record store), occasional performance and interesting totally vegan food served with few frills by friendly staff. Organic ales/wines. 7 days 12noon-8/9pm (bar 12midnight).

583 2/XF3
2/XA5
<£15

Tapa Bakehouse www.tapabakehouse.com · 0141 554 9981 · 21 Whitehill Street, Dennistoun **Tapa Coffeehouse** 0141 423 9494 · 721 Pollokshaws Road Two organic caffs, the original in the East End producing their artisan bread and bakes and with a smattering of seats, the larger laid-back deli and proper café way down Pollokshaws Rd in the South Side. Soups and mezze sold here and cakes. Both dispense some of the best coffee in Glasgow and good for breakfast. 8am-6pm. Thu-Sat till 9pm with supper specials and all organic and wine. Sun 9am-5pm.

584 2/E4
<£15

The 13th Note www.13thnote.co.uk · 0141 553 1638 · 50-60 King Street Old-style veggie hangout – a good attitude/good vibes café-bar with live music downstairs. Menu unexceptional but honest, from vegeburgers to Indian, Greek meze dishes. Some dairy, otherwise vegan. Organic booze on offer, but also normal Glasgow bevvy. 7 days, 12noon-12midnight. Food 9pm (10pm Fri/Sat).

585 2/C2
<£15

Heavenly www.heavenlyglasgow.co.uk · 0141 353 0884 · 185 Hope Street That unusual thing, a vegetarian – no, actually vegan, diner and bar that you wouldn't expect until you'd bitten into their marinated tofu burger and possibly not even then. Deliberate, not-laying-it-on-you approach though most dishes are vegetarian versions rather than creations. Airy, contemporary room with mellow indie soundtrack. Organic beers, ciders. 7 days 12noon-12midnight, food till 8pm then bar.

Tchai-Ovna www.tchaiovna.com · 0141 357 4524 · Otago Lane Old-style vegetarian caff for modern people; boasts best boho credentials. 597/TEAROOMS.

Restaurants serving particularly good vegetarian food but not exclusively vegetarian. NB: some ethnic restaurants will subscribe to halal practices.

The Ubiquitous Chip Report: 486/BEST RESTAURANTS.
Baby Grand Report: 612/LATE-NIGHT RESTAURANTS.
Mother India, Dakhin Report: 543/550/INDIAN RESTAURANTS.
Café Gandolfi Report: 586/TEAROOMS.
Banana Leaf Report: 549/INDIAN RESTAURANTS.
Alla Turca Report: 572/OTHER ETHNIC RESTAURANTS.
Persia Report: 574/ETHNIC RESTAURANTS.

The Best Tearooms & Coffee Shops

586 2/E4
ATMOS
✓✓**Café Gandolfi** www.cafegandolfi.com · 0141 552 6813 · **64 Albion Street** For well over a quarter of a century, Seumas MacInnes's definitive and landmark meeting/eating place has occupied a pivotal corner of the Merchant City. A bistro menu, but the casual, boho ambience of a tearoom or coffee shop. Long ago now the stained glass and heavy, over-sized wooden furniture created an ideal ambience that has withstood the vagaries of Glasgow style. The food is light and imaginative and served all day. You may have to queue. 7 days, 9am-11.30pm, Sun from 12noon (619/SUNDAY BREAKFAST). The Bar upstairs (513/GASTROPUBS) and Fish restaurant next door contribute to a unique and exemplary Glasgow experience. Won *The List* readers award 2011.

587 2/XA1
✓✓**Kember & Jones** www.kemberandjones.co.uk · 0141 337 3851 · **134 Byres Road** A deli with well-sourced nibbles and the stuff of the good life. Of all those places with piles of pies and meringues and cupcakes, this is the real deal. They roast the coffee, they bake the bread. Tables outside and on the mezzanine. Great sandwiches and the best tartes and tortes and quiche in town. How they do all that baking from that small kitchen is a triumph of cookability. 7 days, 8am-9pm (9am-10pm Sat, 9am-5pm Sun).

588 2/XA2
✓✓**Hidden Lane Tearoom** 0141 237 4391 · **1103 Argyle Street** The lane next to Tesco leads to another lane then at the end, as it says, the Hidden Tearoom. Kirsty Fitzgerald was born to do tea and cakes and the rest. Small downstairs and upstairs parlour quiet and civilised. Hot dishes of the maccy cheese variety, sandwiches, soup and top cakes especially combined in a brilliant afternoon tea (588/TEAROOMS) served from noon on. I'd say: 'go find'. 10am-6pm.

589 2/XA1
✓✓**Artisan Roast** www.artisanroast.co.uk · 07776 428409 · **15 Gibson Street** Follow that aroma that blew over from Edinburgh where they dispense the same indispensible coffee in a similar neighbourhood (275/EDINBURGH COFFEE SHOPS). A bit fancier here but the same blend and stripped-back offering. Probably the best coffee in the West (End). Check for opening hours.

590 2/XA1
✓**Sonny & Vito's** 0141 357 0640 · **52 Park Road** On a West End corner between Great Western Rd and Gibson St, a daytime deli-caff with excellent home baking, light menus and tartlettes to eat in or take away. Not many tables, always busy; those outside have interesting urban aspects. Nice for breakfast. 7 days 9am-6pm. Sun from 10am.

591 2/D3
2/C3
✓**Fifi and Ally** www.fifiandally.com · 0141 229 0386 · **Princes Square** More a lifestyle experience than a mere tearoom but they do it well. On the top floor of this indoor mall now flooded with eateries. F&A did this contemporary tearoom thing first. Good for hot snacks, sandwiches and cakes, especially the now-ubiquitous meringues. Many ladies lunch! Afternoon tea 2-5pm with the 3-tier treatment. 7 days; Sun-Wed till 6pm; till 11pm Thu-Sat.

592 2/XA2
✓**Coffee, Chocolate & Tea** www.coffeechocolateandtea.com · 0141 204 3161 · **944 Argyle Street** Among many others, this stands out: they make the chocolates and they blend and roast their own coffee (5 different beans) and there's home-made daily muffins and chocolate tart. No surprise that CC&T comes from folk who know and care about food though a bit of a departure for the MacCallums of Troon (1318/SEAFOOD). 40 teas and unquestionably good cuppas of C, C & T.

593 2/XA1 **Cup** 0141 357 2525 · **311 Byres Road** A caff in the middle of busy Byres Rd where 'cup' refers to what you eat rather than what you drink out of. Taking the rise and rise of the cupcake to perhaps its icing on the-cake conclusion, they are here in their multi-iced and festooned glory. Sandwiches, soup, afternoon tea: God knows how they do it, but it's all home baked. Delightful, really. 7 days 10am-6pm.

594 2/XA1 **Auntie M's Cake Lounge** De Courcy's Arcade, Cresswell Lane Upstairs in arcade off Byres Rd. Michelle Aaron used to make the cakes for Heart Buchanan (624/TAKEAWAYS) and is now here in this midst of this fascinating boho emporium. Her paean to the '50s does exactly what it says on the cake tin. It's a post-war world with mix 'n' match kitchen units, knick knacks and a rockabilly soundtrack. And of course the non-rationed eggs, butter and sugared cakes we love. More real and relaxed than most in this quarter. 11am-5.30pm, Sun 12noon-5pm. Closed Mon.

595 2/XA1 **Tinderbox** 0141 339 3108 · **189 Byres Road & 14 Ingram Street** · 0141 552
   2/E3 **6907 & Princes Square**Stylish, shiny coffee shops. Snacks and Elektra, the good-looking coffee machine. Great people-watching potential especially at Byres Rd, the original. Better sandwiches and cakey things than others of this ilk. Daily soups, pies, etc (methinks their hot food not so hot). Tinderbox made the leap to London and Aberdeen. 7 days, 7.15am-10pm, 10.40pm Byres Rd. Both Sun from 8am.

596 2/XA1 **Epicures of Hyndland** 0141 334 3599 · **157 Hyndland Road** By the makers of La Vallée Blanche, a very Hyndland coffeeshop/bistro in the heart of the territory. Breakfast through lunch, snacks and dinner on the airy ground floor or more intimate mezzanine. Pain Quotidien style. 7 days 8am-9.45pm, bar till 11pm.

597 2/XA1 **Tchai-ovna** www.tchaiovna.com · 0141 357 4524 · **42 Otago Lane** A 'house of tea' hidden away off Otago St on the banks of the Kelvin with verandah and garden terrace. A decidedly gap-year tearoom which could be Eastern Europe, North Africa or Kathmandu but the vibe mainly Middle Eastern. Hookahs are smoked. 70 kinds of tea, soup, organic sandwiches and cakes. Impromptu performances likely. A real find but suits and ladies who lunch may not be quite so chilled out here. 7 days 11am-10pm.

598 2/C2 **The Tearooms** 0141 243 2459 ·**151 Bath Street** Upstairs and part of The Butterfly and The Pig, this very tea kind of room has fully embraced the T-come-back. But it's on the go from breakfast (traditional with twists) through soup and super 'sanner' lunch to the all-important tier of afternoon tea then, of course, high tea. All very much in-period, owing something to the good eyes of Ruby Tuesdays, the vintage boutique upstairs. 7 days 8.30am-8pm. Sun from 11am.

The Best Caffs

599 2/XA1 ✓✓**University Café** 87 Byres Road 'People have been coming here for
   ATMOS generations to sit at the "kneesy" tables and share the salt and vinegar. Run by the Verecchia family who administer advice, sympathy and pie, beans and chips with equal aplomb.' And have done apparently since 1918! 6 booths only; it resists all change. BYOB; no corkage. Daily 9am-10pm (weekends till 10.30pm). Sun from 10am.

600 2/XF3 ✓**Coia's Café** www.coiascafe.co.uk · 0141 554 3822 · **473 Duke Street** Since 1928, Coia's has been supplying this East End high street with ice cream, great-deal breakfasts and the kind of comforting lunch that any neighbourhood needs. Some years back a substantial makeover and expansion turned this caff into a full-blown food operation with deli counter, takeaway and restaurant. So now it's traditional grub and ice cream along with the olive-oil niceties. They still do the Havana cigars. 7 days. 10am-9pm (10pm Fri/Sat).

601 2/XA5 ✓ **Brooklyn Café** 0141 632 3427 · **21 Minard Road** Here just off Pollokshaws Rd since 1931, the kind of all-purpose caff any neighbourhood would be proud of. More tratt perhaps than caff, with pasta/pizza, risottos, salads, excellent puds and great ice cream. It will, of course, never die, like their Empire biscuits. 7 days 8am-9pm (weekends 10pm). Sun from 9am. Can BYO.

602 2/XA1 **Biblocafé** 0141 339 7645 · **262 Woodlands Road** At St George's Cross. Boho second-hand bookshop and coffeestop; soup, sandwich and the internet. Cool spot! 8am-8.30pm, Sat/Sun from 9.30am.

603 2/C1 **CCA** www.cca-glasgow.com · 0141 332 7521 · **350 Sauchiehall Street** Glasgow arts institution and all-round studio and gallery spaces with a calm, airy coffee shop in its lofty atrium to plot and muse and while away an afternoon. Food by Encore Catering who also do The Tramway (608/KID-FRIENDLY) ain't bad: soup, salads, pasta. 10am-7.30pm, Fri/Sat till 9pm.

604 2/XF3 **7 Grams** 0141 554 9404 · **27 Hillfoot Street, Dennistoun** Off Duke St. Neighbourhood soup 'n' sandwich caff in the East End. Funky furnishings; it's a living room! Home bakes. Nothing flash or frenzied here, just a mellow vibe for slow days in the east (end). 10am-7pm. Closed either Sun or Tue (still deciding at TGP).

605 2/E4 **Trans-Europe Café** 0141 552 7999 · **25 Parnie Street** Easygoing caff near Glasgow Cross off Trongate with neighbourhood atmosphere and home-made food individually prepared in Tony Sinclair's mad gantry kitchen. Light food, especially bespoke sandwiches and more meal-like at night (Thu-Sat only). A friendly vibe. 10am-5pm (weekends till 10pm).

▪▪▪▪ Kid-Friendly Places

606 2/XA1 ✓ **Rio Café** 0141 334 9909 · **27 Hyndland Street, Partick** A kid-friendly caff that's cool – cool for parents that is, with decent food and service for both from breakfast fry-ups to sustaining suppers. Here there's also DJs, 'spoken word' nights, jazz on Thursdays, poker on Sundays and sweeties, sweeties, sweeties. An all-round neighbourhood place for all Jock Tamson's bairns. 7 days 9am-9pm (bar 11pm/12midnight).

607 2/XA1 **Di Maggio's** www.dimaggios.co.uk · 0141 334 8560 · **61 Ruthven Lane off** 2/XA5 **Byres Road & 1038 Pollokshaws Road** · 0141 632 4194 & **21 Royal Exchange** 2/D3 **Square** · 0141 248 2111 'Our family serving your family' they say and they do (in the extending DM family of restaurants). These are all bustling, friendly pizza joints with a good Italian attitude to brats. There's a choice to defy the most finicky kid. High chairs, special menu. Handy outdoor section in Exchange Sq for runaround kids. 7 days.

608 2/XA5 **Tramway Café** 0141 422 2023 · **25 Albert Drive** Caff at Tramway arts venue on the South Side. Venue itself cavernous and contemporary with changing programme always worth visiting. Caff well run with great healthy grub and facing on to the Hidden Garden (1519/GARDENS). Play area. Snack bags for kids and lots of freshly made fruit and vegetable juices. 10am-8pm, Sun 12noon-6pm. Closed Mon.

609 2/XA5 **Brooklyn Café** 0141 632 3427 · 21 Minard Road The unassuming, long-established South Side (off Pollokshaws Rd) caff where families are very welcome for the carbo and the cones and the jars of sweeties on the shelf. Report: 601/CAFFS

610 2/XA1 **The Big Blue** 0141 357 1038 · 445 Great Western Road Downstairs on Kelvin Bridge corner. Accessible, Italian-led menu but main attraction is the family-friendly open-air terrace overlooking the river. 7 days lunch and dinner. More drink-driven later.

611 2/D3 **Princes Square** Buchanan Street Glasgow's downtown mall almost taken over by eateries with 'outside' tables and suitable kids' choices. There's a central mosaic in the basement where kids can play. Several options to choose from.

Bella Napoli Family-run and run for families: a tratt with the standard Italian grub we've all loved ever since we could keep spaghetti on a spoon. Report: 524/TRUSTY TRATTS.

▓▓▓ The Best Late-Night Restaurants

612 2/A2
ATMOS
✓ **Baby Grand** www.babygrandglasgow.com · 0141 248 4942 · Elmbank Gardens It's not easy to find by Charing Cross Station and Premier Lodge skyscraper hotel behind King's Theatre, but persevere – this is a useful bar/diner at any time of day but comes into its own after 10pm when just about everywhere that's decent is closing. A grazing menu à la mode. Piano player Wed-Sat; nighttime people. **Daily till 12midnight, Fri/Sat 2am.**

613 2/XA1
ATMOS
✓ **Asia Style** 0141 332 8828 · 185 St George's Road Simple, authentic Chinese and Malaysian café/canteen with familiar sweet 'n' sour, curry and satays, 4 kinds of noodle, exotic specials and 5 kinds of porridge. Only open evenings. **7 days 5pm-3am** (may close 2am if quiet).

614 2/B1 **Glasgow Noodle Bar** 0141 333 1883 · 482 Sauchiehall Street The stripped-down noodle bar in Sauchiehall St where and when you need it. Authentic, fast, no-frills Chinese (ticket service and eezee-kleen tables). The noodle is 'king'; but cooking is taken seriously. Report: 561/FAR-EASTERN RESTAURANTS. **7 days, 12noon-4am.** The arriviste Wok to Walk (562/FAR-EASTERN RESTAURANTS) nearby at number 304 is open **till 1am and also 4am (Thu-Sat).**

615 2/XA1 **Stravaigin & Stravaigin 2** www.stravaigin.5pm.co.uk · 0141 334 2665 · Gibson Street & 0141 334 7165 Ruthven Lane, off Byres Road Worth remembering that both these excellent restaurants (492/FINE-DINING RESTAURANTS and 496/BISTROS) serve food **till 11pm.** It is later than most in 'cosmopolitan' Glasgow.

✓✓ **Ubiquitous Chip** www.ubiquitouschip.co.uk · 0141 334 5007 · Ashton Lane 486/FINE-DINING RESTAURANTS. **7 days till 11pm.** Best late choice in the West End.

✓✓ **Guy's Restaurant & Bar** 494/BISTROS. **11.30pm Fri/Sat.** Best late choice in the Merchant City.

Good Places For Sunday Breakfast

616 2/XA1 ✓✓ **Cafézique** 0141 339 7180 · 66 Hyndland Street This award-winning,
ATMOS hard-to-fault, two-level bistro/caff opens at 9am every day for snacking or more ambitious breakfast. A very civilised start to the day; fills up quickly. **From 9am.**

617 2/XA1 ✓ **The Left Bank** www.theleftbank.co.uk · 0141 339 5969 · 33 Gibson Street Classy and popular café-bar-restaurant in student and luvvyland. From great granola to eggs mornay and beans on toast. 502/BISTROS. From 9am weekdays, **Sun from 10am.**

618 2/F3 ✓ **Babbity Bowster** 0141 552 5055 · 16 Blackfriars Street The seminal Merchant City bar/hotel recommended for many things (540/SCOTTISH RESTAURANTS, 672/DRINKING OUTDOORS), but worth remembering as one of the best and earliest spots for Sunday breakfast. **From 10am.**

619 2/E4 ✓ **Café Gandolfi** www.cafegandolfi.com · 0141 552 6813 · 64 Albion Street Atmospheric room, with daylight filtering through stained glass and comforting, oversized wooden furniture. A pleasant start to a Sunday, that day of rest and more shopping made even better with pastrami, a pot of tea and the papers. 586/BEST TEAROOMS. Bar upstairs has all-day menu. **Both from 12noon.**

620 2/XA1 ✓ **Sonny & Vito's** www.sonnyandvitosdeli.co.uk · 0141 357 0640 · 52 Park Road Much-loved West End brunch rendezvous. A deli-caff with home baking from scones and muffins to Mediterranean platefuls. Outside tables and takeaway. 590/BEST COFFEE SHOPS. **From 10am.**

621 2/XF3 ✓ **Coia's Café** 473 Duke Street They've been doing breakfast here for over 75 years. Goes like a fair and still damned good. The full-fry monty lasts all day (vegetarian too). The East End choice. 600/BEST CAFFS. **From 10am.**

622 2/XA1 ✓ **Stravaigin** www.stravaigin.5pm.co.uk · 0141 334 2665 · 28 Gibson Street Same care and flair given to breakfast menu as the rest (492/BEST RESTAURANTS). Cramped maybe, but reflects appetite for Sunday breakfast from home-made granola to French toast, the Ayrshire bacon. Served till 5pm. **From 11am.**

623 2/XA1 **Tinderbox** 0141 339 3108 · 189 Byres Road · 14 Ingram Street · 0141 552 6907 & Princes Square Great café/diner open early to late. Probably the earliest decent breakfast for out-all-nighters. Porridge, muesli and cake. 595/COFFEE SHOPS. Weekdays from 7.15am. Weekends **from 8am.**

The Best Takeaway Places

624 2/XA1 ✓ ✓ **Heart Buchanan** www.heartbuchanan.co.uk · 0141 334 7626 · **380 Byres Road** Traiteur and adjacent **Café**: Fiona Buchanan demonstrates the French idea that excellent food can be pre-prepared to take home. Certainly an extraordinary and changing menu (every 2 weeks) is produced in the kitchens downstairs according to a published list. Many pestos and lots of other selected goodies to go. Fiona puts her 'heart' into this place. Every urban neighbourhood should have some heart and a Buchanan. 7 days 8.30am-8pm. Sun 10am-6pm. Café LO 4pm; Fri/Sat till 9pm. BYO (free if you buy next door).

625 2/XA1 ✓ ✓ **Delizique** www.delizique.co.uk · 0141 339 2000 · **70 Hyndland Street** Down from Cottier's and two doors up from their original corner, a larger, busy emporium serving the luvvies, loaded and long-term denizens of Hyndland and beyond. In-house bakery with top breads. Fruit, vegetables, cheese counter; the unusual alongside dinner-party essentials including the de rigeur cookbooks. Gorgeous food to go includes salads, tarts and scrumptious cakes. 7 days 9am-7pm (till 8pm Sat/Sun).

626 2/XA1 ✓ **Cottonrake Bakery** 07951 734089 · **31 Hyndland Street** Michelin-experienced Stefan Spicknell's superlative bakery brings proper pâtisserie and top takeaway tarts, galettes and the sausage roll extraordinaire to Partick. You better be quick! Tue-Sat 9am-5pm.

627 2/XA5 ✓ **Cherry and Heather** www.cherryandheather.co.uk · 0141 427 0272 · **7 North Gower Street, Cessnock** Just off Paisley Rd West near Ibrox and next to Bellahouston Post Office. A perfect wee takeaway with integrity food and a great range of soups, casseroles and truly gourmet sandwiches. Artisan bread, unusual combos. A few stools. Cherry represents Japan (where the cook comes from) and Heather Scotland, where she and her Indonesian partner have settled. It's a happy combination. 10am-5pm (Sat 11am-4pm). Closed Sun.

628 2/XA1 ✓ **Roots & Fruits** 0141 339 3077 · **Great Western Road & 351 Byres Road & 1137 Argyle Street** A row of wholefood provisioner shops near Kelvinbridge (and branches), famously where to go for fruit and veg in the West End. GW Rd branch has traiteur section and a couple of chairs by one of the windows, but the delicious home-made food (paellas, tortillas, salads) and bakery (bread from Tapa) is mainly to take home. 7 days. 8.30/9am-6.30pm (7pm Thu/Fri), 10am-6.30pm Sun.

629 2/XA2 ✓ **Piece** 0141 221 7975 · **1056 Argyle Street** Neat and nifty, hard-working sandwich bar in interminable Argyle St (western end). Infinite choice of bespoke fillings (all better than most), daily soup and rather good proof-of-the-pudding tartes. Shows you what a difference a difference makes! 8am-6pm Mon-Fri, Sat from 10am.

630 2/E3 **Fressh** 0141 552 5532 · **51 Cochrane Street** A takeaway with a soupçon of integrity in the Merchant City, at George Sq along (in every sense) from Greggs. Healthy soups and good juice. Sandwiches made up or ready-to-go. Much vegetarian. Both dolphin- and people-friendly. 9am-5pm. Closed Sun.

631 2/XA1 **Grassroots** www.grassrootsorganic.com · 0141 353 3278 · **20 Woodlands Road** Near Charing Cross. Food to go, but mainly big organic deli. Vegetarian ready meals, bespoke sandwiches and the fatrias. 7 days 8.30am-6/7pm, Sat 9am-6pm, Sun 11am-5pm.

The Best Delis

632 2/XA1 ✓ ✓ **Grassroots Organic** 48 Woodlands Road Long-established, seminal and original organic provisioner. Food one side, rest of your life the other. Everything chemically unaltered and environmentally friendly. Great breads and salads for lunch and their signature nutty pastries called fatrias. Best organic fruit and veg range in town. 7 days 8.30am-6pm (Thu/Fri till 7pm, Sun till 5pm).

633 2/XA1 ✓ ✓ **Delizique** 70 Hyndland Street Excellent neighbourhood deli for the affluent Hyndlanders and others who roam and graze round here. Counters, kitchen and bakery. Great prepared meals (in-house chef), tarts, pasta and gorgeous cakes. Other hand-picked goodies include oils, hams, flowers and Mellis cheeses. Open till 9pm Mon-Fri, till 8 weekends. 625/TAKEAWAY. Cafézique at no. 66, the original location, is the top café-bistro in the west (493/BISTROS).

634 2/XA1 ✓ ✓ **Heart Buchanan** 380 Byres Road Great deli and first-rate takeaway. Report: 624/TAKEAWAY.

635 2/XA1 ✓ ✓ **Roots & Fruits** 0141 339 3077 · Great Western Road This the main branch (see 628/TAKEAWAYS) of the all-round, all-good-things-in-life provisioner of the West End: the flower shop, the deli and the fruit and veg together offering a superlative service. Makes you wonder why all things can't be as good as this. 8.30am-6.30pm (till 7pm Thu/Fri). Sun from 10am.

636 2/XA1 ✓ ✓ **I.J. Mellis** www.mellischeese.co.uk · 0141 339 8998 · 492 Great Western Road Started out as the cheese guy, now more of a very select deli for food that's good and 'slow'. Coffees, Iberico hams, sausages, olives and seasonal stuff like apples and mushrooms (branches vary), so smells mingle. Irresistible! Branches also in Edinburgh (325/EDINBURGH DELIS), St Andrews (1441/DELIS) and Aberdeen. 7 days though times vary. See also 1468/CHEESES. He's still the cheese guy!

637 2/XA5 ✓ **Eat Deli** 0141 638 7123 · 16 Busby Road Deep south of the city, the last good food stop before and after East Kilbride. A café-cum-deli and outside-catering outfit; essentially great home-cooked food to go. From antipasti to wholesome meals and sweet and savoury bakes. 7 days 8am-7pm, Sun 11am-5pm.

638 2/XA5 ✓ **Gusto and Relish** www.gustoandrelish.com · 0141 424 1233 · 729 Pollokshaws Road More perhaps a caff than a deli. They cure their own ham, make sausages etc, so brill for breakfast. Other wholesome options and nice salads. Book for their supper club on the last Thursday of the month. All to go. 7 days 9am-6pm, Sat 10am-5pm, Sun from 10.30am.

639 2/XA5 ✓ **Deli 1901** www.deli1901.co.uk · 0141 632 1630 · 11 Skirving Street Just off Kilmarnock Rd at the Granary. South Side traiteur with meals, pies and bakes to go. Lots for starters. Good cheese selection. Big on outside catering. They also have The Pelican across from the Art Gallery; 501/BISTROS. 7 days 9am-7pm, Sun 10am-5pm.

640 2/XF3 ✓ **Eusebi Deli** 0141 763 0399 · 793 Shettleston Road A long way down the Shettleston Rd but customers travel here from way beyond the neighbourhood. Great Italian wine and deli ranges but especially notable for Giovanna Eusebi's home-made food to go. A real traiteur; a passion for food and for Italy written all over it. Tue-Sat 9am-6pm.

Unique Glasgow Pubs

641 2/XA1
ATMOS
✓ ✓ **Oran Mor** www.oran-mor.co.uk · Corner of Byres & Great Western Roads This is the epitome of all the things you can do with a pub and you could spend your (Glasgow) life here. A huge and hugely popular emporium of drink and divertissements in a converted church on a prominent West End corner, the always-evolving vision of Colin Beattie. Drinking on all levels (and outside) but also good pub food (516/GASTROPUBS) and separate brasserie, the only bit which for some reason has not set the heather alight. Big entertainment programme from DJs to comedy in the club and home of the brilliant 'A Play and a Pint'. They thought of everything. From lunch till very late, this is a hostelry of happiness and hope. 7 days till 12midnight.

642 2/D5
ATMOS
✓ ✓ **Scotia Bar** 112 Stockwell Street Probably Scotland's oldest continually running pub, established 1792, Tudor-style with a low-beamed ceiling and intimate, woody snug. Long the haunt of folk musicians, writers and raconteurs. Music and poetry sessions, folk and blues Wed-Sun. Open till 12midnight. A must-visit for true pub lovers.

643 2/D3
ATMOS
✓ ✓ **The Horseshoe** 17 Drury Street A mighty pub since the 19th century in a small street between West Nile and Renfield Sts near Central Station. Early example of this style of pub, dubbed 'gin palaces'. Island rather than horseshoe bar ('longest in the UK'), impressive range of alcohols and an upstairs lounge where they serve lunch and high tea and karaoke till midnight (no, really!). Food is amazing value (541/SCOTTISH RESTAURANTS). All kinds of folk. Daily till 12midnight.

644 2/E1
✓ **Corinthian** www.g1group.co.uk · 191 Ingram Street Mega makeover of impressive listed building to form a restaurant and comfy lounge/cocktail bar, The Gaming Room casino and a night club downstairs, all in glorious surroundings. Awesome ceiling in main room. The flagship unit of the mighty (Glasgow-based) G1 Group, this in both senses mirrors Glasgow perfectly (see me!). More or less all of the day and all of the night.

645 2/E4
✓ **Arta** www.arta.co.uk · Old Cheesemarket, Walls Street In the Merchant City; near and sharing ownership and scale of vision with Corinthian (above). Dated and a tad trashed now but this massive, OTT bar/restaurant/club somewhere between old Madrid and new Barcelona could only happen in Glasgow at the turn of the century (this one!). Tapas menu upstairs till 10pm (Thu-Sat) and below, the full-on Glasgow drinking, dressing-up and chatting-up experience. Closed Mon/Tue. Bar 3am.

646 2/D5
✓ **Victoria Bar** 157 Bridgegate The Vicky and the Clutha are in two of the city's oldest streets, near the Victoria Bridge over the Clyde. Once a pub for the fishmarket and open odd hours, now it's a howff for all those who like an atmosphere that's old, friendly and uncontrived. Ales. Mon-Sat till 12midnight, Sun 11pm.

647 2/D5
✓ **Clutha Vaults** 167 Stockwell Street Same owner, joined at the hip and sharing a common courtyard or beer garden through the back. The Clutha (ancient name for the Clyde) has a Victorian-style interior and an even longer history. Both feature live music (Wed-Sun). Mon-Sat till 12midnight, Sun till 11pm.

648 2/XA1
The Halt Bar 160 Woodlands Road Edwardian pub largely unspoiled and unchanged since at least the 1970s. Original counter and snug intact. Always great atmosphere – though may be a tad grungy for some. Live music and DJs Thu-Sun, football on the telly. Open mic nights. The quiz et al. Open till 11pm/12midnight.

649   2/XA1   **Lismore**   206 Dumbarton RoadLismore/Lios mor named after the long island
ATMOS   off Oban. Great neighbourhood (Partick) bar that welcomes all sorts. There's just
something about this place from the stained glass to the floor and the walls that's
good to be in. Gives good atmosphere, succour and malts. Occasional music. Daily
till 12midnight.

650   2/XA2   **Ben Nevis**   1147 Argyle Street Owned by the same people as Lismore and Òran
Mór (above) but run by others. An excellent makeover in contemporary but not
faux-Scottish style. Small and pubby, the Deuchars is spot-on and great malt list. A
calm and civilised corner of the West End.

Hummingbird   186 Bath Street 670/COOL BARS. Glasgow style loud and proud.

▬▬▬ The Best Real-Ale Pubs

651   2/A2   ✓**Bon Accord**   www.thebonaccord.com · 153 North Street On the road
above the motorway near the Mitchell Library. One of the first real-ale pubs in
Glasgow. Great atmosphere for drinking. Good selection of malts and up to 12
beers; always Deuchars and IPA plus many guest ales on hand pump. Food at
lunchtime and till 7.45pm. Light, easy-going atmosphere but they do take their ale
to heart. Quiz night on Wed, live band on Sat. Till 12midnight, Sun till 11pm.

652   2/XF5   ✓**WEST**   www.westbeer.com · 4 Binnie Place, Templeton Building,
Glasgow Green First find the People's Palace (677/MAIN ATTRACTIONS) then
gaze at the fabulous exterior of the Templeton edifice where on the bottom corner
the UK's first German brewery brews its award-winning beers (4 ingredients only:
water, malt, hops and yeast). 8 in total in a beerhall setting and garden overlooking
the Green. St Mungo for starters and a massive selection of imports. 'Simple,
hearty' food with a German slant till 9pm. Decent wine list. 11am-11pm, Fri/Sat
12midnight.

653   2/B1   ✓**The State**   148 Holland Street Off Sauchiehall St at the West End. No-
ATMOS   compromising, old-style pub, all wood and old pictures. 8 guest ales. No fancy
extras. Will probably outlive the many makeovers around here. Food at lunchtime.
Some music. 7 days till 12midnight.

654   2/XA1   **Tennent's**   191 Byres Road Near the always-red traffic lights at University Ave, a
big, booming watering-hole of a place where you're never far away from the horseshoe bar and its dozen excellent hand-pumped ales, including up to 4 guests. In
2011, 1500 regulars petitioned against a plan to give it a makeover: the seabass and
the risotto are on hold for now! So, basic bar meals including 'the steak pie' till
9pm. Till 12midnight at weekends.

655   2/F3   **Babbity Bowster**   16 Blackfriars Street In a pedestrianised part of the
Merchant City and just off the High St, a highly successful pub/restaurant/hotel
(475/INDIVIDUAL HOTELS); but the pub comes first. Caledonian, Deuchars, IPA and
well-chosen guests. Many malts and cask cider. Food all day (540/SCOTTISH
RESTAURANTS), occasional folk music, outside patio (660/DRINK OUTDOORS).

656   2/D3   **The Horseshoe**   17 Drury Street Great for lots of reasons (643/UNIQUE GLAS-
GOW PUBS), not the least of which is its range of beers in exactly the right surroundings to drink them. Sky sports.

Places To Drink Outdoors

657 2/XA1 ✓**Cottier's** www.thecottier.com · 93 **Hyndland Street** First on the left
after the swing park on Highburgh Rd (going west) and the converted church
is on your right, around the corner. Heart of West End location. Cottier Theatre
reopened after refurbishment with lovely upstairs restaurant. Think: a cold beer on
a hot day sitting in the leafy shade of a churchyard. On summer weekends, the
barbeque is full-on: steaks, fish, halloumi, the lot! It's a Hyndland kind of life! Bar
12noon-12midnight, food till 10pm. Restaurant 5 10pm.

658 2/XA1 **Lock 27** www.lock27.com · **1100 Crow Road** At the very north end of Crow Rd
beyond Anniesland, an unusual boozer for Glasgow: a canalside pub on a lock of
the Forth & Clyde Canal (691/WALKS IN THE CITY), a (very wee) touch English, where
of a summer's day you can sit outside. Slightly worn around the edges but excellent bar food and always busy.

659 2/XA1 **Bar Brel & others in Ashton Lane** www.brelbarrestaurant.com As soon
as the sun comes out, so do the punters. With numerous watering holes, benches
suddenly appear and Ashton Lane becomes a cobbled, alfresco pub. The nearest
Glasgow gets to Euro or even Dublin drinking. Brel has the hill out the back.

660 2/F3 **Babbity Bowster** 16 **Blackfriars Street** Unique in the Merchant City for several reasons (655/REAL-ALE PUBS, 540/SCOTTISH RESTAURANTS), but in summer certainly for its napkin of garden in an area bereft of greenery. Though enclosed by
surrounding streets, it's a concrete oasis. And always good craic.

The Big Blue Outside terrace overlooks the murky Kelvin. 532/PIZZA.

The Goat Not the cleanest air but clear views from this corner all the way into
town. 667/COOL BARS.

Clutha Vaults & The Victoria Two of Glasgow's most venerated pubs share a
common beer garden. 647/646/UNIQUE PUBS.

McPhabbs Back 'n' front. 661/BARS WITH GOOD FOOD.

Chinaski's 239 **North Street** Above the M8 and the flyover outside at the back
(conservatory and courtyard) in this great post-work watering hole.

Bars With Good Food

See also Gastropubs, p. 98.

661 2/XA1 ✓ **McPhabbs** www.mcphabbs.com · **22 Sandyford Place** Sauchiehall St west of Charing Cross. Long-standing great Glasgow pub with loyal following. Tables in front garden and on back decks. Standard home-made pub-grub menu and great specials. Food till 12noon-9pm. Bar 11pm/12midnight. Bit of a West End secret.

662 2/C2 ✓ **The Butterfly And The Pig** www.thebutterflyandthepig.com · **153 Bath Street** Among many style-heavy bars and eateries the BF&P arrived (oh, aeons ago now) as quite the latest thing but neatly avoided the gastropub bandwagon by being more real than just recherché and cooler than contrived. Colloquial food descriptions but what comes is imaginative and fun to eat. They do proper afternoon tea and upstairs is the proper Tearooms (598/TEA-ROOMS). 7 days 12noon-9pm, Sun till 6pm. Bar till 3am.

663 2/D3 **Vroni's** www.vronis.co.uk · **47 West Nile Street** Not a pub by any means, rather a dark but welcoming wine bar from the days when wine bars were where we went after work. So, great list, champagne and interesting 'small plates' to snack and graze. May have been a blokes-in-suits place in the past, now ladies also linger over a Sancerre. 11am-12midnight. Food 9pm.

664 2/XA1 **Brel** www.barbrelrestaurant.com · **Ashton Lane** Always-busy bar in West End lane where teams of students and the rest of us teem, especially at weekends. Pots of moules/frites help the many euro brews go down. Popular, stuff-your-face type of lunches and serried ranks of outside tables up the back. Lunch and food till 9.45pm (10.30pm weekends), bar 12midnight. Outside is the hill. 659/OUTSIDE DRINKING.

665 2/D3 **Bar Soba** www.barsoba.co.uk · **11 Mitchell Lane** Up the narrow lane off Buchanan St and next to the Lighthouse design centre, a bright, contemporary room and an ambitious fusion menu: Japanese and Malaysian staples reasonably accomplished. 7 days 12noon-10pm. Bar 12midnight.

Babbity Bowster See 655/REAL-ALE PUBS and 660/OUTDOORS.

Cottier's See 657/OUTDOORS.

Bier Halle See 533/PIZZAS.

Cool Bars

666 2/C3 ✓ **Arches** www.theaiches.co.uk · 0141 565 8900 (box office) · 253 Argyle Street The boho bar/café of the essential Arches Theatre, the club and experimental theatre space refurbished a while ago now with Millennium money, its vitality undiminished. Design by Timorous/Taller, this is an obvious pre-club pre-theatre space, but works at any time. Food and DJs and lots going on. Even if you're only in Glasgow for the weekend, you should come here for the vibe. Food has upped its game and Scottish credential of late. Served 12noon-9pm. Bar till 12midnight/1am.

667 2/XA1 ✓ **The Goat** www.thegoat.co.uk · 0141 357 7373 · 1287 Argyle Street Up west near Kelvingrove Gallery, a comfortable, friendly, sitting-room pub (with mezzanine and upstairs snug), not obviously 'cool' but known for its laid-back vibe and reasonable food. Big windows and pavement terrace look down Argyle St; a great corner for people gazing and a Glasgow-affirming experience. 7 days. Food 12noon-9pm, bar 12midnight.

668 2/E4 ✓ **The Brunswick Hotel Bar** www.brunswickhotel.co.uk · 0141 552 0001 · 104 Brunswick Street This small Merchant City hotel and its ground-level bar/restaurant has stood the style test of times and 20 years on is still a cool hangout for a mixed crowd, especially at Sunday brunch and all over the weekend. Very decent grub (530/PIZZA).

669 2/XA2 ✓ **Brewdog** www.brewdog.com · 01346 519009 · 1397 Argyle Street Opposite Kelvingrove Art Gallery, the Glasgow Brewdog; others in Edinburgh (669/COOL BARS) and Aberdeen. The 'craft-beer revolution': hand-made, often very strong beers (9 and counting, from signature Trashy Blonde to their infamous End of History), here in a big-window, spacious room that's not only for drinking. Food till 10pm. Live music Sun.

670 2/E3 ✓ **Hummingbird** www.socialanimal.co.uk · 186 Bath Street The bird hummed into vibrant view with no expense spared by the G1 group in 2009; it still invites its youngish and up-for-it clientele to sup the nectar of life. There are 3 floors of theme and thin people with great haircuts (upstairs manly private parties). Downstairs kicks in later. Food is burger-dominated. The lighting is proper; makes you look good. 5pm-3am.

671 2/D3 **Bar 10** 10 Mitchell Lane Halfway up Buchanan St pedestrian precinct on the left in the narrow lane that also houses the Lighthouse design centre. There's an NYC look about this joint that is so loved by its habitués, they still pack it at weekends over 15 years after it arrived. Ben Kelly design has worn well. Food till 7pm, DJs and pre-club preparations. 7 days till midnight. **Bar Soba**, great for cocktails and its pan-Asian menu, is opposite in the lane.

672 2/D3 **The Lab** Springfield Court, off Buchanan Street The lane between Office and Russell & Bromley shops. Not cool in a haircut kind of way, but a smartly turned-out and -run bar with food and an outdoor courtyard. Table service; a little gem.

The Main Attractions

673 2/XA4
FREE
✓ ✓ ✓ **The Riverside Museum** www.glasgowlife.org.uk · 0141 287 2720 · By Clydeside Expressway Beyond the SECC; across the Clyde from Govan. Glasgow's newest and most spectacular attraction, the Zaha Hadid-designed relocated and reborn Museum of Transport. Entirely at home here. 3,000 objects from trains and trams to paddlesteamers and prams are skilfully and imaginatively arranged and displayed in the battleship-grey big, wavy shed. A 'Tall Ship' on the river and the New Glasgow emerging in the distance and getting closer. Given Scotland's and in particular Glasgow's pre-eminence in the invention and manufacture of so many forms of transport, it's heartening that this museum is such an impressive showcase. Like much of its contents, it's world class! Not just for boys! 10am-5pm (from 11am Fri and Sun).

674 2/XA1
ATMOS
FREE
✓ ✓ **Kelvingrove Art Gallery & Museum** 0141 276 9599 · Argyle Street · www.glasgowlife.org.uk Huge Victorian sandstone edifice with awesome atrium. On the ground floor is a natural history/Scottish history museum. The upper salons contain the city's superb British and European art collection. A prodigious success, with literally millions of visitors since it reopened '06 after major refurbishment. Endless interest and people-friendly presentations. See the world from a Glasgow point of view! (You go through 'Glasgow Stones' to get to 'Ancient Egypt'.) And it's all free, folks! 7 days. 10am-5pm (Fri/Sun from 11am).

675 2/XA5
FREE/
ADMISSION
NTS
✓ ✓ **The Burrell Collection, Pollok Park & Pollok House** 0141 287 2550 · www.nts.org.uk South of the river via A77 Kilmarnock Rd (over Jamaica St Bridge from the city centre) or M77, well signed. Set in rural parkland, this award-winning modern gallery was built to house the eclectic acquisitions of Sir William Burrell. Showing a preference for medieval works, among the 8,500 items the magpie magnate donated to the city in 1944 are artefacts from Ancient Egypt and the Romans to Rodin. The building itself integrates old doorways and whole rooms reconstructed from Hutton Castle. Self-serve café and restaurant on the ground floor (Mon-Thu, Sat 10am-5pm, Fri and Sun 11am-5pm). **Pollok House** (0141 616 6410) and gardens further into the park (with works by Goya, El Greco and William Blake) is worth a detour and has, below stairs, the better tearooms; gardens to the river. Both open 7 days. 10am-5pm. 692/WALKS IN THE CITY.

676 2/XF3
FREE
✓ **Glasgow Cathedral & Provand's Lordship** 0141 552 6891/553 2557 · www.glasgowcathedral.org.uk · Castle Street Across the road from one another, they represent what remains of the oldest part of the city, which (as can be seen in the People's Palace; see below) was, as late as the early 18th century, merely a ribbon of streets from here to the river. The present cathedral, though established by St Mungo in AD 543, dates from the 12th century and is a fine example of very real, if gloomy, Gothic. The house, built in 1471, is a museum which strives to convey a sense of late-medieval life. Don't get run over when you re-emerge into the 21st century and try to cross the street. In the background, the Necropolis piled on the hill invites inspection and offers a viewpoint and full Gothic perspective (though may be don't go alone). Easy to do all these and St Mungo's Museum (below) together; allow half a day. Open 7 days. Times vary slightly.

677 2/XF5
ATMOS
FREE
✓ **The People's Palace** www.glasgowlife.org.uk · 0141 276 0788 Approach via Glasgow Cross and London Rd, then turn right into Glasgow Green. This has long been a folk museum *par excellence* wherein, since 1898, the history, folklore and artefacts of a proud city have been gathered, cherished and displayed. But this is much more than a mere museum; it is part of the heart and soul of the city and together with the Winter Gardens adjacent, shouldn't be

missed, to know what Glasgow's about. Tearoom in the Tropics, among the palms and ferns of the Winter Gardens. Opening times as most other museums: Tue-Thu, Sat 10am-5pm, Fri & Sun 11am-5pm. Closed Mon.

678 2/XA5
ADMISSION
✓ **Glasgow Science Centre** www.gsc.org.uk · 0141 420 5000 On south side of the Clyde opposite the SECC. Built with Millennium dosh. Approach via the Clyde Arc ('squinty') Bridge or walk from SECC complex by Bell's Bridge. Impressive, titanium-clad mall, Imax cinema and 127m-high tower. 4 floors of interactive exhibitions, planetarium and theatre. Separate tickets or combos. Book slot for the on-again, off-again tower (closed on windy days). Closed 2011 for maintenance; check for times in 2012/13. Museum 7 days 10am-5pm.

679 2/XF3
FREE
St Mungo Museum of Religious Life & Art www.glasgowlife.org.uk · 0141 276 1625 · Castle Street Part of the lovely and not-cherished-enough cathedral precinct (see above), this houses art and artefacts representing the world's 6 major religions arranged tactfully in an attractive stone building with a Zen garden in the courtyard. 3 floors, 4 exhibition areas. The assemblage seems like a good and worthwhile vision not quite realised, but in a time and place where sectarianism is still an issue and a problem, this is a telling and informative display. 7 days 10am-5pm (Fri/Sun from 11am).

680 2/XA1
FREE
Hunterian Museum & Art Gallery www.hunterian.gla.ac.uk · 0141 276 1625 · University Avenue On one side of the street, Scotland's oldest museum with geological, archaeological and social history displayed in a venerable building. The **University Chapel** and cloisters should not be missed. Across the street, a modern block holds part of Glasgow's exceptional civic collection: Rembrandt to the Colourists and the Glasgow Boys, as well as one of the most complete collections of any artist's work and personal effects to be found anywhere, viz that of Whistler. Fascinating stuff, even if you're not a fan. There's also a print gallery and superb **Mackintosh House** (718/MACKINTOSH). Mon-Sat 9.30am-5pm. Closed Sun.

■■■ The Other Attractions

681 2/XA1
FREE
✓✓ **Botanic Gardens & Kibble Palace** www.glasgow.gov.uk · 0141 276 1614 · Great Western Road Smallish park close to River Kelvin with riverside walks (690/WALKS IN THE CITY), and pretty much the 'Dear Green Place'. Kibble Palace (built 1873; major renovation 2006) is the distinctive domed glasshouse with statues set among lush ferns and shrubbery from around the (mostly temperate) world. Killer Plant House especially popular. Main range arranged through smell and colour and seasonality. A wonderful place to muse and wander. Gardens open from 7am till dusk; palace 10am-6pm (4.15pm in winter).

682 2/D3
FREE
✓✓ **Gallery of Modern Art** www.glasgowlife.org.uk · 0141 287 3050 · Queen Street Central, accessible and housed in former Stirling's Library, Glasgow's big visual arts attraction opened in a hail of art-world bickering in 1996. Main point is: does it reflect Glasgow's eminence as a provenance of cutting edge or conceptual work (all those Turner and Becks Prize nominees and winners?). Murmurs stilled of late by more representative exhibitions and new acquisition fund. It should definitely be on your Glasgow hit list. Mon-Wed, Sat 10am-5pm, Thu 10am-8pm, Fri & Sun 11am-5pm.

683 2/F4
✓ **The Barrows** East End The sprawling street and indoor market area around the Gallowgate. 20 years ago when I first wrote this book, the Barras,

as it's called, was pure dead brilliant, a real slab of Glasgow life. Its glory days are over but, as with all great markets, it's full of character and characters and it's still just about possible to find bargains if not collectibles. Everything from clairvoyants to the latest scam. Sat and Sun only 10am-5pm.

684 2/B1 **The Tenement House** www.nts.org.uk · 0844 493 2197 · **145 Buccleuch**
NTS **Street** Near Charing Cross but can approach from near the end of Sauchiehall St
ADMISSION and over the hill. Typical 'respectable' Glasgow tenement, kept under a bell-jar since Our Agnes moved out in 1965. She lived there with her mother since 1911 and wasn't one for new-fangled things. It's a touch claustrophobic when busy and is distinctly voyeuristic, but, well... your house would be interesting, too, in 50 years if the clock were stopped. Daily, Mar-Oct 1-5pm. Reception on ground floor.

685 2/E4 **Sharmanka Kinetic Theatre** www.sharmanka.com · 0141 552 7080 ·
ADMISSION **64 Osborne Street** Off King St in the Merchant City. A small and intimate experi-ence cf most others on this page, but an extraordinary one. The gallery/theatre of Russian emigré Eduard Bersindsky shows his meticulous and amazing mechanical sculptures. Short performance (35 minutes) Wed-Fri 3pm, Sat and Sun 1pm and 3pm. Full performances Thu 7pm, Sun 7pm.

686 2/XA5 **Greenbank Gardens** www.nts.org.uk · 0844 493 2201 · **Clarkston**
NTS 10km southwest of centre via Kilmarnock Road, Eastwood Toll, Clarkston Toll and Mearns Road, then signposted (3km). A spacious oasis in the suburbs; formal gar-dens and 'working' walled garden, parterre and woodland walks around elegant Georgian house. Very Scottish. Gardens open all year 9.30am-dusk, shop/tearoom Apr-Oct 11am-5pm, Nov-Mar Sat and Sun 1-4pm.

687 2/E3 **City Chambers** www.glasgow.gov.uk · 0141 287 4018 · **George Square**
FREE The hugely impressive building along the whole east side of Glasgow's municipal central square. This is a wonderfully evocative monument of the days when Glasgow was the Second City of the Empire. Guided tours Mon-Fri 10.30am and 2.30pm (subject to availability).

688 9/L25 **Finlaystone Country Estate** www.finlaystone.co.uk · 01475 540505 ·
ADMISSION **30km west of city centre via M8/A8** Signed off the dual carriageway just before Port Glasgow. Delightful gardens and woods around mansion house with many pottering places and longer trails (and ranger service). Estate open all year round 10am-5pm. Visitor centre and the Finlaystone tearoom. Spectacular blue-bells in May, colour therapy in autumn.

689 2/A4 **The Waverley** www.waverleyexcursions.co.uk · 0845 130 4647 'The
ADMISSION World's Last Sea-going Paddle Steamer' which plied the Clyde in the glorious 'Doon the Watter' days had a £7M lottery-funded refit. Definitely the way to see the West Coast. Sailings from Glasgow's Science Centre to Rothesay, Kyles of Bute, Arran. Other days leaves from Ayr or Greenock, many destinations. Call for complex timetable. Bar, restaurants, live bands: it's a party!

Paisley Abbey Report: 1904/ABBEYS.

Bothwell Castle, Uddingston Report: 1799/RUINS.

The Best Walks In The City

See p. 12 for walk codes.

690 2/XA1 **Kelvin Walkway** A path along the banks of Glasgow's other river, the Kelvin,
2/XB1 which enters the Clyde unobtrusively at Yorkhill but first meanders through some
2/XC1 of the most interesting parts and parks of the northwest city. Walk starts at
2-13+KM Kelvingrove Park through the university and Hillhead district under Kelvin Bridge
XCIRC and on to the celebrated Botanic Gardens (68/OTHER ATTRACTIONS). The trail then
BIKES goes north, under the Forth and Clyde Canal (see below) to the Arcadian fields of
1-A-1 Dawsholm Park (5km), Killermont (posh golf course) and Kirkintilloch (13km from
start). Since the river and the canal shadow each other for much of their routes,
it's possible, with a map, to go out by one waterway and return by the other (e.g.
start at Great Western Road, return Maryhill Road).
START Usual start at the Eildon St (off Woodlands Road) gate of Kelvingrove Park
or Kelvin Bridge. Street parking only.

691 2/XC1 **Forth & Clyde Canal Towpath** The canal, opened in 1790, reopened 2002 as
ANY KM the Millennium Link. Once a major short cut for fishing boats and trade between
XCIRC Europe and America, it provides a fascinating look round the back of the city from
BIKES a pathway that stretches on a spur from Port Dundas just north of the M8 to the
1-A-1 main canal at the end of Lochburn Rd off Maryhill Rd, and then east all the way to
Kirkintilloch and Falkirk (Falkirk Wheel: 08700 500208; 4/BIG ATTRACTIONS), and
west through Maryhill and Drumchapel to Bowling and the Clyde (60km). A good
option is go as far as Croy and take the very regular train service back. Much of the
route is through the forsaken or redeveloped industrial heart of the city, past waste
ground, warehouses and high flats, but there are open stretches and curious corners and, by Bishopbriggs, it's a rural waterway. More info from British Waterways
(0141 332 6936).
START (1) Top of Firhill Rd (great view of city from Ruchill Park, 100m further on –
703/BEST VIEWS). (2) Lochburn Rd (see above) at the confluence from which to go
east or west to the Clyde. (3) Top of Crow Rd, Anniesland where there is a canalside pub, **Lock 27** (658/DRINK OUTDOORS), with tables outside, real ale and food
(12noon-evening). (4) Bishopbriggs Sports Centre, Balmuildy Rd. From here it is
6km to Maryhill and 1km in other direction to the country churchyard of Cadder or
3km to Kirkintilloch. All starts have some parking.

692 2/XA5 **Pollok Country Park** www.glasgow.gov.uk The park that (apart from the
area around the gallery and the house – 675/MAIN ATTRACTIONS) most feels like a
real country park. Numerous trails through woods and meadows. The leisurely
guided walks with the park rangers can be educative and more fun than you would
think (0141 276 0924 for details). Burrell Collection and Pollok House and Gardens
are obvious highlights. The better (old-fashioned) tearoom is in the basement of
the latter serving an excellent range of hot, home-made dishes, soups, salads,
sandwiches as well as the usual cakes and tasties. 7 days 10am-5pm (0844 493
2202). Enter by Haggs Rd or by Haggs Castle Golf Course. Well signed for cars
including from Pollokshaws Rd and then to the car park in front of the Burrell.

693 10/L25 **Mugdock Country Park** www.mugdock-country-park.org.uk · 0141 956
5-20KM 6100 Not perhaps within the city, but one of the nearest and easiest escapes.
CAN BE CIRC Park which includes Mugdock Woods (SSSI) and 2 castles is northwest of
BIKES Milngavie. Regular train from Queen St Station takes 20 minutes, then follow route
1-A-2 of the West Highland Way for 4km across Drumclog Moor to south edge of the
park. By car to Milngavie by A81 park is 5km north. Well signed. 5 car parks; the

main one includes Craigend Visitor Centre (9am-9pm; closes 6pm Nov-Mar), Stables Tearoom (10am-5pm daily), craft gallery and theatre. There's also a garden centre and farm shop. Many trails marked out and further afield rambles. This is a godsend between Glasgow and the Highland hills.

Cathkin Braes South edge of city with views. Report: 701/BEST VIEWS.

Easy Walks Outside The City

See p. 12 for walk codes.

694 10/M25 **Campsie Fells** www.eastdunbarton.gov.uk Range of hills 25km north of city
10+KM best reached via Kirkintilloch or Cumbernauld/Kilsyth. Encompasses area that
CAN BE CIRC includes the Kilsyth Hills, Fintry Hills and Carron Valley between. (1) Good approach
MTBIKES from A803, Kilsyth main street up the Tak-me-Doon (*sic*) road. Park by the golf
2-B-2 club and follow path by the burn. It's possible to take in the two hills to left as well
as Tomtain (453m), the most easterly of the tops, in a good afternoon; views to the
east. (2) Small car park on the south side of the B818 road to Fintry at the west end
of the Carron Valley reservoir opposite the access road to Todholes Farm and the
wind farm. Follow tracks along reservoir to ascend Meikle Bin (570m) to the right,
the second-highest peak in the Campsies. (3) The bonny village of Fintry is a good
start/base for the Fintry Hills and Earl's Seat (578m). (4) Campsie Glen – a sliver of
glen in the hills. Approach via Clachan of Campsie on A81 (decent tearoom) or from
viewpoint high on the hill on B822 from Lennoxtown-Fintry. This is the easy
Campsie introduction.

695 10/L26 **Gleniffer Braes** www.renfrewshire.gov.uk · **Paisley** Ridge to the south of
2-10KM Paisley (15km from Glasgow) has been a favourite walking-place for centuries. M8
CAN BE CIRC or Paisley Road West to town centre then south via B774/B775 (Causeyside St
MTBIKES then Neilston Rd) and sharp right after 3km to Glenfield Rd. Park/start at
1-A-2 Robertson Park (signed). Here there are superb views and walks marked to east
and west. 500m along Glenfield Rd is a car park/ranger centre (0141 884 3794).
Walk up through gardens and formal parkland and then west along marked paths
and trails.

696 9/K25 **Greenock Cut** www.clydemuirshiel.co.uk 45km west of Glasgow. Can
15/16KM approach via Port Glasgow but simplest route is from A78 road to Largs. Travelling
CIRC south from Greenock take first left after IBM, brown-signed Loch Thom. Lochside
MTBIKES 5km up winding road. Park at Greenock Cut Centre (01475 521458). Walk left along
1-B-2 lochside road to Overton (5km) then path is signed. The Cut, an aqueduct built in
1827 to supply water to Greenock and its 31 mills, is now a historic monument.
Great views from the mast along the Cut though it is a detour. Another route to
the right from the centre leads through a glen of birch, rowan and oak to the Kelly
Cut. Both trails described on board at the car park.

697 9/K25 **Clyde Muirshiel** www.clydemuirshiel.co.uk General name for vast area of
Inverclyde west of city, including Greenock Cut (see above), Lochwinnoch, Castle
Semple Country Park and Lunderston Bay, a stretch of coastline near the Cloch
Lighthouse on the A770 south of Gourock for littoral amblings. Best wildish bit is
around Muirshiel Centre itself, Muirshiel Country Park (01505 614791), with trails, a
waterfall and Windy Hill (350m). Nothing arduous, but a breath of air. The hen har-
rier hunts here. From M8 junction 29, take A737 Lochwinnoch, then B786 to top
of Calder Glen Road. Follow brown signs.

698 10/L25 **Dumgoyne** near **Blanefield** Close to Glasgow and almost a mountain, so a
2-A-2 popular non-strenuous hike. Huge presence, sits above A81 and Glengoyne
Distillery (open to public). Approach from Strathblane War Memorial via Campsie
Dene road. 7km track, allow 3–4 hours (or take the steep way up from the
distillery). Refresh/replenish in Killearn (1299/PUB FOOD).

699 10/L25 **The Whangie** On A809 north from Bearsden about 8km after last roundabout
5KM and 2km after the Carbeth Inn, is the car park for the Queen's View (702/BEST
CIRC VIEWS). Once you get to the summit of Auchineden Hill, take the path that drops
XBIKES down to the W (a half right angle) and look for crags on your right. This is the 'back
NO DOGS door' of The Whangie. Carry on and you'll suddenly find yourself in a deep cleft in
1-A-1 the rock face with sheer walls rising over 10m on either side. The Whangie is more
than 100m long and at one point the walls narrow to less than 1m. Local
mythology has it that The Whangie was made by the Devil, who lashed his tail in
anticipation of a witchy rendezvous somewhere in the north, and carved a slice
through the rock, where the path now goes.

700 10/M26 **Chatelherault** **www.southlanarkshire.gov.uk** · near **Hamilton** Junction 6
2 7KM off M74, well signposted into Hamilton, follow road into centre, then bear left
CIRC away from main road where it's signed for A723. The gates to the 'château' are
BIKES about 3km outside town. A drive leads to the William Adam-designed hunting
1-A-2 lodge of the dukes of Hamilton, set amid ornamental gardens with a notable
parterre and extensive grounds. Tracks along the deep, wooded gorge of the Avon
(ruins of Cadzow Castle) lead to distant glades. Good walks and ranger service
(01698 426213). House open Mon-Thu and Sat 10am-4.30pm (Sun 12noon-
4.30pm); walks at all times. Café, gift shop, visitor centre 10am-5pm Mon-Sat,
12noon-5pm Sun. The circular walk from the visitor centre is about 8km.

▪▪▪ The Best Views Of The City & Beyond

701 2/XF5 **Cathkin Braes, Queen Mary's Seat** The southern ridge of the city on the
B759 from Carmunnock to Cambuslang, about 12km from centre. Go south of river
by Albert Bridge to Aikenhead Road which continues south as Carmunnock Rd.
Follow to Carmunnock, a delightfully rural village, and pick up the Cathkin Rd. 2km
along on the right is the Cathkin Braes Golf Club and 100m further on the left is
the park. Marvellous views to north of the Campsies, Kilpatrick Hills, Ben Lomond
and as far as Ben Ledi. Walks on the Braes on both sides of the road.

702 10/L25 **Queen's View** **Auchineden** Not so much a view of the city, more a perspective
1-A-1 on Glasgow's Highland hinterland, this short walk and sweeping vista to the north
has been a Glaswegian pilgrimage for generations. On A809 north from Bearsden
about 8km after last roundabout and 2km after the Carbeth Inn, a very decent pub
to repair to. Busy car park attests to popularity. The walk, along a path cut into rid-
geside, takes 40-50 minutes to the cairn, from which you can see The Cobbler
(1952/HILLS), that other Glasgow favourite, Ben Ledi and sometimes as far as Ben
Chonzie 50km away. The fine views of Loch Lomond are what Queen Victoria came
for. Further on is The Whangie (699/EASY WALKS).

703 2/XC1 **Ruchill Park** **Glasgow** An unlikely but splendid panorama from this overlooked
but well-kept park to the north of the city near Possilpark housing estate. Go to
top of Firhill Road (past Partick Thistle football ground) over Forth and Clyde Canal
(691/WALKS IN THE CITY) off Garscube Rd where it becomes Maryhill Rd. Best view
is from around the flagpole; the whole city among its surrounding hills, from the
Campsies to Gleniffer and Cathkin Braes (see above), becomes clear.

704 10/M25   **Bar Hill** Twechar, near Kirkintilloch 22km north of city, taking A803
  1-A-2   Kirkintilloch turnoff from M8, then the low road to Kilsyth, the B8023, bearing left
at the black-and-white bridge. Next to Twechar Quarry Inn, a path is signed for Bar
Hill and the Antonine Wall. Steepish climb for 2km; ignore the strange dome of
grass. Over to left in copse of trees are the remains of one of the forts on the
Roman wall which was built across Scotland in the 2nd century AD. Ground plan
explained on a board. This is a special place with strong history vibes and airy
views over the plain to the city which came a long time after.

705 10/M26   **Blackhill** near Lesmahagow 28km south of city. Another marvellous outlook,
  1-A-2   but in the opposite direction from above. Take junction 10/11 on M74, then off the
B7078 signed Lanark, take the B7018. 4km along past Clarkston Farm, head uphill
for 1km and park by Water Board mound. Walk uphill through fields to right for
about 1km. Unprepossessing hill that unexpectedly reveals a vast vista of most of
east-central Scotland.

706 10/L26   **Paisley Abbey** www.paisleyabbey.org.uk · 0141 889 7654 · Paisley M8 to
Paisley; frequent trains from Central Station. Abbey Mon-Sat 10am-3.30pm. Every
so often on Abbey 'open days', the tower of this amazing edifice can be climbed.
The tower (restored 1926) is 50m high and from the top there's a grand view of the
Clyde. This is a rare experience, but phone the tourist information centre (0141 889
0711) or abbey itself (mornings) for details; it could be your lucky day. Guided tours
by arrangement. 1904/GREAT ABBEYS.

707 9/K25   **Lyle Hill** Gourock Via M8 west to Greenock, then round the coast to relatively
genteel old resort of Gourock where the Free French worked in the yards during
the war. A monument has been erected to their memory on the top of Lyle Hill
above the town, from where you get one of the most dramatic views of the great
crossroads of the Clyde (Holy Loch, Gare Loch and Loch Long). Best vantage-point
is further along the road on other side by trig point. Follow British Rail station
signs, then Lyle Hill. There's another great view of the Clyde further down the
water at **Haylie, Largs**, the hill 3km from town reached via the A760 road to
Kilbirnie and Paisley. The island of Cumbrae lies in the sound and the sunset.

Campsie Fells & Gleniffer Braes Reports: 694/695/WALKS OUTSIDE THE CITY.

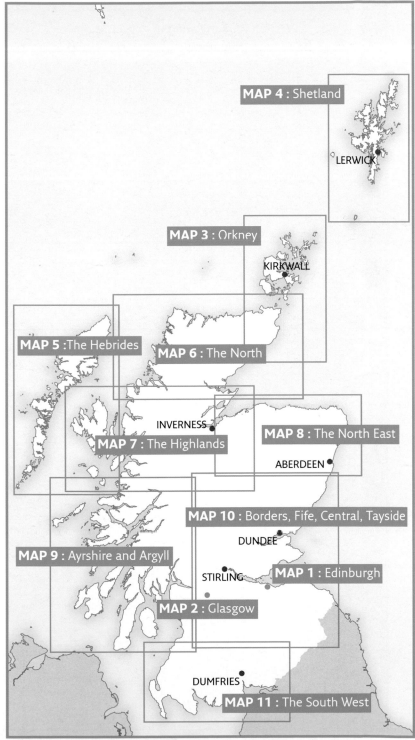

MAP 4 : Shetland

LERWICK

MAP 3 : Orkney

KIRKWALL

MAP 5 :The Hebrides

MAP 6 : The North

MAP 7 : The Highlands

INVERNESS

MAP 8 : The North East

ABERDEEN

MAP 10 : Borders, Fife, Central, Tayside

DUNDEE

MAP 9 : Ayrshire and Argyll

STIRLING

MAP 1 : Edinburgh

MAP 2 : Glasgow

DUMFRIES

MAP 11 : The South West

Locations numbered below 1490 on the maps generally refer to places to eat and stay

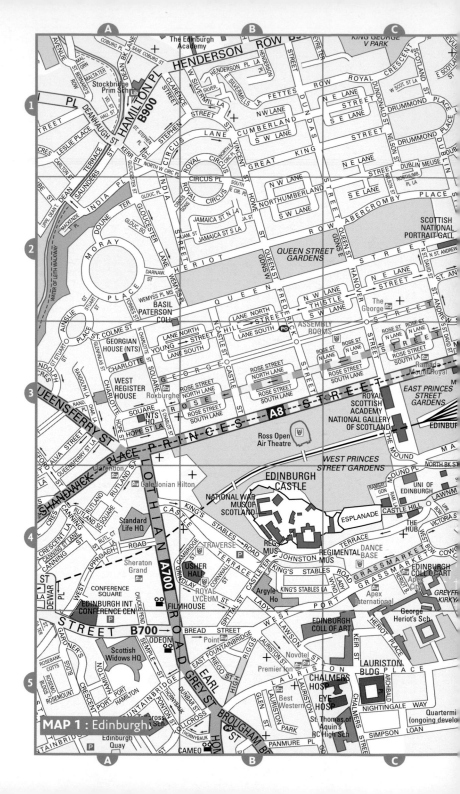

MAP 1 : Edinburgh

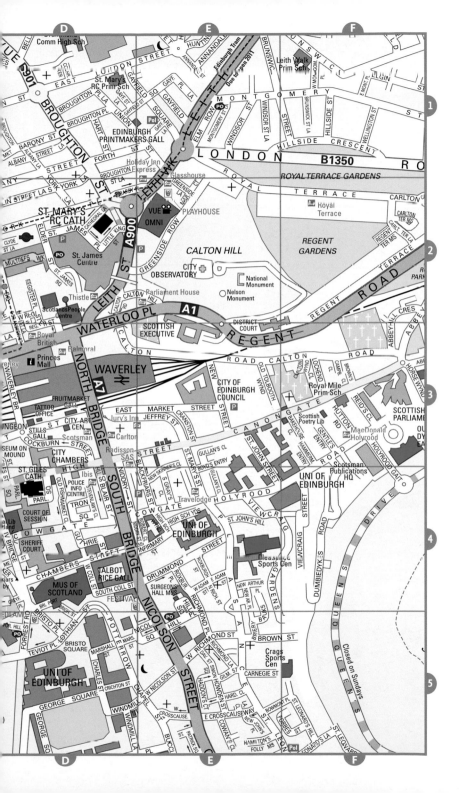

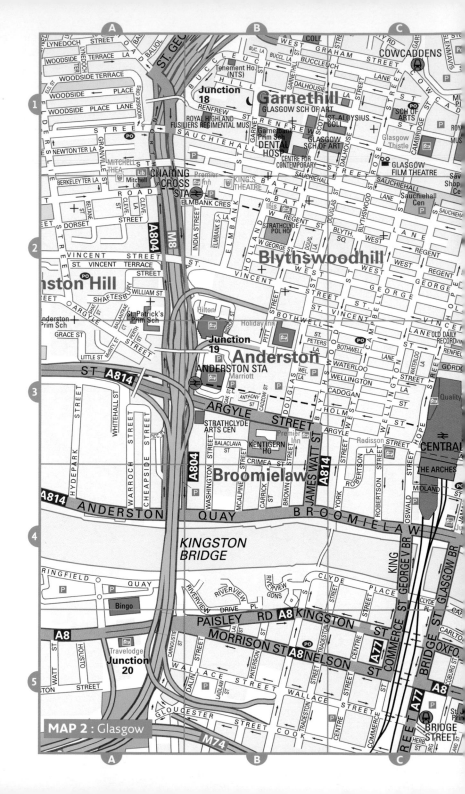

MAP 2 : Glasgow

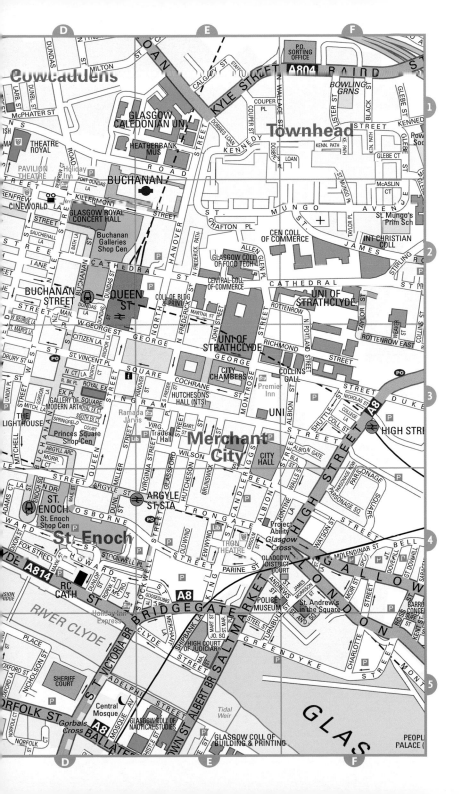

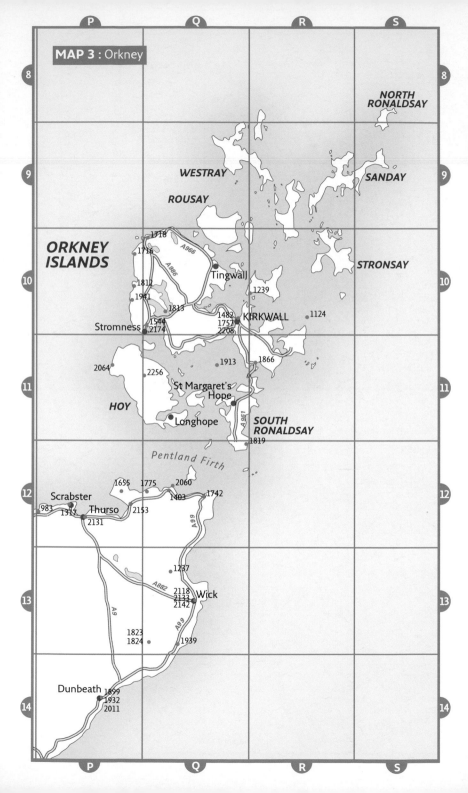

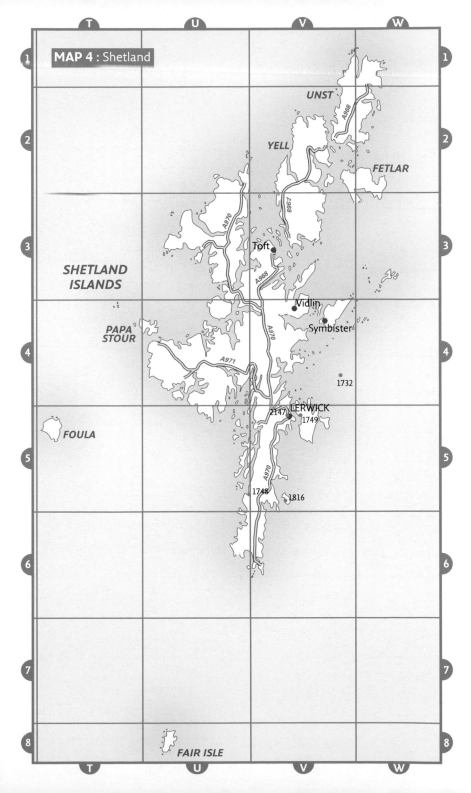

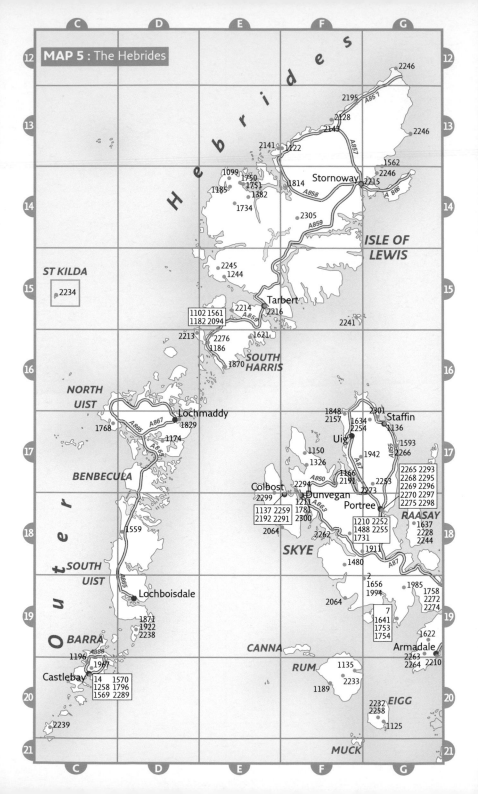

MAP 5 : The Hebrides

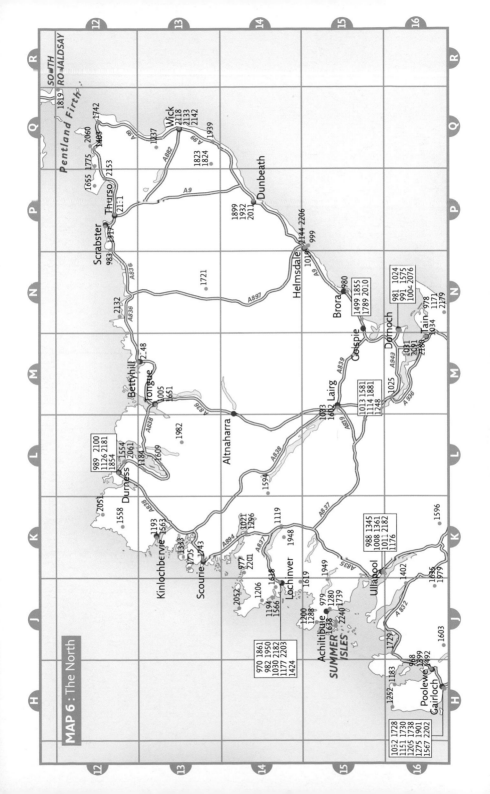

MAP 6 : The North

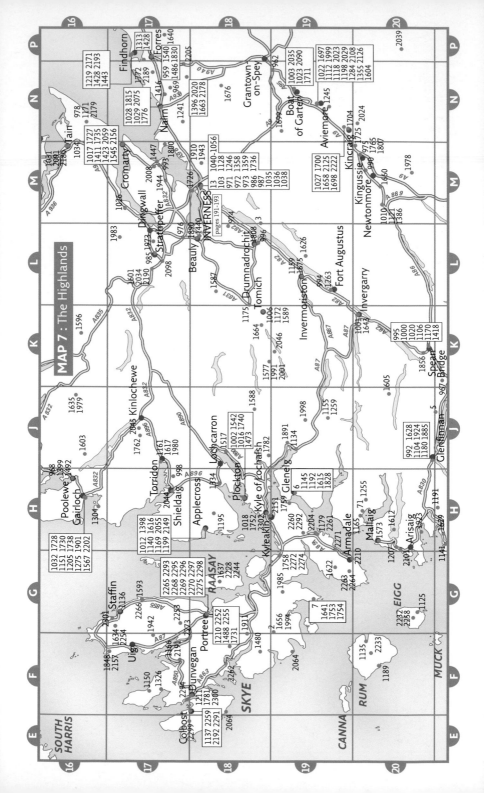

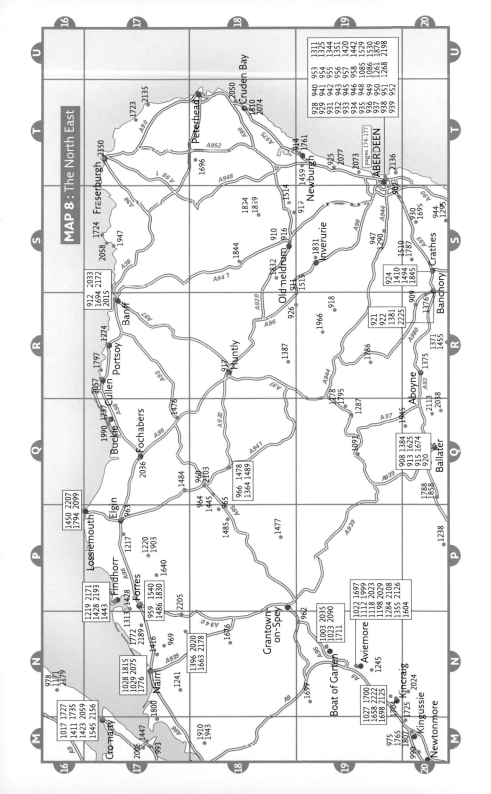

MAP 8: The North East

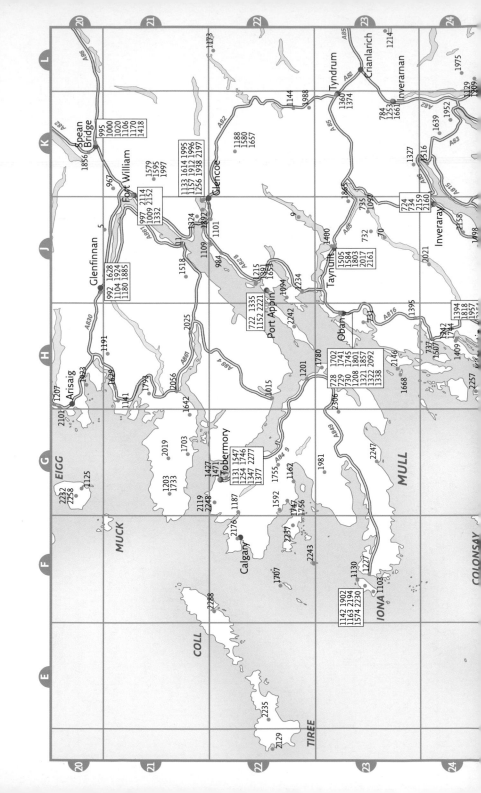

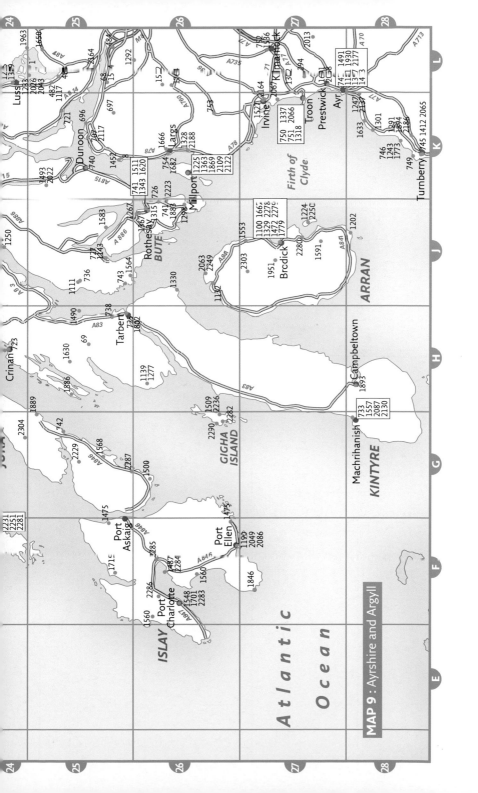

MAP 9 : Ayrshire and Argyll

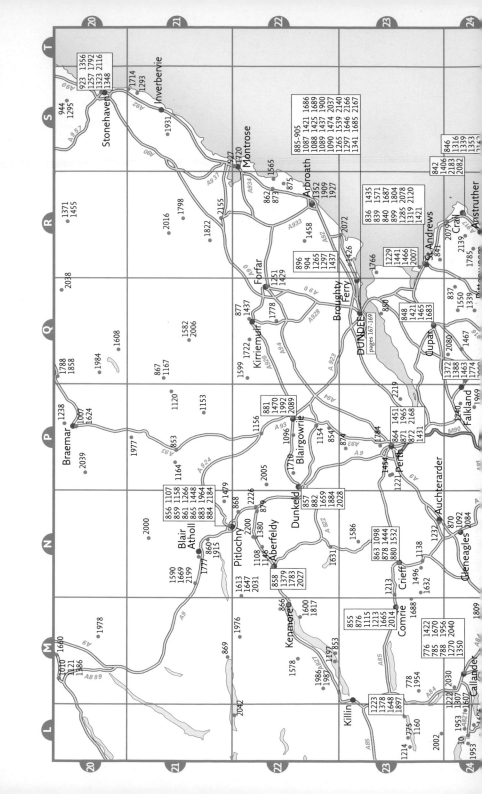

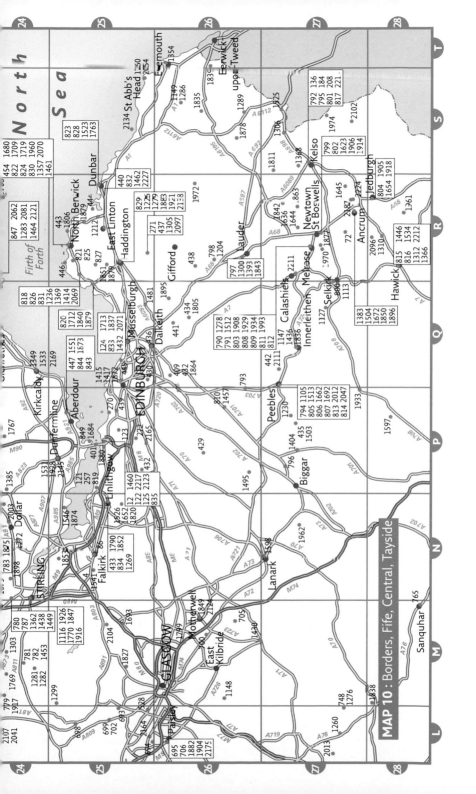

MAP 10 : Borders, Fife, Central, Tayside

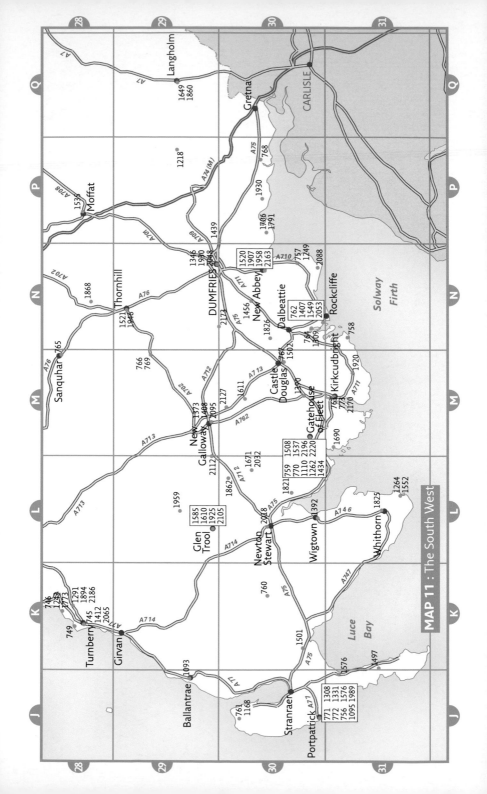

The Best Small Galleries

Apart from those listed in Main Attractions and Other Attractions, the following galleries are always worth looking into. The Glasgow Gallery Guide, free from any of them, lists current exhibitions.

708 2/E4 ✓✓ **Glasgow Print Studio** www.gpsart.co.uk · 0141 552 0704 · Trongate 103 Influential and accessible gallery in Glasgow's contemporary-art centre with print work on view and for sale from many of Scotland's leading and rising artists. Gallery Tue-Sat 10am-5.30pm, Sun 12noon 5pm. Closed Mon. Workshop 10am-9pm Tue-Thu, 10am-5.30pm Fri/Sat.

709 2/E4 ✓✓ **Transmission Gallery** www.transmissiongallery.org · 0141 552 7141 · 28 King Street Cutting-edge and often off-the-wall work from contemporary Scottish and international artists. Reflects Glasgow's increasing importance as a hot spot of conceptual art. Stuff you might disagree with. 11am-5pm Tue-Sat. Closed Sun/Mon.

710 2/C4 ✓✓ **The Modern Institute** www.themoderninstitute.com · 0141 248 3711 · 14-20 Osborne Street Not really a gallery – more a concept. International reputation for cutting-edge art ideas and occasional events. MI shows at London's pre-eminent, highly selective Frieze Art Fair. Gallery 10am-6pm Mon-Fri, 12noon-5pm Sat.

711 2/XF3 ✓ **Sorcha Dallas** www.sorchadallas.com · 0141 553 2662 · 5-9 St Margaret's Place Deep in the East End, the secret salon of La Dallas where interesting new artists first come into the light. Phone first. Sorcha also usually does Frieze (see MI above). Gallery (during exhibition) 11am-5pm Tue-Sat.

712 2/D4 ✓ **Mary Mary** www.marymarygallery.co.uk · 0141 226 2257 · 6 Dixon Street Cool, always interesting gallery showing the kind of work that keeps Glasgow pre-eminent as a UK centre of edgy, contemporary work. Tue-Sat 11am-6pm. Closed Aug.

713 2/C2 ✓ **Compass Gallery** www.compassgallery.co.uk · 0141 221 6370 · 178 West Regent Street Glasgow's oldest established commercial contemporary art gallery. Their New Generation exhibition in Jul-Aug shows work from new graduates of the art colleges and has heralded many a career. Combine with the other Gerber gallery (see below). Closed Sun.

714 2/C2 ✓ **Cyril Gerber Fine Art** www.gerberfineart.co.uk · 0141 221 3095 · 148 West Regent Street British paintings and especially the Scottish Colourists and 'name' contemporaries. Gerber and the Compass (see above) have Christmas exhibitions where small, accessible paintings can be bought for reasonable prices. Closed Sun.

715 2/C2 **Roger Billcliffe Gallery** www.billcliffegallery.com · 0141 332 4027 · 134 Blythswood Street Big, long-established gallery on 5 floors specialising in painting and decorative arts of the last 100 years. Roger, obviously this page was incomplete without you!

The Mackintosh Trail

Architect and designer Charles Rennie Mackintosh (1868–1928) had an extra-ordinary influence on contemporary design. Visit www.crmsociety.com

716 2/B1
ATMOS

✓ ✓ ✓ **Glasgow School of Art** www.gsa.ac.uk · 0141 353 4500 · 167 Renfrew Street Mackintosh's supreme architectural triumph and 'Britain's Most Admired Building' 2009. It's enough almost to admire it from the street (and maybe best – is very much a working college) but there are guided tours at 11am and 3pm (also 5pm Apr-Oct; Sat 10.30am, 11.30am) of the sombre yet light interior, halls and library. You may wonder if the building itself is partly responsible for its remarkable output of acclaimed artists. Temporary exhibitions in the Mackintosh Gallery. The Tenement House (684/OTHER ATTRACTIONS) is nearby.

717 2/XC1
ADMISSION

✓ ✓ **Queen's Cross Church** www.queenscrosschurch.org.uk · 0141 946 6600 · 870 Garscube Road at Maryhill Road Built 1896-99. Calm and simple, the antithesis of Victorian Gothic. If all churches had been built like this, we'd go more often. The HQ of the Charles Rennie Mackintosh Society which was founded in 1973. Mar-Oct Mon-Fri 10am-5pm, Sun 2-5pm (summer only). Nov-Feb Mon-Fri 10am-5pm.

718 2/C2
ADMISSION

✓ ✓ **The Mackintosh House** www.hunterian.gla.ac.uk · 0141 330 5431 · University Avenue Opposite and part of the Hunterian Art Gallery (680/MAIN ATTRACTIONS) within the university campus. The master's house has been transplanted and methodically reconstructed from the next street (they say even the light is the same). If you've ever wondered what the fuss is about, go and see how innovative and complete an artist, designer and architect he was, in this inspiring yet habitable set of rooms. Mon-Sat 9.30am-5pm. Closed Sun.

719 2/XA5
ATMOS
FREE

✓ ✓ **Scotland Street School Museum** www.glasgowlife.org.uk · 0141 287 0500 · 225 Scotland Street Opposite Shields Rd underground station; best approach by car from Eglinton St (A77 Kilmarnock Rd over Jamaica St Bridge). Entire school (from 1906) preserved as museum of education through Victorian/Edwardian and wartimes. Original, exquisite Mackintosh features, especially tiling, and powerfully redolent of happy school days. This is a uniquely evocative time capsule. Café and temporary exhibitions. Tue-Thu, Sat 10am-5pm, Fri and Sun 11am-5pm. Closed Mon.

720 2/D3
ADMISSION

✓ **The Lighthouse** www.glasgow.gov.uk · 0141 276 5360 · 11 Mitchell Lane, off Buchanan Street Glasgow's legacy from its year as UK City of Architecture and Design. Changing exhibitions in Mackintosh's 1893-95 building for the *Glasgow Herald* newspaper. It houses, over 6 floors, a shop and books, a café-bar, an interpretation centre and exhibition space. Fantastic rooftop views. Mon-Sat 10.30am-5pm. Closed Sun.

721 9/K25
NTS
ATMOS
ADMISSION

✓ **The Hill House** www.nts.org.uk · 0844 493 2208 · Upper Colquhoun Street, Helensburgh Take Sinclair St off Princes St (at Romanesque tower and tourist information centre) and go 2km uphill, taking left into Kennedy Dr and follow signs. A complete house incorporating Mackintosh's typical total unity of design, built for publisher Walter Blackie in 1902-4. Does have a bit of a damp problem (so check opening hours) but much to marvel over and wish that everybody else would go away and you could stay for the night. There's a library full of books to keep you occupied. Tearoom; gardens and two shops. Apr-Oct 1.30-5.30pm. Helensburgh is 45km northwest of city centre via Dumbarton (A82) and A814 up the north Clyde coast.

Regional Hotels & Restaurants

The Best Hotels & Restaurants In Argyll

722 9/J22
11 ROOMS
+ COTTAGE
TEL · TV
NO PETS
EXP

✓✓ **Airds Hotel** www.airds-hotel.com · 01631 730236 · Port Appin 32km north of Oban, 4km off A828. Airds has long been one of the foremost northern hostelries and a legendary gourmet experience. Shaun and Jenny McKivragan continue this tradition and with care and attention, ongoing refurbishment and a great team, Airds remains at the forefront of the 'civilised escape in a hectic world' market. Contemporary-cosy might describe bedrooms and lounges (and conservatory dining room). Dinner is the culmination of a hard day on the croquet lawn or gazing over the bay. Unobtrusive service and a new chef at TGP but Robert Macpherson has a strong track record. Tasting menu and à la carte. 2 elegant suites, one with patio, one with balcony. Port Appin is one of Scotland's most charming places. The Lismore passenger ferry is 2km away (2242/MAGIC ISLANDS). Bring a bike (or hire locally) and come home to Airds!

£35+   **EAT** Has always been one of the best meals in the North, a destination in itself.

723 9/H24
20 ROOMS
TEL · TV
DF · LL
EXP

✓✓ **Crinan Hotel** www.crinanhotel.com · 01546 830261 · Crinan 8km off A816. On coast, 60km south of Oban (Lochgilphead 12km) at head of the Crinan Canal which joins Loch Fyne with the sea. Nick Ryan's landmark hotel in a stunning setting and some of the best sea views in the UK. Outside on the quay is the boat which landed those massive prawns, sweet clams and other creatures with legs or valves that are cooked very simply and brought to your table. This hotel has long housed one of the UK's great seafood restaurants. Nick's wife's (notable artist Frances Macdonald) pictures of these shorelines and those of son, Ross, are hung around you and for sale; the rooftop lounge regularly shows other curated pictures from significant Scottish artists. This is also the perfect sunset setting for your aperitif. Last but not least, there are always beautiful flowers.

£32+/ £15   **EAT** Choice of Westward dining room or perfect pub grub in Mainbrace bar.

724 9/J24
25 ROOMS
TEL · TV
DF
ATMOS
MED.INX-
MED.EX

✓✓ **George Hotel** www.thegeorgehotel.co.uk · 01499 302111 · Inveraray On the main street of an interesting town on Loch Fyne with credible attractions both here (the castle, the *Arctic Penguin*, etc) and nearby, The George gets 2 ticks because this ancient inn (1770), still in the capable and friendly hands of the Clark family, has fantastic atmosphere, especially in the bars. Rooms refurbished tastefully in a Highland-chic kind of way. Downstairs open fire, great grub; all Scottish towns on the visitors' map have a place like this. The First House adjacent (actually the first house in the town) has 8 of the 25 rooms with some great loch views. Very much part of the local community, the main bar is surprisingly cosmopolitan: memories of Scotland are made of this!
EAT Gastropub grub in multichambered stone and wood setting. Good ales, wines and staple/classic-led menu.

725 9/G25
5 ROOMS
APR-OCT
MED.EX

✓✓ **Kilberry Inn** 01880 770223 · near Tarbert Small Knapdale roadside inn with famously good food. Simple, stylish cottage-courtyard rooms. Beautiful drive out on B8024 off the Tarbert-Lochgilphead coast road. 2-tick gastropub food as good as it gets. David out front, Clare in the kitchen. Hotel deal includes dinner. Report: 1277/GASTROPUBS.

726 9/J26
5 ROOMS
TV
NO KIDS
NO PETS
EXP

✓ **Balmory Hall** www.balmoryhall.com · 01700 500669 · Ascog, Isle of Bute 6km Rothesay towards Mount Stuart (1833/COUNTRY HOUSES). Grand, liveable, lived-in big hoose up road 150m from 30mph sign. A country-house hotel with guest-house intimacy. Deer on the lawn. 5 grand rooms and a sweet little lodge at foot of the drive. Impeccable appointments, pictures, fabulous bathrooms! All home-made breakfast from the Aga, supper at the Smiddy (1305/GASTROPUBS) 7km or Mount Stuart (741/ARGYLL RESTAURANTS). Balmory is *the* top stay on Bute.

727 9/J25
11 ROOMS
TEL · TV
NO KIDS
INX-EXP

✓**The Royal Hotel** 01700 811239 · Tighnabruaich The Royal is back! For a while it turned into An Lochan, a brand that over inflated then burst, and the Bettises found it (you may have seen their search on *Location, Location, Location*) and restored the name of this grand old seaside mansion. Lovely rooms, many looking over to Bute, comfy furnishings and a plethora of pictures. Lots of public space and the lovely wee Shinty Bar. Food in bar or conservatory. Time moves slow in Tighnabruaich!

728 9/H23
6 ROOMS
TEL
CLOSED DEC
MED.EX

✓**Alt Na Craig House** www.altnacraighouse.com · 01631 564524 · Oban The MacArthurs took over this historic house sitting above the town (a steep pull up from the Gallanach south coast road out of town beyond the ferry terminal) and turned it into a boutique B&B of a very high standard. Calm and contemporary with underfloor heating and big rooms, most with superb views. They're quite pleased with themselves but so would you be.

729 9/H23
11 ROOMS
TEL · TV
MED.EX

✓**The Manor House** www.manorhouseoban.com · 01631 562087 · Oban On south coast road out of town towards Kerrera ferry, overlooking bay. Understated elegance in contemporary style and a restaurant that serves (in an intimate dining room) probably the most fine-dining dinner in town. Daily changing menu. Bedrooms small but cosy: it is a civilised lodging. More delightful than merely deluxe. Nice bar.

730 9/H23
12 ROOMS
MAR-NOV
TV
CHP

✓**Glenburnie Hotel** www.glenburnie.co.uk · 01631 562089 · Oban Corran Esplanade. In the middle of a broad sweep of hotels overlooking the bay, this probably the best! Amiable Graeme Strachan's a natural innkeeper so everything in his seaside mansion is welcoming and easy on the eye. Great detail: home-made muesli and fruit for breakfast; nice furnishings. No dinner but he'll tell you where to go. Book.

731 9/H23
5 ROOMS
FEB-NOV
TV · NO KIDS
NO PETS
MED.INX

✓**Lerags House** www.leragshouse.com · 01631 563381 · near Oban 7km south of Oban. 4km from A816, a very particular guest house unobtrusively brilliant (even the sign off the road is low-key). Mansion in deep country with contemporary feel and style. Lovely gardens in almost estuarine setting. Charlie and Bella Miller from Australia do good rooms and excellent food. Dinner inclusive, though B&B also possible as is exclusive use (a good house-party spot). Fixed menu; neat wine list including selected Oz wines. A cool and calming place.

732 9/J23
3 ROOMS
TV
CHP

✓**Roineabhal** www.roineabhal.com · 01866 833207 · Kilchrenan Another great place to stay near Kilchrenan (see Taychreggan below and Ardanaiseig, 1097/COUNTRY HOUSE HOTELS) deep in the Loch Awe interior (10km from the A85 Oban road, near Taynuilt). This is a good deal less expensive. Roger and Maria Soep call this a Highland country house (pronounced Ron-ay-val) – it is really a gorgeous guest house in a family home; good pictures (they are quite arty). Intimate (you eat round the same table) but all in excellent taste, especially the set-menu dinner. You don't have to have it but you should (one day I will) and there's an excellent breakfast (that porridge!). Wine provided but you can BYOB.

733 9/G28

✓**Macrihanish Dunes** www.macrihanishdunes.com · 01586 810000 · Kintyre Over the wide ocean from America comes a new golf course and resort adjacent to the time-honoured and Old Tom Morris-designed Macrihanish; some dunes, some strand. Cottages and a hotel at TGP plus the refurbished Royal Hotel in Campbeltown bring a new standard of accommodation not yet tried by *StB*; but glowing reports.
EAT The Old Clubhouse bar and restaurant for family-friendly top dining. Not tried.

734 9/J24   **Loch Fyne Hotel** www.crerarhotels.com · 01499 302148 · **Inveraray** A sur-
74 ROOMS   prisingly large and decidedly decent hotel in this charming town. On main A83
TEL · TV   towards Lochgilphead overlooking loch. Part of the Crerar Group, the remains of
MED.INX   British Trust Hotels; this one of their best. Pleasing, simple design makeover with
a touch of tartan. Bistro. Pool and modest spa facilities. They do take coach
parties.

735 9/J23   **Taychreggan** www.taychregganhotel.co.uk · 01866 833211 · **Kilchrenan**
18 ROOMS   Signed off A85 just before Taynuilt, 30km from Oban and nestling on a bluff by
TEL · TV   Loch Awe in imposing countryside. Quay of the old Portsonachan ferry is nearby.
EXP   The hotel has boats. Stylish internal courtyard, decent rooms (especially the junior
suites) and water lapping at garden's edge, this remains a good getaway prospect:
everybody remarks on the tranquillity (it's often not busy) and the lochside views.
Table d'hôte menu under chef Colin Cairns. American owners also have Culloden
House (973/BEST HIGHLAND HOTELS).

736 9/J25   **Kilfinan Hotel** www.kilfinan.com · 01700 821201 · **Kilfinan** 13km from
10 ROOMS   Tighnabruaich on B8000. A much-loved inn on the beautiful single-track road that
TEL · TV   skirts Loch Fyne. The Wyatts run this classic, quiet getaway inn (quiet as the adja-
MED.INX   cent graveyard) with long-standing manager and people person, Madalon.
Relaxing rooms (most have recently been refurbished), great cooking from Helen
Wyatt in dining room or bar; sensible wine list. For a not-too-expensive retreat on
a quiet peninsula, this is a good bet. They make a virtue of the poor mobile-phone
and TV reception. And it's a very nice place to bring kids. 1111/HOTELS THAT WEL-
COME KIDS.

737 9/H24   **Loch Melfort Hotel** www.lochmelfort.co.uk · 01852 200233 · **Arduaine**
25 ROOMS   30km south of Oban on A816. This landmark hotel on the beautiful road between
FEB-DEC   Oban and Campbeltown has had its ups and downs in the past (my last visit was
TEL · TV   cancelled because part of the roof blew off) but owners Calum and Rachel Ross
MED.EX   are restoring it to its rightful place. You start with the view of Loch Shuna which
you get from most rooms (including all those in extension; they come with either
balcony or patio). Those in the main mansion are more traditional but are pleasantly large. Same view dominates the dining room (chef, David Bell) and the Chart-
room bar with pub-food menu (seafood specials). Hotel has the same access road
as **Arduaine**, an extraordinary back garden in which to wander (1507/GARDENS).

738 9/H25   **Stonefield Castle Hotel** www.stonefieldhotels.com · 01880 820836 ·
32 ROOMS   **Tarbert** Just outside town on the A83, a castle evoking the 20th more than pre-
TEL · TV   ceding centuries. Splendid luxuriant gardens leading down to Loch Fyne. Rhodies
DF   in spring, hydrangeas in summer. Dining room with baronial splendour and stag-
L   gering views. Friendly, flexible staff; overall, it seems quintessentially Scottish and
MED.INX   ok, especially for families. Refurbishments by owners Oxford Hotels have tidied
things up. 4 principal rooms, but standards with £10 premium loch views are fine.

√√ **Isle of Eriska** 01631 720371 20km north of Oban. 1094/COUNTRY-
HOUSE HOTELS.

√√ **Ardanaiseig** 01866 833333 · **Loch Awe** 1097/COUNTRY-HOUSE
HOTELS.

√ **Kames Hotel** 01700 811489by · **Tighnabruaich** Report: 1143/SEASIDE
INNS.

RESTAURANTS

739 9/J24 ✓ **Inver Cottage** www.invercottage.co.uk · **01369 860537** ·
£15-25 **Strathlachlan, Loch Fyne** South of Strachur on B8000, the scenic south road by Loch Fyne, a cottage bar/bistro overlooking loch and ruins of Castle Lachlan. Home baking and cooking at its best, from local sources: the scallops, Gigha halibut, venison from the hill. Comfort food and surroundings. Lovely walk to the ruins (40 minutes return) before or after. A real find! 10.30am-8.30pm in summer, Sun till 5pm. Closed Mon-Wed in winter.

740 9/K25 ✓ **Chatters** www.chattersdunoon.co.uk · **01369 706402** · **58 John Street,**
£25-35 **Dunoon** Rosie Macinnes's long-established and excellent restaurant is a good reason to take a ferry to Dunoon; the Cowal peninsula awaits your explorations (and Younger Gardens: 1503/GARDENS). Bar menu and à la carte, a small garden for drinks or lunch on a good day and a garden room when not. Chatters is an all-round dining-out experience: just delightful. Wed-Sat dinner, Thu-Sat lunch.

741 9/J26 ✓ **Mount Stuart** 01700 505276 · **Bute** The restaurant at fabulous Mount
ATMOS Stuart (1833/COUNTRY HOUSES) is the top place to eat on Bute (EatBute, as
<£15 they say). Always a great café in the modern-build visitor centre, now up a notch under chef Jason McNelly. A destination in itself with impeccably sourced and presented light, healthy food. 10am-6pm and Thu-Sat for dinner (check winter hours).

742 9/G25 **Starfish** 01880 820733 · **Castle Street, Tarbert** Just off the quayside. New
£25-35 (2011) restaurant-gallery by one of the gals from the great Café Fish in Tobermory. Pics so-so but pleasant bistro settling in at TGP. Extensive menu all home-made including bread and ice cream. Looks good. Lunch and dinner. Closed Sun/Mon.

743 9/J25 **Portavadie Marina** www.portavadiemarina.com · **01700 811075** Off the
£15-25 B8000. The new, sheltered marina that's popped up at the mouth of Loch Fyne opposite Tarbert, with a steel-and-glass restaurant and yachty complex that serves ok food from breakfast to late. For people messing about off boats and the legions who for some reason go just to look at them. 7 days 9am-11pm (12midnight weekends).

If you're in Oban...

744 9/H23 **WHERE TO STAY**
✓ **The Manor House** www.manorhouseoban.com · **01631 562087** ·
Gallanach Road South of centre and ferry terminal. Quietly posh. Report: 729/BEST ARGYLL.

✓ **Alt Na Craig House** www.altnacraighouse.com · **01631 564524** The classiest accommodation in town in a fab converted house overlooking the bay. Report: 728/BEST ARGYLL.

✓ **Glenburnie Hotel** www.glenburnie.co.uk · **01631 562089** · **Corran Esplanade** From tea and shortbread on arrival and lovely rooms, it's clear this is a superior bed for the night. See 730/ARGYLL HOTELS.

59 ROOMS **Caledonian Hotel** www.obancaledonian.com · **01855 821582** Lashings of
TEL · TV dosh spent on this refurbished seafront hotel. Can't beat the captain's rooms –
MED.EX comfort and contemporary facilities. Dining room and café and bar. In the centre of things, the port and the people, so it can be noisy but it's the best of the main hotels.

13 ROOMS TV CHP	**Alltavona** www.alltavona.co.uk · 01631 565067 · **Corran Esplanade** Another (and surprisingly large) good guest house/hotel on the Esplanade over- looking the bay. Contemporary rooms. Good breakfast.

S.Y. Hostel 01631 562025 · **Esplanade** Good location on the front.

WHERE TO EAT

£25-35
L
✓**Ee-Usk** www.eeusk.com · 01631 565666 & **Piazza** 01631 563628 ·
North Pier These 2 adjacent identical contemporary steel-and-glass houses
on the corner of the bay are both the ambitious creation and abiding passion of
the Macleod family. They epitomise the new open Oban. Macleod père runs a
tight ship at Ee-Usk, a bright, modern seafood café with great views. Wild halibut,
haddock and cod locally sourced (they know its origins and the fishermen personally), hand-cut chips; home-made starters and puds. **Piazza** run by Callum
Macleod purveys standard though good standard Italian fare. Both are routinely
packed. 7 days lunch and LO 9.30pm. All year.

£25-35
✓**The Waterfront At The Pier** www.waterfrontoban.co.uk · 01631
563110 In the port, by the station, in the midst of all, a place that's serious
about seafood. 'From pier to pan' is about right. Blackboard (well, TV-screen)
menu and the usuals à la carte. Big on oysters and scallops. Airy upstairs diner
and large ground-floor café/bar (a seafood, ie fish 'n' chips, bar-meal menu,
though not at all bad). Many locals, many tourists. New branch on the Tobermory
waterfront: 2306/MULL. Open lunch and LO 9pm-ish. All year.

£25-35
✓**Coast** 01631 569900 · **104 George Street** Main street on corner of John
St. Richard (in the kitchen) and Nicola (out front) Fowler run the best (non-
seafood) restaurant in Oban. Modern British menu by a pedigree chef in contemporary, laid-back room. Excellent value for this quality and no fuss. Menu changes
seasonally. Open all year. 7 days lunch and LO 9.30pm.Closed Sun in winter.

>£35
✓**The Manor House** The best hotel dining room in town. Creative cuisines,
fresh seafood and other good things in an elevated location. Book. 729/
ARGYLL HOTELS

✓**Fish & Chips In Oban** Oban has called itself the 'seafood capital of
Scotland' and for good reason. Not only is there a choice of seafood restau-
rants (above), there are 3 good fish 'n' chip shops, 2 with cafés: **Nories**, the **Oban
Fish & Chip Shop** and the **George St Fish 'n' Chip Shop**. See 1338/FISH & CHIPS.

<£15
✓**Julie's Coffee House** 01631 565952 · **33 Stafford Street** Opposite Oban
Whisky Visitor Centre. Only 10 tables, so fills up. Nice approach to food (excellent home baking, soups and snacks) and customers. Best coffee shop and best
cakes in town. 7 days 10am-5pm.

£15-25
The Seafood Temple 01631 566000 · **Gallanach Road** Along the bay adja-
cent to Oban Sailing Club. Great location with dreamy views, this is The Seafood
Temple which built a cult following in its short tenure. Now run by Eilidh Smith
who makes/bakes everything. Still seafood here not only. Rebuilding reputation at
TGP. Dinner only. Closed Mon. Check winter hours. Reports, please!

<£15
Oban Chocolate Coffeeshop 01631 566099 · **Corran Esplanade** The place
to go for coffee, cake and of course chocolate. Chocs are made on the premises.
You can have the hot variety. Croissants for breakfast. 10am-5pm, Sun 10.30-4pm.

<£15 The Kitchen Garden www.kitchengardenoban.co.uk · **01631 566332** · **14 George Street** Deli-café that's often busy; you may have to queue for the upstairs gallery caff. Not a bad cup of coffee, a sandwich and hot dishes. Great whisky selection and a plethora of cheese. 7 days 9am-5.30pm, Sun 10.15am-4.30pm. Deli has some great munchies, kitchen stuff and a good cheese counter.

£15-25 Cuan Mor www.cuanmor.co.uk · **01631 565078** · **George Street** On the bay, very central and busy bar bistro attached to Oban Brewery. They say 'contemporary Scottish' and that's about right. Perfectly good pit or quay stop. 7 days 12noon-9pm, bar later.

<£15 Waypoint Bar & Grill 07840 650669 · **Kerrara Island** Now for something refreshingly different: al fresco and over there, ie the (Oban) marina on Kerrara, 8 minutes away by a free ferry from the North Pier (by Piazza), 10 minutes past the hour. Set up in a tent with a BBQ pit, this is casual dining, seafood and sandwiches (well, banquettes). Fun and can be fab. 7 days 12noon-9pm May-Sep.

<£15 Little Bay Café www.littlebaycafe.com · **01631 569583** On the bay right enough: very central, near Columba Hotel. Sandwich bar/takeaway, all bespoke and better than the rest. They have pizza. 7.30am-evening (10pm Fri/Sat).

Tourist Office 01631 563122 · **Argyll Square** Open all year.

745 9/K28
130 ROOMS
+ LODGES
TEL · TV
LL
LOTS

✔ ✔ **Turnberry** www.turnberry.co.uk · 01655 331000 · Turnberry Not just a splendid hotel on the Ayrshire coast, more a way of life centred on golf. Looks over the 2 celebrated courses (home to the Open '09) and Ailsa Craig, the enigmatic lump of rock in the sea (2065/GREAT GOLF COURSES). A 'Luxury Collection Resort' owned by Dubai Inc. (my appurtenance). No expense has been spared on its recent substantial upgrading of bedrooms and public rooms, and for once the word 'luxury' is completely appropriate, from clubhouse to spa (ESPA treatments, good gym, stunning swimming-pool pavilion). The principal impression is one of calm and discreet efficiency. Also, they've gone back to their roots: the central hub is the Grand Tea Lounge (1412/AFTERNOON TEAS), the main restaurant 1906 (the year the hotel opened) opens for dinner at 6 minutes past 7. Everywhere subtle, contemporary design underlines original features and public rooms and many bedrooms (several categories, gorgeous bathrooms) have spectacular views of the Ailsa and Kintyre Courses and the coast. Every day a different sunset!

£25-35+ **EAT** Main restaurant 1906 offers fine dining in grand style. Cheerful Australian chef Justin Galea in charge of a top team and a richly varied, almost brasserie-style menu. Adjacent Ailsa Bar does cocktails etc and a lighter, grazing menu of flights (small plates). Tappie Toorie daytime dining in The Clubhouse.

746 9/K28
6 SUITES
+ COTTAGES
APR-OCT
TEL · NO PETS
LL
LOTS

✔ **Culzean Castle** www.culzeanexperience.org · 01655 760615 · near Maybole 18km south of Ayr, this accommodation in the suites of Culzean (1773/CASTLES), including the famous and recently refurbished Eisenhower apartment, now presents itself more as a hotel. In any case, a bed for the night rarely comes as historically posh. The second floor (you enter by the original 1920s lift and there's a very grand staircase) has some fabulous views. Rates are expensive but include afternoon tea. Dinner is available. Bookable for individual or exclusive use (where you won't find strangers in the drawing room); 1243/HOUSE PARTIES. The cliff-top setting, the gardens and the vast grounds are superb.

747 9/K26
38 ROOMS
TEL · TV
NO PETS
MED.EX

✔ **Lochgreen House** www.costley.biz · 01292 313343 · Troon Top hotel of the Bill Costley group which is so preeminent in this neck of the woods, Lochgreen (adjacent to and overlooking Royal Troon Golf Course) is a comfortable, spacious yet homely country house with big bedrooms looking out to the green. Chef Lesley McQuistan in charge of smart brasserie-type menu in chandeliered but clubbable dining room; lounges can be tight pre/après. The **Brig o' Doon** at Alloway is the romance-and-Rabbie Burns hotel (01292 442466), with a fabulous self-catering house, Doonbrae, opposite (1247/HOUSE PARTIES) in gorgeous gardens, while **Highgrove** (01292 312511), more intimate and with great coastal views, is just outside Troon. All operate at a high standard. The Costleys also have the Ellisland Hotel in Ayr (755/AYR) and 2 excellent roadside inns, the Cochrane at Gatehead (1302/GASTROPUBS) and the new Soutar Johnnie's (1291/GASTROPUBS).

£35+ **EAT** Lochgreen: The top restaurant here but consistently high quality throughout the group. Executive chef informs all.

748 10/L27
4 ROOMS
TEL · TV
MED.INX

✔ **The Sorn Inn** www.sorninn.com · 01290 551305 · 35 Main Street, Sorn 8km east of Mauchline on the B743 off the A76. Traditional inn in rural setting and pleasant village in deepest Ayrshire. The Grant family have established a big reputation for food with a continuing clutch of awards including consecutive Michelin Bib Gourmands. There are 4 delightful, great-value rooms with WiFi, etc.

£15-25 **EAT** People travel from miles around to eat here. Restaurant and pub meals. Craig Grant a nice guy in the kitchen. See 1276/GASTROPUBS.

749 9/K28
11 RMS · TV
TEL · NO PETS
MED INY
£25-35

✓ **Wilding's Hotel & Restaurant** 01655 331401 · Maidens Chef/patron and consummate restauranteur Brian Sage's restaurant with rooms above. Contemporary and comfortable, they overlook a serene harbour in this coastal village near Turnberry (and a fraction of the cost of the course)

EAT A beautiful spot and excellent gastropub-style menu in 2 large, buzzing rooms. Food LO 9pm. They come from all over the county, so book at weekends. This place, in troubled times, going from strength to strength.

750 9/L28
6 ROOMS
+LODGES
TEL · TV
LOTS

Enterkine House www.enterkine.com · 01292 520608 · near Annbank 10km from Ayr in beautiful grounds. Self-consciously upmarket, informally formal country-house hotel with pleasantly traditional public rooms. Paul Moffat presides over Browne's conservatory restaurant with long-standing local reputation. Occasionally a piano is played. Woodland Lodge under the trees is a quirky, romantic hideaway and a permanent marquee indicates a concerted effort in the wedding market.

751 9/K27
37 ROOMS
TEL · TV
NO PETS
MED.EX

Piersland Hotel www.piersland.co.uk · 01292 314747 · Craig End Road, **Troon** Opposite Portland Golf Course which is next to Royal Troon (2066/GREAT GOLF). Mansion house of character and ambience much favoured for weddings. Wood-panelling, open fires, lovely gardens only a 'drive' away from the courses (no preferential booking on Royal, but Portland usually possible) and lots of great golf nearby. New garden block has added 7 rooms; some shiny modernising not so sympatico. Eat in the Redbowl Restaurant. Local reputation also for bar meals.

752 9/L27
50 ROOMS
TEL · TV
MED.INX

The Park Hotel www.theparkhotel.uk.com · 01563 545999 · Kilmarnock Rugby Park ie adjacent Kilmarnock's football stadium and owned by the football club. Contemporary business and family hotel much better than chains of Travelodge ilk. Good café/restaurant. Small gym and sports facilities at the ground opposite. Weddings and dinner-dances do occur.

✓✓ **Glenapp Castle** www.glenappcastle.com · 01465 831212 Discreet and distinguished. A jewel in the Scottish crown; discreetly here in deepest South Ayrshire. Report: 1093/SUPERLATIVE COUNTRY-HOUSE HOTELS.

6 ROOMS
TV · L
MED.INX

Dunure Inn www.dunureinn.co.uk · 01292 500549 · Dunure On the A719, the minor but beautiful coast road south of Ayr. Harbourside pub with contemporary rooms (3 doubles, 3 suites). Report: 1301/GASTROPUBS.

RESTAURANTS

753 9/K26
>£35

✓✓ **Braidwoods** www.braidwoods.co.uk · 01294 833544 · near Dalry Simplest approach is from the section of A78 north of Irvine; take B714 for Dalry. Cottage restaurant discreetly signed 5km on left. Michelin-star dining doesn't get more casually accomplished. Keith and Nicola Braidwood here almost 20 years with their impeccably sourced (long before it was de rigeur; they use eg., the local farm shop at Auchendree on A737), everything made on the premises (bread, chocolates). With its own quiet dignity, Braidwoods remains the best meal in the shire. Wed/Sun lunch (not Sun lunch in summer) and Tue-Sat dinner.

754 9/K26
£15-25

✓ **Nardini** www.nardinis.co.uk · 01475 675000 · Largs On the Esplanade. This legendary seaside salon is back after a million-dollar refit, trading somewhat on its glory days. Still, in a town now hoaching with eateries (including the estimable **Lounge** above RBS), I'm with the new Nardini which has nowt to do with the original family. Its big rooms usually packed; the cafeteria and Tony Macaroni trattoria. Snowdrifts of ice cream. Go back too! 12noon-10pm.

✓MacCallums 01292 319339 · **Troon** Report: 1318/SEAFOOD RESTAURANTS.

Fins 01475 568989 · **Fairlie near Largs** Report: 1328/SEAFOOD RESTAURANTS.

GASTROPUB GRUB IN AYRSHIRE
Ayrshire has many good gastropubs (mostly down to the Costleys).
All are routinely packed with happy Ayrshire eaters. Book at weekends.

✓The Sorn Inn 01290 551305 · **Mauchline** Report: 748/AYRSHIRE HOTELS.

✓Souter Johnnie's 01655 760653 · **Kirkoswald** Report: 1291/GASTROPUBS.

✓Carrick Lodge Hotel 01292 262846 · **Ayr** Report: 755/AYR.

The Cochrane 01563 570122 · **Gatehead** Report: 1302/GASTROPUBS.

Dunure Inn 01292 500547 · **Dunure** Report: 1301/GASTROPUBS.

The Wheatsheaf 01563 830307 · **Symington** Village inn off main A77. Report: 1289/GASTROPUBS.

If you're in Ayr...

755 9/K27 WHERE TO STAY

44 ROOMS
TEL · TV
MED.INX
Fairfield House www.fairfieldhotel.co.uk · 01292 267461 · **Fairfield Road** 1km centre on the front. Solid, decent, suburban. 'Deluxe' facilities include pool/ sauna/steam, and conservatory brasserie. 3 rooms have sea view.

49 ROOMS
TEL · TV
MED.EX
Western House Hotel 08700 555510 · **Craigie Road** Very much part of Ayr Racecourse. Close to the big roundabout into Ayr on A77 from north. Former jockey dorm, now a contemporary bed for the night. 10 rooms in old mansion, the rest in 2 adjacent blocks. Lacking a little in charm but a good business bet.

9 ROOMS
TEL · TV
MED.EX
The Ellisland www.costley.biz · 01292 260111 · **19 Racecourse Road** On road to Alloway. Another makeover by the Costley group who have Lochgreen (see below) and many bar/restaurant options (see above). Rooms vary but mostly large and well appointed. Decent restaurant with the Costleys' irresistible comfort food.

Piersland 01292 314747 · **Troon** 12km north of Ayr. 751/AYRSHIRE HOTELS.

Enterkine House 01292 521608 · **Annbank** 12km Ayr town centre across ring road. Country house comforts. 750/AYRSHIRE HOTELS.

✓The Sorn Inn 01290 551305 · **near Mauchline** 25km east. Top gourmet pub with rooms. 748/AYRSHIRE HOTELS.

✓Lochgreen House 01292 313343 · **Monktonhall Road, Troon** White seaside mansion near famous golf courses. Flagship hotel of Costley family (see below and all over Ayrshire). Report: 747/AYRSHIRE HOTELS.

✓Savoy Park 01292 266112 · **16 Racecourse Road** Interesting period mansion run by the hard-working Hendersons. Very Scots, very Ayrshire. 1181/SCOTTISH HOTELS.

WHERE TO EAT

£15-25 ✓**Carrick Lodge Hotel** www.carricklodgehotel.co.uk · 01292 262846 ·
46 Carrick Road On main road out of town in Alloway direction. Jim and
Tracey Murdoch have created probably the most popular dining rooms in town
(there's a lot of them). Big kitchen team producing à la carte menu of wholesome
pub food. 7 very pleasant rooms above. Book Fri/Sat. Lunch & 5.30-9pm.

£15-25 ✓**Beresford Wine Bar** www.costley.biz · **2 Academy Street** Another
venture from the unstoppable Costleys (of Lochgreen and Ellisland above); this
contemporary Main St bistro bar is most definitely the only wine bar in Ayr. Great
wine selection and grazing menu all day. Always busy; it is well done. Costley
senior's art on the walls and for sale in the gallery upstairs. How does he find the
time? 7 days 9am-12midnight.

<£15 **The Lido** www.lido-troon.com · 01292 310088 · **11 West Portland Street,
Troon** Contemporary Italo-American café-bar that buzzes from breakfast to supper. Massive-choice menu and a stylish spot by the Blairs who have their finger
completely on the button around here. 7 days 9am-10/10.30pm. They also have:

£15-25 **Scott's** www.scotts-troon.com · 01292 315315 · **Troon** Harbour road in the
marina about 2km from Troon centre. A self-consciously stylish but seriously well
thought-out contemporary bar/restaurant upstairs overlooking the surprisingly
packed marina. Same people have **Elliots** in **Prestwick**, The Lido (above) and
spreading to Largs at TGP. Food ok, bling in evidence. 7 days. All day LO 10/11pm.

£15-25 **Saffy's** www.saffys-ayr.com · 01292 288598 · **2 Dalbair Road** Opposite the
Ramada Inn. Honest, home-made, do-the-lot cookery: seafood, meat, game and
good vegetarian. Ayr is the better for this! Lunch and LO 9pm. Sun 12noon-8pm.

£15-25 **Cecchini's** www.cecchinis.com · 01292 317171 · **72 Fort Street, Ayr &
39 Portland Street, Troon & Clyde Marina, Ardrossan** Excellent Italian and
Med restaurants run by the estimable Cecchini family. Recent flash refurbishment
in Ayr. In Ardrossan where the Arran ferry comes in. Mon-Sat, lunch & LO 10pm.

£15-25 **The Rupee Room** 01292 283002 · **Wellington Square** Ordinary-looking restaurant on the square serving the denizens of Ayr; they do fish 'n' chips but also
rather good Indian food that's exactly what they want. 7 days. Lunch & LO 11pm.

Ayr India 01292 261026 · **1A Alloway Place & 01292 263731 · 10 Seafield
Road** Cleverly named, serviceable Indian restaurants in the centre and seafront,

✓✓**MacCallum's of Troon Oyster Bar** This faraway dock on the bay
has both the best restaurant hereabouts and also the best fish 'n' chip
takeaway in the Wee Hurrie (see below). Report: 1318/SEAFOOD RESTAURANTS.

✓✓**The Wee Hurrie** Ayr The best fish 'n' chips on the coast. See
MacCallum (above) and report: 1337/FISH & CHIPS.

✓✓**Mancini's** Ayr Ice cream and a' that. Report: 1433/ICE CREAM.

✓**The Tudor Restaurant** 8 Beresford Terrace Good little (and large) all-
round caff. They don't make 'em like this any more! Report: 1397/TEAROOMS.

Tourist Office 01292 290300 Open all year.

756 11/J30
10 ROOMS
TEL · TV
DF · LL
LOTS

>£35

✓✓ **Knockinaam Lodge** www.knockinaamlodge.com · 01776 810471 ·
Portpatrick Tucked away on dream cove, historic country house full of
fresh flowers, great food, sea air and sympatico but smart service. Sian and David
Ibbotson balance a family home and a top-class get-away-from-it-all hotel.
Rooms traditional but top-drawer. The famous Churchill suite recently refur-
bished. Family suite with high tea for kids at 6pm. 1095/COUNTRY-HOUSE HOTELS.
EAT Best meal in the South from the outstanding and long-established Michelin
chef in Scotland, Tony Pierce. Fixed menu – lots of unexpected treats.

757 11/N30
8 ROOMS
NO KIDS
TEL · TV
MED.INX

✓ **Cavens** www.cavens.com · 01387 880234 · **Kirkbean** 20km south Dumfries via A710, Cavens is signed from Kirkbean. This elegant mansion now in 20
landscaped acres has been converted by Angus and Jane Fordyce into a homely,
informal Caven-haven of peace and quiet – great base for touring the South West.
Lots of public space so you can even get away from each other. Angus's honest,
good cooking using locally sourced ingredients: lots from Loch Arthur (1460/FARM
SHOPS) including the excellent granola for breakfast. Gardens to wander: new cottage garden supplies dinner. Inexpensive to take over the lot: 1249/HOUSE PARTIES.
EAT Best food in the quarter. Straightforward daily-changing menu like going to a
dinner party but without having to get on with the guests.

757A
11/K30
20 ROOMS
NO PETS

✓ **Penninghame House** www.penninghame.org · 01671 401414 ·
Newton Stewart 5km north of Newton Stewart on A715 to Girvan. Ray and
Marie Butler's impressive country house and estate has been on the go for 10
years but only recently reached my radar. So recently in fact that it's not in the
right *StB* category – it should be with Retreats (p. 221). But there was no room
there so here it squeezes in, a great place to stay in southwest Scotland. You will
need to sign up for one of their 30 courses (weekends or weeks) in matters of
health and wellbeing: the macrobiotic and holistic life. Everything about this place
is beautifully done, most especially the cookery courses and food throughout your
stay. Rooms in the antiqueful house, stable block or six lodges. Certainly you will
feel better here. Prices vary.

758 11/N31
20 ROOMS
FEB-NOV
TEL · TV
DF
LL
EXP

✓ **Balcary Bay** www.balcary-bay-hotel.co.uk · 01556 640311 · **Auchencairn** 20km south of Castle Douglas and Dalbeattie. Off A711 at end of shore
road and as close to the shimmering Solway as you can get. I haven't stayed here
for years but on a recent visit, it's obvious that this is a well-cared-for and well-
loved (by its regulars) hideaway and romantic retreat (like the weekend magazines
like). Ideal for walking, bird watching, outdoor pursuits (dogs welcome). Kitchen
continues a strong commitment to local produce. 100-strong wine list. Afternoon
tea by the sea in lounge or conservatory. Location, location!

759 11/M30
10 ROOMS
TEL · TV
NO PETS
FEB-DEC
MED.INX

✓ **The Ship Inn** 01557 814217 · **Gatehouse of Fleet** Main street of the best
of Galloway villages with good forest walking all round. Refurbished to a good
contemporary standard by the Stewart family who know what they're doing hereabouts (and have taken over the **Murray Arms**) so expect good things here '12/13.
Nothing ostentatious but functional and nice bathrooms in simple, elegant rooms
above. Decent pub/bistro food make this the best all-round stay in the village.

760 11/K30
17 ROOMS
FEB-DEC
TEL · TV
NO PETS
LOTS

Kirroughtree Hotel www.kirroughtreehouse.co.uk · 01671 402141 · **Newton Stewart** On A712. Built 1719, Rabbie Burns was once here. Extensive country house draped and plushed up by the people who have a small chain of carefully run hotels and gorgeous Glenapp (1093/COUNTRY-HOUSE HOTELS). For a long time now the stand-out hotel in the region. Original panelled hall and stairs, some spacious rooms the epitome of traditional country-house living; nice grounds. Gracious dining. Closed 6 weeks in January; no leisure facilities.

761 11/J30
9 ROOMS
TEL · TV
LL
ATMOS
EXP

Corsewall Lighthouse Hotel www.lighthousehotel.co.uk · 01776 853220 · **Stranraer** A718 to Kirkcolm 3km, B738 to Corsewall 6km (follow signs). Wild location on cliff top. Cosily furnished clever but snug don't say cramped – just go with someone you like. The adjacent fully functioning lighthouse (since 1817) makes for surreal evenings. 3 suites are outside the lighthouse and 2 are further away. All suites have the sea and sky views (though only half the hotel rooms do). Small dining room. Food fine (it's a long way to the chipper).

762 11/N30
15 ROOMS
TEL · TV
DF
MED.INX

Clonyard House www.clonyardhotel.co.uk · 01556 630372 · **Colvend** On Solway Coast road near Rockcliffe and Kippford (1549/COASTAL VILLAGES; 2053/COASTAL WALKS) but not on sea. Extension to house provides 11 somewhat utilitarian bedrooms adjacent patio garden, though shaded. Friendly family, good for kids; decent pub grub. The old building has old-style charm; the parrot is long gone.

763 11/M31

Good Spots in Kirkcudbright Pronounced Cur-*Coo*-Bree; a gem of a town. On a High Street filled with posh B&Bs, the Cowans' **Gladstone House** (01557 331734) stands out. Only 3 (lovely attic) rooms so book well ahead.

16 ROOMS
TEL · TV
MED.INX

Selkirk Arms www.selkirkarmshotel.co.uk · 01557 330402 · **High Street** Much more your 'proper hotel' (a Best Western). They set out to turn this Kirkcudbright townhouse into the best hotel and dining in the district, and they did! 16 of the best medium-expensive rooms in this most interesting of southwest towns. Artistas dining room with strong local menu and informal bistro; garden.

764 11/N30
5 ROOMS
TV · L
CHP

Anchor Hotel 01556 620205 · **Kippford** Seaside hotel in cute village 3km off main A710. Basic accommodation but great pub atmosphere and extensive food operation; seafood menu (local lobster, pints of prawns). See 1309/GASTROPUBS. Though 'gastro' it ain't.

Cally Palace 01557 814341 Report: 1110/KID-FRIENDLY HOTELS.
Aston Hotel 01387 272410 Report: 774/DUMFRIES.

RESTAURANTS

765 11/M28
£25-35

✓ **Blackaddie Hotel** www.blackaddiehotel.co.uk · 01659 50270 · **Sanquhar** This foodie destination hotel is as far-flung as it's sensible to be; first find Sanquhar then left at gas station (Glasgow end of village), through a small industrial estate; surprisingly, it's on a river (the Nith). Notable once-Michelin chef/patron Ian McAndrew (a mentor to many others) carries the cook's blowtorch here with dogged determination. Hotel itself (9 rooms) not quite up the quality of the cooking but this is a bold bothy in unforgiving hills (Wanlockhead and Leadhills are also worth discovering). Hail to the chef!

766 11/M29
ATMOS
<£15

✓ **Green Tea House** 07752 099193 · **Moniaive** Down a side street in couthy Moniaive, a tea house right enough with an old-schoolroom ambience that goes like a country fair inside and in the garden. Catherine Braid has created a caff/bistro in the back of beyond that's kinda brilliant. 5 daily soups, toasties (her signature haggis, cheese and peach chutney) and loadsa hot dishes and baking from a tiny kitchen. Daily till 5pm and in summer – Bistro Nights Mon-Fri 6-9pm.

767 11/M30 ✓ **Carlo's** 01556 503977 · 211 King Street, Castle Douglas Here over 20
£15-25 years, the Bignami family restaurant with Carlo in the kitchen is your absolute
best option in town. Bustling tratt atmosphere – probably the best Italian food in
the South. Open Tue-Sat 6-9pm. **The Style's Scrumptious** next door is open
during the day for decent home-made takeaway food using local produce.

768 11/P30 **Del Amitri** www.del-amitri.co.uk · 01461 201999 · Annan I don't know (for
£15-25 sure) but I've been told this is the new pearl of the South. Traditional Scottish-
Euro cooking. Reports, please. Tue-Sat 6-10pm. Sun lunch and dinner in summer.

769 **Little Italy at The Three Glens** 01848 200057 · Moniaive Surprising that
11/M29 there are 2 places to eat in Moniaive: Green Tea (above) and this contemporary
£25-35 cottage conversion with a pasta/wood-ovened-pizza place and interesting daily
specials. Sat/Sun lunch. Dinner Wed-Sun.

770 11/M30 **The Masonic Arms** www.themasonic-arms.co.uk · 01557 814335 · Gate-
£15-25 **house of Fleet** This place always had a big reputation for food but some changes
of management later it's hard to say where it's going. Always a good local atmosphere. Let's watch (also the **Murray Arms** next door, now in reliable old hands).

771 11/J30 **Campbell's** www.campbellsrestaurant.co.uk · 01776 810314 · Portpatrick
£15-25 Robert and Diane Campbell's café since 1998. Unpretentious fishy fare with something for everyone including vegetarians. Crab and lobster from their boat a good,
fresh bet. Invariably get a Michelin mention. Lunch and LO 9.30pm. Closed Mon.

772 11/J30 **The Crown** www.crownportpatrick.com · 01776 810261 · Portpatrick
£15-25 Harbourside hotel and pub with better-than-average grub. Goes like a fair in
summer. 7 days. LO 10pm. Competition from the **Waterfront** (01776 810800)
next door. The Crown has better atmosphere and decidedly better seafood.

773 11/M31 **In Kirkcudbright: Kirkpatrick's** 01557 330888 Scottish restaurant much
£15-25 welcomed in this much-visited town; upstairs and round corner from main street.
Dinner is where Tom Kirkpatrick shows his stuff and names his sources. Hours
vary.
Castle Restaurant 01557 330569 · 5 Castle Street Opposite the said
Maclellan's Castle. Haven't tried. Dinner only and Sun lunch. And further along:
Masterpiece 24 Castle Street Stuart and Alina Graham's snack bar of home-
made food to go. 7am-3pm, Sat 8am-2pm. Closed Sun.

✓ ✓ **Kitty's** New Galloway A definitive tearoom in the definitive Galloway
town. Report: 1373/TEAROOMS.

✓ **The Schoolhouse** Ringford An excellent roadside (A75) café/bistro.
Report: 1390/TEAROOMS.

If you're in Dumfries...

WHERE TO STAY

)1 ROOMS **Aston Hotel** ·1387 272410 · Bankend Road. Newish hotel in the Crichton
TEL · TV Estate (signposted from centre), a curious 100-acre campus of listed sandstone
MED.INX buildings including a conference centre. Contemporary-furnished hotel with bras-
serie. A bit far to walk to town but best bet for modern facilities and decent food.

4/7 ROOMS **Criffel Inn** www.criffel-inn.co.uk · 01387 850305 · New Abbey &
TV **Abbey Arms** 01387 850489 · New Abbey 12 km south of Dumfries A710. 2
CHP old-style pubs on either side of the green in this lovely wee village where Sweet-
heart Abbey is the main attraction (1907/ABBEYS). At Criffel, big changes afoot at
TGP. Locals seem to patronise the bar in both. But very basic accommodation.

 Cavens www.cavens.com · 01387 880234 · Kirkbean 20km from
Dumfries by A710. Report: 757/SOUTHWEST HOTELS. And very civilised dining!

WHERE TO EAT

Auld Alliance www.auldalliancedumfries.com · 01387 256800 · 60 Moffat
Road At Marchills, parallel to the main Edinburgh road out of (and on the edge
of) town. A French/Scottish fusion of approach and produce as they say, in a modern barn-type room with bistro down and finer dining up. Best all-round bet! 7
days. LO 9.30pm.

£15-25 **Hullabaloo** www.hullabaloorestaurant.co.uk · 01387 259679 At the Robert
Burns Centre, also home to an art-house cinema. Hard to reach by car, so walk
across the bridge over the river. Lighter food by day. Some say it's not as good as
you'd wish. Summer Sunday BBQs a nice idea! Closing time varies but usually
11am-8.30pm. Closed Sun/Mon dinner.

£15-25 **The Brasserie @ The Aston** 01387 272410 On edge of town near the university and infirmary; follow signs for the Crichton (see Aston Hotel above). Pleasant
room with bar. Contemporary menu. 7 days. Lunch & LO 9.30pm.

£15-25 **Bruno's** 01387 255757 · 3 Balmoral Road Off Annan Rd. Very long-established
old-style Italian eaterie. Most folks attest to this being the most reliable albeit old-
style eating-out in town.

Balmoral Balmoral Road Chippy adjacent Bruno's above but not related; the
best in or out choices are next to one another. Interior (they close the blinds) but
home cooking and real. 6-10pm, closed Tue. See 1346/FISH & CHIPS.

£15-25 **Pizzeria Il Fiume** www.pizzeriailfiume.co.uk · 01387 265154 · Dock Park
Near St Michael's Bridge, underneath Riverside pub. Usual Italian menu but this
town's best pizzas. (Last time I was here, the family were out unloading the bogs.)
Cosy tratt atmosphere. A long-standing Italian gem. 5.30-10pm daily.

<£15 **Globe Inn** www.globeinndumfries.co.uk · 01387 252335 · 56 High Street
Historic (17th century) pub made internationally famous as Robert Burns' howff
(1915/BURNS). Decent lunches and suppers by arrangement. Best found on foot.

Cavens www.cavens.com · 01387 880234 · Kirkbean In a town not tops
for eating out, Cavens is only 20 minutes away (757/BEST SOUTHWEST).

The Best Hotels & Restaurants In Central Scotland

775 10/L23 ✓✓ **Monachyle Mhor** www.monachylemhor.com · 01877 384622 ·
14 ROOMS **near Balquhidder** Along the ribbon of road that skirts Loch Voil 7 km
TEL · TV beyond the village (which is 4km) from the A84 Callander-Crianlarich road. Rela-
LL tively remote (1152/GET-AWAY HOTELS) and splendid backdrop for this informal and
ATMOS pink farmhouse hotel with great food, fabulous sexy, contemporary rooms and
LOTS altogether good vibes. An urbane back of beyond.
>£35 **EAT** It's a long way for dinner but some of the best dining in Scotland is to be had
here. The wee bar before for the craic, dinner in the conservatory, drawing room
craic after. Tom Lewis and team out back; Black Betty and Angel in attendance.

776 10/M24 ✓✓ **The Roman Camp** www.romancamphotel.co.uk · 01877 330003 ·
14 ROOMS **Callander** Nothing much changes nor needs to in Ian and Marion
TEL · TV Brown's top-of-the-Trossachs hotel, though bedrooms have been recently ruched:
ATMOS bathrooms with underfloor heating, flat-screen TVs, wi-fi etc. Behind the main
LOTS street (at east end), away from the tourist throng and with extensive gardens on
the River Teith; another, more elegant world. Roman ruins are nearby. The house,
built for the dukes of Perth, has been a hotel since the war. Rooms low-ceilinged
and snug; some small. Magnificent period furnishings. Candlelight and log fires! In
the old building corridors do creak. Delightful drawing room and conservatory.
Oval dining room very sympatico. Private chapel should a prayer come on and, of
course, some weddings. Rods for fishing – the river swishes past the lawn.
>£35 **EAT** Dining room effortlessly the best food in town with a great and long-standing
chef – Ian McNaught. Nice for Sunday lunch.

777 10/M24 ✓✓ **Cromlix House** www.cromlixhouse.com · 01786 822125 · **Dunblane**
14 ROOMS 3km from A9 and 4km from town on B8033; follow signs for Perth, then
(8 SUITES) Kinbuck. A leisurely drive through old estate with splendid mature woods to this
TEL · TV spacious mansion both sumptuous and homely. Not much changes in its old-
L style atmosphere but best to leave well alone. No leisure facilities but woods to
ATMOS walk and 3,000 acres of meadows and fishing lochs. House Loch is serenity itself.
LOTS Private chapel. Cromlix is one of Scotland's great and truly country house hotels.
>£35 **EAT** Chef Steve Rooney has upped the game here considerably of late. Great con-
servatory and cosy dining rooms.

778 10/M23 ✓ **Creagan House** www.creaganhouse.co.uk · 01877 384638 · **Strathyre**
5 ROOMS End of the village on main A84 for Crianlarich. Gordon & Cherry Gunn's very
TEL · TV personally run Creagan farmhouse is the place to eat in Rob Roy and Callander
MED.EX country. Rooms are small and inexpensive in an old-fashioned home from home.
You eat in an impressive baronial dining room (stone fireplace, vaulted ceiling).
There are many hills to walk and forest trails start in the lovely garden (1954/HILLS).
£25-35 **EAT** Gordon's been in that kitchen creatively cooking for 25 years. They do take
Wednesday nights off (which I think we can allow), so check.

779 10/M24 ✓ **Lake Hotel** www.lake-hotel.com · 01877 385258 · **Port of Menteith**
16 ROOMS A very lake-side hotel on the Lake of Menteith in the Trossachs' purple heart.
TEL · TV A good centre for touring, walking and fishing (adjacent; 01877 385664): the lake
LL swarms with fishermen in wee boats. The Inchmahome ferry leaves from nearby
MED.EX (1902/MARY, CHARLIE & BOB). A kind of New England feel pervades (they also have
a hotel on Chesapeake Bay). Conservatory restaurant for sunset supper or lazy
lunch; also bar menu. All rooms are light and quiet. A great hotel if you are in love.
£15-25 **EAT** Different menus in bar and conservatory, all stylish and well done. LO 9.30pm.

780 10/N24
10 RMS · TEL
TV · NO PETS
MED.INV

✓ **Adamo Hotel** www.adamohotels.com · 01786 833268 · Bridge of Allan Main street of pleasant town (good shops and restaurants) and suburb of Stirling. Surprisingly and self-consciously stylish and modern with cool interiors. Fine-ish dining good value in an urbane setting. And nice bar.

781 10/M24
3 ROOMS
TEL · DF
CHP

✓ **Cross Keys** www.kippencrosskeys.com · 01786 870293 · Kippen Main street of dreamy little village above the Forth flood plain not far from Stirling. 3 pleasant, airy rooms above a homely pub with a great reputation for a warm welcome and excellent food (1281/GASTROPUBS).

782 10/M24
3 ROOMS · TV
NO PETS
MED.INX

✓ **The Inn at Kippen** www.theinnatkippen.co.uk · 01786 871010 · Kippen In the middle of the village, a village-inn experience stylishly and smartly done and a foodie destination on some scale (1282/GASTROPUBS). With the Cross Keys (above), this wee village is on the foodie map. Rooms are good value.

783 10/M24
200 ROOMS
TEL · TV
DF
MED.EX
£15-25

✓ **Doubletree Dunblane** www.doubletreedunblane.com · 01786 825800 · Dunblane One of the huge hydro hotels left over from the last health and holiday-at-home boom, refurbished at vast expense (£12m) in 2009 by Hilton to create a massive urban edifice on the edge of this small town. Nice views for some and a long walk down corridors for most. Leisure facilities include pool. **EAT** Celebrity chef Nick Nairn has created a couthy contemporary menu in the Kailyard restaurant/dining room. A vast improvement on hydrocatering of yore.

784 9/K23
14+16
ROOMS
L
ATMOS
CHP

Inverarnan Hotel/The Drover's Inn & Lodge www.thedroversinn.co.uk · 01301 704234 · Inverarnan North of Ardlui on Loch Lomond and 12km south of Crianlarich on the A82. Much the same now as when it was pub of the year 1705: bare floors, open fires and heavy drinking (1253/BLOODY GOOD PUBS). The lodge on the other side of the road is modern. Highland hoolies here much recommended (live music Saturdays). Bar staff wearing kilts look like they're meant to. Rooms highly individual: traditional in the hotel, contrasting contemporary in the lodge. Some surprises (1 in hotel, 5 in lodge house have jacuzzis and 4-posters). A wild place in the wilderness. Expect atmosphere not service. Neither places have phones, only a couple have TV and mobiles probably don't work. Hey, you're away!

785 10/M24
6 ROOMS
MAR-NOV · GF
NO PETS/KIDS
MED.INX

Arden House www.ardenhouse.org.uk · 01877 330235 · Callander Bracklinn Rd off Main St at Stirling end and uphill. Superior B&B in elegant mansion that featured in the seminal Sunday night series, *Dr Finlay's Casebook*: for oldies it is still redolent of Tannochbrae. Expect old-fashioned graces but no airs. Good breakfast.

✓ ✓ **DeVere Cameron House** 01389 755565 · Loch Lomond Report: 482/OUTSIDE TOWN HOTELS.

✓ **Lodge on Loch Lomond** 01436 860201 · Loch Lomond Report: 485/OUTSIDE TOWN HOTELS.

RESTAURANTS

786 10/N25
£15->£35

✓ **Glenskirlie House & Castle** www.glenskirliehouse.com · 01324 840201 · Banknock On A803 Kilsyth-Bonnybridge road, junction 4 off M80 Glasgow-Stirling. The Macaloney family have one of Central Scotland's foodie destinations in this many-roomed mansion in an unlikely spot. Victorian house and Castle Grill offer dining options informal and finer. House for lunch and dinner (not Mon), the castle evenings only (not Wed). It's all wonderfully weegie!

787 10/N24 **The Allan Water Café** www.bridgeofallan.com · Bridge of Allan · Caff
<£15 that's been here forever at end of the main street in Bridge of Allan with big
brassy, glassy extension. Original features and clientele still remain in the old bit.
It's all down to fish 'n' chips and the family ice cream (Bechelli's). 1438/ICE CREAM.
7 days, 8am-8.30pm.

788 **Callander Meadows** www.callandermeadows.co.uk · 01877 330181 ·
10/M24 **24 Main Street, Callander** Bang in the middle of the tourist-thronged main
£15-25 street, this is your best bet by far for home-made, well presented contemporary
food. The Parkes preside over 3 townhouse dining rooms; nice local girls. Excellent
puds (the wave!). Lunch and dinner. Closed Tue/Wed, and Mon in winter.

✓ ✓ **Roman Camp** Callander Report: 776/CENTRAL HOTELS.

✓ ✓ **Monachyle Mhor** Balquhidder Report: 775/CENTRAL HOTELS.

✓ ✓ **Cromlix House** Dunblane Report: 777/CENTRAL HOTELS.

✓ **Creagan House** Strathyre Report: 778/CENTRAL HOTELS.

✓ **Lake Hotel** Port of Menteith Report: 779/CENTRAL HOTELS.

✓ **Cross Keys** Kippen Report: 1281/GASTROPUBS.

✓ **The Inn at Kippen** Kippen Report: 1281/GASTROPUBS.

✓ **The Lion & The Unicorn** Thornhill Report: 1303/GASTROPUBS.

If you're in Stirling...

789 10/N24 **WHERE TO STAY**
Two new hotels are planned to open 2012/13. At TGP, these are
recommended:

✓ **Adamo** www.adamohotels.com · 01786 833268 · Bridge of Allan Near
Stirling and probably the best place to be. Report: 780/CENTRAL HOTELS.

7 ROOMS **Osta** www.adamohotels.com · 01786 430890 · 78 Upper Craigs In the cen-
TEL · TV tre of the town and its hard-to-fathom road system, a former bank transformed
MED.INX by the emerging Adamo group (above) into the most contemporary hotel in town.
The main thing here is the busy, brasserie-style restaurant, The Bank (see below).

9 ROOMS **Park Lodge** www.parklodge.net · 01786 474862 · 32 Park Terrace Off
TEL · TV main King's Park Rd, 500m from centre. Quite posh hotel in Victorian/Georgian
MED.INX town (they say country) house near the park and golf course. Objets and lawns.
French chef/proprietor. Michelin-mentioned. Some weddings.

4 ROOMS **Portcullis Hotel** www.theportcullishotel.com · 01786 472290 · Castle
TEL · TV Wynd Jim and Lynne Walker's pub with rooms in one of the best locations in
MED.INX town, no more than a cannonball's throw from the castle. Pub and pub food
(home-made and popular though basic); 4 rooms upstairs, 3 with brilliant views of
the town, graveyard and plain and 1 of the castle. Food till 8pm (9pm weekends).

Stirling Management Centre www.smc.stir.ac.uk · 01786 451712 Not a hotel, but as good as. Fully serviced rooms on university campus (7km from centre in Bridge of Allan which has a good choice of restaurants). Excellent leisure facilities nearby. No atmosphere but a great business like option on a budget.

S.Y. Hostel 01786 473442 On road up to the castle in a great location is this new-style hostel, still very SYH (1116/HOSTELS). **Willy Wallace Hostel**, 77 Murray Pl at Friars St (01786 446773) is more funky. Upstairs in busy centre with caffs and pubs nearby. Unimposing entrance but bunkrooms for 54.

WHERE TO EAT

£25-35 ✓**Hermann's** www.hermanns.co.uk · 01786 450632 · Mar Place After many a year, probably still Stirling's best. A house on road up (and very close) to the castle. Hermann Aschaber's (with Scottish wife, Kay) corner of Austria where schnitzels and strudels figure along with Scottish fare. 2-floor, ambient, well-run rooms. Conservatory best. LO 9.30pm.

£15-25 **Ziggy Forelles** www.ziggyforelles.com · 01786 463222 · 52 Port Street The contemporary café/bar/restaurant place in town: pasta, pizza, risotto; the rest. Good enough, though. 9am-9pm. Bar later.

£15-25 **Mamma Mia** www.mammamiastirling.co.uk · 01786 446124 · 52 Spittal Street The road to the castle, near the top. Italian restaurant run by Italians who make an effort. Better than your average tratt. Lunch and dinner. Closed Tue.

<£15 **Corrieri's** 01786 472089 On the road to Bridge of Allan at Causewayhead. For 70 years this excellent café/restaurant near busy corner below the Wallace Monument serving pasta/pizza and ice cream probably as it should be. A genuine family caff. LO 9.30pm. Closed Tue.

£15-25 **La Cucina** www.lacucinabridgeofallan.co.uk · 01786 834679 · Bridge of Allan On the main (Henderson) street. Contemporary, reasonably authentic Italian place. Once again, B of A is where 2B. Lunch and dinner LO 9.30pm.

£15-25 **Khushis** www.dine@khushis.com · 01786 470999 · 50 Upper Craigs Town-centre location for the expanding Khushis chain from Edinburgh (237/EDINBURGH INDIAN RESTAURANTS). Characteristic contemporary blingy interior but the curries are hot. Big attraction is the BYO. 7 days lunch and LO 11pm (10pm Sun).

£15-25 **Birds & Bees** www.thebirdsandthebees-stirling.com · 01786 473663 Between Stirling and Bridge of Allan at Causewayhead. Going towards Stirling from B of A it's first on the right (Easter Cornton Rd). A local secret and a hugely popular pub-grub destination in the burbs. This unlikely roadhouse is also the Scottish *pétanque* (*boules*) centre. Good for kids. Terrace. 7 days LO 9.15/10pm.

<£15 **Allan Water Café** www.bridgeofallan.com · Bridge of Allan On the main street near the bridge itself. Great café, the best fish 'n' chips 'n' ice cream. A local institution. See 1438/ICE CREAM.

Osta www.osta.uk.com · 01786 430890 City-centre modern grazing and dining. See *Where To Stay* (above).

Tourist Office 01786 479901 Open all year.

The Best Hotels & Restaurants In The Borders

790 10/R27
11 ROOMS
TEL · TV
MED.EX

✓ **The Townhouse** www.thetownhousemelrose.co.uk · 01896 822645 · **Melrose** Longstanding Burt's (below) spawned a stylish little sister across the street. Charming and boutiqueish with a coherent, elegant look by Michael Vee Decor (from down the street); it's very Melrose! In the whole of the Borders, this is probably the only hotel you could call contemporary. Dining room and busy brasserie confidently positioned between Burt's' fine dining and its gastrogrub bar. The Hendersons here and over the road continue to put their town on the map.

791 10/R27
20 ROOMS
TEL · TV
DF
MED.INX

<£15->£35

✓ **Burt's** www.burtshotel.co.uk · 01896 822285 · **Melrose** In Market Sq/main street; some (double-glazed) rooms overlook. Busy bars, especially for food; it's easy to see why. The dining room is where to fine dine in this part of the Borders. Cosy in winter, it looks out to the garden and is summery in summer. Traditional but comfortably modernised small town hotel, though some rooms do feel small. Convenient location for Borders roving (1908/ABBEYS; 1970/HILL WALKS; 1512/GARDENS). Where to stay for the Sevens or the Book Festival. **EAT** Bar, an AA Pub of the Year, serves top gastropub food (1278/GASTROPUBS). It and the main restaurant are in a class of their own hereabouts.

792 10/S27
4 ROOMS
TV
NO PETS
L
MED.INX

£25-35

✓ **Edenwater House** www.edenwaterhouse.co.uk · 01573 224070 · **Ednam** Find Ednam on Kelso–Swinton road B6461, 4 km. Discreet manse-type house beside old kirk and graveyard overlooking Eden Water, the lovely garden and tranquil green countryside. Bucolic is the word. You have the run of the home of Jeff and Jacqui Kelly. Jacqui's flair in the kitchen and Jeff's carefully wrought wine list (he has a wine shed in the old coachouse and once a week there's a wine-themed dinner) make this the secret Borders dinner destination. **EAT** Best cook in the counties? Jacqui Kelly is longstanding, unassuming and underestimated. Non-residents must book.

793 10/Q26
8 ROOMS
TEL · TV
NO PETS
MED.INX

£25-35

✓ **Horseshoe Inn** www.horseshoeinn.co.uk · 01721 730225 · **Eddleston near Peebles** On the A703 (8km Peebles, 30km Edinburgh), a recreated, reconstructed coaching inn and a convivial and contemporary stopover with famously good food that continues to win awards for chef/proprietor Patrick Bardoulet. Rooms in the old village school behind are peaceful and better than anything down the road in Peebles. Stumble there replete after dinner. **EAT** A destination for dinner. Bistro and dining room both on the formal side (white-gloved waiters!). Tasting menu and à la carte; all gloriously gastro.

794 10/Q27
13 ROOMS
TEL · TV
LOTS

>£35

✓ **Cringletie House** www.cringletie.com · 01721 725750 · **Peebles** Privately owned and carefully tended country-house hotel 5km from town just off A703 Edinburgh road (35km). Late-19th-century Scottish baronial house in 28 acres. Quintessential Peeblesshire: comfortable and civilised with an imperturbable air of calm. Well-loved local art. Restful garden view from every room. Top disabled facilities including a lift! Conservatory, lounges up and downstairs; gracious dining room. Walled kitchen garden. **EAT** Craig Gibb has forged a strong local reputation in the upstairs, fabulously frescoed Sutherland Restaurant. Peebles's top dine-out!

795 10/S27
22 ROOMS
TEL · TV
MED.EX

✓ **Roxburghe Hotel** www.roxburghe.net · 01573 450331 · **near Kelso** *The* consummate country-house hotel in the Borders. Owned by the Duke and Duchess of Roxburgh who have a personal input. Rooms distinctive, all light with garden views. Owls hoot at night and once – no, twice, a crow fell down my chimney. This was good luck! The 18-hole golf course has major appeal – it's challenging and championship-standard and in a beautiful riverside setting. Non-residents can play (2085/GREAT GOLF). 2 treatment rooms and Health and Beauty Suite in the courtyard for golf widows. Game, meat and fish from the estate inform an improved menu of late under Ross Miller. Compared with other country-house hotels, the Roxburghe is good value. Serene garden, perfect policies!

796 10/P27
6 ROOMS
MAR–DEC
TV
MED.INX

✓ **Skirling House** www.skirlinghouse.com · 01899 860274 · Skirling On A72. 3km from Biggar as you come into Skirling village. In an Arts and Crafts house (by Ramsay Traquair, son of Phoebe), Bob and Isobel Hunter have created a rural guest house which is the epitome of taste. From the toiletries to the white doves in the doocot, the hens from which your breakfast eggs come and the garden produce, it's just perfect. Bob cooks (set menu), Isobel out front. This is a very superior B&B (&D). Though I haven't been of late, I wish...

797 10/R26
8+2 ROOMS
MAR–JAN
TEL · TV · DF
CHP

Black Bull 01578 722208 · Lauder Main street near the clock of strip of town on A68 that leads to the real Border country. Food reputation slightly diminished of late but a good find here (1300/GASTROPUBS); it also has 8 (and 2 family) very pleasant rooms above the many-chambered pub. A popular local with charming, helpful young staff.

798 10/R26
10 ROOMS
TEL · TV
L
MED.INX

Lodge At Carfraemill www.carfraemill.co.uk · 01578 750750 · near Lauder On A68 roundabout 8km north of Lauder. Old coaching-type lodging. Rooms are old-style and all different – it sure beats a motel! Old-style cooking, a good stop on the road for grub (Jo's Kitchen LO 9pm, all-day menu Sat/Sun) and a gateway to the Borders. Nice for kids.

799 10/R27
38 ROOMS
TEL · TV
LL
MED.EX

Dryburgh Abbey Hotel www.dryburgh.co.uk · 01835 822261 · near St Boswells Secluded, elegant 19th-century house in abbey (1906/ABBEYS) grounds by the Tweed (with trout-fishing rights). A peaceful, beautiful location. Not big on atmosphere despite surroundings. Dining in very pink room improved a lot of late and Abbey Bistro 12noon-9pm. Afternoon tea a speciality. Lovely riverside strolling. And the abbey: pure romance especially by moonlight.

800 10/Q27
12 ROOMS
+5 LODGES
TEL · TV
MED.EX

Philipburn www.philipburnhousehotel.co.uk · 01750 720747 · Selkirk 1km from town centre. Excellent, privately owned Best Western hotel for families, walkers, a weekend away from it all. Selkirk is a good Borders base. Restaurant and bar-bistro and comfy rooms, some more luxurious than others. Spa and pool (still!) underway at TGP. 1113/HOTELS THAT WELCOME KIDS.

801 10/S27
32 ROOMS
TEL · TV
MED.INX

Ednam House www.ednamhouse.com · 01573 224168 · Kelso Just off town square overlooking River Tweed; a majestic Georgian mansion with very old original features including some of the guests! In the same family (the Brooks) since 1928, it has dated in a comforting way: guests quietly getting on with the main business of fishing and dozing in an old armchair. The restaurant's river view is the main attraction in a great garden room with an unfortunate carpet. Half the bedrooms have a view. In contrast to this old-style ambience, the new Pharlanne deli and bistro at the gateway and on the street is bright and contemporary and makes much of its local and artisan producers. Bistro, lunch only and until 4pm.

802 10/R27
5 ROOMS
TV
MED.INX

Clint Lodge www.clintlodge.co.uk · 01835 822027 · St Boswells On B6356 (1623/SCENIC ROUTES) between Dryburgh Abbey (1906/ABBEYS) and Smailholm Tower (1863/MONUMENTS). Small country guest house in great border country with tranquil views from rooms. Nice conservatory pre dinner. Very good home cooking and service from Bill and Heather Walker then a splendid Border breakfast.

803 10/R27 · **Fauhope** www.fauhopehouse.com · 01896 823184 · **Melrose** Borders house
3 ROOMS · in sylvan setting overlooking Tweed. Lovely front rooms, terrace and terraced
TV · lawns. Only 3 rooms but in more guides than mine (*Best B&Bs, Michelin*), so must
CHP · book. Family dogs much in evidence.

804 10/R28 · **Hundalee House** www.accommodation-scotland.org · 01835 863011 ·
5 RMS · TV · **Jedburgh** 1km south of Jedburgh off A68. Lovely 1700 manor house in 10-acre
CLOSED MAR · garden. Brilliant value, great base, views of Cheviot hills. Near the famously old
NO C/ CARDS · Capon Tree. Big garden.
CHP

S.Y. Hostels Very good in the Borders. Report: 1127/HOSTELS.
Wheatsheaf Swinton Report: 1289/GASTROPUBS.
Traquair Arms Innerleithen Report: 1147/ROADSIDE INNS.

RESTAURANTS

805 10/Q27 · ✓ **Coltman's** www.coltmans.co.uk · 01721 720405 · **Peebles** Bridge end
£15-25 · of main street. A light, contemporary deli and café with restaurant through
the back. Ken Coltman (Prestonfield, Edinburgh) set up shop here in 2010 and
well, it's just what Peebles needed. Exudes confidence and class. Weekly changing
menus, dining area small; so book. Lovely breakfasts and puds. Deli counter out
front with café tables. 10am-7pm, Sun 12noon-4pm. Dinner Fri/Sat only.

806 10/Q27 · ✓ **Osso** 01721 724477 · **Innerleithen Road, Peebles** Aka the main street.
£15-35 · Ally McGrath's perfectly judged and effective bistro/tearoom/restaurant
changes through the day from lightsome lunch to scones and cakes to superb
dining-out experience at night. With local staff and no city prices or pretensions,
Osso is perfectly Peebles. Lunch 7 days through to dinner (Tue-Sat). LO 8.45pm.

807 10/Q27 · ✓ **The Restaurant @ Kailzie Gardens** 01721 722807 · **Peebles** ·
L · www.therestaurantatkailziegardens.co.uk 4km from town on B7062. In
<£15 · the estate outbuildings by the gardens (807/KIDS), Stuart and Amanda Clink have
restored and surpassed the reputation of the Kailzie (pronounced Kaylee) tearoom.
Light, organic where possible and largely locally sourced menu. Smorrebrod a speciality (on home-made bread). 7 days 10am-5pm. Sat night dinners.

808 10/R27 · ✓ **Marmion's** www.marmionsbrasserie.co.uk · 01896 822245 ·
£15-25 · **Buccleuch Street, Melrose** Near the abbey. Local fave bistro for a long
time, its original formula and atmosphere reassuringly unchanged. Open for
breakfast, lunch and dinner in a brasserie-type room with bistro-type menu, if you
know what I mean. Good vegetarian. The reliably good repast in the Borders
foodie capital. LO 8.45pm. Closed Sun.

809 10/R27 · ✓ **Chapters** www.melrose.bordernet.co.uk · 01896 823217 · **Gattonside**
£25-35 · near **Melrose** Over the River Tweed (you could walk by footbridge as quick
as going round by car). Kevin and Nicki Winsland's surprising bistro is a real find.
Huge choice from à la carte and daily seafood specials in a periodically changing
menu. Great dessert list. Locally best atmos! Tue-Sat dinner only.

✓ **Burts & Townhouse** Melrose · **Cringletie** Peebles Burt's for best dining (including the gastropub and brasserie at the Townhouse), Cringletie for a
very special treat. Reports: 791/790/BORDERS HOTELS, 1278/GASTROPUBS.

810 10/P26 ✓ **Whitmuir Farm** www.whitmuirorganics.co.uk · 01968 661147 ·
<£15 Lamancha Off A701 15 minutes from Peebles. Ambitious farm shop (1457/
FARM SHOPS), food hall, gallery and café/restaurant in contemporary build on a real
farm in the best kind of middle of nowhere. Food is taken seriously on a light,
largely organic menu with fish, meat and vegetarian. Dinner once a month. Trying
to make things better; we need more farms like this! 10am-6pm, 5pm weekends.

<£15 ✓ **Turnbulls** 01450 372020 · Hawick By 'the Horse', ie Oliver Place, this
foodie oasis is thought by some to be the best thing to happen to Hawick
this century. This may be true. 9.30am-5.30pm (café LO 4pm). Report: 1450/DELIS.

811 10/R27 **The Hoebridge Inn** www.thehoebridgeinn.com · 01896 823082 · Gatton-
£15-25 side At Earlston end of village, signed towards the river (or from Melrose by footbridge). Kerr and Elaine Marrian's superior, slightly formal bistro/dining room (with
a snack menu); good, though. Lunch Tue-Sun, dinner Tue-Sat. LO 9.30pm.

812 10/R27 **Monte Cassino** 01896 820082 · Melrose Great setting just up from the main
£15-25 square in the old station and station master's house. Cheerful, non-pretentious
and popular Italian – often Neapolitan – with pasta/pizza staples and the odd ok
special. The place is packed; that tells you something! LO 9.30pm. Closed Mon.

813 10/Q27 **Courthouse** 01721 723537 · Peebles Facing the end of the High St near the
£15-25 bridge. Upstairs in the former courthouse, an odd layout but a vaulted main room
with terrace and garden. Popular, with an eclectic menu, especially their big burgers. 10.30am-5pm, Thu-Sun till 9.30pm. Closed Tue.

814 10/Q27 **Sunflower Restaurant** www.thesunflower.net · 01721 722420 · Bridge-
£15-25 gate, Peebles Off the main street at Veitches corner. Gorgeous wee Sunflower is
a local fave. 3 small rooms, so book for dinner at weekends. Integrity and design
in the café menu during day and nice for kids. They take vegetarian food seriously
(and have their own cookbook). Thu/Fri/Sat for dinner 7-9 pm. Lunch 7 days.

815 10/R28 **Brydons** 01450 372672 · 16 High Street, Hawick Once Brydons were bakers,
<£15 now they have this oddly funky family caff-cum-restaurant. Home cooking, good
folk – this is a totally Hawick experience. 7.30am-4pm. Closed Sun. 1377/CAFÉS.

816 10/R28 **Damascus Drum Café & Books** 0786 7530709 · 2 Silver Street, Hawick
<£15 Near tourist office. Surprisingly contemporary, laid-back second-hand bookshop
and caff in a Hawick backstreet. Comfy seats. Home-made soups, quiche and
bagels (1312/VEGETARIAN RESTAURANTS)... and rugs. Mon-Sat 10am-5pm.

817 10/S27 **The Cobbles Inn** 01573 223548 · Kelso Off the main square behind the Cross
£15-25 Keys Hotel. Popular local pub-grub (more grub than pub) restaurant. The Meikle-
johns run a tight and friendly ship and care about their (mostly local) suppliers.
Bar and restaurant menu (evenings). Good ales. Lunch and LO 9pm. Closed Mon.

£15-25 **Giacopazzi's & Oblo's** 01890 752527 · Eyemouth Great fish 'n' chips and ice
cream plus upstairs bistro near Eyemouth harbour. Report: 1354/FISH & CHIPS.

Auld Crosskeys Inn Denholm Report: 1281/GASTROPUBS.
The Craw Inn Auchencrow Report: 1149/ROADSIDE INNS.
Woodside near Ancrum Report: 1383/TEAROOMS.
Under The Sun Kelso Report: 1365/CAFÉS.

The Best Hotels & Restaurants In The Lothians

See Section 2 for Edinburgh Hotels & Restaurants just outside the city.

818 10/R25
23 ROOMS
TEL · TV
LL
LOTS
£25-£35

✓✓ **Greywalls** www.greywalls.co.uk · 01620 842144 · **Gullane** Outside the village on the North Berwick road 36km east of Edinburgh, a classic country-house hotel in 4 superb acres of garden especially convenient for golfing. There are 12 courses nearby, including 3 championship (2069/2071/GOLF) and the hotel overlooks Muirfield (though no right of access). No grey walls here but warm sandstone and light, summery (cosy in winter) rooms: a manor house designed by Lutyens, the garden by Gertrude Jekyll – a rather winning combination. The roses are legendary and what could be nicer than afternoon tea... well, dinner probably, in the Albert Roux-managed (and very branded) restaurant. Unsurprisingly expensive, the hotel and adjacent Colonel's House can be taken for exclusive use. The evening light from the western sky on the terrace pre or post prandial is priceless. **EAT** Dining rooms, drawing rooms and conservatory for bar and à la carte menu; both it and the wine list characteristically (of Roux outstations) good value. Chef Derek Johnstone at the helm of a hard-to-fault team.

819 10/P25
16 ROOMS
TEL · TV
NO KIDS
NO PETS
MED.EX
>£35

✓✓ **Champany Inn** www.champany.com · 01506 834532 · near **Linlithgow** Excellent restaurant with rooms near M9 junction 3, 30 minutes from Edinburgh city centre, 15 minutes from the airport. Convenient high-standard hotel adjacent to nationally famous restaurant (121/HOTELS OUTSIDE EDINBURGH) especially if you love your meat properly hung (3 weeks, butchered on the premises) and presented. Superlative wine list, especially South African vintages also available to buy from The Cellar (12noon-10pm, 7 days). **EAT** Accolades confirm the best meal in West Lothian. Casual dining in the Chop 'n' Ale House. Angus beef, home-made sausages, the right oysters.

820 10/Q25
26 ROOMS
TEL · TV
MED.INX

✓ **Kilspindie House** www.kilspindie.co.uk · 01875 870682 · **Aberlady** Old-style village inn taken over by Edinburgh restauranteur of repute, Malcolm Duck. Rooms adequate and upgraded but hotel excels not surprisingly in the food department. Bistro menu and proper dining. Excellent wine list. **EAT** Amusingly, the options are bistro dining across the bar and several rooms at **Donald's** or finer dining at **Ducks**. Integrity throughout and very much part of the East Lothian Food Group (sources listed). Gastronomic without being histrionic. Bistro 7 days 12noon-9.30pm. Ducks lunch and dinner.

821 10/R25
5 ROOMS
TEL · TV
NO PETS · L
MED.INX
£15-25

✓ **Castle Inn** www.castleinndirleton.com · 01620 850221 · **Dirleton** Close to the castle ruins on the corner of the green in this lovely wee village 4km from Gullane and 30 minutes from Edinburgh. Only a few rooms; individual, well-chosen period furnishings – you do feel like you're in an inn and great food downstairs. A new top stop in the county. **EAT** Comfortable gastropub/bistro busy and buzzing so book weekends. Outside terrace and dining room (same menu). Daily and seasonal. 7 days 12noon-9pm.

822 10/R25
83 ROOMS
TEL · TV
MED.EX

Marine Hotel www.macdonaldhotels.co.uk · 01620 892406 · **North Berwick** A few years back the old seaside hotel of North Berwick underwent an extensive re-fit and re-emerged as a spa and conference centre. Done in the sombre/elegant, corporate style à la mode with lots of public space and everywhere (except the leisure area) the great views of the Links and the sea. There are 20 golf courses on your doorstep. Fine-ish dining in the plush restaurant; chef: John Paul. Links bar less formal and there's a drawing room for that afternoon tea. Small pool and other vital facilities. It's still all very North Berwick.

823 10/R25
11 ROOMS
TEL · TV
CHP
£15-25

The Rocks www.experiencetherocks.co.uk · 01368 862287 · Dunbar Not signed but at the east and John Muir Park end of Dunbar (take a right at Marine Dr) with great views across to the rocky harbour area, a hotel with big local reputation for food. Rooms vary but most have a view.
EAT They come from across the country to Jim Findlay's gastropub rooms. Seafood and the rest in bar and Piano Room. They just do it well. Book weekends.

824 10/R25
12 RMS · TEL
TV · NO PETS
MED.EX

Nether Abbey www.netherabbey.co.uk · 01620 892802 · 20 Dirleton Avenue, North Berwick On the Coastal Trail from Gullane. Long-established family seaside hotel with major drop-in bar/restaurant operation – the Fly-Half Bar and Grill (locally and well-sourced dishes). Busy downstairs, comfy up.

825 10/R25
12 ROOMS
TEL · TV
MED.EX

Open Arms www.openarmshotel.com · 01620 850241 · Dirleton The other comfortable, cosy and countrified hotel in this tiny village opposite ancient ruins. If this were in France it might be a Hotel du Charme, but is in need of a little TLC. Location means it's a golfers' haven; special packages available. Nice public rooms with much lounging space. Deveaus Restaurant LO 9pm.

✓✓ **The Dakota** 0870 423 4293 · South Queensferry Report: 122/HOTELS OUTSIDE EDINBURGH. Designed for travellers.
✓ **Orocco Pier** 0131 331 1298 · South Queensferry Report: 125/HOTELS OUTSIDE EDINBURGH. Boutique on the water. And the bridge.

RESTAURANTS: EAST LOTHIAN

826 10/R25
>£35

✓✓ **La Potinière** www.la-potiniere.co.uk · 01620 843214 · Gullane On the main street of a golfing mecca, this small, discreet restaurant has been an East Lothian destination for decades. Keith Marley and Mary Runciman, who share the cooking, have consolidated its reputation since 2003. The room is not bustling but is just right for gentle, perhaps genteel, appreciation of their simply excellent 2-choice, locally sourced menu. By far the best dining in East Lothian. I wrote this for the last edition and after a recent visit I stick by it word for word. Lunch Wed-Sun, Dinner Wed-Sat (Sun in summer). LO 8.30pm. Closed Jan.

827 10/R25
<£15

✓ **Fenton Barns** www.fentonbarnsfarmshop.com · 01620 850294 · near Drem Farmshop/deli but also a great café with delicious food home-made from the mainly local produce they sell; hot dishes till 3.30pm then scrumptious cake. Not licensed. Café 10am-4pm, shop 5pm. See 1461/FARMSHOPS.

828 10/R25
±25-35

✓ **Creel** www.creelrestaurant.co.uk · 01368 863279 · Lamer Street, Dunbar Logan Thorburn's meticulously run but informal bistro on a discreet corner of old Dunbar near the harbour; from a tiny kitchen he produces sound and simple, almost rustic menus. Local of course and not just seafood. It's close-up and personal. Wed-Sun lunch dinner (Sun till 5.30pm).

829 10/R25
L
£15-25

✓ **Waterside Bistro** www.watersidebistro.co.uk · 01620 825674 · Haddington Long a food find on the Tyne, of mixed fortunes recently but now under new, experienced ownership and reinstated as a classic... waterside bistro. Separate chambers and ambience options but the same menu throughout. This smartly operated riverside gastropub, easy on the eye and pocket, puts Haddington back on the East Lothian food trail.

830 10/R25
£15-25

✓ **Osteria** 01620 890589 · High Street, North Berwick A classic Italian restaurant in downtown small town set up by the legendary Italian chef from Edinburgh, called just simply Cosmo, at age 75. The family run it but its old-fashioned values in menu and service make this the smart and reliably good place to eat in North Berwick. Good Italian wine list. Closed Sun and Mon lunch. LO 10pm.

831 10/R25 £15-25 ✓ **The Old Clubhouse** www.oldclubhouse.com · 01620 842008 · **East Links Road, Gullane** Behind main street, on corner of Green. Large, woody clubhouse; a bar/bistro serving a long menu (of the burgers/pasta/nachos variety) and daily specials all day till 9.30pm. Obliging, reliable. Great busy atmosphere. Surprising wine selection.

832 10/R25 <£15 **The Linton** www.lintonhotel.com · 01620 860202 · **East Linton** Family-run small country village hotel; friendly and welcoming. Simple, quiet rooms and notable locally for bar meals and dining. Has an unusual upstairs walled garden.

833 10/Q25 £15-25 **Lanna Thai** www.thaifood-scotland.com · 0131 653 2788 · **32 Bridge Street, Musselburgh** Edinburgh end of the bridge opposite the theatre. Here a long time but a new entry in *StB*. I realise this honest neighbourhood Thai bistro in the Honest Town is just what's needed here and it has been well liked, providing a strong alternative to burgers and ice cream. The food is good. 7 days lunch and LO 10pm. Also takeaway.

Goblin Ha' Hotel 01620 810244 · Gifford Report: 1305/GASTROPUBS, 271/EDINBURGH KID-FRIENDLY.

RESTAURANTS: WEST LOTHIAN

834 10/N25 £15-25 ✓ **Livingston's** www.livingstons-restaurant.co.uk · 01506 846565 · **Linlithgow** Through arch at east end of High St, now sitting a bit uncomfortably behind a brash Italian tratt. Cottage conversion with conservatory and garden – a bistro with imaginative modern Franco-Scottish cuisine (4 starters, mains, desserts) holding on to its reserve and still the best in town and shire. Straightforward menu; good vegetarian. Tue-Sat, lunch and dinner. Closed Jan.

835 10/P25 £15-25 ✓ **The Boathouse** 0131 331 5429 · South Queensferry Enter from main street or down steps to terrace overlooking shingly beach and excellent views of the bridge (401/MAIN ATTRACTIONS). Bistro serving all day from noon and restaurant room in evenings. Nothing too fancy but mainly seafood in a lucky location.

 **Champany Inn** 01506 834532 · South Queensferry See *Hotels In The Lothians*, above.

 **The Dakota** 0870 423 4293 · South Queensferry Report: 122/HOTELS OUTSIDE EDINBURGH.

✓ **Orocco Pier** 0131 331 1298 · South Queensferry Report: 125/HOTELS OUTSIDE EDINBURGH.

836 10/R23
144 ROOMS
TEL · TV
NO PETS
LL
LOTS

✓ ✓ **Old Course** www.oldcoursehotel.co.uk · 01334 474371 · St Andrews Arriving in St Andrews on the A91, you come to the Old Course and this world-renowned hotel first. An elegant presence on the hallowed greens, it's full of golfers coming and going. It was designed by NY architects with Americans in mind. Rooms, most overlooking the famous course and sea, are immaculate and tastefully done with no facility or expense spared, as with the Sands Grill and fine-dining Road Hole Restaurant up top. Bar here also for lingering views and a big choice of drams. Truly great for golf, but anyone could unwind here, towelled in luxury. Excellent Kohler (the hotel's US owners) water spa with 20m pool, thermal suite and some top treatments (1229/BEST SPAS). No preferential treatment on the Old Course adjacent but the hotel has its own course, Dukes, 5km away and there are 10 others nearby.

>£35

EAT Road Hole Restaurant for spectacular dinner, especially on late light summer nights. Sands is, as they say, a grill. Nice afternoon tea in the conservatory.

£25-35

837 10/Q24
8 ROOMS
TEL · TV
NO PETS
LOTS

✓ **The Peat Inn** www.thepeatinn.co.uk · 01334 840206 · near Cupar & St Andrews A luxurious restaurant with rooms at a historic crossroads 20 minutes from St Andrews (by Leven road or Strathkinness Rd). Long a foodie destination. The Smeddles have upgraded the rooms and transformed The Residence into a comfortable, contemporary and quiet retreat rather than just a place to kip so you don't have to drive anywhere after dinner. 7 of the rooms on 2 floors, breakfast discreetly delivered (from pre-order) to your upstairs dining room so you can start your day relaxed. Flowers in the room which look out to the flowers in the serene gardens. It goes without saying that dinner is top (see below).

838 10/Q24
30 ROOMS
TEL · TV
DF
EXP

✓ **Balbirnie House** www.balbirnie.co.uk · 01592 610066 · Markinch Signed from the road system around Glenrothes (3km) in surprisingly sylvan setting of Balbirnie Country Park. One of the most sociable and comfortable country-house hotels in the land, with high, if traditional, standards in service and decor personally overseen by the Russell family. Library Bar leads on to tranquil garden. Lots of luxury space. Choice of dining and a good wine list. No leisure facilities. Nice wedding/honeymoon destination (many of). Good golf in the park.

>£35

EAT An elegant hotel for lunch and dinner in Orangery or downstairs bistro.

839 10/R23
24 ROOMS
+2 LODGES
TEL · TV
L
LOTS

✓ **Rufflets** www.rufflets.co.uk · 01334 472594 · St Andrews 4km from centre along Strathkinness Low Rd past campus buildings and playing fields. The Murray-Smiths' calm, elegant country-house hotel on edge of town is the epitome of comfort. The celebrated gardens are not just a joy, they're among the most beautiful hotel grounds in the land. Garden-restaurant fine dining; lovely lounges, especially for afternoon tea. Cosy rooms, half overlook garden: 2 in the garden, 3 on the drive. New conference/wedding suite but it's in a separate building so the serenity remains mainly intact (except for photo calls on the lawns).

840 10/R23
209 ROOMS
+2 LODGES
TEL · TV
L
LOTS

✓ **Fairmont St Andrews (aka St Andrews Bay)** 01334 837000 · near St Andrews 8km east on A917 to Crail overlooking eponymous bay. Smart modern edifice in rolling greens by international hotel group. Soulless perhaps, but every facility a golfing family could need. It does have a championship course and service at the Fairmont is top. There's a Mediterranean approach to the menu in The Squire, a brasserie-type restaurant in an immense atrium (feels a bit like a municipal leisure facility but for the bold clashing carpet). Fine dining in evenings in windowless Esperante: the name sounds universal but the lingo is Scottish; and The Clubhouse on the green has its signature fish 'n' chips. Spa has 12 treatment rooms with Kerstin Florian and Pure Lochside products.

841 10/R23 ✓ **Old Station** www.theoldstation.co.uk · 01334 880505 · **near St**
8 ROOMS **Andrews** On B9131 (Anstruther road) off A917 from St Andrews. Individualist
TV contemporary makeover of old station with themed rooms. Great consideration
MED.INX for guests: library, putting green, snooker, ping-pong. Conservatory dining room,
comfy lounge. 2 garden suites in a railway carriage! Nice for kids. B&B only.

842 10/R24 **Cambo Estate** www.camboestate.com · 01333 450054 · **near Crail** 2km
17 ROOMS east of Crail on A917. Huge country pile in glorious gardens on the St Andrews-
+2 COTTAGES Crail coastal road. Hugely individual, even quirky. Rooms arranged in apartments
L (and 2 cottages). This is home-stay in the grand manner, especially for groups. A
VARIES real period piece and not so expensive. Grounds are superb, especially in spring
(the snowdrops!) and an event programme makes the most of the gardens. Great
walks and Kingsbarns golf and beach adjacent (2079/GREAT GOLF). Rattle around,
pretend you're house guests and be grateful you don't have to pay the bills.

843 10/P25 **Woodside Hotel** www.thewoodsidehotel.co.uk · 01383 860328 · **Aberdour**
20 ROOMS Historic inn in main street of pleasant village with prize-winning floral rail station,
TEL · TV castle and church (1873/CHURCHES), coastal walk and beach. This is where to
MED.INX come from Edinburgh (30 minutes), arriving at the station with your bit on the
side. Old-style accommodation, friendly staff.

844 10/P25 **Forth View** www.forthviewhotel.co.uk · 01383 860402 · **Aberdour** Over the
5 ROOMS sea from Edinburgh, an old-fashioned hideaway on the point and the undercliff
TV just outside Aberdour. A jagged pier and view of the water and the sunset. A
L Room With A View is the well regarded seafood dining room though some kitchen
MED.INX smell pervades; public area small. Family-run historic house. Steep approach by
car from Silver Sands car park or they pick you up from the station.

For accommodation in St Andrews, see p. 160.

For accommodation in St Andrews, see p. 160.

RESTAURANTS

845 10/Q24 ✓✓ **The Peat Inn** www.thepeatinn.co.uk · 01334 840206 · **near**
>£35 **Cupar & St Andrews** Legendary restaurant (with 8 suites; see above)
ATMOS at the eponymous crossroads. Geoffrey and Katherine Smeddle have further developed it as one of the great Scots dining-out experiences. A tasting menu, seasonal à la carte and good-value menu du jour offer loads of hard choice. Tables
comfortably spread through many chambered, cosmo rather than just cosy cottage
rooms. Unlike some top chefs, Michelin-starred chef-patron Geoffrey Smeddle is
always there (*and* somehow writes a column in the *Sunday Herald*). The Peat Inn,
handily close to St Andrews, is still the top spot in an area not short of foodie
choices. Superb wine list, especially French. Lunch & LO 9pm Tue-Sat.

846 10/R24 ✓✓ **The Cellar** 01333 310378 · **Anstruther** For over 30 years, this classic
>£35 bistro has pioneered and served some of the best fish you'll eat in Scot-
ATMOS land. I couldn't visit for this edition but no need – you know it's always going to be
great. Off a courtyard behind the Fisheries Museum in this busy East Neuk town
(1563/COASTAL VILLAGES). You'd never think it was a restaurant from the approach
but inside is a comforting oasis of epicurean delight. Peter Jukes sources only the
best produce and he does mean *the best*. Even the Anstruther crabs want to crawl
in here. One meat dish, excellent complementary wine list. Pure, simple food and
timeless atmosphere. Lunch Fri/Sat, dinner Tue-Sat. 1316/SEAFOOD RESTAURANTS.

847 10/R24 ✓ **Sangster's** www.sangsters.co.uk · 01333 331001 · **Main Street, Elie**
>£35 Michelin-starred chef and the missus' unobtrusive and unpretentious restau-

rant is perfect for charmed and charming little Elie, the secret neuk of many a moneyed Edinburger and other lovers of the good life. Usually 3 choices, simply described and presented; the chef's signature elegant pairings of fine ingredients. And stand-out value for money among the best of Michelin standard in the UK. Only a few tables so must book, especially for dinner. Tue-Sat and Sun lunch.

848 10/Q23
£25-35

✓ **Ostler's Close** www.ostlersclose.co.uk · 01334 655574 · **Temperance Close, Cupar** Down a close off the main street, Amanda and Jimmy Graham run a bistro/restaurant that has been on the gastronomic map and a reason for coming to Cupar for 30 years. Intimate, cottagey rooms. Amanda out front also does puds, Jimmy a star in the kitchen. Long before it was de rigeur they pioneered local and personal sourcing. Often organic and from their garden, big on mushrooms and other wild things, lots of fish choice – the hand-written menu sums up their approach. Cupar is only 20 minutes from St Andrews. Go to it! Sat lunch & Tue-Sat dinner LO 9.30pm. Must book.

849 10/P25
£25-35

✓ **The Wee Restaurant** www.theweerestaurant.co.uk · 01383 616263 · **Main Street, North Queensferry** Just over the Road Bridge from Edinburgh and in the shadow of the Rail Bridge (401/MAIN ATTRACTIONS). Oh, this is a busy wee restaurant (in a quiet wee town) with only a few tables up a few stairs from the street. Owner/chef Craig Wood and missus, Vicki, live through the back, bake the bread in the morning and prepare their no-fuss menu with commitment (to good food) and aplomb. Somehow Craig finds the time to revitalise Aberdour Golf Clubhouse. There's nowhere as good as this anywhere nearby except Edinburgh. Neat wine list. Lunch Tue-Sun, dinner Tue-Sat.

850 10/Q23
£15-25

The View www.view-restaurant.co.uk · 01382 542287 · **Wormit** On the main road in or out of Wormit next to the PO, it has a great view right enough (of the Tay Bridge and bonny Dundee). Steve and Karen Robertson (of the much-respected Glasshouse Restaurant in Granton) upped sticks and tables in 2011 and took over the local pub, turning it into a lovely non-city but almost urban dining lounge. The menu is based on the grazing, tasting, tapas principle of small, inexpensive dishes: you order 2 or 3. Steve's good so this should work well and there ain't nothing like it in Dundee so come on over. Lunch and dinner but check hours.

<£15

Fish & Chips In Fife: Valente's Kirkcaldy, The Anstruther Fish Bar, The Wee Chippie, The Pittenweem Fish & Chip Bar 4 great fish 'n' chip shops in Fife, mostly with queues every day. They're all very good and a change from the fancier foodie places above. 1349/1353/1339/FISH & CHIPS.

851 10/R24
<£15

Wok & Spice 01333 730888 · **St Monans** On A917 turning past St Monans. Not a caff but a takeaway. Sizzling woks, proper rice, a taste of real Malaysian food (please don't have the chips). This would work anywhere but when in Fife, order here (they deliver between Largo and Crail). 7 days 4.30pm till whenever.

✓✓ **The Seafood Restaurant** St Andrews Report: 1319/SEAFOOD RESTAURANTS.

✓ **Craig Millar** St Monans Report: 1320/SEAFOOD RESTAURANTS.

✓ **The Grange Inn** St Andrews Report: 1285/GASTROPUBS.

✓ **The Ship Inn** Elie Report: 1283/GASTROPUBS.

✓ **The Vine Leaf** St Andrews See Where to Eat in St Andrews, p. 161.

If you're in St Andrews...

Many of the places below are listed in Scotland- or Fife-wide categories.

852 10/R23 **WHERE TO STAY**

✓ ✓ **Old Course Hotel** 01334 474371 Report: 836/FIFE HOTELS.

✓ **Rufflets** 01334 472594 Report: 839/FIFE HOTELS.

✓ **Fairmont (St Andrews Bay)** 01334 837000 Report: 840/FIFE HOTELS.

✓ **Old Station** 01334 880505 Report: 841/FIFE HOTELS.

68 ROOMS **Rusacks** www.rusacks-hotel.co.uk · 01334 474321 · **Pilmour Links** Long-
TEL · TV standing golfy hotel near all courses and overlooking the 1st and 18th of the Old.
EXP You're at the heart of the matter here. Nice sun-lounge and breakfast overlooking
the greens. Jack Nicklaus looms large. Reliable and quite classy Macdonald Hotel.
Restaurant (Italianate) recently ruched. Good packages.

22 ROOMS **Albany Hotel** 01334 477737 · **56 North Street** Townhouse hotel with
TEL · TV surprising number of rooms and beautiful back garden. 50% of rooms overlook
NO PETS and are individually (though not in a boutique sense) done; 3 have outside decks
MED.EX and there's a suite with a patio. Bar and basement restaurant, The Garden. A very
St Andrews kind of a hostelry.

13 ROOMS **Ogstons On North Street** www.ogstonsonnorthst.com · 01334 473387 ·
TEL · TV **127 North Street** Corner of Murray Park where there are numerous guest-house
MED.INX options. Boutique-ish rooms above restaurant and often-busy bar. Club room in
basement, the Oakrooms on street level is quite civilised café-bar. Comfy, contemporary rooms, perhaps best for students and their mates, rather than their
parents (club kicks in from 10pm, though the room is soundproofed).

20 RMS · TEL **Greyfriars** 01334 474906 · **129 North Street** And immediately adjacent to
TV · NO KIDS Ogstons (above), another bar/restaurant with rooms above with a similar offering.
NO PETS Perhaps even more self-consciously contemporary: a more recent makeover.
MED.INX Restaurant not bad; a busy, sports-on-TV kind of a billet for the night.

8 ROOMS **Dunvegan Hotel** www.dunvegan-hotel.com · 01334 473105 · **7 Pilmour**
TV **Place** If you like golf you'll like the Dunvegan and if you're on that kind of a holi-
MED.EX day, this, a stroll to both town and greens, is for you (of a modest budget). The
Willoughbys run a tidy and friendly house, bar and (The Claret Jug) restaurant. It's
well TripAdvised.

6 ROOMS **5 Pilmour Place** www.5pilmourplace.com · 01334 478665 Adjacent 18th
TV · NO PETS green of Old Course (and Dunvegan Hotel, above). Contemporary-style guest
MED.INX house with lounge. The Wrights have got it, well... right, and are notably obliging.
Great breakfast choice.

4 ROOMS **West Port** www.westport.co.uk · 01334 473186 Bottom of South St near the
CHP arch. Busy bar/restaurant with rooms; very St Andrews. Only 4 so book ahead. You
don't need to leave the premises to get the student-and-their-mates experience.
A Maclays Inn.

WHERE TO EAT

£25-35 ✓ **The Vine Leaf** 01334 477497 · 131 South Street Inauspicious entrance belies what has been for ooh, a very long time the best all-round restaurant in town. Eclectic menu covers all bases, including vegetarian and wines. Morag and Ian Hamilton know how to look after you and what you like (especially for pud). David Joy's calming pictures around the walls are for sale. Tue-Sat from 6.30pm.

£15-25 ✓ **Nahm-Jim** www.nahm-jim.co.uk · 01334 474000 · 62 Market Street Sandy and Bee's Thai (and Japanese) upstairs bistro with L'Orient lounge below put St Andrews itself on the food map when they were finalised in Gordon Ramsay's Best Thai UK programme in 2010. May be why it's always packed but authentic food and great service also underpin its reputation. Many famous visitors (well, golfers) in Bee's gallery. 7 days 12noon-12midnight (can close earlier).

<£15 ✓ **The Tailend Fish Bar** www.tailendrestaurant.co.uk · 01334 474070 · 130 Market Street The well-loved Tailend of Edinburgh's Leith Walk (216/EDINBURGH FISH & CHIPS) flipped over to St Andrews with a similar look and feel and commitment to good F&C served sizzling fresh. Contemporary design, takeaway out front, surprisingly spacious caff through the back and outside terrace. Many choices but it's haddock/cod 'n' chips, aint' it? 11.30am-10pm. 7 days.

£15-25 **The Doll's House** www.houserestaurants.com · 01334 477422 · Church Square Very central café/restaurant that caters well for kids (and their parents). Eclectic range, smiley people and tables outside in summer. Same people have **The Grill House** in St Mary's Place, a real townhouse with 3 different rooms and young staff. Both these bistros are routinely rammed. And they also have:

£15-25 **The Glasshouse** www.houserestaurants.com · 01334 473673 · 80 North Street Contemporary building with few tables downstairs and a few up. Bright, buzzy surroundings of metal, brick and glass. Mainly Italian (pasta and thin stoneoven pizza and specials). 7 days noon-10pm.

£25-35 **Balaka Bangladeshi Restaurant** www.balaka.com · 01334 474825 · 3 Alexandra Place One of those 'Best Curry in Scotland' winners. But as good as many in Edinburgh or Glasgow (they have Dil Se in Dundee; 902/DUNDEE RESTAURANTS). Methinks due a makeover (2011). Celebrated herb and spice garden out back which supplies others in St Andrews. Handily open later than most.

<£15 **Maisha** www.maisharestaurant.co.uk · 01334 476666 · 5 College Street Small Indian restaurant specialising in seafood. Haven't tried but seems a real deal. Reports, please. 7 days lunch and dinner (not Sun lunch).

<£15 **North Point** North Street Top of the street. Great little caff. Coffee, salads, home-made stuff – soup, scones, hot dishes; good vibe. 8.30am-5pm.

✓✓ **The Peat Inn** 01334 840206 15km southwest. Only 20 minutes to the best meal around. Report: 845/FIFE RESTAURANTS.

✓✓ **The Seafood Restaurant** 01334 479475 Top seafood, top view (Old Course and the sea). Report: 1319/SEAFOOD RESTAURANTS.

✓ **Grange Inn** 01334 472670 4km east off Anstruther road A917. Popular country pub with local reputation and new owners. Report: 1285/GASTROPUBS.

Janetta's 31 South Street Popular caff. 7 days till 5pm. Report: 1435/ICE CREAM.

853 10/P21
17 ROOMS
TEL · TV
DF
L
MED.EX-LOTS

✓✓ **Dalmunzie Castle** www.dalmunzie.com · 01250 885224 · Spittal o' Glenshee 3 km from Perth-Braemar road close to Glenshee ski slopes and good base for Royal Deeside without Deeside prices. 9-hole golf course for fun and the air. Highland-lodge feel: tasteful, comfortable, great attention to detail; a semi-chic retreat! Hills all around and burn besides; a truly peaceful outlook. Food mention in Michelin, notable wine list, bar-billiards room, great whisky bar. A fire in the hall!

854 10/P22
25+16
ROOMS
TEL · TV
DF
L
MED.EX-LOTS

>£35

✓ **Ballathie House** www.ballathiehousehotel.com · 01250 883268 · near Perth A true country-house hotel on the Tay that you fall in love with, especially if you hunt, shoot, fish. Comfortingly old-style, the river and the astonishing trees are the thing. Good dining, great fishing; good for a weekend away. 'Riverside' rooms are over the lawn (150m walk for breakfast; or room service) and uniform but you taste the Tay. Also cheaper, motel-like Sportsman's Lodge adjacent main house. Love the approach: red squirrels, copper beeches, golden corn. They're working hard to titivate the perhaps too lived-in splendour. **EAT** Chef Andrew Wilkie. Local and estate produce, especially beef/lamb.

855 10/M23
11 ROOMS
TEL · TV
DF
MED.EX

✓ **Royal Hotel** www.royalhotel.co.uk · 01764 679200 · Comrie Central square of cosy town, a surprisingly stylish small-town hotel. Refurbished 10 years ago so perhaps a tad TLC wouldn't go amiss. Excellent restaurant with good light, a bar and also a pub out back with ale and atmosphere. Bar food menu available all over and à la carte and specials in the dining room. Nice rugs and pictures. A pleasing touch of understated class in the county bit of the country. Both restaurant and bar food LO 9pm. Pub later.

856 10/N21
13 ROOMS
TV
NO KIDS
MED.INX

✓ **Craigatin House** www.craigatinhouse.co.uk · 01796 472478 · Pitlochry Gorgeous boutique B&B in, as they say, Highland Perthshire on main street (but the road north) of this tourist town. The house and courtyard (1820s) now transformed into a smart contemporary and comfortable retreat from Pitlochry's less tasteful aspects. Martin and Andrea Anderson are your obliging hosts. Rooms in both mansion and courtyard; great bathrooms. New breakfast and guest lounge built around a wood-burning stove. Patio and serene garden.

857 10/P22
98 ROOMS
TEL · TV
EXP

✓ **(Hilton) Dunkeld House** www.hilton.co.uk/dunkeld · 01350 727771 · Dunkeld Former home of Duke of Atholl, a very large, impressive country house on the banks of the Tay in beautiful grounds (some time-share) outside Dunkeld. Leisure complex with good pool, etc and many other activities laid on, eg. quad bikes, clay pigeons. Traditional dining. Fine for kids. Pleasant walks. Not cheap but often deals available. Rooms in old house best. Many weddings.

858 10/N22
11 ROOMS
TEL · TV
EXP

✓ **Fortingall House** 01887 830367 · near Aberfeldy Historic roadhouse hotel on the road to gorgeous Glen Lyon, 8km from Aberfeldy, one of the most beautiful Arts and Crafts villages in Scotland. Refurbished to a high, boutique-style standard. Adjacent the kirkyard and famous Fortingall Yew, the oldest tree in Europe. It has long had a big reputation for top gastro-pub dining and recently appointed chef Paul Newman (sic) continues the tradition in a delightful dining room. The Ewe Bar at the side is a sympatico spot. Sunday lunch.

859 10/N21
13 ROOMS
TEL · TV
DF
EXP

✓ **East Haugh House** www.easthaugh.co.uk · 01796 473121 · near Pitlochry On south approach to Pitlochry from A9, a mansion house built in the 18th century; part of the Atholl estate. Notable for hunting/shooting and especially fishing with a beat on the Tay and a full time ghillie, and for very decent food in dining room or Cosy Fisherman's bar. Family-run with popular proprietor Neil McGown cheffing for the Two Sisters restaurant and one of those daughters out front. Nice themed rooms especially up top, romantic with it (8 rooms have 4-posters). A top retreat near the Tay.
EAT Food taken seriously here. Fish/game: good sourcing; seasonality.

860 10/N21
10 ROOMS
MAR–NOV
TEL · TV
DF
L
MED.EX

✓ **Killiecrankie Hotel** www.killiecrankiehotel.co.uk · 01796 473220 · Killiecrankie 5km north of Pitlochry off A9 on B8079 signed Killiecrankie; near Blair Castle. Roadside inn long known for food with cosy rooms. Delightful garden supplying kitchen. Conscientiously run with a simple good taste. Henrietta Ferguson's cottage home from home will also be yours.
EAT Bar and conservatory seasonal menus and dining room with daily menu. All proper good food from chef Mark Easton.

861 10/N21
5 ROOMS
TV
MED.INX

✓ **Torrdarach House** www.torrdarach.co.uk · 01796 472136 · Pitlochry The big pink house above town (via Larchwood Rd off north main street) and almost in the country: they have their own wee woody glen. Complete contemporary makeover of old established B&B: light, modern rooms; lots of pictures. Free-range hens in garden and eggs for breakfast. Competitively priced. Family friendly.

862 10/R22
3 ROOMS
ATMOS
MED.INX

✓ **Ethie Castle** 01241 830434 · Inverkeilor near Arbroath 10km north of Arbroath off the A92 on the backroad to Lunan at a bend on the road marked Ethiebarns. An ancient sandstone castle dating from the 14th century and in very good nick. Home of the de Morgan family and also of the ghost of Cardinal Beaton. Fabulous public and bedrooms at your disposal; breakfast in the Tudor kitchen. Dinner by arrangement but Gordons and the But 'n' Ben are nearby (see below). Lovely gardens. This is a very superior guest house!

863 10/N23
6 ROOMS
TEL · DF
MED.INX

✓ **Yann's** 01764 650111 · Crieff Yannick and Shari Grospellier's restaurant with rooms: a bistro and a small mansion-house hotel on the Perth road out of town. This really is where to eat around here. Very French (Yann from Chamonix). A la carte, specials, grill menu and the très popular *pierrade* hot slates. Rooms lovely and not expensive. Book eating weekends, well in advance. Lunch and LO 9pm. Bistro closed Mon/Tue.

864 10/P23
34 ROOMS
TEL · TV
MED.INX

Huntingtower Hotel www.huntingtowerhotel.co uk · 01738 583771 near Perth Crieff road (1km off A85, 3km west of ring route A9 signed). Elegant, modernised mansionhouse outside town. Good gardens with spectacular copper beech and other trees. The tartan carpet. Subdued, panelled restaurant with traditional menu (ok lunch) and wine list. Businesslike service.

865 10/N21
20 ROOMS
TEL · TV
NO PETS
MED.INX

Pine Trees Hotel www.pinetreeshotel.co.uk · 01796 472121 · Pitlochry A safe and sophisticated haven in visitor-ville – it's above the town and above all that (there are many mansions here). Take Larchwood Rd off north end of main street. Woody gardens, woody interior. Scots owners. Very traditional but with taste (nice rugs).

866 10/M22
40 ROOMS
TEL · TV
L
MED.INX

Kenmore Hotel www.kenmorehotel.com · 01887 830205 · Kenmore
Ancient coaching inn (16th century) in quaint conservation village. Good prospect
for golfing with preferential rates at the adjacent Taymouth Castle and fishing. On
the river (Tay) itself with terrace and restaurant overlooking it. Layout bitty, food
so-so but real fires (and Robert Burns was definitely here).

867 10/Q21
10 ROOMS
TEL · TV
NO PETS · L
CHP

Glen Clova Hotel www.clova.com · 01575 550350 Near end of Glen Clova,
one of the great Angus glens (1582/GLENS) on B955 25km north of Kirriemuir. A
walk/climb/country-retreat hotel; very comfy. Superb walking nearby. Often full.
Also bunkhouse accommodation behind. 3 luxury lodges out back have hot tubs
and fluffy downies. This place a very civilised Scottish inn in the hills and great
value. The lovely Claire is everywhere.

868 10/N22
7 ROOMS
TEL · DF
CHP

Dalshian Guest House www.dalshian.co.uk · 01796 472173 · near
Pitlochry Historic house in lovely gardens just off the A9 6km south towards
Ballinluig (road signed Croftinloan and Dalshian). Martin and Heather Walls' old
hoose and their hospitalities make for a very civilised retreat. Good fishing prospect. Logierait Inn nearby for dinner (see below). Family friendly. Very good value.

869 10/M21
28 ROOMS
TEL · TV
L
MED.INX

Dunalastair Hotel www.dunalastair.co.uk · 01882 632323 · Kinloch
Rannoch Dominates one side of cute Victorian village square on this road
(B8019) that stabs into the wild heart of Scotland. 30km Pitlochry on A9 (station
for Edinburgh train) and 30km Rannoch station further up (station for Glasgow
train). Schiehallion overlooks and must be climbed (1976/MUNROS); many other
easy hikes. Welcoming Highland lodge that can point you in the direction of many
outdoor activities. Good bar.

√ √ √**Gleneagles** 01764 662231 Report: 1092/COUNTRY-HOUSE HOTELS.

√ √ √**Crieff Hydro** 01764 655555 Superb, especially for kids.
Quintessentially Scottish. Report: 1098/HOTELS THAT WELCOME KIDS.

√ √**Kinloch House** 01250 884237 · Blairgowrie 5km west of Blairgowrie
on A923 to Dunkeld. Quintessential Perthshire comfort and joy. Report:
1096/COUNTRY-HOUSE HOTELS.

√ √**The Bield at Blackruthven** 01738 583238 Report: 1221/RETREATS.

√ √**The Barley Bree** Muthill · 01764 681451 Report: 1138/ROADSIDE INNS.

√**The Inn on the Tay** Grandtully · 01887 840760 Report: 1146/ROADSIDE
INNS.

RESTAURANTS

870 10/N24
>£35

√ √+ **Andrew Fairlie at Gleneagles** www.gleneagles.com · 01764
694267 The two-Michelin landmark restaurant where you'd expect to
find it, in Scotland's best hotel (1092/COUNTRY-HOUSE HOTELS). Deep in the interior, well laid out and lit, a room where we come to experience as well as eat
ingredients that seem both effortlessly and masterfully matched, dish after dish.
Tasting menus and à la carte. With perfectly judged, mouth-watering morsels, tea
and après. Andrew, always there, both in the kitchen and on the wall in a portrait
among the Archie Forrests. You're in those good (big) hands. Dinner only. Closed
Sun and Jan.

871 10/P23
£25-35

✓ ✓ **Deans @ Let's Eat** www.letseatperth.co.uk · 01738 643377 · **Kinnoull Street, Perth** Perth's long-established premier and probably most popular eaterie. Fine contemporary dining and great value – the business-lunch deal (£14 for 2 courses) is the business and there's a great 4-course set-menu dinner for £16 at TGP. Must book weekends. Chef/patron Willie Deans very much in charge. Tue-Sat lunch and LO 9.30pm.

872 10/P23
£25-35

✓ **63 Tay Street** www.63taystreet.co.uk · 01738 441451 · **Perth** On the new riverside road and walk. Graeme Pallister from Parklands hotel (see Perth) where there is another 63, took over this premier Perth food stop some time ago and it continues to win awards. Their 5-course dinner with fancy bits (£35) is a must-book at weekends. Tue–Sat lunch, LO 9pm.

873 10/P22
£25-35

✓ **Gordon's** www.gordonsrestaurant.co.uk · 01241 830364 · **Inverkeilor** Halfway between Arbroath and Montrose on the main street. A restaurant with rooms (4) which has won loadsa accolades for Gordon and son Gary in the kitchen (including no. 1 TripAdvisor restaurant in Inverkeilor!). It's been here for 25 seriously good years! Splendid people doing good Franco-Scot cooking. Seasonal menu. May lack atmosphere but it's the best meal for miles. Lunch (Wed-Fri and Sun) and dinner. Closed Mon (Sun in winter). LO 8.45pm. Best book.

874 10/P23
£15-25

✓ **Apron Stage** 01738 8288885 · **King Street, Stanley** 3km from A9 just north of Perth. Shona and Jane's tiny local but magic bistro in the main street of sleepy village. It was chef Shona Drysdale who along with Tony Heath established Let's Eat (above) – this is where Shona came for a quieter life. Only 6 tables, so tight space and limited choices, but simply good. Fri lunch and dinner Wed-Sat.

875 10/R22
LL
£15-25

✓ **The But 'n' Ben** 01241 877223 · **Auchmithie** 2km off A92 north from Arbroath, 8km to town or 4km by cliff-top walk. Village on cliff top where a ravine leads to a small cove and quay. Adjacent cottages converted into a cosy restaurant. Menus vary but all very Scottish and informal, emphasising fresh fish and seafood. The brilliant couthy creation of Margaret Horn after 30 years and still in the family, it's now run by son Angus (in the kitchen) and Margo out front assuring a warm welcome and consistency for a huge loyal following. Lunch and dinner with famous Sunday high tea (may have to book). Closed Tue.

876 10/M23
£15-25

✓ **Deil's Cauldron** www.deilscauldron.co.uk · 01764 670352 · **Comrie** On bend of the A85 main road through town and corner of the Glen Lednock road. For night on 10 years Katy and Brian Healy have run their cottage restaurant quietly and effectively. A hugely popular destination for lunch, dinner (especially steaks) and the eclectic tapas menu in the bar. Seriously good wine list; cosy ambience. Don't know why I took so long to tick it. Lunch Tue-Sun, dinner Tue-Sat.

877 10/Q22
<£15

✓ **88º** 01575 57888 · **17 High Street, Kirriemuir** Actually on main square. Johanna and Philip Woodhead's labour of love deli/café is a very welcome find hereabouts. Artisan and proper cheese, chocolates, hand-made specials and great coffee. Hot food and deli platters all conscientiously done. (Also opened in Forfar with the same format in summer '11). 9.30am-5pm (from 10am Sun). Closed Mon/Tue. Till 9pm every other Fri.

878 10/N23
£15-25

✓ **Delivino** 01764 655665 · **6 King Street, Crieff** Just off the main street. As it says on the tin, a deli counter and wine bar, but mainly an Italian bistro where ladies may lunch. Great thin, crispy, wood-oven pizza. Perfectly Crieff! 9.30am-7pm (8pm Fri/Sat, earlier in winter). Sun 11-4pm.

879 10/N22 ✓ **Logierait Inn** 01796 482423 · near Ballinluig 8km south of Pitlochry. An
<£15 inn (and self-catering lodges) by the River Tay 2km from the main A9 on
A827 to Aberfeldy. Reputation for food is such that it has fairly limited opening
hours but its many rooms are always busy and you may have to book. Excellent
gastropub grub. Wed-Sun. Evenings only LO 8.30pm; Sun lunch.

880 10/N23 **Lounge** 01764 654407 · Crieff West end of main street. As it says, a lounge,
<£15 the uptown extension of Yann's (see Hotels, above) keeping even more Perthshire
people happy and well fed. Here you come to graze and sup, not pig out. Has that
black, purple and mirrored look. Another good thing about Crieff.

881 10/P22 **Cargill's** 01250 876735 · Lower Mill Street, Blairgowrie The fact that this
£15-25 bistro, tucked away behind the square, not quite on the riverside, has been here
for nigh on 10 years and has survived, never mind thrived, says a lot. It clearly
works and on a recent visit I liked everything on its classic bistro blackboard (and
wished I could have stayed for dinner). 7 days. Lunch and LO 9pm.

882 10/P22 **Howie's Bistro** www.howiesbistro.com · 01350 728847 · Dunkeld No
£15-25 relation to the Scottish Howie's chain but the *soi-disant* and, in Dunkeld, much-
needed creation of Graham Howie. Serving reliably good fare all day and seasonal
evening menu, all home-made. 7 days 10.30am-10pm.

883 10/N21 **Fern Cottage** 01796 473840 · Ferry Road, Pitlochry 100m from the south
£15-25 end of main street. It's been here a while but I always missed it. There's a couple
of good B&Bs in Pitlochry (see above) so you'll need somewhere decent to eat and
this is it. Scottish-Mediterranean. It is a cottage. Lunch and dinner.

884 10/N21 **Port-na-Craig** www.portnacraig.com · 01796 472777 · Pitlochry Just by
£25-35 the Pitlochry Theatre, cottage-style bistro with courtyard in a 17th-century inn.
Informal and friendly with a Modern European menu. Especially handy pre- and
post-theatre.

The Best Places To Stay In & Around Dundee

This is perhaps a controversial statement but as of writing I don't feel there is much to recommend among the hotels of Dundee. There were only 7 in the last edition but having looked at them all again (1 had closed), I've decided to incur the wrath of Dundonians and declare that there are only a couple of places that measure up (until the Malmaison opens).

885 10/Q23
151 ROOMS
TEL · TV
NO PETS
EXP

✓ **The Apex** www.apexhotels.co.uk · 01382 202404 · West Victoria Dock Road There are 4 Apex hotels in Edinburgh (75/MAJOR HOTELS) and 3 in London, all good 4/5-star business and leisure options. Here in Dundee this 21st-century edifice is still in a league of its own and after some years now it's still the only place to stay. Overlooking both bridge and new dock and with good detail in the modern facilities, including the Yu spa and pool. As a business stopover it's good value compared to elsewhere. Metro restaurant also one of the city's reliably good eats. Rooms facing the firth and out to sea are best. Big waterfront developments are coming, mostly nearer the bridge, including the much-heralded V&A. Apex will service all you new visitors. The beauty of the Apex location is its urban serenity with dreamy views of a still non-bustling waterfront.

886 10/Q23
11 ROOMS
(9 EN SUITE)
CHP

Fisherman's Tavern www.fishermanstavern.co.uk · 01382 775941 · Fort Street, Broughty Ferry Not a hotel, it's a pub but in the absence of others, repair to the Ferry (20 minutes by car) down by the river and the sea. These modest 17th-century fisherman's cottages were converted to a pub in 1827. Rooms above and adjacent cottages. Excellent real ales and pub menu, but also near the Ship Inn (894/DUNDEE RESTAURANTS) which is preferred for eats.

The Best Places To Eat In & Around Dundee

887
10/Q23
£15-25

✓ **Jute at Dundee Contemporary Arts** www.dca.org.uk · 01382 909246 · Perth Road Jute, the downstairs bar/restaurant of Dundee's acclaimed arts centre, DCA, is the most convivial place in town to eat – no contest. Chef Chris Wilson offers a menu far superior to any old arts venue, especially one which is all things to all people. Bar and restaurant: your rendezvous in Dundee. A good kids' menu. Book weekends. All day 10.30am-9.30pm.

888
10/Q23
£15-25

✓ **Bon Appétit** www.bonappetit-dundee.com · 01382 809000 · Exchange Street Near Commercial St. Owners Audrey and John Batchelor spent years in France then returned to Dundee to 'make a difference'. Well, they have: in a culinary desert and with no French chefs they created an authentic French café with food as good as any bistro de la gare. All Francophile faves from croques to crèmes done comme ça. Menu changes every 6 weeks. All excellent value, especially their early-evening menu. Lunch and LO 10pm. Closed Sun.

889
10/Q23
£25-35

✓ **Blue Marlin** www.thebluemarlin.co.uk · 01382 534001 · Camperdown Street, City Quay Part of the city's emerging Quayside quarter and its only proper seafood restaurant. Decamped from an unlikely location in Monifieth and too early to review at TGP but Steve Hyatt comes with fishy and foodie credentials so expect to dine well. Check hours.

890
10/Q23
£15-25

✓ **The Playwright** www.theplaywright.co.uk · 01382 223113 · Tay Square
On the square adjacent and taking its point of reference from the estimable
Dundee Repertory Theatre, this upstairs bistro has plugged the informal but in-
formed contemporary-dining gap in Dundee and gets good notices from public
and critics alike. Dundee's Brian Cox has pride of place (and he does, too). Good
Modern British cookery. Lunch and LO 9/10pm. Closed Sun.

891
10/Q23
£15-35

✓ **The Tasting Rooms** www.thetastingrooms.com · 01382 224188 ·
2 Whitehall Crescent Behind the Caird Hall. A 2-floor wine bar/restaurant
on a central corner. Decent contemporary food simply put; this is foodie territory.
Lunch, pre-theatre and LO 9.30pm.

892
10/Q23
£25-35

✓ **Piccolo** www.piccolodundee.co.uk · 01382 207149 · 210 Perth Road An
intimate dining experience with chef/patron Athol Shepherd in the hot
kitchen, cramped but civilised out front. Italian-ish including pizza, kind of place to
go and many do, so book. Dinner only. Closed Sun/Mon.

893
10/Q23
£15-25

✓ **The Agacan** 01382 644227 · 113 Perth Road Fabled bistro for Turkish
eats and wine (though only 'red' or 'white'). OTT frontage, much (rotated) art
on the walls; and the furniture. Bohemian ambience. You smell the meat (veggies
go meze). 5-9/10pm. Closed Mon.

894
10/Q23
£15-25
ATMOS

✓ **The Ship Inn** 01382 779176 · Broughty Ferry On the front. Weathered by
the River Tay since the 1800s, this cosy pub has sustained smugglers, fishermen and foody folk alike. Bar and upstairs restaurant; no-nonsense Scottish menu
and a fabulous picture window overlooking the Tay. Lunch and bar food till
7.30pm, restaurant 8.30pm (9.30pm weekends). Small but...

895
10/Q23
£15-25

✓ **Malabar** www.malabardundee.co.uk · 01382 646888 · 304 Perth Road
Quite far up the road. More than a few Indian restaurants in Dundee, including Dil Se (below), but for authenticity and sympatico service and surroundings,
Malabar has the (soft) edge. Avowedly south of the subcontinent, so mellow
sauces and good seafood curries. Evenings only. LO 10pm. Closed Mon.

896
10/R23
>£35

✓ **Fraser's** 01382 730890 · 594 Brook Street, Broughty Ferry Here for
years but something of a local secret. Chef/owner Dick Fraser and family keep
this place almost as a hobby, only opening on Fri/Sat for set-price (£38 at TGP) 5-
course dinner: salad, soup and 4 choice starters, mains, etc. Top cheeses! Modern
Scottish dining real good and excellent wine selection. Must book.

897
10/Q23
<£15

✓ **The Parrot Café** 01382 206277 · 91 Perth Road Many caffs around here
but Val Ireland holds her own coz she makes her own (bread, cakes, scones,
soups, specials) with a regular following of students and ladies who lunch and tea.
No cellophaned muffins in sight. 2 delicious hot-lunch options. The craft of home
baking is alive here and one day, I'll be back. Tue-Sat 10am-5pm (4pm Sat).

898
10/Q23
<£15

✓ **T. Ann Cake** 01382 540138 · 27 Exchange Street In a street of good food
options (Bon Appétit above and the Cheesery), this charmingly named caff
(owned by Ann, of course) has good cred and good crit, both savoury and sweet.
Individual and cool as. 10am-5pm (4pm Sat). Closed Sun/Mon.

899
10/Q23
<£15

✓ **Fisher & Donaldson** www.fisheranddonaldson.com · Whitehall
Street, off Nethergate The best traditional bakers in Scotland (1425/BAK-
ERS) with busy tearoom and 2 other Dundee branches. Snacks and all their fine
fare from maccy cheese to chocolates. Mon-Sat 8am-4.45pm (shop till 5.15pm).

900
10/Q23
<£15

Visocchi's 01382 779297 · 40 Gray Street, Broughty Ferry Following from the original Kirriemuir caff (now no relation): a busy tratt and ice-cream parlour. Over 3 generations they've made mouth-watering Italian ice creams (amaretto, **marsala, etc.**) alongside home-made pasta (and less good pizza) and snacks. Hard work and integrity evident here. Till 8pm (4pm Tue, 10pm Fri/Sat). Closed Mon.

901
10/Q23
<£15

The Parlour 01382 203588 · West Port Opposite the Globe Bar, this wee caff at the end of the row of shops is easily missed but loyal locals and students pack it for home-made light food, soups, salads and big slabs of cakes. Lunch and LO 5pm, 7pm Sat. Closed Sun. Good vegetarian and they have their own cookbook.

902
10/Q23
£15-£25

Dil Se www.dilse-restaurant.co.uk · 01382 221501 · 99-101 Perth Road Bangladeshi restaurant; on two floors and food from all over the subcontinent but it's for curries, ain't it? Related to Balaka in St Andrews, this is just a bit smarter than the competition. Lunch and dinner Sun-Thu, all day Fri and Sat. Till late!

903
10/Q23
£15-£25

The Byzantium www.byzantiumrestaurant.com · 01382 221946 · 13 Hawkshill In a modern glass case in the West Port area, a contemporary-kinda-predictable Mediterranean menu but with good service and not so steep prices. Lunch and LO 10pm. Closed Mon/Tue.

904
10/R23
L
£15-25

The Glass Pavilion 01382 732738 · The Esplanade, Broughty Ferry Over-looking the Tay but tricky to find and maybe easier to walk east from Broughty Ferry Castle and harbour, about 1.5km. Food so-so but the glass pavilion is a modern reconstruction of an Art Deco gem. Pictures of old Broughty Ferry beach and Esplanade are worth the trip alone. Nice coffee and terrace. 7 days. 9.30am-10pm.

905
10/Q23
£15-25

Dundee Rep Café Bar Restaurant 01382 206699 · Tay Square Part of the celebrated Rep, a café in the foyer worth a visit in its own right for food and civilised surroundings. Loads better than many cultural caffs with serious options in à la carte and blackboard specials. Lunch and LO 9pm. Closed Sun/Mon (if no show).

If you're in Perth...

906 10/P23
34 ROOMS
TEL · TV
MED.INX

WHERE TO STAY
Huntingtower Hotel www.huntingtowerhotel.co.uk · 01738 583771 Crieff road (1km off A85, 3km west of ring route A9 signed). Decent modernised mansion-house hotel outside town. Good gardens. Subdued, panelled restaurant; decent menu (folk come for lunch) and wine list. Business-like service.

15 ROOMS
TEL · TV
MED.EX

£25-35

Parklands www.theparklandshotel.com · 01738 622451 · 2 St Leonard's Bank Near station overlooking expansive green parkland of North Inch. Reasonable town mansion hotel with a reputation for food under chef/proprietor Graeme Pallister who cooks at 63 Tay Street (872/PERTHSHIRE).
EAT Smaller, 63-type set-price menu (£35; must book). The larger room, No. 1 The Bank, has eclectic menu; fusion going on. Top hotel dining in this town.

23 ROOMS
MED.INX

New County Hotel www.newcountyhotel.com · 01738 623355 · 22 County Place And new it is, all spruced up and probably as close as Perth hotels come to 'boutique'. Comfy bedrooms and public areas include Gavin's, the pub and the estimable Opus One restaurant (2 AA Rosettes and tries hard to keep them). Busy street and tricky parking but fine in a county-town-chic kind of way.

39 ROOMS
TEL · TV
MED.INX

Royal George www.theroyalgeorgehotel.co.uk · 01738 624455 · Tay Street By Perth Bridge over the Tay to the A93 to Blairgowrie. Georgian proportions and nostalgic niceties, all unapologetically old-style. Big on high tea, especially on Sundays. Mums, farmers and visiting clergy get comfy here.

WHERE TO EAT

£25-35 ✓ **Café Tabou** 01738 446698 · 4 St John's Place Central corner of a pedestrianised square; from outside and in, it feels like an unassuming café de la place; locals love it. French staff, French wine and a reasonable pass at French country food. Mon-Sat lunch and LO 9.30pm.

£15-25 ✓ **Sante** www.sante-winebar.co.uk · 01738 449710 · 10 South St John's Place From the makers of Breizh (Les Tabourels) comes, with a new partner, a wine bar/restaurant that gives Perth a chic place to hang out and graze. Open all day, brasserie-style, from coffee to nightcap (great by-the-glass selection) and excellent plats and plats du jour. 7 days 9.30am-10/11pm.

£15-25 ✓ **Breizh** 01738 444427 · 28 High Street Breizh (pronounced Brez), the Breton name for Brittany, is a buzzy eaterie: galettes galore, salads, grillades, good pizza and home-made puds. Good food all-round. 7 days 9am-9/9.30pm.

£15-25 **Reids** 01738 636310 · 32 High Street Next to Breizh, another good cafe/restaurant but with a Scottish – and unlike others in this town, an authentic Scottish – flavour. Food though is eclectic, including Italian and all home-made including the bread (which is for sale). Great casual dining! 7 days early-late.

£15-25 **Keracher's** www.kerachers-restaurant.co.uk · 01738 449777 · Corner of South & Scott Streets Upstairs diner a surprisingly pleasant room given the unprepossessing entrance. Run by notable local seafood supplier. Great fish and seafood of course; some meat and vegetarian choice. The right ingredients and service. Dinner only Tue-Sat. LO 'depends'.

£25-35 **The North Port** www.thenorthport.co.uk · 01738 580867 · 8 North Port Small, cosy, pub-like bistro behind the Concert Hall. Good, family traditional home cooking goes down a treat: excellent chips, for example, with a well-hung steak. Tue-Sat, lunch and LO 9/10pm.

£15-25 **Tabla** 01738 444630 · 173 South Street Credible Indian under the Kumars. North and south cuisine. Farm-grown spices from family in India. Open kitchen. A big plus for ethnic eating in Perth. 7 days lunch and LO 10.30pm (Sun from 3pm).

£15-25 **Grand'Italia** 01738 626016 · 33 George Street Mario Digna's excellent ristorante in the town centre does all that it says on the tin, ie the menu outside. Possibly the best Italian food in the shire. 7 days 12noon-9.30pm.

<£15 **Holdgate's Fish Teas** South Street Here for over 100 years! Through the back an unreconstructed classic. Well sourced haddock; their fritters making a comeback. 12noon-8.30pm.

✓✓ **Deans @ Let's Eat** 01738 643377 871/PERTHSHIRE RESTAURANTS.

✓ **63 Tay Street** 01738 441451 872/PERTHSHIRE RESTAURANTS.

Tourist Office 01738 636103 · Lower City Mills Open all year.

The Best Hotels & Restaurants In The North East

Excludes Aberdeen (except Marcliffe), see p. 174. Speyside listings on p. 178.

907 8/S19
42 ROOMS
TEL · TV
MED.EX-LOTS

✓ ✓ **Marcliffe of Pitfodels** www.marcliffe.com · 01224 861000 · **North Deeside Road** En route to Royal Deeside 5km from Union St. On the edge of town, a successful mix of intimate and spacious, the old (mansion house) and the newer wing. Personally run by the Spence family: Stewart Spence the consummate hotelier. His many pics on the piano with the famous (both Margarets – the princess and Mrs Thatcher; and that other T, The Trump) attest to this hotel's enduring primacy. Excellent restaurant and breakfast in light conservatory with nice courtyard and terrace overlooking gardens. Spa facilities but no pool. Honeymoon suites are fab and there are many weddings and rollicking Aberdonian functions. This understated hotel caters for all and is unquestionably one of the best all-round hotels in Scotland. I should declare that Stuart always ensures I'm very well and discreetly looked after when I'm here but it is always a pleasure.

908 8/Q20
12 ROOMS
FEB-DEC
TEL · TV
EXP-LOTS

>£35

✓ ✓ **Darroch Learg** www.darrochlearg.co.uk · 01339 755443 · **Ballater** On main A93 at edge of town. The family Franks maintain high standards at this Deeside mansion, continuing their longtime reputation for food. With a relaxed ambience, understated style and excellent conservatory dining room, it's a Deeside destination. Oft-awarded chef David Mutter has been there since '95, a long time in chef world. Some great views of grounds (8 rooms at the front) and Grampians. No bar, but civilised drinks before and après. They work hard but for us it's effortless comfort and style, an antidote to the manufactured hospitality so commonplace. They also run the Station Restaurant in Ballater (1384/TEAROOMS). **EAT** One of best restaurants in the North East. Great wine list. Nice garden view.

909 8/R20
20 ROOMS
+ SELF-
CATERING
TEL · TV
DF
ATMOS
MED.EX

✓ ✓ **Raemoir House** www.raemoir.com · 01330 824884 · **Banchory** 5km north from town via A980 off main street. Romantic, quirky country mansion with old-fashioned, very individual comfy rooms given contemporary details. Flowers everywhere, candles at night. Stable annex and self-catering apartments. Extensive grounds (helicopter pad). New owner Neil Rae breathing fresh life, is very hands-on; you will be looked after. In the kitchen David Littlewood devises uncomplicated, delicious dining. There's lots of public space to slouch in. Staff largely local and all friendly! This place has the perfect peace and quiet.

910 8/S18
22 ROOMS
(5 IN LODGE)
TEL · TV
MED.EX

✓ ✓ **Meldrum House** www.meldrumhousegolf.co.uk · 01651 872294 · **Oldmeldrum** 1km from village, 30km north of Aberdeen via A947 Banff road. Immediately impressive chunk of Scottish baronial set amid new 18-hole golf course (private membership, but guests can use) and a lake with swans. Rooms large with atmosphere and nice furnishings, many original antiques and period pictures. New lodge with contemporary rooms in stable block opposite. A lot of cash has gone into restoring this landmark Aberdeenshire hotel to its former glory: the deluxe choice for business (especially whisky industry) and the golfing fraternity. Expect weddings. Nice afternoon tea. Surprisingly inexpensive.

911 8/R19
30 ROOMS
TEL · TV
L
EXP

✓ **Pittodrie House** www.macdonaldhotels.co.uk · 01467 681444 · **Pitcaple** A large family mansion house on an estate in one of the best bits of Aberdeenshire with Bennachie above (1966/HILLS). 30km Aberdeen; well signed. Comfortable rooms look out on verdant lawns and great trees. Exquisite walled garden 500m from house (911/GARDENS) and many walks around. A Macdonald hotel (possibly their best) with very individual rooms in old house and a new extension out back. Period pictures, great whisky bar. Many weddings!

912
8/R17
5 ROOMS
TV · DF
MED.INX

£15-25

✓ **The County Hotel** www.thecountyhotel.com · 01261 815353 · **Banff** Eric and Vida Pantel's love letter from France. Notable mainly for food in dear sleepy Banff. Bistro, restaurant and bar (lunches and bar suppers Mon-Sat). Menu has tartiflette, proper terrine and salade champêtre. Burgers et al in the bar but the food here is quite a find; an appreciative letter from Alex Salmond is one of many flapping on the noticeboard by the door. Rooms basic but charmant.
EAT Where to eat on this long stretch of coast. Eric makes and bakes everything.

913 8/Q20
6 ROOMS
TEL · TV
GF · DF
MED.INX

✓ **The Auld Kirk** 01339 755762 · **Ballater** On Braemar road heading out of town. It is indeed an auld kirk and Peter Graydon and Tony Fuell make the most of the ecclesiastical shapes and ambience. Bedrooms (2 standards) are taste-ful, contemporary boutique-style. Good reputation for dinner in purply-chande-liered vestry (closed Sun). AK is a good find but was for sale at TGP.

914 8/T19
30 ROOMS
TV · TEL
MED.INX
£25-35

Udny Arms 01358 789444 · **Newburgh** A975 off A90. Village pub once and now again, famous for food. New, independent owners rebuilding reputation and improving rooms. Golf course Cruden Bay (2074/GREAT GOLF) 16km north and walks beside Ythan estuary (1761/WILDLIFE).
EAT Lunch Thu-Mon, dinner LO 9pm. Sticky Toffee Pudding said to be invented here.

915 8/Q20
45 ROOMS
TEL · TV
NO PETS
MED.INX-EX

Hilton Craigendarroch www.hilton.co.uk/craigendarroch · 01339 755858 · **Ballater** On the Braemar road (A93). Part of a country-club/time-share operation with elegant dining, good leisure facilities and discreet resort-in-the-woods feel. 2 restaurants: an informal one by the pool (like a leisure-centre caff) and the self-conscious Oaks (Thu-Sun) – no Topshop tops here, please. Lodges can be available on short lets, a good idea for a group holiday or weekend. All nice for kids.

916 8/S18
3 ROOMS
TEL · TV · CHP

The Red Garth www.redgarth.com · 01651 872353 · **Oldmeldrum** This family-run inn (signed from main road system) has only 3 rooms but it's great value; bar meals are very popular locally. Nice flowers. Very Aberdeenshire.

917 8/R18
18 RMS · TEL
TV · NO PETS
MED.INX

Castle Hotel www.castlehotel.uk.com · 01466 792696 · **Huntly** Behind the spooky, eyeless ruin of Huntly Castle; take the B9022 Portsoy road off the A96 for 2km, then signed. Former dowager house of the Dukes of Gordon, family-run and not bad value for the faded grandeur and the setting. Nice period feel.

918 8/R19
12 ROOMS
TEL · TV
CHP

Grant Arms www.grantarmshotel.com · 01467 651226 · **Monymusk** This village inn on a remarkable square is a good base for walking, the Castle Trail (1786/CASTLES; 1844/COUNTRY HOUSES) and fishing (rights on the Don). Rooms in hotel and 6 chalets around a courtyard. Good ambience; decent grub in the pub.

RESTAURANTS

919
8/T18
>£35

✓ ✓ **Eat On The Green** www.eatonthegreen.co.uk · 01651 842337 · **Udny Green** Former pub, now a restaurant on a cute village green. Folk come from miles for this celebratory, unpretentious food that's great value. Chef/proprietor Craig Wilson has cooked for Alex Salmond, Sir Sean and Scotland but he's always here to cook for you (though see 943/ABERDEEN RESTAURANTS). Book especially for Saturday night prix fixe: £49 at TGP. Wed-Sun lunch, LO 9pm.

920
8/Q20
£25-35

✓ ✓ **The Green Inn** www.green-inn.com · 01339 755701 · **Victoria Road, Ballater** Small frontage opens into conservatory out back. The O'Hallorans maintain and continue to raise the reputation of this Deeside destina-tion for dining. Understated and dependable. Simple, excellent, proper food. Book weekends. 3 inexpensive rooms upstairs. Dinner only Mon-Sat 7-9pm.

921 8/S20
£15-25
✓ **Cowshed** www.cowshedrestaurant.co.uk · 01330 820813 · Banchory Just outside this expanding Deeside hub on Raemore road, essentially in the country – you look to the hills. Graham Buchan's light restaurant and cook school has a no-frills menu ('beef', 'salmon', 'quiche') described with ingredients. Local and lovely! Lunch and LO 9.30pm (Sun 7pm). Closed Mon/Tue.

922 8/S20
£15-25
✓ **Buchanan's** www.buchananfood.com · 01330 826530 · Banchory Turn right at Tesco as you enter town from Aberdeen; 1km signed. Adjacent Woodend Barn arts centre (home to an eclectic, quality mix of music, theatre and film), the bistro in the barn is a contemporary, urbane, informed eaterie on the edge of Banchory, the prospering heart of Royal Deeside. Val and Calum Buchanan have an enlightened and shop/grow approach (there are allotments out back) and this airy bistro demonstrates the best kind of rural re-creation. 7 days. 9am-10pm.

923 8/S20
£25-35
✓ **The (Art Deco) Carron Restaurant** www.carron-restaurant.co.uk · 01569 760460 · 20 Carron Street, Stonehaven Discreet location off main street in a fantastic and faithfully restored Art Deco building, now for sale at TGP. The lighting could be softer but they don't make 'em like that any more. A Modern Scottish menu, and friendly and efficient service. Closed Sun/Mon.

924 8/S20
£15-25
✓ **Milton Restaurant** www.themilton.co.uk · 01330 844566 On A93 Royal Deeside road 4km east of Banchory opposite the entrance to Crathes (1494/GARDENS; 1845/COUNTRY HOUSES). Contemporary restaurant in old steading adjacent craft village, event field and railway (sic). Light and pleasant space. All-day menu so they cater for everything (and rather well). Mon-Sat 9.30am-9pm (later weekends, 5pm Mon/Tue). Sun 10am-5pm. Can be awash with weddings.

925 8/T19
L
£15-25
Cock & Bull www.thecockandbull.co.uk · 01358 743249 · Balmedie On A90, 20km north of Aberdeen. Atmospheric roadside pub long a fixture here but increasing reputation for grub and winning awards; a strong team in the kitchen. Very pubby and intimate, oak beams, etc. Always busy. Food 12noon-9pm 7 days.

926 8/R19
£15-25
Gadies www.gadiesrestaurant.com · 01464 851573 · Oyne 3km from A96 north of Inverurie. Robin and Jan Hobbs's delightful café/restaurant in wide countryside below Bennachie. Informal dining in airy room adjacent their shop/gallery. Local sourcing. Menu easy on the eye and pocket. I was happy to eventually find this place; so will you be. 10am-5pm (9pm Thu-Sat); 11.30am-7pm Sun.

927 10/S22
£15-25
The Quay 01674 672821 · 1 Wharf Street, Montrose The road leading to the harbour. Montrose has a contemporary bistro which hits all the spots (although I haven't tried it). Open surprisingly late: is there something about Montrose we don't know? 11.30am-12midnight (till 1am Fri/Sat). Closed Mon/Tue.

✓ **Tolbooth** Stonehaven Report: 1323/SEAFOOD RESTAURANTS.

✓ **Lairhillock Inn** near Stonehaven Report: 944/ABERDEEN RESTAURANTS; 1295/GASTROPUBS.

✓ **The Black-Faced Sheep** Aboyne Report: 1388/TEAROOMS.

✓ **The Creel Inn** Catterline Report: 1293/GASTROPUBS.

✓ **The Raemoir Garden Centre** Report: 2225/GARDEN CENTRES.

✓ **The Falls of Feugh** Banchory Report: 1381/TEAROOMS.

The Best Places To Stay In & Around Aberdeen

✓ ✓ **Marcliffe of Pitfodels** www.marcliffe.com · 01224 861000 · **North Deeside Road** Aberdeen's premier hotel: nothing else is remotely close for comfort and service. Report: 907/NORTHEAST HOTELS.

928 8/T19
79 RMS · TEL
TV · NO PETS
LOTS
£25-35

✓ **Malmaison** www.malmaison.com · 01224 327370 · **49 Queen's Road** Main road west from Union St, 2km from centre, a welcome find in Aberdeen. Usual design values of the brand here put to notably good use. Excellent, ambient. ESPA spa, no pool. Rooms cosy and cool; you might say seductive. **EAT** Large, well-laid-out brasserie: you dine surrounded by wine; meat in the larder. Charcoal grill and signature home-grown and local menu.

929 8/T19
7 ROOMS
TEL · TV
NO KIDS
NO PETS
CHP

✓ **The Globe Inn** www.travelodge.co.uk · 01224 624258 · **15 Silver Street** Rooms above the Globe, the civilised pub in a street off Union St (1320/GASTROPUBS). Pub has good reputation for ales, food (and does live music Tuesday and weekends, so no early to bed). Accommodation is reasonably priced and very serviceable. Breakfast is continental and comes on a pre-packed tray with flasks – not a strong point. Since decent value and individuality are hard to find in Aberdeen, book ahead. Parking is cheap inside nearby square.

930 8/S20
39 ROOMS
TEL · TV
NO PETS · L
MED.EX

Maryculter House Hotel www.maryculterhousehotel.com · 01224 732124 · **Maryculter** Excellent setting on banks of Dee: riverside walks and an old graveyard and ruined chapel in the priory. The hotel is on the site of a 13th-century preceptory. Newer annex; rooms overlook river. Poacher's Bar is special, dining room not; food is not their strong point. At weekends this hotel can be a wedding factory! Fishing rights on Dee (though further up river).

931 8/T19
50 ROOMS
TEL · TV
NO PETS
MED.INX-EXP

Carmelite www.carmelitehotels.com · 01224 589101 · **Stirling Street** Aberdeen's 'boutique' hotel. Very central in the Merchant Quarter below Union St near the port. 3 types of room (including 6 suites), all very modern. Most have good light, including bathrooms. Suites themed: Japanese, antique, etc. Bar and restaurant. Not that smart but not that expensive, either.

932 8/T19
17 RMS · TEL
TV · NO PETS
CHP-MED.INX

City Centre Hotel www.aberdeencitycentrehotel.co.uk · 01224 658406 · **Belmont Street** Beneath and part of the Vodka Bar in a busy street off Union St. Opened '09, an upmarket bedbox for urban sophisticates and whoever you meet in the night. All somewhat subterranean – voddy-fuelled sessions await.

933 8/T19
77 ROOMS
TEL · TV
MED.INX

Thistle Caledonian Hotel www.thistlehotels.com · 01224 640233 · **Union Terrace** Victorian edifice, one of 3 Thistles in the city and of several city centre hotels off Union St, The Caley always somehow seems the easiest to deal with; the most likely to be calm and efficient. Dining room and on-street bar/brasserie. Some nice suites overlooking the gardens.

934 8/T19
34 ROOMS
TEL · TV
NO PETS
MED.INX

Atholl Hotel www.atholl-aberdeen.com · 01224 323505 · **54 King's Gate** On a busy road in west towards Hazelhead. An Aberdeen stalwart. I've never stayed, but many an Aberdonian would attest that this is the best among many mansions. Woody and traddy rather than fit and trendy but perfect perhaps for ladies of *un certain* age and their blokes. It's a comfort.

935 8/T19
155 ROOMS
TEL · TV
NO PETS
CHP-MED.EX

Express by Holiday Inn www.hieaberdeen.co.uk · 01224 623500 · **Chapel Street** In the middle of West End nightlife zone. A chain, of course, but a better than average bedbox in a central location for, say, urban weekend breakers. Contemporary and convenient. You'd eat out (there's plenty to choose from) and there's the legendary all-night bakery opposite. Room price varies a lot.

936 8/T19

Hostels SYHA www.syha.org.uk · **8 Queen's Road** On an arterial road to west. Grade 1 hostel 2km from centre (plenty buses). No café. Rooms mainly for 4-6 people. You can stay out late. Other hostels and self-catering flats c/o University, of which the best is the **Robert Gordon** (01224 262134). Campus in Old Aberdeen is a good place to be though 2km city centre; has university-halls accommodation (01224 273444). Both these vacation-times only.

The Best Places To Eat In Aberdeen

BISTROS & CAFÉ BARS

937 8/T19
ATMOS
£15-25

✓ **Café 52** www.cafe52.net · 01224 590094 · **52 The Green** Below the east end of Union St in the Merchant Quarter: go down the steps or approach via Market St. A sliver of a cosy bistro with outside terrace. It has a kind of boho chic. Chef/owner Steve Bothwell keeps customers happy with unusual dishes but comforting combinations prevail. Mum does the puds. Busy at (good-value) lunch. Lunch then tapas and dinner. LO 9.30pm (bar 12midnight). 4.30pm Sun.

938 8/T19
£25-35

✓ **La Stella** www.lastella.co.uk · 01224 211414 · **28 Adelphi** In a lane off the east end of Union St. Chris Tonner's breakout bistro, a small room (10 or so tables) opening directly onto this discreet lane. Perfectly judged and routinely full. Big-choice menu with many (mainly fish) specials. From amuse bouche to petit fours, this is fine bistro dining at great prices. Within 2 years, it spawned:

939 8/T19
£25-35

✓ **The Courtyard** www.courtyardaberdeen.co.uk · 01224 589100 · **Alford Lane** In another lane, off the other (west) end of Union St. Similar formula; larger room. Many specials. Also great value for this standard. Haven't eaten here but unquestionably Chris is on a roll. Both open lunch and LO 9.30pm. Closed Sun.

940 8/T19
£25-35

✓ **Fusion** www.fusionbistro.com · 01224 652959 · **10 North Silver Street** Fusion burst like tastebuds onto the Aberdeen dining and foodie-night-out scene with serious cheffing, tasting menus and no expense spared. 2 years later it's settled in somewhere between fine living and fine dining: a top choice. Cocktails, interesting wine and an eclectic menu under Derek Malcolm with a straightforward 3 choices changing monthly. Not fusion food in the conventional sense but diverse and creative. Good value. Dinner only Tue-Sat. LO 10pm.

941 8/T19
ATMOS
£15-25

✓ **Le Café Bohème** 01224 210677 · **Windmill Brae** Authentic French bistro, atmosphere and food behind a discreet frontage in an area that gets drunk at weekends. Here all is calm with style and good service. Food proper French, à la carte and plats du jour (especially seafood). Best place to eat by far in this part of the city centre. Lunch and LO 9pm. Closed Sun/Mon.

942 8/T19
£15-25

✓ **The Foyer** www.aberdeenfoyer.com · 01224 582277 · **82a Crown Street** Remarkable in that this busy, contemporary restaurant with good Modern British seasonal menu and great service is part of a local charity helping homeless and disadvantaged people. No hint of charity evident but you can satisfy your conscience as well as your appetite in airy, spacious surroundings. Lunch till LO 9.30pm. Closed Sun/Mon.

943 8/T19 **Cocoa** www.cocoa-aberdeen.co.uk · 01224 211319 · 11 Market Street
£25-35 ✓ Self-consciously stylish bar restaurant still establishing at TGP. But the menu is created and overseen by estimable Craig Wilson of Eat on the Green (919/ NORTHEAST RESTAURANTS) so expect credible cuisine. Street-level cocktail bar and café; on the mezz, the affordable urban bistro fare we sophisticates love to share and compare. Lunch and LO 9.30pm, bar 11am-12midnight. Closed Sun/Mon.

944 8/T19 **The Lairhillock Inn** www.lairhillock.co.uk · 01569 730001 Not in the
ATMOS ✓ city at all but a roadside inn at a country crossroads to the south. Head south
£15-25/ on A92, turn off at Durris then 5km. Famous for food (1295/GASTROPUBS) and infor-
£25-35 mal atmosphere in conservatory lounge and bar (same menu). Restaurant adja- cent, **Crynoch**, with more ambitious menu, excellent cheeseboard and malts. Restaurant open weekends for dinner. Inn 7 days lunch & LO 9pm (10pm Fri/Sat).

945 8/T19 **Moonfish** www.moonfishcafe.co.uk · 01224 644166 · 9 Connection
£15-25 ✓ Wynd Down steps from east end of Union St. Discreet location and an bit of an Aberdeen secret, this easy-on-the-eye and pocket (2-course dinner £21) caff/ restaurant turns out simple good food with some panache. Leans to seafood but 2 meat and vegetarian choices. Lunch Tue-Sat, dinner Wed-Sat. LO 9.30pm.

946 8/T19 **Stage Door** www.pbdevco.com · 01224 642111 · 26 North Silver Street
£15-25 ✓ A strange url – this the restaurant of an Aberdeen company who own pubs, clubs and a casino. I somehow missed Stage Door in past editions of *StB*. It's up 2 flights of stairs in a cul de sac off Golden Sq, but this is an Aberdeen fave. Title coz it's between 2 theatres and has a theatre-restaurant buzz and ambience, bistro- type menu, linen cloths, fastidious placements and service. A smart but far from corporate stylee operation. Sorry I missed it till now. Dinner only, LO 9.30/10pm.

947 8/S19 **The Broadstraik Inn** www.broadstraikinn.co.uk · 01224 743217 ·
ATMOS ✓ Elrick Not in the city but on the main A944 to Alford at Elrick near Westhill,
£15-25 about 12km city centre. Roadside pub since 1905 now gastrofied and civilised and a destination with a reputation for good food and smart service (1290/GASTRO- PUBS). Great for families early evening. 7 days lunch, LO 9/9.30pm.

948 8/T19 **The Victoria** 01224 621381 · Upstairs at 140 Union Street Not a bistro
ATMOS ✓ or café-bar as such, more a luncheon- and tearoom. Excellent as always on a
£15-25 recent visit. Upstairs from busy street with same staircase and foyer as adjacent jewellery-and-gift emporium so an odd alliance. Great light and seasonal menu, everything home- and terribly well-made including the bread and the biscuits. Authentic and conscientious, the antithesis of high street eating – a real Aberdeen asset. See 1420/AFTERNOON TEAS. 9am-5pm (6.30pm Thu). Closed Sun.

949 8/T19 **Howie's** www.howies.uk.com · 01224 639500 · 50 Chapel Street Follows
£15-25 successful formula once made in Edinburgh in classic/contemporary bistro style, this discreetly fronted restaurant presses all the right Aberdonian buttons (includ- ing the price!). A reliable redoubt. 7 days, lunch and LO 10pm.

950 8/T19 **Food Story** 01224 622293 · 22 Rose Street Central café/takeaway with arti-
<£15 san, ethical approach and well-sourced produce. Daytime only; they also do out- side catering. 7.30am-5pm (from 8.30am Sat, 9.30am Sun).

951 8/T19 **Beautiful Mountain** www.thebeautifulmountain.com · 01224 645353 ·
<£15 11 Belmont Street In an area of many eateries, this unpretentious caff stands out. Takeaway and tables jammed together in 2 rooms upstairs. Great combos and ingredients. Home bakes. Tapas menu daytime and also Thu-Sat till 11pm.

SEAFOOD

952 8/T19
LLL
>£35+
ATMOS

Silver Darling www.silverdarling.co.uk · 01224 576229 · Pocra Quay
Didier Dejean still on the stoves in this exemplary seafood bistro in a perfect spot. Not so easy to find: head for Beach Esplanade, the lighthouse and harbour mouth (Pocra Quay). The light winks and ghostly boats glide past. Upstairs dining room not large and you so want to be by the window. Different menu for lunch and dinner varies with catch and season. Apposite wines; every one a winner. Due desserts. Long-serving but still the best and most dynamic location of any seafood restaurant in the land. Mon-Fri lunch, Mon-Sat dinner 7-9.30pm (best to book).

953 8/T19
£25-35

Atlantis at the Mariner Hotel www.themarinerhotel.co.uk · 01224 591403 · 349 Great Western Road Those that know where to go in Aberdeen for excellent fish and seafood may not necessarily go to Silver Darling, but come here off centre and in a hotel but always busy. Hotel dining room atmosphere is not too evident (tables in conservatory) and the fish very good. Also bar menu. Moderately priced wines. Lunch (not Sat) and dinner LO 9pm. Sunday carvery.

ITALIAN

954 8/T19
£15-25

Rustico 01224 658444 · Corner of Union Row & Summer Street 50m from Union St. If this were French I'd say it had the *je ne sais quoi*, but it is most definitely Italian (Sicilian actually). Tony and Niko's love for Sicily evident (their brill photos on the walls) though Niko is Greek. And the food is well above the tratt average: everything home made, including the puds. As good a tratt as you'll find. Lunch and LO 10pm. Closed Sun lunch.

955 8/T19
<£15

Carmine's Pizza 01224 624145 · 32 Union Terrace A tiny slice of a room for *the* best pizza in town and behind, slaving over a hot stove, the eponymous, much-loved, curvy Carmine. Take away (to the gardens opposite). Real pasta in basic spag/tag/penne variants in no-frills caff. Brill! Lunch and 4.30-6.45pm. Closed Sun.

EASTERN

956 8/T19
£15-25

Yorokobi www.yorokobibycj.com · 01224 566002 · 51 Huntly Street Authentic Japanese/Korean restaurant by chef/proprietor Jang – that's Chef Jang to you and me. Sushi, sashimi and maki rolls, this is a share-and-savour kind of place but there are teriyakis and even curry. Setting perhaps less inspired than the food. Lunch and LO 10pm. Closed Sun.

957 8/T19
£15-25

Jewel In The Crown www.thejewelinthecrown.com · 01224 210288 · 145 Crown Street Way down the street on corner with Affleck. Great North Indian food all home made and authentic. Possibly the best curry in town – always arguments about that, natch, though not from the sons of Farooq Ahmed who work like a football team to make this place a top spot. Lunch and LO 11pm. 7 days.

958 8/T19
£25-35

Nargile www.nargile.co.uk · 01224 636093 · 77 Skene Street Turkish survivor that has made regulars happy for almost 30 years. The newer **Rendezvous @ Nargile**, 106 Forest Ave (01224 323700), is the lighter, brighter version on a suburban corner whose constant buzz attests to destination status. Ms Iridag, wife of the original owner, cooks here. Lunch and LO 9.30pm. 7 days. Both do definitive and enormously popular meze. Lunch Fri/Sat. Dinner only LO 11pm. Closed Sun.

Hammerton Stores 1442/GOOD DELIS.

The Globe 1311/GASTROPUBS.

The Best Hotels & Restaurants In Speyside

959 8/P17
15 ROOMS
TEL · TV · DF
MED.EX

✓ **Knockomie** www.knockomie.co.uk · 01309 673146 · Forres 2km south of town on A940 to Grantown, well placed for the Moray Coast, Inverness and your golfing and Speyside meanderings. Gavin and Penny Ellis are discreet, fastidious hosts in this comfortable but contemporary mansion house which is more a gastropub with rooms than a stuffy manor with manners. Informal dining, nice bar. Comfortable in its country self, though the suburbs are coming.

960 8/Q18
26 ROOMS
TEL · TV
NO PETS · L
MED.EX

Craigellachie Hotel www.craigellachie.com · 01340 881204 · Craigellachie The quintessential Speyside hotel, off A941 Elgin to Perth. Trading a bit on past glory but very good for fishing, walking (Speyside Way at the bottom of the garden; 1990/LONG WALKS) and distillery visits (1478/WHISKY). Rooms ok – you want one of the master rooms overlooking the river. The food is sufficient and the Quaich bar is for whisky lovers – probably one of Scotland's best places for a dram.

961 8/Q18
5 ROOMS
TEL · TV
MED.INX

The Mash Tun www.mashtun-aberlour.com · 01340 881771 · 8 Broomfield Square, Aberlour Off main street behind the church by a lovely river meadow park. A restaurant/pub with rooms above (all named after whiskies). This is a very Malt Trail destination that's boutique standard, informal and better value than most. Pub has nice ambience and good grub. LO 9pm.

962 8/N19
12 ROOMS
TEL · TV · L
MED.EX

Muckrach Lodge 01479 851257 · Dulnain Bridge Off Carrbridge road out of Dulnain Bridge which is off the A95. Country manor presiding over bucolic demesne to the river. Andy Picheta and Rebecca Ferrand's labour of country-house love on Speyside. 2 rooms in The Steading. Nice bar leading on to deck terrace and conservatory restaurant. I haven't visited this time, so reports, please.

963 8/P17
23 ROOMS
TEL · TV
NO PETS
MED.EX

Mansion House www.mansionhousehotel.co.uk · 01343 548811 · Elgin This mansion house in small green grounds below a monument to the last Duke of Gordon is also now overshadowed by a 24-hour Tesco in a suburb somewhat encroaching on its serenity. Comfy enough. Leisure facilities include a small pool, gym and drop-in bistro. Nice dining room. Where else are you gonna stay in Elgin?

964 8/Q18
16 ROOMS
TEL · TV
MED.INX

Dowan's Hotel www.dowanshotel.com · 01340 871488 · Aberlour Above river and charming town signed off the A85 from Grantown. Solid mansion and solid Speyside hospitality though oddly you approach from the back. Inside all is pleasant and comfortable and there are 150 malts in the bar. Fishermen–friendly and inexpensive. Scottish menu, of course.

965 8/P18
11 ROOMS
TEL · TV · L
MED.INX

Archiestown Hotel www.archiestownhotel.co.uk · 0870 950 6282 · Archiestown Main street of village in the heart of Speyside near Cardhu Distillery (1485/WHISKY). Over the years I've warmed to Jane and Alan Hunter's village inn/hotel with comfortable rooms and bistro (LO 8.30pm) which comes with a long-standing reputation for good food. All very lived-in especially by fishers. A plethora of armchairs to lounge in and take a dram (with very many to choose from).

RESTAURANTS

966 8/Q18
£15-25

✓ **La Faisanderie** 01340 821273 · Dufftown A small Franco-Scots affair: the Whisky Trail with Eric Obry's French twist. On the corner of the square and Balvenie St. A welcome departure for these parts and well known as *the place* to eat. Last time I was here, Eric had been out 'hunting chanterelles'. Simple 4-choice menu. Excellent early-evening deal. Lunch and dinner LO 8.30pm. Closed Tue.

The Best Hotels & Restaurants In The Highlands

See also Inverness, p. 191, Skye, p. 381 and 385, Outer Hebrides, p. 393.

967 9/K21
17 ROOMS
+ LODGE
TEL · TV
DF · LL
ATMOS
LOTS

✓ ✓ **Inverlochy Castle** www.inverlochycastlehotel.com · 01397 702177 · **Fort William** 5km from town on A82 Inverness road, Scotland's flagship Highland hotel is filled with sumptuous furnishings, elegant decor and occasional film stars, luminaries and royalty. Owner Mr KC Chai insists on old-style hospitality. Inverlochy is the anchor hotel of expanding ICMI group which also owns Rocpool, Inverness (see below), the contemporary antithesis of this, and manages Greywalls near Edinburgh (818/LOTHIANS). As you sit in the atrium after dinner, perhaps with someone tinkling the piano, marvelling at the ceiling and stylish people swish up and down the staircase, you know this is no ordinary country-house hotel. And it has all you expect of a castle; the epitome of grandeur and service. Huge comfortable bedrooms, the antlered billiard room, acres of rhododendrons, trout in the lake, tennis and a lovely terrace; though no spa or pool. Kennel for dogs. The big Ben is over there.
EAT A dining destination open to non residents. Michelin-starred Philip Carnegie almost 10 years on these sacred stoves. J&T for dinner in an old-style setting.

968 7/H16
7 ROOMS
TEL · TV
NO KIDS
ATMOS
LOTS

✓ ✓ **Pool House Hotel** www.poolhousehotel.com · 01445 781272 · **Poolewe** Once owned by Osgood MacKenzie who founded the nearby gardens (1492/GARDENS). With immaculate style and determination the Harrisons have transformed this Highland home into one of Scotland's must-do stopovers. Their dream of creating something truly special has grown over years and still doesn't stop. In 2012/13 they're creating a new Chinese suite to add to the others, all fastidiously themed, including the Indian suite with amazing bed; the Boathouse overlooking the river mouth and the bay; the Titanic (house connection); the Osgood; and the Astrology. All rooms are meticulously assembled and hand-painted by daughter Liz. Bathrooms are fabulous. This has been a labour of love for the whole family and for this standard, is great value. Son-in-law John Moir in the kitchen. On summer Sundays there's a BBQ in the pavilion in the lovely kitchen garden. Go luxuriate in their remarkable achievement. They close Mon.

969 8/N17
9 ROOMS
(2 SUITES)
TEL · TV
LOTS

✓ ✓ **The Boath House** www.boath-house.com · 01667 454896 · **Auldearn** Signed from A96 3km east of Nairn. A small country-house hotel in a classic, immaculately restored mansion: Don and Wendy Matheson's family home with superb landscaped grounds, and a much-deserved Michelin star. Comfy public rooms with local artists' pics. Bedrooms (3 woodland, 2 lake, 2 downstairs with their own conservatory and a cottage over-by) are home-from-home with great bathrooms. Chef Charlie Lockley's 6-course (no choice, so declare diet first) dinner is the finest (and in no way overstated) dining in the north, much of it foraged and farmed nearby. You'll have had your afternoon tea (1416/AFTERNOON TEA). Service impeccable; friendly and local. Delightful grounds a long work in progress with Wendy's immaculate walled garden (from whence your salad), a lake where deer come to drink and a big heron waits motionless for its dinner; you watch while having yours. Beautiful Brodie nearby (1772/CASTLES).
EAT Mr Lockley: intuitive, great judgement, Michelin-starred and 4 AA rosettes. Cooking: organic, slow and from the kitchen garden. Set menu. The Boath experience: this dinner, those gardens. Good life in a nutshell.

970 6/J14
5 ROOMS
MAR-DEC

✓ ✓ **The Albannach** www.thealbannach.co.uk · 01571 844407 · **Lochinver** 2km up road to Baddidarach as you enter Lochinver on the A837. Lesley and Colin's uniquely beautiful boutique hotel in the north: ancient splendid landscape around you, contemporary splendid comfort to return to. The Byre suite overlooks the Croft from its own conservatory and hot tub. The Penthouse has its own terrace. Colin has put these immaculate rooms together and a shoreline cottage is on the way at TGP. Your stay revolves around Lesley's 5-course fixed (so declare diets up front): locally sourced and seasonal and fabulous. Non-residents can also dine. Suilven is the big mountain over there as you linger in the conservatory or on a relatively midge-free terrace contemplating its grandeur. EAT Maybe the smallest team (Lesley and Colin) and smallest kitchen in the Michelin galaxy, so even more remarkable. Laid-back and inexpensive for this standard.

TEL · TV
NO KIDS
NO PETS
LL
LOTS

---

971 7/M18
11 ROOMS
TEL · TV
NO PETS
LOTS

✓ ✓ **Rocpool Reserve** www.rocpool.com · 01463 240089 · Culduthel Road, Inverness Above the town, a determinably urbane hotel now owned by the people who have Inverlochy (above). Though look and feel are poles apart, service is similarly top. Room categories somewhat offputting ('extra decadence', anyone? see 1035/INVERNESS HOTELS) but do exceed expectations. EAT Albert Roux's no-nonsense French food brilliantly done for a fraction of what you'd pay in London. Report: 1045/INVERNESS RESTAURANTS.

---

972 7/M18
30 ROOMS
TEL · TV
LOTS

✓ ✓ **Glenmoriston Townhouse** www.glenmoristontownhouse.com · 01463 223777 · 20 Nessbank, Inverness Along the riverside opposite Eden Court Theatre. No expense was spared in the conversion of this long-reputed hotel (and the one next door) into a chic boutique and urban hotel in the early-21st-century ascendance of Inverness. Rooms split 50/50 between main hotel and adjacent Windsor House, the latter refurbished to urban-chic standard; with rooms overlooking the river, the old building more traditional. Plans to insert a new block of rooms in between the 2 at TGP. Top restaurant is Abstract and bistro/brasserie Contrast where breakfast is served. All a smart, well-oiled operation. EAT Both restaurants in main house. Abstract fine dining; piano at weekends. Contrast is buzzier and more casual.

---

973 7/M18
28 ROOMS
TEL · TV
LL
LOTS

✓ ✓ **Culloden House** www.cullodenhouse.co.uk · 01463 790461 · Inverness 5km east of town near A9, follow signs for Culloden village, not the battlefield. Easiest approach from A96 Nairn road, turn right at first roundabout after the mall. Hugely impressive Georgian mansion and lawn a big green duvet on edge of suburbia and, of course, history. Near town and airport. Demonstrates that sometimes old-style is the best style. Lovely big bedrooms overlooking the policies. Some fab suites in separate garden house. Elegant dining in beautifully conserved room under long-serving chef Michael Simpson. Garden House is adjacent to an immaculately restored 4-acre walled garden, yours to wander. Fabulous trees include redwoods. Tennis courts. A true country house (but close to town) courtesy of Culloden's caring American owners.

---

974 7/L18
7 ROOMS
+5 COTTAGES
TEL · TV
LL
LOTS

✓ ✓ **Loch Ness Lodge** www.loch-ness-lodge.com · 01456 459469 · near Abriachan On the A82, 18km south of Inverness by the Clansman Hotel which you can't miss on the road. The Lodge is set back above the road and loch, a new build and labour of love of the Sutherland family – siblings Scott and Iona. Their haven of hospitality is well out of the tourist tide that washes down to Drumnadrochit. Comfortable, bright rooms in the main building and cottages alongside, all overlooking the garden and that famous stretch of water. 2-choice fine-dining menu from assured, perhaps underestimated chef Ross Fraser; a strong, not predictable wine list. Surprising spa and hot tub. All in all a new and discreet lochside lodging to discover. EAT Best dining south of Inverness by some distance. Non-residents go find.

975 7/M20
8 ROOMS
FEB-DEC
TEL · TV
NO PETS
MED.INX

✓ **The Cross** www.thecross.co.uk · 01540 661166 · Kingussie Off main street at traffic lights 200m uphill then left. Tasteful hotel and superb restaurant in converted tweed mill by the river which gurgles outside most windows. Comfy rooms. David and Katie Young, considerate hosts, help you get the most from this wonderful area. Alas they were 'out with the dogs' last time I called.

✓ ✓ **EAT** Deal probably includes dinner which is so what you want. But also open to non-residents for what is after all these years still the best restaurant in the region. David and long-standing Beca on the stoves. Fabulous wine list! Closed most Sun/Mon.

976 7/L17
4 ROOMS
TFI · TV
NO KIDS
MED.INX
£22-32

✓ **Dower House** www.thedowerhouse.co.uk · 01463 870090 · near Muir of Ord On A862 between Beauly and Dingwall, 18km northwest of Inverness and 2km north of village after the railway bridge. Charming, personal place; you are the house guest of Robyn (in the kitchen) and Mena Aitchison, your consummate hosts. Cottagey-style, lived-in, small country house, with comfy public rooms and lovely garden with pond for G&T moments. Packed lunch for those gone fishing (not available to non-residents).

977 6/K14
4 ROOMS
TV
NO PETS
MED.EX

✓ **Blar Na Leisg, Drumbeg House** www.blarnaleisg.com · 01571 833325 Drumbeg No signage to help you find this fabulous restaurant with rooms behind the Drumbeg Hotel in the village between Kylesku and Lochinver (1618/ SCENIC ROUTES). Eddie and Anne Strachan keep out of sight but foodies now beating a path (including Michelin). Have to admit I haven't eaten but my antennae tell me this is good, very good. Fixed 4-course menu so discuss fads up front. Eddie's small but selective wine list. You eat round the expandable table. Good contemporary art surrounds you (some of it Eddie's); rooms are modest and modish. A stylish home from home in the back of a beautiful beyond (with otters, pine martin and deer). Sounds good (I know, I've used the word 4 times), doesn't it?

978 7/N16
6 ROOMS
+3 COTTAGES
TEL · NO PETS
LOTS

✓ **Glenmorangie House at Cadboll** www.theglenmorangiehouse.com · 01862 871671 · near Fearn South of Tain 10km east of A9. Old mansion in open grounds overlooking a distant sea. Owned, like the distillery, by Louis Vuitton Moët Hennessy so expect some luxury (understated in public areas but all-embracing in bedrooms after a £300k refurbishment). No leisure facilities but no shortage of distraction around (the 'seaboard villages', the dolphins, Anta/Tain Pottery; 2179/2180/SHOPPING). Open fires and communal, house-party atmosphere. Afternoon tea; fixed dinner round one table, honesty bar; great service.

979 6/J15
15 ROOMS
APR-OCT
TEL · TV
DF · LL
LOTS

✓ **The Summer Isles Hotel** www.summerisleshotel.co.uk · 01854 622202 Achiltibuie 40km from Ullapool with extraordinary views over the isles; Stac Polly and Suilven are close to climb. A long-established romantic retreat on the strand at Achiltibuie with a range of comfortable, contemporary rooms in the main hotel (11) and adjacent cottage conversions. Chef Chris Firth-Bernard here almost 25 years, still turning out some of the best food you'll eat in the North. Local sourcing here means scallops from the bay, lamb and beet from fastidious manager Jody Marshall's own croft, veg and salad leaves from his hydroponic garden. You couldn't get fresher and lighter than this. Fixed menu with their famous cheeseboard of mainly Scottish cheeses (all in perfect condition; they offer a cheese flight with selected libations) and Chris's to-die-for desserts. Adjacent pub offers similar quality food at half the price (1280/GASTROPUBS). Lots to do outdoors including boat trips (Summer Isles Cruises, 1739/SEALIFE CRUISES) and don't miss some of the best views of Scotland nearby (1638/VIEWS).

EAT Superb fine dining. Fixed (truly individual) menu, trolley of puds and cheese. And the sunset over the Isles. Bar menu is great value.

980 6/N15
22 ROOMS
TEL · TV
MED.EX

✓ **Royal Marine Hotel** www.royalmarinehotel.co.uk · 01408 621252 · **Golf Road, Brora** Turn-of-century mansion house by Robert Lorimer overlooking the harbour and self-catering apartment block newly built overlooking the golf course. Great for golfers, a civilised stopover for the rest of us. Contemporary public rooms; bedrooms vary. Spa has decent pool. Restaurant in dining room, Lorimer's, and the bar have similar menus and complementary atmosphere.

981 6/N16
22 ROOMS
TEL · TV
MED.EX

✓ **Royal Golf Hotel** www.royalgolfhoteldornoch.co.uk · 01862 810283 · **Dornoch** Comfy, not-too-golfy golfing hotel by Dornoch's famously fabulous golf course. On a much more human scale than others of the ilk further south. Casual dining.

982 6/J14
22 ROOMS
TEL · TV
DF · LL
MED.EX

✓ **Inver Lodge** www.inverlodge.com · 01571 844496 · **Lochinver** Here a long time on the hill overlooking the bay and the harbour but not in *StB* until taken over by the never-less-than-excellent ICMI group who have Inverlochy Castle and Greywalls (967/HIGHLAND HOTELS, 818/LOTHIAN HOTELS). House here is a bit austere though comfortable, but it's dinner and that view that you probably come for. Albert Roux's menu and the estimable manager Nicholas Gotten hereabouts these 20 odd years.

983 6/P12
14 ROOMS
TEL · TV
MED.EX

✓ **Forss House Hotel** www.forsshousehotel.co.uk · 01847 861201 · **near Thurso** 8km west on A836. Georgian mansion house set in 20 (rare in these parts) woodland acres by the meandering River Forss. This stretch of the river and the foot of the lawn with its perfect pool and waterfall is yours to contemplate and (if fortunate) to fish. It is quite exceptional and the main reason for the *StB* tick. Rooms are spacious and comfortable (4 in separate River House, 2 in cottages), conservatory is nice and the bar has an impressive malt list. Though long the only decent hotel in the northeast corner, there is complacency and house rules: dinner strictly 7-8.30pm, lights out at 10.30pm, service short of polite and a long way from giving a toss (my 8.35pm arrival was not well received). But fishermen will always throw a line into this river and if you, passing-through tourist, toe theirs you can enjoy their well-located if inconsistent hospitality.

984 9/J22
20 ROOMS
+5 LODGES
TEL · TV · DF
MED.EX

✓ **Holly Tree** www.hollytreehotel.co.uk · 01631 740292 · **Kentallen** On A828 Fort William (Ballachulish)–Oban road, 8km south of Ballachulish Bridge. On road and sea and once the railway; it was formerly a station. Convenient location and superb setting on Loch Linnhe with views from all bedrooms (some balconies) and dining room. Appropriate location for surf 'n' turf menu. Nice for kids. New pool and the jetty on the sea outside. 1132/HOTELS THAT WELCOME KIDS.

985 7/L17
21 ROOMS
TEL · TV
DF
MED.INX

Coul House Contin www.coulhousehotel.com · 01997 421487 · **near Strathpeffer** Comfortable country-house hotel on the edge of the wilds with some lovely public rooms refurbished with elegance intact (especially the octagonal dining room). On a recent visit I got (in mine host Stuart Macpherson's words), 'the worst room in the house'; I believe most are quite nice, though. Well-kept lawns with bog garden and duck pond. An accessible, not-too-posh country-house retreat. Varied menu under chef Garry Kenley. Well-priced wines. All great value.

986 7/M18
11 ROOMS
+2 COTTAGES
TEL · TV · DF
MED.INX-EXP

Loch Ness Country House Hotel www.lnchh.co.uk · 01463 230512 ·
Inverness 6km southwest of town on A82 Fort William road. Formerly Dunain
Park, now rebranded with the magic Loch Ness moniker but still the same lived-
in, civilised, old-style mansion-house alternative to hotels in town. Gorgeous gar
dens; real countryside beyond. The Park restaurant in various cosy dining rooms
with sound Scottish menu. Excellent wine and malt list. Enviro-friendly garden
(where the cottages are) and a great deck/terrace for that warmer evening.

987 7/M18
16 ROOMS
TEL · TV
MED.INX

Bunchrew House www.bunchrew-inverness.co.uk · 01463 234917 · near
Inverness On A862 Beauly road only 5km from Inverness yet completely
removed from town; on the wooded shore of the Beauly Firth. Mentioned here as
a historic and atmospheric billet for the night, but it mainly functions as a wedding hotel (midweek stays more likely).

 **The Torridon** www.lochtorridonhotel.com · 01445 791242 · Loch
Torridon near Kinlochewe At the end of Glen Torridon in immense
scenery. Highland Lodge atmosphere, big hills to climb. Now with adjacent
Torridon Inn (inexpensive, with bar and bistro). Report: 1161/GET-AWAY HOTELS.

✓✓ **Ackergill Tower** 01955 603556 · near Wick Report: 1237/HOUSE
PARTIES.

✓✓ **House Over-By** 01470 571258 · Skye Report: 2259/SKYE HOTELS.

✓ **Eilean Iarmain** 01470 833332 · Skye Report: 2261/SKYE HOTELS.

✓ **Kinloch Lodge** 01470 833333 · Skye Report: 2260/SKYE HOTELS.

✓ **Scarista House** 01859 550238 · South Harris Report: 2276/ISLAND
HOTELS.

Best Less Expensive Highland Hotels

988 6/K15
13 ROOMS
+20 BUNKS
TEL
ATMOS
CHP-MED.EX

✓ ✓ **The Ceilidh Place** www.ceilidhplace.com · 01854 612103 · **Ullapool** 'Books, Music, Art' and Life: Jean Urquhart's oasis of hospitality, craic and culture in the Highlands with daughter Rebecca in charge as Jean is now an MSP and has a larger house to contend with. What started out in the 1970s as a coffee/exhibition shop in a boat shed, spread along the row of cottages and now comprises a restaurant, bookshop, café/bar (and performance) area with bedrooms upstairs. Bar and restaurant go all day from famously good breakfast to dinner menu from 6.30pm (LO 9pm). The amazing truth is it's hardly changed a bit but it's still on the button. Bunkhouse across the road offers cheaper accommodation: stay 'luxuriously rough'. Live music and events through the year (check the website) or you can simply sit in the downstairs parlour or, if you're a hotel guest, in the lounge upstairs with honesty bar or on the terrace overlooking Ullapool where the boats come in.

£25-35 **EAT** Bar and restaurant areas in one big, happy room. All-day menu then supper. Puts the craic into casual dining.

989 6/L12
7 ROOMS
APR-OCT
TV · L
NO PETS
MED.INX

✓ ✓ **Mackay's** www.visitmackays.com · 01971 511202 · **Durness** Far-away north in the centre and at the heart of a straggled-out township. Small (7 rooms, 8 tables) but perfectly conceived and formed hotel at the corner of northwest Scotland (literally where the road turns south again). In the Mackay family for generations. Fiona and Robbie have transformed this solid old house into the coolest spot in this northern hemisphere where in summer the light lingers forever. Wood and slate. Discreet but efficient service. Comfy beds in calm, stylish rooms. No bar but all-day food; LO 8.30pm. Many interesting distractions nearby (2100/GOLF, 1854/MONUMENTS, Smoo Cave, etc). As well as the adjacent bunkhouse (1126/HOSTELS), they now have 2 fabulous state-of-play new-build eco cottages at Lade 9km east, overlooking Loch Eriboll (1609/LOCHS). Sex, romance, nature. Go treat yourself in splendid isolation. 2181/SHOPPING, 1554/BEACHES.

990 5/M20
5 ROOMS
TV
CHP

✓ **Coig na Shee** www.coignashee.co.uk · 01540 670109 · **Newtonmore** Road out of Newtonmore (which is just off the A9) for Fort William. Mansion house with light, contemporary feel and furnishings. Nice breakfast (they have free-range hens and evening meals on request. (The Letterbox in the village also has good food.) Friendly proprietors, the Bords. Exceptional value.

991 6/N16
3 RMS · TEL
TV · NO PETS
INX

✓ **2 Quail** www.2quail.com · 01862 811811 · **Castle Street, Dornoch** As you arrive from south. For a long time a pre-eminent destination in the region, especially for the restaurant which is no more. The rooms above and the breakfast, however, remain, and Kerensa Carr will make you very comfortable and welcome. Eat at Luigi's next door; 1024/RESTAURANTS.

992 9/J20
13 ROOMS
MAR-NOV
LL
ATMOS
MED.INX-EX

✓ **Glenfinnan House Hotel** www.glenfinnanhouse.com · 01397 722235 · **Glenfinnan** Victorian mansion with lawns down to Loch Shiel and the Glenfinnan Monument over the water. No shortbread-tin twee or tartan carpet here; instead a warm welcome from the MacFarlanes and managers the Gibsons. Everything is just right here. Bar with atmosphere, craic and music (Thu). A cruise on this stunning loch (01687 470322) or row boat at the foot of the lawn! Great for kids. 1180/SCOTTISH HOTELS.

993 7/M17
9 ROOMS · TV
ATMOS
MED.INX

✓ **The Anderson** www.theanderson.co.uk · 01381 620236 · **Fortrose** Main street of town in the middle of the Black Isle. Restaurant, bar and reasonable rooms in very individual hotel notable for an extraordinary bottled-ales and whisky collection and then the grub. Rooms have a certain and well-chosen

charm; in fact this place exudes boho-chic with a tartan trim. US owners diligent in their pursuit of approvals. Many accolades, including mine.
EAT Anne Anderson manages a perhaps unfeasibly long daily-changing menu in atmospheric bar and dining room.

994 7/L19
27 ROOMS
TEL · TV
MED.INX

✓**The Lovat** www.thelovat.com · 0845 450 1100 · **Fort Augustus** On edge of town, the road to Fort William. Refurbished and rebranded (they dropped their 'Arms') by the family of the people who brought us Torridon (1183/GET-AWAY HOTELS) into a contemporary, comfortable roadside hotel, unquestionably the best hereabouts. Brasserie menu and lovely, light dining rooms for table d'hôte and breakfast. Good looks and smart service in the heart of the Great Glen.

995 9/K20
4 ROOMS · TV
MAR-OCT
NO PETS · L
CHP

✓**Corriechoille Lodge** www.corriechoille.com · 01397 712002 · **Spean Bridge** 4 (riverside) km out of Spean Bridge on the small road by the station. Justin and Lucy Swabey's hideaway house facing the mountains. Beautiful corner of the country with spectacular views to the Grey Corries and Aonach Mor. Lovely set dinner, very simple cosy rooms. (No kids under 7 years.) 2 turf-roofed self-catering chalets over by. Great walks begin here. Also 1170/GET-AWAY HOTELS.

996 7/L18
12 ROOMS
NO PETS
MED.INX

✓**The Loch Ness Inn** 01456 450991 · **Lewiston by Drumnadrochit** Just off the A82 1km from the monster mash of Drumnadrochit. A functional roadhouse hotel, quite the best in the area and with a notable restaurant that's invariably full. The estimable Judy Fish from the Applecross Inn (1169/GETAWAY HOTELS) has a hand in this and supplies the langoustines etc.
EAT Lewiston Restaurant, the best casual meal between Inverness and Fort Augustus; may have to book. Garden menu in summer; the garden is out the back.

997 9/K21
9 ROOMS
MED.INX

✓**Lime Tree Studios** 01397 701806 · **Achintore Road, Fort William** At the roundabout as you come from the south. Regional and local art gallery (owner David Wilson's work on some walls) with rooms above and a very good restaurant that makes you feel better about Fort William. Simple, contemporary, convivial atmosphere in tasteful public rooms of the Old Manse.

998 7/H17
11 ROOMS
APR-OCT
DF · LL
MED.EX

✓**Tigh-an-Eilean** 01520 755251 · **Shieldaig** Lovely, cosily furnished hotel on waterfront overlooks Scots Pine island on loch. The Fields run a charming house and adjacent Coastal Kitchen pub, transformed with upstairs bistro and deck overlooking the loch. Live music weekends. Dining room and the Kitchen busy with people, pizzas and specials, pulling off the tricky combination of populist, popular and something more refined. A cool spot at the heart of a Highland village.

999 6/P15
16 ROOMS
TEL · TV
MED.INX

✓**Bridge Hotel** 01431 821100 · **Dunrobin Street, Helmsdale** End of the main street and along from the Mirage (1019/HIGHLAND RESTAURANTS) in this historic, atmospheric village which coyly reveals its considerable charm if you look. There's the bridge, glen and sentinel church, a pub called the Bohemian, a shop called 20th Century Collectibles (2206/SHOPPING) and Timespan (2144/HERITAGE). The hotel is surprisingly commodious. Animals, art and science everywhere; antlertastic (more deer here than in your average glen). Eclectic staff; service varies. Spacious public rooms and cosy bar. Eat in the Green Stag or the Red Lobster.

1000 9/K20
8 ROOMS
TEL · TV
MED.INX

✓**Old Pines** www.oldpines.co.uk · 01397 712324 · **near Spean Bridge** 3km Spean Bridge via B8004 for Garlochy at Commando Monument. Open-plan pine cabin with wood stove, neat bedrooms and a huge polytunnel (where bits of your dinner come from). A very comfy, unpretentious hotel with great food; à la carte menu open to non-residents lunch and dinner. Chickens run, the pines are old! And see 1106/HOTELS THAT WELCOME KIDS.

1001 7/K20 ✔ **Glengarry Castle** www.glengarry.net · 01809 501254 · **Invergarry**
26 ROOMS A family-run hotel in the Highlands for over 50 years, in the charge of the
MAR–NOV younger MacCallums. Rhodies, honeysuckle as you walk to the loch. Magnificent
TEL · TV trees and a newly restored ruined castle in the grounds the stronghold of the
L Macdonells: you may remember the famous portrait by Raeburn – the epitome of
MED.INX the fashionable Highland chief. 2 rowboats at your disposal (and the brown trout).
A romantic destination in every way. Big rooms.

1002 7/H18 **The Plockton Inn** www.plocktoninn.co.uk · 01599 544222 · **Plockton**
14/15 **The Plockton Hotel** www.plocktonhotel.co.uk · 01599 544274 · **Plockton**
ROOMS Two stays in perfect Plockton (1542/COASTAL VILLAGES). The village is why we come.
TEL · TV The inn is away from the front. Some good cask ale in bar. Very basic rooms. 7
MED.INX rooms in hotel and 7 in more contemporary annex over the street. Bistro: mainly
seafood. Tables on terrace in summer, back garden for kids. Probably best for food.
The Plockton Hotel is by the water's edge and is busier and buzzier. Pub and pub
meals seem always packed. May be noisy weekends.

1003 8/N19 **Boat Hotel** www.boathotel.co.uk · 01479 831258 · **Boat of Garten** Centre
34 ROOMS of village overlooking the steam train line and near golf course (2090/GOOD GOLF).
TEL · TV Great old-style (Victorian/1920s) hotel in rolling refurbishment with a big variety of
MED.INX-EXP varied rooms. There are also 6 chalet-type garden rooms: ok and quiet. Decent
food in very pleasant bar and bistro and dining room.

1004 6/N16 **Dornoch Castle Hotel** 01862 810216 · **Dornoch** Main street of delightful
24 ROOMS northern town with nice beaches, great golf and a cathedral made famous by
TEL · TV Madonna who once got married here. Very castle-like (from 15th century), up-and-
MED.INX-EX down building where rooms vary hugely, as do prices. Garden Restaurant (yes, on
the garden) is up and down (for food) too, but overall there is charm.

1005 6/M13 **Tongue Hotel** www.tonguehotel.co.uk · 01847 611206 · **Tongue** One of 2
19 ROOMS hotels in Tongue at the centre of the north coast where Ben Loyal rises. This the
TEL · TV most presentable at present though a little more expensive. Nicely turned-out
MED.INX rooms. Lounge bar and candlelit dining room. Very Highland. The Brass Tap pub
downstairs has atmosphere and many locals.

1006 7/K18 **Tomich Hotel** www.tomichhotel.co.uk · 01456 415399 · **Tomich near**
8 ROOMS **Drumnadrochit** The inn of a quiet conservation village, part of an old estate on
TEL · TV the edge of Guisachan Forest. Near fantastic Plodda Falls (1589/WATERFALLS) and
L Glen Affric (1577/GLENS). Rooms pleasant and cosy. Use of pool nearby in farm
MED.INX steading (9am-9pm); especially good for fishing holidays. 25km drive from
Drumnadrochit by A831. Nice bar.

1007 **Clunie Lodge** www.clunielodge.com · 01339 741330 · **Braemar** If you want
10/P20 somewhere to stay in this royal stamping ground much favoured by bus parties
5 ROOMS (but hey, the scenery is immense), this tidy Victorian mansion house on the edge
NO PETS of town (well, 200m from the Fife Arms) and looking into the hills is a good bet.
CHP Between the church and the woods and far enough from the ravening hordes in
search of coasters and tea towels, the Hampsons maintain a discreet distance.

1008 6/K15 **The Arch Inn** www.thearchinn.co.uk · 01854 612454 · **Ullapool** On the
10 ROOMS shore of Loch Broom along from the ferry, heart of the town and especially its
TV · DF music scene and festivals (Loopallu and Feis). Most rooms have a view and may be
CHP on the street. Great pub food and separate finer dining seafood restaurant. An all-
round good base and place to know and you sleep by the sea.

EAT Long-established, locally popular pub for food with patio and upstairs their restaurant notable for seafood (dinner only).

 The Smiddy House 01397 712335 · Spean Bridge A notable restaurant with rooms. Report: 1020/BEST HIGHLAND RESTAURANTS.

3 GREAT HIGHLAND B&Bs

And 3 on Skye; see p. 383

1009 9/K21
3 ROOMS
MAR-NOV
MED.INX

✓✓ **The Grange** www.thegrange-scotland.co.uk · 01397 705516 · Fort William Probably the best rooms for the night in Fort William. All in the best possible taste and with views of Loch Linnhe. Reports: 1080/FORT WILLIAM.

1010 7/M20
3 ROOMS
FEB-NOV
CHP

✓ **The Rumblie** www.rumblie.com · 01528 544766 · Laggan near Newtonmore Off the A9 on the A86 midway between Dalwhinnie and Newtonmore to this eco-friendly and people-friendly B&B which takes its green agenda seriously. Organic breakfast; evening meal by arrangement (or go to The Laggan, former pottery and now pizza place; 1386/TEAROOMS in Newtonmore, below). Nice garden; bike hire nearby at Wolftrax.

1011 6/K15
3 ROOMS
TV
NO C/CARDS
MED.INX

Tanglewood House www.tanglewoodhouse.co.uk · 01854 612059 · Ullapool Just outside town on A835 south overlook Loch Broom. Family guest house very personally run by Anne Holloway who reckons she serves the best dinner to be had in Ullapool. Not a tough contest, you say, but hey, she's probably right. And it's available to non-residents. All rooms have great view of lovely Loch Broom; there's a boat if you feel like a row on it (or to visit the Prince's Cove).
EAT Fixed-menu (so phone fads ahead), delicious 4-course dinner overlooking the loch. You join other guests like a dinner party. Sunset and supper to savour.

The Best Restaurants In The Highlands

1012 7/H18 — **The Potting Shed** 01520 744440 · Applecross In north Applecross along
L — the strand at the back of a gorgeous walled garden. Ongoing restoration after
<£15 — 50 years of neglect – enter via a pergola of roses (in summer). A destination coffee
shop/restaurant like the Inn (1169/GET-AWAY HOTELS), making that harrowing drive
worthwhile. Everything home made and often from the garden. Full menu lunch
and dinner and Martin's excellent cakes. 7 days 11am-9pm, Sun till 8pm. Mar-Oct.

1013 6/L15 — **Carron Restaurant** www.carronrestaurant.co.uk · 01520 722488 ·
£15-25 — Strathcarron On A890 round Loch Carron (joins A87 Kyle of Lochalsh road)
just south of Strathcarron. Peter and Michelle Teago's roadside diner and grill
started by Peter's dad over 30 years ago is a destination and not just locally.
Couldn't visit for this edition but I know what I say still holds. With absolutely
everything home made, including the bread, the puds, the chips, and sourced
locally as a matter of course (salad leaves from Attadale Gardens down the road;
(1517/GARDENS), this place looks like just another caff but is far from it. 'Honest to
goodness' it is. Apr-Nov, 10.30am-9pm. Closed Sun.

1014 8/P17 — **The Bakehouse** 01309 691826 · Findhorn Follow the one-way system
<£15 — round end-of-the-road village – you can't and mustn't miss it. Jan Boultree
and David Boyle once with the deli at the Findhorn Community (1443/DELIS, 1219/
RETREATS). This is a brilliant coffee shop/restaurant where you eat ethically and
really well. Home made/home grown/organic naturally and part of the slow-food
movement so all individually prepared. Mostly vegetarian though they do great
burgers. 7 days. 10am-5pm. Bakery behind where David bakes (1428/BAKERS).

1015 9/H22 — **Whitehouse** www.thewhitehouserestaurant.co.uk · 01967 421777 ·
L — Lochaline, Ardnamurchan Sits above the ferry port as the Mull boats come
£25-35 — in, a restaurant adjacent the village shop with all the right/best principles: local
produce, organic, imaginative cooking. Ingredients from Mull and Lochaber – bay,
woods and hedgerow in Sarah and Jane's brilliant, back-of-beyond bistro. Quiet
days in Ardnamurchan begin here. Pan-fried Lochaber stag's liver with Oban
whisky and capers, anyone? Lovely tartines. Perfect! Apr-Oct. 11am-afternoon tea-
dinner LO 9.30pm. Closed Sun.

1016 7/H18 — **Plockton Shores** 01599 544263 · Plockton On the foreshore of lovely
L — little Plockton, an all-purpose eaterie with fine home cooking making the
£15-25 — most of location and hinterland (for ingredients). Breakfast, lunch and dinner Tue-
Sat, (LO 9pm), Sun till 6pm, Mon till 5pm. Decent vegetarian choice.

1017 5/M17 — **Sutor Creek** www.sutorcreek.co.uk · 01381 600855 · 21 Bank Street,
L — Cromarty Near the seafront. An end-of-the-road (across the Black Isle) diner
£15-25 — in Cromarty (1545/COASTAL VILLAGES). Both a destination and a neighbourhood
caff. Now under the Foxes, more focus on seasonal- and local-produce specials.
Wood-fired oven turning out great crispy pizza. 11am-9.30pm. Winter hours vary.

1018 7/H18 — **The Seafood Restaurant** 01599 534813 · Kyle of Lochalsh ·
LL — www.theseafoodrestaurant.com Not quayside, more platform-side by the
ATMOS — busy port, off the road to Skye and with that bridge in the distance. *Brief Encounter*
£25-35 — location; being actually on the platform at the end of the line lends distinction.
Seafood from Kyle/Mallaig/Skye, ie very local, and vegetarian selection. Dinner
only 6-8.30pm. Closed Sun/Mon.

1019 6/P15
£15-25
✓ **La Mirage** www.lamirage.org · 01431 821615 · Dunrobin Street, Helmsdale Near the Bridge Hotel (999/HIGHLAND HOTELS). A bright little gem in the Sutherland straths and once a homage to Barbara Cartland, the romantic novelist, who lived nearby in this gorgeous wee village by the sea and strath. Snacks of every kind all day and great home cooking and baking from Don, son-in-law of Nancy Sinclair who famously put this caff on the map (her pic's on the wall). Great fish and chips (can takeaway). All year 11am-9pm.

1020 9/K20
L
£15-25
✓ **Russell's @ Smiddy House** www.smiddyhouse.co.uk · 01397 712335 · Spean Bridge Near junction of A82 for Skye on A86 for Laggan, Messrs Bryson and Russell's carefully run guest house or restaurant with 4 rooms (and cottage). Excellent, unpretentious fare all home made. Fish selection and great chargrill steaks. Especially good for vegetarian food and diets. Best in a wide area (including Fort William) so best to book. Afternoon tea in light lounge with great choice of teas and tier of tea things (1418/AFTERNOON TEA). Book that too. 7 days in summer, lunch & LO 9.30pm. Wed-Sun winter.

1021 6/K14
II
MAR-OCT
£15-25
✓ **Kylesku Hotel** www.kyleskuhotel.co.uk · 01971 502231 · near Kylestrome On A894, tucked down by Loch Glencoul where the boat leaves to see Britain's highest waterfall (1594/WATERFALLS). Tanja and Sonia's small quay-side pub/hotel (8 pretty and basic rooms, 4 with sea views) serves great seafood in fabulous waterside setting with mighty Quinag behind (1950/HILLS). Food in bar or residents-only dining room. 12noon-9pm. See also 1296/GASTROPUBS.

1022 7/N19
<£15
✓ **The Mountain Café** www.mountaincafe-aviemore.co.uk · 01479 812473 · Aviemore On the main street above an outdoor shop, definitely the best bet for food in this activity hub town with a touch of New Zealand in menus and presentation. Great for breakfast and home baking (especially bread). Good vegetarian: they make everything and have own-branded deli. Big big helpings for hungry outdoorsy types. But they ain't open for dinner. 7 days 8.30am-5pm (5.30pm Sat-Mon).

1023 8/N19
£15-25
Andersons www.andersonsrestaurant.co.uk · 01479 831466 · Boat of Garten On the main road from Aviemore/Carrbridge. The Andersons' family-run restaurant (Steve in the kitchen), a welcome dine-out around here where there are lots of visitors and not much good food on the go. All home made, nothing fancy but an eclectic choice. 'Fishy Fridays'. Lunch and dinner LO 9pm.

1024 6/N16
£15-25
Luigi www.luigidornoch.com · 01862 810893 · Castle Street, Dornoch On the way into town. Smart-looking café/restaurant, a welcome find in dreamy Dornoch. Drop-in snack place by day with good Lavazza coffee, Euro-Scottish menu in evenings. 10am-10/11pm.

1025 6/M16
£15-25
Crannag www.crannag.com · 01863 766111 · Bonar Bridge A brill bistro where you might least expect one in faraway Sutherland. Scottish, local as usual these days but with more than a soupçon of spice: Ian and Kathy Smith also have the Caledonian Curry Co., so venison etc. with a twist. Might say 'a culinary oasis'; and in this quarter there's nowhere else. Tue-Sat 5-9pm.

1026 7/M17
<£15
☕
The Storehouse near Evanton · 01349 830038 Roadside farm shop/deli but mainly destination diner on A9 north of Inverness south of Alness overlooking the firth. Locally sourced meats and various olives/mugs/haggis (you get the picture). However, there's no doubting that they've got the food right – the self-service restaurant goes like a fair with all things irresistible though not necessarily good for you. Often queues. Lashings of cream. 7 days 9am-6pm, Sun 10am-5pm.

1027 7/N19   **The Boathouse** www.kincraig.com · 01540 651394 · **Kincraig** 2km from
LL   village towards Feshiebridge along Loch Insh. Part of Loch Insh Water Sports (2125/
<£15   WATER SPORTS), a balcony restaurant overlooking beach and loch. Serene setting
and ambience, friendly young staff. Some vegetarian; home-made puds. Bar menu
and home baking till 5.30pm; supper till 9pm, bar 11pm. Check winter hours.

1028 7/N17   **Kist** 01667 459412 · **Basil Harbour Café** Nairn Two small restaurants half a
<£15-25   mile apart (Kist at top of the High St, Basil on the harbour) by the Barron boys,
Dave and Jamie. Kist a simple, inexpensive bistro; Basil more caff-like but with hot
meals, home- and locally made cakes and the best coffee in town. Integrity but
not at a price. Kist lunch & LO 8.45pm. Closed Sun/Mon. Basil 10-6pm.

1029 7/N17   **The Classroom** 01667 455999 · **Cawdor Street, Nairn** At top end of main
<£15-25   shopping street; Cawdor St is a continuation. Contemporary makeover in this con-
servative, golfy town. An airy bar/restaurant; feels like a real brasserie. Good for
kids, for afternoon tea and grown-up dinner. 7 days. LO 9.30pm.

1030 6/J14   **Riverside Bistro** www.piesbypost.co.uk · 01571 844356 · **Lochinver** On the
£15-25   way into town on A837. This Lochinver larder is notable mainly for the vast array
of Ian Stewart's home-made pies and calorific cakes. The banoffi pie here is truly
wicked. You can eat in or take away. Conservatories out front and back. Bistro on
riverside serves very popular meals at night; using local seafood, venison and vegetarian – we won't mention Michael Winner again. Evening menu from 6.30pm.
The **Caberfeidh** pub (01571 844391) next door, with great Scottish (haddock 'n'
chips, mince 'n' tatties) pub grub, all home made and locally sourced, adds to the
excellent Lochinver options (Albannach and Inver Lodge).

1031 7/M16   **The Oystercatcher** www.the-oystercatcher.co.uk · 01862 871560 ·
L   **Portmahomack** On promontory of the Dornoch Firth (Tain 15km), this hidden
£25-35   seaside village (the only east-coast village that faces west) could bring back beach-
plootering memories. Restaurant (a bistro by day – they switch rooms) is a destination in itself, the wine list and malt choice truly extraordinary. Food is inventive,
multi-ingredient, always interesting. Bistro does 'hearty' or 'ample' portions. A la
carte and prix fixe menu for dinner. Closed Nov-Feb and Mon/Tue. Best book.

1032 7/H16   **Na Mara** 01445 712397 · **Gairloch** Main part of strung-out village opposite
£15-25   Mountain Coffee Co. Contemporary café/restaurant, really the only decent place to
eat around here; a welcome find. Café lunch then evening menu Thu-Tue, 7 days
in summer. Beachcomber takeaway behind not related.

1033 6/M15   **Falls of Shin Visitor Centre** www.fallsofshin.co.uk · 01549 402231 · **near**
L   **Lairg** Self-serve café/restaurant in visitor centre and shop across the road from
<£15   the Falls of Shin 8km south of Lairg (1602/WATERFALLS). Home-made food better
than it probably has to be in what was an unlikely outpost of Harrods: Mohammed
al Fayed's Highland estate is here. (He's erected a statue of himself – a not-unex-
pected vanity and a bit of a hoot.) Somebody in that kitchen knows how to cook.
Menu updated 2011. 9.30am-6pm; winter 10am-5pm. Food LO 4.30pm.

1034 7/M16   **Carnegie Lodge** 01862 894039 · **Tain** At top of the town signed from A9 (and
£15-25   toon bypass). It's a Tain thing, but the Wynes have turned this curiously suburban
roadhouse/motel into *the* place to eat around here. Straight-up scrumptious food,
big helpings, great value. They also have 8 rooms. Lunch and LO 9pm.

The Best Places To Stay In & Around Inverness

1035 7/M18
11 ROOMS
TEL · TV
NO PETS
LOTS

 Rocpool Reserve www.rocpool.com · 01463 240089 · Culduthel Road Looking down on the centre from above (great view from terrace), this self-consciously presented boutique hotel followed Rocpool Restaurant (see below). Owned by the expanding superlative ICMI group who have Inverlochy Castle (993/HIGHLAND HOTELS) and Greywalls (818/LOTHIANS HOTELS). Each room a design statement, divided into Hip, Chic or Decadent. You may feel you have to live up to the titles. 2 rooms have hot tubs on outdoor decks. Probably best to have someone to shag in these circumstances. As with others in the group, a restaurant under Albert Roux who has assembled a great team and a great menu most definitely worth sampling even as a non-resident. Solicitous service; a top stay.

 Glenmoriston 01463 223777 · Ness Bank Smart riverside hotel with 2 restaurant choices (fine dining and informal). Independently owned and personally run with excellent service. 972/HIGHLAND HOTELS.

Boath House 01667 454896 · Auldearn Half an hour east on A96. Excellence, elegance and very fine dining! 969/HIGHLAND HOTELS.

Culloden House 01463 790461 5km east near (but not adjacent) the battlefield. Gracious living, splendid grounds. 973/HIGHLANDS HOTELS.

1036 7/M18
8 ROOMS
TEL · TV
MED.INX

The Heathmount www.heathmounthotel.com · 01463 235877 Kingsmills, then centre (from Eastgate Mall). Fiona Newton's quite groovy boutique-style hotel with popular, and at weekends very busy, bar/restaurant. High standard of mod-con; rich boudoir decor with personal attention to detail. Famously, some rooms have TVs in the shower. Good value at the price.

1037 7/M18
76 ROOMS
TEL · TV
MED.INX

Columba Hotel 01463 231391 · 7 Ness Walk An excellent central location overlooking the main bridge over the Ness and across the river to the castle. Pleasant and friendly, contemporary feel. Rooms vary, some small; river views best. Nice bar with good grub and outside tables.

1038 7/M18
70 ROOMS
TEL · TV · L
MED.EX

Royal Highland Hotel www.royalhighlandhotel.co.uk · 01463 231926 · Academy Street Literally on top of the station. Nice staircase and a recherché charm but rooms rather average. A surreal start to the day in the very interior breakfast room. Very much in the centre of things, def more functional than flash.

1039 7/M18
83 ROOMS
TEL · TV
MED.EX

Kingsmill Hotel www.kingsmillhotel.com · 01463 237166 · Culcabock Road In suburban area south of centre near A9. Modern, very well-appointed with pleasant garden. Best of the chain hotels. 3 room categories. Leisure facilities include gym, sauna/steam and small pool.

1040 7/M18
11 ROOMS
TV · NO PETS
CHP

The Alexander www.thealexander.net · 01463 231151 On Ness Bank opposite the cathedral and Eden Court. Of many options in this central, pleasant street, the Alexander stands out. 3 rooms out back more contemporary, main house individual. A landlady who will help you get the best out of this town. B&B only.

1041 7/M18
6 ROOMS
IV
INX

Moyness House www.moyness.co.uk · 01463 233836 · 6 Bruce Gardens Accolade-gathering and TripAdvisor-rated suburban guest house over bridge south of river but 10 minutes' walk to centre; on-street parking Jenny Jones's friendly family house. B&B only. Writer Neil Gunn lived here; rooms named after his canon.

Loch Ness Country House Hotel 01463 230512 6km southwest on A82 Fort William road. Comfy country house just outside town. 986/HIGHLANDS HOTELS.

Bunchrew House Hotel 01463 234917 4km north on the road to Beauly on the firth shore. Wedding hotel but weekdays possible. 987/HIGHLAND HOTELS.

1042 7/M18 **3 Good Hostels: SY Hostel** www.syha.org.uk · 01463 231771 · **Victoria Drive** Large official hostel (SYHA). More funky are the **Student Hostel**, 8 Culduthel Rd (01463 236556), and 3 doors down **Bazpackers** (01463 717663).

The Best Places To Eat In Inverness

>£35 ✓ ✓+ **Boath House** www.boath-house.com · 01667 454896 · **Auldearn** Well out of town off A96 3km east of Nairn 30 minutes from Inverness. 2-plus ticks from me to make the distinction that in the Highlands Michelin-star chef Charlie Lockley is cooking at another level. 969/HIGHLAND HOTELS.

1043 7/M18 ✓ ✓ **Rocpool** www.rocpool.com · 01463 717274 · **Ness Walk** Corner of
£15-25 main bridge over river. Stephen Devlin's excellent bright, buzzy diner with accent on inexpensive daytime and eclectic evening menu. Still the consistently good place to eat in the centre of Inverness. Look no further – if you can get in! Forerunner of the Reserve (below). 7 days. LO 9.45pm. Closed Sun lunch.

1044 7/M18 ✓ ✓ **Café One** www.cafe1.net · 01463 226200 · **10 Castle Street** For
£15-25 almost 10 years Norman Macdonald has been running one of the most in-tune with its clientele restaurants in Scotland. I kinda missed this revelation before but on a recent visit in the newish expanded dining rooms with wine bar out front it's quite apparent that this is Inverness's number one choice for an affordable dinner out. Seasonally changing menu, superb well-informed wine list (with huge by-the-glass choice) at almost jawdrop prices. Café One and Rocpool are the par excellence eateries in this ville. Breakfast, lunch, dinner LO 9.30pm. Closed Sun.

1045 7/M18 ✓ ✓ **Rocpool Reserve Chez Roux** www.rocpool.com · 01463 240089 ·
£25-35 **Culduthel Road** 3 rooms, private dining and terrace overlooking town. The Albert Roux experience is classic French à la carte at great prices. The £25 3-course dinner is superb value and includes his signature floating souffle. He ain't here of course (though he phones every week and comes several times a year) but the kitchen team are top. A real treat! 7 days. Lunch & LO 10pm.

1046 7/M18 ✓ **Abstract @ The Glenmoriston** 01463 223777 · **20 Nessbank** ·
>£35 www.abstractrestaurant.com Along the river. The top-end restaurant in town, part of Barry Larsen's Glenmoriston Hotel (see above). A sophisticated dining experience – the 8-course tasting menu or à la carte under South African chef Raynor Muller. Dinner Tue-Sat. LO 9.30pm.

1047 7/M18 ✓ **Contrast** 01463 227889 · **Ness Bank** Also in the Glenmoriston Hotel
£15-25 (above), the bistro/brasserie contrasts with fine-dining Abstract in the other room. Genuinely quite French, informal and light à la carte. Outside tables overlook the river. Lunch and LO 9.30pm.

1048 7/M18 ✓ **The Mustard Seed** 01463 220220 · **16 Fraser Street** Catriona Bissett's
£15-25 cool restaurant in architectural riverside room with good attitude and buzz.

Contemporary menu, ok wine. A restaurant that would not be out of place in any city on the up. 7 days lunch and LO 10pm.

£15-25 ✓ **Girvans** Stephens Brae Behind M&S. Fast-turnover food for all folks. Home-made, on the button. All towns should have an easy drop-in, reliable eaterie like this. 7 days 9am-9pm. Report: 1359/CAFÉS.

1049 7/M18 **The Kitchen** 01463 259119 · 15 Huntly Street In a new building on the river
<£15 almost opposite its parent, The Mustard Seed (see above). On 3 floors so waiters work hard up and down those staircases as does the kitchen which you can watch on screen. Often all 3 floors (though small) are packed. It's coz of the exceptional value (and a good burger). 7 days lunch & LO 10pm.

1050 7/M18 **Riva & Pizza Place** 01463 237377 · 4 Ness Walk Prominent (by main bridge)
£25-35/ Italian restaurant and (upstairs) tratt. Probably best in town. By the Girvans (see
£15-25 below). Contemporary room overlooking riverside. Decent Italian menu. Riva lunch and LO 9.30pm, upstairs evenings only (pasta and pizza); lively room. LO 10pm.

1051 7/M18 **Riverhouse Restaurant** 01463 222033 · Greig Street Over the pedestrian
£25-35 bridge. Intimate restaurant with contemporary food (mainly fish) from Alan Little, who knows his oysters, in an open kitchen. Gets busy so can feel cramped but excellent reputation. Lunch Tue-Sat, dinner Tue-Sun, LO 9pm. Closed Sun in winter.

1052 7/M18 **River Café** www.rivercafeandrestaurant.co.uk · 01463 714884 · Bank
£15-25 Street On town side of the river near pedestrian bridge. Small, friendly café/ restaurant – a high-tea kind of place. Solid and unpretentious evening menu and ladies who lunch. All home made. 7 days LO 9pm. May close Sun in winter.

1053 7/M18 **Clachnaharry Inn** www.clachnaharryinn.co.uk · 01463 239806 On A862
£15-25 Beauly road outside town 4km from the centre. Old-style, long-established road-side pub well known for its ales (usually 5, all interesting), now gaining a big reputation for food under chef David Aspin. Pub staples but specials more gastrotastic. Good terrace; view of the firth. Lunch and LO 9pm. Closed Mon.

1054 7/M18 **Little Italy** 01463 712963 · 8 Stephen Brae Up the brae from the Eastgate
£15-25 Centre end of main street. Small, we do mean small, family-run (the De Vitas) tratt that folk like (see TripAdvisor, or on second thoughts, don't). Authentic menu of everything you'd want that ends in a vowel. 11am-9.30pm. Closed Sun.

1055 7/M18 **Raja** 01463 237190 · Post Office Lane Downstairs in the lane (between Church
£15-25 and Academy Sts, behind Queensgate), the best of several curry houses. Here since 1982 and usually packed. Says it all! Will probably see off all the nouveau Indians.

1056 7/M18 **La Tortilla Asesina** www.latortillaasesina.co.uk · 01463 709809 · Top of
£15-25 Castle Street Near castle and hostels (see above). Reasonably authentic Spanish restaurant serving the UK version of tapas ie 2/3 portions as a meal. All the faves and some variants are here with lots de dia. The rioja and the beers are here, of course. 7 days. LO 10pm (bar later).

✓ **Castle Restaurant** Castle Street Legendary caff of the Highlands. Hardest-working kitchen in the North. Report: 1358/CAFÉS.

If you're in Fort William...

WHERE TO STAY

9 ROOMS
TV
MED.INX

✓ **Lime Tree Studios** www.limetreefortwilliam.co.uk · 01397 701806
Achintore road as you come from south, the last hotel of many near the end of main street. Combines regional art-gallery space in the old manse with (Victorian) rooms above and a (modern, rustic) newer extension. Bar/restaurant with open kitchen and terrace. David Wilson (his art on the walls) and Charlotte Wright run a convivial, cosmopolitan inn.

3 ROOMS
MAR-NOV
TV
NO KIDS
NO PETS
MED.INX

✓ **The Grange** www.thegrange-scotland.co.uk · 01397 705516 · **Grange Road** Overlooks the loch and the main road south. Look for Ashburn House on main A82 turning into Ashburn Lane. Joan and John Campbell have been running this superlative, contemporary B&B in bereft Fort William for years. Discreet, almost suburban house but great views from garden terrace and fresh, modern rooms with great bathrooms. **Ashburn House** (01397 706000) on the main road and water's edge has 7 rooms and gets a Michelin mench.

20 ROOMS
TEL · TV
NO PETS
MED.EX

✓ **Nevis Bank Inn** www.nevisbankinn.co.uk · 01397 705721 On the main A82 to Inverness near the roundabout and road into Glen Nevis. Extensively refurbished hotel in contemporary style: neutrals, browns, wood with busy bistro. Better by far than several very dated stopovers in this town.

S.Y. Hostel 0870 004 1120 · Glen Nevis 5km from Fort William by picturesque but busy Glen Nevis road. The Ben is above. Grade 1. Many other hostels in area (ask for list at tourist information centre) but especially **FW Backpackers** 01397 700711 · Alma Road.

Achintee Farm 01397 702240 On approach to Ben Nevis main route and adjacent Ben Nevis Inn (see below). Guest house/self catering and bunkhouse in walkers' haven.

Camping/Caravan Site 01397 702191 · Glen Nevis Near hostel. Well-run site, mainly caravans (also for rent). Many facilities including restaurants.

✓ ✓ **Inverlochy Castle** 01397 702177 5km out on A82 Inverness road. In the forefront of hotels in Scotland. Victorian elegance, classically stylish and impeccable service. The restaurant is open to non-residents but this is not casual dining. 967/HIGHLANDS HOTELS.

WHERE TO EAT

✓ **Loch Leven Seafood Café** 01855 821048 From the A82 15km south at Ballachulish, take the lochside road to this award-winning seafood caff. Simply worth the drive. 1324/SEAFOOD RESTAURANTS.

£15-25

✓ **Russell's @ Smiddy House** 01397 712335 · Spean Bridge 14km north by main A82. Busy bistro dining at busy Highland corner. Good vegetarian; afternoon teas. 1020/HIGHLAND RESTAURANTS.

L
£15-25

✓ **Lime Tree Restaurant** 01397 701806 · Cameron Square Achintore Rd at roundabout as you arrive from south, or at the south end of the main street. Restaurant of boutiquey hotel (see above) with good atmosphere, open kitchen and terrace. 4 starters/mains/desserts. Cheeky wee amuse bouche. Local sourcing and Scottish cheeses, neat wine list. Lunch and LO 9pm.

£15-25 **Crannog At The Waterfront aka The Seafood Restaurant** 01397 705589 · www.oceanandoak.co.uk Finlay Finlayson's long-established landmark restaurant on the waterfront. Freshly caught seafood mainly (one meat/one vegetarian) in informal bistro setting. Good wine list. All year. 7 days. Lunch & LO 9pm.

<£15 **Ben Nevis Inn** www.ben-nevis-inn.co.uk · 01397 701227 · Achintee On
ATMOS main approach to the Ben itself. Reach across river by footbridge from visitor centre or by road on right after Inverlochy/Glen Nevis roundabout on A82 (marked Claggan and Achintee; 3km). Excellent atmosphere inn in converted farm building. Good grub/ale and walking chat. LO 9pm; bar 10.45pm. Thu-Sun in winter.

If you're around Wick & Thurso...

1058 6/Q13 **WHERE TO STAY**
13 ROOMS ✓ **Ulbster Arms Hotel** www.ulbsterarmshotel.co.uk · 01847 831641 ·
TEL · TV **Halkirk** In middle of village off A9 10km south of Thurso. By the river which
MED.INX is there to be fished (the hotel has 13 beats). Refurbished to comfy and country-stylish standard, unusually contemporary up Caithness way. Dining more traditional in atmospheric bar or dining room.

14 ROOMS ✓ **Forss House** www.forsshousehotel.co.uk · 01847 861201 · near Thurso
TEL · TV 8km west to Tongue off A836. Old established mansion by a magic river in
MED.EX woody policies in a region where you may long for a tree. Report: 983/HIGHLAND HOTELS.

S.Y. Hostel 0870 004119 · Canisbay John o' Groats (7km). Wick 25km. Regular bus service. Furthest-flung youth hostel on the mainland. Thurso has **Sandra's** at 24-26 Princes Street (01847 894575). Cheap 'n' cheerful with snack bar adjacent.

WHERE TO EAT
£15-25 ✓✓ **Captain's Galley** www.captainsgalley.co.uk · 01847 894999 ·
Scrabster The best dinner to be had on this coast. Seafood with simplicity and integrity. Report: 1317/SEAFOOD RESTAURANTS.

✓ **The Tempest Café** 01847 892500 · Thurso On the harbour, a damned good café/tearoom, the best on this long, wavy coast.

Le Bistro 01847 893737 · Trail Street, Thurso On the main road through at the end of the pedestrianised main street. If you have to eat in Thurso, this is the long-established local choice. A' things to a' folk, they have a bit of everything. Lunch and dinner. Closed Sun/Mon.

£25-35 **Bord de L'Eau** 01955 604400 · Market Street, Wick By the bridge – bord de l'eau, as they say. Passably French bistro with chef Chretien a long way from Paris. Best in town but not a lot of bistro atmosphere. Lunch Tue-Sat, dinner Tue-Sun.

Tourist Offices 01847 893155 · Whitechapel Road, Wick Open all year. Riverside, Thurso Apr-Oct.

EDINBURGH
BARS & CLUBS

1059 1/D2 ✔ ✔ **New Town Bar** www.newtownbar.co.uk · 26 Dublin Street · 0131 538 7775 Grown-up and cosmo watering hole for mixed, mainly older crowd. Bear-friendly (especially 3rd Sat of the month). Basement club area Fri-Sat. Bar, outside smokers' terrace. 7 days till 12midnight/3am, weekends till 4am. Food 12noon-5pm; Sunday roast (food, that is!).

1060 1/XE1 ✔ **Priscilla's** 0131 554 8962 · Albert Place On right of Leith Walk going down. Cabaret bar quite Leith-like, good fun karaoke and very mixed crowd: some yoofs, some oldies, some roughies; many smokers. Liza would love it. Till 1am.

1061 1/D2 ✔ **GHQ** 0131 550 1780 · 4 Picardy Place Basement bar and club by Glasgow's G1 Group in the heart of the Pink Triangle. Various club nights with dance depending on crowd and DJs. Banquettes can be booked (for watching and gossip). 7 days 5pm-3am. Young crowd with haircuts.

1062 1/E2 **CC Bloom's** 0131 556 9331 · Greenside Place Kind to call it enduring, the long-established last stand now a bit worse for wear, like much of the clientele. Bar and small dancefloors up and downstairs. Cruisy, of course (your last chance before The Gardens). 7 days till 3am.

1063 1/E1 **Planet Out** 0131 556 5551 · Greenside Place/Baxter's Place Clubby and pre-club crowd dominate later but an unthreatening vibe in this long bar below the Playhouse; gals will out! Till 1am.

1064 1/E2 **Café Habana** www.cafehabanaeh1.com · 0131 558 1270 · 22 Greenside Place Adjacent CCs above. Banging music. Young crowd. Quite tiny really, so usually rammed. Line-up on the mezzanine so coming in is like arriving on the beach at Mykonos: you are immediately checked out, ie probably dismissed, then you can relax. Many outside tables. 7 days noon-1am.

1065 1/B3 **Frenchie's** 0131 225 7651 · Rose Street Lane North Near Castle St. Oldest gay bar, quite removed from the East End Pink Triangle. Hence more intimate but no less trashy. Age before beauty so suits all. 7 days till 11pm; 1am Fri/Sat.

1066 1/F2 **The Regent** 0131 661 8198 · Corner of Abbeyhill Adjacent well-known cruising gardens. Friendly locals, relaxed, straight-friendly. They even have ales (Deuchars, Cally 80/- and guests). 7 days till 1am.

OTHER PLACES

1067 1/D1 ✔ **Blue Moon Café** www.bluemooncafe.co.uk · 0131 556 2788 · Barony
<£15 Street Long-running neighbourhood caff with juice bar (Sejuiced) attached; enter round the corner on Broughton St. Always busy with lively mixed crowd for food and drink and goss. **Q Store** gay accessories and book shop next door (11am-7pm). If you arrive in Edinburgh and don't know anybody, come here first. Food 7 days till 10-ish; bar 11/11.30pm. See 296/EDINBURGH CAFÉS.

1068 1/D1 ✔ **Café Nom de Plume** 0131 478 1372 · 60 Broughton Street Part of the
<£15 LGBT Centre. Proper café-bistro with changing à la carte home-made food and nice people sitting around. So 2 civilised caffs within 100 metres at the heart of the gay zone. 7 days 12noon-9.30/10pm food, bar later.

1069 1/D1   **No. 18** 0131 553 3222 · 18 Albert Place Sauna for gentlemen (mainly older). Discreet doorway halfway down Leith Walk, next to Priscilla's (above). Dark room. 7 days 12noon-10pm; Fri-Sun till 11pm. Cheaper after 8pm each night.

1070 1/D1   **Steamworks** 0131 477 3567 · Broughton Market At the end of Barony St off Broughton St at the Blue Moon. Modern, Euro-style wet and dry areas. Cubies and lockers. Café. Dark room and cruise area. Mixed crowd. Part of the Village Apartments (see below). 7 days 11am-10pm.

GUEST HOUSES

1071 1/E1   ✓**Ardmor House** www.ardmorhouse.com · 0131 554 4944 · 74 Pilrig
5 ROOMS · TV   Street Quiet mix of contemporary and original design meet in this stylish
MED.INX   guest house run by Robin and Lola the doggie. Family room so straight-friendly. They have very nice flats to rent, too.

1072 1/D1   ✓**Village Apartments** www.villageapartments.co.uk · 0131 556 5094 ·
4 ROOMS · TV   Broughton Market Attached to Steamworks (above), 4 well turned-out
CHP   rooms (2 deluxe), central especially for the gay village (between the New Town and the Blue Moon). Is ticked though I have never stayed (nor been invited). Men only.

1073 1/E1   **Garlands** www.garlands.demon.co.uk · 0131 554 4205 · 48 Pilrig Street
6 ROOMS · TV   Another guest house on Pilrig St, similarly central. Garlands is more old style and
CHP   probably more gay than Ardmor (above).

GLASGOW
BARS & CLUBS

1074 2/E3   ✓**Delmonica's** 0141 552 4802 · 68 Virginia Street Del's has been on the corner of this quiet lane at the heart of the Merchant City gay quarter for over 20 years (can it be that long?). Glasgow-stylish pub with long bar and open plan. Pleasant and airy by day but busy and sceney at night, especially weekends. It's nice if your face fits. Themed nights. 7 days till 12midnight (then the PL, below).

1075 2/E3   ✓**Moda** 0141 553 2553 · 58 Virginia Street Another young gay bar by the G1 group between Delmonica's and the Polo Lounge so you're on the same beat even if it is theirs. 5pm-1am, 3am weekends.

1076 2/E3   ✓**Polo Lounge** 0141 553 1221 · 84 Wilson Street Long-established late-night venue with stylish decor. Smart service, themed nights downstairs. Gents' club meets Euro-lounge ambience. 3am licence; otherwise till 1am. Downstairs disco (with admission).

1077 2/C3   **Waterloo Bar** 0141 248 7216 · 306 Argyle Street Scotland's oldest gay bar and it tells. But an unpretentious down-to-earth vibe, refreshing in its way. Long-established, like its clientele. Good soundtrack, Sunday bingo! You might not fancy anybody but they're a friendly old bunch. 7 days till 12midnight.

1078 2/E4   **Court Bar** 0141 552 2463 · 69 Hutcheson Street Centre of Merchant City area. Long-going LGBT-friendly small bar that's fairly straight till mid evening then turns into a friendly fairy. 7 days till 12midnight.

1079 2/E4   **Bennet's** www.bennetsnightclub.co.uk · 0141 552 5761 · 80 Glassford Street In the beginning and in the end... Bennet's. Relentless, unashamed disco fun without attitude on 2 dance floors. Wed-Sun 11pm-3am, Tue is traditionally straight night, first Fri of the month is ladies' night.

1080
2/E3
Revolver www.revolverglasgow.com · 0141 553 2456 · 6a John Street In basement opposite Italian Centre. Civilised subterranea. Free juke box, pool, ale. Some uniform nights. Most of the men will be men. 7 days all day to 12midnight.

OTHER PLACES

1081
2/D4
✓ **The Pipeworks** 0141 552 5502 · 5 Metropole Lane East of St Enoch Centre, near Slater Menswear, down an unlikely lane. Glasgow's most full-on (and modern) sauna labyrinth. 7 days 12noon-11pm, all night Sat/Sun.

1082
2/D2
Babylon 0141 332 1377 · 28 Bath Street Street Recent arrival in Glasgow: sauna with all the usual heat. 12noon-8pm.

1083
2/C4
The Lane 0141 221 1802 · 60 Robertson Street Near Waterloo (above), across Argyle St, lane on right. You look for the green light. Sauna, private club with dark room. You wouldn't call it upmarket, that cabin fever! 7 days, afternoons till 7/8pm.

1084
2/D3
Relax Central 0141 221 0415 · 27 Union Street Between Central Station and Argyle St, way up on the third floor. Small, friendly sauna. Limited facilities but regular clientele. 11.30am-10pm, Sun 12noon-8.30pm.

ABERDEEN

1085
8/T19
Cheerz 01224 594511 · 2 Exchange Street Evening gay bar and (next door) club later on. A cheeky z but a cheery kind of (local) gay as gay bar. 7 days 6pm-12midnight. Club till 2/3am.

1086
8/T19
Wellman's Health Studio www.wellmans-health-studio.co.uk · 01224 211441 · 218 Holburn Street Through the archway half-way down Holburn St, west end of Union. A sauna with all you could want: jacuzzi, steam, sauna and cabins. Very cruisy! 12noon-10pm (earlier Sat/Sun).

DUNDEE

1087
10/Q23
Out 01382 200660 · 124 Seagate Bar and dancefloor. Everybody knows everybody else, but not you. This may have its advantages. Wed-Sun till 2.30am. Also ...

1088
10/Q23
Brooks Bar 01382 200660 · St Andrews Lane Behind and above Out (above). Refurbished bar, a pre-club bar on disco nights (reduced tickets available at bar). Tue-Thu 5pm-12midnight, weekends 3pm-2.30am, Sun till 12midnight.

1089
10/Q23
The Clozet 01382 226840 · 75 Seagate Formerly Gauger and new at TGP. Reports, please.

1090
10/Q23
Jock's Health Club 01382 451986 · 11 Princes Street Not so easy to find if you're a stranger which most of the clientele are not. Smallish steam and sauna with some room to roam; new faces (and other bits) welcome! 12noon-10pm.

HOTELS ELSEWHERE

1091
8/Q19
10 ROOMS
TV · GF · DF
CHP
Colquhonnie House Hotel www.thecolquhonniehotel.co.uk · 01975 651210 · Strathdon In the Don valley, an unlikely find in the Highlands, this roadside (A944) lodge adjacent Lonach village hall takes all sorts but is positively gay-friendly (they fly the flag and the saltire). Good base for the Castle Trail, active stuff (fishing rights on the Don) or just chilling. Small, comfy, inexpensive rooms. Local bar is, you will understand, not a gay bar (though some local lads are fit).

Particular Places
To Eat & Stay

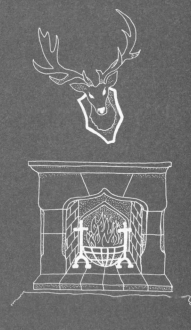

Superlative Country-House Hotels

1092
10/N24
232 ROOMS
TEL · TV
L
LOTS

✓✓✓ **Gleneagles** Auchterarder · www.gleneagles.com · 01764 662231 Off A9 Perth-Stirling road and signed. Scotland's truly luxurious resort hotel. For facilities on the grand scale others pale into insignificance; this is an international destination. Comfort and style and they've thought of everything. And surprisingly human and welcoming – they make you feel special from arrival (I'm sure this is not just me). Sport and leisure activities include shooting, riding, fishing, gun-dog school, off-roading (even kids' jeeps), 2 pools (one for lengths) with outdoor tub and for inactivity the ESPA spa is gorgeous (1232/SPAS). Gleneagles golf (3 courses plus 1 9-hole) is world-renowned; the 40th Ryder Cup is coming 2014. Rooms both traditional luxurious and contemporary luxurious (by Amanda Rosa) in the main house; the new wing Braid House contemporary and remote (in the 'handset to control temperature, lights, curtains and fireplace' sense). Strathearn Restaurant is a foodie heaven, a bustling brasserie feel with state-of-the-sector service. Casual dining in Deseo: lighter, brighter Mediterranean; there are 2 other restaurants. Andrew Fairlie's intimate dining room is considered by many to offer Scotland's best fine dining (870/PERTHSHIRE RESTAURANTS). Gleneagles could be anywhere but it is quintessentially Scottish. It has airs and graces but it's still a friendly old place. It is all right!

1093
11/J29
17 ROOMS
MAR–DEC
TEL · TV
DA
LOTS

✓✓ **Glenapp Castle** near Ballantrae · www.glenappcastle.com · 01465 831212 Relais and Chateaux luxury in South Ayrshire south of Ballantrae. Very discreet entrance (first right turn after village: no sign, and entryphone system – don't bother without a reservation or appointment). Home of Inchcape family for most of 20th century, opened as a hotel in first year of 21st. Run by Graham and Fay Cowan (Fay's family has several much larger hotels but this is very special). Fabulous restoration on a house that fell into disuse in the 1990s. Excellent and considerate service, top-notch food, impeccable interiors. The rooms are all individually beautiful, the suites are enormous. Quality costs but the price includes just about everything, so relax and join this effortless house party. Kids can have separate high tea. Tennis, lovely walks in superb grounds (especially May and September) kept by almost as many gardeners as there are chefs. No leisure facilities as such but access to Pebbles Spa 5 minutes away, with 15m infinity pool. A southern secret though with many accolades.
EAT Adam Stokes: a Michelin omission! 6-course gourmet dinner open to non-residents (must book).

1094
9/J22
16 ROOMS
5 SUITES
2 COTTAGES
FEB–DEC
TEL · TV
LL
LOTS

✓✓ **Isle of Eriska** Ledaig · www.eriska-hotel.co.uk · 01631 720371 20km north of Oban (signed from A85 near Benderloch Castle). Hotel, spa and they do say, island! As you drive over the Victorian iron bridge, you enter a more tranquil and gracious world. Its 300 acres are a sanctuary for wildlife; you are not the only guests. The famous badgers come almost every night to the door of the refurbished, now conservatory bar for their milk and peanuts. Comfortable baronial house with fastidious service and facilities. Rooms (named after islands) are very individual. Two 2-bedroom and five 1-bedroom suites in spa outbuilding are more contemporary, with private terraces and hot tubs. Picturesque 9-hole golf, great 17m pool and gym excellent in summer when it opens on to the garden. No slouch himself, patron Beppo Buchanan-Smith recently raising the Eriska resort status by building an adjacent games barn where you can play (when it's raining, as it does) indoor tennis, squash, bowls and ping-pong. ESPA treatment rooms (3) and Verandah Café with deck adjacent for lunch. Dining, with a Scottish flavour and local flava from a rich backyard and bay, in elegantly remodelled dining room. Though perhaps one wouldn't say that Eriska rocks, it certainly rolls with the times. Top stay in the west!

1095
11/J30
9 ROOMS
MAR-DEC
TEL · TV
DF · LL
LOTS

✓ ✓ **Knockinaam Lodge** Portpatrick · www.knockinaamlodge.com · 01776 810471 An ideal place to lie low; a historic Victorian house nestled on a cove. The Irish coastline is the only thing on the horizon, apart from discreet service and excellent food. Winston Churchill was once very comfortable here, too! (His room recently refurbished.) Superb wine (especially French) and whisky list. 15km south of Stranraer, off A77 near Lochans but get directions. Further report 756/SOUTH-WEST HOTELS.
EAT Tony Pierce – Scotland's longest-standing Michelin chef. Tasting set menu (advise requirements). Understated foodie fabulousness.

1096
10/P22
18 ROOMS
TEL · TV
DF
LOTS

✓ ✓ **Kinloch House** near Blairgowrie · www.kinlochhouse.com · 01250 884237 5km west on A923 to Dunkeld. Quintessential rural Scottish comfort and joy. Beautiful mansion among the green fields and woods of Perthshire, home to exemplary hosts and consummate hoteliers the Allen family. Always welcoming: open fires, oak-panelled hall and portrait gallery with comfy rooms and informal but sure service. Fine south-facing views.
EAT Excellent food: Graeme Allen and the guys in the kitchen. Top wine list (especially French). Classy dining as always, since Airds.

1097
9/J23
16 ROOMS
FEB-DEC
TEL · TV
DF · LL
LOTS
ATMOS

✓ **Ardanaiseig** Loch Awe · www.ardanaiseig.com · 01866 833333 16km from Taynuilt signed from main A85 to Oban down a beautiful winding road and 7km from Kilchrenan. In sheltered landscaped gardens dotted with ongoing sculpture project to complement this rambling gothic mansion's collection of selected antiques (proprietor owns antique business in London) overlooking an enchanting loch. Peaty water on tap, splendid trees on the grounds, the omnipresent loch; deer wander and bats flap at dusk. This is pure romance. Chef Gary Goldie gets it just right. The Boatshed suite, with its boat and its loch, is simply idyllic. Not surprisingly, there are many weddings.

✓ ✓ **Cromlix House** Dunblane · www.cromlixhouse.com · 01786 822125 Near A9 north of Perth, 4km Dunblane. Quintessential country-house hotel in the most beautiful grounds. Report: 777/CENTRAL HOTELS.

✓ ✓ **Raemoir House** Banchory · 01330 824884 5km north from town via A980. A gem in the North East. Historical with contemporary comforts and excellent dining. Report: 909/NORTHEAST HOTELS.

✓ **Ballathie House** Kinclaven near Blairgowrie & Perth · 01250 883268 · www.ballathiehousehotel.com Superb situation on River Tay. Handy for Perth and probably the best place to stay near the town. Full report and codes: 854/PERTHSHIRE HOTELS.

Hotels That Welcome Kids

1098
10/N23
214 ROOMS
+51 LODGES
TEL · TV
MED.INX-EXP

✓ ✓ ✓ **Crieff Hydro** Crieff · www.crieffhydro.com · 01764 655555
A national institution and still a family business. I hadn't visited for a couple of years but when I did in the summer of 2011 and saw their recent improvements, especially the new foyer and reception, I realised that more than ever this is a truly great family hotel, moving with the times, and a superb holistic experience. So along with only 2 other hotels in this book I've decided to elevate Crieff Hydro to 3 ticks: uniquely good in the world! A vast Victorian pile still run by the Leckies from hydropathic beginnings. The continuous refurbishments include the fabulous winter gardens moving graciously with the times (fine coffee shop: freshly squeezed OJ and must-have donuts). New sports hall (the Hub), café and kids' centre; the entranceway; the rooms. Formal chandeliered dining room (Meikle's) and the Brasserie (best for food Med-style; open all day). There are 7 restaurant choices. Activities seem endless: great tennis courts, riding school, 2 pools including 1 for adults only. Tiny cinema shows family movies; nature talks, donkey rides. Kids entertained (even while you eat) with a high tea just for them. Chalets in the grounds are among the best in Scotland. Great for family get-togethers. It occurs to me that actually it's also brilliant for adults on their own. Populism with probity and no preciousness: when in doubt, resort to this resort!

1099
7/E14
7 ROOMS
MAY-SEP
LLL
MED.INX-EXP

✓ ✓ **Baile-Na-Cille** Timsgarry, Lewis · www.bailenacille.com · 01851 672242 Far, far into the sunset on the west of Lewis. 60km Stornoway so a plane/ferry and drive to somewhere you and the kids can leave all your other baggage behind. Exquisite, vast beach and many others nearby, garden, tennis, games room. No TV, phone or mobile reception (but WiFi in the lounge). Plenty books. There are a couple of places nearby for lunch (2305/HEBRIDES) and a great tearoom (2305/HEBRIDES). The kids will never forget you brought them here.

1100
9/J27
36 ROOMS
TEL · TV
MED.INX

✓ **Auchrannie** Brodick, Arran · www.auchrannie.co.uk · 01770 302234
Much expanded from the original house, the new block is perfect for a family holiday. You may have the run of both. Loadsa activities on tap including 2 pools, racquet court, spa and outdoor stuff (c/o Arran Adventures out back) on rivers, trails and hills of Arran. Many rooms can take 2 adults and 2 kids. Main restaurant is a bit motorway services but 2 other options include fine-ish dining in Eighteen69 (phone-monitoring service and the hotel can arrange babysitting). This is where kids will begin their lifelong love of Arran.

1101
9/J22
59 ROOMS
TEL · TV
L
MED.INX

✓ **Isles of Glencoe Hotel** Ballachulish · www.islesofglencoe.com ·
01855 811602 Beside the A82 Crianlarich to Fort William: a modern hotel and leisure centre jutting out onto Loch Leven. Adventure playground outside and nature trails. Conservatory restaurant overlooking the water. Lochaber Watersports next door have all kind of boats from pedalos to kayaks and bikes. 10% off for hotel guests. Hotel has pool. Almost 50% are family rooms (Deck Dens work well). Snacks in the restaurant all day. Glencoe and 2 ski areas nearby.

1102
7/E15
6 ROOMS
MAR-DEC
LL
EXP

✓ **Scarista House** Harris · www.scaristahouse.com · 01859 550238
20km south of Tarbert on west coast of South Harris, just over an hour to Stornoway. Big, comfortable former manse overlooking amazing beach (1561/BEACHES); and golf course (2094/GOOD GOLF). Lots of other great country-side around. The Martins have 3 school-age kids and yours are very welcome; separate supper at 6pm. A laid-back, far from Alton Towers experience.

1103
9/F23
16 & 27
ROOMS
APR-OCT
MED.INX

✓ **Argyll Hotel** & **St Columba Hotels** Iona · www.argyllhoteliona.co.uk & www.stcolumba-hotel.co.uk · 01681 700334 & 01681 700304 The 2 Iona hotels owned by a consortium of local people on this charmed and blessed little island. Holidays here are remembered forever. Argyll has more atmosphere, St Columba is basic but more spacious, both child- and people-in-general-friendly. Unhurried, hassle-free; beautiful organic gardens; kids run free. Both Apr-Oct.

1104
9/J20
13 ROOMS
MAR-NOV
MED.INX-EX
L
ATMOS

✓ **Glenfinnan House** Glenfinnan · www.glenfinnanhouse.com · 01397 722235 Just off the Road to the Isles (the A830 from Fort William to Mallaig; 1628/SCENIC ROUTES). Very large Highland hoose with so many rooms and such big gardens you can be as noisy as you like. Great introduction to the Highland heartland; music, scenery and local characters. Comfy rooms: no phone or TV but fresh flowers; you won't need a room key. Row on the loch from the foot of the lawn. Midge-eater in the garden is welcome. 992/INEXPENSIVE HIGHLAND HOTELS.

1105
10/Q27
132 ROOMS
TEL · TV
MED.EX

✓ **Peebles Hydro** Peebles · www.peebleshydro.co.uk · 01721 720602 One of the first Victorian hydros (1881, rebuilt 1907) and a complete resort for families; it has that well-worn look but it doesn't matter too much if they run amok. Huge grounds, corridors (you get lost) and floors of rooms. Pool and leisure facilities. Entertainment and baby-sitting services. Now being extensively refurbished by McMillan Hotels, the very effective people who have Glenapp (1093/COUNTRY-HOUSE HOTELS) and Kirroughtree (760/SOUTHWEST HOTELS); they seem to be keeping it traditional and refreshingly untrendy. Rooms vary. Dining room is vast and hotel-like. Lazels downstairs is light, contemporary for lunch and tea for the kids (5-6.30pm). Many family rooms.

1106
9/K20
8 ROOMS
TEL · TV
MED.INX

✓ **Old Pines** near Spean Bridge · www.oldpines.co.uk · 01397 712324 3km Spean Bridge via B8004 for Gairlochy at Commando Monument. A ranch-like hotel in a good spot north of Fort William. This hotel has long had a big reputation not only for food but also for welcoming kids. The Dalleys have kids too and welcome yours. Separate mealtimes with Imogen's proper family-food menu then a great dinner for the adults. Very safe, easy environment with chickens and woods (those pines!) to run. Nice stroll to the old Spean Bridge.

1107
10/N21
5 ROOMS
TV
MED.INX

✓ **Torrdarach House** Pitlochry · www.torrdarrach.co.uk · 01796 472136 In a town of many mansions and hotel/guest houses, this is fresh, contemporary and welcomes kids. Big pink house above the town (150m to main street via Larchwood Rd). The Lothians have kids and chickens and a great garden that merges with the countryside. An easy-on-the-eye (and pocket) B&B.

1100
10/N22
6 ROOMS
TV
MED.INX

Inn on the Tay Grandtully · www.theinnonthetay.co.uk · 01887 840760 Road and riverside inn in small village near Aberfeldy. This stretch of river famous for its rapids so usually plenty of raft and canoe action. Josie and Geoff make this place family-friendly. Some rooms have 3 beds but only adults pay. 4 overlook and you are soothed to sleep by the river. Nice lounge and café/bar with river deck.

1109
9/J22
20 ROOMS
TEL · TV
MED.EX

Holly Tree Hotel Kentallen · www.hollytreehotel.co.uk · 01631 740292 On A828 Fort William-Oban road south of Ballachulish. Long-established roadside and seaside hotel in great setting. All rooms have the view. Garden on the shore with pier. Former railway station with Mackintosh references (sic). Surf 'n' turf restaurant, bar and surprising swimming pool.

1110   **The Cally Palace** Gatehouse of Fleet · www.callypalace.co.uk · 01557
11/M30   814341 The big, all-round family and golf hotel in the South West in charming
56 ROOMS   village with safe, woody walks in the grounds and beaches nearby. Old-style ambi-
TEL · TV   ence (let's not say tired); a piano is played at dinner. Leisure facilities include pool
DF   and tennis. 500 acres of forest good for cycling (bike hire can be arranged). There
MED.INX   are allegedly red squirrels. 10 family rooms. Kids' tea at 5pm. See 1508/GARDENS.

1111   **Kilfinan Hotel** Kilfinan · www.kilfinan.com · 01700 821201 North of
9/J25   Tignabruaich on B8000 close to but not on Loch Fyne in the country heart of
10 ROOMS   Cowal and Argyll. On a quiet road, a long-established coaching inn with a good
TEL · TV   reputation for food. The Wyatts have 3 kids and there's a proper kids' menu. Lots
L   of chickens and ducks and a fairy bridge; wild walks nearby (they loan their dogs
MED.INX   out). A relaxing and easy place for the whole bunch.

1112   **Hilton Coylumbridge** near Aviemore · www.hilton.co.uk/coylumbridge ·
7/N19   01479 810661 8km from Aviemore Centre on B970 road to ski slopes and nearest
175 ROOMS   hotel to them. 2 pools of decent size, sauna, flume, etc. Plenty to do in summer
TEL · TV   and winter (1697/KIDS) and enough to do when it rains. Best of the often-criticised
MED.INX-EXP   Aviemore concrete blocks with the most facilities. Huge shed with kids' play area
(the Funhouse). Nice family rooms. Whole hotel a playground in school hols.

1113   **Philipburn** Selkirk · www.philipburnhousehotel.co.uk · 01750 720747
10/Q27   1km town centre on Peebles Rd. Privately owned (and Best Western) and well-run
12 ROOMS   hotel in middle of Borders. Comfy rooms and easy-eat bistro restaurant with sepa-
+ 5 LODGES   rate kids' mealtime. Giant chess in the garden, indoor pool (and spa) on the way at
TEL · TV   TGP. Other physical (kids' adventure playground in woods at Bowhill, salmon-leap-
MED.EX   ing and -watching centre 2km up the road) and more energetic pursuits at St
Mary's Loch/Grey Mare's Tail (1597/WATERFALLS) nearby.

✓ **Comrie Croft** near Comrie Hostel accommodation on a working farm
with basic or quite posh camping in the woods in beautiful heart of
Perthshire setting. Report 1115/HOSTELS.

Stonefield Castle Hotel Tarbert On A83 on slopes of Loch Fyne with wonderful views. A real castle in 60 acres of woody grounds. Report: 738/ARGYLL HOTELS.

Pier House Port Appin · 01631 730302 Report: 1152/SEASIDE INNS.

▉▉▉▉ The Best Hostels

*For hostels in Edinburgh, see p. 36; for Glasgow, see p. 92. SYHA Info: 01786
891400. Central reservations (SYHA) 0870 155 3255. www.syha.org.uk*

1114   ✓ ✓ ✓ **Carbisdale Castle SYH** Culrain, near Bonar Bridge · 01549
6/L15   421232 · www.syha.org The flagship hostel of the SYHA reopened
L   after refurbishment for 2012. An Edwardian castle in terraced gardens overlooking
the Kyle of Sutherland on the edge of the Highlands. Once the home of the exiled
king of Norway, it still contains original works of art (nothing of great value though
the sculptures lend elegance). The library, ballroom, lounges are all in use and it's
only a few quid a night. Some private rooms. Kitchens and café. Bike hire in summer; lots of scenic walks. Station (from Inverness) 1km up steep hill. Buses:
Inverness/Thurso/Lairg. 75km Inverness, 330km Edinburgh. You can hire the
whole place for parties; it has its own ghost 1248/HOUSE PARTIES.

1115
10/M23

✓ ✓ **Comrie Croft** near Comrie · www.comriecroft.com · 01764 670140
On A85 Comrie-Crieff/Perth road 3km before Comrie. 2 self-contained
buildings: the Farmhouse and the Lodge and courtyard of a working farm in beautiful countryside including a millpond and a mountain. Excellent facilities: shop,
games barn, kitchen, lounges. Mountain bikes for hire or sale and a brilliant 3.5km
nature trail with views. Eco-friendly camping in the woods, including 5 Swedish
katas for hire with own wood-burning stoves. Cool for kids, great for grown-ups!

1116
10/N24

✓ **Stirling SYH** Stirling · www.syha.org · 01786 473442 Modern conversion in great part of town, close to castle, adjacent ancient graveyard and
with fine views from some rooms. One of the new hotel-like hostels with student-hall standard and facilities. Many oldies and international tourists. Breakfast
included or self-catering. Access till 2am.

1117
9/L25

✓ **Loch Lomond SYH** Alexandria · www.syha.org.uk Built in 1866 by
George Martin (tobacco baron, not Beatles' producer), this is grand-scale
hostelling. Towers and turrets, galleried upper-hall, space for banqueting and a
splendid view across the loch. 30km Glasgow. Station (Balloch) 4km. Buses 200m.
Access till 12midnight. Some private accommodation (not cheap).

1118
7/N19

✓ **Aviemore Bunkhouse** Aviemore · www.aviemore-bunkhouse.com ·
01479 811181 Main road into Aviemore from south (A95) near station and by
the river. Part of Old Bridge Inn (1284/GASTROPUBS) so great food adjacent. Ensuite
rooms for 6/8 and family rooms available. Can accommodate 44. All year.

1119
6/K14
LL

✓ **Inchnadamph Lodge** Assynt · www.inch-lodge.co.uk · 01571 822218
25km north of Ullapool on A837 road to Lochinver and Sutherland. Well
appointed mansion house for individuals or groups in geology-gazing, hill-walking,
mountain-rearing Assynt. Kitchen, canteen (dinner not provided but self-service
breakfast). Commune with nature, then with each other. Some twin rooms.

1120
10/P21
LL

✓ **Prosen SYH** Glen Prosen · www.syha.org · 01575 540238 Glen Prosen,
the gentlest, most beautiful and wooded of the Angus glens (1582/GLENS).
10km from start of glen at Dykehead and part of tiny Prosen village (well, church)
at the end of the road. An SYH 'green' hostel; wood-burning stove, internet. Tidy
rooms for 4 and 6. Grassy sward, lovely terrace and red squirrels.

1121
7/M20

✓ **Pottery Bunkhouse** Laggan Bridge · www.potterybunkhouse.co.uk ·
01851 643316 On A889 near Loch Laggan 12km from A9 at Dalwhinnie.
Homely bunkhouse, great home-bakes caff (1386/TEAROOMS) and new 2012, the
pizza barn. Lounge overlooks hills and has TV; wood stove, hot tub on deck. All year.

1122
5/F13
L

✓ **2 Hebridean Hostels: Na Gearrannan** near Carloway, North Lewis ·
www.syha.org · 01575 540238 The remarkable hostel in a village of black-houses is an idyllic spot. It was closed 2011; hopefully, 'heating issues' will be
resolved – it is quite unique. See 2141/MUSEUMS. Also:
Am Bothan Harris · www.ambothan.com · 01859 520251 At Leverburgh in
the south of South Harris, a bunkhouse handbuilt and personally run – a bright,
cool building with well-lived-in feel. Good disabled facilities. Caff, shop nearby.

1123
7
ATMOS
LL

✓ **Hostelling in the Hebrides** www.syha.org.uk Simple hostelling in the
crofting communities of Lewis, Harris and the Uists. Run by a trust to maintain standards of Highland hospitality; local crofters act as wardens. Lewis, Harris,
North and South Uist. The Black House cottages on Lewis at Gearrannan (above)
are exceptional. Check local tourist info centres for details (2305/OUTER HEBRIDES).

1124
3/R10
L

✓ **Bis Geos** Isle of Westray, Orkney · www.bisgeos.co.uk · 01857 677420
Remote and fabulous: this is how this traditionally rebuilt croft is described, because I still haven't been. Sounds like perhaps 2 ticks may be due. Exceptional standard with nautical theme. Conservatory overlooks the wild ocean. Minibus from the ferry. Sleeps 12. 2 cottages.

1125
7/G20
L

✓ **The Glebe Barn** Eigg · www.glebebarn.co.uk On fabulously good Eigg, a haven in a haven (sailings from Mallaig and Arisaig; 2232/ISLANDS). Civilised, comfy, wood-burning, well-furnished; duvets and linen provided. Just what you and the island needs. Apr-Oct. Exclusive use possible.

1126
6/L12

✓ **Lazy Crofter Bunkhouse** Durness · www.durnesshostel.com · 07803 927642 Adjacent (and with the same owners as) Mackay's Hotel (989/LESS EXPENSIVE HIGHLANDS). A small, woody chalet (sleeps 12 in 4 rooms) in good location for exploring Durness, Cape Wrath, etc (2051/2061/COASTAL WALKS, 1554/BEACHES) and the caffs at Balnakeil nearby (2181/SHOPPING). No pub in the hotel but great eats all day. Kitchen and outdoor terrace. Open all year.

1127
10/Q27

The Borders SYH www.syha.org.uk There are some ideal wee hostels in this hill-walking tract of Scotland where it all began. These 2 are especially good, one grand, one very small.
Melrose 01896 822521 Grade 1, 81 beds, very popular. Well-appointed mansion on meadow 250m by riverside from the abbey. Nice pub nearby (The Ship).
Broadmeadows 8km from Selkirk off A708, the first hostel in Scotland (1931) is a cosy howff with a stove and a view.

1128
7/M18

Inverness Student Hostel 8 Culduthel Road · www.scotlands-top-hostels.com · 01463 236556 Best independent hostel in town uphill from town centre. Run by same folk who have the great Edinburgh one (117/HOSTELS) with similar laid-back atmosphere and camaraderie. **Bazpackers** 100m downhill, similar vibe.

1129
9/L24

Rowardennan SYH Loch Lomond · www.syha.co.uk · 01360 870259 The hostel at the end of the road up the east (less touristy) side of Loch Lomond from Balmaha and Drymen. Large, well managed and modernised and on a water-side site. On West Highland Way and obvious base for climbing Ben Lomond (1975/MUNROS). Good all-round activity centre and lawns to the loch of your dreams. Rowardennan Hotel boozer nearby. Can do private rooms.

1130
9/F23

Iona Hostel Iona · www.ionahostel.co.uk · 01681 700781 Bunkhouse in north 2km from ferry on John Maclean's farm. Feels like the edge of the world looking over to Staffa and beyond; beach besides. Open-plan space with wood stove. Open all year. 5 rooms, sleeps 21. Iona of course is very special (2230/ISLANDS).

1131
9/G22

Tobermory SYH Mull · www.syha.org.uk · 0870 004 1151 Looks out to Tobermory Bay. Central, highly rated hostel, very busy in summer. 5/6 bunks in 7 rooms (4 on front). Kitchen. Internet. Sweet garden terrace. Near ferry to Ardnamurchan; main Oban ferry 35km away (1547/COASTAL VILLAGES). Mar-Oct.

1132
9/J26

Lochranza Youth Hostel SYH Lochranza · www.syha.org.uk · 01770 830631 On left coming from south. Refurbished Victorian house overlooking fab bay, castle ruins. Swans dip at dawn. Full self catering. Comfortable sitting room. Mar-Nov.

1133
9/J21
L

Glencoe SYH Glencoe · www.syha.org.uk · 01855 811219 Deep in the glen itself, 3km off A82, 4km by back road from Glencoe village and 33km from Fort William. Modern timber house near river; especially handy for climbers and walkers. Laundry, drying room. Clachaig pub, 2km for good food and craic. (Also

1614/SCENIC ROUTES; 1938/ENCHANTING PLACES; 1912/BATTLEGROUNDS; 1256/PUBS; 1996/SERIOUS WALKS.)

1134
7/J19
L

Ratagan SYH www.syha.org.uk · 0870 004 1147 29km from Kyle of Lochalsh, 3km Shiel Bridge (on A87). A much-loved Highland hostel on the shore of Loch Duich, well situated for walking and exploring some of Scotland's most celebrated scenery, eg 5 Sisters of Kintail/Cluanie Ridge (1998/LONG WALKS), Glenelg (1615/SCENIC ROUTES; 1828/PREHISTORIC SITES), Falls of Glomach (1588/WATERFALLS). From Glenelg there's the short and dramatic crossing to Skye through the Kylerhea narrows (continuous, summer only), quite the best way to go.

1135
7/F20
LL
ATMOS

Kinloch Castle Rum · www.isleofrum.com · 01687 462037 The hostel in the servants' quarters in one of the most opulent castle-fantasies in the Highlands though you don't get to use those bathrooms. Hostel operates to allow visitors to experience the rich natural wildlife, grandeur and peace of Rum. Bistro in summer or self-catering. But check for 2012/13. See Rum: 2233/ISLANDS.

1136
7/G17
APR-OCT
LL

Dun Flodigarry near Staffin, Skye · www.hostelflodigarry.co.uk · 01470 552212 In far north 32km from Portree in big, big scenery beside Flodigarry Country House Hotel, which has a decent bistro, pub. Overlooks sea. Bunkrooms for 6-8 and 3 doubles (holds up to 40) and great refectory. Wind-powered by 2012.

The Best Roadside, Seaside & Countryside Inns

1137
7/F18
6 ROOMS
TEL · TV
LOTS

✓ ✓ **The Three Chimneys** Colbost, Skye · www.threechimneys.co.uk · 01470 511258 7km west of Dunvegan on B884 to Glendale. Rooms in a new build, **The House Over-by** across yard from the much-loved, much-awarded Three Chimneys restaurant (2291/SKYE RESTAURANTS). Roadside yes but not so many cars come by and there's the smell of the sea. Calm and contemporary split-level rooms with own doors to the sward. Little treats and nice touches. Breakfast lounge doubles as a pre-dinner lounge in the evening. There are a few gorgeous places like this in the Highlands now; this was the first! Be sure to book for dinner!

1138
10/N23
6 ROOMS
TV
MED.INX
ATMOS

✓ ✓ **The Barley Bree** Muthill near Crieff · www.barleybree.com · 01764 681451 Stylish, excellent-value restaurant with rooms above on main road through village. Great food; tasteful, comfortable rooms. Chef/patron Fabrice Bouteloup a great chef and patron and all-round nice guy. Bar/restaurant open for lunch (Wed-Sat) and dinner (closed Mon). Not much to do in Muthill itself but the amazing Drummond Gardens are nearby (1496/GARDENS). Last year I sent them incognito a supermodel – she loved it too.

1139 9/H26
5 ROOMS
APR-OCT
TV · DF
MED.EX

✓ ✓ **Kilberry Inn** near Tarbert, Argyll · www.kilberryinn.com · 01880 770223 Half-way round the Knapdale peninsula on the single-track B8024 (1139/SCENIC ROUTES), the long and breathtaking way to Lochgilphead. Homely roadside inn with simple, classy rooms and excellent cooking (1277/GASTROPUBS) that comes fresh and local. Michelin Bib Gourmand.

1140
7/H18
7 ROOMS
MED.INX

✓ ✓ **The Applecross Inn** Applecross · www.applecross.uk.com/inn · 01520 744262 The end of the legendary road to a definitive seaside inn on the Applecross strand. Spectacular journey to get here (1616/scenic routes) and not for the faint-hearted driver; hit the shoreline and settle in (though only 7 small and not so cheap rooms. They all face the sea, which is what you do here. Then eat at Judy Fish's seafood table and get forever Applecrossed (2055/WALKS, 2149/HERITAGE, 1398/COFFEE SHOPS). Report: 1169/GET AWAY HOTELS.

1141
9/H21
7 ROOMS
DF
MED.INX

✓ **Glenuig Inn** Glenuig · www.glenuig.com · 01687 470219 Just off A861 between Lochailort on the Road to the Isles from Fort William (1628/SCENIC ROUTES) and Kinlochmoidart, a perfect Highland road and seaside inn. Extensively refurbished, light and contemporary to gold-standard in the green-tourism code (sustainable materials, solar-powered, etc). Bunkhouse above pub and lounge, 7 simple rooms adjacent. Good base for sea kayaking. Locally sourced organic grub.

1142
9/F23
16 ROOMS
APR-OCT
LL
MED.EX

✓ **Argyll Hotel** Iona · www.argyllhoteliona.co.uk · 01681 700334 On beautiful, turquoise bay between Iona and Mull on road between ferry and abbey. Day trippers come and go; you should stay! A charming hotel on a remarkable island. Cosy rooms quite fabulous (1 suite). Excellent, all-home-made food (especially vegetarian) from organic garden. Real peace and quiet and that's just sitting in the sun lounge or on the bench outside. It's Colourist country and this is where they would have stayed too. Nice for kids (1103/HOTELS THAT WELCOME KIDS).

1143 9/J25
10 RMS · TV
L
MED.EX
ATMOS

✓ **The Kames Hotel** by Tighnabruaich · www.kames-hotel.com · 01700 811489 Frequented by passing yachtsmen (hotel has its own free moorings) who can pop up for lunch. Great seaside setting overlooking the Doon-the-Water shore, and atmospheric bar busy with locals. Owners Shelley and Pat at the helm: a calming colour scheme, friendly staff and Philippa Elliott's photography along with other well-chosen pictures. Simply, reasonably stylish and a good vibe.

1144
9/K22
10 ROOMS
TEL · TV
MED.EX

✓ **Bridge of Orchy Hotel** Bridge of Orchy · www.bridgeoforchy.co.uk · 01838 400208 Unmissable on the A82 (the road to Glencoe, Fort William and Skye) 11km north of Tyndrum. Old inn extensively refurbished and a great stopover for motorists and walkers. Simple, quite stylish rooms. A la carte menu and specials in pub/conservatory. Good spot for the malt or a munch on the West Highland Way (1988/LONG WALKS). Food LO 9pm. The 46-bed bunkhouse is cheap.

1145
7/H19
6 ROOMS
L
MED.INX
ATMOS

✓ **Glenelg Inn** Glenelg · www.glenelg-inn.com · 01599 522273 At the end of that great road over the hill from Shiel Bridge on the A87 (1615/SCENIC ROUTES)... well, not quite the end because you can drive further round to ethereal Loch Hourn, but this halt has always been a civilised hostelry and often a whole lot of fun. Decent food, good drinking, snug lounge. Garden with tables and views. Rooms basic but it all has the atmosphere that a lineage of estimable proprietors has conferred and now in the very capable hands of Sheila Condi. From Glenelg, take the best route to Skye (6/FAVOURITE JOURNEYS).

1146
10/N22
6 ROOMS
TV
MED.INX

✓ **Inn on the Tay** Grandtully · www.theinnonthetay.co.uk · 01887 840760 Recent conversion of roadside inn that also has a commanding position on the riverbank where rapids tax legions of helmeted rafters and canoeists; so constant entertainment. Contemporary café/bar with good food, residents' lounge, outside deck and comfortable modern bedrooms – some with 3 beds, so a good family or ménage à trois option.

1147
10/Q27
14 ROOMS
+3 COTTAGES
TV · DF
MED.INX

✓ **Traquair Arms** Innerleithen · www.traquairarmshotel.co.uk · 01896 830229 100m from the A72 Gala–Peebles road towards Traquair, a popular village and country inn that caters for all kinds of folk (and, at weekends, large numbers of them). Notable for bar meals (Scottish emphasis), real ale and family facilities. Rooms refurbished to a decent standard. David and Jane Roger making a fair go of it here. Beer garden out back. Much cycling nearby and the Tweed.

1148 **Eglinton Arms Hotel** www.eglintonarms.co.uk · 01355 302631 ·
10/M26 Eaglesham Sprawling inn in a charming conservation village, a quiet contrast to
35 ROOMS downtown Glasgow but surprisingly close – only 20 minutes on a good day. A dif-
TEL · TV ferent green world and gurgling brook besides. Recent major makeover of the
CHP locally popular bar/grill restaurant, and a surprisingly stylish stay for much less
than anywhere comparable in the city.

1149 **Craw Inn** Auchencrow, near Reston · www.thecrawinn.co.uk · 01890
10/S26 761253 5 km A1 and well worth the short detour into Berwickshire countryside.
5 ROOMS Quintessential inn with cosy pub and dining room. Funky furniture, simple rooms.
MED.INX Food decent, wines extraordinary. Lunch and dinner. 1286/GASTROPUBS.

1150 **The Stein Inn** Waternish, Skye · www.stein-inn.co.uk · 01470 592362
7/F17 Off B886 the Dunvegan-Portree road, about 10km Dunvegan. In row of cottages
5 ROOMS on water side. The 'oldest inn on Skye' with great pub (open fire, ok grub lunch
L and dinner). Rooms above are cottagey, small and cosy and Waternish is a very
INX special spot. Excellent seafood restaurant adjacent (2294/SEAFOOD RESTAURANTS).

1151 **Old Inn** Gairloch · www.theoldinn.net · 01445 712006 Southern approach
7/H16 on A832, tucked away by river and old bridge. Excellent pub for food in bar, lounge
17 ROOMS and restaurant and tables by the river. Music (Tue/Sat or as advertised). Nice, sim-
TEL · TV · DF ple rooms (and the pub goes like a fair). Routinely recommended in pub guides;
MED.INX their ale is good (and includes their own Blind Piper).

1152 10/M24 **Pier House** Port Appin · www.pierhousehotel.co.uk · 01631 730302 Inn at
11 ROOMS the end of the road (minor road that leads off A828 Oban-Fort William) and at end
+COTT of the pier where the tiny Lismore passenger ferry leaves (2242/MAGIC ISLANDS). A
TEL · TV bistro restaurant with decent seafood (1335/SEAFOOD RESTAURANTS) in a great set-
NO PETS · LL ting. Comfy motel-type rooms (more expensive overlook the sea and island) and
MED.INX conservatory restaurant, lounge. Good place to take kids and a great yachty stop.

1153 **Glenisla Hotel** Kirkton of Glenisla · www.glenisla-hotel.com · 01575
10/P21 582223 20km northwest of Kirriemuir via B951 at head of secluded story-book
6 ROOMS glen. A home from home: hearty food, real ale and local colour. Fishers, stalkers,
DF trekkers and walkers (a stopover on the Cateran Trail; 1992/LONG WALKS) all come
CHP by for grub, grog and a chat along the way (pub closed Mon). Neat rooms look into
countryside but haven't visited recently to see if they've had that wee makeover.

1154 **Meikleour Hotel** Meikleour · www.meikleour-inn.co.uk · 01250 883206
10/P22 Just off A93 Perth-Blairgowrie road (on B984) by and behind famously high beech
5 ROOMS · TV hedge (a Perthshire landmark). Roadside inn with quiet accommodation; food in
MED.INX dining room or (more convivially) the bar. Rooms recently refurbished. Simply rural!

1155 7/J19 **Cluanie Inn** Glenmoriston · www.cluanieinn.com · 01320 340238 On road
12 ROOMS to Skye 15km before Shiel Bridge, a traditional inn surrounded by mountain sum-
+BUNKHOUSE mits (they say 21 Munros within reach) that attract walkers and travellers: 5 Sisters,
TEL Ridge and Saddle (1998/LONG WALKS). Club house adjacent has some group
L accommodation while inn rooms can be high-spec: 1 with sauna, 1 with jacuzzi!
CHP-MED.EX Dining room and bar food all wholesome. LO 9pm. Rooms do vary. Friendly staff.

1156 **Bridge of Cally Hotel** Bridge of Cally · www.bridgeofcallyhotel.com ·
10/P22 01250 886231 Wayside pub on a bend of road between Blairgowrie and Glenshee/
18 ROOMS· Braemar (ski zone and Royal Deeside). Cosy and inexpensive between gentle Perth-
TV · DA shire and the wilder Grampians. Staging post on the Cateran Trail (1992/LONG
CHP WALKS). Rooms quiet, pleasant and good value. Restaurant and bar meals till 9pm.

1157 9/J21 **Clachaig Inn** Glencoe · www.clachaig.com · **01855 811252** Basic accommo-
23 ROOMS dation but you will sleep well here especially after walking/climbing/drinking,
TV · NO PETS which is what most people are doing here. Great atmosphere both inside and out.
L Food (very basic too) available bar/lounge and dining room till 9pm. Ales aplenty;
MED.INX 1256/PUBS. 4 lodges out back. Harry Potter and film crew were once here.

1158 10/N21 **Moulin Hotel** Pitlochry · www.moulinhotel.co.uk · **01796 472196**
16 RMS · TEL Kirkmichael Rd; at the landmark crossroads on the A924. Basic rooms above and
TV · DA· CHP beside notable pub for food and especially ales – they brew their own out the
ATMOS back. (1266/REAL ALES). There is an annexe across the street.

1159 7/L19 **Glenmoriston Arms Hotel** Invermoriston, Loch Ness · **01320 351206** ·
11 ROOMS www.glenmoriston-arms-hotel.co.uk On main A82 between Inverness (45km)
TEL · TV and Fort Augustus (10km) at the Glen Moriston corner, and a worthwhile corner of
MED.INX this famous loch side to explore. Busy local bar, fishermen's tales. Bar meals look
ok and extensive malt list – certainly a good place to drink them. Inn-like bedrooms with 3 cottagey rooms over-by.

√ **The Ship Inn** Gatehouse of Fleet · **01557 814217** Old inn on main street
corner of this charming Galloway town. Report: 759/SOUTHWEST HOTELS.

√ **The Harbour Inn** Islay · **01496 810330** & **The Port Charlotte Hotel**
01496 850360 2 waterfront inns on faraway Islay: one in town, the other in
charming Port Charlotte. 2284/2283/ISLAND HOTELS.

√ **The Sorn Inn** Sorn, Ayrshire · **01290 551305** 1276/GASTROPUBS.

Anchor Hotel Kippford · **01556 620205** Pub grub with rooms in superb
Solway setting. 764/SOUTHWEST HOTELS & RESTAURANTS.

The Best Restaurants With Rooms

√ √ **The Peat Inn** near Cupar · **01334 840206** At eponymous Fife
crossroads. Long-established brilliant restaurant under masterchef
Geoffrey Smeddle. And swish suites. 845/FIFE RESTAURANTS.

√ √ **The Sorn Inn** Sorn · **01290 551305** 8km east of Mauchline on the
B743, half an hour from Ayr. 748/AYRSHIRE HOTELS.

√ √ **The Three Chimneys** Colbost, Skye · **01470 511258** State-of-the-
art dining and contemporary rooms far away in the west. Near
Dunvegan. But you'll be lucky to get in. 2259/SKYE HOTELS.

√ √ **The Barley Bree** Muthill near Crieff · **01764 681451** French guy in
the kitchen, Scots partner on decor and design have transformed this old
pub in a sleepy village to a destination. 1138/ROADSIDE INNS.

√ √ **The Horseshoe Inn** Eddleston near Peebles · **01721 730225**
New-ish Borders destination. Bistro and restaurant and rooms in old
school behind. Designed to impress. 793/BORDERS HOTELS.

✓ ✓ **The Cross** Kingussie · 01540 661166 Rooms upstairs in converted tweed mill. Downstairs the best restaurant and wine list in the region. 975/HIGHLAND HOTELS.

✓ ✓ **Mackay's** Durness · 01971 511202 Contemporary makeover of long-established far North West hotel. 989/LESS EXPENSIVE HIGHLAND HOTELS.

✓ ✓ **The Cross Keys** Kippen · 01786 870293 Long-established gastropub with rooms in foodie village main street. 1281/GASTROPUBS.

✓ ✓ **The Inn At Kippen** Kippen · 01786 871010 Excellent bar, restaurant in village just off Stirling-Loch Lomond road. 782/CENTRAL HOTELS.

✓ ✓ **Kilberry Inn** Kilberry near Tarbert · 01880 770223 1139/ROADSIDE INNS.

✓ **Blar Na Leisg** Drumbeg · 01571 833325 Artistic, historic and unbelievably picturesque surroundings. 977/HIGHLAND HOTELS.

✓ **The Creel Inn** St Margaret's Hope, Orkney · 01856 831311 Long-established, great location, excellent good-value food. 2307/ORKNEY.

✓ **Yann's At Glenearn House** Crieff · 01764 650111 Victorian mansion with 5 rooms above best bistro in the county. 863/PERTHSHIRE RESTAURANTS.

✓ **The Mash Tun** Aberlour · 01340 881771 Boutique-style rooms above pub in whisky country. 961/SPEYSIDE.

✓ **The Green Inn** Ballater · 01339 755701 Long-established best restaurant in Deeside tourist town. 920/NORTHEAST RESTAURANTS.

✓ **The Inn on the Tay** Grandtully · 01887 840760 A made-over inn on the banks of the rushing River Tay. Great for kids. 1146/ROADSIDE INNS.

✓ **Creagan House** Strathyre · 01877 384638 Rob Roy and Trossachs country. On the road west and to the islands. 778/CENTRAL HOTELS.

✓ **Smiddy House** Spean Bridge · 01397 712335 Comfy roadside inn and best casual food in Fort William area. 1020/BEST HIGHLAND RESTAURANTS.

✓ **Wildings Hotel** Maidens · 01655 331401 Huge local reputation for food; refurbished rooms overlook the sea. 749/AYRSHIRE HOTELS.

✓ **The Wheatsheaf** Swinton, Berwickshire · 01890 860257 10 all-different bedrooms above gastropub of long standing. 1289/GASTROPUBS.

Dunure Inn Dunure · 01292 500549 South of Ayr. 1301/GASTROPUBS.

Kilspindie House Aberlady · 01875 870682 Main street of East Lothian village. 820/LOTHIAN HOTELS.

The Rocks Dunbar · 01368 862287 At east end of town. Overlooking harbour area. Big local reputation for food. 823/LOTHIAN HOTELS.

The Great Get-Away-From-It-All Hotels

1160
10/L23
14 ROOMS
TEL · TV
LL
ATMOS
EXP

✓ ✓ **Monachyle Mhor** near Balquhidder · www.monachylemhor.com · 01877 384622 Though only 11km from the A84 Callander-Crianlarich road as you follow a thread of road along Loch Voilside with the Balquhidder Braes above you know you're leaving those urban blues behind. Once you're inside the old pink farmhouse you could be in a boutique hotel in NYC or more aptly Glasgow, except your window looks over the farm to big, beautiful countryside. Contemporary, calm and sexy. 7 rooms in courtyard annexe, 6 (a bit smaller) in main building, 1 out back. All completely gorgeous, especially the baths and bathrooms. A bar that locals and visitors use. Tom Lewis on stoves (when he's not food festing) cooking up some of the best food in the North. Friendly, cosy, inexpensive for this standard; a place to relax summer or winter. The shop that stocks the selected stuff, part of what Tom, Dick and Madeleine have turned into the Mhor brand which includes the Library Tearoom in Balquhidder (1378/TEAROOMS) and the bakers and café in Callander (1422/BAKERS, 1350/FISH & CHIPS). Like me, you will always want to come back for Mhor. See also 1214/GLAMPING.

1161
7/J17
19 ROOMS
TEL · TV
NO KIDS · DF
LL
LOTS

✓ ✓ **The Torridon** Glen Torridon near Kinlochewe · 01445 791242 · www.lochtorridonhotel.com Impressive former hunting lodge on lochside, surrounded by the pick of the peaks of the Scottish mountains. Deluxe comfort and taste in this family-run (the Rose-Bristows) baronial house with relaxed atmosphere: an all-round Highland experience. Focuses on outdoor activities like clay-pigeon shoots, kayaking, gorge-scrambling, mountain biking or fishing with 2 full-time guides/instructors. Lots of walking possibilities nearby including the Torridon big 3: Beinn Alligin (1980/MUNROS), Liathach right in front of the hotel and the easier Beinn Eighe. This great hotel has spawned a cheaper travel-lodge option: **The Torridon Inn** in adjacent block with own bar and bistro. An excellent budget choice (12 rooms). Main hotel has elegant dining room under 3-rosette chef Bruno Birbeck (5-course rustic but delicate, fine-dining menu) who also oversees the inn menu. Nice afternoon tea after the exertions and a fantastic malts bar for a dram in the dwindling day (See Whisky, p. 263). Hotel closed Jan.

1162 9/G22
9 ROOMS
+3 COTTAGES
EASTER-OCT
TV
LOTS

✓ **Tiroran House** Isle of Mull · tiroran.com · 01681 705232 Southwest corner on road to Iona from Craignure then B8035 round Loch na Keal, or more scenic and sometimes scary via Salen. 1 hour Tobermory. Family-friendly small country house in fabulous gardens by the sea, under conscientious owners Laurence and Katie Mackay (Katie, a Cordon Bleu cook, is executive chef). Near Iona and Ulva ferry; you won't miss Tobermory. Excellent food from sea and organic kitchen garden. Traditional rooms. Sea eagles fly over, otters flop in the bay.

1163 9/F23
15 ROOMS
(1 SUITE)
APR-OCT · LL
MED.EX

✓ **Argyll Hotel** Iona · www.argyllhoteliona.co.uk · 01681 700334 Quintessential island hotel on the best of small islands just large enough to get away for walks and explore (2230/ISLANDS). You can hire bikes (or bring). Abbey is nearby (1902/ABBEYS). 3 lounges (1 with TV, 1 with sun) and 1 lovely suite (with wood-burning stove). Good home-grown/made food from their organic garden.

1164
10/P21
17 ROOMS
TEL · TV · DF
L
MED.EX-LOTS

✓ **Dalmunzie Castle** www.dalmunzie.com · 01250 885224 · Spittal of Glenshee 3km off Blairgowrie-Braemar road and near Glenshee skiing. By riverside and surrounded by bare hills, this laird's house is warm and welcoming but splendidly remote. Some great rooms, Michelin-mentioned dining, bar and 9-hole golf course. Good aesthetic, comfy yet stylish. You wanna be here! See also 853/PERTHSHIRE.

1165 7/H20
4 ROOMS
+ LODGE
APR-SEP
NO PETS
CHP

✓ **Doune Stone Lodge** www.doune-knoydart.co.uk/stlodge.html ·
01687 462667 · Knoydart On the wonderful and wild and remote peninsula
of Knoydart (71/DISCOVER) and this great spot on the west tip overlooking a bay on
the Sound of Sleat. They have own boats so pick you up from Mallaig and drop you
round the inlets for walking. Otherwise 10km from Inverie, the village with brilliant
pub. Lodge mainly for groups (shared bathroom area) and 4 individual rooms
100m round the bay with dining room adjacent. Excellent fixed menu (diets
advise), home-made dinner to a high standard; wine list. Breakfast and packed
lunch. This whole place is an impressive labour of love.

1166 7/F17
8 ROOMS
MAR-DEC
L
MED.EX

✓ **Greshornish Country House** www.greshornishhouse.com · 01470
582345 · Skye Off A850 Portree-Dunvegan road about half-way then 6km
along Loch Greshornish to delightful isolation. It's a long way to another good dinner so you're expected to eat in (but lovely menu from Greshornish Loch starters
to impressive Scottish cheese). Comfy, airy rooms presented with great taste (nice
pics) by the Colquhouns. Log fires, billiard room, candlelit dinners. A superb retreat
(available for exclusive use). 2 nights' minimum stay. Pronounced Grish-nish.

1167
10/Q21
10 ROOMS
TEL · TV
NO PETS
L
CHP

✓ **Glen Clova Hotel** www.clova.com · 01575 550350 · near Kirriemuir
Well, not that near Kirriemuir: 25km north up the glen on B955 from Dykehead. Rooms surprisingly well appointed. Climbers' bar (till all hours). Superb walking (eg Loch Brandy and classic path to Loch Muick). A laid-back get-away though
lots of families drive up on Sunday for lunch. Also has a bunkhouse (cheap) and 3
luxury lodges with hot tubs. Great value, great craic! Calmer, greener and more
basic is **Prosen Hostel** at the head of Glen Prosen, probably the most beautiful
and unspoiled of the glens. No pub, no interference (1120/HOSTELS).

1168 11/J30
6 ROOMS
+ SUITES
TEL · TV · LL
MED.EXP

✓ **Corsewall Lighthouse Hotel** www.lighthousehotel.co.uk · 01776
853220 · near Stranraer 20 minutes from Stranraer (via A718 to Kirkcolm)
and follow signs, but way up on the peninsula and as it suggests a hotel made out
of a working lighthouse. Romantic and offbeat, but only ok food. Local attractions
include Portpatrick, 30 minutes by quiet backroads. Report 761/SOUTHWEST HOTELS.

1169 7/H18
7 ROOMS
LL
MED.INX

✓ **Applecross Inn** www.applecross.uk.com/inn · 01520 744262 ·
Applecross At the end of the road (the Pass of the Cattle which is often
snowed up in winter), you can really disappear north of Kyle of Lochalsh and west
of Strathcarron. After a spectacular journey, this waterside inn is a haven of hospitality. Buzzes all seasons. Rooms small and well, no' cheap. Judy Fish, a great team
and a real chef, the returned Roddy Macrae, to look after you. Poignant visitor centre (2140/HERITAGE), walled garden, lovely walks (2055/COASTAL WALKS) and even a
real pizza hut in summer (1398/COFFEE SHOPS) easily enough to keep you happy in
faraway Applecross for days.

1170 9/K20
5 ROOMS · TV
MAR-OCT
NO PETS · LL
CHP

✓ **Corriechoille Lodge** www.corriechoille.com · 01397 712002 · by
Spean Bridge 3km from south Bridge via road by station. Lovely road and
spectacularly situated; it's great to arrive. Justin and Lucy share their perfect
retreat with you in house and 2 turf-covered chalets out back. Rooms simple. Set-
menu dinner. All round serenity! Report 995/HIGHLAND HOTELS.

1171 7/N16
9 ROOMS
TEL · NO PETS
LOTS

✓ **Glenmorangie House** www.theglenmorangiehouse.com · Cadboll by
Fearn · 01862 871671 On the little peninsula east of Tain off A9 (10km).
Luxurious but laid-back mansion; house-party atmosphere with communal-style
delectable dining. Owned by LVMH. Report: 978/HIGHLAND HOTELS.

1172 7/K20
9 ROOMS
L
CHP-MED.INX

Tomdoun Hotel www.tomdoun.com · 01809 511218 · near Invergarry
20km from Invergarry, 9km off A87 to Kyle of Lochalsh. Ivy-covered Victorian
coaching inn off the beaten track but perfect (we do mean perfect) for fishing and
walking (River Garr, Loch Quoich and Knoydart, the last wilderness). Superb views
over Glengarry and Bonnie Prince Charlie Country. House-party ambience, panelled public rooms, mix-match furniture, loadsa malts. Not all bedrooms with view
or en suite but this is an inexpensive Highland retreat (no phones or TV to disturb).

1173 9/L22
5 ROOMS
MID FEB-OCT
LL
CHP

Moor of Rannoch Hotel Rannoch Station · www.moorofrannoch.co.uk
01882 633238 Beyond Pitlochry and the Trossachs and far west via Loch Tummel
and Loch Rannoch (B8019 and B8846) so a wonderful journey to the edge of
Rannoch Moor and adjacent station (so you could get the sleeper from London
and be here for breakfast. 4 trains either way each day via Glasgow). Literally the
end of the road but an exceptional find in the middle of nowhere. Cosy, wood-
panelled rooms, ok restaurant, though gourmets may grumble. Nevertheless a
great-value quintessential Highland inn. Superb walking.

1174 5/D17
11 ROOMS
MAR-JAN
DF
MED.INX-EX

Langass Lodge North Uist · www.langasslodge.co.uk · 01876 580285 On
the A867 which runs through the middle of the Uists, 7km south of Lochmaddy,
500m from the road. Small, hideaway hotel with garden and island outlook,
though the entrance ain't so lovely. Half of rooms in extension to stylish standard
but others in hotel ok. Nice bar and dining overlooking the garden. Kid-friendly
and you can bring the dog. Uists are wonderful to explore and there's prehistoric
stuff nearby and a great (2.5km) walk. 1829/PREHISTORIC, 1559/BEACHES.

1175 7/K18
8 ROOMS
TEL · TV
MED.INX

Tomich Hotel www.tomichhotel.co.uk · 01456 415399 · near Cannich
8km from Cannich which is 25km from Drumnadrochit. Fabulous Plodda Falls
nearby (1589/WATERFALLS). Cosy country inn in conservation village with bonus of
use of swimming pool in nearby steading. Faraway feel, surprising bar round the
back where what's left of the locals do linger. Good base for outdoorsy weekend.
Glen Affric across the way and this is the nearest good place to stay.

 Knockinaam Lodge near Portpatrick · 01776 810471 Report:
756/SOUTH WEST HOTELS.

 Glenapp Castle Ballantrae · 01465 831212 Report: 1093/COUNTRY-
HOUSE HOTELS.

 Three Chimneys Skye · 01470 511258 Report: 1137/ROADSIDE INNS,
2291/SKYE RESTAURANTS.

Mackay's Durness · 01971 511202 Report: 989/LESS EXPENSIVE HIGH-
LAND HOTELS.

Glenelg Inn Glenelg · 01599 522273 Report: 1145/ROADSIDE INNS.

Broad Bay House Lewis · 01851 820990 Report: 2305/HEBRIDES.

Balcary Bay Auchencairn · 01556 640311 Report: 758/SOUTHWEST
HOTELS.

The Best Very Scottish Hotels

1176 6/K15
23 ROOMS
TEL
ATMOS
CHP-MED.EX

✓✓ **The Ceilidh Place** Ullapool · www.ceilidhplace.com · 01854 612103 Off main street near port for the Hebrides. Inimitable Jean Urquhart's place (and also daughter Rebecca) which, more than any other in the Highlands, encapsulates Scottish traditional culture and hospitality. Caters for all sorts: hotel rooms are above (with a truly comfortable lounge – you help yourself to drinks) and a bistro/bar below often with live music and performance (ceilidh-style). A bunkhouse across the way with cheap and cheerful accommodation and a bookshop where you can browse through the best of all Scottish literature. Though it was long ago that the Ceilidh Place put Ullapool on the must-visit map of Scotland, it has moved effortlessly with the times. Now and forever, as they say. More detail: 988/LESS EXPENSIVE HIGHLAND HOTELS.

1177 6/J14
5 ROOMS
MAR-DEC
TEL · TV
LL
LOTS

✓✓ **The Albannach** Lochinver · www.thealbannach.co.uk · 01571 844407 2km up road to Baddidarach as you come from south into Lochinver on A837, at the bridge. Lovely 18th-century house in one of Scotland's most scenic areas, Assynt, where the mountains take your breath away (1948/1950/FAVOURITE HILLS). The Byre overlooking the croft is the latest of their gorgeous 3 suites. There's also the Loft and the Penthouse with outside cliff-enclosed terrace. Great walk behind house to Archemelvich beach – otters on the way – and Colin's 'secret' beach nearby (1566/BEACHES). Non-residents can, and should, eat. Fixed-menu dinner with Michelin star (hard-won but shouldn't be your reason for coming here; Lesley's food has always been fab): it's nature on a plate. All in all, a highly individual urban-boutique-hotel experience in a glorious landscape.

1178 8/Q18
16 ROOMS
FEB-DEC
TEL · TV
EXP

✓ **Kildrummy Castle Hotel** www.kildrummycastlehotel.co.uk · 01975 571288 · near Alford 6okm west of Aberdeen via A944 through some fine bucolic scenery and the green Don valley to this spectacular location with real Highlands aura. Well placed if you're on the Castle Trail, this comfortable chunk of Scottish Baronial has the redolent ruins of Kildrummy Castle on the opposite bluff and a gorgeful of gardens between. Some rooms small; all very Scottish. Romantic in autumn when the gardens are good. Faber family preside. Fran's in the kitchen.

1179 7/H19
12 ROOMS
+4 SUITES
TEL · TV
LL
MED.EX
ATMOS

✓ **Eilean Iarmain** Skye · www.eilean-iarmain.co.uk · 01471 833332 Sleat area in south of Skye, this snug Gaelic inn nestles in the bay and is the classic island hostelry: the word 'location' does come to mind. Bedrooms in hotel best but garden rooms over-by are quieter. The 2-floor suites in adjacent steading are more expensive, like being in your own Highland cottage. Food decent in dining room and with more atmosphere in the bar. Mystic shore walks. Gallery with selected exhibitions and shop by the quay (2204/SPECIAL SHOPS). The El is very Highland and very Scottish, its voice is Gaelic, its charm subtle and totally engaging.

1180 9/J20
13 ROOMS
MAR-NOV
LL
MED.INX-EX
ATMOS

✓ **Glenfinnan House Hotel** Glenfinnan · www.glenfinnanhouse.com · 01397 722235 Off the Road to the Isles (A830 Fort William to Mallaig; 1628/SCENIC ROUTES). The MacFarlanes have owned this legendary hotel in this historic house for over 30 years (1924/MARY, CHARLIE & BOB); managers, the Gibsons keep it soundly sympatico. Refurbishment has retained its charm; the huge rooms remain yet intimate and cosy with open fires. Impromptu sessions and ceilidhs in the bar especially on Thursdays. Bar food and à la carte in dining room. Fishing or dreaming on Loch Shiel at foot of the lawn (row boat and a cruise boat nearby; 5/JOURNEYS). Day trips to Skye and the small islands. Quintessential!

1181 9/L28 · **Savoy Park** 16 Racecourse Road, Ayr · www.savoypark.com · 01292 266112
15 ROOMS · In a street and area of indifferent hotels this one, owned and run by the Henderson
TEL · TV · family for approaching 50 years, is a real Scottish gem. Many wedding guests will
MED.INX · agree. Period features, lovely garden; not too much tartan. A warm, cosy, home-
spun atmosphere. And round one of the fireplaces: 'blessed be God for his giftis'.

✓ ✓ ✓ **Crieff Hydro** Crieff · 01764 655555 *The* Scottish family hotel.
Report: 1098/ HOTELS FOR KIDS.

✓ ✓ **George Hotel** Inveraray · 01499 502111 Happy memories of
Scotland are made of this. Report: 724/ARGYLL HOTELS.

✓ **Glengarry Castle** Invergarry · 01809 501254 In the Great Glen, lochside
grounds. Centuries of history. Report: 1001/LESS EXPENSIVE HIGHLANDS.

Stonefield Castle Tarbert · 01880 820836 Report: 738/ARGYLL HOTELS.

Luxurious Isolation

*In StB there is no category for self-catering accommodation – there's too
much to choose from and it's not possible to try them out and then select the
best but these cottages in exceptional locations are too special to go
unmentioned.*

1182 5/E15 · ✓ **Blue Reef Cottages** South Harris · www.stay-hebrides.com · 01859
LL · 550370 1 km from Scarista House (2276/ISLAND HOTELS) and overlooking the
same idyllic beach (1561/BEACHES). 2 exceptional cottages, probably first of a new
wave of luxury-in-good-location lodges. For couples only though the study could
be another bedroom at a pinch. Stylish, good facilities, amazing view. Gourmet
meals from lady nearby or eat at Scarista House. 2-day minimum stay in winter.

1183 6/H16 · ✓ **Blue Cabin by the Sea** Cove · www.bluecabinbythesea.co.uk · 07999
LL · 755825 It's blue and it's 10m from its own little beach near perfect little
Cove harbour in Berwickshire. You reach the cottage through a rock-cut smuggling
tunnel and across the beach. Owned by Ben Tindall, the architect who did the
Queen's Gallery at Holyrood Palace; we can expect a uniquely, even quirkily com-
fortable abode and in this case perfect isolation. Sleeps 4 from £500-750pw.

1184 6/L13 · ✓ **Croft 103** near Durness · www.neverwanttoleave.co.uk · 01971
L · 511202 2 state-of-the-eco-art lochside cottages by the people who have
Mackay's in Durness (10km along beautiful coast; 1554/BEACHES). Hill and sea cottages overlooking Loch Eriboll (1609/LOCHS) with their own wind turbine and solar
panels so carbon negative. Merging into the rocky, watery landscape with big big
windows, underfloor heating, outside tubs and high-tech appliances. Well... you'll
never want to leave. One bedroom. All year round. Around £1200 a week.

1185 5/E14 · ✓ **Beach Bay Cottage** www.beachbaycottage.co.uk · Carnish near Uig,
LL · Lewis · 0845 2680801 Way out west to the Atlantic and the sunset, about
45 minutes from Stornoway, a new build – stone, glass, turf roof, nestling into the
hillside 150m above a truly spectacular beach (1562/BEACHES). 180º windows,
sauna, totally mod con. 2 bedrooms. Though you're in seemingly splendid isolation, the rather good Auberge (2305/HEBRIDES) is right next door for meals and
further accommodation. From £1100. The phone number is an agency number.

Great Wild Camping Up North

In StB we don't do caravans. In fact, because I spend a lot of time behind them on Highland roads, WE HATE CARAVANS and ain't mad about camper-vans, either. Wild camping is different, provided you are sensitive to the environment and respect the rights of farmers and landowners. All sites are LL.

1186 5/E16 ✓ **South Harris** West coast south of Tarbert where the boat comes in. 35km to Stornoway. Follow road and you reach some truly splendid beaches (eg Scarista 1561/BEACHES). You could treat yourself to dinner at Scarista House (2276/ISLAND HOTELS). Gaze on your own private sunset and swim in a turquoise sea.

1187 9/G22 ✓ **Calgary Beach** Mull 10km from Dervaig, where there are toilets, picnic tables and BBQs but no other facilities – this is classic wild camping but you won't be alone. Also on Mull south of Killiechronan on the gentle shore of **Loch na Keal**, there is nothing but the sky and the sea and you have it all to yourself. Ben More is in the background (1981/MUNROS). Both sublime!

1188 9/K22 ✓ **Glen Etive** near Ballachulish & Glencoe One of Scotland's great unofficial camping grounds. Along the road/river side in a classic glen (1580/GLENS) guarded where it joins the pass into Glencoe by the awesome Buachaille Etive Mor. Innumerable grassy terraces and small meadows on which climbers and walkers have camped for generations, and pools to bathe in (1657/WILD SWIMMING). The famous Kingshouse Pub is 2km from the foot of the glen for sustenance, malt whisky and comparing midge bites.

1189 7/F20 ✓ **Lickisto Blackhouse Camping** Harris · 01859 530485 On east coast (see 1621/SCENIC ROUTES) of South Harris, a beautiful natural campsite, not so wild because there are showers and a 180-year-old blackhouse for warmth and wash-up facilities. Not many pitches (10) so phone first; also a couple of yurts for hire. Unlikely as it may seem, there's a great caff nearby (2305/HEBRIDES).

1190 9/F26 **Kintra** Islay Bowmore-Port Ellen road, take Oa turn-off then follow signs 7km. A long beach one way, a wild coastal walk the other. Camping (and room for a few campervans) on grassy strand looking out to sea; basic facilities in farmyard – shower, toilet, washing machine.

1191 9/H21 **Lochailort** A 12km stretch south from Lochailort on the A861, along the southern shore of the sea loch itself. A flat, rocky and grassy foreshore with a splendid seascape and backed by brooding mountains. Nearby is Loch nan Uamh where Bonnie Prince Charlie landed (1923/MARY, CHARLIE & BOB). Once past the salmon farm laboratories, you're in calendar scenery; the excellent Glenuig Inn at the southern end is the pub to repair to (1141/INNS). No facilities except the sea.

1192 7/H19 **Glenelg** Near Glenelg village which is over the amazing hill from Shiel Bridge (1615/SCENIC ROUTES). Village has great pub, the Glenelg Inn (1145/INNS) and a shop. Best spots to camp are 1km from village on road to Skye ferry on the strand.

1193 6/K13 **Oldshoremore** near Kinlochbervie 3km from village and supplies. Gorgeous beach (1563/BEACHES) and **Polin**, next cove. On the way to **Sandwood Bay** where the camping is legendary (but you have to carry everything 7km).

1194 6/J14 **Achmelvich** near Lochinver Signed off the fabulous Lochinver-Drumbeg road (1618/SCENIC ROUTES) or walk from village 3km via Ardroe (a great spot to watch otters that have been there for generations). There is an official campsite adjacent horrible caravan park, but walk further north towards Stoer. The beach at **Alltan na Bradhan** with the ruins of the old mill is fabulous. Best sea-swimming on this coast. Directions: 1566/BEACHES.

1195
7/H18
On the Road to Applecross The road that winds up the mountain from the A896 that takes you to Applecross (1616/SCENIC ROUTES) is one of the most dramatic in Scotland or anywhere. At the plateau before you descend to the coast, the landscape is lunar and the views to die for. Camp here (wind permitting) with the gods. Once over and 8km downhill there's the foreshore for more leisurely camping and proper (quite lovely) campsite with caff (see below).

1196
5/C20
Barra www.isleofbarra.com Lots of quiet places but you may as well be next to an amazing beach – one by 'the airport' where the little Otters come and go has added interest (and mobile phone reception – unlike rest of the island) but the twin crescent beaches on **Vatersay** are too beautiful to miss (1569/BEACHES).

1197
10/M22
Loch Tay South bank between Kenmore and Killin. A single-track road. Stunning views of the loch and Ben Lawers. Very woody in places. Great variety of potential pitches. Great inn and restaurant half-way, the Ardeonaig Hotel (though closed at TGP, awaiting new ownership).

Camping With The Kids

Caravan sites and camp grounds that are especially kid-friendly, with good facilities and a range of things to do (including a good pub).

1198
7/N19
✓ **Glen More Camp Site** near Aviemore · 01479 861271 9km Aviemore on the road to the ski slopes, B970. Across the road from Glen More Visitor Centre and adjacent to Loch Morlich Watersports Centre (2126/WATER SPORTS). Extensive grassy site on lochside with trees and mountain views. Loads of activities include watery ones, reindeer (1697/KIDS) and at the Coylumbridge Hotel (1112/HOTELS THAT WELCOME KIDS) there's a pool and the Fun House, a separate building full of stuff to amuse kids of all ages. Shop at site entrance; café (does breakfast).

1199
7/H18
APR-OCT
✓ **Applecross Campsite** www.applecross.uk.com/campsite · 01520 744268 First thing you come to as you approach the coast after a hair-raising drive over the *bealach*, the mountain pass. Grassy meadow in farm setting 1km sea. Some wigwam wooden cabins (and trailers further in). Usual facilities; Flower Tunnel café (1398/COFFEE SHOPS) Apr-Oct till 9pm. A green, grassy, safe landing.

1200
6/J15
✓ **Port A Bhaigh Campsite** Altandhu near Achiltibuie · 01854 622339 Wild yet civilised camping on grassy sward gently sloping to a wee beach on one of Scotland's secretly celebrated foreshores with an immense and forever memorable view of the Summer Isles. Add the pub (who run the site), the **An Fuaran** with its great grub and it would be hard to find a more perfect spot. Cruise to the isles, climb something, gaze at the sunset.

1201
9/H22
APR-MID OCT
✓ **Shieling Holidays** Craignure, Mull · www.shielingholidays.co.uk · 01680 812496 35km from Tobermory right where the ferry docks. Great views and a no-nonsense, thought-of-everything camp park. Self-catering shielings (carpeted cottage tents with heaters and ensuite facilities) or hostel beds. Loads to do and see (though mainly by car), including nearby Duart Castle (1780/CASTLES); and a pool at the Isle of Mull Hostel open to the plebs (1km).

1202
9/J28
APR-OCT
✓ **Seal Shore** Kildonan, Arran · 01770 820320 In the south of the island, the emerging fun place to be, Kildonan (2303/ARRAN HOTELS) with a long littoral to wander and open views to Pladda Island. Smallish, intimate greenfield site (40+) for campers and caravans. BBQ, dayroom and hotel adjacent for grub and pub. 'We're always in the UK top 20,' says Mr Deighton who will brook no nonsense from naughty kids or naughty parents. Sleep with the seals!

1203
9/G21
APR-OCT
✓ **Resipole Farm** Loch Sunart, Ardnamurchan · www.resipole.co.uk · 01967 431235 Arrive via Corran Ferry (11/JOURNEYS) or from Mallaig or Fort William route via Lochailort (1629/SCENIC ROUTES). Extensive grassy landing on lochside with all mod cons including shop, dishwashers, washing machines. A bit caravan-cluttered but quiet days in Ardnamurchan are all around you. Adventurous may kayak on the loch.

1204
10/R26
MAR-NOV
Carfraemill Camping & Caravanning Site aka Lauder Camping & Caravanning Club www.campingandcaravanningclub.co.uk · 01578 750697 Just off A697 where it joins the A68 near Oxton. Small, sheltered and friendly campsite in the green countryside with a buttercup meadow and a trickling burn. 4 chalets for hire on site. Good gateway to the Borders (Melrose 20km). The Lodge (or Jo's Kitchen as it is also known) adjacent has great family restaurant where kids made very welcome (play area and the food they like, etc).

1205
7/H16
APR-OCT
✓ **Sands Holiday Centre** www.highlandcaravancamping.co.uk · 01445 712152 · Gairloch 4km Gairloch (road to Melvaig) with island views, a large grassy park with dunes and its own long, sandy beach (1567/BEACHES). Separate camping area. 10 wooden wigwams named after islands. Kids' play area. Lots to do and see in Gairloch: a great pub, the **Old Inn** (1151/ROADSIDE INNS); well-equipped shop, mountain bikes for hire; great camping in dunes plus walking, fishing, etc.

1206
6/J14
JAN-DEC
Clachtoll Beach Campsite near Lochinver · www.tomichhotel.co.uk Friendly family grassy beachsite in spectacular scenery (1619/SCENIC ROUTES). Camping, caravan hook-ups and chalets: all usual facilities in a great wild place.

1207
7/H20
MAR-OCT
Camusdarach near Arisaig · 01687 450221 Friendly, natural campsite sheltered by big trees near splendid beach and looking on to the islands. It's on the Road to the Isles (the A830; 1628/SCENIC ROUTES): turn left, signed Camusdarrach 6km after Arisaig then 3km. Small (42 pitches) so book in summer. Decent shower block. No shop; free-range eggs available. Beaches are the thing (1573/BEACHES).

1208
9/H23
MAR-OCT
Roseview Caravan Park Oban · www.roseviewoban.co.uk · 01631 562755 3km out of Oban. Quiet, clean and friendly ground with stream running through. All sorts of extras such as undercover cooking area, BBQ, playpark. No bar. No dogs. The **Oban Caravan & Camping Park** www.obancaravanpark.com · 01631 562425 is adjacent at Gallanachmore overlooking the sea and easier to find. Well-run C&C Club family site with shop and ducks!

1209
9/L24
MAR-OCT
Cashel Caravan & Campsite Rowardennan · www.forestholidays.co.uk · 01360 870234 Forestry Commission site on the quieter shores of Loch Lomond in Queen Elizabeth Forest Park. Jumbo pitches and pre-pitched tents. Excellent facilities including shop, takeaway and play area and tons to do in the surrounding area which includes Ben Lomond and plootering on or by the loch.

1210 7/F18
LL
JAN-DEC
Sligachan Skye · 01478 650204 The camp site you see at the major bend in the road on the A87 going north to Portree from the bridge and the ferries. Sligachan is major hotel landmark and all its facilities include all-day bistro/

Seumas' bar. Lovely site by river with many walks from here. Free choice. Just pitch up and they'll come round. Laundry facilities. Adventure playground by hotel and the adventure playground of Skye all around.

1211
7/F18
APR-OCT

Kinloch Campsite Dunvegan, Skye · www.kinloch-campsite.co.uk · 01470 521531 Friendly, family-run grassy campsite on Glendale road by Dunvegan. Not so caravan heavy; choose your own pitch from many. Good location for northwest Skye wanderings and eating-out options in Dunvegan, especially Jann's (2300/SKYE).

Glorious Glamping

1212
10/R25
L

✓ **Lochhouses Farm** www.harvestmoonholidays.com · 07785 394026 · near North Berwick From A1 south of Haddington, A198 to North Berwick through Tyninghame; Lochhouses signed on right. 1km to farmyard, check in. 7 safari tents (can take 8) under trees in beautiful farmland near beach. Fabulous light and a microclimate of one of the driest places in Scotland. Shop, BBQ and cock-a-doodle kids' corner. All mod glamping cons. Can hire for exclusive use.

1213
10/M23

✓ **Comrie Croft** near Comrie · www.comriecroft.com · 01764 670140 On A85 Comrie-Crieff road, essentially a hostel (1115/HOSTELS) and camp ground but they have 5 Swedish katas, canvas yurt-type things beautifully situated up the hill in the woods. Wood stoves, platform to sleep, picnic tables. Millpond nearby and superb walking. Bike hire (and sales) on premises. Shop, games barn; good eating-out options in Comrie (876/PERTHSHIRE) and Crieff (863/880/ PERTHSHIRE).

1214
10/L23
L

✓ **Lovestruck @ Monachyle Mhor** near Balquhidder · 01877 384622 · www.monachylemhor.com 11km from Balquhidder along Loch Voil. The irrepressible Lewis family get on the glamping bandwagon and in this case it really is a wagon, parked overlooking the amazing loch beneath the Braes a discreet distance from their fabulous hotel (1160/GET-AWAY HOTELS) where you will want to eat and hang out in the bar or lounge. Only one lovestruck at TGP. Roomy it ain't but romantic – no question. Verandah and wood stove. You will want to be in love!

1215
9/J22

Ecopods near Port Appin · www.domesweetdome.co.uk · 07725 409003 On A828 between Oban and Fort William at the Castle Stalker café and viewpoint (1391/COFFEE SHOPS). Jim and Nicola who have the café (and can give you breakfast) have built 2 (so far) futuristic dome structures (by Zendome of Berlin) full of light, space and mod cons in what they call a boutique retreat. Tucked away in the rhododendron and birch woods they have maximum privacy though none of the view. A very intimate hideaway, couples or real close friends only.

1216
10/M24

Mains Farm Thornhill · www.mainsfarmwigwams.com · 01786 850735 On edge of this not terrifically interesting town in very central Scotland 20 minutes northwest of Stirling but close to the Trossachs. Take Kippen road B822 from town crossroads; farm is on the right. A wigwam right enough but mainly 10 wooden barnlets (looking like tiny individual barns) with minimal comforts, picnic tables outside. Shower block. Proper camping over-by. I haven't sold this very well, have I, but it is a good base: Flanders Moss 3km (1769/WILDLIFE RESERVES), great pub food in Kippen (1281/1282/GASTROPUBS) and Thornhill itself (1303/GASTRO-PUBS), and 20 minutes to Callendar and beyond. And it's cheap (£15pp). Go sleep.

1217
8/P17

Woodlands Aldroughty Woods near Elgin · www.aldroughtywoods.co.uk
I haven't managed to visit these privately owned woods but they're near Elgin and the main A96. Not clear if it's only one yurt they have but it looks good: wood-burning stove etc in a woody and wildlife setting. Reports, please.

Real Retreats

1218
11/P29
LL
ATMOS

✓ ✓ ✓ **Samye Ling** Eskdalemuir near Lockerbie & Dumfries · www.samyeling.org · 01387 373232 Bus or train to Lockerbie/ Carlisle then bus (Mon-Sat 0871 200 2233) or taxi (01576 470480). Community consists of an extraordinary and inspiring temple incongruous in these Border parts. The complex comprises main house (with some accommodation), dorm and guest-house blocks many single rooms, a café (open 7 days 9am-5pm) and shop. Further up the hill, longer retreats in annexes. Much of Samye Ling, a world centre for Tibetan Buddhism, is still under construction under the supervision of Tibetan masters, but they offer daily and longer stays (£24 dorm to £37 single room, '11) and courses in all aspects of Buddhism, meditation, tai chi, yoga, etc. Daily time-table from prayers at 6am and work period. Breakfast/lunch; light supper at 6pm, all vegetarian. Busy, thriving community atmosphere; some holier-than-thous but rewarding and unique and thriving. This is Buddhism, pure and simple. See also World Peace Centre (below).

1219
8/P17

✓ ✓ ✓ **Findhorn Community & Park** Findhorn near Forres · 01309 690311 · www.findhorn.org The world-famous and world-class spiritual community and foundation begun by Peter and Eileen Caddy and Dorothy Maclean in 1962, a village of caravans, cabins and brilliant houses on the way into Findhorn on B9011. Visitors can join the community as short-term guests eating and working on-site but probably staying at recommended B&Bs. This sprawling, always-growing eco village is fascinating and a joy just to pass through. Programme of courses and residential workshops in spiritual growth/dance/healing, etc. Many other aspects and facilities available in a cosmopolitan and well-organised community. Casual visitors can take a tour. Excellent shop (1443/DELIS), pottery (2193/ SHOPPING) and café – the Blue Angel (1313/VEGETARIAN); the Universal Hall has a great music and performance programme featuring many of Scotland's finest.

1220
8/P17
ATMOS

✓ ✓ **Pluscarden** between Forres & Elgin · www.pluscardenabbey.org · fax: 01343 890258 Signed from the main A96 (11km from Elgin) in a sheltered glen south-facing with a background of wooded hillside, this is the only medieval monastery in the UK still inhabited by monks. It's a deeply calming place. The Benedictine community keep walled gardens and bees. 8 services a day in the glorious chapel (1903/ABBEYS) which visitors can attend. Retreat for men (14 places) and women (separate, self-catering) with 2-week maximum and no obligatory charge. Write to the Guest Master, Pluscarden Abbey, by Elgin IV30 8VA; no telephone bookings. Men eat with the monks (mainly vegetarian). Restoration/ building work always in progress (of the abbey and of the spirit).

1221
10/P23

✓ ✓ **The Bield at Blackruthven** www.bieldatblackruthven.org.uk · Tibbermore · 01738 583238 Take Crieff road (A85) from Perth and A9/ ring road past Huntingtower then left for Tibbermore. 2km. Bield is an old Scottish word for a place of refuge and shelter; also means to nurture, succour, encourage. All are possible here. A Georgian home with outbuildings containing accommoda-tion, lounges, meeting rooms in 30 gorgeous garden acres (a lovely labyrinth) with a swimming pool and chapel (in old carpenter's workshop); they're always open.

More like a country-house hotel but there are prayers, courses and support if you want it. No guests on Monday, so 6 days max. Very cheap for this level of comfort. It is beautiful, peaceful and all very tasteful. Meals and self catering. Serenity!

1222 ✓ **Lendrick Lodge** Brig o' Turk · www.lendricklodge.com · 01877
10/L24   376263 On A821 scenic road through the Trossachs, 15km from Callander. Near road but in beautiful grounds with gurgling river. An organised retreat and get-away-from-it-all yoga and healing centre. Yoga, reiki and shamanic teaching throughout year (they even do fire walking!). Can take up to 50 people and run 2 courses at the same time. Individual rooms and full board if required. River Retreat in separate building overlooking the river has a pool and 2 ensuite rooms.

1223 ✓ **Dhanakosa** Balquhidder · www.dhanakosa.com · 01877 384213
10/L23   3km village on Loch Voilside 9km from A84 Callander-Crianlarich road. Gentle Buddhist place with ongoing retreat programmes (Introductory or Regular; 1 week or weekends in winter). Guidance and group sessions. Yoga and tai chi. Meditation room. Rooms hold 2–6 and are ensuite. Vegetarian food. Beautiful serene setting on Balquhidder Braes: you will 'radiate love'.

1224 ✓ **The World Peace Centre** Holy Island · www.holyisle.org · 01770
9/J27   601100 Take a ferry from Lamlash on Arran (ferry 01770 700463/600998) to
LL   find yourself part of a Tibetan (albeit contemporary) mystery. Escape from the madding crowd on the mainland and compose your spirit or just refresh. Built by Samye Ling abbots on this tiny Celtic refuge, the centre offers a range of activities to help purge the soul or restore the faith. Day trippers, holiday-breakers and multifaiths welcome. Can accommodate 60. Conference/gathering centre. Do phone ahead. And there's a hill to climb (2251/ISLAND WALKS). Ferries very limited in winter.

1225 **College of the Holy Spirit** Millport, Isle of Cumbrae · 01475 530353 ·
9/K26   www.island-retreats.org Continuous ferry service from Largs (every 15 minutes or 30 minutes in winter) then 6km bus journey to Millport. Off main street through a gate in the wall, into grounds of the Cathedral of the Isles (1869/CHURCHES) and another more peaceful world. A retreat for the Episcopal Church since 1884. Available for groups but there are 16 comfortable rooms, all renovated 2003, some ensuite, with B&B. Also half/full board. Morning and night prayer each day, Eucharist on Sunday and delightful concerts in summer. Fine library. Bike hire available on island. And the island's great café (1363/CAFÉS).

1226 **Nunraw Abbey** Garvald near Haddington · www.nunraw.org.uk · 01620
10/R25   830223 Cistercian community earning its daily bread with a working farm in the land surrounding the abbey but visitors can come and stay for a while or for a day in the Sancta Maria Guest House (a house for visitors is part of the Cistercian doctrine). Payment by donation. Very Catholic monastic ambience throughout. Guest house is 1km from the monastery, a modern complex built to a traditional Cistercian pattern. Services in the abbey are open to visitors. Guests often attend 8.30am service and Compline at 7.30pm with its traditional chant.

1227 **Camas Adventure Centre** Mull · www.iona.org.uk/camas_home.php ·
9/F25   01681 700404 Part of Iona Community near Fionnphort in south of island. Good
LL   bus service then a 20-minute yomp over the moor. On a rocky coast with limited electricity (candlelight), no cars, TV or noise except the waves and the gulls. Outdoor activities (eg canoeing, hillwalking) and creative ones. 2 dorms; share chores. Week-long stays. Individuals or groups. You'll probably have to relate, but this spiritual place invokes the simple outdoor life and reminds you that you are not alone. May-Sep.

The Best Spas

All these spas offer day visits and specific treatments.

1228
10/P25

✓✓ **One Spa** Sheraton Grand Hotel, Edinburgh · www.one-spa.net · 0131 221 7777 Considered the best spa in the city and on loads of national/international lists. And probably the best thing about the hotel which is centrally situated on Festival Sq opposite the Usher Hall (79/EDINBURGH HOTELS). As well as the usual (reasonably spacious) pool there's another which extends outdoors dangling infinity-style over Conference Sq behind the hotel. Decent gym. Exotic hydrotherapy and a host of treatments. ESPA and the Australian Li'tya products. Range of day and half-day tickets and gift vouchers available.

1229
10/R23

✓✓ **The Kohler Waters Spa** The Old Course Hotel, St Andrews · www.oldcoursehotel.co.uk · 01334 474371 In the mega Old Course golfing resort (836/FIFE HOTELS), this beautifully designed leisure and treatment suite, though small, is another reason for staying. The spa was designed by the team who created the original Cow Shed at Babington House. Owners of the hotel, the Kohler Company produces iconic kitchens and bathrooms in the US and own a slew of luxury resorts. Here the gym looks out over the Old Course (there's a roof-top hot tub). In the main suite there's a 20m pool, monsoon showers, saunas, crystal steam rooms and treatment rooms. Non-residents welcome.

1230
10/P27

✓✓ **Stobo Castle** Stobo near Peebles · www.stobocastle.co.uk · 01721 725300 Border baronial mansion 10km south of Peebles in beautiful countryside of towering trees and trickling burns. Dawyck Botanic Gardens nearby (1503/GARDENS) and there are Japanese Water Gardens in the grounds. Mainly a hotel but day visits possible; the spa is the heart of the pampering experience. Over 70 treatments. Not too much emphasis on exercise. Different categories of rooms and suites; also lodges. Bespoke and every conceivable and currently fashionable treatment for men and women. They know what they are doing; all medical peculiarities accounted for. Decent dining: 'healthy' of course but no denial of carbs or cream. Coffee shop/juice bar. Deals often available for days and half days.

1231
2/C2

✓✓ **The Spa at Blythswood Square** Glasgow · 0141 240 1662 In the basement of Glasgow's fab new townhouse hotel in the city centre, a top spa and destination in itself. Hugely popular with Glasgow lasses for individual treatments and day packages using ila and Anne Semonin products. Great lighting and pool; seductive, indulgent as they say. Pure (as well as purifying) Glasgow.

1232
10/N23

✓✓ **The Spa** Gleneagles Hotel, Auchterarder · www.gleneagles.com · 01764 662231 The leisure suites at Gleneagles have always offered one of the best spa experiences. Now with ESPA, 20 treatment rooms, 28 therapists and built-in soothing atmosphere, it is practically irresistible with or without golf fatigue. Suites for men and women, vitality pool, heated beds and a long menu of tantalising treatments. Only branded ESPA in Scotland. 9.30am-7.30pm.

1233
9/L25

✓✓ **The Spa** Cameron House Hotel, Loch Lomond · 01389 713659 · www.devere.co.uk The spa of De Vere Cameron House Hotel is 5km along the road and lochside at the Carrick, the new 18-hole golf course (shuttle service). New building complex incorporates golf clubhouse facilities, shop and recommended Claret Jug bar/restaurant. Very professional service. 17 treatment rooms, many therapists; 3 different spa products in use. There's a pool, a rooftop infinity pool, an outside (sheltered) deck, bar and restaurant. When you've made enough dosh to afford this (or somebody treats you), you really can relax.

1234
9/J22

✓ **The Spa** Isle of Eriska Hotel, Ledaig · www.eriska-hotel.co.uk · 01631 720371 The Isle of Eriska ('hotel/spa/island') is one of Scotland's most comfy country-house hotels (1094/COUNTRY-HOUSE HOTELS), 20km north of Oban. Apart from other activities and the usual indulgences they have created a lovely spa in the gardens overlooking the surprising 9-hole golf course. There's a pool and gym, the Verandah Café with terrace and 3 treatment rooms using ESPA products. Unlikely to be crowded; enjoy perfect tranquillity.

1235
9/L24

✓ **The Spa In The Walled Garden** Luss · www.lochlomond.com · 01436 655315 The more leisurely side of Loch Lomond Golf Club, this stunning contemporary spa suite (designed by Donna Vallone) is what it says on the tin. Thermal suites, treatment and relaxation rooms open on to small, private gardens and the walled garden itself with its fabulous glass houses, a visit to which is relaxation in itself. ESPA products. Technogym. Day 'experiences' to be had.

For The Best House Parties

Rent these for families or friends and have to yourselves: exclusive use.

1236
10/R25
ATMOS

✓ ✓ **Greywalls** Gullane · www.greywalls.co.uk · 01620 842144 36km east of Edinburgh off A198 beyond Gullane towards North Berwick. Though now (after a 4-year lapse) fully reinstated as a fabulous country-house hotel (818/LOTHIANS HOTELS), Greywalls is also available for exclusive use. Overlooks Muirfield, the championship course, and is close to several of Scotland's top courses. The Lutyens-designed manor house and the gardens attributed to Gertrude Jekyll are simply superb, especially in summer, and the public rooms are the epitome of taste and comfiness at all times. Dining c/o the Albert Roux team. The Colonel's House adjacent is also available (takes 8). 23 rooms in the hotel and lodges in the garden where dogs are welcome. £6k approximately; £1.2k for the House at TGP. This is house-party living as it's supposed to be.

1237
6/Q13
L
ATMOS

✓ ✓ **Ackergill Tower** near Wick · www.ackergilltower.co.uk · 01955 603556 New ownership since last edition but same fabulous formula and facilities. Deluxe retreat totally geared for parties and groups (mostly corporates). 5 times a year, eg Valentine's/Hogmanay, you can join their house parties. Fixed price (3-night minimum stay around £900 at TGP), all-inclusive: this means atmospheric dinners (huge fires, candlelight); you may not eat in the same place twice. Host of activities (there's even an opera house) and outside, the wild coast. A perfect treat/retreat. Individual prices on request. You'll probably have to mingle.

1238
8/P20
LL

✓ ✓ **Mar Lodge Estate** near Braemar · www.ntsholidays.com · 0844 493 2173 For exclusive use, there are several remarkable properties including apartments in the big hoose in the NTS-run, extensive (ie 8% of the entire Cairngorm National Park) 72,000-acre estate 15km from Braemar. Classic Highland scenery superb in any season; the upper waters of the Dee. 5 apartments in main mansion (takes 4–15) and 2 other houses (sleep 8 and 10). Public rooms including library, billiard room and ballroom can be hired separately. Expensive of course but not, divided between all your mates. Live like the royals down the road, without the servants (unless you bring with). Otherwise it's all sorted!

1239
3/R10
LLL

✓ ✓ **Balfour Castle** Orkney · 01856 711282 · www.balfourcastle.co.uk Lording it though sympathetically so over the 300 souls of Shapinsay (they built them a pub), this is as far as you can get in the UK to gracious living from the city or the City whence many guests will come (by plane or helicopter). Castle launch from Kirkwall or regular ferry. Up to 18 guests, unbridled luxury, dedicated chef, the esteemed Jean Baptiste Bady. In summer, the light! 2307/ORKNEY.

1240
10/P24
✓ **Myres Castle** near Auchtermuchty · www.myrescastle.com · 01337 828350 2 km Auchtermuchty on Falkland road. Well-preserved castle/family home in stunningly beautiful gardens. High country life though at a price. 9 rooms individually refurbished to exceptional standard. Formal dining room, evocative Victorian kitchen and impressive billiard room. The perfect setting for a murder-mystery shindig. Central to Fife attractions, Falkland and St Andrews. Takes 18.

1241
8/N17
✓ **Drynachan Lodge** near Nairn · www.cawdor.com · 01667 402402 This fab 19th-century hunting lodge is on the Cawdor Estate south of Nairn. The castle is signed from all over (1776/CASTLES). While there are many cottages here for let this is the big house (sleeps 22) and was personally decked out by Lady Isabella Cawdor. Like all things on the estate it's done with great taste. Fully staffed and catered, it's like a hip shooting lodge. But it'll cost ya.

1242
9/H24
✓ **Lunga House** Ardfern · www.lungahouse.co.uk · 01852 500237 Take Craobh Haven (marina) turnoff the A816 Oban-Lochgilphead road. Long with a boho-chic, Lunga-time reputation among those who know, this rambling big hoose is less crumbly and chaotic of late and is perfect for parties and gatherings. Great public space includes a ballroom. 18 bedrooms and many cottages. Here, you really can call it your own! Catering provided. £2000 for basic exclusive use.

1243
9/K28
NTS
LL
✓ **Culzean Castle: Eisenhower Apartment** South Ayrshire · 01655 760615 · www.culzeanexperience.org The second-floor apartment once stayed in by the wartime Supreme Allied Commander in Europe and later president of the United States. It has 6 suites and public rooms available singly or for exclusive use. Spectacular both in and out with great easy walking. Dinner can be provided; the grounds are superb (1773/CASTLES). Near Turnberry.

1244
5/E15
ATMOS
✓ **Amhuinnsuidhe Castle** Harris · www.amhuinnsuidhe.com · 01859 560200 North from Tarbert then west to faraway strand (directions: see Lost Glen 2245/FANTASTIC ISLAND WALKS). Staffed, fab food and gothic Victorian castle/shooting and fishing lodge (salmon arrive in a foaming mass at the river mouth). 12 bedrooms; mainly sporting and fishing weeks but individuals can join at certain times for mixed house party. Grand interiors and top fishing on 9 lochs and rivers.

1245
8/N19
✓ **Inshriach House** near Aviemore · www.inshriachhouse.com · 01540 651341 On B970 back road between Inverdrurie and Feshiebridge 8km south of Aviemore. Atmospheric, comfy, lived-in Edwardian country house with gorgeous public rooms, highly individual bedrooms, gardens and small estate. Close to spectacular Loch an Eilean (1604/LOCHS) and Inshriach (2222/GARDEN CENTRES) with its famous cakes and bird-watching, but loads to do round here. Self-catering or chef or Old Bridge Inn (1284/GASTROPUBS) nearby. Up to 17 can stay. From £2k-3.5k per week. One of the most laid-back options on this page. They have fishing! Great wee festival, The Insider, in the grounds in June.

1246
7/M17
✓ **Castle Stuart** Inverness · www.castlestuart.com · 01463 790745 15 minutes city centre on airport road via A96 Aberdeen road. Authentic pile of 17th-century history; a real castle experience complete with ghost, open fires, flowers, portraits: antique in every sense. Guided tour on arrival. 8 bedrooms (can take 16). £2k per night. Naughty houseguests may not be welcome here.

1247
9/K28

✓**Doonbrae** Alloway · www.costley.biz · 01292 442466 In heart of unspoilt village still evocative of Burns whose birthplace, gardens and Tam o' Shanter graveyard are nearby. Opposite and part of **Brig o' Doon Hotel** (747/AYR-SHIRE HOTELS), much favoured for weddings. This refurbished mansion is separate and you have it to yourself (group bookings only). There are also 2 cottages. On Doon banks in delightful gardens. Self-catering or eat at hotel. 5 suites.

✓**Greshornish Country House** Skye · www.greshornishhouse.com · 01470 582345 Comfy, artful country house to yourself; lovely rooms. Lochside in the middle of Skye. Report: 1166/GET-AWAY-FROM-IT-ALL.

1248
6/L15
L

Carbisdale Castle Culrain near Bonar Bridge · www.carbisdale.org · 01549 421232 Another castle and hugely impressive but on a per-head basis, very inexpensive. Carbisdale is the flagship hostel of the SYHA (1114/BEST HOSTELS for directions). From Nov-Feb you can hire the whole place so big Highland hoolies over Xmas/Hogmanay are an option. Up to 140 people can stay in the 32 rooms (from singles to 12-bed dorms). Per-night price around £2,500-4,250. Bring your own chef or muck in. Other SYHA hostels can be hired Oct-May (www.rentahostel.com).

1249
11/N30

Cavens Kirkbean · www.cavens.com · 01387 880234 Off A710 Solway Coast road 20km south Dumfries. Well-appointed mansion in gorgeous grounds near beach. Sleeps up to 22 in house (16) and lodges. Very reasonable compared to other grand manors. Angus's dinner-party cooking. 757/SOUTHWEST HOTELS.

1250
9/J24
L

Castle Lachlan Loch Fyne · www.castlelachlan.com · 01369 860669 For directions see Inver Cottage, the tearoom on the estate (739/ARGYLL RESTAU-RANTS). Stunning setting in heart of Scotland scenery, the 18th-century ancestral home of the Clan Maclachlan. Snooker room; all-weather tennis. Self-catering but dining can be arranged. Sleeps up to 15 (22 for dinner). £2-3K per week. Sumptuous surroundings for rock stars and weddings and the like.

1251
10/Q22

Kinettles Castle Forfar · www.amazingretreats.com Haven't visited Kinettles yet (so no tick); it's part of the emerging Amazing Retreats group who have Ackergill (above). Baronial, castellate, impressive, Kinettles is deep in Angus (though they say 30 minutes from Dundee Airport). Can sleep 28 in 11 suites. Lots of public space with billiards room, 2 games rooms, 2 dining and many acres to besport yourself. 2 nights for £3700 includes some butler/maid service.

1252
6/H16
L

Rua Reidh Lighthouse Melvaig near Gairloch · www.ruareidh.co.uk · 01445 771263 End of the road 20km from Gairloch but yes, you can have this lighthouse to yourself. Sleeps up to 24 in 9 bedrooms (from £500 for 2 nights low season to £1900 7 nights New Year at TGP). Gairloch has good food/pub options but you do or arrange your own catering. Plus the sea and the scenery!

Cambo near Crail · www.camboestate.com · 01333 450313 Old, interesting mansion in beautiful grounds near St Andrews. Up to 17 separate rooms available and B&B. Very reasonable rates. Report: 842/FIFE HOTELS.

National Trust for Scotland has many interesting properties they rent out for weekends or longer. 0131 243 9331 or www.nts.org.uk for details.
The Landmark Trust also have 19 mostly fabulous properties in Scotland including **The Pineapple** (1853/MONUMENTS), **Auchenleck House** in Ayrshire which sleeps 13 and the wonderful **Ascog House** or **Meikle House** on the Isle of Bute which sleep 9 and 10 respectively. Phone 01628 825925 to get their beautiful handbook (properties throughout the UK) or see www.landmarktrust.org.uk

Scotland's Great Guest Houses

Balmory Hall Isle of Bute · 01700 500669 In Ascog, 6km from Rothesay towards Mount Stuart. Top! Report: 726/ARGYLL HOTELS.

Skirling House near Biggar · 01899 860274 On the A72 3km from Biggar. Arts and Crafts and excellent food. Report: 796/BORDERS HOTELS.

Lerags House near Oban · 01631 563381 7km south of Oban and 4 km from the main A816. Quiet spot. Excellent food. Report: 731/ARGYLL HOTELS.

Edenwater House Ednam near Kelso · 01733 224370 On Kelso-Swinton road B6461 1km from Kelso. The *best* food. Report: 792/BORDERS HOTELS.

Coig Na Shee Newtonmore · 01540 670109 Just outside the village towards Fort William, off the A9. Report: 990/INEXPENSIVE HIGHLAND HOTELS.

Roineabhal near Kilchrenan, Loch Awe · 01866 833207 10km from the A85 road to Oban near Taynuilt. Home and away! Report: 732/ARGYLL HOTELS.

Blar Na Leisg Drumbeg · 01571 833325 Faraway house in spectacular Assynt. Fabulous food. Report: 977/HIGHLAND.

Broad Bay House Lewis · 01851 820990 New-build house 20 minutes north of Stornoway on Broad Bay. Report: 2305/HEBRIDES.

Old Station near St Andrews · 01334 880505 On B9131, the Anstruther road off the A917 St Andrews-Crail (3km). Report: 841/FIFE HOTELS.

Doune Stone Lodge Knoydart · 01687 462667 Remote but comfy house on this faraway peninsula. Will collect from Mallaig. Boat excursions and wonderful walks. Great food. Report: 1165/GET-AWAY HOTELS.

The Bield Tibbermore near Perth · 01738 583238 Crieff road, from Perth off the ring road. Spiral staircase. Report: 1221/RETREATS.

Torrdarach House Pitlochry · 01796 472136 New life in an old mansion in tourist town. Great for kids. Report: 861/PERTHSHIRE.

Craigatin House Pitlochry · 01796 472470 Surprisingly stylish guest house in this traditional tourist town. Report: 856/PERTHSHIRE HOTELS.

Tanglewood House near Ullapool · 01854 612059 Beautiful house overlooking Loch Broom. Great dining and the view. Report: 1011/HIGHLAND.

Clint Lodge near St Boswells · 01899 860274 Near Dryburgh Abbey in rolling, green Scott country. Report: 802/BORDERS HOTELS.

Good Food & Drink

Bloody Good Pubs

Pubs in Edinburgh and Glasgow are listed in their own sections.

1253
9/K23
L
ATMOS
✓✓**Drover's Inn** Inverarnan · www.thedroversinn.co.uk A famously Scottish drinking den/hotel on the edge of the Highlands just north of Ardlui at the head of Loch Lomond and 12km south of Crianlarich on the A82. Smoky, low-ceilinged rooms, open ranges, whisky in the jar, stuffed animals in the hall and kilted barmen; this is nevertheless the antithesis of the contrived Scottish tourist pub. Food till 9pm. Also see 784/HOTELS CENTRAL.

1254
9/G22
LL
ATMOS
✓✓**The Mishnish** Tobermory · www.mishnish.co.uk For many, the Mish has always been the real Tobermory; it's been in the Macleod family since, well, since 1869 so they are somewhat connected to Mull. So will you be in this classic island hostelry with rooms (8), a restaurant adjacent, The Mishdish (2306/MULL) but most importantly – the pub. 7 days till late. Often live music from Scottish traditional to DJs and indie especially Saturdays. Different rooms, nooks and crannies. Great pub grub, open fire. Something, as they say, for everybody.

1255
7/H20
LL
ATMOS
✓**Old Forge** Inverie, Knoydart · www.theoldforge.co.uk 01687 462267 A warm haven for visitors who have found their way to this pristine peninsula. Suddenly you're part of the community; real ales and real characters, excellent pub grub. Pub for sale at TGP but the community will ensure its survival intact. Lunch and LO 9pm. Stay along the road (well, 10km) at the brilliant Doune Stone Lodge (1165/GET-AWAY HOTELS) or bunk nearer by (info@knoydart-foundation.com).

1256
9/J21
L
ATMOS
✓**Clachaig Inn** Glencoe · www.clachaig.com · 01855 811252 Deep in the glen itself down the road signed off the A82, 5km from Glencoe village. Both the pub with its wood-burning stove and the lounge are woody and welcoming. Backdoor best for muddy boots or those averse to leather-studded sofas. Real ale and real climbers and walkers. Handy if you're in the hostel 2km down road or camping. Walking-fuel food in bar/lounge and good, inexpensive accommodation including lodges. A plethora of ales and a beer fest in October.

1257
10/S20
L
✓**Marine Hotel** Stonehaven · www.marinehotelstonehaven.co.uk Popular local on a great harbour with seats outside and always a crowd. 7/8 guest ales, big Belgian and wheat-beer selection and food till 9pm. Upstairs dining room overlooks the boat-bobbing bay. Same menu; local fish specials. Open all day.

1258
5/C20
LL
ATMOS
Castlebay Bar Barra · www.castlebay-hotel.co.uk Adjacent to Castlebay Hotel. A deceptively average-seeming but brilliant bar. All human life is here. More Irish than all the Irish makeovers on the mainland. Occasional live music including the Vatersay Boys; conversations with strangers. Report: 2289/ISLAND HOTELS.

1259
7/J19
L
Cluanie Inn Loch Cluanie · www.cluanieinn.com · 01320 340238 On A87 at head of Loch Cluanie 15km before Shiel Bridge on the long road to Kyle of Lochalsh (and Skye). A wayside inn with good pub food, a restaurant and the (both bunkhouse and hotel) accommodation walkers want (1155/ROADSIDE INNS). Good base for climbing/walking (especially the 5 Sisters of Kintail, 1998/SERIOUS WALKS). A cosy refuge. LO 9pm for food.

1260
10/L27
ATMOS
Poosie Nansie's Mauchline Main street of this Ayrshire village where Burns lived in 1788. This pub there then, those characters still there at the bar. 4 of his children buried (yes, 4) in the churchyard opposite. A room in the pub left as was. Living heritage at its most real! Lunch and 6-8pm Fri/Sat. Otherwise the ale.

1261
8/T19
Under the Hammer North Silver Street, Aberdeen Time-served basement bar. Forever and a day favourite (and certainly mine) in Aberdeen. No snooker, no sports, no food; just the vibe.

1262
11/M30
The Murray Arms & **The Masonic Arms** Gatehouse of Fleet 2 adjacent unrelated pubs that just fit perfectly into the life of this great wee town. The Masonic has had the reputation for best food but many changes of management later, this is changing; good atmosphere, though. Masonic symbols still on the walls of the upstairs rooms. The Murray Arms has a Burns *Scots Wha' Ha'e* connection. Now owned by the people who have **The Ship Inn** (759/SOUTHWEST HOTELS) on the main street, the newer, more stylish kid on the block, expect a refurbishment and much-improved food offering '12 at The Murray.

1263
7/L19
L
Lock Inn Fort Augustus Busy canalside (Caledonian Canal which joins Loch Ness in the distance) pub for locals and visitors. Good grub downstairs or up if you want (overlooking lock). Pub staples; reasonable malts. Food LO 9.30pm. Occasional live music. Seats on the canal in summer where boats go by very slowly.

1264
11/L31
LL
ATMOS
The Steampacket Inn www.steampacketinn.com · 01988 500334 · Isle of Whithorn The hub of this atmospheric wee village at the end of the road south (1552/COASTAL VILLAGES). On harbour that fills and empties with the tide. Great for ales and food (brunch and LO 9pm all year). 7 inexpensive rooms upstairs (£45). An all-round happy hostelry.

Great Pubs For Real Ale

For real-ale pubs in Edinburgh, see p. 71-2, Glasgow p. 118.

1265
10/Q23
ATMOS
✓**Fisherman's Tavern** Broughty Ferry · www.fishermanstavern.co.uk In Dundee, but not too far to go for great atmosphere and great collection of ales (6). In Fort St near the seafront. Regular IPAs and many guests. Low-ceilinged and friendly. Inexpensive accommodation adjacent and pub grub as you like (886/DUNDEE HOTELS).

1266
10/N21
ATMOS
✓**Moulin Inn/Hotel** Pitlochry · www.moulinhotel.co.uk 4km uphill from main street on road to Bridge of Cally, an inn at a picturesque crossroads since 1695. Some rooms and (mixed) reputation for pub grub but loved for cosy bar and brewery out back from which comes Moulin Light, Ale of Atholl and others. Live music some Sundays. Food (LO 9.30pm).

1267
9/J26
✓**The Port Royal** Port Bannatyne near Rothesay Seafront on Kames Bay in Bute. A 'Russian' tavern with latkas and sauerkraut with your stroganoff. Some live music. 5 rooms upstairs and a great selection of ales. Brill atmosphere.

1268
8/T19
✓**The Prince of Wales** Aberdeen St Nicholas Lane, just off Union St at George St. An all-round great pub (by Belhaven) always mentioned in guides and one of the best places in the city for ale: Old Peculier, Caledonian 80/- and guests. Very cheap self-service food till 8.30pm. Wood, flagstones, booths. Large and very pub-like; gets very crowded. 7 days, 11am-12midnight (11pm Sun).

1269
10/N25
The Four Marys Linlithgow · www.thefourmarys.co.uk Main street near road up to palace (1790/RUINS) so handy for a pint after schlepping around the historical attractions. Mentioned in most beer guides. 7 ales, usually guests. Beer

festivals May and October. Notable malt whisky collection and popular locally for lunches (daily) and evening meals (LO 8.45pm); weekends 12noon-food LO.

1270
10/M24
The Lade Inn Callander At Kilmahog, western approach to town at the start of road into the Trossachs, so a good place to stop. Inn brews its own ale (Waylade, Ladeback, Lade Out). Ale shop adjacent with well over 100 of Scotland's finest. Shop 12noon-6pm. Big pubfood operation though reports vary (served till 8.45pm).

1271
10/J26
The Tappit Hen Dunblane By the cathedral. Good ales (usually Deuchars and 5 guests and many malts), atmosphere and occasional live music. A good find in these parts; it's a man's kind of pub!

1272
10/N24
The Woolpack Tillicoultry Via Upper Mill St (signed Mill Glen) from main street on your way to the Ochils. They come far and wide to this ancient pub. Changing selection of ales which they know how to keep. Sup after a stroll. The Staniforths have improved the bar meals a lot (weekends only).

1273
7/M18
Clachnaharry Inn Inverness On A862 Inverness-Beauly road just outside Inverness overlooking firth and railway, with beer garden. Long list of regulars posted, 5 on tap. Food much improved of late (1053/INVERNESS).

1274
8/R17
L
The Shore Inn Portsoy Down at the harbour, good atmosphere (and ales). Food: lunch only weekends in summer. Plays centre stage at the Traditional Boats fest (42/EVENTS). May be quiet other times, but a great pub on the quayside corner though its location is its principal charm.

1275
7/H16
The Old Inn Gairloch Southern approach on A832 near golf course, an old inn across an old bridge; a goodly selection of malts and ales including their own Blind Piper and other Scottish regional. Tourists and locals mix in season, live music Tuesdays and Saturdays. Rooms above make this an all-round good reason to stop in Gairloch (1151/ROADSIDE INNS).

The Masonic Arms Gatehouse of Fleet 770/SOUTHWEST RESTAURANTS.
The Steampacket Inn Isle of Whithorn 1264/BLOODY GOOD PUBS.
The 2 pubs in the South West that look after their ale (and their drinkers).

The Best Gastropubs

Gastropubs in Edinburgh and Glasgow are listed in their own sections.

1276
10/L27
ATMOS
✓✓**The Sorn Inn** Sorn · www.sorninn.com · 01290 551305 Village main street, 8km east of Mauchline, 25km Ayr. Pub with rooms and big reputation for food. Restaurants and tables in bar. Family-run (the Grants with chef Craig Grant). Michelin Bib Gourmand. All just-so and made to order. An exemplary rural gastropub experience. Lunch and LO 9pm. All day Sat/Sun. LO Sun 8.30pm.

1277
9/H26
✓✓**Kilberry Inn** near Tarbert, Argyll · 01880 770223 On the single-track B8024 that follows the coast of the Knapdale peninsula between Lochgilphead and Tarbert, this is out on its own. Bib Gourmand and a treat to eat. Clare Johnson is a great cook, all her ingredients properly sourced; the lounges have a smart, pubby ambience with relaxed, unobtrusive service led by Clare's bloke David. Make that journey (1630/SCENIC ROUTES) and discover Knapdale. (69/DISCOVER). Lunch and dinner. LO 9pm. Closed Mon. Apr-Oct. Weekends Nov/Dec.

1278
10/R27

✓ ✓ **Burt's** Melrose · www.burtshotel.co.uk · 01896 822285 The bar of the estimable hotel on Melrose's main street (791/BORDER HOTELS) and some might say even better than their fine-dining restaurant. A la carte specials with pub faves like fish 'n' chips and beef olives and chef's specials. Big rugby-player helpings. 7 days lunch and LO 9.30pm.

1279
10/R25
L

✓ ✓ **Waterside Bistro** Haddington · www.watersidebistro.co.uk · 01620 825674 On the banks of the River Tyne near Lamp of the Lothians (1883/CHURCHES). This great multi-chambered gastropub is back! Best pub grub on this or any nearby river. Report: 829/LOTHIANS.

1280
6/J15
LL

✓ ✓ **The Summer Isles Hotel Bar** www.summerisleshotel.co.uk · Achiltibuie · 01854 622282 The adjacent bar of this romantic hotel on the foreshore faces the isles and the sunset (979/HIGHLAND HOTELS). All the superior qualities of their famous food operation available at less than half the price in the cosy bistro-like bar with tiny terrace; occasional traditional music. Great seafood and vegetarian. Apr-Oct, lunch and LO 8.30pm (bar Thu-Sun in winter).

1281
10/M24
DF

✓ ✓ **The Cross Keys** Kippen · www.kippencrosskeys.co.uk · 01786 870293 Here forever in this quiet town off A811 15km west of Stirling. Debby Macgregor and Brian Horsburgh transformed this dependable pub for grub into a stopover not just for Sunday lunch but for a weekend stay. 3 rooms upstairs, open fires, great food in bar or lounge areas below. Seriously thought-over and irresistible gastropub food. Some live music. Beer garden. Lunch and LO 9/9.30pm.

1282
10/M24

✓ ✓ **The Inn at Kippen** Kippen · www.theinnatkippen.co.uk · 01786 871010 Amazingly, this couthie village above the Forth plain has 2 great gastropubs. This is the one that first put Kippen on the foodie map and after a dip it's back as a serious pub-dining destination. Lotsa space but often full. Garden terrace has pizza oven. 3 good-value rooms. 7 days lunch and LO 9pm. Bar 11pm/1am.

1283
10/R24
ATMOS
L

✓ ✓ **Ship Inn** Elie · www.ship-elie.com · 01333 330246 Pub on the bay at Elie, the perfect toon in the picturesque East Neuk of Fife (1550/COASTAL VILLAGES). In summer a huge food operation: bar, back room, next door and upstairs (the latter has good view; book weekends). Same menu throughout; all home-made blackboard specials. On warm days the terrace overlooking the beach goes like Bondi. LO 9/9.30pm. They love cricket (played on the beach).

1284
7/N19

✓ ✓ **Old Bridge Inn** Aviemore · www.oldbridgeinn.co.uk/aviemore Off Coylumbridge road at south end of Aviemore as you come in from A9 or Kincraig. 100m from main street by the river. An old inn like it says but with excellent eclectic menu under chef Chris McCall. 3 cask ales on tap. Kids' menu not just pizza and chips; ski bums welcome. Good music, good vibes. Lunch and 6-9pm. In summer, tables over road by the river. Hostel adjacent (1118/HOSTELS). LO 9.30pm.

1285
10/R23
ATMOS

✓ **The Grange Inn** St Andrews · www.thegrangeatstandrews.com · 01334 472670 4km out of town off Anstruther/Crail road A917. This perennially popular country pub on the edge of town had new owners 2011 and I hadn't tried at TGP. However, they're the people who have the hugely successful Nahm-Jim in Market St (852/ST ANDREWS) and the long reputation of the Grange is in good hands. Gastropub classics order of the day. Lunch Fri-Sun, dinner Wed-Sat.

1286
10/S26

✓ **Craw Inn** Auchencrow · www.thecrawinn.co.uk · 01890 761253 Off A1 near Reston and Eyemouth – actually 4km off the A1 and further than they sign but near enough for a swift detour and the best place to eat between Berwick and the Lothians: a real destination for great food (proper chefs) and amazing wine in classic pub atmosphere. A great deck out the back. Go find! Lunch and LO 9pm.

1287
8/Q19

✓**The Glenkindie Arms** between Alford & Strathdon · 01975 641288
Taking over a run-down roadhouse hotel in the Don valley 60km west of Aberdeen was a bold venture for chef/patron (once a Masterchef contestant) Ian Simpson. But he loves to cook and this is evident in his no-frills, small former bar and in the menu. He worked with a lot of name chefs; here he's on his own, but there is money in those hills and an appetite for his careful Scottish cookery with un peu Français. 3 very basic rooms upstairs. Lunch and dinner. Closed Mon. Best book.

1288
6/J15

LL

✓**An Fuaran** Altdhu · 01854 622339 Along from Achiltibuie, this pub has an elevated, elevating view of the Summer Isles from its terrace. Inside is dark and pub-like and welcoming. I know their food is good from recommendations but I haven't tried. They also have a fab wee campsite on the foreshore (1200/CAMPING). Lunch and dinner LO 8.30pm (8pm Sun).

1289
10/S26

✓**The Wheatsheaf** Swinton · www.wheatsheaf-swinton.co.uk · 01890 860257 A village hotel pub about halfway between Kelso and Berwick (18km) on B6461. In deepest, flattest Berwickshire, owners Chris and Jan Winson serve up the best pub grub you've had since England (they're also involved in the Fisherman's Arms at Birgham; see below). 10 rooms adjacent and in cottages with great dinner, B&B deals. An all-round good hostelry. Lunch (Sat/Sun) and 6-9pm.

1290
8/S19

✓**The Broadstraik Inn** Westhill · www.broadstraikinn.co.uk · 01224 743217 On main A944 Aberdeen-Alford road, 12km from city centre and well worth the drive. This long-running roadside pub was transformed into an all-round pub and pub-food destination. Bar and restaurant area. Great for families: real food kids' menu. Blackboard specials. Busy weekends. 7 days lunch and LO 9/9.30pm.

1291
9/K28

✓**Souter Johnnie's Inn** Kirkoswald · www.costley.biz · 01655 760653 On A77 between Girvan and Ayr. Contemporary and ambitious transformation of old hotel and adjacent buildings to form a smart, modern complex that includes a tearoom, deli/shop, ice-cream factory and bakers (2186/SCOTTISH SHOPPING). Created by the estimable Costley family (see Cochrane Inn below and many other Ayrshire winners), the pub here offers the usual sound gastropub menu with a Scottish emphasis. Restaurant open all day for snacks, hot meals – the chocolates, the ice cream – the brand. All good stuff 7 days, lunch and LO 9pm.

1292
9/L26

✓**Fox and Hounds** Houston · www.foxandhoundshouston.co.uk On B790 village main street in Renfrewshire, 30km west of Glasgow by M8 junction 29 (A726), then cross back under motorway on B790. Village pub, home to Houston brewery with great ales, excellent pub food and dining room upstairs for family meals and suppers. Folk come from miles. Sunday roasts. Fine for kids. Lunch and LO 8.45pm (later Fri/Sat). Restaurant: 01505 612448. Bar till 12midnight.

1293
10/S21

L

✓**The Creel Inn** Catterline near Stonehaven · 01569 750254 2km from main A92 8km south Stonehaven (signed) perching above the bay from where the lobsters come. And lots of other seafood. Good wine; huge speciality beer selection. Cove itself has a haunting beauty. Catterline is Joan Eardley (notable artist) territory. It's also famous for this pub; it's always buzzing. 7 days lunch and LO 9pm.

1294
9/L27
✓ **Wheatsheaf Inn** Symington · www.wheatsheafsymington.co.uk · 01563 830307 2km A77. Pleasant village off the unpleasant A77 with this busy coaching inn opposite the church. Folk come from miles around to eat (book at weekends) honest-to-goodness pub fare in various rooms (roast beef every Sunday). Menu on boards. Beer garden. LO 10pm but open 11am-11pm.

1295
8/S20
ATMOS
✓ **Lairhillock Inn** near Netherley, Stonehaven · www.lairhillock.co.uk · 01569 730001 Long a landmark pub for good grub in the country south of Aberdeen. 7 days lunch and dinner. Fine for kids. Superb cheese selection, notable malts and ales. Can approach from South Deeside road (signed), but simplest direction for strangers is: 15km south of Aberdeen by main A92 towards Stonehaven, then signed Durris, go 5km to country crossroads. From south take Netherley road from edge of Stonehaven. **The Crynoch Restaurant** (open weekends) is adjacent (944/ABERDEEN RESTAURANTS).

1296
6/K14
LL
✓ **Kylesku Hotel** Kylesku · www.kyleskuhotel.co.uk · 01971 502231 Off A894 between Scourie and Lochinver. A hotel and pub with a great quayside location on Loch Glencoul where boats leave for trips to see the 'highest waterfall in Europe' (1594/WATERFALLS). Tanja's and Sonia's friendly bar/bistro atmosphere with local fish, seafood including interesting specials, eg spineys (the tails of squat lobsters) and their signature seafood platter, everything from waters within reach; yummy desserts. Lunch and 6-9pm Mar-Oct (food 12noon onwards July/Aug).

1297
10/Q23
L
✓ **The Ship Inn** Broughty Ferry · Excellent seafront snug pub with food in upstairs attic and down (best tables at window upstairs). Famous for clootie dumpling, other classic gastropub fare. There are sometimes dolphins in the estuary (binoculars available). 7 days, lunch and 5-9pm (894/DUNDEE RESTAURANTS).

1298
9/J26
✓ **Smiddy Bar at the Kingarth Hotel** Isle of Bute · 01700 831662 · www.kingarthhotel.com 13km Rothesay, 4km after Mount Stuart (1833/COUNTRY HOUSES). Good, friendly old inn serving the best pub food on the island. Blackboard menu and à la carte. The atmosphere is just right. Outside deck. Open all year. Food LO 8pm (9pm Fri/Sat).

1299
10/M25
✓ **Old Mill** Killearn · www.old-mill-killearn.co.uk · 01360 550068 More than one inn in this village but this one on the Main St is the cosy, friendly one and all that an old pub should be (old here is from 1774). Pub and restaurant. Log fires, brilliant for kids. Garden. All home made! 7 days 12noon-9pm (Sun 8pm).

1300
10/R26
Black Bull Lauder · www.blackbull-lauder.com · 01578 722208 Main street of A68 ribbon town between Edinburgh and the Borders. Not quite the gastro gold standard it once was but near enough the city to be a destination meal. 8 individual rooms above, different dining areas below. Some great Modern British cooking; good wine list. 7 days. LO 9pm.

1301
9/K28
L
Dunure Inn Dunure · www.dunureinn.co.uk · 01292 500549 Just off A719 coast road 10km south of Ayr. Inn of a charming wee village, not much more than a ruined castle and an old harbour on this picturesque coast (1633/SCENIC ROUTES). A family affair (the Munros), this restaurant with rooms overlooks the harbour and has built a good reputation for food, especially seafood. Good atmosphere inside and out in the garden. Occasional live music. 7 days, lunch and LO 8.30pm.

1302
9/L27
Cochrane Inn Gatehead · www.costley.biz · 01563 570122 Part of the Costley hotel empire (747/HOTELS IN AYRSHIRE). A trim and cosy ivy-covered, very inn-like inn – most agreeable. On A759 Troon to Kilmarnock and 2km A71

Kilmarnock-Irvine road. A bugger to get to (locals know how), but excellent gourmet pub with huge local reputation; must book weekends. Lunch and LO 9.30pm.

1303
10/M24

Lion & Unicorn Thornhill · www.lion-unicorn.co.uk · 01786 850204
On A873 off A84 road between the M9 and Callander and near Lake of Menteith in the Trossachs. On main road through the village. They come from miles around for pub grub and sizzling steaks. 3 cosy dining areas, open fires and garden. Changing menu (including a gluten-free one), not too fancy, just nice. 7 days. LO 9pm.

1304
7/H16
LL

Badachro Inn Badachro near Gairloch · 01445 741255 South of Gairloch off A832, then B8056 to Redpoint. A spectacular road and fantastic setting for this waterside pub. Great beer and wine list with lots by the glass and home-made pub grub. A great deck overlooks the rocky bay. 7 days 12noon-9pm in summer, earlier in winter (and closed Mon/Tue). This pub is where it first occurred to me to introduce the LLL code (see p. 12). Go see why!

1305
10/R26

Goblin Ha' Hotel Gifford · www.goblinha.com · 01620 810244 Twee village in East Lothian heartland; one of 2 hotels. This one, with the great name, serves a decent pub lunch and supper (6-9pm; 9.30pm on Fri and Sat) in lounge and pub, conservatory, terrace and beer garden. Latter rooms good for kids and grown-ups. A well-run Punch Tavern.

1306
10/S27

Fisherman's Arms Birgham near Kelso · 01890 830230 In small Tweedside village 6km from Kelso on Coldstream road. A very village pub, friendly and local. Decent food, no pretence. Garden terrace. Sunday carvery.

1307
10/L24

The Byre Brig o' Turk · 01877 376292 Off A821 at Callander end of the village by Loch Achray. Country inn in deepest Trossachs. Basic pub grub in cosy, firelit rooms with outside decks in summer. Inexpensive wine list. LO 9pm, pub till 11pm. Can walk from here to Duke's Pass (1627/SCENIC ROUTES).

1308
11/J30
L

The Crown Portpatrick · 01776 810261 Popular, busy pub on harbour with tables outside in summer and everywhere else (it's huge!). Light, airy conservatory. Freshly caught fish their speciality. 12 rooms above. Locals and Irish who sail over. Lunch till 9.30pm.

1309
11/N30
LL

The Anchor Kippford · 01556 620205 A defining pub of this popular coastal village on the 'Scottish Riviera'. The plate of sauce sachets lets you know this ain't gastro territory but it's hearty and old-style with a huge throughput in bar and lounges and especially outside tables. Overlooking the tranquil cove and the sunset. Lunch and LO 9pm.

1310
10/R28

The Auld Cross Keys Inn Denholm · 01450 870305 Not a lot to recommend in Hawick, so this village pub with rooms is worth the 8km journey on A698 Jedburgh road. On the Green, with pub and dining lounges and new patio. A la carte and blackboard menu; heaps of choice. Real fire, candles. Sunday carvery. Denholm Folk Club meets here. Food LO 8pm. 12 well-appointed good-value rooms.

1311
8/T19

The Globe Inn Aberdeen Urban and urbane bar in North Silver Street – a place to drink coffee as well as lager, but without any self-conscious, pretentious café-bar atmosphere. Lovely stained-glass rooflight; patio. Known for its food (12noon-9pm; 8.30pm weekends) and for live music at weekends – jazz and blues in the corner traditional on Tuesdays. The Globe Inn has rooms upstairs (929/ABERDEEN HOTELS) so not a bad place to base a weekend in Aberdeen.

The Best Vegetarian Restaurants

Not surprisingly perhaps, there are few completely vegetarian restaurants in Scotland. However, there are lots in Edinburgh (see p. 53-4) and some in Glasgow (see p. 109).

1312
10/R28
ATMOS
<£15

✓ **Damascus Drum** Hawick · 07707 856123 One of the notable cafés of the Borders (816/BORDER RESTAURANTS), Chris Ryan's bookshop and haven of civilisation is not strictly vegetarian but is mostly, and it gets a tick a) coz it's quirky and good and b) for sticking it out in this least favourite of towns where men and rugby and meat still rule. Coffee/cake, hot dish of the day, quiches and borek (sic). Great atmosphere. Mon-Sat 9am-5pm.

1313
8/P17
<£15

✓ **Blue Angel at Findhorn Community** Findhorn You will go a long way in the North to find real vegetarian food, so it may be worth the detour from the main A96 Inverness-Elgin road, to Findhorn and the famous community (1219/RETREATS) where there is a great deli (1443/DELIS) and this always vibrant caff by the hall at the end of the (old) runway. 7 days till 5pm and evenings if event in the hall (hot food till 3pm).

1314
8/P17
£15-25

✓ **The Bakehouse** Findhorn · 01309 691826 Same neck of the woods as Blue Angel (above) and its owners loosely connected. Not strictly vegetarian either but lots of vegetarian choice; all ethical and 'slow'. Bread and cakes from the bakery behind. Lovely, conscientious cookery. 7 days 10am-5pm.

1315
9/J26
<£15

✓ **Musicker** High Street, Rothesay · 01700 502287 Beside the castle, up from the ferry. Great pastries, paninis and soup, range of coffee all the same price! Totally vegetarian! Nice books, old juke box, newspapers, bluesy: jazz CDs for sale. Friendly, relaxed. Loyal clientele. Mon-Sat 10am-5pm.

✓ **Woodside** near Ancrum On B6400 near Monteviot House, a tearoom in a walled garden (1504/GARDENS). Organic, simple food. Report: 1383/TEAROOMS.

The Best Vegetarian-Friendly Places

HIGHLANDS
The Ceilidh Place Ullapool · 01854 612103 988/HIGHLAND HOTELS.
Café One Inverness · 01463 226200 1044/INVERNESS.
Three Chimneys Skye · 01470 511258 2291/SKYE RESTAURANTS.
Café Arriba Skye · 01478 611830 2297/SKYE RESTAURANTS.
Mountain Café Aviemore 1022/HIGHLAND RESTAURANTS.
Riverside Bistro Lochinver · 01571 844356 1030/HIGHLAND RESTAURANTS.
Old Pines near Spean Bridge · 01397 712324 1000/HIGHLAND HOTELS.
Russell's @ Smiddy House Spean Bridge · 01397 712335 1020/HIGHLAND RESTAURANTS.
Carron Restaurant Loch Carron · 01520 722488 1013/HIGHLAND RESTAURANTS.
Plockton Shores Plockton · 01599 544263 1016/HIGHLAND RESTAURANTS.

NORTH EAST
The Foyer Aberdeen · 01224 582277 942/ABERDEEN RESTAURANTS.
Beautiful Mountain Aberdeen · 01224 645353 951/ABERDEEN RESTAURANTS.

Milton Restaurant Crathes · 01330 844566 924/NORTH-EAST HOTELS.
Rendezvous @ Nargile Aberdeen · 01224 323700 958/ABERDEEN
RESTAURANTS.
Buchanan's Banchory · 01330 826530 922/NORTH-EAST RESTAURANTS.

ARGYLL & ISLES
Argyll Hotel Iona · 01681 700334 1139/SEASIDE INNS.
St Columba Hotel Iona · 01681 700304 2306/MULL.
Inver Cottage Loch Fyne · 01369 860537 739/ARGYLL RESTAURANTS.
The Green Welly Stop Tyndrum · 01838 400271 1374/TEAROOMS.
Julie's Coffee House Oban · 01631 565952 744/OBAN.
Kilmartin House Café Kilmartin · 01546 510278 1394/TEAROOMS.
Mount Stuart Restaurant Isle of Bute · 01700 505276 741/ARGYLL.

FIFE & LOTHIANS
Pillars of Hercules near Falkland · 01337 857749 1388/TEAROOMS.
Ostler's Close Cupar · 01334 655574 848/FIFE RESTAURANTS.
The Vine Leaf St Andrews · 01334 477497 852/ST ANDREWS.
Old Clubhouse Gullane · 01620 842008 831/EAST LOTHIAN RESTAURANTS.
Livingston's Linlithgow · 01506 846565 834/WEST LOTHIAN RESTAURANTS.

CENTRAL
Deans @ Let's Eat Perth · 01738 643377 871/PERTHSHIRE RESTAURANTS.
Monachyle Mhor near Balquhidder · 01877 384622 1160/GET-AWAY HOTELS.
Parrot Café Dundee · 01382 206277 897/DUNDEE RESTAURANTS.
T. Ann Café Dundee · 01382 540138 898/DUNDEE RESTAURANTS.
Jute Dundee · 01382 909246 887/DUNDEE RESTAURANTS.
The Parlour Dundee · 01382 203588 901/DUNDEE RESTAURANTS.
Malabar Dundee · 01382 646888 895/DUNDEE RESTAURANTS.
The Inn at Kippen Kippen · 01786 871010 1282/INNS.
Cargills Blairgowrie · 01250 876735 881/PERTHSHIRE RESTAURANTS.
88º Kirriemuir & Forfar · 01575 570888 877/PERTHSHIRE RESTAURANTS.

SOUTH & SOUTH WEST
Marmions Melrose · 01896 822245 808/BORDERS RESTAURANTS.
Philipburn Selkirk · 01750 20747 800/BORDERS HOTELS.
The Sunflower Peebles · 01721 722420 814/BORDERS RESTAURANTS.
Osso Peebles · 01721 724477 806/BORDERS RESTAURANTS.
The Restaurant at Kailzie Gardens 01721 722807 807/BORDERS
RESTAURANTS.
Whitmuir Farm near Peebles · 01968 661908 810/BORDERS RESTAURANTS.
Saffy's Ayr · 01292 288598 755/AYR RESTAURANTS.

The Best Seafood Restaurants

For seafood restaurants in Edinburgh, see p. 51-2; for Glasgow, see p. 108.

1316
10/R24
£25-35
ATMOS

✓✓ **The Cellar** Anstruther · 01333 310378 From a time when seafood restaurants were few, the Cellar has set a shining example from its cosy neuk of Fife of how assiduously sourced ingredients (and especially the seafood) served simply is what makes a restaurant meal great. And of all those shiny diners that have since lit up the coasts, the Cellar's darker but timeless atmosphere still sets exactly the right tone for the fish supper you won't forget. Can't say better than that. Peter (Jukes), chef/patron. 846/FIFE RESTAURANTS.

1317
6/P12
£25-35
LL

✓✓ **The Captain's Galley** Scrabster · www.captainsgalley.co.uk · 01847 894999 In the Galley there is a very firm and sure hand on the tiller. This is the place to eat on the north coast and a reputation built on total integrity with a conservation, sustainability and slow-food ethos throughout. Chef/proprietor Jim Cowie and his missus know exactly where everything comes from: salad from their poly tunnel and daily-landed fish from the boats and bay is all personally selected (and from a 50-mile radius). Those crabs actually choose Jim's creels. Menu short (usually 4 choices) and to the point, as are opening hours. Dinner only Tue-Sat 7-9pm. Best book: this was UK Seafood Restaurant of the Year 2009. This entry virtually unchanged since last edition – it's all still true!

1318
9/K27
£25-35
L

✓✓ **MacCallum's of Troon Oyster Bar** Troon · 01292 319339 Down at the quayside 3km from centre. Follow signs for ferry, past the woodpiles and fishmarket. Red-brick building with discreet sign, so eyes peeled. MacCallum's long-time suppliers to the restaurants of Edinburgh and Glasgow (home to their impressive and extensive fish shop in Finnieston), here on their home quay, literally over the tanks where langoustines lurk. Lovely fish (big on oysters and catch of the day), great atmosphere and unpretentious. They keep it admirably simple. Tue-Sat lunch and LO 9.30pm. Sun lunch only. Adjacent fish 'n' chip shop is the best in the west (1337/FISH & CHIPS).

1319
10/R23
£25-35
LL

✓ **The Seafood Restaurant** www.theseafoodrestaurant.com · 01334 479475 · St Andrews In a landmark position overlooking the Old Course and bay, this glass-walled pavilion is the top spot in the town and for a sunset supper is hard to beat. And food even better here of late. Great wines, nice puds but mainly fish pure and simple (usually 1 meat option). 7 days lunch and dinner LO 10pm.

1320
10/R24
£25-35
L

✓ **Craig Millar 16 West End** St Monans · www.16westend.com · 01333 730327 Title sounds like a cosmo upmarket bistro in a city somewhere but this is a street up from the harbour in a sleepy East Neuk Village. It is smart though and a destination dinner. Conservatory and terrace overlooks sea, waves lap, gulls mew, etc. Superb, out-of-the-way setting. Chef/proprietor Craig Millar rattles the pans. Seasonal menu Wed-Sun lunch and dinner LO 9pm.

1321
9/H23
£25-35

✓ **The Waterfront** Oban · www.waterfrontoban.co.uk · 01631 563110 On the waterfront at the station and upstairs from unimposing entrance a light, airy room (formerly the Seaman's Mission) above the busy bar, both serving some of the best seafood around in an authentic setting and their game upped again 2011. Specials change daily. The fish leap upstairs and onto your plate. And oysters and scallops (hot or cold) are a speciality. Good chips, by the way! Somewhere in Oban to linger on the way to the ferry. And The Waterfront now in Tobermory (2306/MULL). Open all year. Lunch and LO 9pm.

1322
9/H23
£25-35
L

✓ **Ee-Usk** Oban · www.eeusk.com · 01631 565666 Landmark new-build on the north pier by the hospitable Macleods (adjacent an Italian restaurant in a similar building which they also run – the Piazza). A full-on seafront caff with urban bistro feel, great views and fish from that sea. Goes like a ferry. Good wee wine list. No kids in the evening – t'usk, t'usk! 7 days lunch and LO 9.30pm.

1323
10/S20
£25-35
LL

✓ **The Tolbooth** Stonehaven · 01569 762287 On a corner of the harbour, long one of the best restaurants in the area in a great setting (reputedly the oldest building in town) under chef Craig Sommers. Upstairs bistro, a light room with picture windows on to beach and harbour no longer landing much fish but local fishermen do supply crab, langoustine, great lobster and the odd halibut. In summer, this sea still hoaches with mackerel. Fresh, simple and decent value. Tue-Sat, lunch and dinner (also Sun May-Sep).

1324
9/J21
£25-35
L

✓ **Loch Leven Seafood Café** near Kinlochleven · 01855 821048 · www.lochlevenseafoodcafe.co.uk Leave the A82 at north Ballachulish, 15km south of Fort William, then 7km on B863 down the side of Loch Leven to this shellfish tankery, shop and bright, airy restaurant. A la carte of scallops, mussels, clams, lobster, crab and specials. Excellent wine list. Reciprocal fine products from places they export to, like Spain. Best food in the area. Lunch and 6-9pm. 7 days in summer. Wed-Sat, and Sun lunch, in winter.

1325 8/T19
£25-35
LLL ATMOS

✓ **Silver Darling** Aberdeen · www.silverdarling.co.uk · 01224 576229 Down by the harbour. For a long time now one of the best restaurants in the city and the North East; an ethereal location. 952/ABERDEEN RESTAURANTS.

1326
7/F17
£25-35
LL
ATMOS

✓ **Lochbay Seafood** Skye · www.lochbay-seafood-restaurant.co.uk · 01470 592235 12km north Dunvegan; A850 to Portree, B886 Waternish peninsula coastal route. A scenic Skye drive leads you to the door of this small cottage at end of the village row where David and Alison Wilkinson have been cooking up their simply sublime seafood for many seasons now. Overlooks the water where your scallops, prawns and oysters are surfaced. Main dishes served unfussily with puds like clootie dumpling. Small, with nice bistro atmosphere; you feel this is exactly where you want to be to eat seafood. Best book. Apr-Oct; lunch and LO 8.30pm-ish. Tue-Sat.

1327
9/K23
£15-25

✓ **Loch Fyne Oysters** Loch Fyne · 01499 600264 On A83 the Loch Lomond to Inveraray road, 20km Inveraray/11km Rest and Be Thankful. Landmark roadside restaurant and all-round seafood experience on the way out west. Though Loch Fyne Seafood is a huge UK chain, this is the original (and not actually in the chain after a management buy-out). People come from afar for the oysters and the smokery fare, especially the kippers. Spacious and with many banquettes though somewhat refectory-ish! House white (other whites and whisky) well chosen. Same menu all day; LO 8pm (later in summer). Shop sells every conceivable packaging of salmon and other Scots produce; shop 7.30pm.

1328
9/K26
£15-25

✓ **Fins** Fairlie near Largs · www.fencebay.co.uk · 01475 568989 On main A78 south of Fairlie a seafood bistro, smokery (Fencebay), shop and craft/cookshop (2188/SHOPPING). Roadside fish farm, bistro, farmshop and cookshop: an all-round day-out and love-food experience. Best place to eat for miles in either direction. Simple, straightforward good cookin' and the wine list is similarly to the point. Nice conservatory; and geraniums. Lunch and dinner LO 8.30/9pm. Closed Mon. Farmers market here last Sunday of the month.

1329 **√Creelers** Brodick, Arran · www.creelers.co.uk · 01770 302810 Just out-
9/L26 side Brodick on road north to castle beside Aromatics-led gift plaza; the
£25-35 cheese shop is nice (1472/CHEESES). Excellent seafood bistro, the original of the
one in Edinburgh (212/SEAFOOD RESTAURANTS), this is where they have the smokery and Tim plies his boat in nearby waters. You don't get more direct sea- or
smokehouse-to-plate than this. Easter-Oct. Closed Mon.

1330 **√The Seafood Cabin** Skipness · 01880 760207 Adjacent Skipness Castle,
9/J26 signed from Claonaig where the CalMac ferry from Lochranza arrives. Sophie
<£15 James's famous wee cabin with outdoor seating and indoor options in perfect spot
LL for their fresh and local seafood, snacks and cakes. Mussels come further (Loch
Etive). Smoked stuff from Creelers (above) in Arran. Jun-Sep 11am-6pm. Closed Sat.

1331 **Campbell's** Portpatrick · www.campbellsrestaurant.co.uk · 01776 810314
11/J30 Friendly, harbourside restaurant in much-visited Portpatrick. Some meat dishes,
£25-35 but mainly seafood. Their own boat brings back crab and lobster (and sea bass and
pollack). 7 days lunch and LO 10pm. Closed Jan-Mar and Mon.

1332 **Crannog at the Waterfront** Fort William · www.oceanandoak.co.uk ·
9/K21 01397 705589 Long-established landmark and destination restaurant. Nice bright
£25-35 contemporary setting, not only great seafood but a real sense of place in this rainy
L town. 7 days, lunch and LO 9pm (later weekends).

1333 **Shorehouse Café** Tarbet near Scourie · 01971 502251 Charming conserva-
6/K13 tory restaurant on cove where boats leave for Handa Island bird reserve
£15-25 (1705/BIRDS). Julian catches your seafood from his boat and Jackie cooks it; they
LL have the Rick Stein seal of approval. Home-made puds. Located at end of unclassified road off the A894 between Laxford Bridge and Scourie; best phone to check
openings. Apr-Sep: Mon-Sat 12-8pm. Closed Sun.

1334 **Kishorn Seafood Bar** Kishorn · www.kishornseafoodbar.co.uk · 01520
7/H18 733240 Conveniently located on A896 at Kishorn on the road between
£25-35 Lochcarron (Inverness) and Sheildaig near the road over the hill to Applecross
(1616/SCENIC ROUTES). Fresh local seafood in a roadside diner: Kishorn oysters,
Applecross crab; lobsters in a tank out back. Light, bright and a real find in the
middle of beautiful nowhere courtesy of the ebullient Viv Rollo. Mar-Nov daily
10am-5pm (9pm Jul/Aug). Sun 12noon-5pm.

1335 **The Pierhouse** Port Appin · www.pierhousehotel.co.uk · 01631 730302 At
9/J22 the end of the minor road and 3km from the A828 Oban–Fort William road in Port
£15-25 Appin village right by the tiny pier where the passenger ferry leaves for Lismore;
LL the setting is everything. A hotel and bistro with bar and dining room. Ingredients
come fresh to the door by boat and many local suppliers: oysters, mussels, crab.
Chowders and platters. Lively atmosphere, wine and the wonderful view. Report:
1152/INNS.

√ √**Applecross Inn** 01520 744262 · Applecross The inn at the end of
the road. Great seafood; classic fish 'n' chips. 1169/GET-AWAY HOTELS.

√**Café Fish** Tobermory · 01688 301253 2306/MULL RESTAURANTS.

The Best Fish & Chip Shops

1336
1/B1

✓ ✓ **L'Alba D'Oro** Henderson Row, Edinburgh Near corner with Dundas St. Large selection of deep-fried goodies, including vegetarian savouries. Inexpensive proper pasta, real pizzas and superb, surprising Italian wine to go in adjacent takeaway **Anima**, a stools-at-the-window diner (316/TAKEAWAYS). L'Alba in Alba; a more civilised chip. Open till 12midnight. 195/EDINBURGH PIZZA.

1337
9/K27
L

✓ ✓ **The Wee Hurrie** Troon · 01292 319340 Famed and fabulous, the Wee Hurrie is part of MacCallum's oyster and fish restaurant (see 1318/SEAFOOD RESTAURANTS for directions because it's a fair walk from the town centre). Big range of fresh daily fish displayed and to select. Light tempuras, even salads to go in veg oil. Tue-Sun 12noon-8pm (9pm Fri/Sat). Best in the west, we say!

1338
9/H23

✓ ✓ **Fish & Chips in Oban** Oban has declared itself the Seafood Capital of Scotland, with 3 good seafood restaurants but also these 3 great chip shops. All are in George St near the bay. **Nories** at 88 has been here over 50 years. They are uncompromising about the lard but they do great F&C (12noon-10.30/11.30pm). **Oban Fish & Chip Shop** is the fancy newcomer at 116 with coley, hake and home-made fishcakes along with sustainable haddock and cod. They do use vegetable oil (11.30am-11pm 7 days). Both Nories and the Oban have sit-in caffs. Some locals say the best fish 'n' chips in town is from the **George St Fish & Chip Shop** behind the Caledonian Hotel near the square. All here is bright and fresh. They do use beef dripping and keep the menu small. 7 days 10am-11pm. Wherever you go, Oban's waterfront is the perfect place to scoff 'em.

1339
10/Q24

✓ **Fish & Chips in Fife** Apart from the estimable Valente's in Kirkcaldy and the much-vaunted Anstruther Fish Bar (in the Lard section; see below), Fife has 2 less celebrated but damned good fish 'n' chip shops. **The Wee Chippie** in Anstruther is on the harbour west of the AFB. They have a caff with home baking – **The Bakehouse** up the alley; open till 8pm. The takeaway out front is open till 10pm. Go on, give it a try: the word on the waterfront is that it's better. Along the road, the even better-kept secret is the **Pittenweem Fish & Chip Bar**, a door in the wall at the end of the High St next to the clock tower. 6-10pm (Sun from 5pm). Closed Mon.

1340
1/E1

✓ **The Deep Sea** Leith Walk, Edinburgh Opposite Playhouse. Open late and often has queues (which are quickly dispatched). Haddock has to be of a certain size. Traditional menu. One of the best fish suppers with which to feed a hangover. 2am-ish (3am Fri/Sat).

1341
10/Q23

✓ **Deep Sea** 81 Nethergate, Dundee At bottom end of Perth Rd; very central. The Sterpaio family have been serving the Dundonians excellent fish 'n' chips for 75 years (you read that correctly); great range of fish in groundnut (the most expensive) oil. Café with aproned waitress service is a classic. So very traditional, so very tasty. Mon-Sat, morning till early evening.

1342
2/XA1

✓ **Philadelphia** 445 Great Western Road, Glasgow Adjacent Big Blue (531/PIZZA) and La Parmigiana (517/BEST ITALIAN RESTAURANTS), owned by same family. Since 1930, a Glasgow fixture and fresher fryer than most. 7 days 12noon-12midnight (Fri/Sat 4am).

1343
9/J26

✓ **West End** 1 Gallowgate, Rothesay Remains a Rothesay must-do and always a queue. Only haddock but a wide range of other fries and fresh pizza. We can't make head nor tail of their hours, but they're mostly open (not 2-4pm).

1344
8/P17

✓ **The Ashvale** Aberdeen, Elgin, Inverurie, Ellon, Banchory, Brechin Original restaurant (1985) at 46 Great Western Rd; 3 other city branches. Restaurant/takeaway à la Harry Ramsden (stuck to dripping for long enough but changed to vegetable oil in '09). Various sizes of haddock, sole, plaice. Home-made stovies, etc, all served fresh so you do wait. From 12noon but hours vary.

1345
6/K15

Seaforth Chippy Ullapool Adjacent ferry terminal. Part of Seaforth Hotel with upstairs seafood bistro but probably best to stick to fish and chips and walk the harbour. Some question in Ullapool whether it's the Seaforth or the one round the corner but I'll stick with this. Chips often pale but fish don't get any fresher. 7 days till 10pm, 8.30pm in winter.

1346
11/N29

Balmoral Balmoral Road, Dumfries Seems as old and essential as the Bard himself. Using rapeseed oil, it's the best chip in the south. Out the Annan road heading east, 1km from centre. LO 10pm (9pm Sun/Mon).

1347
9/G22
L

The Fish & Chip Van aka The Fisherman's Pier Tobermory By the clock on Fisherman's Pier, this van has almost achieved destination-restaurant status. Always a queue. Fresh and al fresco. All year. 12.30-9pm. Closed Sun in winter.

1348
10/S20

Sandy's Market Square, Stonehaven The established Stoney chipper, and always busy despite interlopers (see The Bay, below). Daily, LO 10pm, 9pm Sun. Big haddock like the old days (and the smaller 'haddock bites').

AND THESE THAT STICK TO LARD

1349
10/Q24

✓ ✓ **Valente's** 73 Overton Road, Kirkcaldy · 01592 651991 Ask directions or satnav to this superb chippy in east of town (not the high street one); worth the detour and the queue when you get there. They also make ice cream. LO 10.25pm. Branch at 73 Henry Rd (01592 203600). Closed Wed.

1350
10/M24

✓ ✓ **Mhor Fish** Callander · www.mhor.net Main street near square. Legendary café taken over by the ambitious and industrious Lewis family of Monachyle Mhor (1160/GET-AWAY HOTELS). Unprepossessing frontage but here, Dick Lewis adds a fresh-fish counter and general panache but doesn't tamper with the basic product: the fish tea with fresh Scrabster-landed fish and great chips. Fish here is to love; they have demonstrations of filleting and oyster-opening and other fishy stories regularly in the upstairs room. They use dripping but they tell you why. 12noon-9pm. Closed Mon. The takeaway next door is open later.

1351
8/T19

✓ **The Dolphin** Chapel Street, Aberdeen Despite the pre-eminence of the Ashvale in Aberdeen, many would rather swear by this small, always-busy place just off Union St. Previous owner Graeme Herd has returned to restore its recently tarnished reputation. Till 1am; 3/4am weekends.

1352
10/R22

✓ **Peppo's** 53 Ladybridge Street, Arbroath By the harbour where those fish come in. Fresh as that and chips in dripping. Peppo here since 1951; John and Frank Orsi carry on a great family tradition feeding the hordes. 7 days 4pm-8pm (it's a teatime thing).

1353
10/R24

✓ **The Anstruther Fish Bar** Anstruther · www.anstrutherfishbar.co.uk On the front (1550/COASTAL VILLAGES). Often listed as the best fish 'n' chips in Scotland/UK/Universe and the continuous queue suggests that either: a) we believe that; or b) they may be right. Sit in or walk round the harbour. There's also the ice cream. 7 days 11.30am-10pm.

1354
10/T26

✓ **Giacopazzi's** Eyemouth Harbour by the fish market (or what's left of it). A caff and takeaway with the catch on its doorstep. For over 100 years, the home of the now oft-cited Eyemouth-landed haddock and their award-winning ice cream. Takeaways eaten on boat-filled harbour, probably attended by very pushy gulls. 7 days 12noon-9pm. Upstairs to flashier **Oblo's Bistro** (01890 752527). Sun-Thu 10am-12midnight, Fri and Sat 10am-1am.

1355
7/N19

✓ **Harkai's** Aviemore On main street at south end as you come in from A9. Aka The Happy Haggis. Here since 1965 with a big local reputation. A long way from the sea but this a chipper (and café) takes itself seriously (although no obvious sustainable fish policy). 7 days LO 8.30pm (9pm Jul/Aug).

1356
10/S20

✓ **The Bay** Stonehaven On the prom towards the open-air pool (2116/SWIM-MING POOLS), a newer chip shop to add to Sandy's (above) in this well-fried town. Everything cooked to order. Bay is the local choice. 7 days till 10pm.

1357
10/R25

The North Berwick Fry 11 Quality Street, North Berwick Adjacent tourist information centre. Here forever in this seaside town. A long, thin 'diner' and next door, the chippie. Best to take your poke (or box) to the front (or to the gardens opposite). Big reputation, always busy. 7 days 11am-11pm (approximately).

Great Cafés

For cafés in Edinburgh, see p. 64-65, Glasgow, p. 111-12.

1358
7/M18

✓✓ **The Castle Restaurant** Inverness On road that winds up to the castle from the main street, near the tourist information centre and the hostels. No pandering to tourists here, but this great caff has been serving chips with everything for 40 years though these (crinkle cuts) are not their strong point. Pork chops, perfect fried eggs, prawn cocktail to crumbles. They work damned hard. In Inverness or anywhere nearby, you'll be pushed to find better-value grub than this (but see below). 9am-8pm. Closed Sun.

1359
7/M17

✓✓ **Girvans** 2 Stephens Brae, Inverness Behind M&S at end of pedestrian street. A different proposition to the Castle (above), more up-market – more perhaps a restaurant, but the atmosphere is of a good, unpretentious caff serving everything from omelettes to full-blown comfort meals. Great all-day Sunday breakfast. Tempting cream-laden cakes. Always busy but no need to book. I never go to Inverness without going here. 7 days 9am-9pm (Sun from 10am).

1360
9/K23

✓✓ **The Real Food Café** Tyndrum · www.therealfoodcafe.com Created from a Little Chef on the main A82 just before the junction Oban/Fort William and what a difference. May appear like a chip shop but this is excellent food for the road, conscientiously sourced, seriously sustainable fish and the antithesis of frozen, fast and couldn't-care-less. Fish 'n' chips, burgers, breakfasts, pies – all home-made. Lounge with wood-burning stove. Birds to watch. No ordinary pitstop! 7 days 11.30am-9pm, Fri 10pm.

1361
6/K15

✓ **The Tea Store** Argyll Street, Ullapool · www.theteastore.co.uk In the street parallel to and one up from the waterfront. Excellent, unpretentious café serving all-day fry-ups and other snacks. Great home baking including those strawberry tarts in season. Best caff in Ullapool (or Lewis where you might be heading). All year. 8.30am-4.30pm. Sun 9am-3pm; winter hours vary.

1362
10/N24

✓ **Allan Water Café** Henderson Street, Bridge of Allan The main street, beside the eponymous bridge. Worth coming over from Stirling (8km) for a takeaway or a seat in the caff (a steel-and-glass extension somewhat lacking in charm) for great fish 'n' chips and the ice cream (1438/ICE CREAM). In BoA the AWC is a bit of a must! 7 days, 8am-8.30pm.

1363
9/K26
ATMOS
L

✓ **The Ritz Café** 01475 530459 · Millport See Millport, see the Ritz. Since 1906 (though pure 1960s) and now in its fourth generation, the classic café on the Clyde. Once overshadowed by Nardini's and a short ferry journey away (from Largs, continuous; then 6km), it should be an essential part of any visit to this part of the coast, and Millport is not entirely without charm. Toasties, rolls, the famous hot peas. Exellent ice cream (especially with melted marshmallow). Something of 'things past'. 7 days, 10am-9pm in season. Must also mention here **The Cumbrae Bistro**, Stuart St (01475 531227). A different thing, a bistro of course, al fresco, fresh and nice.

1364
8/Q18
<£15

Glenfiddich Restaurant 01340 820363 · Church Street, Dufftown Near the town clock. Enough to send some modern Scots gibbering into their Irn Bru cocktail, others may be in unreconstructed heaven. They say it's a restaurant, but it's a proper caff. Self-proclaimed award-winning, the food is fairly ghastly but this is as camp as the Black Watch on manoeuvres. Packed with paraphernalia (one room a homage to Elvis and the Beatles) and yes, happy punters. 7 days all day. LO 9pm, winter hours vary.

1365
10/S27

Under The Sun Roxburgh Street, Kelso · 01573 225179 Just off the square. Fraser and Kirstin Murray's café and Fair-trade centre Under the Sun has been something of a Kelso fixture for nigh on 20 years. Curious mix of kids' stuff for sale and busy caff. Home baking, hot dishes, big-choice menu with integrity. 9.30am-6pm (5pm Sat). Closed Sun.

1366
10/R18

Brydons 16 High Street, Hawick · 01877 376267 Family-run and friendly caff in Hawick main street serving breakfast through to tea. Has a real caff atmosphere. Hot food like mince 'n' tatties, macaroni cheese. This was the food I was brought up on and I went to that damned high school. Surprising collection of teapots. 7.30am-5pm. Closed Sun.

1367
9/J26
L

Ettrick Bay Café Bute End of the road from Port Bannatyne near Rothesay. In the middle of the bay and the beach looking over to Arran-Kintyre – this is the caff with the view. Here forever, a family fixture from seaside days gone by. Honest, home-made menu including their famous garlic mussels and Alec's rather large cakes. 7 days 10am-5pm.

� The Best Tearooms & Coffee Shops

For Edinburgh, see p. 61-3, for Glasgow, p. 110-11.

1368
10/S27
L

✓ ✓ **The Terrace** Floors Castle, Kelso Top garden tearoom inside and out an old outbuilding that forms one side of the estate walled garden (2218/GARDEN CENTRES) some distance from the castle (1841/COUNTRY HOUSES). Superb, home-made, unpretentious hot dishes and baking: home-cured ham, salads and irresistible cakes and puds and pies. Shop with deli stuff. And the terrace: bliss. 7 days 10am-5pm, hot food till 2.30pm then toasties. Open all year.

1369
10/R25

✓ ✓ **Falko** Gullane Main street of genteel village (though too much house building seems likely to lower the dulcet tone) on corner. A bakery/coffee shop (though the bakery is actually in Edinburgh) that calls itself a konditerai because those gorgeous cakes and breads are German, Austrian and Swiss and they change with the seasons (stollen comes in October). Soup and 'cheese tongues' come hot. The cake is simply irresistible. Master baker and proprietor Falko in command. 9am-5.30pm, Sun from 10am. Closed Tue.

1370
10/N23

✓ ✓ **Indulge** Auchterarder · 01764 660033 Aptly named and as befits the town where Gleneagles presides, a top tearoom/restaurant at the bottom end of the long main street. Eclectic, comforting hot-meal menu, irresistible desserts and some good old-fashioned cakes to wash down with Darjeeling. 9am-4pm. Closed Sun. Just a pity they weren't open longer!

1371
8/R20

✓ ✓ **Finzean Tearoom** Finzean · www.finzean.com · 01330 850710 The tearoom and farmshop of the Finzean (pronounced Fing-In) estate on backroad between Aboyne and Banchory, a very worthwhile detour. Great food, great views. Report: 1455/FARMSHOPS. 7 days 9am-5pm. Sun from 11am.

1372
10/Q24

✓ ✓ **Kind Kyttock's Kitchen** Falkland Folk come to Falkland (1774/CASTLES; 1969/HILL WALKS) for many reasons, not least for afternoon tea at KKK: Quentin Dalrymple keeping it in the family with great attention to detail and to you. Omelettes, pizza, toasties, baked potatoes, top cake list. A visit to Falkland wouldn't be the same without it! 10.30am-5.30pm (4.30pm in winter). Closed Mon.

1373
11/M29

✓ ✓ **Kitty's Tearoom** New Galloway Main street of town in the forest. Absolutely splendid. Sylvia Brown's steady hand in the kitchen. Lovely teas, lovely china, lovely cakes! Conversation. Great salads. High tea 4-6pm very popular, including 'a roast'. All this but you must take cake. It's an Alan Bennett world. 10am-5pm (6.30pm Thu-Sun). Closed Mon.

1374
9/K23
L

✓ ✓ **The Green Welly Stop** Tyndrum · www.thegreenwellystop.co.uk On A82, a strategically placed all-round super services on the drive to Oban or Fort William (just before the road divides), with a Scottish produce shop, a gas station, a snack stop which does pizzas and a self-service restaurant: great comfort food at a much higher standard than any motorway in the land. Food prepared to order, excellent cakes and puds, fresh OJ and fast, friendly service. Shops stuffed with everything Scottish you possibly don't need. 7 days, 8.30am-5.30pm (5pm in winter). Snack stop 7am-9pm.

1375
8/R20

✓ ✓ **The Black-Faced Sheep** Aboyne · 01339 887311 Near main Royal Deeside road through Aboyne (A93) and Mark Ronson's excellent coffee shop/gift shop is well-loved by locals (and regulars from all over) but is thankfully missed by the bus parties hurtling towards Balmoral. Sylvie bakes the breads and cakes. Light specials and good coffee (real capp and espresso from Elektra machine). Their love affair with Italy means own-label wines (excellent exclusive house red) and olive oil. 10am-5pm, Sun from 11am. Fascinating furniture and objets, way better than the usual knick-knacks.

1376
8/R20

✓ ✓ **Raemoir Garden Centre** Banchory On A980, the Deeside road through town, about 3km to a garden centre that has grown into a house-and-gardens megastore. Self-service caff with salad bar, quiches etc. and cream-laden cakes (though not a good coffee machine) and beyond the packed emporium a waitress-service restaurant with extensive menu and more cakes. Always packed; where did they go before? 7 days 9am-5pm (caff), 4pm restaurant.

1377
9/G22
✓ ✓ **Glengorm Farm Coffee Shop** near Tobermory · 01688 302321
First right on Tobermory-Dervaig road (7km). Organic food served in well refurbished stable block. Soups, cakes, staples (mac cheese, steak pie), specials and delicious salads from their famous garden (they supply other Mull restaurants). All you need after a walk in the grounds of this great estate (2306/MULL HOTELS, 2248/WALKS) ...and the *best* cappuccino on Mull. Easter-Oct. LO 4.30pm.

1378
10/L23
L
✓ ✓ **Library Tearoom** Balquhidder Centre of village opposite the church (1897/GRAVEYARDS) where many walks start. Includes great view (1648/VIEWS) and near long walk to Brig o' Turk (2002/GLEN WALKS). This corner-of-the-country caff is by the Mhor people from along the loch (1160/GET-AWAY HOTELS). Excellent bakes, soup, salad and impossible-to-resist cake. Mighty leaf tea. Only a few tables. Apr-Oct, 10am-5pm. Closed Tue.

1379
10/S22
✓ ✓ **The Watermill** Aberfeldy · www.aberfeldywatermill.com · 01887 822896 Off Main St direction Kenmore near the Birks (2012/WOODLAND WALKS). Downstairs caff on riverside in a conserved mill. Much more than this, though: the top independent bookshop in the Highlands, a remarkable art gallery upstairs with Scottish artists and international print work for sale and Homer, a selective, always-interesting homes-and-gardens shop (they have opened another Homer in Howe St, Edinburgh). Waiter service in busy caff with inside and terrace seating. Soups, quiches, home baking. 10am-5.30pm (Sun 11am-5pm). Signed from all over, this is your destination for the good life in Aberfeldy!

1380
10/N22
✓ **Legends & The Highland Chocolatier** Grandtully Main street of village on the Tay where rivers are as busy with rafters as the road with traffic. Gifts and, even in the now-crowded chocolate-making world, Iain Burnett's famously good home-made-chocolate shop. Through the back a good tearoom for light snacks, home-made stuff, great tea list and of course hot chocolate. 10am-5pm.

1381
8/S20
L
✓ **The Falls of Feugh** Banchory · www.fallsoffeugh.com · 01330 822123
Over bridge south from town, the B974 for Fettercairn (signed), a restaurant-cum-tearoom by a local beauty spot, the tumbling falls. Ann Taylor's labour of love with à la carte menu, specials and great scones.Here on the Deeside teaside there are more than a few places to choose from (see above and below), so stiff competition; this is your old-style with luncheon, afternoon and then high tea. All year. 7 days till 6.30pm (4pm in winter). Closed Mon/Tue.

1382
5/E14
L
✓ **Loch Croistean** Uig, Lewis · 01851 672772 Further west than all the rest (30 minutes from Stornoway by A8110), Marianne Campbell's homely oasis in an unforgiving landscape. Further on the amazing beaches and the sunset, here home-made, lovely food (the soda bread and soup). Buffet supper Fri/Sat in summer. Mon-Sat from 12noon (Wed-Sat in that long winter).

1383
10/R27
L
✓ **Woodside** near Ancrum On B6400 off A68 at Ancrum turnoff. The caff in the shack at the back of the Woodside Garden Centre in the walled garden of Monteviot House (1504/GARDENS). Simple, delicious, mostly organic and locally sourced home baking: soup, sandwiches, quiche and cakes. Outside tables on sheltered lawn. Change of management '11. 10am-5pm.

1384
8/Q20
✓ **Station Restaurant** Ballater Part of the old station (terminus for Balmoral) made famous by Queen Vic, now a museum to her, and the royals now loved again as then. A proper tea and luncheon room by the Franks who have the estimable Darroch Learg (908/NORTH-EAST HOTELS). Menu informed by chef David Muller so nice touches with (home-made) chips, great wine list. 7 days 10am-5pm.

1385
10/P24

✓ **The Powmill Milkbar** near Kinross On A977 Kinross (on the M90, junction 6) to Kincardine Bridge road, a real milk bar and real slice of Scottish craic and cake. Apple pie, moist fly cemeteries, big meringues: an essential stop on any Sunday run (but open every day). The paper plates do little justice to the confections they bear, but they are part of the deal, so don't complain! Hot meals, great old-style salads. Local girls! Good place to take kids. An unreconstructed heaven. 7 days 9am-5pm (6pm summer, 4pm winter). And then: 2004/GLEN & RIVER WALKS.

1386
7/M20

✓ **Laggan Coffeeshop** near Laggan · www.potterybunkhouse.co.uk · 01528 544231 On A889 from Dalwhinnie on A9 that leads to A86, the road west to Spean Bridge and Kyle. Lovely Linda's road sign points you to this former pottery, craft shop and bunkhouse (1121/HOSTELS) and now pizza barn. Great home baking, scones, soup, sarnies and the most yummy cakes. Near great spot for forest walks and river swimming (1660/WILD SWIMMING). Open all year, ring for hours.

1387
8/R18

✓ **The Tearoom at Clatt** near Alford & Inverurie Since 1985, in the village hall in hamlet of Clatt where local ladies display great home-made Scottish baking – like a weekly sale of work. Take A96 north of Inverurie then B9002; follow sign for Auchleven, then Clatt. Great countryside. Weekends Apr-Oct 12noon-4pm. One of the great tea-and-scone experiences in the world (you'll see what I mean).

1388
10/Q24

✓ **Pillars of Hercules** near Falkland · www.pillars.co.uk · 01337 857749 Rustic tearoom on organic farm on A912 2km from village towards Strathmiglo and the motorway. Excellent, homely place and fare and ethical. Home-made cakes, soup, etc. They also have a bothy and you can camp around them. See also 1463/FARM SHOPS. 7 days 10am-5pm (shop till 6pm).

1389
9/L24

✓ **The Coach House** Luss, Loch Lomond · www.lochlomondtrading.com Long after the soap *Take The High Road* which was set here ended, this village still throngs with visitors happy with twee. Rowena Ferguson's lovely caff goes like a proverbial fair. Not all home-made but good soups and quiches. Big tea selection, lashings of cream. Some outside seating. Nice loos. 7 days 10am-5pm.

1390
11/M30

✓ **The Schoolhouse** Ringford On A75 10km west of Castle Douglas. A busy road and a perenially busy foodstop where passers-by and a legion of regulars love fresh, home-made cooking done with integrity and commitment. It's all made here (except the bread). Can take away. 10am-6pm. Closed Wed except Jul/Aug.

1391
9/J22
L

✓ **Castle Stalker View** Portnacroish · www.castlestalkerview.co.uk On A828 Oban-Fort William about halfway. Modern build café/gift shop with soup 'n' salad menu and home baking. Breakfast till 11.30am. Nice people so a popular local rendezvous as well as passers-through. Extraordinary view (1653/VIEWS) and in the woods, Ecopods (1215/GLAMPING). Mar-Oct 9.30am-5.30pm, winter Thu-Sun 10am-4pm. Closed Jan.

1392
11/L30

✓ **Readinglasses** Wigtown Few good eating places in Wigtown Booktown but this tiny caff at the back of yet another bookshop is a rest and respite from all that browsing. 3-lovely-wifie operation (Gerrie, Susan and Bex) with named, locally sourced ingredients, soup with Creetown's Wigwam bread, signature Homity pie, salad leaves from garden and home-made cakes. Can be as packed as a bookshelf. 7 days Easter-Oct. 10am-7pm.

1393
10/R26

✓ **Flat Cat Gallery Coffee Shop** Lauder · www.flatgallery.co.uk Opposite Eagle Hotel on Market St. Speeding through Lauder (don't: speed camera at Edinburgh end) you might miss Annette and Jacqui's cool coffee spot and serious gallery. Always interesting work including furniture from Harestanes down the road; and ethnic things. Soup and sandwiches, home baking. 7 days till 5pm.

1394 ✓**Kilmartin House Café** Kilmartin · 01546 510278 Attached to early-
9/H24 peoples' museum (2154/MUSEUMS) in Kilmartin Glen and on main road north of Lochgilphead. Totally worth swinging in here from road or glen walk for home-made, conscientiously prepared light food. Down steps to bright conservatory with pastoral outlook. Organic garden produce. Good vegetarian choices and creative cooking. 7 days, hot food till 3pm, cakes till 5pm and dinner Thu-Sat in summer.

1395 ✓**The Quaich Café** Kilmelford · 01852 200271 On road south from Oban
9/H23 to Campbeltown, Anne Saunders' village store and through the back, upstairs an unlikely great wee café; in the evenings, a restaurant. Home baking and snack meals by day 10.30am-4.30pm, then lovely home-made comfort food/local-produce-driven menu. 2 cosy dining rooms, candlelit at night. A hidden gem methinks! Supper Thu-Sat 6-9pm.

1396 ✓**Logie Steading** near Forres South of town towards Grantown (A940) –
8/N17 10km. Or from Carrbridge via B9007. See 2020/WOODLAND WALKS (**Randolph's Leap**). In a lovely spot near the River Findhorn, a courtyard of fine things (2178/ SHOPPING) and **The Olive Tree Tearoom** – home bakes and snacks; sound local sourcing. Hot food till 3pm. Tables in the courtyard. All in a vital place to visit. 7 days 10.30am-5pm (winter hours vary).

1397 **Tudor Restaurant** 8 Beresford Terrace, Ayr Near Odeon and Burns
9/L28 Monument Sq. High tea from 3.15pm, breakfast all day. Roomy, well-used, full of life. Bakery counter at front (fab cream donuts and bacon butties) and locals from bairns to OAPs in the body of the kirk. 10am-9pm Mon-Sat, 12noon-8pm Sun.

1398 **The Flower Tunnel** Applecross · www.applecross.uk.com/flower_tunnel
7/H18 In campsite (1199/CAMPING WITH KIDS) as you arrive in Applecross after an amaz-
L ing journey (1616/SCENIC ROUTES). Laid-back, summer coffee shop in greenhouse full of plants and with outdoor seating. Snacks, hot specials and their quite famous pizzas (evenings only). Apr-Oct. 7 days till 9pm.

1399 **Bridge Cottage** Poolewe In village and near Inverewe Gardens (1492/
7/H16 GARDENS), a cottage right enough with crafts/pictures up stairs and parlour teashop down. Salads, soups, baked potatoes, big cakes; nearby produce. Neighbouring artists; the Inmans shop and support local. 10.30am-4.30pm (winter hours vary). All year 10.30am-5.30pm. Weekends only in winter.

1400 **Robin's Nest** Main Street, Taynuilt Off A85 (to Bonawe 2140/MUSEUMS and
9/J23 Glen Etive Cruises). Tiny home-baking caff with unusual soups and snacks as well as the good WRI kind of cakes. Easter-Oct 7 days 10am-5pm, Thu-Sun in winter.

1401 **Crinan Coffee Shop** Crinan · www.crinanhotel.com Run by the hotel people
9/H25 (732/BEST HOTELS ARGYLL) in this fascinating village for yachties and anyone with
LL time to while away. The café overlooks canal basin with boats always going through. Excellent cakes, bread and scones. Easter-Oct 9am-5.30pm.

1402 **Maggie's Tearoom** Dundonnell On A832 in Wester Ross, the road to
6/J16 Inverewe Gardens and Gairloch. Actually Ishbel's, this well-placed bistro and craft shop in a roadside cottage, though small inside, has a great deck and garden. Home-made hot dishes, salads and bakes. Apr-Oct 10am-5pm. Closed Sun.

1403   **Tea Cosy**   East Mey near John o' Groats   From Thurso follow signs for Jo'G and
6/Q12   Castle of Mey (1775/CASTLES). 2km further on, signed 200m from the road. Lindy
L   Brooks Crowson flies the (Union) flag (well, Prince Charles does walk this way) and
runs a cute tearoom/shop/gallery – a toastie and cake kind of place, the most
northerly tearoom on the British mainland; views to Dunnet Head and Orkney.
Stock up and head for Scotland's Haven (2060/COASTAL WALKS). Easter-Sep,
10.30am-5.30pm.

1404   **Laurel Bank**   Broughton · 01899 830462   On A701 near Biggar. Cottage tea-
10/P27   room, bistro and bar; local, friendly and a tad traditional. Nice coffee, home baking
and Broughton Ales. 9am-11pm in summer, winter hours may vary.

1405   **The Cocoa Tree Shop & Café**   Pittenweem   Near end of the high street, a
10/R24   chocolate emporium and through the back a busy tea/coffee/choc room with hot
snacks, soups, crêpes, cakes and naturally hot choco. Nice spot. 10am-6pm.

1406   **Crail Harbour Tearoom**   Crail   At last in cute little Crail, a tearoom where you
10/R24   need it on the road going down to the harbour. Gallery with pics from the owner.
Lovely, sheltered terrace overlooking the shore. Dressed crab from harbour, herring
and dill, flaky salmon and cakes. Perfect! 7 days 10.30am-5pm. Closed Dec/Jan.

1407   **Garden Room Teashop**   Rockcliffe   On main road in/out of this seaside cul de
11/N30   sac. Best on sunny days when you can sit in the sheltered garden. Snacks and
cakes (though not all home made); and pizza? 10.30am-5.30pm. Closed Mon/Tue.

1408   **The Smithy**   New Galloway   This village has long been a tearoom terminus
11/M29   because of Kitty's (above) but the Smithy has a brilliant location by the burn (with
outside terrace) and there's home baking, soups, omelettes. Mar-Oct 10am-5pm.

1409   **Crafty Kitchen**   Ardfern   Down the Ardfern B8002 road (4km) from A816 Oban-
9/H24   Lochgilphead road, the classier yachty haven of the Craignish peninsula. More
kitchen craft than crafty craft: great home-made cakes and special hot dishes
emerge along with superior burgers and fries. Tue-Sun 10am-5pm. Weekends only
Nov/Dec. Closed Jan-Mar.

1410   **Horsemill Restaurant**   Crathes Castle near Banchory · 01330 844525
8/S20   Adjacent magnificent Crathes (1845/COUNTRY HOUSES; 1494/GARDENS) so lots of
reasons to go off the Deeside road (A93) and up the drive. More tearoom than
restaurant in contemporary conversion of steadings around a pleasant courtyard.
Soup 'n' sandwich kinda menu. Gets mobbed. Open all year till 4.30pm.

1411   **The Pantry**   Cromarty   In great wee town in Black Isle 45km northeast of
7/M17   Inverness (1545/COASTAL VILLAGES) on corner of Church St. Excellent home baking,
soups and a decent cup of coffee. Easter-end Oct 10.30am-4.30pm. Closed Fri.

✓✓ **Gloagburn Farm & Coffee Shop**   Tibbermore near Perth
1454/FARM SHOPS.

✓ **The Corn Kist**   Milton Haugh, near Arbroath   1458/FARM SHOPS.

✓ **Inshriach**   Aviemore   2222/GARDEN CENTRES.

✓ **The Potting Shed**   Applecross   1012/HIGHLAND RESTAURANTS.

The Best Afternoon Teas

1412
9/K28
✓✓ **Turnberry** 01655 331000 · www.turnberry.co.uk It was at Turnberry that I was alerted to the extent of the revival of this English tradition. In their recent refurbishment Turnberry reinstated the Grand Tea Lounge at the centre of their classic, now très contemporary public space with mesmerising view over the links and sea and Ailsa Craig always there. Chef Justin Galea gives as much attention to his tier of afternoon treats as to the dinners that follow: aesthetic, delicate, irresistible; consuming mine *after* dinner at 11pm in the kitchens. 7 days 2-5pm. £26pp (champagne version with Möet or Krug available).

1413
2/XA3
✓ **The Hidden Lane Tearoom** 1103 Argyle Street, Glasgow · 0141 237 4391 Beyond Kelvingrove under an arch at the west end of Argyle St where there are many other coffee shops and grazing places, to the end of a backstreet lane which is pure Glasgow, a truly hidden but once found, oft-revisited tearoom. Old style and very new style at the same time. Kirsty Fitzgerald and girls up and downstairs with hot dishes, sandwiches and great cakes turned out miraculously from a tiny kitchen. Tier of tea 12noon-5pm, otherwise 10am-6pm. Hidden but not for long!

1414
10/R25
✓ **Greywalls** Gullane · www.greywalls.co.uk · 01620 842144 The Lutyens manor house and Gertrude Jekyll gardens at this country-house hotel 40 minutes east of Edinburgh is the perfect setting for genteel afternoon tea. It's a Roux restaurant (818/EAST LOTHIAN HOTELS) so expect well thought-out, smartly delivered niceties at a good price (£17 at TGP). Comfy lounges, the gorgeous gardens; and croquet! 2.30-5pm.

1415
10/Q25
1/XE5
✓ **Prestonfield** Edinburgh · www.prestonfield.com · 0131 668 3346 This superlative country-house hotel and restaurant on the edge of the city (83/INDIVIDUAL HOTELS), the epitome of gracious living and an ideal prospect for a proper tea. An artpiece of knitted cakes in the hallway may also put you in the mood. A number of sumptuous lounges and locations, tea options and of course, champagne. 3-6pm (£17). In town, another of James Thomson's esteemed establishments, **The Tower** (0131 225 3003) above and adjacent to the museum, serves tea 3-5pm (£16) with some wonderful views of the Old Town from the terrace.

1416
8/N17
✓ **Boath House** Auldearn near Nairn · 01667 454896 On A96 3km east, this is one of the great country-house hotels of the north, on the food map of Scotland for Charlie Lockley's Michelin magic. Now he also knocks out afternoon tea! You can bet it's rather good but the point of coming here for your scone and cake is that the grounds, walled garden and lakeside are a joy to walk in before or after. So this is a civilised way to pass an afternoon in the (sometimes) summer, blowy autumn (in the trees) or blazing fireside winter. It is, however, a short mid-afternoon interlude: 2.30-4pm. Champagne also served. 969/HIGHLANDS.

1417
10/Q25
1/D3
✓ **Palm Court at The Balmoral Hotel** Edinburgh · 0131 556 2412 · www.thebalmoralhotel.com The grande dame of afternoon tea in the Bollinger Palm Court beyond the foyer of Edinburgh's landmark hotel. Urbane and soothing (there is a harpist) at the very heart of the city. The cake stand with everything you would expect. £23pp or with champagne from £37 at TGP. 2.30-5.30pm. You should probably book. See also 73/EDINBURGH HOTELS.

1418
9/K20
Russell's @ Smiddy House Spean Bridge · www.smiddyhouse.co.uk · 01397 712335 On A82 14km north of Fort William. Guest house and hugely popular bistro with big local reputation that (pre-booked) does a top afternoon tea, all

specially made for you in a cosy afternoon-tea-type parlour. Bakewell tart, whisky cake, fruit tarts and an eclectic range of teas. Climb something nearby and then treat yourself! Arrange your own time. £18.50 (or with champagne). 1029/HIGH-LAND RESTAURANTS.

1419 **The Tearooms** 151 Bath Street, Glasgow · 0141 243 2459 Upstairs at 151.
2/C2 The less pub-like, more tearoom-like tearoom of The Butterfly and The Pig (662/PUB FOOD) somewhat sips the zeitgeist but on ever-changing style-driven Bath St, this is a more reflective space. From breakfast to supper but it's in afternoon and high-tea sessions that it comes into its own. Forget cocktails. 8.30am-8pm. Sun from 11am.

1420 **The Victoria** Union Street, Aberdeen 01224 621381 Upstairs adjacent the
8/T19 jewellers at no. 140, near the gardens. This trad and teriffic tearoom doesn't actually do an afternoon tea of tiered cakes and mini sandwiches but it's a teatime fave of mine. Gillian and Gordon Harold bake and make everything including spiffing lemonades. And in summer they serve a classic strawberry tea with pot of tea, strawberry lemonade or royale with cava, local strawberries of course and delicious cake. Till 5pm, 6.30pm Thu. Closed Sun. Also 948/ABERDEEN RESTAURANTS.

The Best Scotch Bakers

1421 ✓✓**Fisher & Donaldson** www.fisheranddonaldson.com · Dundee, St
10/Q23 Andrews & Cupar Main or original branch in main square, Cupar and a kind of factory outlet up by Tesco, 3 in Dundee (Whitehall St, 300 Perth Rd and Lochee) and Church St, St Andrews. Superior contemporary bakers along traditional lines (born 1919). Surprising (and a pity) that they haven't gone further but they do supply selected outlets with pastries and most excellent Dr Floyd's bread which is as good as anything you could make yourself. Sample also their yum yums, coffee trees, other breads and signature mini apple and rhubarb pies. Dundee Whitehall and Cupar have good tearooms (899/BEST DUNDEE) and the factory one is fab.

1422 ✓✓**Mhor Bread** Callander West end of main street in busy touristy town.
10/M24 Here forever but taken on by Dick of the food-loving Lewis family of Monachyle Mhor (1160/GET-AWAY HOTELS) so those pies, cakes, the biggest, possibly the best, tattie scones and sublime doughnuts in Scotland have all been thrust into the 21st century; your picnic on the Braes is sorted. Adjacent café does bake stuff plus sandwiches, omelettes and always, the scone. Callander transforming (but still some way to go)! 7 days 7am-5pm (Sun from 9am, tearoom till 4.30pm).

1423 ✓**Cromarty Bakery** Bank Street, Cromarty One of the many reasons to
7/M17 visit this picturesque seaside town. A wee shop but an abundance of speciality cakes, organic bread, rolls and pies, baked daily on premises. Top oatcakes! Also tea, coffee, hot savouries and takeaway. CB have also expanded to Fortrose. Produce available elsewhere in the area, eg the Storehouse at Evanton. 8.30am-5.30pm; Sat till 4pm. Closed Sun.

1424 ✓**Riverside Bistro, The Lochinver Larder** www.piesbypost.co.uk ·
6/J14 Lochinver On way into town from Ullapool, etc. A bistro/restaurant rightly famous for their brilliant pies from takeaway counter. Huge variety of savoury and fruit from traditional to exotic. And irresistible puds. Ready sustenance or merely indulgence; you can also get 'em by post. 7 days.

1425 **Goodfellow & Steven** Dundee, Perth & Fife The other bakers in the Fife/
10/Q23 Dundee belt (not a patch on Fisher & Donaldson, but hey). G&S have several branches. Good commercial Scotch baking with the kind of cakes that used to be a treat.

1426 **JM Bakery** Reform Street, Monifieth · www.jmbakery.co.uk · 01224
10/R23 621381 Off the high street. Specialising in wedding and designer cakes, the Robbs are also purveyors of bread and traditional savoury and sweet things. They do well at the Scotch Pie Championships. Keeping the craft alive! They're also in Carnoustie. 7am-5pm (4pm Sat). Closed Sun.

1427 **Island Bakery** Tobermory · 01688 302225 In the middle of the postcard
9/G22 houses and shops around Tobermory Bay, this is very much the island bakery. Bread, pies, quiches, even pizza and an array of old-style fancies and cakes including the bright yellow pineapple jobs. Some deli stuff. 8.30am-4.30pm (Sun from 10am, summer).

1428 **The Bakehouse** Findhorn The bakery behind the excellent Bakehouse café
8/P17 (1014/HIGHLAND RESTAURANTS) where David Boyle turns out a huge range of breads, scones etc. to supply the caff, the deli and the Findhorn community (1443/DELIS) and other places further and wide. Ryes, spelt, gluten-free and from French country to foccacia. Until the caff opens at 10am you can buy from the bakery door. 7 days.

1429 **McLaren's** Forfar Town centre next to Queens Hotel; also Kirriemuir. Best in
10/Q22 town (and only here because of it) to sample the famous Forfar bridie, a large, meaty shortcrust pastie hugely underestimated as a national delicacy. It's so much better than the gross and grossly overhyped Cornish pasty but it has never progressed beyond its (beefy) Angus heartland; one of the best copies is the home-made bridie that can be found in the café at Glamis (1778/CASTLES). 8am-4.15pm, closed Sun and Thu afternoon.

1430 **Waterside Bakery** Strathaven Alexander Taylor's long established (1820)
10/M26 bakery in Strathaven was omitted last edition. I got letters! Some people say Taylors is one of the reasons for living here. Ok, they do good breads, croissants, bics and cakes and the Flour Store Gallery is upstairs – you wouldn't find that at Greggs. 8am-5.30pm, from 7am Sat. Closed Sun (though caff adjacent open).

1431 **Murray's** 114 South Street, Perth In Perth and far and wide they know that
10/P23 Murray's Scotch pies are the business. Baked continuously from early till afternoon; there's often a queue. Their sausage rolls and plain and onion bridies are also top, followed possibly with a perfect pineapple cake. Closed Sun.

The Best Ice Cream

1432
10/Q25

✓✓ **Luca's** www.s-luca.co.uk · 32 High Street, Musselburgh & Edinburgh Queues out the door in the middle of a Sunday afternoon in February are testament to the enduring popularity of this much-loved ice-cream parlour. The classic flavours (vanilla, choc and strawberry), many arrivistes and a plethora of sorbets. For many, Luca's is simply the best and folk come from Edinburgh (14km) though there is a branch in town at 16 Morningside Rd (293/EDINBURGH CAFÉS). In café through the back, The Olympia, basic and always busy, the usual caff snax; and you may have to wait. In Edinburgh café upstairs more pizza/pasta and sandwiches. Mon-Sat 9am-10pm, Sun 10.30am-10pm. Edinburgh hours: 7 days 9am-10pm. Luca's (wholesale) spreading everywhere.

1433
9/L28

✓✓ **Mancini's, The Royal Café** Ayr · www.mancinisicecream.co.uk On New Rd, the road to Prestwick. Ice cream that's taken seriously, entered for competitions and often wins UK awards. Since 1913 a family biz, now amazingly in its fourth generation. Massive number of flavours at their disposal, always new ones. Home-made ice-cream cakes. Also caff in **Prestwick** on the esplanade. Their sorbets taste better than the fruit they're made from. They were first with ice-cream toasties and diabetic ice cream. These Mancinis are surely the kings and princes of ice cream. 7 days till 10.30pm. Caff has great pasta and the fish 'n' chips are to go.

1434
11/M30

✓ **Cream o' Galloway** Rainton near Gatehouse Of Fleet · 01557 814040 · www.creamogalloway.co.uk A75 take Sandgreen exit 2km then left at sign for Carrick. Originally a dairy farm producing cheese, now you can watch them make the creamy concoctions that you find all over. Nature trail, fab kids' adventure-play area (1690/KIDS; they could spend a day here) and decent organic-type café and Burger Barn with Galloway beef. All year 10am-6pm (till 5pm winter).

1435
10/R23

✓ **Janetta's** 31 South Street, St Andrews Family firm since 1908. There are two Janetta's, but the one to adore is top-end South St. Look for the queue. Once only vanilla, then Americans at the Open asked for other flavours. Now there are over 40, sorbets and frozen yoghurt and numerous awards. Janetta's is another good reason for being a student at St Andrews. Good café adjacent, family fare, outside tables. LO 5pm and takeaway. 7 days till 9.30pm.

1436
10/Q27

✓ **Caldwell's** High Street, Innerleithen On the High St in this ribbon of a town between Peebles and Gala. 2011 was their centenary – yes, they've been making ice cream since 1911. Purists may bemoan the fact that they've exploded into flavours in the 21st century, but their vanilla is still best. Many jars of sweeties. And get this – they open every day 6am-7.30pm. True old-style hours.

1437
10/Q22

Visocchi's Broughty Ferry, Kirriemuir Originally from St Andrews; ice-cream makers for 75 years with legendary caff in Kirriemuir (now no longer connected). So here in Dundee's seaside suburb, a trusty tratt with home-made pasta as well as the peach melba and a perfectly creamy vanilla. On a sunny day you queue! Closed Mon. Also: 900/DUNDEE EAT & DRINK.

1438
10/N24

The Allan Water Café Bridge of Allan In early editions of this book this was an old-fashioned café in an old-fashioned town in the main street (since 1902). Fabulously good fish 'n' chips and ice cream. Now it's taken over the whole block and has a glass-and-metal extension; the ice cream has many new flavours. Plus ça change – the ice cream is still great. 7 days 8am-8pm.

1439 **Drummuir Farm** Collin near Dumfries · www.drummuirfarm.co.uk 5km
11/P30 off A75 (Carlisle/Annan) road east of Dumfries on B724 (near Clarencefield). A real
farm producing real ice cream – still does supersmooth original and honeycomb,
seasonal specials; on a fine day, sit out and chill. Indoor and outdoor play areas.
Easter-Sep daily till 5.30pm; Oct-Dec Sat/Sun till 5pm.

The Really Good Delis

For Edinburgh and Glasgow delis, see p. 68 and p. 116.

1440 ✓✓**The Corner on the Square** 1 High Street, Beauly · 01463 783000 ·
7/L18 www.corneronthesquare.co.uk On said corner of the square. For
☕ passers-through a good find hereabouts mainly because of its sit-in coffee-shop
fare including great baking, quiches, scones, soups, etc. But also Gary
Williamson's well-cared-for cheeses, Cromarty bakes (1423/BAKERIES) and an
eclectic wine selection. Lunch 12noon-3pm, shop and snacks 9am-5.30pm (Sat
5pm). Sun 11am-5pm.

1441 ✓✓**I.J. Mellis** St Andrews · www.mellischeese.co.uk Started out as
10/R23 the cheese guy, now more of a very select deli for food that's good and
'slow'. Coffees, hams, sausages, olives and seasonal stuff like apples and mushrooms (branches vary), so smells mingle. Irresistible! Branches also in Edinburgh
(325/EDINBURGH DELIS), Glasgow (636/GLASGOW DELIS) and Aberdeen. 7 days
though times vary. See also 1468/CHEESES.

1442 ✓✓**Hammerton Stores** Aberdeen · www.hammertonstore.co.uk ·
8/T19 01224 324449 Not a deli as such though many ingredients of good life
☕ are here. A corner shop par excellence described more fully at 2198/SPECIAL SHOPS.

1443 ✓**Phoenix Findhorn Community** Findhorn · www.phoenixshop.co.uk
8/P17 Serving the eco village (1219/RETREATS) and wider community and pursuing a
conscientious approach long before it was de rigueur, this is an exemplary and
very high-quality deli worth the detour from A96 Inverness-Elgin road. Packed and
carefully selected shelves; as much for pleasurable eating as for healthy. Best
organic fruit and veg in the North East. The excellent **Bakehouse** café in Findhorn
itself owned by the folk who used be here; superb ethical eats (1014/LESS EXPEN-
SIVE HIGHLAND RESTAURANTS). Their breads on sale here. Till 6pm (weekends 5pm).

1444 ✓**2 Damned Fine Delis in Crieff: McNee's** Main Street Near the town
10/N23 clock. Deli/bakers/chocolatiers. More like an old-fashioned grocer and they
make things: great home-baking and ready-made meals, home-roasted meats;
some sweety and touristy stuff creeping in… 9am-6pm (Sun 9.30am-4pm).
J.L. Gill West end near turn to Crianlarich And the real McCoy, here over 70
years. Unpredictable choice of provisions: honey, 10 kinds of oatcakes, lotsa whisky
and wine. This genuine old-style, still the best style. 8.45am-5.30pm. Closed Sun.

1445 ✓**Spey Larder** Main Street, Aberlour · www.speylarder.com In deepest
8/Q18 Speyside. Beautiful old shop (1864), spacious and full of great, often local
produce (honeys, bread, game in winter, Speyside chanterelles and of course
whisky). Nice cheese counter. All year. Closed Sun. 9am-5.30pm.

1446
10/R28

✓ **Turnbull's** Hawick · 01450 372020 By The Horse in main street, a much-needed shot in the foodie arm in old Hawick which waited a long time for olive oil to drip into the diet. Now this attractive, eclectic deli/café supplies the lot and makes life better. Tables a bit cramped for soup/salad/sandwich menu but where else would you go (perhaps Damascus Drum; 809/BORDERS RESTAURANTS)? 9.30am-5.30pm (food till 4pm). Closed Sun.

1447
7/M17

✓ **Comfort Food** Rosemarkie · 01381 620814 When you love food and your name's Comfort, you really do have to open a deli (in the Black Isle). More like a village store-cum-butcher's, cheeserie, wine shop and greengrocer's; with ready-made meals. All great stuff! The Comforts have also taken over the defunct **Station Hotel** in **Avoch**, the next village, a new pub-food destination in the making (also has 8 rooms). Deli 7am-6pm. Closed Sun.

1448
10/N21

✓ **The Scottish Delis** www.scottish-deli.co.uk · 01796 473322 · Pitlochry & 01350 7280828 · Dunkeld Pitlochry shop is on the main street; Dunkeld also. Both have great takeaway food and ready meals: traiteur-style and cafés with home baking. Charcuterie, cheese, etc and great coffee. 7 days, daytime only.

1449
10/N24

Clive Ramsay Main Street, Bridge of Allan · www.cliveramsay.com Here for years but both this and the café/bistro adjacent have fallen into other (both different) hands and Mr Ramsay has moved on. Still a decent deli in pleasant B of A for fruit/veg, cheese, olives, seeds and well-chosen usuals. 7 days 7am-7pm.

1450
8/P17

Gordon & MacPhail South Street, Elgin Whisky HQ and purveyors of fine wines, cheeses, meats, Mediterranean goodies, unusual breads and other epicurean delights to the good burghers of Elgin for nigh on a century. Traditional shopkeeping, in the style of the family grocer. G & M are widely known as bottlers of lesser-known high-quality malts (Connoisseurs' range) – on sale here as well as every other whisky you've ever heard of and many you ain't. Some rare real ales by the bottle too. Mon-Sat 8.30am-5pm.

1451
10/P23

Provender Brown 23 George Street, Perth · 01738 587300 As we might expect, a decent deli in the town/city where several good restaurants reside, there's a big farmers' market (first in Scotland) and many folk aren't short of a bob or two. P&B are good for olives, vacuum-packed products and especially cheese. 9am-5pm (till 5.30pm Thu-Sat). Closed Sun.

1452
9/K25

Mearns T. McCaskie Wemyss Bay Now in its third generation, a butcher of integrity and repute: home-cured bacon, sausages, pies, cheeses, fine wines and other delights. Picnic, anyone? 8am-5.30pm (5pm Sat). Closed Sun.

1453
10/M24

Berits & Brown Kippen · 01786 870077 The first of the deli and coffee-shop franchise (in Glasgow, Edinburgh, etc.). Not hugely original but nice enough. Café with bespoke sandwiches from counter, soup, etc. Adds to Kippen's foodie-village credentials (and a great butcher's, Skinner's, opposite). 10am-5pm.

✓ ✓ **Gloagburn Farm & Coffee Shop** Tibbermore, near Perth Excellent sit-in coffee shop/restaurant but also deli with selected local/organic produce. Report: 1454/FARM SHOPS.

✓ ✓ **The Pillars of Hercules** near Falkland · 01337 857749 Organic grocers with tearoom (1388/TEAROOMS) and outstanding farm shop. Report: 1463/FARM SHOPS.

The Really Good Farm Shops

1454
10/P23

✓✓ **Gloagburn Farm & Coffee Shop** Tibbermore Off A85 Perth-Methven and Crieff road from A9 and ring road at Huntingtower, signed Tibbermore (Tibbermore also signed off A9 from Stirling just before Perth). Through village, second farm on right: a family (the Nivens') farm shop (it all started with a free-range egg) with ducks on the pond and Tamworth pigs out back – excellent fresh produce and inside a deli and café where food (hot dishes, cakes, etc.) is exemplary. Hot and other food till 5pm. Vacuum-packed meats, frozen meals, fruit 'n' veg, home-made bread and their own oats. A destination place only 15 minutes from Perth. Open all year 9am-5.30pm (4pm winter). 7 days.

1455
8/R20

✓✓ **Finzean Farm Shop & Tearoom** Deeside · 01330 850710 On the south side of the river on B976 between Banchory and Aboyne on the Farquerson family's Finzean estate. Kate and Catriona's foodie haven in glorious open countryside with views to the hills from the terrace. Local and carefully sourced produce beautifully presented fresh and frozen. Meat and game from the estate. Cool cookbooks. Hot dishes till 3pm. Cakes that don't rely on cream. 7 days 9am-5pm (Sun from 11am).

1456
11/N30

✓✓ **Loch Arthur Creamery & Farm Shop** Beeswing near Dumfries Run by Camphill Trust, this is the genuine article tucked away in a work-ing dairy farm with a strong organic agenda. Great baking (bread, cakes and pies), famous organic veg, those cheeses (see p. 258, Scottish Cheeses) and the UK's best granola. Meats and eggs. From Beeswing take New Abbey road 1km. Mon-Fri 9am-5.30pm, Sat 10am-3pm. Closed Sun.

1457
10/P26

✓✓ **Whitmuir, the Organic Place** Lamancha near Peebles · 01968 661908 · www.whitmuirorganics.co.uk All-round foodie destination and fully realised good-life emporium, with shop, serious art gallery and café/restaurant. Farm supplies own beef, lamb, pork, eggs and up to 32 different veg and fruit. Own butchery. A light, well-run place with good attidue. Only 40 min-utes from Edinburgh. 10am-6pm, weekends 5pm (occasional foodie evenings).

1458
10/R22

✓✓ **Milton Haugh Farm Shop** Carmyllie · www.miltonhaugh.com · 01241 860579 Off A92 Dundee-Arbroath road at Carnoustie, follow Forfar road then signs. Faraway farm on B961 that's enormously popular. Great range of fruit and veg, meats and selected deli fare with own-label meals, jams, etc. Many different oatcakes. Excellent Corn Kist Coffee Shop with home-made cakes, soups and specials, so from far and wide you come. 9am-5pm (Sun from 10am). Café 10am-4pm.

1459
8/T19

✓ **The Store** Westfield, Foveran near Udny Station · 01358 788083 Off A90 at Foveran (1km), this beautiful farm shop is a food-lovers' haven and a base for the Booth family (in their fourth generation), their Aberdeen Angus (well-hung and tender) operation and more recent café. Vacuum-packed meats, cooked meals and the stuff including fruit and veg to go with them. 7 days 10am-5pm.

1460
10/P25

✓ **West Craigie Farm** near South Queensferry · 0131 319 1048 Take the South Queensferry exit from dual carriageway north from Edinburgh, A90 to Forth Road Bridge. Farm is signed 2km. Like many on these pages, these guys saw the potential in farm shopping and grew rapidly from a PYO farm on the edge of town to a visitor magnet. You can still PYO strawbs and rasps and other soft fruit (Jun-Aug) but there's a self-service caff and an emporium of food. Best is their own butchery section but the real attraction is to sit on a terrace taking tea and cake overlooking rows and fields of fruit like vineyards in France while the city shimmers in the distance. All year 9-5pm.

1461
10/R25

✓ **Fenton Barns Farm Shop** near North Berwick · 01620 850294 · www.fentonbarns.co.uk Off A1 for Dirleton, Mhairi and Roy's country emporium/caff is between Drem and Dirleton on Fenton Barns retail and craft parklet, an old airfield complex. They also look after the Fruitmarket Gallery Café in Edinburgh (279/TEAROOMS) and St Giles' Cathedral coffee shop – they never flag (or go on holiday). Organic meats, free-range eggs, home-made pies, soups, terrines, selected fruit and veg, Roy's great coffee and their home-made just-about-everything coffee shop in the back. 827/EAST LOTHIAN RESTAURANTS. 7 days 10am-5pm. **The Gosford Bothy Farmshop** nearby (Edinburgh side of Aberlady) is especially good for meats, pies etc. 7 days 10am-4pm.

1462
10/R25

✓ **Knowes Farm Shop Farm** near East Linton · 01620 860010 Close to A1 on A198 to North Berwick just before Tyninghame (well signed). Farm cottage converted into spacious, integrity food store. Organic veg and herbs, home-made pâtés, pavlova. Lots of eggs; the chickens in the field. All year 9.30am-5pm. They supply many other farm shops, restaurants, etc. with their excellent 'sun and dung' home-grown veg.

1463
10/Q24

✓ **The Pillars of Hercules** near Falkland · www.pillars.co.uk · 01337 857749 On A912 2km from town towards Strathmiglo and motorway. A pillar of the organic community and a more ethical way of life. Grocers with tearoom (1388/TEAROOMS) on farm/nursery where you can PYO herbs and flowers. Always fruit/veg and great selection of dry goods that's a long way from Sainsbury's and here long before the organic boom. They have a bothy and camping; it's pretty nice around here. 7 days 10-6pm.

1464
10/R24

✓ **Ardross Farm** near Elie · 01333 330415 Between St Monans and Elie on the A917 Fife coastal route. East Neuk farm shop an all-round highly selective provisioner from home farm produces meats to a vast array of seasonal dug vegetables, Fiona's pies, ready-made meals. The Pollock family have been here over a century and they're big supporters of UK farm produce as well as their own. 7 days 9am-5.30pm, Sun 9am-4pm. Closed Mon/Tue in winter.

1465
10/Q23

✓ **Cairnie Fruit Farm (and Maze)** near Cupar · 01334 655610 A truly a(maze)ing conversion of a fruit farm into major family attraction (1683/KIDS), demonstrating if nothing else the inexorable rise of the strawberry. This and other berries can be picked, purchased and eaten in all manner of cakes with other farm produce and snack food. Main thing though is the kids' area outside. Apr-Oct 10am-5pm, 9.30am-5.30pm Jul-Aug. Maze: Jul-Oct. Farm is 4km north of Cupar on minor road past the hospital or 3km from main A92, signed near Kilmany.

1466
10/R23

Allanhill near St Andrews · 01334 477998 6km out of town off Anstruther/Crail road A917 past the Grange (1285/GASTROPUBS). Simple farm shop mainly and café with tables in the field. Kids' stuff includes animals, hay bales. Great views to St Andrews Bay. Known for excellent soft fruits including the elusive blueberry. Tearoom has excellent strawberry cakes and a top scone. Open 100 days, May-Sep.

1467
10/Q24

Muddy Boots Balmalcolm · 07843 630762 On A914 from A92 south of Cupar, a farm shop with kitchen and crafts and some integrity over their produce; and now a full-on kids' playground. Their home-grown fruit and veg is high quality (the *best* raspberries) and they're keen to educate and inspire kids into good country practice. All year 7 days 9am-4.30pm (from 10am Sun).

Scottish Cheeses

Mull or Tobermory Cheddar www.isleofmullcheese.co.uk From Sgriob-Ruadh Farm (pronounced Skibrua). Comes in big 50lb cheeses and 1lb truckles. Good, strong cheddar, one of the very best in UK. And their new **Hebridean Blue** (about time, too).

Dunsyre Blue/Lanark Blue Carnwath Made by Humphrey Errington. Next to Stilton, **Dunsyre** (made from the unpasteurised milk of Ayrshire cows) is the best blue in the UK. It is soft, rather like Dolcelatte. **Lanark**, the original, is Scotland's Roquefort and made from ewe's milk. Both can vary seasonally but are always excellent. Go on, live dangerously – unpasteurise your life.

Locharthur Cheese www.locharthur.org.uk Anything from this (Camphill Trust) South West creamery is worth a nibble: the cheddar, **Criffel** (mild), **Kebbuck** (shaped like a dinosaur's tooth, semi-soft). Widely available but have their own shop (see below).

The Dunlop Dairy Stewarton Anne Dorwood's West Clerkland Farm in Ayrshire producing award-winning cow's-, sheep's- and goat's-milk cheeses. **Ayrshire Dunlop** The traditional version, this is a signature Scottish cheddar (moist and soft and fruity). **Bonnet** Crumbly, dry, goat's-milk cheese. **Swinzie** Named after a local burn is their harder-to-find, creamy, nutty ewe's-milk cheese.

Wester Lawrenceton Farm Cheeses Forres Pam Rodway's excellent organic cheeses: **Carola**, **Califer** (goat's milk) and the hard-to-get **Sweetmilk Cheddar**. On sale Findhorn shop and Gordon & MacPhail (1450/DELIS).

Highland Fine Cheeses Tain From the Stone family. Half a dozen cheeses including **Crowdie** (traditional curd cheese), most notably **Caboc** and **Strathdon Blue** (award winner) and their excellent cheddar **Blairliath**.
Blue Monday The cool blue cheese named after a New Order hit by Julie Harbutt and the Blur guy-turned-farmer Alex James. Made from cow's milk; mild and creamy.

St Andrews Farmhouse Cheeses Bishop Kennedy A semi-soft, runny, cow's-milk cheese that hums. Note also **Anster** – crumbly, white and tasty but harder to find.

Arran Cheeses Award-winning and a big variety. See their cheese shop outside Brodick, below.

And Where To Find Scottish Cheeses...

The delis on pp. 68, 116 and 254–5 will have good selections (especially Valvona's in Edinburgh and Delizique in Glasgow).

1468
1/X5B
2/X1A
10/R23
8/T19

✓ ✓ **I.J. Mellis** Edinburgh, Glasgow, St Andrews & Aberdeen · www.mellischeese.co.uk 30a Victoria St, far end of Morningside Rd and Baker's Pl, Stockbridge (Edinburgh), 492 Great Western Rd (Glasgow), 149 South St (St Andrews), 201 Rosemount Pl (Aberdeen). A real cheesemonger. Smell and taste before you buy. Cheeses from all over the UK in prime condition. Daily and seasonal specials. (325/EDINBURGH DELIS, 636/GLASGOW DELIS, 1441/DELIS.)

1469
1/XA1

✓ **Herbie** 66 Raeburn Place, Edinburgh · www.herbieofedinburgh.co.uk
Excellent selection – everything here is the right stuff. Great bread, bagels, etc from independent baker, home-made houmous and Scottish cheeses. Impossible here to find a Brie or a blue in less than perfect condition.

1470
10/P22

✓ **McDonald's Cheese Shop** Rattray near Blairgowrie · 01250 872493
Long-established emporium of cheese (80 varieties selected by owner Caroline Robertson): great blues, 'crumblier' and especially Swiss. You can buy a whole wheel of Gruyère. 9am-5pm. Sun 10am-4pm. Closed Mon.

1471
9/G22
L

✓ **Sgriob-Ruadh Farm** Tobermory Head out on road to Dervaig, take turning for Glengorm (great coffee shop; 1377/TEAROOMS) and watch for sign and track to farm. Past big glass barn where they live in some kind of blissful bohemia and follow path to distant doorway into the cheese factory and farm shop (though all there is usually are lovely shit-covered fresh eggs and the cheddar, their new blue and a bit of sausage). Honesty box when nobody working.

1472
9/J27

Arran Cheeseshop Arran 5km Brodick, road to castle and Corrie. Excellent selection of their own (the well-known cheddars) but many others especially crowdie, Camembert, Brie, Arran white (like Cheshire) and award-winning blue. Selected others. See them being made. 7 days. 9.30am-5.30pm (5pm in winter).

1473
7/H18

West Highland Dairy www.westhighlanddairy.co.uk · 01599 577203 · Achmore near Plockton Charming and shuffly Mr and Mrs Biss still running their great farm dairy shop selling their own cheeses (goats' and cows' milk), yoghurt, ice cream, cranachan cheesecake. Mar-Dec. Signed from village. Highland sylvan setting but no cows in sight. If you're making the trip specially, phone first to check they're open (usually 10am-4.30pm).

1474
10/Q23

The Cheesery Dundee · www.thecheesery.co.uk · 01382 202160
In Exchange St where there are good caff/restaurants (see DUNDEE RESTAURANTS, p. 167-69) and Sa'vor next door for takeaway food with integrity, this cheese place is a foody oasis in downtown Dundee. Scottish, continental, artisan. Tue-Sat 9.30am-5.30pm.

Loch Arthur Creamery Beeswing Off A75, A711 to New Abbey. 1456/FARM SHOPS.

House of Bruar near Blair Atholl Roadside emporium. 2199/SHOPPING.

Peter MacLennan 28 High Street, Fort William.

Scottish Speciality Food North Ballachulish By Leven Hotel.

The Kitchen Garden Oban 744/OBAN.

Corner on the Square Main Street, Beauly 1440/DELIS.

Whisky: The Best Distillery Tours

The process is basically the same in every distillery, but some are more atmospheric and some have more interesting tours, like these below. www.scotchwhisky.net is a great site on all things whisky.

1475
9/F25
ATMOS

✓✓ **The Islay Malts** www.islaywhiskysociety.com Plenty to choose from including, in the north:
Caol Ila (Mon-Fri, tour times vary Feb-Nov; 01496 302769);
the wholly independent **Bruichladdich** (3 tours daily Mon-Fri, twice daily on Sat, 01496 850221); and
Kilchoman, the brand new Wills kid, daily tours Mon-Sat (Mon-Fri in winter) with great café; 2304/ISLAY (01496 850156).
In the south near Port Ellen, 3 of the world's great malts all in a row on a mystic coast. The distilleries here look like distilleries should.

LLL **Lagavulin** (01496 302749) and **Laphroaig** (01496 302418) offer fascinating tours where your guide will lay on the anecdotes as well as the process and you get a feel for the life and history as well as the product of these world-famous places. At Laphroaig there are enhanced (cost and effect) tours especially on Friday. All year round, more frequent in summer. Times vary.
Ardbeg (01496 302244) is perhaps the most visitor-oriented and has a really good café (2304/ISLAY) and makes the most of its (dark olive) brand. All these distilleries are in settings that entirely justify the romantic hyperbole of their advertising. Worth seeing from the outside as well as the factory floor.
Bowmore (01496 810441) has a slick operation with peat-bog standard and Craftsman's Tours (£40). All year round.

1476
8/Q17
ATMOS

✓ **Strathisla** Keith · 01542 783044 Oldest working distillery in the Highlands, literally on the strath of the Isla River; methinks the most evocative atmosphere of all the Speyside distilleries. Tastefully reconstructed, this is a very classy halt for the malt. Used as the heart of Chivas Regal, the Strathisla though not commonly available is still a fine dram. You wait for a tour group to gather; there's a dram at the beginning and the end. Apr-Oct 9.30am-4pm (Sun from 12noon).

1477
8/P18
LL

✓ **The Glenlivet** Minmore · www.theglenlivet.com · 01340 821720 Starting as an illicit dram celebrated as far south as Edinburgh, George Smith licensed the brand in 1824 and founded this distillery in 1858, registering the already mighty name so anyone else had to use a prefix. After successions and mergers, independence was lost in 1978 when Seagrams took over. Now owned by Pernod Ricard. The famous Josie's Well, from which the water springs, is underground. Small parties and a walk-through which is not on a gantry make the tour satisfying and as popular, especially with Americans, as the product. Excellent reception centre with bar/restaurant and shop; the tour on the website's so good, you probably don't need to go at all though you won't then get a dram in those hallowed surroundings. Apr-Oct 9.30am-4pm. Sun 12noon-4pm.

1478
8/Q18
LL

✓ **Glenfiddich** Dufftown · www.glenfiddich.com · 01340 820373 Outside town on A941 to Craigellachie by Balvenie Castle ruins. Well-oiled tourist operation and the only distillery where you can see the whole process from barley to bar (well, not the bottlery). The only major distillery that's free (including dram). Also runs artists-in-residence scheme with changing exhibitions in summer; gallery by car park (details 01340 821565). All year 9.30am-4.30pm. Good restaurant.
On the same road you can see a whisky-related craft that hasn't changed.
Speyside Cooperage is 1km from Craigellachie. See those poor guys from the gantry (no chance to slack). All year Mon-Fri 9.30am-4.30pm. Good coffee shop.

1479 ✓ **Edradour** near Pitlochry · www.edradour.co.uk · **01796 472095**

10/N21 Picturesque and as romantic as you can imagine the smallest distillery in

L Scotland to be, producing single malts for blends since 1825 and limited quantities of the Edradour (only 12 casks a week then laid for 10 years, so not easy to find; see website for stockists) as well as the House of Lords' own brand. Guided tour of charming cottage complex every 20 minutes. 4km from Pitlochry off Kirkmichael road, A924; signed after Moulin village. Complex opening hours though open all year, 7 days.

1480 **Talisker** Carbost, Isle of Skye From Sligachan-Dunvegan road (A863) take

7/F18 B8009 for Carbost and Glen Brittle along the south side of Loch Harport for 5km.

L Skye's only distillery; since 1830 they've been making this classic after-dinner malt from barley and the burn that runs off the Hawkhill behind. A dram before the In-formative 40-minute tour. Good visitor centre. Apr-Oct 9.30am-5pm (set times in winter; 01478 614308). Great gifts nearby (2192/SHOPPING). Nice pub for grub and music nearby: the Old Inn at Carbost.

1481 **Glenkinchie** Pencaitland near Edinburgh · **01875 342004** Only 25km from

10/Q25 city centre (via A68 and A6093 before Pathhead), signposted; very popular. Founded in 1837 in a pastoral place watered from the Lammermuirs, 3km from vil-lage, with its own bowling green; a country trip and a whisky tour. State-of-the-art visitor centre. Open all year round but times vary.

1482 **Highland Park** Kirkwall, Orkney · www.highlandpark.co.uk · **01856 874619**

3/Q10 2km from town on main A961 road south to South Ronaldsay. The whisky is great and the award-winning tour one of the best. The most northerly whisky in a class and a bottle of its own. You walk through the floor maltings and you can touch the warm barley and fair smell the peat. Good combination of the industrial and the traditional. Tours every half hour. Open all year Mon-Fri 10am-5pm. Afternoons only in winter.

1483 **Scotch Whisky Heritage Centre** Edinburgh · **0131 220 0441** ·

1/C4 www.whisky-heritage.co.uk On Castlehill on last stretch to castle (you cannot miss it). Not a distillery of course, but a visitor attraction to celebrate all things a tourist can take in about Scotland's main export. Shop has huge range. 7 days 10am-5pm (extended hours in summer).

THE BEST OF THE SPEYSIDE WHISKY TRAIL

1484 **Glen Grant** Rothes · **01340 832118** In Rothes on the A941 Elgin to Perth road.

8/Q17 Not the most picturesque but a distillery tour with an added attraction, viz the gardens and orchard reconstructed around the shallow bowl of the glen of the burn that runs through the distillery: there's a lime-tree-lined walk (15 minutes) and delightful Dram Pavilion. Now owned by Campari, you will be immersed in the history as well as the process with a word from the founder in a replica of his study and then 2 tastings before you leave. Feb-Dec 9.30am-5pm, Sun from 12noon.

1485 **Cardhu (or Cardow)** Carron · **01340 872555** Off B9102 from Craigellachie to

8/P18 Grantown through deepest Speyside, a small if charming distillery with its own community, a millpond, picnic tables, etc. Owned by Diageo, Cardhu is the 'heart of Johnnie Walker' (which, amazingly, has another 30 malts in it). Open all year round, Mon-Fri (7 days Jul/Aug). Hours vary.

1486
8/P17 **Benromach** Forres · www.benromach.com · 01309 675968 Signed from A96 at Forres. The smallest working distillery so no bus tours or big tourist operation. Human beings with time for a chat. Rescued by Gordon & MacPhail (1450/DELIS) and reopened 1999. A great introduction to whisky. Apr-Sep 9.30am-5pm (and Sun Jun-Aug only 12noon-4pm). Winter 10am-4pm.

Whisky: The Best Malts Selections

EDINBURGH

✓ ✓ **Scotch Malt Whisky Society** 28 Queen Street · www.smws.com
Your search will end here. More a club (with membership), and top restaurant.

✓ ✓ **Vintners Rooms** Giles Street, Leith Extraordinary collection of 1,500 whiskies arranged around the walls in alphabetical order including 24 different Ardbegs and bottles from 10 distilleries that have closed. Available by the glass at the bar or in atmospheric candlelit restaurant. 148/EDINBURGH BISTROS.

Bennet's 8 Leven Street · www.bennets.co.uk 334/UNIQUE EDINBURGH PUBS.

Kay's Bar 39 Jamaica Street 339/UNIQUE EDINBURGH PUBS.

The Bow Bar 80 West Bow · www.bowbar.com 355/EDINBURGH REAL-ALE PUBS.

Cadenhead's 172 Canongate · www.wmcadenhead.com The shrine.

Canny Man 237 Morningside Road 157/EDINBURGH PUBS.

The Malt Shovel 11 Cockburn Street Unpretentious pub.

Blue Blazer Corner Spittal & Bread Streets 359/EDINBURGH REAL-ALE PUBS.

GLASGOW

✓ ✓ **The Pot Still** 154 Hope Street · www.thepotstill.co.uk 450 different bottles of single malt. And proud of it.

The Bon Accord 153 North Street · www.thebonaccord.com 651/GLASGOW REAL-ALE PUBS.

The Lismore 206 Dumbarton Road 649/UNIQUE GLASGOW PUBS.

Ubiquitous Chip Ashton Lane · www.ubiquitouschip.co.uk Restaurant, bistro and great bar on the corner.

Ben Nevis Argyle Street Far west end of street. 650/UNIQUE GLASGOW PUBS.

REST OF SCOTLAND

1487
9/F26 **Lochside Hotel** Bowmore, Islay · www.lochsidehotel.co.uk More Islay malts than you ever imagined in a friendly local near the Bowmore Distillery. And on the lochside.

✓ ✓ **Torridon Inn** near **Kinlochewe** Classic Highland hotel bar with 300 malts shelf by shelf. And the mountains! 1161/GET-AWAY HOTELS.

✓ ✓ **Clachaig Inn** Glencoe Over 100 malts to go with the range of ales and the range of thirsty hillwalkers. 1256/BLOODY GOOD PUBS.

✓ ✓ **The Drover's Inn** Inverarnan Classic roadhouse hostelry with around 75 drams to choose from and the right atmosphere to drink them in. Kilty barmen. 1253/BLOODY GOOD PUBS.

✓ ✓ **The Oystercatcher** Portmahomack Gordon Robertson's exceptional malt (and wine) collection in far-flung coastal village. 1031/HIGHLAND RESTAURANTS.

✓ ✓ **Forss House** near **Thurso** Hotel on north coast. Often a wee wind outside; warm up with one of 300 well-presented malts. 983/HIGHLAND.

✓ **The Quaich Bar** at The Craigellachie Hotel Whiskies arranged around cosy bar of this essential Speyside hotel, the river below. 960/SPEYSIDE.

✓ **Knockinaam Lodge** Portpatrick Comfortable country-house hotel; especially good Lowland selection includes the local Bladnoch. 756/SOUTH WEST HOTELS.

✓ **The Piano Bar at the Glenmoriston Townhouse** Inverness Easy-to-decipher malt list in superior, stylish surroundings. 972/HIGHLAND HOTELS.

✓ **The Anderson** Fortrose Amazing collection of malts (and beers) in small town hotel bar. 993/LESS EXPENSIVE HIGHLANDS.

✓ **Ardanaiseig Hotel** Loch Awe A dram's a must after dinner in the bar looking over the lawn to the loch. 1097/COUNTRY-HOUSE HOTELS.

1488
7/F18 ✓ **Sligachan Hotel** Skye · www.sligachan.co.uk · 01478 650204 On A87 (A850) 11km south of Portree. Over 250 malts in Seamus' huge cabin bar. Good ale selection, including their own (the Cuillin Brewery is here).

✓ **Gordon & MacPhail** Elgin The whisky provisioner and bottlers of the Connoisseurs brand you see in other shops and bars all over. From these humble beginnings over 100 years ago they now supply their exclusive and rarity range to the world. Mon-Sat till 5.15pm (5pm Wed). Closed Sun. 1450/DELIS.

1489
8/Q18 ✓ **The Whisky Shop Dufftown** www.whiskyshopdufftown.co.uk · **Dufftown** The whisky shop in the main street (by the clock tower) at the heart of whisky country. Within a few miles of numerous distilleries and their sales operations, this place stocks all the product (including many halfs). 10am-5pm Mon-Sat, 2-4pm Sun.

1490
9/H25 **Loch Fyne Whiskies** Inveraray · www.lfw.co.uk Beyond the church on the A83, a shop with 400 malts to choose from; quaichs and other whisky ware.

1491
9/L27 **Robbie's Drams** Sandgate, Ayr · www.robbiesdrams.com Robin Russell's impressive emporium. Bottle or case. Huge selection; also beers and wines.

Outdoor Places

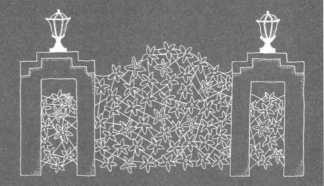

The Best Gardens

1492
7/H16
NTS
ADMISSION
☐
L

✓✓ **Inverewe** www.nts.org.uk · **Poolewe** 80km south of Ullapool on A832. World-famous gardens on a Loch Ewe promontory. Beginning in 1862, Osgood Mackenzie made it his life's work and since then people have come from all over the world to admire his efforts. Helped by the ameliorating effect of the Gulf Stream, the wild garden became the model for many others. The walled garden is beyond immaculate: if you were a flower or vegetable, you'd want to be here sheltered, nurtured and inclined to the southern sun (terrace best viewed from the top path by James Reid bench). Guided tours (1.30pm Mon-Sat, Mar-Oct) to get the most out of this vast garden or go in the evening when it's quiet! Shop, visitor centre. Café 10am-4.30pm; hot meals till 3pm. Gardens all year till dusk.

1493
9/K25
ADMISSION
☐
L

✓✓ **Benmore Botanic Garden** www.rbge.org.uk · **Benmore near Dunoon** 12km on A815 to Strachur. An outstation of the Royal Botanic in Edinburgh, gifted to the nation by Harry Younger in 1928, but the first plantations date from 1820. Marked walks through formal gardens, woody grounds and pinetum where the air is often so sweet and spicy it seems like the elixir of life (I said this in my first edition). Redwood avenue, terraced hill sides, views; a garden of different moods and fine proportions. Newly restored ferry. Good walk, Puck's Glen, nearby (2022/WOODLAND WALKS). Café. Mar-Oct 10am-6pm (5pm Oct-Mar).

1494
8/S20
NTS
ADMISSION
☐
L

✓✓ **Crathes** www.nts.org.uk · **near Banchory** 25km west of Aberdeen, just off A93. One of the most interesting tower houses (1834/COUNTRY HOUSES) surrounded by terrific topiary and walled gardens of inspired design and tranquillity (though you're unlikely to have any part of it to yourself). Keen gardeners will be in their scented heaven. The Golden Garden (after Gertrude Jekyll) works particularly well and there's a wild garden beyond the old wall that many people miss. A very *House & Garden* experience though in summer it's stuffed with people as well as plants. Grounds all year 9.30am-sunset. See 1410/TEAROOMS.

1495
10/P26
ATMOS
LL

✓✓ **Little Sparta** www.littlesparta.co.uk · **07826 495677** · **near Dunsyre** Near Biggar off A702 (5km), go through village then signed. House in bare hill country the home of conceptual artist and national treasure, Ian Hamilton Finlay who died 2006. Gardens lovingly created over years, full of thought-provoking art/sculpture/perspectives (over 250 separate artworks). Unlike anywhere else. A privilege to visit but it is fragile; no dogs or little kids. Jun-Sep, Wed/Fri/Sun 2.30-5pm, but check the website as the Trust may change times.

1496
10/N23
ADMISSION

✓✓ **Drummond Castle Gardens** www.drummondcastlegardens.co.uk · **Muthill** Near Crieff; signed from A822, 2km from Muthill then up an avenue of fabulous trees to the most exquisite formal gardens viewed first from the terrace by the house. A boxwood parterre of a vast St Andrew's Cross in yellow and red (especially antirrhinums and roses), the Drummond colours, with extraordinary sundial centrepiece; 5 gardeners keep every leaf in place. 7 days Easter and May-Oct 1-5pm (last admission). House not open to public.

1497
11/K31
ADMISSION
☐
L

✓✓ **Logan Botanical Gardens** www.rbge.org.uk · **near Sandhead** 16km south of Stranraer by A77/A716 and 2km on from Sandhead. Remarkable outstation of the Edinburgh Botanics amongst sheltering woodland in the mild South West. Compact and full of pleasant southern surprises. Less crowded than other exotic gardens. Walled and woodland gardens and the

Tasmanian Creek. The Gunnera Bog is quite extraterrestrial. Coffee shop decent. Mar-Oct; 7 days, 10am-5pm (6pm Apr-Sep).

1498
9/J24
NTS
ADMISSION
✓ ✓ **Crarae** www.nts.org.uk · **Inverary** 16km southeast on A83 to Loch-gilphead. Most gorgeous of the famed gardens of Argyll, in any season. The wooded banks of Loch Fyne with the gushing Crarae burn are as lush as the Himalayan gorges where many of the plants originate. Follow the footsteps of plant-hunters and pandas! All year 9.30am-dusk. Visitor centre Apr-Sep. Walks 0.5-2km.

1499
6/N15
ADMISSION
LL
✓ ✓ **Dunrobin Castle Gardens** Golspie On A9 1km north of town. The Versailles-inspired gardens that sit below the opulent Highland chateau of the dukes of Sutherland (1789/CASTLES). Terraced, parterred and immaculate, they stretch to the sea. 30 gardeners once tended them, now there are 4 but little has changed since they impressed a more exclusive clientele. Castle Apr-Oct 10.30am-last admission 4pm (5pm Jun-Aug). Garden gate open later.

1500
9/G26
ATMOS
ADMISSION
✓ ✓ **Jura House Walled Garden** www.jurahouseandgardens.co.uk · **Ardfin, Jura** Around 8km from the ferry on the only road. Park opposite and follow track into woods. The most beautiful not-overtended walled garden can be part of a walk that takes you ultimately (though steep) to the beach and the Misty Pools. Beautiful in rain (frequent) or shine and a place of utmost serenity. New owners 2011 and closed at TGP; possible new arrangements 2012.

1501
11/K30
✓ **Glenwhan** www.glenwhangardens.org.uk · **near Glen Luce near Solway Coast** Signed from A75 and close to more famous **Castle Kennedy** (also very much worth a visit), this the more edifying labour of love. Up through beechy (and in May) bluebell woods and through backyards to horticultural haven teased from bracken and gorse moorland from 1979. Open moorland still beckons at the top of the network of trails through a carefully planted but wild botanical wonder. Many seats for contemplations, some sculpture. Easter-Sep 10am-5pm.

1502
11/M30
NTS
✓ **Threave** near **Castle Douglas** 64 acres of magnificent Victorian landsca-ping in incomparable setting overlooking Galloway coastline. Gardeners should not miss the walled kitchen garden. Horticulturally inspiring and daunting. Garden is part of a vast estate which includes the castle and a wildfowl reserve. Various walks: a circular Estate Walk 4km with spur (2km return) to the castle. Threave is a bat reserve. You can hire a bat detector with deposit and return next day. Centre open Feb-Dec 10am-dusk (other access points for estate all year round).

1503
10/P27
ADMISSION
✓ **Dawyck** www.rgbe.org.uk · **Stobo** On B712 Moffat road off A72 Biggar/Peebles road, 2km from Stobo. An outstation of the Edinburgh Botanics, though tree planting here goes back 300 years. Sloping grounds around the gur-gling Scrape burn which trickles into the Tweed. Landscaped woody pathways for meditative walks. Famous for shrubs, blue Himalayan poppies and Douglas Firs. Rare Plant Trail and great walk on drovers' road nearby, 2km off Stobo Rd before Dawyck entrance. Visitor centre with café and shop. Mar-Oct 10am-5pm (Feb/Nov till 4pm, Apr/Sep till 6pm).

1504
10/R27
ADMISSION
✓ **Monteviot House Garden & Woodside Nursery** near **Ancrum & Jedburgh** Off A68 at Ancrum, the B6400 to Nisbet (3km), first there's Woodside on left (Victorian walled garden for the house; separate but don't miss) then the mainly formal gardens of the house (home of the Marquess of Lothian); terraced to the river (Teviot). All extraordinarily pleasant. Woodside has an organic demonstrations section, other events and a great tearoom (1383/TEAROOMS, 2224/GARDEN CENTRES). House: 2 weeks in Jul. Gardens: Apr-Oct 12noon-5pm.

1505
9/J23
HONESTY BOX

Angus's Garden www.barguillean.co.uk · Taynuilt 7km from village (12km from Oban on the A85) along the Glen Lonan road. Take first right after Barguillean Farm. A garden laid out by the family who own the farm in memory of their son Angus, a reporter killed reporting on the war in Cyprus. On the slopes around Angus's Loch, brimful of lilies and ducks and (rescued) swans. Informal mix of tended and uncultivated (though wild prevails), a more poignant remembrance is hard to imagine as you while an hour away in this peaceful place. Open all year.

1506
1/XF4
ADMISSION
L

Dr Neil's (Secret) Garden Edinburgh Not quite the secret it was (sorry!) but this garden can still feel like your private demesne on the shores of Duddingston Loch. End of the road through Holyrood Park just past Duddingston church; enter through manse gates. Turn right. At end of the manse lawn a corner gate leads to an extraordinary terraced garden bordering the loch. With wild Arthur's Seat above, you'd swear you were in Argyll. The labour of love of Claudia Poitier and volunteers, this is an enchanting corner of the city. 7 days dawn-dusk. The skating minister of the Raeburn painting took off from the restored tower here.

1507
9/H24
NTS
ADMISSION

Arduaine Garden www.arduaine-garden.org.uk · near Kilmelford 28km south of Oban on A816, one of Argyll's undiscovered arcadias gifted to the NTS who in the current climate struggle to keep it open (in winter get tickets at the hotel). The creation of this (micro) climate in which the rich, diverse vegetation flourished, was influenced by Osgood Mackenzie of Inverewe (above) and its restoration is a testimony to the 20 years' hard labour of the famous Wright brothers. Enter/park by Loch Melfort Hotel (737/ARGYLL HOTELS), gate 100m. Until dusk.

1508
11/M30
ADMISSION

Cally Gardens www.callygardens.co.uk · Gatehouse of Fleet Off A75 at Gatehouse and through the gateway to Cally Palace Hotel (1110/HOTELS THAT WELCOME KIDS), this walled garden is signed off to the left before you reach the hotel. Built in the 1770s as the kitchen garden of the big house, it was rescued in 1987 by Michael Wickenden who has transformed it into a haven for gardeners and has meticulously gathered, introduced, nurtured and recorded herbaceous plants (over 3,000), many of which you can't find anywhere else. Serious stuff but a joy to visit. Easter-Sep. Tue-Fri 2-5.30pm. Sat/Sun 10am-5.30pm.

1509
9/G26
ADMISSION

Achamore Gardens www.gigha.org.uk · Isle of Gigha 1km from ferry. Walk or cycle (bike hire by ferry); an easy 2km trip. The big house (which does top B&B; 2282/ISLAND HOTELS) on the island set in 54 acres. Lush tropical plants mingle with early-flourishing rhodies (Feb-Mar): all due to the mild climate and the devotion of a long rollcall of gardeners; now Micky Little. 2 marked walks (40 minutes/2 hours) start from the walled garden (green route takes in the sea view of Islay and Jura). Density and variety of shrubs, pond plants and trees revealed as you meander in this enchanting spot. Leaflet guides at entrance. New interpretation centre 2010. Open all year dawn to dusk. Honesty box. 2236/MAGICAL ISLANDS.

1510
8/S20

Drum Castle Rose Garden www.nts.org.uk · near Banchory 1km from A93. In the grounds of Drum Castle (the Irvine ancestral home, though nothing to do with my Irvines; 1787/CASTLES), a superb walled garden that pays homage to the rose and encapsulates 4 centuries of its horticulture. 4 areas (17th-20th centuries). Fabulous, Jul/Aug especially. Open Easter-Oct 11am-5pm.

1511
9/J26
ADMISSION

Ascog Hall Fernery www.ascoghallfernery.co.uk · Rothesay Outside town on road to Mount Stuart (1833/COUNTRY HOUSES), worth stopping at this small garden and very small Victorian Fern House. Green and lush and dripping! Easter-Oct, 10am-5pm. Closed Mon/Tue. And don't miss Rothesay's Victorian men's loos (which women can visit, too); they are not small.

1512 **Priorwood** www.nts.org.uk · **Melrose** Next to Melrose Abbey, this tranquil
10/R27 secret garden behind high walls specialises in growing flowers and plants for drying.
ADMISSION Picking, drying and arranging continuously in progress. Samples for sale. Run by
NTS enthusiasts on behalf of the NTS, they're always willing to talk stamens with you.
Includes a historical apple orchard with trees through the ages. Mon-Sat 10am-
5pm; Sun 1-5pm. Closed 4pm winter. Dried flower demos and a superior shop.

1513 **Kailzie Gardens** www.kailziegardens.com · **Peebles** On B7062 Traquair road.
10/Q27 Spacious, well-kept walled garden with informal glasshouses and perfect hedges.
ADMISSION Informal woodland gardens all eminently strollable. Old-fashioned roses, wilder
bits. Excellent courtyard teashop (807/BORDERS RESTAURANTS). Kids' corner and
ospreys (Apr-Aug). Fishing ponds. Apr-Oct 11am-5.30pm (restricted winter access).

1514 **Pitmedden Garden** www.nts.org.uk · **near Ellon** 35km north of Aberdeen,
8/S18 10km west of A92. Formal French gardens recreated in 1950s on site of Sir Alex
ADMISSION Seaton's 17th-century ones. The 4 great parterres, 3 based on designs for Holyrood
NTS Palace gardens, are best viewed from the terrace. Charming farmhouse museum
☕ seems transplanted. For lovers of symmetry and an orderly universe (but there is a
woodland walk with wildlife garden area). May-Sep 10am-5.30pm; last entry 5pm.

1515 **Pittodrie House** www.macdonaldhotels.co.uk · **near Inverurie** An excep-
8/R19 tional walled garden in the grounds of Pittodrie House Hotel at Chapel of Garioch
(911/NORTHEAST HOTELS). Different gardens compartmentalised by hedges. 500m
from house and curiously unvisited by many of the guests, this secret and sheltered haven is both a kitchen garden and a place for meditations and reflections
(and those wedding photos); chances are you'll have this haven to yourself.

1516 **Ardkinglas Woodland** www.ardkinglass.com · **Cairndow** Off the A83 Loch
9/K24 Lomond to Inveraray road. Through village to signed car park and these mature
ADMISSION woodlands in the grounds of Ardkinglas House on the southern bank near the
head of Loch Fyne. Fine pines include the tallest tree in Britain. Magical at dawn or
dusk. 2km Loch Fyne Oysters (1327/SEAFOOD RESTAURANTS) where there is also a
tree-shop garden centre especially for trees and shrubs.

1517 **Attadale Gardens** www.attadale.com · **Strathcarron** On A890 from Kyle of
7/J18 Lochalsh and A87 just south of Strathcarron. Lovely West Highland home (to the
ADMISSION Macphersons) and (painters') gardens near Loch Carron. Exotic specials, water gar-
dens, sculpture, great rhodies May/Jun. Nursery and kitchen garden. Fern and
Japanese gardens. Good café/restaurant nearby (1013/HIGHLAND RESTAURANTS).
Apr-Oct 10am-5.30pm. Closed Sun.

1518 **Ard-Daraich Hill Garden** www.arddaraich.co.uk · 01855 841348 · **Ardgour**
9/J21 3 km south Ardgour at Corran Ferry (8/JOURNEYS) on A861 to Strontian. Private,
labour of love hill and wild garden where you are at liberty to wander. Shores of
Loch Linhe with great views of Ben Nevis and Glencoe. Once the home of
Constance Spry. Specialising in rhodies, shrubs, trees. Nursery/small garden centre. Open all year, 7 days. 2 lovely rooms to stay over; home-garden produce.

1519 **The Hidden Gardens** www.thehiddengardens.org.uk · **Glasgow** This
2/XA5 garden oasis in the asphalt jungle of Glasgow's South Side was created in the disused wasteland behind The Tramway performance and studio space, a project of
environmental theatre group nva working with landscape architects City Design
Co-operative, this is a very modern approach to an age-old challenge – how to
make and keep a sanctuary in the city! It's ageing gracefully. Nice caff (608/GLAS-
GOW KIDS). Open 10am-8pm (winter hours vary). Closed Mon.

1520 **Shambellie Walled Garden** New Abbey near Dumfries Near but not part
11/N30 of Shambellie House, the National Museum of Costume. Leaving village towards
ADMISSION Dumfries, turn left on the road for Beeswing; the garden is on the right 150m. Few
gardens on these pages are quite such a labour of love as this, the walled garden
rescued by Sheila Cameron for no other reason than that 'she had to' and transformed with cash and graft into this lovingly tended oasis. See the pics of what
she and her brother started with. 6 years on, they made it – beautiful! Some plant
sales. Sat/Sun/Mon 10am-4pm in season.

All the following host exceptional gardens.

Royal Botanic Garden Edinburgh 410/OTHER ATTRACTIONS.
Botanic Garden & Kibble Palace Glasgow 681/OTHER ATTRACTIONS.
Kildrummy Castle Hotel 1178/SCOTTISH HOTELS.
Stonefield Castle 738/ARGYLL HOTELS.
Castle of Mey 1775/CASTLES.
Cawdor Castle 1776/CASTLES.
Brodick Castle 1779/CASTLES.
Dunvegan Castle 1781/CASTLES.
Mount Stuart 1833/COUNTRY HOUSES.
Manderston 1835/COUNTRY HOUSES.
Floors Castle 1841/COUNTRY HOUSES.

*If you want to learn more about all these gardens and many others,
I would recommend* Scotland for Gardeners *by Kenneth Cox, published
by Birlinn.*

▌▌ The Best Country Parks

1521 ✓✓ **Drumlanrig Castle** www.drumlanrig.com · 01848 330248 ·
11/N29 Thornhill On A76, 7km north of Thornhill in the west Borders in whose
☕ romance and history it's steeped, much more than merely a country park; spend a
good day, both inside the castle and in the grounds. Apart from *that* art collection
(Rembrandt, Holbein and you may remember the Leonardo got stolen, recovered
but not back at TGP) and the courtyard of shops, the delights include a wee tearoom, an adventure playground and regular events programme. Main outdoor
focus is on extensive trails for walking (4) and cycling (7) up to 15km round the
estate lochs and silvery Nith. Courtyard also houses the Scottish Cycle Museum
for serious bikenuts. Open Apr-Sep 10am-5pm. (House: Apr-Aug 11am-4pm.)

1522 ✓ **Muirshiel** www.clydemuirsheil.co.uk · near Lochwinnoch Via Largs
9/L26 (A760) or Glasgow (M8, junction 29 A737 then A760 5km south of Johns-
L tone). North from village on Kilmacolm road for 3km then signed. Muirshiel is
name given to wider area but park proper begins 6km on road along the Calder
valley. Despite proximity to the conurbation, this is a wild and enchanting place for
walks, picnics, etc. Trails marked to waterfall and summit views. Extensive events
programme. Go look for hen harriers. See also 697/GLASGOW WALKS. Escape!

1523 **John Muir Country Park** www.eastlothian.gov.uk · near Dunbar Named
10/R25 after the 19th-century conservationist who founded America's national parks (and
the Sierra Club) and who was born in Dunbar (his birthplace is now an interactive
museum at 126 High St). This swathe of coastline to the west of the town (partly
known locally as Tyninghame) is an important estuarine nature reserve but is good

for family walks and beachcombing. Various entry points: main one is from Dunbar roundabout on A1 back towards North Berwick, then A1087, 1km; by clifftop trail from Dunbar; or from car park on road into Dunbar from west at West Barns (1763/WILDLIFE).

1524
9/L25
☕

Finlaystone Estate www.finlaystone.co.uk · **Langbank** A8 to Greenock, Houston direction at Langbank, then signed. Grand mansion home to chief of Clan Macmillan set in formal gardens in wooded estate. Lots of facilities, craft shop, leafy walks, walled garden and rather good tearoom. Oct-Mar weekends only, Apr-Sep daily until 5pm. An all-round get oot o' the house experience and kinda vital!

1525
10/S27

Hirsel Country Park www.hirselcountrypark.co.uk · **Coldstream** On A697, north edge town (direction Kelso). 3,000 acres the grounds of Hirsel House (not open to public). 2-4km walks through farmland and woods including lovely languid lake. Museum, tearoom (10.30am-4.30pm) and craft units at the Homestead.

1526
10/N25

Muiravonside Country Park near Linlithgow 4km southwest of Linlithgow on B825 or signed from junction 4 of M9 Edinburgh/Stirling. Former farm estate and a park just where you need it with 170 acres of woodland walks, parkland, picnic sites and a visitor centre for school parties or anyone else with an interest in birds, bees and badgers. Ranger service; guided walks (01324 506119). Great place to walk off that lunch at the not-too-distant Champany Inn (257/BURGERS).

1527
9/K27

Eglinton near Irvine By main A78 Largs/Ayr road signed from Irvine/Kilwinning intersection. Spacious lungful of Ayrshire. Visitor centre with interpretation of absolutely everything. Park always open, visitor centre Easter-Oct. Network of walks.

✓✓ **Culzean Castle Park** Ayrshire Superb and hugely popular. 1773/CASTLES.

✓ **Haddo House** Aberdeenshire Beautiful grounds. 1834/COUNTRY HOUSES.

Mugdock Country Park near Milngavie Marvellous, vast. 693/CITY WALKS.
Tentsmuir near Tayport Estuarine; John Muir, on Tay. 1766/WILDLIFE.
Kelburne Country Centre Largs 1684/KIDS.

▨ The Best Town Parks

1528
1/C3

✓✓ **Princes Street Gardens** Edinburgh South side of Princes St. The greenery that launched a thousand postcards, now under threat from a thousand events. This former loch, drained when the New Town was built, is divided by the Mound. The eastern half has pitch and putt, Winter Wonderland and the Scott Monument (452/BEST VIEWS), the western has its much-photographed fountain, open-air café, space for locals and tourists to sprawl on the grass when sunny, and the Ross Bandstand – heart of Edinburgh's Hogmanay (68/BEST EVENTS) and the International Festival's fireworks concert (53/EVENTS). Louts with lager, senior citizens on benches, dazed tourists: all our lives are here. Till dusk. And as I often rediscover: **The Meadows** is also an exceptional asset to the city.

1529
8/T19

✓✓ **Hazelhead Park** Aberdeen Via Queens Rd, 3km centre. Extraordinary park where the Aberdonians' mysterious gardening skills are magnificently in evidence. Many facilities including a maze, pets' corner, tearoom and there are lawns, memorials and botanical splendours aplenty especially azalea garden in spring and roses in summer. Sculpture and serenity!

1530
8/T19
✔ **Duthie Park** Aberdeen Riverside Dr along River Dee from the bridge carrying main A92 Stonehaven road. The other large well-kept park with duck pond, bandstand, hugely impressive summer rose gardens, carved sculptures and the famous David Welch Winter Garden of subtropical palms/ferns and the UK's biggest collection of cacti (9.30am-6.30pm, 3.30pm in winter). Gardens from 8am.

1531
10/P25
✔ **Pittencrieff Park** Dunfermline Extensive park alongside the abbey and palace ruins gifted to the town in 1903 by Carnegie. Open areas, glasshouses, pavilion (more a function room) but most notably a deep verdant glen criss-crossed with pathways. Great kids' play area. Lush, full of birds, good after rain.

1532
10/N23
✔ **Macrosty Park** www.perthshire.co.uk · Crieff On your left as you leave Crieff for Comrie and Crianlarich; for parking ask locally. A perfect green place on sloping ground to the River Earn (good level walk – Lady Mary's Walk) with tea-rooms, innovative kids' area, mature trees and superb bandstand. A fine old park.

1533
10/Q24
Beveridge Park Kirkcaldy Also in Fife, another big municipal park with a duck and boat pond, wide-open spaces and many amusements (eg bowling, tennis, putting, plootering). **Ravenscraig**, a coastal park on the main road east to Dysart, is an excellent place to walk. Great prospect of the firth and its coves and cruise.

1534
10/R28
Wilton Lodge Park Hawick Hawick not overfull of visitor attractions but it does have a nice park with facilities and diversions enough for everyone, eg the civic gallery, rugby pitches (they quite like rugby in Hawick), a large kids' play-ground, a seasonal café and lots of riverside walks by the Teviot. Lots of my school friends lost their virginity in the shed here. All-round open-air recreation centre. South end of town by A7. PS: the shed, like our virginities, is long gone.

1535
11/P28
Station Park www.visitmoffat.co.uk · Moffat On your right as you enter the town from the M74. Well-proportioned people's park; boating pond (with giant swans) main feature. Annan water alongside offers nice walking. Notable also for the monument to Air Chief Marshall Hugh Dowding, Commander in Chief during the Battle of Britain. 'Never... was so much owed by so many to so few'.

1536
9/L27
Dean Castle Park www.deancastle.com · Kilmarnock A77 south first turnoff for Kilmarnock then signed; from Ayr A77 north, 3rd turnoff. Surprising green and woody oasis in suburban Kilmarnock; lawns and woods around restored castle and courtyard. Riding centre. Burns Rose Garden.

1537
11/M30
Garries Park Gatehouse of Fleet Notable for its tiny perfect garden which you enter under an arch from the village main street. A wee gem especially for its large flowers. Leads to bigger public space, but pause in the garden and smell those roses. Then go to the Ship (759/SOUTHWEST HOTELS) or the Murray Arms.

1538
2/XC5
Rouken Glen & Linn Park Glasgow Both on south side of river. Rouken Glen via Pollokshaws/Kilmarnock Rd to Eastwood Toll then right. Visitor area with info centre, garden centre, a café, kids' play area and woodland walks. Linn Park via Aikenhead and Carmunnock road. It's a journey but worth it; this is one of the undiscovered Elysiums of a city which boasts 60 parks. Activities, wildlife walks, kids' nature trails, horse-riding and Alexander Greek Thomson's **Holmwood House**; open Easter-Oct 12noon-5pm (NTS).

1539
10/Q23
Camperdown Park www.camperdownpark.com · Dundee Calling itself a country park, Camperdown is the main recreational breathing space for the city and hosts a plethora of distractions (a golf course, a wildlife complex, mansion

house, etc). Situated beyond Kingsway, the ring-route; go via Coupar Angus turnoff. Best walks across the A923 in **Templeton Woods** (2037/WOODLAND WALKS). **Balgay Park** also excellent.

1540
8/P17

Grant Park Forres Frequent winner of the Bonny Bloom competitions (a board proclaims their awards) and with its balance of ornamental gardens, open parkland and woody hill side, this is obviously a carefully tended rose. Good municipal facilities like pitch and putt, playground. Cricket in summer and topping topiary. Through woods on Cluny Hill to the Nelson Tower for exercise and view.

1541
10/N25

Callander Park Falkirk Park on edge of town centre, signed from all over. Overlooked by high-rise blocks and near a busy road system, this is nevertheless a beautiful green space with a big hoose (heritage museum), woods and lawns. You can't help feeling they could do with it here.

▉ The Most Interesting Coastal Villages

1542
7/H18
L

✔ **Plockton** www.plockton.com · near Kyle of Lochalsh A Highland gem of a place 8km over the hill from Kyle, clustered around inlets of a wooded bay on Loch Carron. Cottage gardens down to the bay and the palm trees! Some great walks over headlands. Plockton Inn and on the front the Plockton Hotel offer reasonable rooms and pub grub (1002/LESS EXPENSIVE HIGHLAND HOTELS) and there's also the estimable Plockton Shores (1016/BEST HIGHLAND RESTAURANTS). Calum's Seal Trips are a treat (seals and dolphins almost guaranteed; 1740/SEALIFE CRUISES). It's not hard to feel at one with this village (as generations do).

1543
8/R17
LL

✔ **Moray Coast Fishing Villages** From Speybay (where the Spey slips into the sea) to Fraserburgh: some of Scotland's best coastal scenery with interesting villages in cliff/cove and beach settings. See 1556/BEACHES for the best beaches. Especially notable are **Portsoy** with 17th-century harbour (and see 42/EVENTS, 1274/PUBS); **Sandend** with its own beach and a fabulous one nearby at Sunnyside (1556/BEACHES); **Pennan**, famous from the film *Local Hero*; **Gardenstown** with a walk along the water's edge to **Crovie** (pronounced Crivee) the epitome of a coast-clinging community (near Troup Head; 1724/BIRDS); and **Cullen**, a village on the main road with average accommodation and a great wide beach.

1544
3/Q10

✔ **Stromness** Orkney Mainland 24km from Kirkwall and a different kettle of fish. Hugging the shore and with narrow streets and wynds, it has a unique atmosphere, both maritime and oddly European. Some of the most singular shops you'll see anywhere and the Orkney folk going about their business. Park near harbour and walk down the cobbled main street if you don't want to scrape your paintwork (2307/ORKNEY; 2174/GALLERIES).

1545
7/M17

✔ **Cromarty** near Inverness At end of road across Black Isle from Inverness (45km northeast), does take longer than you think (well, 30 minutes). Village with dreamy times-gone-by atmosphere, without being twee. Lots of kids running about and a pink strand of beach. Delights to discover include: the East Kirk, plain and aesthetic with countryside through the windows behind the altar; Hugh (the geologist) Miller's cottage/Courthouse museum (2156/BEST HISTORY & HERITAGE); The Pantry (1411/TEAROOMS); Cromarty Bakery (1423/BEST SCOTCH BAKERS); a perfect, wee restaurant Sutor Creek (1017/BEST HIGHLAND RESTAURANTS); the shore and cliff walk (2059/COASTAL WALKS); the Pirates' Cemetery and of course the obliging dolphins (1727/DOLPHINS).

1546
10/N25
Culross near Dunfermline By A994 from Dunfermline or junction 1 of M90 just over Forth Road Bridge (15km). Old centre conserved and restored by NTS. Mainly residential and not awash with craft and coffee shops. More historical than quaint; a community of careful custodians (including one Dougie Vipond of the telly) lives in the white and yellow red-pantiled houses. Footsteps echo in the cobbled wynds. Palace and Town House open Easter-Oct 12noon-5pm, weekends Sep/Oct. Interesting back gardens and lovely church at top of hill (1874/CHURCHES).

1547
9/G22
L
Tobermory Mull Postcard/calendar village with painted houses round the bay but also the main town of Mull. Ferry port for Ardnamurchan, but main Oban ferry is 35km away at Craignure. Usually a bustling harbour front with quieter streets behind; a quintessential island atmosphere. Some good inexpensive hotels (and quayside hostel) well situated to explore the whole Island. 2306/MULL; 1131/BEST HOSTELS.

1548
9/F26
Port Charlotte Islay A township on the Rhinns of Islay, the western peninsula. By A846 from the ports, Askaig and Ellen via Bridgend then A847. Rows of white-washed, well-kept cottages along and back from shoreline. On the road in, there's an island museum and a coffee shop. Also a town beach and one between Port Charlotte and Bruichladdich (the war memorial nearby). Quiet and charming, not merely quaint. 2304/ISLAY; 2283/ISLAND HOTELS.

1549
11/N30
Rockcliffe near Dumfries 25km south on Solway Coast road, A710. On the Scottish Riviera, the rocky part of the coast around to Kippford (2053/COASTAL WALKS). A good rock-scrambling foreshore though not so clean, and a village with few houses and Baron's Craig hotel; set back with views (27 moderately expensive rooms) but a somewhat gloomy presence. Garden Tearoom in village (1407/TEA-ROOMS) is nice or repair to the Anchor (1309/GASTROPUBS) in Kippford.

1550
10/R24
East Neuk Villages www.eastneukwide.co.uk The quintessential quaint wee fishing villages along the bit of Fife that forms the mouth of the Firth of Forth. **Crail, Anstruther, Pittenweem, St Monans** and **Elie** have different characters and attractions especially Crail (1406/TEAROOMS) and Pittenweem harbours, Anstruther is main centre and home of Fisheries Museum (see also 1353/FISH & CHIPS; 1708/ BIRDS) and perfect Elie (842/FIFE HOTELS; 1283/GASTROPUBS; 2081/GREAT GOLF). Also St Andrews, p. 160–1. Cycling good, traffic in summer not.

1551
10/P25
Aberdour www.aberdour.org.uk Between Dunfermline and Kirkcaldy, 10km east from junction 1 of M90) or go by train from Edinburgh (frequent service: Dundee or Kirkcaldy); delightful station. Walks round harbour and to headland, Silver Sands beach 1km (447/EDINBURGH BEACHES), castle ruins. 1873/CHURCHES.

1552
11/L31
Isle of Whithorn www.isleofwhithorn.com Strange faraway village at end of the road, 35km south Newton Stewart, 6km Whithorn (1825/PREHISTORIC SITES). Mystical harbour where low tide does mean low, saintly shoreline, a sea angler's pub, the Steam Packet – very good pub grub (1264/BLOODY GOOD PUBS). Ninian's chapel round the headland underwhelming but you pass the poignant memorial to the *Solway Harvester*. Everybody visiting IoW seems to walk this way.

1553
9/J27
LL
Corrie www.arran.uk.com · Arran Last but not least, the bonniest bit of Arran (apart from Kildonan and the glens and the rest), best reached by bike from Brodick. Many walks from here including Goat Fell but nice just to sit or potter on the foreshore. Hotel has never quite been up to expectations. The village shop is an art gallery like most of the village itself: animal sculptures on the foreshore and even the boats in the slips of harbours are aesthetic.

Fantastic Beaches & Bays

All those listed below are in L, LL *and* LLL *settings, obviously.*

1554
6/L12

✓ ✓ **Pete's Beach near Durness** The One of many great beaches on the North Coast (see 1572 below) that I've called my own. The hill above it is called Ceannabeinne; you find it 7km east of Durness. Coming from Tongue it's just after where Loch Eriboll comes out to the sea and the road hits the coast again (there's a layby opposite). It's a small perfect cove flanked by walls of coral-pink rock and shallow turquoise sea. Splendid from above (land rises to a bluff with a huge boulder) and from below. Revisiting (summer '11) even though there's more people there now, I saw it in several aspects (of weather and light); it's never short of magnificent. There's a great coastal walk to the Ceannabeinne Township (2061/COASTAL WALKS) nearby. All in all, the coast with the most (great beaches!).

1555
9/F24

✓ ✓ **Kiloran Beach** Colonsay 9km from quay and hotel, past Colonsay House; parking and access on hill side. Often described as the finest beach in the Hebrides, it doesn't disappoint though it has changed character recently (a shallower sandbar traps tidal run-off). Craggy cliffs on one side, negotiable rocks on the other, tiers of grassy dunes between. Do go to the end! The island was once bought as a picnic spot. This beach was probably the reason why.

1556
8

✓ ✓ **Moray Coast** www.moray.gov.uk Many great beaches along coast from Spey Bay to Fraserburgh, notably **Cullen** and **Lossiemouth** (town beaches) and **New Aberdour** (1km from New Aberdour village on B9031, 15km west of Fraserburgh) and **Rosehearty** (8km west of Fraserburgh) both quieter places for walks and picnics. 2 of the great secret beaches on this coast are:

✓ ✓ **Sunnyside** Where you walk past the incredible ruins of Findlater Castle on the cliff top (how did they build it? A place, on its grassed-over roof, for a picnic) and down to a cove which on my sunny day was simply perfect. Signed (Findlater) from A98. Take a left from Sandend 16km west of Banff, follow road for 2km. Park in the farmyard. Walk from here past dovecote, 1km to cliff, then left from the ruin viewpoint. See also 1797/RUINS or 2057/COASTAL WALKS. **Cullykhan Bay** East of Gardenstown signed from the coast road (200m to small car park). A small beach but great littoral for beach scrambling and full of surprises (1947/ENCHANTING PLACES).

1557
9/G28

✓ ✓ **Macrihanish** Foot of the Kintyre peninsula 10km from Campbeltown. Walk north from Machrihanish village or golf course, or from the car park on A83 to Tayinloan and Tarbert at point where it hits/leaves the coast. A joyously long strand (8km) of unspoiled orange-pink sand backed by dunes and facing the 'steepe Atlantic Stream' all the way to Newfoundland (2087/GOLF). Great accommodation and eats at **The Village of Macrihanish Dunes** (733/ARGYLL).

1558
6/K12

✓ ✓ **Sandwood Bay** Kinlochbervie This mile-long sandy strand with its old Stack is legendary but there's the problem: too many people like us come here and you may have to share its glorious isolation. Inaccessibility is its saving grace: it's a 7km walk from the sign off the road at Balchrick (near the cattle grid) which is 6km from Kinlochbervie; allow 3-4 hours return plus time there. More venturesome is the walk from the north and Cape Wrath (2051/COASTAL WALKS). Go easy and go in summer!

1559
5/D18

✓ ✓ **South Uist** www.southuist.com Deserted but for birds, an almost unbroken strand of beach running for miles down the west coast; the machair is best in early summer (follow the Machair Way). Take any road off the spinal A865; usually less than 2km. Good spot to try is turnoff at Tobha Mor 25km north of Lochboisdale; real blackhouses and a chapel on the way to the sea. Listen to those birds – this is as far away as you can get from Shoreditch

1560
9/F26
✓✓ **Saligo, Machir Bay & The Big Strand** Islay The first two are bays on NW of island via A847 road to Port Charlotte, then B8018 past Loch Gorm. Wide beaches; remains of war fortifications in deep dunes, Machir perhaps best for beach bums but Saligo is one of the most pleasingly aesthetic beaches... anywhere. The Big Strand on Laggan Bay: along Bowmore-Port Ellen road take Oa turnoff, follow Kintra signs. There's camping and great walks in either direction, 8km of glorious sand and dunes (contains the Machrie Golf Course). All these are airy ambles under a wide sky. 2086/GOLF IN GREAT PLACES; 2049/COASTAL WALKS.

1561
5/E15
✓✓ **Scarista Beach & the Beaches of South Harris** On road south of Tarbert (20km) to Rodel. Scarista is so beautiful that people get married here. Hotel over the road is worth staying just for this, but is also a great retreat (2276/ISLAND HOTELS) and there's the hard-to-get-into island luxury cottages (2305/OUTER HEBRIDES). Golf on the links (2094/GOLF IN GREAT PLACES). This coast has many extraordinary beaches. You may want to camp (1186/CAMPING). It's fab here in early evening. The sun also rises.

1562
5/G13
✓ **The Beaches of Lewis** Perhaps less celebrated than Harris (above) but there are numerous enchanting beaches on the Lewis coast; apart from the odd surfie you've likely to have the strand to yourself. Around **Uig** in the west via A8011 especially Timsgary/Ardroil. Great hotel and (separate) bistro and top tearoom on the way (2305/OUTER HEBRIDES). Big sunsets! For the beach at the north end (of the Hebrides), **Port Nis**: keep driving (some interesting stops on the way; 2141/2143/MUSEUMS) until you get to this tiny bay and harbour down the hill at the end of the road. Anthony Barber's Harbour View Gallery full of his own work (which you find in many other galleries and even on postcards) is worth a visit (Mon-Sat 10am-5pm). For refreshment, there's The Beach House (2305/OUTER HEBRIDES). 2 more secret spots via the B895 15km northwest of Stornaway (past Broad Bay) are at the long strand at **Tolsta** and further at the end of the road, **Traig Mhor** and the bridge to nowhere, exquisite Ghearadha (pronounced Gary).

1563
6/K13
✓ **Oldshoremore** The beach you pass on the road to Balchrick, only 3km from Kinlochbervie. It's easy to reach and a beautiful spot: the water is clear and perfect for swimming, and there are rocky walks and quiet places. **Polin**, 500m north, is a cove you might have to yourself. (1193/CAMPING).

1564
9/J25
✓ **Ostal Beach/Kilbride Bay** Millhouse near Tighnabruaich 3km from Millhouse on B8000 signed Ardlamont (not Portvadie, the ferry), a track to right before white house (often with a chain across to restrict access). Park and walk 1.5km, turning right after lochan. You arrive on a perfect white sandy crescent known locally as Ostal and, in certain conditions, a mystical place to swim and picnic. Arran's north coast is like a Greek island in the bay. **Ettrick Bay on Bute** is another good beach with this view and a brilliant wee café (1367/CAFÉS).

1565
10/R22
✓ **Lunan Bay** near Montrose 5km from main A92 road to Aberdeen and 5km of deep red crescent beach under a wide northern sky. But 'n' Ben, Auchmithie, is an excellent place to start or finish (875/PERTHSHIRE EATS) and good approach (from south), although Gordon's restaurant at Inverkeilor is closer (873/PERTHSHIRE EATS). You can climb up to the Red Castle. Lunan is often deserted. Atmospheric accommodation at Ethie Castle (862/TAYSIDE). **St Cyrus** north of Montrose (a nature reserve) also a lovely littoral to wander. Walk 2km south of village.

1566 ✓ **The Secret Beach** near Achmelvich Approach from Archmelvich car
6/J14 park going north (it's the next proper bay round) or Lochinver-Stoer/Drumbeg
road (less of a walk; 1618/SCENIC ROUTES); layby on right 3km after Archmelvich
turnoff, 250m beyond sign for Cathair Estate. Park on the right, cross the road and
walk towards the sea following stream (a sign points to Mill). The path is well
defined. Called **Alltan na Bradhan**, it's the site of an old mill (grinding wheels
still there), perfect for camping and the best sea for swimming in the area. And
pretty special.

1567 ✓ **Gairloch** A beach I missed until one (rare in 2011) sunny July afternoon
7/H16 when lots of people but not (and I imagine never) too many were lying on this
perfect curve of sand, a sheltered bay of Loch Gairloch and swimming in its shallow, shimmering, non-wavy water. There's a tranquil old graveyard behind
(1901/GRAVEYARDS) and the green golf course beside. Parking and toilets. The
longer Big Sand is 4km west by the campsite (1205/CAMPING).

1568 **Lowlandman's Bay** Jura Not in itself a beach but a rocky foreshore with ethe-
9/G25 real atmosphere; great light and space (the **Corran Sands** are adjacent). Only
seals break the spell. Go right at 3-arch bridge to first group of houses
(Knockdrome), through yard on left and right around cottages to track to
Ardmenish. After deer fences, bay is visible on your right, 1km walk away.

1569 **Vatersay** Outer Hebrides The tiny island joined by a causeway to Barra. Twin
5/C20 crescent beaches on either side of the isthmus, one shallow and sheltered visible
from Castlebay, the other an ocean beach with more rollers. Dunes/machair; safe
swimming. Poignant memorial to a 19th-century shipwreck in the Ocean Bay and
another (on the way here) to a plane crash during the war; the wreckage is still
there. There's a helluva hill between Barra and Vatersay if you're cycling.

1570 **Seal Bay** www.isleofbarra.com · Barra 5km Castlebay on west coast, 2km
5/C20 after Isle of Barra Hotel through gate across machair where road right is signed
Allathasdal a Deas (after a sandy then a rockier cove). A flat, rocky Hebridean shore
and skerries where seals flop into the water and eye you with intense curiosity.
The more beach-type beach is next to the hotel that you pass on the way.

1571 **West Sands** St Andrews As a town beach, this is hard to beat; it dominates
10/R23 the view to west. Wide swathe not too unclean and sea just about swimmable.
Golf courses behind. Consistently gets the blue flag, but beach buffs may prefer
Kinshaldy (1766/WILDLIFE) or **Kingsbarns** (10km south on Crail road) where there
is a great beach walk taking in the Cammo Estate (with its gardens) and skirting
the great Kingsbarns Golf Course or **Elie** (28km south).

1572 **North Coast** West of Thurso are some of Britain's most unspoiled and unsung
6 beaches. No beach bums, no Beach Boys. There are many great little coves, you
choose; but those to mention are: **Strathy** and **Armadale** (35km west Thurso),
Farr and **Torrisdale** (48km) and **Coldbackie** (65km). My favourite (in the far
west) is elevated to the top of this category.

1573 **Sands of Morar** near Mallaig 70km west of Fort William and 6km from
7/H20 Mallaig by newly improved road, these easily accessible beaches may seem over-
populated on summer days and the south stretch nearest to Arisaig may have one
too many caravan parks, but they go on for miles and there's enough space for
everybody. The sand's supposed to be silver but in fact it's a very pleasing pink.
Lots of rocky bits for exploration. One of the best beachy bits (the bay before the
estuary) is Camusdarrach, signed from the main road (where *Local Hero* was

filmed); further from the road, it is quieter and a very good swathe of sand. Traigh, the golf course makes good use of the dunes (2101/GOOD GOLF).

1574
9/F23
The Bay at the Back of the Ocean Iona Easy 2km walk from the ferry from Fionnphort, south of Mull (2230/MAGICAL ISLANDS) or bike hire from store on your left as you walk into the village (01681 700357). Mostly track: road straight up from the pier, left at the village hall, uphill to Maol Farm and then across the machair. John Smith, who is buried by the abbey, once told me this was his favourite place. 2 great inexpensive hotels on Iona, the Argyll and St Columba (2306/BEST OF MULL).

1575
6/N16
Dornoch (& Embo Beaches) The wide and extensive sandy beach of this pleasant town at the mouth of the Dornoch Firth famous for its golf links. 4km north, Embo Sands starts with ghastly caravan city, but walk north towards Golspie. Embo is twinned with Kaunakakai, Hawaii. We can dream!

1576
11/J30
2 Beaches in the far South West Killantringan Bay near Portpatrick Off A77 before Portpatrick signed Dunskey Gardens in summer, follow road signed Killantringan Lighthouse (dirt track). Park 1km before lighthouse or walk from Portpatrick following the Southern Upland Way. Beautiful bay for exploration. **Sandhead Beach** A716 south of Stranraer. Shallow, safe waters of Luce Bay (8km of sands). Perfect for families (in their damned caravans).

The Great Glens

All those listed below are in L, LL *and* LLL *settings, obviously.*

1577
7/K18
✓ ✓ ✓ **Glen Affric** www.glenaffric.org Beyond Cannich at end of Glen Urquhart A831, 20km from Drumnadrochit on Loch Ness. A dramatic gorge that strikes westwards into the wild heart of Scotland. Superb for rambles (2001/GLEN & RIVER WALKS), expeditions, Munro-bagging (further in beyond Loch Affric) and even just tootling through in the car. Shaped by the Hydro Board, Loch Benevean also adds to the drama. One of the best places in Scotland to appreciate the beauty of Scots Pine. Cycling good (bike hire in Cannich and at the campsite; 01456 415364) as is the detour to Tomich and Plodda Falls (1589/WATERFALLS). Stop at Dog Falls (1664/PICNICS) but do go to the end of the glen.

1578
10/M22
✓ ✓ ✓ **Glen Lyon** www.glenlyon.org · near Aberfeldy One of Scotland's crucial places historically and geographically, much favoured by fishers/walkers/Munro-baggers. Wordsworth, Tennyson, Gladstone and Baden-Powell all sang its praises. The Lyon is a classic Highland river tumbling through corries, gorges and riverine meadows. Several Munros are within its watershed and rise gloriously on either side. Road all the way to the lochside (30km). Eagles soar over the remoter tops at the head of the glen. The **Post Office Tearoom** half-way round at Bridge of Balgie, does a roaring trade (closed Wed; weekends only in winter) and **Fortingal House** on the way in is excellent (858/PERTHSHIRE).

1579
9/K21
✓ ✓ **Glen Nevis** www.glen-nevis.co.uk · Fort William Used by many a film director and easy to see why. Ben Nevis is only part of the magnificent scenery. Many walks and convenient facilities (1595/WATERFALLS; 1997/SERIOUS WALKS). West Highland Way emerges here. Visitor centre; cross river to climb Ben Nevis and the walkers' Ben Nevis Inn (1057/FORT WILLIAM). **Café Beag** nearby is a pleasant caff (summer only). This woody dramatic glen is a national treasure.

1580   ✓ ✓   **Glen Etive**   Off from more exalted Glencoe and the A82 at Kingshouse,
9/K22   as anyone you meet there will tell you, this truly is a glen of glens. Treat with great respect while you make it your own. (1188/CAMPING, 1657/SWIMMING).

1581   **Strathcarron** www.strathcarron.com · **near Bonar Bridge**   You drive up the
6/L15   north bank of this Highland river from the bridge outside Ardgay (pronounced Ordguy) which is 3km over the bridge from Bonar Bridge. Road goes 15km to Croick and its remarkable church (1881/CHURCHES). The river gurgles and gushes along its rocky course to the Dornoch Firth and further up there are innumerable places to picnic, swim and stroll. Heavenly here on the warm days we long for.

1582   **The Angus Glens** www.angusglens.co.uk **Glen Clova**, **Glen Prosen** and
10/Q21   **Glen Isla**   Isla for drama, Clova for walkers, Prosen for the soul. All via Kirriemuir. Isla to the west is a woody, approachable glen with a deep gorge, on B954 near Alyth (1599/WATERFALLS) and the cosy Glenisla Hotel (1153/INNS). Others via B955, to Dykehead then road bifurcates. Both glens stab into the heart of the Grampians. Minister's Walk goes between them from behind the kirk at Prosen village over the hill to B955 before Clova village (7km). Glen Clova is a walkers' paradise especially from Glendoll 24km from Dykehead; limit of road with new Ranger Centre. Viewpoint. Jock's Road to Braemar and the Capel Mounth to Ballater (both 24km). Clova Hotel (867/PERTHSHIRE HOTELS) with famous Loops of Brandy walk (2 hours, 2-B-2); stark and beautiful. Prosen Hostel at end of the road is a serene stopover (1120/HOSTELS). The Museum of the Glens in Kirriemuir is sweet and has a surprising homage to AC/DC (no, really!).

1583   **Glendaruel** www.glendaruel.com · **Cowal**   On the A886 between Colintraive
9/J25   and Strachur. Humble but perfectly formed glen of River Ruel, from Clachan in
2-B-2   south (a kirk and an inn) through deciduous meadowland to more rugged grandeur 10km north. Easy walking, cycling. West road best. Kilmodan carved stones signed. Inver Cottage on Loch Fyne a great coffee/food stop (739/ARGYLL RESTAURANTS).

1584   **Glen Lonan**   **near Taynuilt**   Between Taynuilt on A85 and A816 south of Oban.
9/J23   Another quiet wee glen, but all the right elements for walking, picnics, cycling and
2-B-2   fishing or just a run in the car. Varying scenery, a bubbling burn (the River Lonan), some standing stones and not many folk. Angus's Garden at the Taynuilt end should not be missed (1505/GARDENS). No marked walks; now get lost!

1585   **Glen Trool**   **near Newton Stewart**   26km north by A714 via Bargrennan which
11/L29   is on the Southern Upland Way (1989/LONG WALKS). A gentle wooded glen within the vast Galloway Forest Park (one of the most charming, accessible parts) visitor centre 5km from Bargrennan. Pick up a walk brochure and walk. Many options. (1925/MARY, CHARLIE & BOB) Start of the Merrick climb (1959/HILLS).

1586   **The Sma' Glen**   **near Crieff**   Off the A85 to Perth, the A822 to Amulree and
10/N23   Aberfeldy. Sma' meaning small, this is the valley of the River Almond where the Mealls (lumpish, shapeless hills) fall steeply down to the road. Where the road turns away from the river, the long distance path to Loch Tay begins (28km). Sma' Glen, 8km, has good picnic spots, but they get busy and midgy in summer.

1587   **Strathfarrar** www.glenaffric.org · **near Beauly or Drumnadrochit**   Rare
7/L18   unspoiled glen accessed from A831 leaving Drumnadrochit on Loch Ness via Cannich (30km) or south from Beauly (15km). Signed at Struy and it's a long (25km) walk in to tackle the celebrated Munros. There may be a curfew so check (www.mcofs.org.uk/strathpeffer.access) before you set off. 22km to the head of glen past the lochs. Good climbing, walking, fishing. The real peace and quiet!

The Most Spectacular Waterfalls

One aspect of Scotland that really is improved by rain. All the walks to these falls are graded 1-A-1 unless otherwise stated (see p. 12 for walk codes).

1588
7/J18
2-C-3

✓✓ **Falls of Glomach** 25km south of Kyle of Lochalsh off A87 near Shiel Bridge, past Kintail Centre at Morvich then 2km further up Glen Croe to bridge. Walk starts other side; there are other ways (eg from the SY Hostel in Glen Affric) but this is most straightforward. Allow 5/7 hours for the pilgrimage to one of Britain's highest falls. Path is steep, can be wet and watch for mist and low cloud. Glomach means gloomy and you might feel so, peering into the ravine; from precipice to pool, it's 200m. Vertigo factor and sense of achievement both fairly high. But don't get lost! Consult *Where to Walk in Kintail, Glenelg & Lochalsh*, sold locally for the Kintail Mountain Rescue Team. Ranger service 01599 511231.

1589
7/K18

✓✓ **Plodda Falls** www.glenaffric.org · near Tomich near Drumnadrochit A831 from Loch Ness to Cannich (20km), then 7km to Tomich, a further 5km up mainly woodland track to car park. 200m walk down through woods of Scots Pine and ancient Douglas Fir to one of the most enchanting woodland sites in Britain and the Victorian iron bridge over the brink of the 150m fall into the churning river below. The dawn chorus here must be amazing (though never heard it. Obviously). Freezes into winter wonderland. Good hotel in village (1006/LESS EXPENSIVE HIGHLAND HOTELS).

1590
10/N21
🖫

✓ **Falls of Bruar** near Blair Atholl Close to the main A9 Perth-Inverness road, 12km north of Blair Atholl near House of Bruar shopping experience. (2199/SHOPPING). Consequently, the short walk to lower falls is very consumer-led but less crowded than you might expect. The lichen-covered walls of the gorge below the upper falls (1km) are less ogled and more dramatic. Circular path is well marked but steep and rocky in places. Tempting to swim on hot days (1669/SWIMMING HOLES). 2.3km circular.

1591
9/J27
1-B-1

✓ **Glenashdale Falls** Arran 5km walk from bridge on main road at Whiting Bay. Signed up the burn side, but uphill and further than you think, so allow 2 hours (return). Series of falls in a rocky gorge in the woods with paths so you get right down to the brim and the pools. Swim here, swim in heaven! There's another waterfall walk, **Eas Mor**, further south off the A841 at the second Kildonan turnoff.

1592
9/G22

Eas Fors Mull On the Dervaig to Fionnphort road 3km from Ulva Ferry; a series of cataracts tumbling down on either side of the road. Easily accessible from small car park on left going south (otherwise unmarked). There's a path down the side to the brink where the river plunges into the sea. On a warm day swimming in the sea below the fall is a rare exhilaration.

1593
7/G17
2-C-2

Lealt Falls Skye Impressive torrent of wild mountain water about 20km north of Portree on the A855. Look for sign: River Lealt. There's a car park on a bend on right (going north). Walk to grassy ledges and look over or go down to the beach. **Kilt Rock**, a viewpoint much favoured by bus parties, is a few km further (you look over and along the cliffs). **Glenview Inn** on this road is great for food (2266/SKYE HOTELS). Also...
Eas Mor Glen Brittle near end of road. 24km from Sligachan. A mountain waterfall with the wild Cuillin behind and views to the sea. Approach as part of a serious scramble or merely a 30-minute Cuillin sampler. Start at the Memorial Hut, cross the road, bear right, cross burn and then follow path uphill.

1594 **Eas A' Chual Aluinn** Kylesku Britain's highest waterfall, near the head of
6/L14 Glencoul, is not easy to reach. Kylesku is between Scourie and Lochinver off the
2-C-3 main A894, 20km south of Scourie. There are 2-hour cruises May-Sep (01971
502345) from outside the hotel (1021/BEST HIGHLAND RESTAURANTS). Falls are a
rather distant prospect but the cruise will do you good; baby seals an added
attraction Jun-Aug. There's also a track to the top of the falls from 5km north of
the Skiag Bridge on the main road (4 hours return) but you will need to get directions locally. The water freefalls for 200m, which is 4 times further than Niagara
(take pinch of salt here). You'll need a head for heights, good footwear (track is
often wet) and a map (folk do get lost – check the number of marker cairns).

1595 **Steall Falls** www.glen-nevis.co.uk · **Glen Nevis, Fort William** Take Glen
9/K21 Nevis road at the roundabout outside town centre and drive to the end (16km)
3-A-3 through glen. Start from the second and final car park, following marked path
uphill through the woody gorge with River Ness thrashing below. Glen eventually
and dramatically opens out and there are great views of the long veils of the falls.
Precarious 3-wire bridge for which you will also need nerves of steel. You can cross
further down or see the falls from a distance. 3km walk, 1.5 hours.

1596 **Corrieshalloch Gorge/Falls of Measach** Junction of A832 and A835, 20km
7/K16 south of Ullapool; possible to walk down into the gorge from both roads. Most
dramatic approach is from the car park on the A832 Gairloch road. Staircase to
swing bridge from whence to consider how such a wee burn could make such
a deep gash. Very impressive. A must-stop on the way to/from Ullapool.

1597 **The Grey Mare's Tail** between Moffat & Selkirk On the wildly scenic A708.
10/P28 About halfway, a car park and signs for waterfall. 8km from **Tibby Shiels Inn**
(refreshments! but not recommended for food). The lower track takes 10/15 minutes to a viewing place still 500m from falls; the higher, on the other side of the
Tail burn, threads between the austere hills and up to Loch Skene from which the
falls overflow (45/60 minutes). Then do the circular trail above you for an all-
round satisfying day in the Borders. Mountain goats scamper.

1598 **The Falls of Clyde** www.swt.org.uk · **New Lanark** Dramatic falls in a long
10/N27 gorge of the Clyde. New Lanark, the conservation village of Robert Owen the social
reformer, is signed from Lanark. It's hard to avoid the award-winning tourist
bazaar, but the riverbank has... a more natural appeal. The path to the power station is about 1km, but the route doesn't get interesting till after it, a 1km climb to
the first fall (Cora Linn) and another 1km to the next (Bonnington Linn). One of the
mills is now a hotel, which seems better than it was. The strange uniformity of
New Lanark is oddly poignant when the other tourists have gone home.

1599 **Reekie Linn** Alyth 8km north of town on back roads to Kirriemuir on B951
10/Q22 between Bridge of Craigisla and Bridge of Lintrathen. A picnic site and car park on
bend of road leads by 200m to the wooded gorge of Glen Isla with precipitous
viewpoints of defile where Isla is squeezed and falls in tiers to 100ft. Walk further
along the glen and look back.

1600 **Falls of Acharn** near Kenmore 5km along south side of Loch Tay on an
10/M22 unclassified road. Walk from just after the bridge going west in township of
Acharn; falls are signed. Steepish start then 1km up side of gorge; waterfalls on
other side. Can be circular route.

1601 **Falls of Rogie** www.ullapool.co.uk · near Strathpeffer Car park on A835
7/L17 Inverness-Ullapool road, 5km Contin/10km Strathpeffer. Accessibility makes short

walk (250m) quite popular to these hurtling falls on the Blackwater River. Bridge (built by the Territorial Army) and salmon ladder (they leap in summer). Woodland trails 1-3km marked, include a circular route to Contin (2034/WOODLAND WALKS).

1602 **Falls of Shin** www.fallsofshin.co.uk · near Lairg 6km east of town on signed
6/M15 road, car park and falls nearby are easily accessible. Not quite up to the splendours
☞ of others here, but one of the best places in Scotland to see Atlantic salmon battling upstream (May-Nov; best late summer). **Visitor centre** with extensive shop; the **café/restaurant** is excellent (1033/BEST RESTAURANTS) and there's an adventure playground and other reasons here to hang around in Sutherland.

The Lochs We Love

All those listed below are in L, LL and LLL settings, obviously.

1603 ✓✓ **Loch Maree** A832 between Kinlochewe and Gairloch. Dotted with
7/J16 islands covered in Scots Pine hiding some of the best examples of Viking graves and apparently a money tree in their midst. Easily viewed from the road which follows its length for 15km. Beinn Eighe rises behind you and the omniscient presence of Slioch is opposite. Aultroy Vistor Centre (5km Kinlochewe), fine walks from lochside car parks, among the largest original Scots Pine woodlands in the West Highlands. See 1762/WILDLIFE RESERVES.

1604 ✓✓ **Loch An Eilean** 4km Inverdruie off the Coylumbridge road from
7/N19 Aviemore. Car park and info board. An enchanted loch in the heart of the Rothiemurchus Forest (2023/WOODLAND WALKS for directions). You can walk right round the loch (5km, allow 1.5 hours). This is classic Highland scenery, a calendar landscape of magnificent Scots Pine. Very special.

1605 ✓ **Loch Arkaig** 25km Fort William. An enigmatic loch long renowned for its
7/J20 fishing. From the A82 beyond Spean Bridge (at the Commando Monument; 1856/MONUMENTS) cross the Caledonian Canal, then on by single-track road through the Clunes Forest and the Dark Mile past the Witches' Pool (a cauldron of dark water below cataracts) to the loch. Bonnie Prince Charlie came this way before and after Culloden; one of his refuge caves is marked on a trail.

1606 **Loch Achray** near Brig o' Turk The small loch at the centre of the Trossachs
10/L24 between **Loch Katrine** (on which SS *Sir Walter Scott* and smaller *Lady of the Lake* sail 4 times a day; the morning one stops at the end of the loch. 01877 376316) and **Loch Venachar**. The A821 from Callander skirts both Venachar and Achray. Many picnic spots and a new fishing centre and Harbour Café on the main road by Loch Venachar. Ben Venue and Ben An rise above: great walks (1953/HILLS) and views. A one-way forest road goes round the other side of Loch Achray through Achray Forest (enter and leave from the Duke's Pass road between Aberfoyle and Brig o' Turk). Trail details from forest visitor centre 3km north Aberfoyle. Bike hire at Loch Katrine (01877 376366), Callander or Aberfoyle – best way to see the lochs.

1607 **Glen Finglas Reservoir** Brig o' Turk And while we're on the subject of lochs
10/L24 in the Trossachs (see above) here's a great one to walk to. Although it's manmade it's a real beauty, surrounded by soft green hills and the odd burn bubbling in. Approach 'through' Brig o' Turk houses (past the caff) and park 2km up road, or from new car park 2km before Brig o' Turk from Callander. It's about 5km to the head of the loch and 18km on the Mell Trail round the hill or 12km to Balquhidder:

a walk across the heart of Scotland (2002/GLEN WALKS). Ranger board gives details. **The Byre** bar/bistro across the road in B of T for refreshment (1307/GASTROPUBS).

1608 **Loch Muick** near Ballater At head of road off B976, the South Dee road at
10/Q20 Ballater. 14km up Glen Muick (pronounced Mick) to the car park and visitor centre and 1km to the lochside. Lochnagar rises above (1984/MUNROS) and walk also begins here for Capel Mounth and Glen Clova (1582/GLENS). 3-hour walk around loch and any number of ambles. The lodge where Vic met John is at the furthest point (well, it would be). Open aspect with grazing deer and not too much forestry. (Ranger's office 01339 755059.)

1609 **Loch Eriboll** North Coast 90km west of Thurso. The long sea loch that indents
6/L13 into the North Coast for 15km and which you drive right round on main A838 (40 minutes). Deepest natural anchorage in the UK, exhibiting every aspect of lochside scenery including, alas, fish cages. Ben Hope stands near the head of the loch and there is a perfect beach (my own private Idaho) on the coast (1554/BEACHES). The people who have Mackay's in nearby Durness now have 2 luxury, high-spec eco lodges overlooking the loch at Laid (1184/LUXURIOUS ISOLATION). Walks from Hope.

1610 **Loch Trool** near Newton Stewart The small, celebrated loch in a bowl of the
11/L29 Galloway Hills reached via Bargrennan 14km north via A714 and 8km to end of road. Woodland visitor centre/café on the way. Get Galloway Forest Park brochure. Good walks but best viewed from Bruce's Stone (1925/MARY, CHARLIE & BOB) and the slopes of Merrick (1959/HILLS). An idyllic place.

1611 **Loch Ken** between Castle Douglas & New Galloway Loch Ken, it's been
11/M30 here a while, how could I have ignored it in all previous editions when so many times I've hurtled up both sides (it's long and thin). Maybe it was the perfect spring day and it shimmered and lots of people were boating and surfing and hanging out and it's clear that this is the loch of life here. Marina, holiday park and Galloway Activity Centre (2127/WATERSPORTS; coffee shop here) all thrive on its banks. Then there's New Galloway. Many trails (and deer) around. And the kites!

1612 **Loch Morar** near Mallaig 70km west of Fort William by A850 (a wildly scenic,
7/H20 much improved route). Morar village is 6km from Mallaig and a single-track road leads from the coast to the loch (only 500m but out of sight) then along it for 5km to Bracora. It's the prettiest part with wooded islets, small beaches, lochside meadows and bobbing boats. The road stops at a turning place but a track continues from Bracorina to Tarbet and it's possible to connect with a boat and sail back to Mallaig on Loch Nevis (check tourist information centre). Boat hire on the loch itself from Ewan MacDonald (01687 462520). Loch Morar, joined to the coast by the shortest river in Britain, also has the deepest water. There is a spookiness about it and just possibly a monster called Morag. www.road-to-the-isles.org.uk

1613 **Loch Tummel** near Pitlochry West from Pitlochry on B8019 to Rannoch (and
10/N22 the end of the road), Loch Tummel comes into view, as it did for Queen Victoria, scintillating beneath you, and on a clear day with Schiehallion beyond (1647/VIEWS). This north side has good walks (2031/WOODLAND WALKS), but the south road from Faskally just outside Pitlochry is the one to take to get down to the lochside to picnic, etc.

Loch Lomond The biggest, not the bonniest (1/BIG ATTRACTIONS) with major visitor centre and retail experience, **Lomond Shores**, at south end near Balloch.

Loch Ness The longest; you haven't heard the last of it (3/BIG ATTRACTIONS).

The Scenic Routes

All those listed below are in L, LL and LLL settings, obviously

1614
9/J21
NTS
ATMOS

✓ ✓ ✓ **Glencoe** www.glencoe-nts.org.uk The A82 from Crianlarich to Ballachulish is a fine drive, but from the extraterrestrial Loch Ba onwards, there can be few roads anywhere that have direct contact with such imposing scenery. After Kingshouse and Buachaille Etive Mor on the left, the mountains and ridges rising on either side of Glencoe proper invoke the correct usage of the word 'awesome'. The new visitor centre sets the topographical and historical scene. (1256/ BLOODY GOOD PUBS; 1996/SERIOUS WALKS; 1912/BATTLE-GROUNDS; 1938/ENCHANTING PLACES; 1133/HOSTELS.)

1615
7/H19

✓ ✓ **Shiel Bridge-Glenelg** The switchback road that climbs from the A87 (Fort William 96km) at Shiel Bridge over the hill and down to the coast opposite the Sleat Peninsula in Skye (short ferry to Kylerhea). As you climb you're almost as high as the surrounding summits and there's the classic view across Loch Duich to the 5 Sisters of Kintail. Coming back you think you're going straight into the loch! It's really worth driving to Glenelg (1828/PREHISTORIC SITES, 1192/CAMPING, 1145/INNS) and beyond to Arnisdale and ethereal Loch Hourn (16km).

1616
7/H18

✓ ✓ **Applecross** www.applecross.uk.com · 120km from Inverness. From Tornapress near Lochcarron for 18km. Leaving the A896 seems like leaving civilisation; the winding ribbon heads into monstrous mountains and the high plateau at the top is another planet. It's not for the faint hearted and Applecross is a relief to arrive in with its campsite/coffee shop and the faraway, almost legendary **Applecross Inn** (1169/GET-AWAY HOTELS). Also see 1398/COFFEE SHOPS, 1195/1199/CAMPING. This awesome road rises 2,000 feet in 6 miles. See how they built it at the **Applecross Heritage Centre** (2149/HERITAGE).

1617
7/J17

✓ ✓ **Glen Torridon** A896 between Torridon and Diabaig with staggering views along the route of the 3 mighty Torridon mountains: Beinn Eighe, Liathach and Beinn Alligin. If you want to climb them, there are various starts along this road – enquire and all other information at the NTS Countryside Centre at the Diabaig turnoff. Excellent two-tier accommodation at **The Torridon** (1161/GET-AWAY HOTELS) and a SYHA tents-only campsite adjacent the Centre. There is much to climb and clamber over here; or merely be amazed. See also 1635/VIEWS.

1618
6/J14

✓ ✓ **Lochinver-Drumbeg-Kylestrome** The coast road north from Lochinver (35km) is marvellous, essential Assynt. Actually best travelled north-south so that you leave the splendid vista of Eddrachilles Bay and pass through lochan, moor and even woodland, touching the coast again by sandy beaches (at Stoer a road leads 7km to the lighthouse and the walk to the Old Man of Stoer, 2052/COASTAL WALKS) past the wonderful Secret Beach (1566/BEACHES) and approach Lochinver (possible detour to Auchmelvich and beaches) with a classic long view of Suilven. Take tea 'n' cake at the teagarden at **Soap 'n' Candles** in Drumbeg. Or stock up at the remarkable **Drumbeg Stores** (2201/SPECIAL SHOPPING). And there's now a brilliant restaurant with rooms at **Drumbeg House** (977/HIGHLAND HOTELS). Or get your pies in Lochinver (1030/LESS EXPENSIVE HIGHLAND HOTELS).

1619
6/J14

✓ **Lochinver-Achiltibuie** And south from Lochinver Achiltibuie is 40km from Ullapool; so this is the route from the north; 28km of winding road/unwinding Highland scenery; through glens, mountains and silver sea. Known locally as the 'wee mad road' (it is maddening if you're in a hurry). Passes

Achin's Bookshop (2203/SHOPPING), the path to Kirkaig Falls and the mighty Suilven. Near Achiltibuie is one of Scotland's most uplifting views (1638/VIEWS).

1620
9/J26

✓ **Rothesay-Tighnabruaich** A886/A8003. The most celebrated part of this route is the latter, the A8003 down the side of Loch Riddon to Tighnabruaich along the hill sides with the breathtaking views of Bute and the Kyles (can be a lot of vegetation in summer – one good layby/viewpoint) but the whole way, with its diverse aspects of lochside, riverine and rocky scenery, is supernatural. Includes short crossing between Rhubodach and Colintraive. Great hotel/restaurants at Tighnabruaich (727/ARGYLL HOTELS) and Kames (1143/SEASIDE INNS).

1621
5/E16
ATMOS

✓ **The Golden Road** South Harris The main road in Harris follows the west coast, notable for bays and beaches (1561/BEACHES). This is the other, winding round a series of coves and inlets with offshore skerries and a treeless, rocky hinterland: classic Hebridean landscape, especially Finsbay. **Skoon Art Café** nearby (2305/HEBRIDES). Tweed is woven; visit the crofts and 2 shops (2213/TWEED).

1622
7/G19

Sleat Peninsula Skye The unclassified road off the A851 (main Sleat road) especially coming from south, ie take road at Ostaig near Gaelic College (great place to stay nearby: 2271/SKYE); it meets the coast after 9km. Affords rare views of the Cuillins from a craggy coast. Returning to 'main' road south of Isleornsay, pop into the great hotel pub there (2261/SKYE HOTELS).

1623
10/R27

Leaderfoot-Clintmains near St Boswells The B6356 between the A68 (look out for Leaderfoot viaduct and signs for Dryburgh) and the B6404 Kelso-St Boswells road. This small road, busy in summer, links Scott's View and Dryburgh Abbey (1906/ABBEYS; find by following abbey signs) and Smailholm Tower, and passes through classic Border/Tweedside scenery. 500m walk to the Wallace Statue is signed. Don't miss Irvine's View if you want to see the best of the Borders (1636/VIEWS). Nice guest house (796/BORDER HOTELS).

1624
10/P20

Braemar-Linn Of Dee 12km of renowned Highland river scenery along the upper valley of the (Royal) Dee. The Linn (rapids) is at the end of the road and the mighty Dee is squeezed until it is no more than 1m wide, but there are river walks and the start of the great Glen Tilt walk to Blair Atholl (2000/GLEN WALKS). Deer abound. The whole road between Ballater and Braemar is fit for a queen and all.

1625
8/Q20

Ballater-Tomintoul The ski road to the Lecht, the A939 which leaves the Royal Deeside road (A93) west of Ballater before it gets really royal. A ribbon of road in the bare Grampians (though starts woody), past the sentinel ruin Corgarff (open to view, 250m walk) and the valley of the trickling Don. Road proceeds seriously uphill and main viewpoints are south of the Lecht. There is just nobody for miles. Walks in Glenlivet estates south of Tomintoul. Nearest good food stop at **Glenkindie Arms** 5km east of Strathdon (1287/GASTROPUBS).

1626
7/L19

Fort Augustus-Dores near Inverness The B862 often single-track road that follows and latterly skirts Loch Ness. Quieter and more interesting than the main west bank A82. Starts in rugged country and follows the straight road built by Wade to tame the Highlands. Reaches the lochside at Foyers and goes all the way to Dores (15km from Inverness) where the music festival, **RockNess**, is held in June (33/EVENTS) and where there's a great and popular pub for grub, the **Dores Inn** (01463 751203). Paths to the shore of the loch. Fabulous untrodden woodlands near Errogie (marked) and the spooky graveyard adjacent Boleskin House where Aleister Crowley did his dark magic and Jimmy Page of Led Zeppelin may have done his. 35km total; worth taking slowly. Great start/finish is the

Boathouse café at the Highland Club at Fort Augustus right at the southern tip of the loch (lunch and dinner in season); 01320 366682.

1627 **The Duke's Pass, Aberfoyle–Brig o' Turk** Of the many roads through the
10/L24 Trossachs, this one is spectacular though gets busy; numerous possibilities for
stopping, exploration and great views. Good viewpoint 4km from Loch Achray
Hotel, above road and lay-by. One-way forest road goes round Loch Achray and 2
other lochs (Drunkie and Vennacher). Good hill walking starts (1953/1954/1955/
FAVOURITE HILLS) and Loch Katrine regular daily sailings (2km) Apr-Oct (01877
376316). Bike hire at Loch Katrine (01877 376366), Aberfoyle and Callander.

1628 **Glenfinnan–Mallaig** www.road-to-the-isles.org.uk The A830, aka the Road
9/J20 to the Isles. Through some of the most impressive and romantic landscapes in the
Highlands, splendid in any weather (it does rain a bit) to the coast at the Sands of
Morar (1573/BEACHES). This is deepest Bonnie Prince Charlie country (1924/MARY,
CHARLIE & BOB) and demonstrates what a misty eye he had for magnificent set-
tings. A full-throttle bikers' dream. The road is shadowed by the West Highland
Railway, an even better way to enjoy the scenery (5/FAVOURITE JOURNEYS).

1629 **Lochailort–Acharacle** Off from the A830 above at Lochailort and turning south
9/H21 on the A861, the coastal section of this great scenery is superb especially in the
setting sun, or in May when the rhodies are out. **Glenuig Inn** is a very green and
greatly improved pub to stop over and eat (1141/INNS). This is the road to the
Castle Tioram shoreline, which should not be missed (1793/RUINS); and glorious
Ardnamurchan.

1630 **Knapdale: Lochgilphead–Tarbert** B8024 off the main A83 follows the coast
9/H25 for most of its route. Views to Jura are immense (and on a clear day, Ireland). Not
much happens here but in the middle in exactly the right place is the superb
Kilberry Inn (1139/INNS, 1277/GASTROPUBS). Take it easy on this very Scottish
35km of single track. Short walk to the Coves 3km before Kilberry. 69/DISCOVER.

1631 **Amulree–Kenmore** Unclassified single-track and very narrow road from the
10/N22 hill-country hamlet of Amulree to cosy Kenmore signed Glen Quaich. Past Loch
Freuchie, a steep climb takes you to a plateau ringed by magnificent (far)
mountains to Loch Tay. Steep descent to Loch Tay and Kenmore. You may have to
open and close the gates.

1632 **Muthill–Comrie** Pure Perthshire. A route which takes you through some of the
10/N23 best scenery in central Scotland and ends up (best this way round) in Comrie with
bar/restaurants and other pleasures (855/876/PERTHSHIRE HOTELS & RESTAURANTS,
1665/WILD SWIMMING). Leave Muthill and the **Barley Bree** (1138/ROADSIDE INNS)
by Crieff road turning left (2km) into **Drummond Castle** grounds up a glorious
avenue of beech trees (gate open 1-5pm). Visit garden (1496/GARDENS); continue
through estate. At gate, go right, following signs for Strowan. First junction, go left
following signs (4km). At T-junction, go left to Comrie (7km). Best have a map or
satnav, but if not, who cares? It's all bonny!

1633 **The Heads of Ayr** The coast road south from Ayr to Culzean (1773/CASTLES) and
9/K28 Turnberry (745/AYRSHIRE HOTELS) includes these headlands, great views of Ailsa
Craig and Arran and some horrible caravan parks. The Electric Brae south of
Dunure village is famously worth stopping on (your car runs the opposite way to
the slope) and the **Dunure Inn** itself is a great food stop in a lovely harbourside
setting (1301/GASTROPUBS). Culzean grounds are simply gorgeous.

The Classic Views

For views of and around Edinburgh and Glasgow see p. 86 and p. 127-28.
No views from hill or mountain tops are included here.

1634
7/G17

✓ ✓ ✓ **The Quirang** Skye Best approach is from Uig direction taking the right-hand unclassified road off the hairpin of the A855 above and 2km from town signed Staffin via Quirang (more usual approach from Staffin side is less of a revelation). View (and walk) from car park, the massive rock formations of a towering, contorted ridge. Solidified lava heaved and eroded into fantastic pinnacles. Fine views also across Staffin Bay to Wester Ross. (2254/ISLAND WALKS.)

1635
7/J16

✓ ✓ ✓ The views of **An Teallach** and **Liathach** An Teallach, that great favourite of Scottish hill walkers (40km south of Ullapool by the A835/A832), is best viewed from the side of Little Loch Broom or the A832 just before you get to Dundonnell (1402/TEAROOMS).
The classic view of the other great Torridon mountains (**Beinn Eighe**, pronounced Ben A, and **Liathach** together, 100km south by road from Ullapool) in Glen Torridon (1617/SCENIC ROUTES) 4km from Kinlochewe. This viewpoint is not marked but it's on the track around Loch Clair which is reached from the entrance to the Coulin estate off the A896, Glen Torridon road (be aware of stalking). Park outside gate; no cars allowed, 1km walk to lochside. These mountains have to be seen to be believed.

1636
10/R27

✓ ✓ **Irvine's View** St Boswells The full panorama from the Cheviots to the Lammermuirs. This the finest view in southern Scotland. It's only a furlong further than Scott's View, below: cross the road from Scott's View layby through the kissing gate, veering left uphill across rough pasture till you reach the double track. Head up till the track divides and take the right, lesser path. You'll see the fallen standing stone where I would like my bench. The telecoms masts aren't pleasant but turn your back on them and gaze across the beautiful Borders to another country... you know, England.

1637
7/G18
2-B-2

✓ ✓ From **Raasay** www.raasay.com There are several fabulous views looking over to Skye from Raasay, the small island reached by ferry from Sconser (2228/MAGICAL ISLANDS). The panorama from Dun Caan, the hill in the centre of the island (444m) is of Munro proportions, producing an elation incommensurate with the small effort required to get there. Start from the road to the North End or ask at the hotel in Inverarish (or at the rebuilt Raasay House, reopening 2013 – great view from the lawn).

1638
6/J15

✓ ✓ **The Summer Isles** www.summer-isles.com · Achiltibuie The Summer Isles are a scattering of islands seen from the coast of Achiltibuie, the lounge of the **Summer Isles Hotel** (979/HIGHLANDS HOTELS), the terrace of the **An Fuaran Bar** (1288/GASTROPUBS) and visited by boat from Ullapool. But the best place to see them and the stunning perspective of this western shore is on that road to Altandhu (has other spellings). Best approach is: from Achiltibuie, veer left through Polbain, past Polbain Stores, on and through Allandhu, past turning for Reiff and Blairbuie, then 500m ascending inland. There's a bench and a new path (sign for Viewpoint) 50m to little plateau with many cairns and this one of the ethereal views of Scotland. On this same road 500m round the corner, the distant mountains of Assynt all in a row: 2 jawdropping perspectives of the Highlands in 5 minutes.

1639   ✓ ✓   **The Rest and Be Thankful**   On A83 Loch Lomond-Inveraray road
9/K24   where it's met by the B828 from Lochgoilhead. In summer the rest may
be from driving stress and you may not be thankful for the camera-toting masses,
but this was always one of the most accessible, rewarding viewpoints in the land.
Surprisingly, none of the encompassing hills are Munros but they are nonetheless
dramatic. Only a few carpets of conifer to smother the grandeur of the crags as
you look down the valley.

1640   ✓   **Califer** near Forres   7km from Forres on A96 to Elgin, turn right signed for
8/P17   Pluscarden, follow this road for 5km back towards Forres. You are unaware
how high above the coastal plain you are and the layby is discreetly located. When
you walk across a small park with young memorial trees you are rewarded with a
truly remarkable sight – down across Findhorn Bay and the wide vista of the Moray
Firth to the Black Isle and Ben Wyvis. There is often fantastic light on this coast.

1641   ✓   **Elgol** Skye   End of the road, the B8083, 22km from Broadford. The classic
7/G19   view of the Cuillin from across Loch Scavaig and of Soay and Rum. Cruises
(Apr-Oct) in the *Bella Jane* (0800 731 3089) or *The Misty Isle* (Apr-Oct, not Sun
01471 866288) to the famous corrie of Loch Coruisk, painted by Turner,
romanticised by Walter Scott. A journey you'll remember. There are great Cuillin
views also from the **Glenbrittle Rd**.

1642   **Camas Nan Geall** Ardnamurchan   12km Salen on B8007. 4km from
9/G21   Ardnamurchan's Natural History Centre (1703/KIDS) 65km Fort William. Coming
especially from the Kilchoan direction, a magnificent bay appears below you,
where the road first meets the sea. Almost symmetrical with high cliffs and a
perfect field (still cultivated) in the bowl fringed by a shingle beach. Car park viewpoint and there is a path down. Amazing Ardnamurchan!

1643   **Glengarry** www.glengarry.net   3km after Tomdoun turnoff on A87, Invergarry-
7/K20   Kyle of Lochalsh road. Layby with viewfinder. An uncluttered vista up and down
loch and glen with not a house in sight (pity about the salmon cages). Distant
peaks of Knoydart are identified, but not Loch Quoich nestling spookily and full of
fish in the wilderness at the head of the glen. Gaelic mouthfuls of mountains on
the board. Bonnie Prince Charlie passed this way. Great hotel at **Invergarry** (1001/
HIGHLAND HOTELS) and by the lochside (1172/GET-AWAY HOTELS) at **Tomdoun**.

1644   **Scott's View** St Boswells   Off A68 at Leaderfoot Bridge near St Boswells,
7/R27   signed Gattonside. The View, old Walter's favourite (the horses still stopped there
long after he'd gone), is 4km along the road (Dryburgh Abbey 3km further;
1906/ABBEYS). Magnificent sweep of his beloved Border country, but only in one
direction. If you cross the road and go through the kissing gate you're on the
approach to **Irvine's View** (see above... and beyond).

1645   **Peniel Heugh** near Ancrum   On the subject of great views in the Borders, look
10/R27   no further than this – the Borders sentinel. Report: 1850/BEST MONUMENTS.

1646   **The Law** Dundee   Few cities have such a single good viewpoint. To north of the
10/Q23   centre, it reveals the panoramic perspective of the city on the estuary of the silvery
Tay. Route to Law Rd not easy to follow but walk from town or satnav/Google.

1647   **Queen's View** Loch Tummel near Pitlochry   8km on B8019 to Kinloch
10/N22   Rannoch. Car park and 100m walk to rocky knoll where pioneers of tourism Queen
Victoria and Prince Albert were 'transported into ecstasies' by view of Loch
Tummel and Schiehallion (1613/LOCHS; 2031/WOODLAND WALKS). Their view was

flooded by a hydro scheme after World War II; more recently it spawned a whole view-driven visitor experience. Well, it... makes you wonder!

1648 **The Rallying Place of the Maclarens** Balquhidder Short climb from
10/L23 behind the church (1897/GRAVEYARDS) along the track 150m then signed Creag an Turc, steep at first. Superb view down Loch Voil, the Balquhidder Braes and the real Rob Roy Country and top caff **The Library** with home baking on your descent (1378/COFFEE SHOPS) by the Monachyle Mhor people (where you could treat your-self and stay; 1160/GET-AWAY HOTELS).

1649 **The Malcolm Memorial** Langholm 3km from Langholm and signed from
11/Q29 main A7, a single-track road leads to a path to this obelisk raised to celebrate the military and masonic achievements of one John Malcolm (d. 1833). The eulogy is fulsome especially compared with that for Hugh MacDiarmid on the cairn by the stunning sculpture at the start of the path (1860/MEMORIALS). Views from the obelisk, however, are among the finest in the south, encompassing a vista from the Lakeland Fells and the Solway Firth to the wild Border hills. Path 1km.

1650 **Duncryne Hill** Gartocharn Gartocharn is between Balloch and Drymen on the
9/L25 A811 and this view was recommended by writer and outdoorsman Tom Weir as 'the finest viewpoint of any small hill in Scotland'. Turn up Duncryne road at the east end of village and park 1km on left by a small wood (a sign reads Woods Reserved for Teddy Bears). The hill is only 470ft high and easy, but the view of Loch Lomond and the Kilpatrick Hills is superb.

1651 **Tongue** From the causeway across the kyle, or better, follow the minor road to
6/M13 **Melness Talmine** (and the **Craggan Hotel** – not listed but I hear, excellent) on the west side, look south to Ben Loyal or north to the small islands.

1652 **Cairnpapple Hill** near Linlithgow Volcanic geology, neolithic henge, east of
10/N25 Scottish agriculture, the Forth plain, the bridges, Grangemouth industrial complex and telecoms masts: not all pretty, but the whole of Scotland at a glance. For directions see 1820/PREHISTORIC SITES.

1653 **Castle Stalker View** Portnacroish Near Port Appin on main A828 Oban-Fort
9/J22 William road. On right going south, the view has been commandeered by the **CSV Café** (1391/TEASHOPS) which ain't bad (closed in evenings) but viewpoint can be accessed at all times 50m away from car park. Always impressive, in certain lights the vista of Port Appin, the castle in the fore and Loch Linnhe, is ethereal. There are ecopods here if you want to stay (1215/GLAMPING).

1654 **Carter Bar** English Border near Jedburgh On the A68 Edinburgh-Newcastle
10/R28 road, the last and first view in Scotland just happens to be superb. The Border hill country spread out before you for many long miles. The tear in my eye is not because of the wind, but because this was the landscape of my youth and where I spent my lightsome days.

1655 **Dunnett Head** between Thurso & John o' Groats Didn't have in *StB* before
6/P12 but for this edition (and like so many) I felt I had to go again. Much more natural than Jo'G and it is the most northerly part of the British mainland. Part of exten-sive RSPB reserve, there are happily more birds than sightseers. View to island of Stoma, Hoy and Orkney Mainland; and those cliffs. **Tea Cosy** (1403/TEAROOMS), walk (2060/COASTAL WALKS), **Mary-Ann's Cottage** (2153/HERITAGE) and the vener-able **Castle of Mey** (1775/CASTLES) are all on or just off the A836 which takes you here.

FROM THE TOP: April 2011 – leaving Edinburgh's New Town for all the other towns and the countrysides of Scotland. Discovering Glasgow's spectacular new Riverside Museum – world class (673/GLASGOW ATTRACTIONS). The rise of the cupcake – by 2011, they were everywhere; these at Cup in Glasgow's Byres Road (593/TEASHOPS). The estimable John MacCallum, champion of crustaceans, by his tanks in Troon (1318/SEAFOOD RESTAURANTS, 1337/FISH AND CHIPS).

FROM THE TOP: Start of the Southern Upland way, Portpatrick. Didn't go very far – 100m (1989/LONG WALKS). The perfect ruin with its moat in the south, southwest; the light is also good (1791/INTERESTING RUINS). As always, and unlike anywhere else summer '11, it wasn't raining on Iona (2230/ISLANDS). John and Carla outside their faraway and fabulous restaurant, Ninth Wave, a long way from Tobermory (2306/MULL).

FROM THE TOP: In the rose garden of my ancestral home, Drum Castle near Banchory, drookit roses around me (1510/GARDENS). Not a great photo, but it's hard to find anyway – the evocative ruin of Findlater Castle near the always Sunnyside Beach (1797/INTERESTING RUINS). Susan Watson in her exemplary emporium, Hammerton Stores, in Aberdeen (2198/SPECIAL SHOPS). No, this isn't a pond, it's a flooded lawn at elegant Culloden House Hotel, the grounds still beautiful (973/HIGHLAND HOTELS).

FROM THE TOP: The plucky ferry that plies
between Islay and Jura, or tries to ply
(it tried several times to berth in a
choppy sea in July); great to be stuck on
Jura though (2304/ISLANDS). The calendar
photo of the calendar island town but
Tobermory always brilliant (2306/MULL).
Lizzie Wilder and Rich, outside their
caff on first visit to Tanera Mor,
their own Summer Isle (2240/ISLANDS).
A chessman in the far, far west of Lewis
and a track to an amazing beach and
sunset (1562/BEACHES).

CLOCKWISE FROM TOP:
Over the sea to Skye
and all that; and one of
the best food trails in
Scotland. The fantastic
Fairy Glen near Uig,
Skye, still light one
late summer's eve (1942/
ENCHANTING PLACES). Could
be the Riviera, but it's
Plockton, palms in a
blue sky (1542/COASTAL
VILLAGES). Scarecrows on
the roadsides, the bus
shelters, hanging off the
trees, near Glen Brittle.
What's that about?

FROM THE TOP: Magnificent, extraterrestrial
Scotland: Glencoe (1614/SCENIC ROUTES).
No monster but there's lots going on around
here that's worth searching for (3/LOCHS).
Monument to the Commandos and the newer
commemorative garden to soldiers in the wars
that still go on; poignant. The Old Pines is
nearby (1856/MONUMENTS, 1000/HIGHLAND HOTELS).

CLOCKWISE FROM TOP: Pristine order, in wonderfully lush Perthshire, from the terrace of Drummond Castle (1496/GARDENS). It's one exciting place after another... Back in the Royal Mile, home in a way (404/EDINBURGH ATTRACTIONS).

FROM THE TOP: The fountain in the gardens in my
city, none of which I ever get tired of (1528/PARKS).
Roslyn Chapel, fully re-emerged 2011, contemplation
here (when the crowds have gone) and in the glen below
(1846/CHURCHES, 432/WALKS). Book finished, off the road
and up Calton Hill to start Hogmanay (68/EVENTS).

The Great Wild Swimming Holes

Take care when swimming in rivers; don't take them for granted. Kids should be watched. Most of these places are traditional local swimming and picnic spots where people have swum for years but rivers continuously change their course and their nature. Wearing sandals or old sports shoes is a good idea.

1656
7/G19
✓ ✓ **The Fairy Pools** Glen Brittle, Skye On that rare hot day, this is one of the best places on Skye to go; swimming in several clear, deep pools with the massif of the Cuillins around you. One pool has a stone bridge you swim under. Head off A863 Dunvegan road from Sligachan Hotel then B8009 and Glenbrittle road. 7km down just as road begins to parallel the glen itself, you'll see a river coming off the hills. Park in layby on right. 1-2km walk. Swim with the fairies!

1657
9/K22
✓ ✓ **The Pools in Glen Etive** Glen Etive is a wild, enchanted place where people have been camping for years to walk and climb in Glencoe area. There are many grassy landings at the river side as well as these perfect pools for bathing. The first is about 5km from the main road, the A82 at Kingshouse, but just follow the river and find your own. Take midge cream for evening wear. Lots.

1658
7/N19
✓ ✓ **Feshiebridge** At the bridge itself on the B970 between Kingussie and Inverdruie near Aviemore. 4km from Kincraig. Great walks here into Glen Feshie and in nearby woodland; under bridge a perfect spot for Highland swimming. Go down to left from south. Rocky ledges, clear water. One of the best but cold even in high summer. Further pools nearb and a sculpture trail.

1659
10/P22
✓ ✓ **Rumbling Bridge & The Braan Walk** near Dunkeld Excellent stretch of cascading river with pools, rocky banks and ledges. Just off A9 heading north opposite first turning for Dunkeld, the A822 for Aberfeldy, Amulree (signed Crieff/Crianlarich). Car park on right after 4km. Connects with forest paths (the Braan Walk) to the Hermitage (2028/WOODLAND WALKS) – 2km. Fab picnic and swimming spot though take great care. This is the nearest Highland-type river to Edinburgh (about 1 hour).

1660
7/M20
ATMOS
✓ ✓ **Strathmashie** www.strathmashie.co.uk · near Newtonmore On A86 Newtonmore-Dalwhinnie (on A9) to Fort William road 7km from Laggan, watch for Forest sign. Car parks on either side of the road; the Druim an Aird car park has finder boards. Great swimming spot, but often campers. Viewpoints, waterfall, pines. If people are here and you want privacy, there are great forest walks and follow the river; there are many other great pools. **Laggan Coffeeshop** with home baking and pizza 5km towards the A9 (1386/TEAROOMS).

1661
9/K23
ATMOS
✓ ✓ **Rob Roy's Bathtub** The Falloch Falls, near Inverarnan A82 north of Ardlui and 3 km past the Drover's Inn (1253/BLOODY GOOD PUBS). Sign on the right (Picnic Area) going north. Park, then follow the path. Some pools on the rocky river course but 500m from car park you reach the main falls and below a perfect round natural pool 30m across. There's an overhanging rock face on one side and smooth slabs at the edge of the falls. Natural suntrap in summer (if there is a summer), but the water is Baltic at all times.

1662
10/Q27
✓ **Neidpath** Peebles 2km from town on A72, Biggar road; sign for castle. Park by Hay Lodge Park and walk upriver or down the track to the castle (now closed) or the layby 100m beyond. Idyllic setting of a broad meander of the Tweed, with medieval Neidpath Castle, a sentinel above. Two pools (3m deep in average summer) linked by shallow rapids which the adventurous chute down on their

backs. Usually a rope-swing on the oak tree at the upper pool. Also see (2012/ GLEN & RIVER WALKS). TAKE CARE.

1663 ✓ **Randolph's Leap** near Forres Spectacular gorge on the mythical
8/N17 Findhorn which carves out some craggy scenery on its way to a gentle coast. This no-longer secret glade and fabulous swimming hole are behind a wall on a bend of the B9007 (see 2020/WOODLAND WALKS for directions) south of Forres and Nairn and near **Logie Steading**, a courtyard of good things (a board there maps out walks) and refreshment (1396/TEAROOMS). One Randolph or Alistair as the new tale tells, may have leapt here; we just bathe and picnic under the trees.

1664 **Dog Falls** Glen Affric Half-way along Glen Affric road from Cannich before you
7/K18 come to the loch, a well-marked picnic spot and great place to swim in the peaty waters surrounded by the Caledonian Forest (with trails). Birds well sussed to picnic potential – your car covered in tits and cheeky chaffinches – Hitchcock or what? (2001/GLEN & RIVER WALKS). Falls (rapids really) to the left.

1665 **Near Comrie** www.comrie.org.uk 2 great pools of different character near
10/M23 the neat little town in deepest Perthshire. **The Linn**, the town pool: go over humpback bridge from main A85 west to Lochearnhead, signed The Ross. Take left fork then after 2km there's a parking place on left. River's relatively wide, very pleasant spot. For more adventurous, **Glenartney**, known locally as The Cliffs: go over bridge, the Braco road after 3km signed Glenartney, past Cultybraggan training camp (no longer in use) and then MoD range on left just before the end-of-the-road sign (200m after boarded-up cottage on right, 5km from Comrie). Park and walk down to river in glen. What with the twin perils of the Army and the Comrie Angling Club, you might feel you have no right to be here, but you do and this stretch of river is marvellous. Respect the farmland. Follow the road further for more great picnic spots. Comrie has a great pub/hotel bistro (855/PERTHSHIRE HOTELS) and the Deil's Cauldron (876/PERTHSHIRE RESTAURANTS).

1666 **Greeto Falls** Gogo Glen, Largs Well known locally so ask to find Flatt Rd. At
9/K26 top there's a car park and you follow the beautiful Gogo Glen path, past Cock-ma-lane Cottage. Superb views of the Clyde. 3 pools to choose from in the Gogo Burn near the bridge. You can also start from the main road near the ferry.

1667 **North Sannox Burn** Arran Park at the North Sannox Bridge on the A841 (road
9/J27 from Lochranza to Sannox Bay) and follow the track west to the deer fence and tree line (1km). Just past there you will find a great pool with small waterfall, dragonflies and perhaps even an eagle or two wheeling above.

1668 **Swimmers' Quarry** Easdale Cross to Easdale on the wee boat (5-minute con-
9/H23 tinuous service); see 2146/HISTORY for details. Do visit the museum but go beyond scattered houses following paths to slate quarries full of seawater since 1881 with clear water like an enormous boutique hotel swimming pool. The L-shaped one with its little bench is easiest; the water can be blue like the Aegean.

1669 **Falls of Bruar** near Blair Atholl Just off A9, 12km north of Blair Atholl. 250m
10/N21 walk from **House of Bruar** car park and shopping experience (2199/SHOPPING) to lower fall (1590/WATERFALLS) where there is an accessible large deep pool by the bridge. Cold, fresh mountain water in a woody gorge. The proximity of the retail experience can make it all the more... naturally exhilarating.

1670 **The Scout Pool & The Bracklinn Falls** Callander The latter are a Callander
10/M24 must-see, easy-to-find (signposted from south end of Main St, up hill to golf
course then next car park up on right – from there it's a 2km walk). The Scout Pool
is a traditional swimming hole on same river, the fabulously named Keltie Water,
so a summer thing only. Follow road further alim from Bracklinn car park till road
goes on through iron gate. Park on right. Downhill 150m cross wooden bridge then
follow river path to right 250m. Access to huge pool dammed by giant boulders. A
beautiful secret spot in the woods. (Thanks to Susan Parr.)

1671 **The Otter's Pool** New Galloway Forest A clearing in the forest reached by a
11/L30 track, the Raider's Road, running from 8km north of Laurieston on the A762, for
16km to Clatteringshaws Loch. The track is only open April to October and gets
busy. It follows the Water of Dee and halfway down the road – the Otter's Pool. A
bronze otter used to mark the spot (it got nicked) and it's a place mainly for kids
and paddling; but when the dam runs off it can be deep enough to swim. Road
closes dusk. 2032/WOODLAND WALKS.

1672 **Ancrum** www.ancrum.com A secret place on the quiet Ale Water (out of vil-
10/R27 lage towards Lilliesleaf, 3km out 250m from farm sign to Hopton – a recessed gate
on the right before a bend and a rough track that locals know). A buttercup
meadow, a Border burn, a surprisingly deep pool to swim. Go to left of rough vegetation in defile, going downhill follow fence on your right. Cross further gate at
bottom (only 100m from road). Arcadia awaits beyond the meadow.

1673 **Paradise** Sheriffmuir, near Dunblane A pool at the foot of an unexpected
10/N24 leafy gorge on the moor between the Ochils and Strathallan. Here the Wharry
Burn is known locally as 'Paradise'. Take road from 'behind' Dunblane or Bridge of
Allan to the Sheriffmuir Inn (ok-ish!); head downhill (back) towards B of A. Park
1km after hump-back bridge. Head for the pylon nearest the river and you'll find
the pool. Only midges (or rain) will infiltrate your paradise.

1674 **Potarch Bridge & Cambus o' May** on The Dee 2 places: the first by the
8/Q20 reconstructed Victorian bridge (and near the hotel) 3km east of Kincardine O'Neill.
Cambus another stretch of river east of Ballater (6km). Locals swim, picnic on
rocks, etc, and there are forest walks on the other side of road. The brave jump off
the bridge at Cambus (in wetsuits). Great tearooms nearby: the Black Faced Sheep
in Aboyne (1375/TEAROOMS) and the Finzean (1455/FARMSHOPS).

1675 **Invermoriston** www.invermoriston.org On main Loch Ness road A82
7/L19 between Inverness and Fort Augustus, this is the best bit. River Moriston tumbles
under an ancient bridge. Perfectly Highland. Ledges for picnics, invigorating pools,
ozone-friendly. Nice beech woods. Follow signs for Columba's Well, go under the
bridge to the wee house. Good tavern nearby (1159/INNS).

1676 **Dulsie Bridge** near Nairn 16km south of Nairn on the A939 to Grantown, this
8/N18 locally revered beauty spot is fabulous for summer swimming (when there is a
summer). The ancient arched bridge spans the rocky gorge of the Findhorn (see
Randolph's Leap, above) and there are ledges and even sandy beaches for picnics
and from which to launch yourself or paddle into the peaty waters.

Strathcarron near Bonar Bridge Pick your spot (1581/GLENS).

Good Places To Take Kids

CENTRAL

1677
1/XA4
✓ ✓ ✓ **Edinburgh Zoo** www.edinburghzoo.org.uk · 0131 334 9171 · **Corstorphine Road, Edinburgh** 4km west of Princes St. A large and long-established zoo which is always evolving and where the natural world from the poles to the plains of Africa is ranged around Corstorphine Hill. Enough huge/exotic/ghastly creatures and friendly, amusing ones to fill an overstimulated day. The Budongo Trail chimp enclosure is first class. The penguins do their famous parade at 2.15pm. The beavers are brill, the koalas are cool as... and coming over the hill at TGP, the pandas. Shop stocked with PC toys and souvenirs. Café. Open all year 7 days, Apr-Sep 9am-6pm, Oct-Mar till 5pm, Nov-Feb till 4.30pm.

✓ ✓ ✓ **Riverside Museum** Glasgow · **Museum of Scotland** Edinburgh World-class and fun and awe. Reports 673/GLASGOW ATTRACTIONS, 400/EDINBURGH ATTRACTIONS.

✓ ✓ **Our Dynamic Earth** 0131 550 7800 · **Holyrood Road, Edinburgh** Edinburgh's major kids' attraction. Report 406/MAIN ATTRACTIONS.

✓ ✓ **Museum of Childhood** 0131 529 414242 · **High Street, Edinburgh** An Aladdin's cave of toys for all ages. 415/OTHER ATTRACTIONS.

1678
10/Q25
✓ **Edinburgh Butterfly Farm & Insect World** 0131 663 4932 · near **Dalkeith** · www.edinburgh-butterfly-world.co.uk On A7 signed Eskbank/Galashiels from ring road (1km). Part of a garden-centre complex. Beauty and the beasties in a creepy-crawly world: delightful butterflies but kids are more impressed by the glowing scorpions, locusts, iguanas and other assorted uglies. Red-kneed tarantula not for the faint hearted. 7 days, 9.30am-5.30pm (10am-5pm in winter)

✓ **Glasgow Science Centre** www.glasgowsciencecentre.org · 0141 420 5000 One of Glasgow's most flash attractions. State-of-the-art interactive, landmark tower and Imax. Report: 678/MAIN ATTRACTIONS.

1679
1/XA4
✓ **Gorgie City Farm** www.gorgiecityfarm.org.uk · 0131 337 4202 · **57 Gorgie Road, Edinburgh** A working farm on busy road in the heart of the city. Friendly domestic animals and people, garden, great playground and café. All year 9am-4.30pm (4pm in winter). Free. Green and fluffy in the concrete jungle.

1680
10/R25
LL
Yellowcraigs near **Dirleton** Beautiful beach 35km east of Edinburgh via A1, the A198, though Dirleton village then right, for 2km. Lovely, scenic beach and dunes (446/EDINBURGH BEACHES). Treasure Island play park in the woods is great for kids. Activity and sea air! Luca's on the way for ice cream (1432/ICE CREAM).

1681
1/D2
The Edinburgh Dungeon www.thedungeons.com · 0131 240 1000 · **31 Market Street, Edinburgh** Slick but très contrived experience takes you through a ghoulish history of Scottish nasties. Hammy of course, but kids will love the monorail. 7 days 10am-5pm.

1682
9/K26
L
Kelburn Country Centre www.kelburncountrycentre.com · 01475 568685 · **Largs** 2km south of Largs on A78. Riding school, gardens, woodland walks up the Kelburn Glen and a visitor section with shops/exhibits/cafés. Wooden stockade for clambering kids; indoor playbarn with quite scary slides. Falconry displays (those long-suffering owls). The Plaisance indeed a pleasant place and the Secret Forest

beckons. Stock up on ice cream at Nardini's famous caff (754/AYRSHIRE RESTAU-RANTS). The graffiti art is... well, something else! 7 days 10am-6pm. Apr-Oct. Grounds only in winter 11-dusk.

 Falkirk Wheel Falkirk 4/MAIN ATTRACTIONS.

FIFE & TAYSIDE

1683
10/Q23 **Cairnie Fruit Farm & Maze** 01334 655610 · near Cupar Leave town by minor road from main street heading past the hospital; signed (4km) or from main A92; signed near Kilmany (3km). A fruit and farm shop/café (1465/FARM SHOPS); hugely poppular due to extensive play area using farm materials to amuse kids and get them countrified. This is the Tayside equivalent of Cream o' Galloway (below), this time built around the strawberry rather than the ice cream. The maze in the maize field is major. There's strawberries for tea and other very good grub. Apr-Oct 10am-5pm (9.30am-5.30pm Jul/Aug).

1684
10/P25 **Deep Sea World** www.deepseaworld.com · 01383 411880 · North Queensferry The aquarium in a quarry which may be reaching its swim-by date. Habitats are viewed from a conveyor belt where you can stare at the fish as diverse divers teem around and above you. Maximum hard sell to this all-weather attraction – the shark capital – but kids like it even when they've been queueing for aeons. Cute seals and sharp sharks! Café is fairly awful, but nice views. Open all year 7 days 10am-5pm; weekends till 6pm (last entry 1 hour before).

1685
10/Q23 **Sensation** www.sensation.org.uk · 01382 228800 · Dundee Green-market across roundabout from Discovery Point and adjacent DCA (2166/GAL-LERIES). Purpose-built indoor info-tainment, this is an innovative and interactive games room with a message. 7 days 10am-5pm. Average visit time 2-3 hours.

1686
10/Q23 **Verdant Works** 01382 225282 · West Henderson's Wynd, Dundee Near Westport. Heritage museum that recreates workings of a jute mill. Sounds dull, but is brilliant for kids and grown-ups. Report: 2140/MUSEUMS.

1687
10/R23 **Craigton Park** 01334 473666 · St Andrews 3km southwest of St Andrews on the Pitscottie road (enter via Dukes Golf Course). An oasis of fun: bouncy castles, trampolines, putting, crazy golf, boating lake, a train through the grounds, adventure playgrounds and glasshouses. A perfect day's amusement especially for nippers. I've found it very hard to get up-to-date info about Craigton. Good luck!. Entrance charge covers all attractions.

1688
10/M23 **Auchingarrich Wildlife Park** www.auchingarrich.co.uk · 01764 679469 · L near Comrie 4km from main street over bridge and signed. Conscientious coralling in the Perthshire hills of fluffy, hairy and feathered things, all friendly. Some exotic creatures but mostly familar. Adventure playground, flying fox. All on a very informal and approachable scale. 7 days 10am-dusk.

1689
10/Q23 **Camperdown Park** www.camperdownpark.com · Dundee Large park just off ring road (Kingsway and A923 to Coupar Angus) with wildlife centre and nearby play complex. Animal-handling at weekends. Over 80 species: bats, bears and the odd wallaby. All year; centre 10am-4.30pm, earlier in winter (1539/TOWN PARKS).

SOUTH & SOUTH WEST

1690 ✓ ✓ **Cream o' Galloway** www.creamogalloway.co.uk · **Rainton** There
11/M31 is something inherently good about a visitor attraction based on the in-
controvertible fact that human beings love ice cream, especially with a 'pure and
simple' message. Organic café, burger barn, herb garden, karting and fab adventure playground in the woods, part of 5km of child-friendly nature trails. Let's hear
it for cows! All year 10am-6pm. Allow a few hours. Report: 1434/ICE CREAM.

1691 ✓ **Kidz Play** www.kidz-play.co.uk · 01292 475215 · **Prestwick** Off main
9/L27 street at Station Road, past station to beach and to right. Big shed soft play
area for kids. Everything the little blighters will like in the throwing-themselves-
around department. Shriek city. Babies-12. 7 days 9.30am-7pm.

1692 ✓ **Kailzie Gardens** 01721 720007 · **Peebles** All-round family destination
10/Q27 4km from Peebles on B7062, with fishing lochan, osprey-watching (Apr-Aug)
L though birds are 2km away (as the osprey flies), great courtyard café (807/BORDERS
RESTAURANTS) and the marvellous, serene, well-tended gardens (walled and wild);
perfectly hedged. Apr-Oct 11am-5.30pm (café 10am-5pm); gardens only, winter.

1693 **Palacerigg Country Park** www.northlanarkshire.gov.uk · 01236 720047 ·
10/M25 **Cumbernauld** 6km southeast of Cumbernauld off A801, 40 minutes from Glasgow.
740 acres of parkland; ranger service, nature trails, picnic area and kids' farm with
rare breeds; the longhouses. Golf course and putting green. Changing exhibits
about forestry, conservation, etc. Open all year 7 days; daylight hours. Café.

 Drumlanrig Castle near **Dumfries** 1521/COUNTRY PARKS.

NORTH EAST

1694 ✓ **Macduff Marine Aquarium** www.macduff-aquarium.org.uk On the
8/R17 seafront east of the harbour, a family attraction for this Moray Firth port.
Small but underrated, perhaps because nearby Banff gets more tourist attention,
though Duff House (2172/GALLERIES) gets fewer visitors than this child-friendly
sea-life centre. All fish seem curiously happy with their lot, content to educate and
entertain. Open all year 10am-5pm (last admission 4.15pm). Check winter hours.

1695 ✓ **Storybook Glen** www.storybookglenaberdeen.co.uk · **near Aberdeen**
8/S20 Fibreglass fantasy land in verdant glen 16km south of Aberdeen via B9077,
the South Deeside road, a nice drive. Characters from every fairy tale and nursery
story dotted around 20-acre park. Their fixed manic stares give them a spooky
resemblance to people you know. Older kids may find it tame: no guns, no big
technology but nice for little 'uns. Indoor play area and quite wonderful gardens.
7 days, 10am-6pm (5pm in winter), weather permitting.

1696 **Aden** www.aberdeenshire.gov.uk · **Mintlaw** (Pronounced Ah-den). Country
8/T18 park just beyond Mintlaw on A950 16km from Peterhead. Former grounds of
mansion with walks and organised activities and events. Farm buildings converted
into Farming Heritage Centre, café, etc. Adventure playground. All year.

HIGHLANDS & ISLANDS

1697 ✓ **Cairngorm Reindeer Herd** 01479 861228 · **Glenmore near Aviemore** ·
7/N19 www.reindeer-company.demon.co.uk At Glenmore Forest Park 12km
Aviemore along Coylumbridge Rd, 100m behind Glenmore visitor centre. Stop at
centre (shop, exhibition) to buy tickets and follow the guide in your vehicle up the

mountain. From here, a 20-minute walk. Real reindeer aplenty in authentic free-ranging habitat (when they come down off the cloudy hillside in winter with snow all around it's very real); they're so... small. 1 hour 30 minute trip. 11am all year and 2.30pm in summer. Wear suitable footwear; phone if weather looks threatening.

1698 ✓ **Leault Farm** www.leaultworkingsheepdogs.co.uk · 01540 651310 ·
7/N19 near **Kincraig** On A9 but easier to find from a sign 1km south of Kincraig on B9152. Working farm with daily sheepdog trials showing an extraordinary facility with dogs and sheep (and ducks). A great spectacle, totally authentic in this setting. Usually 4pm May-Oct (possibly other times). Closed Sat. Sometimes pups to love.

1699 ✓ **Landmark Park** www.landmarkpark.co.uk · 01479 841614 · **Carrbridge**
7/N19 A purpose-built tourist centre based on activities with AV displays and much shopping. Great for kids messing about in the woods on slides, in a maze, etc, in a large adventure playground, Microworld or (especially squealy) the Wildwater Coaster. Fire Tower may be too much for granny but there are fine forest views. All year 7 days till 6pm (5pm in winter, 7pm mid Jul-mid Aug). Disappointing caff.

1700 **The Highland Wildlife Park** www.highlandwildlifepark.org · **Kincraig** ·
7/N19 01540 651270 On B9152 Aviemore-Kingussie. Large drive-through reserve run by Royal Zoological Society with wandering herds of deer, bison, etc and pens of other animals. Some in habitats, but mostly cages. Cute, vicious little wildcats! Walker, the only polar bear in a public collection, does a lot of walking. New animals always arriving. Does feel much more natural than a zoo in this swathe of Highland Scotland. Must be time to bring back bears, let the wolves go free and liven up the caravan parks. Open 10am-5pm (Jul/Aug 6pm, winter 4pm).

1701 **Islay Wildlife Information & Field Centre** www.islay.co.uk · 01496
9/F26 850288 · **Port Charlotte** Fascinating, hands-on wildlife centre, activities and day trips (2304/ISLAY). Excellent for getting kids interested in wildlife. Then go find it! Guided rambles c/o the Islay Natural History Trust, Mon and Fri afternoons in different locations. May-Sep 10am-4.30pm (closes 1pm Mon-Fri for the walks). Closed Sat (Jul/Aug 7 days).

1702 **The Scottish Sealife Sanctuary** www.sealsanctuary.co.uk · 01631 720386 ·
9/H23 **Oban** 16km north on the A828. On the shore of Loch Creran, one of the oldest British waterworlds, still one of the best. Environmentally conscientious, they rescue seals and now turtles and house numerous aquatic beasties. Various aquaria, all kinds of fish going round, multi-level viewing otter enclosure and the seal thing. Feeding times posted: almost a theatrical show. Café/shop/adventure playground. Summer 9am-5pm. Check winter hours.

1703 **Natural History Centre** www.anhc.co.uk · 01972 500209 · **Ardnamurchan**
9/G21 A861 Strontian, B8007 Glenmore 14km. Photographer Michael McGregor's award-winning interactive exhibition (under different owners). Kids enjoy, adults impressed. A walk-through of wildlife including live pine martens (if you're lucky) and CCTV of more cautious creatures. Antler Tearoom. Apr-Oct Mon-Sat 10am-5.30pm, Sun from 11.30am. Winter hours vary.

1704 **Loch Insh** www.lochinsh.com · 01540 651272 · **Kincraig** Watersports centre
8/N19 but much more on B970 2km from Kincraig (near Kingussie and the A9). Beautiful loch and mountain setting, 2 small beaches and gentle water. Lots of instruction available, wildlife boat trips, biking possibilites and Kids' Kingdom small adventure playground. Good café and terrace overlooking loch; the Boathouse (1027/OTHER HIGHLAND RESTAURANTS). All-round active day out; there are chalets to stay longer.

The Best Places To See Birds

See p. 302–3 for Wildlife Reserves, many of which are good for bird-watching. All those listed below are in L, LL and LLL settings.

1705
6/K13

✓✓ **Handa Island** www.swt.org.uk · near Scourie Take the boat from Tarbet Pier 6km off A894 5km north of Scourie or from Scourie itself (both 07780 967800) and land on a beautiful island run as a nature reserve by the Scottish Wildlife Trust. Boats (Apr–early Sep though fewer birds after Aug) are continuous depending on demand. Crossing 30 minutes. Small reception hut and 2.5km walk over island to cliffs which rise 350m and are layered in colonies: fulmars, shags and the UK's largest colony of guillemots. Allow 3–4 hours. Though you must take care not to disturb the birds, you'll be eye to eye with seals and bill to bill with razorbills. Eat at the seafood café on the cove when you return (1333/SEAFOOD RESTAURANTS). Mon-Sat. Last return 5pm.

1706
11/P30
ADMISSION

✓✓ **Caerlaverock** www.wwt.org.uk · near Dumfries 17km south on B725 near Bankend, signed from road. The WWT Caerlaverock Wetlands Centre (01387 770200) is an excellent place to see whooper swans, barnacle geese in their thousands and more (countless hides, observatories, viewing towers). Has Fairtrade café as well as farmhouse-style accommodation with a variety of basic rooms (and a badger feeding station). More than just birds too: natterjack toads, badgers so not just for twitchers. New Sir Peter Scott trail. Centre open daily all year 10am–5pm.

1707
9/F22

✓✓ **Lunga & The Treshnish Islands** www.hebrideantrust.org · off Mull Sail from Iona or Fionnphort or Ulva ferry on Mull to these uninhabited islands on a 5/6-hour excursion which probably takes in Staffa and Fingal's Cave. Best time is May–July when birds are breeding. Talk of pufflings not making it because parents can't find sand eels seems premature here. Some trips allow 3 hours on Lunga. Razorbills, guillemots and a carpet of puffins oblivious to your presence. This is a memorable day. Boat trips (Ulva Ferry 08000 858786; or 01681 700338 from Fionnphort) from Iona or Oban. Trips dependent on sea conditions.

1708
10/R24

✓✓ **Isle of May** www.nlb.org.uk · Firth of Forth Island at mouth of Forth off Crail/Anstruther reached by daily boat trip from Anstruther harbour (01333 311808), Apr-Oct 9am-2.30pm depending on tides. Boats hold 40-50; trip 45 minutes; allows 3 hours ashore. Or quicker, smaller *Osprey Rib*. Can reserve the day before. Island (including isthmus to Rona) 1.5km x 0.5km. Info centre and resident wardens. See guillemots, razorbills and kittiwakes on cliffs and shags, terns and thousands of puffins. Most populations increasing. This place is strange as well as beautiful. The puffins in early summer are, as always, engaging.

1709
10/R25

✓✓ **The Bass Rock** www.nlb.org.uk · 01620 892838 · off North Berwick Temple of gannets. A guano-encrusted massif sticking out of the Forth: their largest island colony in the world. Davie Balfour was imprisoned here in RLS's *Catriona* (aka *Kidnapped II*). A variety of weather-dependent boat trips available May-Sep, including landings and safaris (which sell out first). Extraordinary birds, extraordinary experience. For daily trips on *The Sula*: 0870 118 1866 or enquire at the Seabird Centre (below).

1710
10/P22

✓✓ **Loch of the Lowes** Dunkeld 4km northeast Dunkeld on A923 to Blairgowrie. Superbly managed (Scottish Wildlife Trust) site with double-floored hide (always open) and other hide (same hours as visitor centre) and permanent binoculars. Main attractions are the captivating ospreys (from early

Apr-Aug). Nest 100m over loch and clearly visible. Their revival (almost 300 pairs now in UK) is well documented, including diary of movements, breeding history, etc. Also the near-at-hand endless fascination of watching wild birds including woodpeckers, and red squirrels feeding outside the picture window is a real treat. Great walks nearby (2005/GLEN WALKS) including to the other loch (Ordie).

1711
8/N19
✓ ✓ **Loch Garten** www.lochgarten.co.uk · **Boat of Garten** 3km village off B970 into Abernethy Forest. Famous for the ospreys and signed from all round. Best Apr-Jun. 2 car parks: the first has nature trails through Scots Pine woods and around loch; other has visitor centre with the main hide 250m away: TV screens, binoculars, other wild-bird viewing and informed chat. Here since 1954, that first pair have done wonders for local tourism – in fact, they and the RSPB and the army of determined volunteers practically invented eco tourism! Och, but they are magnificent.

1712
10/Q25
✓ **The Scottish Ornithologists' Club House** www.the-soc.org.uk · **near Aberlady** Waterston House on A198 on the left going into Aberlady from Edinburgh, opposite Gosford Estate. Not a birdwatching site per se (though between the Lagoon and the Seabird Centre, below and near Aberlady Reserve 2km), but an archive and library and resource centre for all things related to and for lovers of Scottish birds. Beautiful, light modern building looks across bay to reserve. Art exhibitions and much to browse. Birdwatching for Beginners courses. Friendly staff. The Society published the definitive book *Birds of Scotland*. Open 10am-4pm (12-6pm weekends in summer). Go in October for Goose Watch, late afternoon, when the geese come in.

1713
10/Q25
✓ **The Lagoons** Musselburgh On east edge of town behind the racecourse (follow road round, take turn-off signed Race Course Parking) at the estuarine mouth of the River Esk. Waders, sea birds, ducks aplenty and often interesting migrants on the mudflats and wide littoral. The Lagoons are man-made ponds behind with hide and attracts big populations (both birds and binocs). This is the nearest diverse-species area to Edinburgh (15km) and is one of the most significant migrant stopovers in the UK.

1714
10/S21
✓ **Fowlsheugh** www.rspb.org.uk · **near Stonehaven** 8km south of Stonehaven and signed from A92 with path from Crawton. Sea-bird city on 2km of red sandstone cliffs up to 200 feet high; take great care. 80,000 pairs of 6 species especially guillemots, kittiwakes, razorbills and also fulmar, shag, puffins. Possible to view the birds without disturbing them and discern the layers they occupy on the cliff face. Best seen May-July and from the *Lady Gail II* (boat trips leaving from Stonehaven harbour); 07780 702831 (Ian Watson).

1715
9/F25
✓ **Loch Gruinart, Loch Indaal** Islay RSPB reserve. Take A847 at Bridgend then B8017 turning north and right for Gruinart. The mudflats and fields at the head of the loch provide winter grazing for huge flocks of Barnacle and Greenland geese. They arrive, as do flocks of fellow bird-watchers, in late Oct. Hides and good vantage points near road. Don't miss beautiful Saligo Bay (1560/BEACHES). The Rhinns and the Oa in the south also sustain a huge variety of bird life.

1716
3/P10
✓ **Marwick Head** www.rspb.org.uk · **Orkney Mainland** 40km northwest of Kirkwall, via Finstown and Dounby; take left at Birsay after Loch of Isbister cross the B9056 and park at Cumlaquoy. A 4km circular walk. Spectacular sea-bird breeding colony on 100m cliffs and nearby at the Loons Reserve, wet meadowland, 8 species of duck and many waders. Orkney sites include the Noup cliffs on Westray, North Hill on Papa Westray and Copinsay, 3km east of the mainland.

1717 **Isle of Mull** www.isle.of.mull.com Sea eagles. Since the reintroduction of
9/H22 these magnificent eagles, there is now a hide with CCTV viewing. By appointment
only. Site changes every year. Contact Forest Enterprise (01631 566155) or ask at
the tourist information centre.

1718 **Orkney Puffins** Wildabout tours (www.wildaboutorkney.com). Or go solo at
3/Q10 Marwick Head (see above), Brough of Birsay and Westray (which gets them first);
check Kirkwall tourist information centre for latest.

1719 **Scottish Seabird Centre** www.seabird.org · 01620 890202 · **North**
10/R25 **Berwick** Award-winning, interactive visitor attraction near the harbour overlooking Bass Rock and Fidra (above). If you don't want to go out there, video and
other state-of-the-art technology makes you feel as if the birds are next to you.
Viewing deck for dramatic perspective of gannets diving (140kmph!) Café and
shopping where puffins prevail. 10am-6pm (4pm winter/5.30pm weekends).

1720 **Montrose Basin Wildlife Centre** www.swt.org.uk · 01674 676336 1.5km
10/S22 south of Montrose on A92 to Arbroath. Accessible Scottish Wildlife Trust centre
overlooks estuarine basin hosting residents and migrants. Good for twitchers, kids.
Autumn geese. Visitor centre Mar-Oct daily 10.30am-5pm. Call for winter hours.

1721 **Forsinard Flows Nature Reserve** www.rspb.org.uk · 01641 571225 44km
6/N13 from Helmsdale on the A897, or train stops en route to Wick/Thurso. RSPB
(proposed World Heritage Site) reserve, acquired after public appeal. 19,000
hectares of the Flow Country and its birds: divers, plovers, merlins and hen harriers
(nest watch in visitor centre). Guided walks available. Reserve open all year; visitor
centre Apr-Oct 9am-5.30pm.

1722 **Loch of Kinnordy** www.rspb.org.uk · **Kirriemuir** 4km west of town on B951,
10/Q22 an easily accessible site with 3 hides overlooking loch and wetland area managed
by RSPB. Geese in late autumn, gulls aplenty; always tickworthy. You may see the
vanishing ruglet butterfly.

1723 **Strathbeg** www.rspb.org.uk · **near Fraserburgh** 12km south off the A952
8/T17 Fraserburgh-Peterhead road, signed Nature Reserve at Crimond. Wide, shallow
loch close to coastline, a 'magnet for migrating wildfowl'. Marsh/fen, dune and
meadow habitats. In winter 30,000 geese/widgeon/mallard/swans and occasional
rarities like cranes and egrets. Binoculars in reception centre and 3 hides.

1724 **Troup Head** between **Macduff and Fraserburgh, Moray Firth** Near the
8/S17 cliff-clinging villages of Crovie and *Local Hero* Pennan on the coastal B9031.
Fantastic airy walk from the former (2058/COASTAL WALKS) or (closer) directly from
the road signed for Northfield following RSPB signs for 2km, then a 1.5km stroll
from car park. Puffins, kittiwakes, the whole shebang; and dolphins.

1725 **Inshriach Garden Centre** www.inshriachnursery.co.uk · **near Aviemore** A
8/M20 (very good) garden centre, yes and tearoom, The Potting Shed (2222/GARDEN CEN-
☕ TRES) but also one of the best places to watch wild birds who swarm round the
feeders hanging in the woods over the gorge. Has been voted the most popular UK
site by RSPB members. Red squirrels and great cakes are other good reasons for
going. Mar-Oct 10am-5pm.

Where To See Dolphins, Whales, Porpoises & Seals

✓ ✓ *The coast around the north of Scotland has some of the best places in Europe to view whales and dolphins and seals. Although you don't have to go on a boat trip, you get closer, the boatman will know where to find them and the trip itself can be exhilarating. Good operators are listed below. Dolphins are most active on a rising tide especially May-September.*

MORAY & CROMARTY FIRTHS (near Inverness)
The best area in Scotland. The population of bottlenose dolphins in this area well exceeds 100 and they can be seen all year (though mostly Jun-Sep, obligingly when most other visitors are here).

1726
7/M18
The Dolphins & Seals of the Moray Firth Centre 01463 731866 Just north of Kessock Bridge on A9. Underwater microphones pick up chatterings of dolphins and porpoises and there's always somebody there to explain. They keep an up-to-date list of recent sightings and all cruises available. Jun-Aug 9.30am-4.30pm (closes for lunch 12.30-1pm). The WDCS also runs a wildlife centre at Speybay at the mouth of the Spey south of the Moray Firth off A96 between Mosstodloch and Fochabers on B9014. 01343 820339. Apr-Oct 10.30am-5pm.

1727
7/M17
Cromarty Any vantage around town is good especially South Sutor for coastal walk and an old lighthouse cottage has been converted into a research station run by Aberdeen University. **Chanonry Point, Fortrose**, through the golf course, east end of point beyond lighthouse is the *best* place to see dolphins from land in Britain. Occasional sightings can also be seen at **Balintore**, opposite Seaboard Memorial Hall; **Tarbert Ness** beyond **Portmahomack**, end of path through reserve further out along the Moray Firth possible at **Burghead**, **Lossiemouth** and **Buckie**, **Spey Bay** and **Portknockie**. Also check the Dolphin Space Programme, an accreditation scheme for boat operators: www.dolphinspace.org

NORTH WEST
On the west coast, especially near **Gairloch** the following places may offer sightings of orcas, dolphins and minke whales mainly in summer.

1728
7/H16
Rubha Reidh near Gairloch 20km north of Melvaig (unclassified road). Near Carn Dearg Youth Hostel west of Lonemore. Where road turns inland is good spot.

1729
6/J16
Greenstone Point north of Laide Off A832 (unclassified road) through Mellon Udrigle round Gruinard Bay. Harbour porpoises Apr-Dec, minke whales May-Oct.

1730
7/H16
Red Point of Gairloch By B8056 via Badachro round Loch Gairloch. High ground looking over North Minch and south to Loch Torridon. Harbour porpoises often seen from all along this coast. Good pub on the way (1304/GASTROPUBS).

1731
7/F18
Rubha Hunish Skye The far northwest finger of Skye. Walk from Duntulm Castle or Flodigarry. Dolphins and minke whales in autumn.

OTHER PLACES
1732 4/V4 **Mousa Sound** Shetland 20km south of Lerwick (1816/PREHISTORIC SITES).

1733 **Ardnamurchan** The Point The most westerly point (and lighthouse) on this
9/G21 wildly beautiful peninsula. Go to end of road or park near Sanna Beach and walk
round. Sanna Beach worth going to just to walk the strand. Visitor centre; tearoom.

1734 **Stornoway** Isle of Lewis Heading out of town for Eye Peninsula, at Holm near
5/E14 Sandwick south of A866 or from Bayble Bay (all within walking distance).

The Most Recommended Sealife Cruises

1735 **Eco Ventures** www.ecoventures.co.uk · 01381 600323 · Cromarty Intimate
7/M17 and informative tours, but pricey. 2 trips per day all year. Booking essential.

1736 **Moray Firth Cruises** www.inverness-dolphin-cruises.co.uk · 01463 717900 ·
7/M18 Inverness 4 trips per day Mar-Oct from Inverness.

1737 **Gemini Explorer** www.geminiexplorer.co.uk · 07747 626280 · Buckie
8/Q17 More Moray Firth cruising in former lifeboat. Good facilities.

1738 **Hebridean Whale Cruises** www.hebridean-whale-cruises.com · 01445
7/H16 712458 · Gairloch Long-established and credible whale- and dolphin-watching
outfit. 1-4 hours. 10-30-mile trips include The Shiants (2241/ISLANDS).

1739 **Summer Isles Cruises** www.summer-isles-seatours.co.uk · 07927 920592 ·
6/J15 Achiltibuie Seals and seabirds abound. 3 trips per day on large MV and land on
Tanera Mór (2240/ISLANDS).

1740 **Calum's Seal & Dolphin Trips** www.calums-sealtrips.com · 01599 544306 ·
7/H18 Plockton Great craic from Calum and a money-back guarantee (certainly on the
seals) and he does know his dolphins.

1741 **Hebridean Wildlife Cruises** www.southernhebrides.com · 01631 740595 ·
9/H23 Oban Company with a choice of bigger boats operating out of Oban and other
west-coast locations. Go all over including St Kilda (2234/MAGICAL ISLANDS).

1742 **Wildlife Cruises** www.jogferry.co.uk · 01955 611353 · John o' Groats Seals,
6/Q12 puffins, seabirds. 2.30pm daily Jun-Sep. Large panoramic boat. Trips to Orkney.

1743 **Scourie Wildlife Cruises** www.scouriewildlifecruises.co.uk · 07780
6/K13 9678000 / 07775 625890 · Scourie From Scourie or Tarbet to Handa Island
(1705/BIRDS); sealife and birdlife.

1744 **Wildlife & Corryvreckan Whirlpool Cruises** www.craignishcruises.co.uk ·
9/H24 01631 740595 / 07747 023038 · Ardfern 2-hour cruises to the famous
whirlpool off Jura and to the Garvellach Isles.

1745 **Sea.Fari Adventures** www.seafari.co.uk · Edinburgh · 0131 331 5000 &
9/H23 Oban · 01852 300003 & Skye · 01471 833316 Sealife adventure: eco tours and
trips in fast, inflatable boats out of **Easdale, Isle of Seil** 25km south Oban.

ON THE ISLANDS
1746 **Sea-Life Surveys** www.sealifesurveys.com · Mull · 01688 302916 Various
9/G22 packages from relaxed half-hour to a more intense 8-hour. Good percentage of
porpoise, dolphin and whale sightings.

1747   **Turus Mara** www.turusmara.com · 08000 858786 · Mull Daytrips from Ulva
9/G22   Ferry. Various itineraries taking in bird colonies of Treshnish Isles, Staffa and Iona.
Dolphins, whales, puffins and seals.

1748   **Shetland Wildlife & The Company of Whales** 01950 422403 Shetland ·
4/U5   www.shetlandwildlife.co.uk From day trips to 7-day wildlife holidays. Sealife,
birds, whales and otters. Very professional adventuring.

1749   **Seabirds-and-seals.com** 01595 540224 · Shetland Award-winning wildlife
4/V5   adventure cruises.

1750   **Island Cruising** www.island-cruising.com · 01851 672381 · Lewis Wildlife,
5/E14   birdwatching and diving around Western Isles and St Kilda (2234/MAGICAL ISLANDS).

1751   **Seatrek** www.seatrek.co.uk · 01851 672469 · Uig, Lewis Various excursions
5/E14   from the far west and into the west, including St Kilda (2234/MAGICAL ISLANDS).

1752   **Seaprobe Atlantis** www.seaprobeatlantis.com · 0800 980 4846 · Skye
7/H18   Based at Kyle; stays around Kyle of Lochalsh (conservation) area. Sit underwater in
the gallery for better viewing.

1753   **Misty Isle Boat Trips** 01477 866288 · Skye From Elgol jetty into Loch Coruisk
7/G19   and the classic view of the Cuillin (1641/VIEWS).

1754   **Bella Jane** 0800 731 3089 · Skye The other and very long-established boat trip
7/G19   to Loch Coruisk, also Eigg, Rum and elsewhere.

WILDLIFE TOURS

1755   **Island Encounter Wildlife Safaris** www.mullwildlife.co.uk · 01680
9/G22   300441 · Mull All-day tour with local expert. Possible sightings of otters, eagles,
seals and falcons. Numerous pick-up points including ferry terminals.

1756   **Isle of Mull Wildlife Expeditions** www.torrbuan.com · 01688 500121 · Mull
9/G22   Long-established day-long trips. Eagles, sea eagles et al. They know where to go.

1757   **Wildabout** www.wildaboutorkney.com · 01856 851011 · Orkney Various
3/Q10   trips with experienced guides. Wildlife plus history and folklore. Interactive.

Otters can be seen all over the northwest Highlands in sheltered inlets,
especially early morning and late evening and on an ebb tide. Skye is one of
best places in Europe to see them. You can go with:

1758   **International Otter Survival Fund** www.otter.org · 01471 822487 ·
7/G19   Broadford They organise courses and trips for small numbers and 1-to-1 for all
wildlife and might point you in the right direction. Mon-Fri.

1759   **Otter Haven** www.forestry.gov.uk · Kylerhea Basically a viewing hide with
7/H19   CCTV, binoculars and a knowledgeable warden (not always there). Seabirds and
seals too and a forest walk. 500m walk along a track from car park signposted on
road out of Kylerhea (and from the ferry from Glenelg; 6/JOURNEYS).

Great Wildlife Reserves

These wildlife reserves are not merely bird-watching places. Most of them are easy to get to from major centres; none requires a permit.

1760
10/S25
NTS

✔ ✔ **St Abb's Head** www.nlb.org.uk · **near Berwick** 9km north of Eyemouth and 10km east of main A1. Spectacular cliff scenery (2054/COASTAL WALKS), a huge sea-bird colony, rich marine life and varied flora. Good view from top of stacks, geos and cliff face full of serried ranks of guillemot, kittiwake, razorbill, etc. Hanging gardens of grasses and campion. Behind cliffs, grassland rolls down to the Mire Loch and its varied habitat of bird, insect, butterfly life and vegetation. Unpretentious art gallery and shop and NTS interpretation centre. Coffee shop at the car park. New Inn in Coldingham (3km) for decent pub grub (01890 771315).

1761
8/T19

✔ ✔ **Sands of Forvie & The Ythan Estuary** www.jncc.gov.uk · **Newburgh** 25km north Aberdeen. Cross bridge outside Newburgh on A975 to Cruden Bay and park. Path follows Ythan estuary, bears north and enters the largest undisturbed dune system in the UK. Dunes in every aspect of formation. Collieston, a 17/18th-century fishing village, is 5km away. These habitats support the largest population of eiders in Britain (especially Jun) and huge numbers of terns. It's easy to get lost here, so get lost! One might say the same to Donald Trump who has turned the nearby dune system into a habitat only for golfers.

1762
7/J17

✔ **Beinn Eighe** Bounded by the A832 south from Gairloch and A896 west of Kinlochewe, this first National Nature Reserve in Britain includes remaining fragments of old Caledonian pinewood on the south shore of Loch Maree (largest in West Highlands) and rises to the rugged tops with their spectacular views and varied geology. Excellent wood and mountain trails with starts on both roads – from A832 on Loch Maree side there are woodland strolls. Starts to the Beinn (easier) and to the mighty Liatach are from the A896 Glen Torridon road (1635/VIEWS, 1617/SCENIC ROUTES). Pronounced Ben-Ah.

1763
10/R25

John Muir Country Park www.eastlothian.gov.uk · **Dunbar** Vast park between Dunbar and North Berwick named after the Dunbar-born father of the conservation movement. Includes estuary of the Tyne; part of the park is also known as Tyninghame, and see 444/EDINBURGH BEACHES. Diverse habitats: cliffs, sand spits and woodland. Many bird species. Crabs, lichens, sea and marsh plants. Enter at east extremity of Dunbar at Belhaven, off the B6370 from A1; or off A198 to North Berwick. Or better, walk from Dunbar by cliff-top trail (2km+).

1764
9/L26
RSPB

Lochwinnoch www.lochwinnoch.info · 01505 842663 30km southwest of Glasgow via M8 junction 28A then A737 past Johnstone onto A760. Also from Largs 20km via A760. Reserve just outside village on lochside and comprises wetland and woodland habitats. A serious nature centre, incorporating an observation tower. Hides and marked trails; and a birds-spotted board. Shop and coffee shop. Events programme. Good for kids. Visitor centre open daily 10am-5pm.

1765
7/M20

Insh Marshes www.rspb.org.uk · **Kingussie** 4km from town along B970 (past Ruthven Barracks, 1807/RUINS), 2,500 acres of Spey floodplain run by RSPB. Trail (3km) marked out through meadow and wetland and a note of species to look out for (including 6 types of orchid, 7 'red list' birds and half the UK population of goldeneye). Also 2 hides (250m and 450m) high above marshes, vantage points to see waterfowl, birds of prey, otters and deer. A National Nature Reserve since 2003.

1766   **Tentsmuir** www.forestry.gov.uk · between Newport & Leuchars North tip
10/R23   of Fife at the mouth of the Tay, reached from Tayport or Leuchars via the B945.
Follow signs for Kinshaldy Beach taking road that winds for 4km over flat then
forested land. Park (car park closes 8.30pm in summer, much earlier in winter) and
cross dunes to broad strand. Walks in both direction: west back to Tayport, east to
Leuchars. Also 4km circular walk of beach and forest. Hide 2km away at Ice House
Pond. Seals often watch from waves and bask in summer. Lots of butterflies.
Waders aplenty and, to the east, one of UK's most significant populations of eider.
Most wildfowl offshore. (Ranger: 07985 707593.)

1767   **Vane Farm** www.rspb.org.uk · Loch Leven RSPB reserve on south shore of
10/P24   Loch Leven, beside and bisected by B9097 off junction 5 of M90. Easily reached
visitor centre with observation lounge and education/orientation facilities. Hide
nearer loch side reached by tunnel under road. Nature trail on hill behind through
heath and birchwood (2km circular). Steep, but has the vista. Good place to introduce kids to nature watching. Centre 10am-5pm. Hides always open. Events:
01577 862355.

1768   **Balranald** www.rspb.org.uk · North Uist West coast of North Uist reached by
5/C17   the road from Lochmaddy, then the Bayhead turnoff at Clachan Stores (10km
north). This most western, most faraway reach is one of the last redoubts of the
disappearing corncrake. Catch its calling while you can.

1769   **Flanders Moss** www.nnr-scotland.org.uk · near Thornhill This curious
10/M24   swathe of the Forth valley on the road between Thornhill and Kippen (1km rough
track from B822 to car park) is a much revered and well interpreted... bog, a kind
of micro ecosystem. It's a raised bog and there's a raised walkway around it (1km)
and an impressive tower to overlook it. Wet-loving wildlife includes adders, dragonflies and a host of other insects and the birds who feed on them. Then there's
the history. This place is a bit of an oddity, central but not overrun. Good grub in
both Kippen (1281/1282/GASTROPUBS) and Thornhill (1303/GASTROPUBS). So a satis-
factory afternoon can be had around here.

Historical Places

The Best Castles

NTS *National Trust for Scotland. Hours vary. Admission.*
HS *Historic Scotland, Standard hours are: Apr-end Sep, 7 days 9.30am-6.30pm. Oct 9.30am-4.30pm. Winter hours vary. Admission.*

1770
10/N24
HS
LLL
✓✓✓ **Stirling Castle** www.historic-scotland.gov.uk · 01786 450000
Dominating town and plain, this like Edinburgh Castle is worth the hype and history. More aesthetically pleasing, it is like Edinburgh a timeless attraction that withstands the waves of tourism as it did the centuries of warfare for which it was built. It does seem a very civilised billet, with gorgeous frescoes, peaceful gardens and cannon-studded rampart walks from which the views are excellent, including the aerial view of the ghost outline of the King's Knot Garden (the Cup and Saucer, as they're known locally). Includes the Renaissance Palace of James V and the Great Hall of James IV restored to full magnificence. Some rock legends have played here and there are many dinners. Unicorn Café is average.

1771
1/B4
HS
LLL
✓✓✓ **Edinburgh Castle** www.historic-scotland.gov.uk City centre.
Impressive from any angle and all the more so from inside. Despite the tides of tourists and time, it still enthrals. Superb perspectives of the city and of Scottish history. Stone of Destiny and the Crown Jewels are the Big Attractions. Café and restaurant (superb views) with efficient but uninspiring catering operation; open only castle hours and to castle visitors. Report: 399/MAIN ATTRACTIONS.

1772
8/N17
NTS
✓✓ **Brodie Castle** www.nts.org.uk · 0844 493 2100 · near Nairn
6-7km west of Forres off main A96. More a (Z-plan) tower house than a castle, dating from 1567. In this century and like Cawdor nearby, the subject of family feuding – now resolved and under the calming influence of the NTS, its guides discreetly passing over any unpleasantness. With a minimum of historical hocum, this 16/17th-century, but mainly Victorian, country house is furnished from rugs to moulded ceilings in excellent taste. Every picture (very few gloomies) bears examination. The nursery and nanny's room, the guest rooms, indeed all the rooms, are eminently habitable. Wonderful library. Tearoom and informal walks in grounds. An avenue leads to a lake; in spring the daffodils are famous. Apr-Oct and last tour (register on arrival) at 3.30pm (4pm July/Aug). Closed Thu-Sat May/Jun and Oct. Grounds open all year till sunset.

1773
9/K28
NTS
LL
✓✓ **Culzean Castle** www.culzeanexperience.org · Maybole 24km
south of Ayr on A719. Impossible to convey here the scale and the scope of the house and the country park. Allow some hours especially for the grounds. Castle is more like a country house and you examine from the other side of a rope. From the 12th century but rebuilt by Robert Adam in 1775, a time of soaring ambition, its grandeur is almost out of place in this exposed cliff-top position. It was designed for entertaining, and the oval staircase is magnificent. Wartime associations (especially with President Eisenhower) plus the enduring fascination of the aristocracy. 560 acres of grounds including cliff-top walk, formal gardens, walled garden, Swan Pond (a must) and Happy Valley. Harmonious home farm is visitor centre with exhibits and shop, etc. Caff could be better. Open Apr-Nov 10.30am-5pm. Park AYR. Many special events. Culzean is pronounced Cullane. And you can stay (746/AYRSHIRE HOTELS).

1774
10/Q24
NTS
✓✓ **Falkland Palace** www.historic-scotland.gov.uk · Falkland Middle
of farming Fife, 15km from M90 junction 8. Not a castle at all, but the hunting palace of the Stewart dynasty. Despite its recreational rather than political role, it's one of the landmark buildings in Scottish history and in the 16th century

was the finest Renaissance building in Britain. They all came here for archery, falconry and hunting boar and deer on the Lomonds; and for Royal Tennis which is displayed and explained. Still occupied by the Crichton-Stewarts, the house is dark and rich and redolent of those days of 'dancin and deray at Falkland on the Grene'. Mar-Oct 10am-5pm. Sun 1-5pm. Plant shop and events programme. Great walks from village (1969/HILL WALKS, 2009/GLEN WALKS). See also 1372/TEAROOMS.

1775
6/Q12
☕
ADMISSION
L
ATMOS

✓ ✓ **Castle of Mey** www.castleofmey.org.uk · 01847 851473 · **near Thurso** Actually near John o' Groats (off A836), castles don't get further-flung than this. Stunted trees, frequent wind and a wild coast but the Queen Mother famously fell in love with this dilapidated house in 1952, filled it with things she found and was given and turned it into one of the most human and endearing of the Royal (if not all aristocratic) residences. Guides tell the story and if you didn't love her already, you will when you leave. Lovely walled garden and animal centre in converted granary with farm animals including North Country sheep – great for kids. A top tearoom. Mey cattle and produce (cottage pie and crumble). Charles and Camilla still visit. May-Sep (closed 2 weeks early Aug).

1776
7/N17
☕
ADMISSION

✓ **Cawdor Castle** www.cawdorcastle.com · **Cawdor, near Nairn & Inverness** The mighty Cawdor of Macbeth fame. Most of the family clear off for the summer and leave their romantic yet habitable and yes... stylish castle, sylvan grounds and gurgling Cawdor Burn to you. Pictures from Claude to Craigie Aitcheson, a modern kitchen as fascinating as the enormous one of yore. Even the tartan passage is nicely done. The burn is the colour of tea. An easy drive (25km) to Brodie (above) means you can see 2 of Scotland's most appealing castles in one day. Courtyard café. 9-hole golf course. These gardens are gorgeous. Mid Apr-early Oct, 7 days, 10am-5pm (last admission).

1777
10/N21
ADMISSION

✓ **Blair Castle** www.blair-castle.co.uk · 01796 481207 · **Blair Atholl** Impressive from the A9, the castle and the landscape of the dukes of Atholl (present duke not present); 10km north of Pitlochry. Hugely popular; almost a holi-day-camp atmosphere. Numbered rooms chock-full of 'collections': costumes, toys, plates, weapons, stag skulls, walking sticks – so many things! Upstairs, the more usual stuffed apartments including the Jacobite bits. Walk in the policies (includes Hercules Garden with tranquil ponds); catch The Whim. Apr-Oct 9.30am-4.30pm (last admission) daily. Tue and Sat in winter (1.30pm last admission).

1778
10/Q22
ADMISSION
LL

✓ **Glamis** www.glamis-castle.co.uk · **Forfar** 8km from Forfar via A94 or off main A929, Dundee-Aberdeen road (turnoff 10km north of Dundee, a picturesque approach). Fairy-tale castle in majestic setting. Seat of the Strathmore family (Queen Mum spent her childhood here) for 600 years; every room an example of the interior of a certain period. Guided tours (continuous/50 minutes' duration). Restaurant/gallery shop haven for tourists (and for an excellent bridie; 1429/BAKERS). Apr-Oct 10am-6pm, Nov/Dec 10.30am-4.30pm; last entry 90 min-utes before. Italian Gardens and nature trail well worth 500m walk.

1779
9/J27
NTS

✓ **Brodick Castle** www.nts.org.uk · **Arran** 4km from town (bike hire 01770 302868). Impressive, well-maintained landmark castle, exotic formal gardens and extensive grounds. Goat Fell (1951/HILLS) in the background and the sea through the trees. Dating from 13th century and until the 1950s the home of the dukes of Hamilton. An over-antlered hall leads to liveable rooms with portraits and heirlooms, an atmosphere of long-ago afternoons. Tangible sense of relief in the kitchens now the entertaining is over. Robert the Bruce's cell less convincing. Easter-Oct; check hours. Marvellous grounds open all year (and Goat Fell).

1780
9/H23
⌨
ADMISSION
LL

✓ **Duart Castle** www.duartcastle.com · Mull A fabulous setting for the 13th-century ancestral seat of the Clan Maclean and home to Sir Lachlan and Lady Maclean. Quite a few modifications over the centuries as methods of defence grew in sophistication but with walls as thick as a truck and the sheer isolation of the place it must have doomed any prospect of attack from the outset. Now a happier, homelier place, the only attacking that gets done these days is on scones in the superior tearoom. Apr Sun-Thu 11am-4pm. May-Oct 10.30am-5.30pm. Diverse event programme in summer months.

1781
7/F18
ADMISSION

Dunvegan Castle www.dunvegancastle.com · Skye 3km Dunvegan village. Romantic history and setting, though more baronial than castellate, the result of mid-19th-century restoration that incorporated the disparate parts. The castle and the 30,000-acre estate now presided over by the 30th MacLeod of MacLeod with the task of repairing the roof, etc from the controversial disposal of the Cuillin. Your visit also helps. Necessary crowd management leads you through a series of rooms where the Fairy Flag, displayed above a table of exquisite marquetry, has pride of place. Gardens, perhaps lovelier than the house, down to the loch; boats leave the jetty to see the seals. Busy café, The Macleod Table (though food disappointing; instead, go to Janns in the village; 2300/SKYE). Open Apr-Oct 10am-5.30pm.

1782
7/J18
ADMISSION
LLL

Eilean Donan www.eileandonancastle.com · Dornie On A87, 13km before Kyle of Lochalsh. A calendar favourite, often depicted illuminated; and once, with a balloon hovering over, an abiding image from a BBC promo. Inside is a generous portion of history (American size). The Banqueting Hall with its Pipers' Gallery must make for splendid dinner parties for the Macraes. Much military regalia amongst the bric-a-brac, but also the impressive Raasay Punchbowl partaken of by Johnson and Boswell. Mystical views from ramparts as well as the human story below the stairs. Apr-Oct 10am-5pm; Mar and Nov 10am-3pm and open from 9am Jul/Aug.

1783
10/N22
ADMISSION

Castle Menzies Weem www.menzies.org · near Aberfeldy In Tay valley with spectacular ridge behind (**Walks In The Weem Forest**, part of the Tummel Valley Forest Park; separate car park). On B846, 5km west of Aberfeldy, through Weem. The 16th-century stronghold of the Menzies (pronounced Mingiss), one of Scotland's oldest clans. Sparsely furnished with odd clan memorabilia, the house nevertheless conveys more of a sense of Jacobite times than many more brimful of bric-a-brac. Bonnie Prince Charlie stopped here on the way to Culloden. Open farmland situation, so manured rather than manicured grounds. No tearoom but tea and Tunnocks. Apr-Oct 10.30am-5pm, Sun 2.30-5pm.

1784
10/P23
ADMISSION

Scone Palace www.scone-palace.co.uk · near Perth On A93 road to Blairgowrie and Braemar. A 'great house', the home to the Earl of Mansfield and gorgeous grounds. Famous for the Stone of Scone (aka The Stone of Destiny) on which the kings of Scots were crowned, and the Queen Vic bedroom. Maze and pinetum. Many contented animals greet you and a plethora of peacocks. Annual Game Fair, horse trials and antique fair. Apr-Oct 7 days 9.30am-5pm (last admission). Fri only in winter 10am-4pm.

1785
10/R24
NTS

Kellie Castle www.nts.org.uk · near Pittenweem Major castle in Fife. Dating from 14th century and restored by Robert Lorimer, his influence evidenced by magnificent plaster ceilings and furniture. Notable mural by Phoebe Anna Traquair. The gardens, nursery and kitchen recall all the old Victorian virtues. The old-fashioned roses still bloom for us. Check website for opening hours.

1786 **Craigievar** www.nts.org.uk · near Banchory 15km north of main A93
8/R19 Aberdeen-Braemar road between Banchory and Aboyne. A classic tower house,
NTS perfect like a porcelain miniature. Random windows, turrets, balustrades. Set
amongst sloping lawns and tall trees. Limited access to halt deterioration means
you are spared the shuffling hordes. Apr-Sep Fri-Tue, 11am-5pm. Daily July/Aug.
No caff.

1787 **Drum Castle (the Irvine Ancestral Home)** www.drum-castle.org · near
8/S20 Banchory Please forgive this, the longest entry in this section. 1km off main A93
NTS Aberdeen-Braemar road between Banchory and Peterculter and 20km from
ATMOS Aberdeen centre. For 24 generations this has been the seat of the Irvines. My lot!
Gifted to one William De Irwin by Robert the Bruce, it combines the original keep
(the oldest intact tower house in Scotland), a Jacobean mansion and Victorian
expansionism. I have 3 times signed the book in the Irvine Room and wandered
through the accumulated history hopeful of identifying with something. Hugh
Irvine, the family 'artist' whose extravagant self-portrait as the Angel Gabriel raised
eyebrows in 1810, does seem like my kind of chap, at least more interesting than
most of my soldiering forebears. Give me a window seat in that library! Grounds
have an exceptional walled rose garden (Easter-Oct 11am-5pm; 1510/GARDENS).
House Thu-Mon 11am-4.45pm. Daily July/Aug. Last admission 4pm. Tower can be
climbed for great views. Some pleasant walks from the car park.

1788 **Balmoral** near Ballater On main A93 between Ballater and Braemar. Limited
8/Q20 house access (ie only the ballroom: public functions are held here when they're in
ADMISSION residence and some corporates). Grounds (open Apr-Jul) with Albert's wonderful
LL trees are more rewarding. For royalty rooters only, and if you like Landseers...
Crathie Church along the main road has a good rose window, an altar of Iona marble. John Brown is somewhere in the old graveyard down track from visitor centre,
the memorial on the hill is worth a climb for a poignant moment and view of the
policies. Crathie services have never been quite the same Sunday attraction since
Di and Fergie on a prince's arm (bring it on, Wills and Kate). Daily 10am-5pm, last
admission 4.30pm. Apr-Jul.

1789 **Dunrobin Castle** Golspie The largest house in the Highlands, the home of the
6/N15 Dukes of Sutherland who once owned more land than anyone else in the British
ADMISSION Empire. It's the first Duke who occupies an accursed place in Scots history for his
LL inhumane replacement, in these vast tracts, of people with sheep. His statue
stands on Ben Bhraggie above the town (1855/MONUMENTS). Living the life of
imperial grandees, the Sutherlands transformed the castle into a *château* and filled
it with their obscene wealth. Once there were 100 servants for a house party of 20
and it had 30 gardeners. Now it's a leisure industry. The gardens are beyond fabulous (1499/GARDENS). The castle and separate museum are open Apr-mid Oct,
usually 10.30am-4.30pm (5.30pm Jun-Aug), Sun from 12noon.

Crathes near Banchory 1494/GARDENS; 1845/COUNTRY HOUSES.
Fyvie Aberdeenshire 1844/COUNTRY HOUSES.

The Most Interesting Ruins

HS *Historic Scotland. Standard hours: Apr-end Sep 7 days 9.30am-5.30pm. Oct-Mar Mon-Sat 9.30am-4.30pm. Some variations with individual properties; call 0131 668 8831 to check. All HS properties carry admission. Friends of Historic Scotland membership: 0131 668 8600 or any manned sites (annual charge then free admission). www.historic-scotland.gov.uk*

1790
10/N25
HS
✓✓✓ **Linlithgow Palace** www.historic-scotland.gov.uk Impressive from the M9 and from the south approach to this most agreeable of West Lothian towns, but don't confuse the magnificent Renaissance edifice with St Michael's Church next door, topped with its controversial crown and spear spire. From the Great Hall, built for James I, King of Scots, with its huge adjacent kitchens, and the North Range with loch views, you get a real impression of the lavish lifestyle of the court. Not as busy as some HS attractions on this page but it is fabulous. King's Fountain restoration added to the palace appeal.

1791
10/P30
HS
LL
✓✓ **Caerlaverock** www.wwt.org.uk · near Dumfries 17km south by B725. Follow signs for Wetlands Reserve (1706/BIRDS) but go past road end (can walk between). Fairy-tale fortress within double moat and manicured lawns, the daunting frontage being the apex of an unusual triangular shape. Since 1270, the bastion of the Maxwells, the Wardens of the West Marches. Destroyed by Bruce, besieged in 1640. The whole castle experience is here. Kids' adventure park.

1792
10/S20
LL
✓ **Dunnottar Castle** www.dunnottarcastle.co.uk · near Stonehaven 3km south of Stonehaven on the coast road just off the A92. Like Slains further north, the ruins are impressively and precariously perched on a cliff top. Historical links with Wallace, Mary, Queen of Scots (the odd night) and even Oliver Cromwell, whose Roundheads besieged it in 1650. Mel Gibson's *Hamlet* was filmed here (bet you don't remember the film) and the Crown Jewels of Scotland were once held here. 400m walk from car park. Can walk along cliff top from Stonehaven (2km). Apr-Oct 9am-6pm, Nov-Mar 10am-5pm.

1793
9/H21
ATMOS
L
✓ **Castle Tioram** www.tioram.org · near Acharacle A romantic ruin where you don't need the saga to sense the place. 5km from A861 just north of Acharacle signed Dorlin. Beautiful drive, 5km then park by Dorlin Cottage. Serenely beautiful shoreline then walk across a short causeway. Pronounced Cheerum. Musical beach at nearby Kentra Bay (2056/COASTAL WALKS).

1794
8/P17
HS
✓ **Elgin Cathedral** www.historic-scotland.gov.uk · Elgin Follow signs in town centre. Set in a meadow by the river, a tranquil corner of this busy market town, the scattered ruins and surrounding graveyard of what was once Scotland's finest cathedral. The nasty Wolf of Badenoch burned it down in 1390, but there are some 13th century and medieval renewals. The octagonal chapterhouse is especially revered, but this is an impressive and evocative slice of history. HS have made great job of restorations. Now tower can be climbed. Around the corner, there's now a biblical garden planted with species mentioned in the Bible. Gardens open Apr-Sep, 9.30am-5.30pm (4.30pm in winter and closed Thu/Fri).

1795
8/Q19
HS
ATMOS
L
✓ **Kildrummy Castle** www.historic-scotland.gov.uk · near Alford 15km southwest of Alford on A97 near the hotel (1178/SCOTTISH HOTELS) and across the gorge from its famous gardens. Most complete 13th-century castle in Scotland, an HQ for the Jacobite uprising of 1715 and an evocative and very Highland site. Here the invitation in the old HS advertising to 'bring your imagination' is truly valid. Apr-Sep 9.30am-5.30pm. Now head for the gardens (400m).

1796
5/C20
HS
LLL

✓ **Kisimull Castle** Isle of Barra · 01871 810313 The medieval fortress, home of the MacNeils that sits on a rocky outcrop in the bay 200m offshore. Originally built in the 11th century, it was burnt in the 18th and restored by the 45th chief, an American architect, but was unfinished when he died in 1970. An essential pilgrimage for all MacNeils, it is fascinating and atmospheric for the rest of us, a grim exterior belying an unusual internal layout – a courtyard that seems unchanged and rooms betwixt renovation and decay. Open every day in season and has a gift shop. Easter-Sep, closes for 1 hour at lunch. Last boat 4.30pm.

1797
8/R17
LLL

✓ **Findlater Castle** Moray Coast Ruin of a marvellous castle on a mystical coast. I don't know why I haven't listed it before because I have gazed on it so often on the way to Sunnyside (1556/BEACHES). Signed off A98 Banff-Inverness (3km): park in farmyard, pass the impressive doocot; you don't see the castle until walking through the cornfields. The 13th-15th century ruin is built into the promontory, fortified by nature. A board at the clifftop viewpoint depicts it in its glory – but how did they build it? This is a ruin of ruins though you can't really reach it.

1798
10/R21
HS

Edzell Castle www.historic-scotland.gov.uk · Edzell 3km village off main street, signed. Pleasing red sandstone ruin in bucolic setting – birds twitter, rabbits run. The notable walled parterre Renaissance garden created by Sir David Lindsay way back in 1604 is the oldest-preserved in Scotland. The wall niches are nice. Lotsa lobelias! Mary, Queen of Scots was here (she so got around). Gate on the road is closed at night.

1799
10/M26
HS

Bothwell Castle www.historic-scotland.gov.uk · Uddingston 15km east of Glasgow via M74, Uddingston turnoff into main street and follow signs. Hugely impressive 13th-century ruin, home of the Black Douglas, overlooking the Clyde; fine walks. Remarkable considering proximity to the city that there is hardly any 21st-century intrusion except you. Pay to go in or just sit and watch the river go by.

1800
7/M17
HS

Fort George www.historic-scotland.gov.uk · near Inverness On promontory of Moray Firth 18km northeast via A96 by Ardersier. A vast site – one of the most outstanding artillery fortifications in Europe. Planned after Culloden as a base for George II's army and completed 1769, it remains unaltered and allows a very complete picture. May provoke palpitations in the nationalist heart, but it's heaven for militarists and altogether impressive (don't miss the museum). It's hardly a ruin of course, still occupied by the Army. 7 days 9.30am-5.30pm (4.30pm in winter).

1801
9/H23

Dunollie Castle Oban Just outside town via Corran Esplanade towards Ganavan. Best to walk to or park on Esplanade and then walk 1km. (Only small layby and broken gate on main road below castle.) Bit of a scramble up and a slither down (and the run itself is not 'safe'), but views are superb. More atmospheric than Dunstaffnage and not commercialised. You can climb one flight up, but the ruin is only a remnant of the great stronghold of the Lorn Kings that it was. The Macdougals, who took it over in the 12th century, still live in the house below.

1802
9/H25

Tarbert Castle www.tarbert-castle.co.uk · Tarbert, Argyll Strategically and dramatically overlooking the sheltered harbour of this epitome of a West Highland port. Unsafe to clamber over, it's for the timeless view rather than an evocation of tangible history that it's worth finding the way up. New access from Harbour Rd.

1803
9/J23
HS
L

Kilchurn Castle www.kilchurncastle.com · Loch Awe Romantic ruin at the head of awesome Loch Awe, reached by a 1km walk from the car park off the main A85 5km east of Lochawe village. You go under the railway line. A very pleasant spot for loch reflections; and your own.

1804
10/R23
HS

St Andrews Cathedral www.standrewscathedral.com · St Andrews
The ruins of the largest church in Scotland before the Reformation, a place of great influence and pilgrimage. St Rule's Tower and the jagged fragment of the huge West Front in their striking position at the convergence of the main streets and overlooking the sea, are remnants of its great glory. Open 7 days all year round.

1805
10/Q26
HS

Crichton Castle www.historic-scotland.gov.uk · near Pathhead 3km west of A68 at Pathhead (28km south of Edinburgh) or via A7 turning east, 3km south of Gorebridge. Massive Border keep dominating the Tyne valley in pristine countryside. Open Apr-Sep. Nearby is the 15th-century collegiate church. Summer Sun only, 2-5pm. They record Radio 3 religious music here. 500m walk from Crichton village. Good picnic spots below by the river though may be overgrown in summer.

1806
10/R25
HS
LL

Tantallon Castle www.historic-scotland.gov.uk · North Berwick 5km east of town by coast road; 500m to dramatic cliff top setting with views to Bass Rock (1709/BIRDS). Dates from 1350 with massive curtain wall to see it through stormy weather and stormy history. The Red Douglases and their friends kept the world at bay. Wonderful beach nearby (443/EDINBURGH BEACHES). Closed Thu/Fri in winter.

1807
7/M20
HS
L

Ruthven Barracks www.historic-scotland.gov.uk · Kingussie 2km along B970 and visible from A9 especially at night when it's illuminated, these former barracks built by the English Redcoats as part of the campaign to tame the Highlands after the first Jacobite rising in 1715, were actually destroyed by the Jacobites in 1746 after Culloden. It was here that Bonnie Prince Charlie sent his final order, 'Let every man seek his own safety', signalling the absolute end of the doomed cause. Life for the soldiers is well described and visualised. Open all year.

1808
7/L18
HS
LLL

Urquhart Castle www.historic-scotland.gov.uk · Drumnadrochit, Loch Ness 28km south of Inverness on A82. The classic Highland fortress on a promontory overlooking Loch Ness visited every year by bus loads and boat loads of tourists. Photo opportunities galore amongst the well-kept lawns and extensive ruins of the once formidable stronghold of the Picts and their scions, finally abandoned in the 18th century. Visitor facilities almost cope with demand.

1809
10/M24
HS

Doune Castle www.historic-scotland.gov.uk · Doune Follow signs from centre of village which is just off A84 Callander-Dunblane road. Overlooking the River Teith, the well-preserved ruin of a late 14th-century courtyard castle with a great hall and another draughty room where Mary, Queen of Scots once slept. Nice walk to the meadow begins on track to left of castle.

1810
8/T18
ATMOS
LL

Slains Castle www.peterhead.org.uk · near Cruden Bay 3akm north of Aberdeen and 2km west of Cruden Bay, from car park (Meikle Partens) on bend of the A795. You see its craggy outline then walk 1km. Obviously because of its location, but also because there's no reception centre/postcard shop or proper signposts, this is a ruin that talks. Your imagination, like Bram Stoker's (who was inspired after staying here, to write *Dracula*), can be cast to the winds. The seat of the earls of Errol, it has been gradually disintegrating since the roof was removed in 1925. Once, it had the finest dining room in Scotland. The waves crash below, as always. Be careful!

1811
10/S27
L

Hume Castle Hume A new entry: how could I have missed this imposing, well-preserved ruin that sits above the road and the countryside between Greenlaw and Kelso? Its impressive walls here since the 18th century from a 13th-century fortification. Marvellous views across the Merse as far as the English border.

The Best Prehistoric Sites

HS *Historic Scotland. Standard hours: Apr-end Sep 7 days 9.30am-5.30pm; Oct-Mar 9.30am-4.30pm. Local and winter variations.*

1812
3/P10
HS
ADMISSION
L

✓ ✓ ✓ **Skara Brae** www.historic-scotland.gov.uk · Orkney Mainland 32km Kirkwall by A965/B9655 via Finstown and Dounby. Excellent visitor and orientation centre. Can be a windy (500m) walk to this remarkable shoreline site, the subterranean remains of a compact village 5,000 years old. It was engulfed by a sandstorm 600 years later and lay perfectly preserved until uncovered by the laird's dog after another storm in 1850. Now it permits one of the most evocative glimpses of truly ancient times in the UK.

1813
3/Q10
HS

✓ ✓ **The Standing Stones of Stenness** www.historic-scotland.gov.uk · Orkney Mainland Together with the **Ring of Brodgar** and the great chambered tomb of **Maes Howe**, all within easy distance of the A965, 18km from Kirkwall, these are as impressive ceremonial sites as you'll find anywhere. From same period as Skara Brae. The individual stones and the scale of the Ring are very imposing and deeply mysterious. The burial cairn is the finest megalithic tomb in the UK. 500m walk from the visitor centre. Guided tour only. Note: tunnel entry is only 1m high! Seen together, they stimulate even the most jaded sense of wonder.

1814
5/F14
HS
ADMISSION
☕

✓ ✓ **The Callanish Stones** www.historic-scotland.gov.uk · Lewis 24km from Stornoway. Take Tarbert road and go right at Leurbost. The best preserved and most unusual combination of standing stones in a ring around a tomb, with radiating arms in cross shape. Predating Stonehenge, they were un-earthed from the peat in the mid-19th century and are the Hebrides' major histori-cal attraction. Other configurations nearby. At least at dawn and dusk, hardly anyone else is there. Visitor centre (out of sight) has a good caff. Closed Sun. Free.

1815
7/N17
HS
FREE
ATMOS

✓ **The Clava Cairns** www.historic-scotland.gov.uk · near Culloden, near Inverness Here long before the most infamous battle in Scottish and other histories; another special atmosphere. Not so well signed but continue along the B9006 towards Cawdor Castle, that other great historical landmark (1776/CASTLES), taking a right at the Culloden Moor Inn; follow signs for Clava Lodge holiday homes, picking up HS sign to right. Chambered cairns in a grove of trees. They're really just piles of stones but the death rattle echo from 5,000 years ago is percep-tible to all especially when no one else is there. Remoteness probably inhibits New Age attentions and allows more private meditations in this extraterrestrial spot.

1816
4/V5
HS
ADMISSION
LL

✓ **The Mousa Broch** www.historic-scotland.gov.uk · Shetland On island of Mousa off Shetland mainland 20km south of Lerwick. To see it properly, take the *Solan IV* from Sandsayre Pier at Leebitton in Sandwick (01950 431367; although boat business for sale at TGP). Takes 15 minutes. Isolated in its island fastness, this is the best-preserved broch in Scotland. Walls are 13m high (origi-nally 15m) and galleries run up the middle, in one case to the top. Solid as a rock, this example of a uniquely Scottish phenomenon would have been a very des res. Also **Jarlshof** in the south next to Sumburgh airport has remnants and ruins from Neolithic to Viking times – 18th century, with especially impressive wheelhouses.

1817
10/M22
ADMISSION

✓ **Crannog Centre** www.crannog.co.uk · Kenmore, near Aberfeldy On south Loch Tay road 1km Kenmore. Superb reconstruction of Iron Age dwelling (there are several under the loch). Credible and worthwhile archaeological project, great for kids: conveys history well. Displays in progress and human story told by pleasant costumed humans. Open Apr-Oct 10am-5.30pm, Nov Sat/Sun 10-4pm.

1818
9/H24
HS
✓ **Kilmartin Glen** www.historic-scotland.gov.uk · near Lochgilphead, Templewood 2km south of Kilmartin and 1km (signed) from A816 and across road from car park, 2 distinct stone circles from a long period of history between 3000-1200 BC. Story and speculations described on boards. Pastoral countryside and wide skies. There are apparently 150 other sites in the vicinity, and an excellent museum/café (2154/MUSEUMS). See also Dunadd (1957/FAVOURITE HILLS) for an elevated perspective of the whole area.

1819
3/Q10
ADMISSION
ATMOS
✓ **Tomb of the Eagles** www.tomboftheeagles.co.uk · Orkney Mainland 33km south of Kirkwall at the foot of South Ronaldsay; signed from Burwick. A relatively recent discovery, the excavation of this cliff cave is on private land. You call in at the visitor centre first and they'll tell you the story. There's a 2km walk then you go in on a skateboard – no, really! Allow time; ethereal stuff. All year, Mar-Oct 9.30am-5.30pm (Mar 10am-12noon) or by appointment; 01856 831339.

1820
10/N25
HS
ADMISSION
Cairnpapple Hill near Linlithgow, West Lothian Approach from the Bee-craigs road off west end of Linlithgow main street. Go past the Beecraigs turnoff and continue for 3km. Cairnpapple is signed. Astonishing Neolithic henge and later burial site on windy hill with views from Highlands to Pentlands. Atmosphere made even more strange by the very 21st-century communications mast next door. Cute visitor centre! Summer only 9.30am-5.30pm but can be accessed any time.

1821
11/L30
FREE
Cairnholy www.cairnholy.co.uk · between Newton Stewart & Gatehouse of Fleet 2km off main A75. Signed from road. A mini Callanish of standing stones around a burial cairn on very human scale and in a serene setting with another site (with chambered tomb) 150m up the farm track. Excellent view – sit and con-template what went on 4,000-6,000 years ago. I have it on good authority that this is a great place to watch the sunrise over the Solway Firth.

1822
10/R21
FREE
L
The Brown and White Caterthuns Kirkton of Menmuir, near Brechin & Edzell 5km uphill from war memorial at Menmuir, then signed 1km: a steep pull. Layby with obvious path to both on either side of the road. White easlest (500m uphill). These Iron Age hill top settlements give tremendous sense of scale and space and afford an impressive panorama of the Highland line. Colours refer to the heather-covered turf and stone of one and the massive collapsed ramparts of the White. Sit here for a while and picture the Pict.

1823
6/Q13
FREE
The Grey Cairns of Canster near Wick 20km south of Wick, a very straight road (signed for Cairns) heads west from the A9 for 8km. The cairns are instantly identifiable near the road and impressively complete. The 'horned cairn' is the best in the UK. In 2,500 BC these stone-piled structures were used for the disposal of the dead. You can crawl inside them if you're agile (or at night, brave). There are many other sights signed off the A9/99 but also interesting and nearby is:

1824
6/Q13
FREE
Hill o' Many Stanes www.stonepages.com · near Wick Aptly named place with extraordinary number of small standing stones; 200 in 22 rows. If fan shape was complete, there would be 600. Their very purposeful layout is enigmatic and strange.

1825
11/L31
FREE
The Whithorn Story www.whithorn.com · Whithorn Excavation site (though not active), medieval priory, shrine of St Ninian, visitor centre and café. More than enough to keep the whole family occupied – enthusiastic staff. Christianity? Look where it got us: this is where it started in Scotland. (Also 1552/COASTAL VILLAGES.) Easter-Oct 10.30am-5pm daily.

1826 **The Motte of Ur** near **Dalbeattie** Off B794 north of Dalbeattie and 6km from
11/N30 main A75 Castle Douglas to Dumfries road. Most extensive bailey earthwork castle
FREE in Scotland dating from 12th century. No walls or excavation visible but a great
sense of scale and place. Go through village of Haugh and on for 2km south of.
Looking down to right at farm buildings the minor road crosses a ford; park here,
cross footbridge and head to right – the hillock is above the ford.

1827 **Bar Hill** near **Kirkintilloch** A fine example of the low ruins of a Roman fort on
10/M25 the Antonine Wall which ran across Scotland for 200 years early AD. Great place for
FREE an out-of-town walk (704/GLASGOW VIEWS).

1828 **The Brochs** www.historic-scotland.gov.uk · **Glenelg** 110km from Fort
7/H19 William. Glenelg is 14km from the A87 at Shiel Bridge (1615/SCENIC ROUTES). 5km
HS from Glenelg village in beautiful Glen Beag. The 2 brochs, Dun Trodden and Dun
Telve, are the best preserved examples on the mainland of these mysterious 1st-
century homesteads. Easy here to distinguish the twin stone walls that kept out
the cold and the more disagreeable neighbours. The Wagon Café next to Dun
Troddon open in summer for tea and cake.

1829 **Barpa Lanyass** North Uist 8km south of Lochmaddy, visible from main A867
5/D17 road, like a stone hat on the hill (200m walk). A squashed beehive burial cairn dat-
FREE ing from 1,000 BC, the tomb of a chieftain. It's largely intact and the small and
nimble can explore inside, crawling through the short entrance tunnel and down
through the years. Nice hotel nearby (1174/GET-AWAY HOTELS) where a circular
walk starts, taking in this site and the loch (direction board 2.5km).

1830 **Sueno's Stone** Forres Signposted from main street at east end just off the
8/P17 A96. More late Dark Age than prehistoric, a 9th- or 10th-century carved stone, 6m
FREE high in its own glass case. Pictish, magnificent; arguments still over what it shows.

1831 **Aberdeenshire Prehistoric Trail: East Aquhorthies Stone Circle** near
8/S18 Inverurie 4km from Inverurie. Signed from B993 from Inverurie to Monymusk. A
FREE circle of pinkish stones with 2 grey sentinels flanking a huge recumbent stone set
in the rolling countryside of the Don Valley. Bennachie over there, then as now
(1966/HILLS)!

1832 **Loanhead of Daviot Stone Circle** near **Inverurie** Head for the village of
8/S18 Daviot on B9001 from Inverurie; or Loanhead, signed off A920 road between
FREE Oldmeldrum and Insch. The site is 500m from top of village. Impressive and
ATMOS spooky circle of 11 stones and one recumbent from 4,000/5,000 BC. Unusual
second circle adjacent encloses a cremation cemetery from 1,500 BC. Remains of
32 people were found here. Obviously, an important place. God knows what they
were up to.

Great Country Houses

NTS *National Trust for Scotland. Hours vary. Admission.*
HS *Historic Scotland. Standard hours: Apr-end Sep 9.30am-5.30pm; Oct-Mar 9.30am-4.30pm. Some local variations. All charge admission.*
☕ *signifies notable café.*

1833
9/J26
☕
ATMOS
L
✓ ✓ ✓ **Mount Stuart** www.mountstuart.com · 01700 503877 · Bute
Unique Victorian Gothic house; echoes 3rd Marquis of Bute's passion for mythology, astronomy, astrology and religion. Amazing splendour in intimate and romantic atmosphere. Italian antiques, notable paintings, fascinating detail with humorous touches. Equally grand gardens with fabulous walks, sea views. Stylish visitor centre with restaurant/coffee shop (741/ARGYLL RESTAURANTS); curated artworks in the wooded grounds. Even the garden centre is tasteful (2223/GARDEN CENTRES) and at both restaurant and courtyard tearoom you **EatBute**. May-Oct 11am-5pm. Sat 10am-2.30pm. Grounds 10am-6pm. Allow enough time here.

1834
8/S18
NTS
☕
L
✓ ✓ **Haddo House** www.nts.org.uk · 01651 851440 · Tarves by Ellon
Designed by William Adam for the Earl of Aberdeen, the Palladian-style mansion itself a bit less accessible after NTS cuts but the serenely superb grounds open always. Not so much a house, more a leisure land in the best possible taste, grounds with bluebells, wild garlic and autumn trees, a pleasant café, estate shop and gentle education. Grand house, full of things; the basements are the places to ponder. Glorious window by Burne-Jones in the chapel. Occasional afternoon teas followed by evening service: heaven (May-Oct)! Limited programme of other events. House: guided tours (must book) 0844 493 2179. Gardens all year till sunset.

1835
10/S26
ATMOS
LL
✓ ✓ **Manderston** www.manderston.co.uk · Duns Off A6105, 2km down Duns-Berwick road. Swan-song of the Great Classical House, one of the UK's finest examples of Edwardian opulence. *The* Edwardian CH of TV fame. The family still lives here. Below stairs as fascinating as up (the silver staircase!); sublime gardens (do see the woodland garden across the lake and the marble dairy). May-Sep, Thu/Sun 1.30pm-4.15pm (last entry). Gardens 11.30am-dusk all year.

1836
10/Q27
L
✓ ✓ **Traquair** www.traquair.co.uk · 01896 830323 · Innerleithen 2km from A72 Peebles-Gala road. Archetypal romantic Border retreat steeped in Jacobite history (ask about the Bear gates). Human proportions, liveability and lots of atmosphere. An enchanting house, a maze (20th century) and tranquil duck pond in the garden. Traquair ale still brewed. 1745 cottage tearoom, pottery and candlemaking. Apr-Oct House 11-5pm (Oct 11am-4pm, Nov weekends only). Cool events programme including fairs in May and the main Traquair Fair in Aug.

1837
10/Q25
NTS
☕
✓ ✓ **Newhailes** www.nts.org.uk · 0131 653 5599 · Musselburgh Well signed from Portobello end of Musselburgh (3km). NTS flagship time-capsule project stabilising the microcosm of 18th-century history encompassed here and uniquely intact. Great rococo interiors, very liveable, especially library. A rural sanctuary near the city: parklands, shell grotto, summer house. Easter and May-Sep, Thu-Mon, 12-5pm. Tours last 1 hour 15 minutes. Book: 0844 493 2125.

1838
10/M28
HS
✓ ✓ **Dumfries House** www.dumfries-house.org.uk · 01290 421742 (to book) · near Cumnock & Auchinleck One of the finest Palladian mansions in the country saved for the nation by a consortium led by the Prince of Wales (and £5M from the Scottish Government). The 750 acres and 18th-century apartments with their priceless Chippendale furniture and pristine artefacts are to open to the public on weekdays. Book first, even on the day.

1839
10/T26

✓ **Paxton** www.paxtonhouse.co.uk · 01289 386291 · near Berwick Off B6461 to Swinton and Kelso, 6km from A1. Country park and Adam mansion with Chippendales and Trotters; the picture gallery is a National Gallery outstation. 80 acres of woodlands to walk. Good adventure playground. Restored Victorian boathouse and salmon fishing museum on the Tweed. Red-squirrel hide. Event programme including indoor and outdoor performance; in September, a Regency Ball. Tours (1 hour) every 45 minutes, Apr-Oct 11am-5pm. Garden 10am-sunset.

1840
10/Q25

Gosford House 01875 870808 · near Aberlady On A198 between Longniddry and Aberlady, Gosford estate is behind a high wall and strangely stunted vegetation. Imposing house with centre block by Robert Adam and the wing you visit by William Young who did Glasgow City Chambers. The Marble Hall houses the remarkable collections of the unbroken line of Earls of Wemyss. Priceless art, informally displayed. Superb grounds. Aug-mid Sep, 1-4pm. Tours.

1841
10/S27
🍵
LL

Floors Castle www.floorscastle.com · 01573 223333 · Kelso More vast mansion than old castle, the ancestral home of the Duke of Roxburghe, overlooks with imposing grandeur the town and the Tweed. 18th-century with later additions. You're led round lofty public rooms past family collections of fine furniture, tapestries and porcelain. Priceless; spectacularly impractical. Good garden centre (2218/GARDEN CENTRES) and excellent tearoom, The Terrace (1368/TEAROOMS); café also on courtyard by the house. Apr-Oct 11am-5pm.

1842
10/R27

Mellerstain www.mellerstain.com · 01573 410225 · near Gordon/Kelso Home of the Earl of Haddington, signed from A6089 (Kelso-Gordon) or A6105 (Earlston-Greenlaw). One of Scotland's great Georgian houses, begun by William Adam in 1725, completed by Robert. Outstanding decorative interiors (the ceilings are *sans pareil*) especially the library and spectacular exterior 1761; it is truly a stately home. Easter weekend and May-Oct but days and hours vary, so check (never open Fri/Sat). Courtyard teahouse and beautiful gardens 11.30am-5pm.

1843
10/R26

Thirlestane www.thirlestanecastle.co.uk · 01578 722430 · Lauder 2km off A68. Castellate/baronial seat of the Earls and Duke of Lauderdale and family home of the Maitlands. Extraordinary staterooms, especially plaster work; once again the ceilings must be seen to be believed. The nurseries (with toy collection), kitchens and laundry are more approachable. Adventure playground. Opening times vary.

1844
8/S18
NTS
🍵

Fyvie www.nts.org.uk · Aberdeenshire 40km northwest of Aberdeen, an important stop on the Castle Trail which links the great houses of Aberdeenshire. Before opulence fatigue sets in, see this pleasant baronial pile first. Lived-in until the 1980s, it feels less remote than most. 13th-century origins, Edwardian interiors. Fantastic roofscape and ceilings. The *best* tearoom. Tree-lined acres; lochside walks. Apr-Oct 12noon-5pm; Sat-Wed July/Aug daily 11am-5pm. Grounds all year.

1845
8/S20
NTS
🍵
L

Crathes www.nts.org.uk · near Banchory 25km west of Aberdeen on A93. In superb gardens (1494/GARDENS), a fairy-tale castle: a tower house which is actually interesting to visit. Up and down spiral staircases and into small but liveable rooms. Timed tickets, one-way system. The notable painted ceilings and the Long Gallery at the top are all worth lingering over. 350 years of the Burnett family are ingrained in this oak. Apr-Oct 10.30am-4.45pm; till 3.45pm winter. Last entry 45 minutes before. Big event programme. Grounds all year 9.30am-dusk. Go Ape playground. Tearoom (1410/TEAROOMS) and adjacent 924/NORTHEAST RESTAURANTS.

Abbotsford near Melrose Home of Walter Scott. 1934/LITERARY PLACES.
Drumlanrig Thornhill The art, the courtyard, the park. 1521/COUNTRY PARKS.

Great Monuments, Memorials & Follies

These sites are open at all times and free unless otherwise stated.

1846
9/F27
1-A-2
ATMOS
LL

✓ ✓ **The American Monument** www.Islayinfo.com · Islay On the southwest peninsula of the island, known as the Oa (pronounced Oh), 10km from Port Ellen. A monument to commemorate the shipwrecks nearby of 2 American ships, the *Tuscania* and the *Ontranto*. The obelisk overlooks this sea – which is often beset by storms – from a spectacular headland, the sort of disquieting place where you could imagine looking round and finding the person you're with has disappeared. Take road from Port Ellen past Maltings marked Mull of Oa, then 8km. Signed off the road. Park, then a spectacular cliff-top walk 1.5km to monument. Can do 6km round trip. Bird life good in Oa area (RSPB reserve).

1847
10/N24
LL

✓ **Wallace Monument** www.nationalwallacemonument.com · 01786 472140 · Stirling Visible for miles and with great views, though not as dramatic as Stirling Castle. Approach from A91 or Bridge of Allan road. 150m walk from car park (or minibus) and 246 steps up. Victorian gothic spire marking the place where Scotland's great patriot swooped down upon the English at the Battle of Stirling Bridge. Mel Gibson's *Braveheart* increased visitors mid 90s. In the 'Hall of Heroes' the heroines section requires a feminist leap of the imagination. The famous sword is very big. Cliff top walk through Abbey Craig woods is worth detour. Monument open daily all year. Caff not great.

1848
7/F17
ADMISSION

The Grave of Flora Macdonald Skye Kilmuir on A855, Uig-Staffin road, 40km north of Portree. A 10ft-high Celtic cross supported against the wind, high on the ridge overlooking the Uists from whence she came. Long after the legendary journey, her funeral in 1790 attracted the biggest crowd since Culloden. The present memorial replaced the original, which was chipped away by souvenir hunters. Dubious though the whole business may have been, she still helped to shape the folklore of the Highlands.

1849
10/M26

Carfin Grotto www.carfin.org.uk · 01698 263308 · Motherwell Between M8 and Motherwell; take the road into Carfin and it's by Newarthill Rd. Gardens and pathways with shrines, pavilion, chapel, memorials and recently a monstrance. Built by out-of-work miners in the 1930s. Many statues: St Peregrine (patron saint of cancer sufferers) and Blessed John Paul II. A major Catholic devotional centre and never less than thought-provoking as the rest of us go station to station. Carfin Pilgrimage Centre adjacent open daily, 10am-5pm all year. Grotto open at all times.

1950
10/R27
LL

Peniel Heugh near Ancrum/Jedburgh (pronounced Pinal-hue) An obelisk visible for miles and on a rise offering some of the most exhilarating views of the Borders. Also known as the Waterloo Monument, it was built on the Marquis of Lothian's estate to commemorate the battle. It's said that woodland on the slopes around represents the positions of Wellington's troops. From A68 opposite Ancrum turnoff on B6400, go 1km past Monteviot Gardens up steep, unmarked road to left (cycle sign; monument not marked) for 150m; sign says Vehicles Prohibited, etc. Park, walk up through woods. Great organic caff nearby (1383/TEAROOMS).

1851
10/R25
L

The Hopetoun Monument Athelstaneford, near Haddington The needle atop a rare rise in East Lothian (Byres Hill) and a great vantage point from which to view the county from the Forth to the Lammermuirs and Edinburgh over there. Off A6737 Haddington to Aberlady road on B1343 to Athelstaneford. Car park and short climb. Tower usually open and viewfinder boards at top but take a torch; it's a dark climb. Good gentle ridge walk east from here.

1852
10/N25

The Tower at the House of the Binns near Linlithgow Off A904 west
from the access road at the Forth Road Bridge. This is the perfect chess-piece castle or tower that sits so proudly on the horizon with its saltire blowing behind the
NTS-managed House of the Binns. The house, home of the Dalyell family since
1612 (including Our Tam who asked the famous West Lothian Question) ain't
remittingly interesting but the view of the Forth from the tower, which was built
for a bet and cost £29 10 shillings, is splendid. Park by the house and walk 250m.
Grounds open all year till 7pm/dusk.

1853
10/N25

The Pineapple www.landmarktrust.org · 01628 825925 · Airth From Airth
north of Grangemouth, take A905 to Stirling and after 1km the B9124 for Cowie. It
sits on the edge of a walled garden at the end of the drive. 45ft high, it was built
in 1761 as a garden retreat by an unknown architect and remained 'undiscovered'
until 1963. How exotic the fruit must have seemed in the 18th century, never
mind this extraordinary folly. Grounds open all year. Oddly enough, you can stay
here (2 bedrooms, Landmark Trust). The gardens are kept by NTS (National Trust
for Scotland) and there's a figure-of-8 walk that takes in Dunmore village and the
River Forth.

1854
6/L12

John Lennon Memorial www.lennon.net · Durness In a garden created in
2002 (a BBC *Beechgrove Garden* project) amazing in itself surviving these harsh,
very northern conditions, an inscribed slate memorial to JL who for many years as
a child came here with his aunt for the hols. 'There are places I'll remember all my
life' from *Rubber Soul*. Who'd have thought that song (*In My Life*) was about here?
There's also a piece by national ceramic artist Lotte Glob who lives locally. Garden
upkept by volunteers.

1855
6/N15
L

The Monument on Ben Bhraggie Golspie Atop the hill (pronounced
Brachee) that surmounts the town, the domineering statue and plinth (over 35m)
of the dreaded first Duke of Sutherland; many have campaigned to have it demol-
ished; yet it survives. Climb from town fountain on marked path. The hill racers go
up in minutes but allow 2 hours return. His private view along the north-east
coast is superb (1789/CASTLES; 1499/GARDENS) and for background,
2148/MUSEUMS.

1856
7/K20
L

The Commando Monument near Spean Bridge On prominent rise by the
A82 Inverness to Fort William road where the B8004 cuts off to Gairlochy 3km
north of Spean Bridge. Commemorates the Commandos who gave their lives in
the '39-45 War and who trained in this area. Spectacular visa and poignant
memorial garden to troops lost in more recent conflicts, including the Iraq and
Afghan wars.

1857
9/H23
L

McCaig's Tower or Folly www.follytowers.com · Oban Oban's great landmark built in 1897 by McCaig, a local banker, to give 'work to the unemployed' and
as a memorial to his family. Built from Bonawe granite, it's like a temple or coli-
seum and time has mellowed whatever incongruous effect it may have had originally. The views of the town and the bay are magnificent and it's easy to get up
from several points in town centre. (744/OBAN)

1858
8/Q20
L

The Victoria Memorial to Albert Balmoral Atop the fir-covered hill behind
the house, she raised a monument, the **Albert Cairn**, whose distinctive pyramid
shape can be seen peeping over the crest from all over the estate. Desolated by
his death, the broken-hearted widow had this memorial built in 1862 and spent so
much time here, she became a recluse and the British Empire trembled. Path

begins at shop on way to Lochnagar distillery, 45 minutes up, 460 feet above sea level. Forget Balmoral (1788/CASTLES), all the longing and love for Scotland can be felt here, the great estate laid out below.

1859
8/S18
L
The Prop of Ythsie near Aberdeen 35km northwest of city near Ellon to west of A92, or pass on the Castle Trail since this monument commemorates one George Gordon of Haddo House nearby, who was prime minister 1852-55 (the good-looking guy in the first portrait you come to in the house; 1834/COUNTRY HOUSES). Tower visible from all of rolling Aberdeenshire and there are reciprocal views should you take the easy but unclear route up. On B999 Aberdeen-Tarves road (Haddo-Pitmeddon on the Castle Trail) and 2km from entrance to house. Take road for the Ythsie (pronounced Icy) farms, car park 100m. Don't miss the stone circle nearby.

1860
11/Q29
The Monument to Hugh MacDiarmid Langholm Sculpture by Jake Harvey depicting an open book with images from MacDiarmid's writing, all rusted on the hill above Langholm 3km from A7 at beginning of path to the Malcolm obelisk from where there are great views (1649/VIEWS). MacDiarmid, our other national poet, was born in Langholm in 1872 and, though they never liked him much after he left, the monument was commissioned and a cairn beside it raised in 1992. The bare hills surround you.

1861
6/J14
Memorial to Norman MacCaig near Lochinver Follow directions for the remarkable Achin's bookshop (2203/SHOPPING) which is at the start of the great walk to Suilven (1948/HILLS). Simple memorial of Torridon sandstone to Scotland's great poet who wrote so much about this landscape he loved: Assynt. Site a bit forlorn but there are some words writ here to guide us on the way.

1862
11/L29
Murray Monument near New Galloway Above A712 road to Newton Stewart about halfway between. A fairly austere needle of granite to commemorate a 'shepherd boy', one Alexander Murray, who rose to become a professor of Oriental Languages at Edinburgh University in the early 19th century. A 10-minute walk up for fine views of Galloway Hills; pleasant waterfall nearby. Just as he, barefoot...

1863
10/R27
HS
ATMOS
L
Smailholm Tower www.historic-scotland.gov.uk · near Kelso & St Boswells The classic Border tower which inspired Walter Scott; plenty of history and romance in a bucolic setting. Picnic or whatever. Good views from its crags. Near main road B6404 or off smaller B6937 – well signposted. Open Apr-Sep 9.30am-6.30pm. But fine to visit at any time (1623/SCENIC ROUTES).

Scott Monument Edinburgh 452/EDINBURGH VIEWS

The Most Interesting Churches

*Generally open unless otherwise stated; those marked * have public services.*

1864
10/Q26
ATMOS
L

✓ ✓ ✓ ***Rosslyn Chapel** www.rosslynchapel.org.uk · Roslin 12km south of Edinburgh city centre. Take A702, then A703 from ring-route road, marked Penicuik. Roslin village 2km from main road and chapel 500m from village crossroads above Roslin Glen. Medieval but firmly on the world map because of *The Da Vinci Code*. Grail seekers have been coming forever but now so many, it's guided tours only in summer. No doubting the atmosphere in this temple to the Templars and all holy meaningful stuff in a *Foucault's Pendulum* sense. But a special place. Recent major restoration. Episcopalian. Mon-Sat 10.30am-5.30pm, 12noon-4.15pm Sun (1 hour earlier in winter). Walk in the glen (432/WALKS OUTSIDE THE CITY). Coffee shop.

1865
9/J23
ATMOS
LL

✓ ✓ ***St Conan's Kirk** Loch Awe A85 33km east of Oban. Perched amongst trees on the side of Loch Awe, this small but spacious church seems to incorporate every ecclesiastical architectural style. Its building was a labour of love for one Walter Campbell who was perhaps striving for beauty rather than consistency. Though modern (begun by him in 1881 and finished by his sister and a board of trustees in 1930), the result is a place of ethereal light and atmosphere, enhanced by and befitting the inherent spirituality of the setting. There's a spooky carved effigy of Robert the Bruce, a cosy cloister and the most amazing flying buttresses. Big atmosphere.

1866
3/R12
ATMOS
LL

✓ ✓ **The Italian Chapel** www.visitorkney.com · Lamb Holm, Orkney 8km south of Kirkwall at Lamb Holm, the first causeway on the way to St Margaret's Hope. In 1943, Italian PoWs transformed a Nissen hut, using the most meagre materials, into this remarkable ornate chapel. The meticulous *trompe l'œil* and wrought-iron work are a touching affirmation of faith. Open all year round, daylight hours. At the other end of the architectural scale, **St Magnus Cathedral** in Kirkwall is a great edifice, but also imbues spirituality.

1867
2/XC1
ADMISSION

✓ ✓ **Queen's Cross Church** www.crmsociety.com · 70 Garscube Road, Glasgow Set where Garscube Rd becomes Maryhill Rd at Springbank St. C.R. Mackintosh's only church. Fascinating and unpredictable in every part of its design. Some elements reminiscent of Glasgow School of Art (built in the same year 1897) and others, like the tower, evoke medieval architecture. Bold and innovative, now restored and functioning as the headquarters of The Mackintosh Society. Mon-Fri 10am-5pm, Sun 2pm-5pm. (Not Sun in winter.) Closed Sat. No services. See 717/MACKINTOSH.

1868
11/N28
ATMOS
L

✓ ***Durisdeer Parish Church** www.churchesinscotland.co.uk · near Abington & Thornhill Off A702 Abington-Thornhill road and near Drumlanrig (1521/COUNTRY PARKS). If I lived near this delightful village in the hills, I'd go to church more often. It's exquisite and the history of Scotland is in the stones. The Queensberry marbles (1709) are displayed in the north transept (enter behind church) and there's a cradle roll and a list of ministers from the 14th century. The plaque to the two brothers who died at Gallipoli is especially touching. Covenanter tales are writ on the gravestones.

1869
9/K26

✓ ***Cathedral Of The Isles** Millport, Isle Of Cumbrae Frequent ferry service from Largs is met by bus for 6km journey to Millport. Lane from main street by Newton pub, 250m then through gate. The smallest cathedral in Europe, one of Butterfield's great works (other is Keble College in Oxford). Here, small is outstandingly beautiful and absolutely quiet except Sundays in summer when there are concerts. 1225/RETREATS; 1363/CAFÉS.

1870 **St Clements** Rodel, South Harris Tarbert 40km. Classic island kirk in
5/E16 Hebridean landscape. Go by the Golden Road (1621/SCENIC ROUTES). Simple cruciform structure with tower, which the adventurous can climb. Probably influenced by Iona. Now an empty but atmospheric shell, with blackened effigies and important monumental sculpture. Goats in the churchyard graze amongst the headstones of all the young Harris lads lost at sea in the Great War. There are other fallen angels on the outside of the tower.

1871 ***St Michael's Chapel** Eriskay, near South Uist/Barra That rare example of
5/D19 an ordinary modern church without history or grand architecture, which has charm and serenity and imbues the sense of well-being that a religious centre should. The focal point of a relatively devout Catholic community who obviously care for it. Overlooking the Sound of Barra. A delight whatever your religion.

1872 ***The Robin Chapel** www.robinchapel.org.uk · Edinburgh Surprising, char-
10/Q25 ming sanctuary in Craigmillar housing estate of south of the city. Built in the early 1950s by doting parents of a son killed in the war. Angels sing on Sunday at 4.30pm to a sublime liturgy. Lovely windows, carvings, tranquillity. Tours 0131 661 3366.

1873 ***St Fillan's Church** Aberdour Behind ruined castle (HS) in this pleasant sea-
10/P25 side village (1551/COASTAL VILLAGES), a more agreeable old kirk would be hard to find. To enter is to worship. Restored from a 12th-century ruin in 1926, the warm stonework and stained glass create a very soothing atmosphere (church open at most times, but if closed the graveyard is very fine). Sun services 10.30am.

1874 ***Culross Abbey Church** www.historic-scotland.gov.uk Top of Forth-side
10/N25 village of interesting buildings and windy streets (1546/COASTAL VILLAGES). Worth
HS hike up hill (signed; ruins adjacent) for views and for this well-loved and cared-for church. Great stained glass (see Sandy's window); often full of flowers.

1875 ***Dunblane Cathedral** www.dunblanecathedral.org.uk Huge nave of a
10/M24 church built around a Norman tower (from David I) on the Allan Water and restored
HS 1892. The wondrously bright stained glass is mostly 20th century. The poisoned sisters buried under the altar helped change the course of Scottish history. A contemplative place! Summer concerts.

1876 ***St Machar's Cathedral** www.stmachar.com · Aberdeen The Chanonry in
8/T19 Old Aberdeen off St Machar's Drive about 2km from centre. Best seen as part of a walk round the old village within the city occupied mainly by the university. The cathedral's fine granite nave and twin-spired West Front date from 15th century, on site of 6th-century Celtic church. Noted for heraldic ceiling and 19/20th-century stained glass. Seaton Park adjacent has pleasant Don-side walks and there's the old Brig o' Balgownie. Church open daily 9am-5pm (10am-4pm in winter).

1877 ***Bowden Kirk** near Melrose & Newtown St Boswells Signed from A68 (the
10/R27 A699), 500m off the main street. Beneath the Eildons (1970/HILL WALKS) in classic rolling Border country, an atmospheric 17th-century kirk of 12th century origin. Beautiful setting in one of southern Scotland's prettiest villages. Sun service 9.30am.

1878 **Fogo Parish Church** Fogo near Greenlaw Go find this sweet historic church by
10/S26 the Blackadder, the quintessential Berwickshire river. 17th century from 12th century origins: lairds' lofts, box pews. Rurality and spirituality; you'll have it to yourself.

1879
10/Q25

*The East Lothian Churches Aberlady, Whitekirk, Athelstaneford &
Garvald 4 charming churches in bucolic settings; quiet corners to explore and
reflect. Easy to find. All have interesting local histories and in the case of
Athelstaneford, a national resonance: a vision in the sky near here inspired the flag
of Scotland, the saltire. The spooky Doocot Heritage Centre behind the church
explains. Aberlady is my favourite, Garvald a days-gone-by village with pub.

1880
10/P25

Abercorn Church near South Queensferry Off A904. 4 km west of roundabout at Forth Bridge, just after village of Newton, Abercorn is signed. 11th-century
kirk nestling among ancient yews in a sleepy hamlet, untouched since Covenanter
days. St Ninian said to have preached to the Picts here and though hard to believe,
Abercorn was once on a par with York and Lindisfarne in religious importance.
Church always open. Walk in woods from corner stile or the Hopetoun Estate.

1881
6/L15
ATMOS
L

Croick Church www.croickchurch.com · Bonar Bridge 16km west of
Ardgay, just over the river from Bonar Bridge and through the splendid glen of
Strathcarron (1581/GLENS). This humble and charming church is remembered for
its place in the story of the Highland Clearances. In May 1845, 90 folk took shelter
in the graveyard around the church after they had been cleared from their homes
in nearby Glencalvie. Not allowed even in the kirk, their plight did not go unnoticed
and was reported in *The Times*. The harrowing account is there to read, and the
messages they scratched on the windows. Sheep graze all around then and now.

1882
10/L26

*Thomas Coates Memorial Church www.paisley.org.uk · Paisley Built by
Coates (of thread fame), an imposing edifice, sometimes called the Baptist cathe-
dral of Europe. A monument to God, prosperity and the Industrial Revolution.
Opening hours vary: 0141 887 2773. Service on Sun at 11am.

1883
10/R25

*The Lamp Of The Lothians St Mary's Collegiate www.stmaryskirk.com ·
Haddington Signed from east main street. A beautiful town church on the River
Tyne, with good stained glass and interesting crypts and corners. Obviously at the
centre of the community, a lamp as it were, in the Lothians. Tours, brass rubbings
(Sat). Summer concert season. Coffee shop and gift shop. Don't miss Lady Kitty's
garden, including the secret medicinal garden, a quiet spot to contemplate (if not
sort out) your condition. Apr-Sep 1.30-4pm (11am-4pm Sat). Daily and Sun service.

1884
10/P22

*Dunkeld Cathedral www.dunkeldcathedral.org.uk In town centre by lane
to the banks of the Tay at its most silvery. Medieval splendour amongst lofty trees.
Notable for 13th-century choir and 15th-century nave and tower. Parish church
open for edifying services and other spiritual purposes. Lovely summer recitals.

1885
9/J20

St Mary & St Finnan Church Glenfinnan On A830 Fort William-Mallaig Road
to the Isles (1628/SCENIC ROUTES), a beautiful (though inside a bit crumbly) Catholic
church in a spectacular setting. Queen Vic said she never saw a lovelier or more romantic spot (bet she said that a lot). Late 19th century. Open daily for meditations.

1886
9/H25
HS
L

Keills Chapel www.historic-scotland.gov.uk · South of Crinan The chapel
at the end of nowhere. From Lochgilphead, drive towards Crinan, but before you
get there, turn south down the B8025 and follow it past lovely little Tayvallich for
nearly 20km to the end. Park at the farm then walk the last 200m. You are 7km
across the Sound from Jura, at the edge of Knapdale. Early-13th-century chapel
houses some remarkable cross slabs, a 7th century cross and ghosts.

St Giles' Cathedral Edinburgh 416/OTHER ATTRACTIONS.
Glasgow Cathedral/University Chapel Glasgow 676/680/MAIN ATTRACTIONS.

The Most Interesting Graveyards

1887
2/XF2
ATMOS
LL

✓ ✓ **Glasgow Necropolis** www.glasgowcathedral.org.uk The vast burial ground at the crest of the ridge, running down to the river, that was the focus of the original settlement of Glasgow. Everything began at the foot of this hill and, ultimately, ended at the top where many of the city's most famous (and infamous) sons and daughters are interred within the reach of the long shadow of John Knox's obelisk. Generally open (official times), but best if you can get the full spooky experience to yourself, though don't go alone. See 676/MAIN ATTRACTIONS.

1888
1
ATMOS

✓ **Edinburgh Canongate** On left of Royal Mile going down to Palace. Adam Smith and the tragic poet Robert Fergusson revered by Rabbie Burns (who raised the memorial stone in 1787 over his pauper's grave) are buried here in the heart of Auld Reekie. Tourists can easily miss this one. **Greyfriars** A place of ancient mystery, famous for the wee dog who guarded his master's grave for 14 years, for the plundering of graves in the early 18th century for the Anatomy School and for the graves of Allan Ramsay (prominent poet and burgher), James Hutton (the father of geology), William McGonagall (the 'world's worst poet') and sundry serious Highlanders. Annals of a great city are written on these stones. **Dean Cemetery** is an Edinburgh secret and my New Town circle won't let me speak of it here.

1889
9/G25

✓ **Isle of Jura** www.theisleofjura.co.uk Killchianaig graveyard in the north. Follow road as far as it goes to Inverlussa, graveyard is on right, just before hamlet. Mairi Ribeach apparently lived until she was 128. In the south at Keils (2km from road north out of Craighouse, bearing left past Keils houses and through the deer fence), her father is buried and he was 180! Both sites are beautiful, isolated and redolent of island history, with much to reflect on, not least the mysterious longevity of the inhabitants and that soon we may all live this long.

1890
7/L18

✓ **Chisholm Graveyard** near Beauly Last resting place of the Chisholms and 3 of the largest Celtic crosses you'll see anywhere in a secret, atmospheric woodland setting. 15km west of Beauly on A831 to Struy after Aigas dam and 5km after golf course on right-hand side; 1km before Cnoc Hotel opposite Erchless Estate and through a white iron gate on right. Walk 150m on mossy path. Sublime!

1891
7/J19
LL

✓ **Clachan Duich** near Inverinate A beautiful stonewalled graveyard at the head of Loch Duich just south of Inverinate, 20km south of Kyle of Lochalsh. A monument on a rise above, a ruined chapel and many, many Macraes, this a delightful place to wander with glorious views to the loch and the mountains.

1892
9/J21

Eilean Munde near Ballachulish The island and graveyard in Loch Leven around the chapel of St Fintan Munnu who travelled here from Iona in the 7th century; the church was rebuilt in the 18th. Notable apart from mystery and history because of the Stewarts buried here and also the Macdonalds and Camerons who maintained it despite their conflicts. Obviously you'll need a wee boat. Enquire Lochaber Watersports adjacent the Isles of Glencoe hotel (1101/KIDS).

1893
9/H28

Campbeltown Cemetery Odd, but one of the nicest things about this end-of-the-line town is the cemetery. It's at the end of a row of fascinating posh houses, the original merchant and mariner owners of which will be interred in the leafy plots next door. Still very much in use after centuries of commerce and seafaring disasters, it has crept up the terraces of a steep and lush overhanging bank. The white cross and row of WW2 headstones are particularly affecting.

1894 **Kirkoswald Kirkyard** near Maybole & Girvan On main road through village
9/K28 between Ayr and Girvan. The graveyard around the ruined kirk and famous as the
burial place of the characters in Burns' most famous poem, *Tam o' Shanter*. A must
for Burns fans and famous-grave seekers with Souter Johnnie and Kirkton Jean
buried here. Pub across the road is a great grub stop and adjacent the House of
Burns, turned the village into a major visitor destination (2186/SHOPPING).

1895 **Humbie Churchyard** Humbie, East Lothian 25km southeast of Edinburgh via
10/Q26 A68 (turnoff at Fala). This is as reassuring a place to be buried as you could wish
for; if you're set on cremation, come here and think of earth. Deep in the woods
with the burn besides; after hours the sprites and the spirits have a hell of a time.

1896 **Ancrum Churchyard** near Jedburgh The quintessential country churchyard;
10/R27 away from the village (2km along B6400), by a lazy river (the Ale Water) crossed to
a farm by a humpback bridge and a chapel in ruins. Elegiac and deeply peaceful.
Great river swimming spot nearby (1672/WILD SWIMMING).

1897 **Balquhidder Churchyard** Chiefly notable as the last resting place of one Rob
10/L23 Roy Macgregor who was buried in 1734 after causing a heap of trouble hereabouts
and raised to immortality by Sir Walter Scott and then Michael Caton-Jones (the
movie). Despite well-trodden path, setting is poignant. For best reflections head
along Loch Voil to Inverlochlarig. Sunday evening concerts have been held in the
kirk Jul/Aug (check with local tourist information centres). Nice walk from back
corner to the waterfall and then to Rallying Place (1648/VIEWS). Great long walk to
Brig o' Turk (2002/GLEN WALKS). Tearoom in **Old Library** in village is a top county
spot, with very good cakes (1378/TEAROOMS).

1898 **Logie Old Kirk** near Stirling A crumbling chapel and an ancient graveyard at
10/N24 the foot of the Ochils. The wall is round to keep out the demons, a burn gurgles
beside and there are some fine and very old stones going back to the 16th century.
Take road for Wallace Monument off A91, 2km from Stirling, then first right. The
old kirk is beyond the new. The interpretation board is sponsored by the enig-
matic-sounding Sons of the Rock. Continuing on this steep narrow road (then right
at the t-junction) takes you onto the Ochils (1971/HILL WALKS).

1899 **Tutnaguail** Dunbeath There are various spellings of this enchanting cemetery
6/P14 5km from Dunbeath, Neil Gunn's birthplace. Found by walking up the strath he
describes in his book *Highland River* (1932/LITERARY PLACES). With a white wall
around it, this graveyard, which before the clearances once served a valley community of 400 souls, can be seen for miles. Ask at heritage centre for route or see
www.dunbeath-heritage.org.uk

1900 **Birkhill Cemetery** Dundee Opened in 1989. Part of the city's Templeton
10/Q23 Woods across the road (to Coupar Angus from the arterial dual carriageway) from
Camperdown Park (1539/TOWN PARKS, 2037/WOODLAND WALKS), this well-laid-out
cemetery is a destination in itself. No other graveyard on these pages seems so
well kept and well used. Extraordinary number of flowers on the graves. An aesthetic as well as reflective place to visit. Many Islamic graves and a woodlands burial section beyond.

1901 **Gairloch Old Graveyard** On the left as you arrive in Gairloch from the south by
7/H16 the golf course (where you park). Looking over the lovely bay and beach (1567/
BEACHES), a green and tranquil spot to explore. Osgood Mackenzie of Inverewe
Gardens (1492/GARDENS) is buried in the bottom-right corner (facing the sea)
under a simple Celtic cross, wild ferns behind, among many other Mackenzies.

The Great Abbeys

NTS *National Trust for Scotland. Hours vary. Admission.*
HS *Historic Scotland. Standard hours are: Apr-end Sep Mon-Sat 9.30am-5.30pm. Oct-Mar 9.30am-4.30pm. Local variations.*

1902
9/F23
HS
ATMOS
✓✓ **Iona Abbey** www.historic-scotland.gov.uk This hugely significant place of pilgrimage for new age and old age pilgrims and tourists alike is reached from Fionnphort, southwest Mull, by frequent CalMac Ferry (a 5-minute crossing). Walk 1km. Here in 563 AD St Columba began his mission for a Celtic church that changed the face of Europe. Cloisters, graveyard of Scottish kings and, marked by a modest stone, the inscription already faded by the weather, the grave of John Smith, the patron saint of New Labour. Ethereal, clear light through the unstained windows may illuminate your contemplations. Great sense of being part of a universal church and community. Regular services. Good shop (2194/SHOPPING) and nearby galleries. Residential courses (MacLeod Centre adjacent, 01681 700404). (2230/MAGICAL ISLANDS). For many, this is the Mull must-visit.

1903
8/P17
ATMOS
✓✓ **Pluscarden Abbey** www.pluscardenabbey.org · between Forres & Elgin The oldest abbey monastic community still working in the UK (1220/RETREATS) in one of the most spiritual of places. Founded by Alexander II in 1230 and being restored since 1948. Benedictine services (starting with Vigil and Lauds at 4.45am through Prime-Terce-Sext-None-Vespers at 5.30pm and Compline at 8pm) open to the public. The ancient honey-coloured walls, brilliant stained glass, monks' Gregorian chant: the whole effect is a truly uplifting experience. The bell rings down the valley. Services aside, open to visitors 4.30am-8.30pm.

1904
10/L26
✓✓ **Paisley Abbey** www.paisleyabbey.org.uk · 0141 889 7654 In the town centre. An abbey founded in 1163, razed (by the English) in 1307 and with successive deteriorations and renovations ever since. Major restoration in the 1920s brought it to present-day cathedral-like magnificence. Exceptional stained glass (the recent window complementing the formidable Strachan East Window), an impressive choir and an edifying sense of space. Sunday services are superb, especially full-dress communion and there are open days; phone for dates. Otherwise Abbey open all year Mon-Sat 10am-3.30pm. Café/shop.

1905
10/R28
HS
✓✓ **Jedburgh Abbey** www.historic-scotland.gov.uk The classic abbey ruin; conveys the most complete impression of the Border abbeys built under the patronage of David I in the 12th century. Its tower and remarkable Catherine window are still intact. Excavations have unearthed example of a 12th-century comb. It's now displayed in the excellent visitor centre which brilliantly illustrates the full story of the abbey's amazing history. Best view from across the Jed in the Glebe. My home town; my abbey! Check HS for hours.

1906
10/R27
HS
ATMOS
✓ **Dryburgh Abbey** www.historic-scotland.gov.uk · near St Boswells One of the most evocative of ruins, an aesthetic attraction since the late 18th century. Sustained innumerable attacks from the English since its inauguration by Premonstratensian Canons in 1150. Celebrated by Sir Walter Scott, buried here in 1832 (with his biographer Lockhart at his feet), its setting, amongst huge cedar trees on the banks of the Tweed is one of pure historical romance. 4km A68. (1644/VIEWS.) Hotel adjacent (799/BORDER HOTELS). Apr-Sep 9.30am-5.30pm, Oct-Mar till 4.30pm, Sun 2-4.30pm.

1907
11/N30
HS

Sweetheart New Abbey, near Dumfries 12km south by A710. The endearing and enduring warm red sandstone abbey in the shadow of Criffel, so named because Devorguilla de Balliol, devoted to her husband (he of the Oxford college), founded the abbey for Cistercian monks and kept his heart in a casket which is buried with her here. No roof, but the tower is intact. OK tearoom (but 'orrible gift shop): you can sit and gaze at the ruins while eating your Cream o' Galloway.

1908
10/R27
HS

Melrose Abbey www.historic-scotland.gov.uk Another romantic setting, the abbey seems to lend class to the whole town. Once again built by David I (what a guy!) for Cistercian monks from Rievaulx from 1136. It once sustained a huge community, as evinced by the widespread excavations. There's a museum of abbey, church and Roman relics; soon to include Robert the Bruce's heart, recently excavated in the gardens. Tempting Tweed walks start here.

1909
10/R22
HS

Arbroath Abbey www.historic-scotland.gov.uk 25km north of Dundee. Founded in 1178 and endowed on an unparalleled scale, this is an important place in Scots history. It's where the Declaration was signed in 1320 to appeal to the Pope to release the Scots from the yoke of the English (you can buy facsimiles of the yellow parchment; the original is in the Scottish Records Office in Edinburgh – oh, and tea towels). It was to Arbroath that the Stone of Destiny (on which Scottish kings were traditionally crowned) was returned after being 'stolen' from Westminster Abbey in the 1950s and is now at Edinburgh Castle. Great interpretation centre before you tour the ruins. All year round 9.30am-5.30pm.

The Great Battlegrounds

NTS *National Trust for Scotland. Hours vary. Admission.*

1910
7/M18
NTS
ATMOS

✓✓**Culloden** www.nts.org.uk · Inverness Signed from A9 and A96 into Inverness and about 8km from town. The new, state-of-the-art visitor centre puts you in the picture, then there's a 10-minute rooftop walk with perspective or a 40-minute through-the-battlefield walk. Positions of the clans and the troops marked out across the moor; flags enable you to get a real sense of scale. If you go in spring you see how wet and miserable the moor can be (the battle took place on 16 April 1746). No matter how many other folk are there wandering down the lines, a visit to this most infamous of battlefields can still leave a pain in the heart. Centre 9am-6pm (winter 10am-4pm). Ground open at all times for more personal Cullodens.

1911
7/F18

Battle of the Braes Skye 10km Portree. Take main A850 road south for 3km then left, marked Braes, for 7km. Monument is on a rise on right. The last battle fought on British soil and a significant place in Scots history. When the Clearances, uninterrupted by any organised opposition, were virtually complete and vast tracts of Scotland had been depopulated for sheep, the Skye crofters finally stood up in 1882 to the Government troops and said enough is enough. A cairn has been erected near the spot where they fought on behalf of 'all the crofters of Gaeldom', a battle which led eventually to the Crofters Act which has guaranteed their rights ever since. At the end of this road at Peinchorran, there are fine views of Raasay (which was devastated by clearances) and Glamaig, the conical Cuillin, across Loch Sligachan. Great B&B at the start of Braes road (2275/SKYE).

1912
9/J21
LLL

Glencoe Not much of a battle, of course, but one of the most infamous massacres in British history. Much has been written (John Prebble's *Glencoe* and others) and a discreetly located visitor centre provides audiovisual scenario. Macdonald monument near Glencoe village and the walk to the more evocative Signal Rock where the bonfire was lit, now a happy woodland trail in this doom-laden landscape. Many other great walks. See 1938/ENCHANTING PLACES, 1256/PUBS.

1913
3/Q11

Scapa Flow www.scapaflow.co.uk · **Orkney Mainland & Hoy** Scapa Flow, surrounded by various of the southern Orkney islands, is one of the most sheltered anchorages in Europe. Hence the huge presence in Orkney of ships and personnel during both wars. The Germans scuttled 54 of their warships here in 1919 and many still lie in the bay. The *Royal Oak* was torpedoed in 1939 with the loss of 833 men. Much still remains of the war years (1913/BATTLEGROUNDS): the rusting hulks, the shore fortifications, the Churchill Barriers and the ghosts of a long-gone army at Scapa and Lyness on Hoy. Evocative visitor centre and naval cemetery at Lyness. Open all year round. Excellent tour on MV *Guide* with remote controlled camera exploring 3 wrecks (01856 811360). May-Sep.

1914
10/R27

Lilliard's Edge near St Boswells On main A68, look for Lilliard's Edge Caravan Park 5km south of St Boswells; park and walk back towards St Boswells to the brim of the hill (about 500m), then cross rough ground on right along ridge, following tree-line hedge. Marvellous view attests to strategic location. 200m along, a cairn marks the grave of Lilliard who, in 1545, joined the Battle of Ancrum Moor against the English 'loons' under the Earl of Angus. 'And when her legs were cuttit off, she fought upon her stumps'. An ancient poem etched on the stone records her legendary... feet.

1915
10/N21
NTS

Killiecrankie near Pitlochry The first battle of the Jacobite Risings where, in Jul 1689, the Highlanders lost their leader Viscount (aka Bonnie) Dundee, but won the battle, using the narrow Pass of Killiecrankie. One escaping soldier made a famous leap. Well-depicted scenario in visitor centre; short walk to 'The Leap'. Battle viewpoint and cairn is further along road to Blair Atholl, turning right and doubling back near the Garry Guesthouse and on, almost to A9 underpass (3km from visitor centre). You get the lie of the land from here. Many good walks and the lovely **Killiecrankie Hotel** (860/PERTHSHIRE) for rest, refreshments and excellent food.

1916
10/N24
NTS

Bannockburn www.nts.org.uk · **near Stirling** 4km town centre via Glasgow road (it's well signposted) or junction 9 of M9 (3km), behind a sad hotel and car-rental centre (though this is set to change at TGP with a relocation and rebuild in time for the 700-year celebration). Some visitors might be perplexed as to why 24 Jun 1314 was such a big deal for the Scots and, apart from the 50m walk to the flag-pole and the huge statue, there's not a lot doing. But the battle against the English did finally secure the place of Robert I (the Bruce) as King of Scots, paving the way for the final settlement with England 15 years later. The best place to see the famous wee burn is from below the magnificent Telford Bridge. Controversies still rage among scholars: eg did the English really scarper after only an hour?

Mary, Charlie & Bob

HS *Historic Scotland. Standard hours are: Apr-end Sep 7 days 9.30am-5.30pm. Oct-Mar 9.30am-4.30pm; and winter variations.*

MARY, QUEEN OF SCOTS (1542–87)

Linlithgow Palace Where she was born. 1790/RUINS.
Holyrood Palace Edinburgh And lived. 403/MAIN ATTRACTIONS.

1917
10/M24
HS
LL
Inchmahome Priory www.historic-scotland.gov.uk · Port of Menteith
Priory ruins on the Isle of Rest in Scotland's only lake. Here the infant queen spent her early years cared for by Augustinian monks. A short boat journey. Signal the ferryman by turning the board to the island, much as she did. Apr-Oct 7 days. Last trip 4.30pm (Oct till 4pm). Lake Hotel adjacent for great food (779/CENTRAL HOTELS).

1918
10/R28
Mary, Queen of Scots' House Jedburgh In gardens via Smiths Wynd off main street. Historians quibble but this long-standing museum claims to be *the* house where she fell ill in 1566 but still made it over to visit the injured Bothwell at Hermitage Castle 50km away. Tower house in good condition; displays and well-told saga. We used to play tennis in the garden. Hours vary.

1919
10/P24
HS
L
Loch Leven Castle www.historic-scotland.gov.uk · near Kinross Well-signed! The ultimate in romantic penitentiaries; on the island in the middle of the loch; visible from the M90. Not much left of the ruin to fill the fantasy, but this is where Mary spent 10 months in 1568 before her famous escape and final attempt to get back the throne. Sailings Apr-Oct, 9.30am-5.30pm (last out 4.30pm, 3.30pm Oct) from pier at the National Game Angling Academy (Pier Bar/café serves as you wait) in small launch from Kirkgate Park. 7-minute trip, return as you like.

1920
11/M31
HS
Dundrennan Abbey www.historic-scotland.gov.uk · near Auchencairn
Mary got around and there are innumerable places where she spent the night. This was where she spent her last one on Scottish soil, leaving next day from Port Mary (nothing to see there but a beach, 2km along the road skirting the sinister MoD range, the pier long gone). The Cistercian abbey (established 1142) which harboured her on her last night is now a tranquil ruin.

'In my end is my beginning,' she said, facing her execution 19 years later.

1921
10/R25
Her 'death mask' is displayed at **Lennoxlove House** near Haddington · www.lennoxlove.com; it does seem small for someone who was supposedly 6 feet tall! Lennoxlove on road to Gifford. Apr-Sep, Wed/Thu/Sun 1.30-3.30pm.

BONNIE PRINCE CHARLIE (1720–88)

1922
5/D19
L
Prince Charlie's Bay or Strand Eriskay The uncelebrated, unmarked and quietly beautiful beach where Charlie first landed in Scotland to begin the Jacobite Rebellion. Nothing much has changed (except the pier for Barra ferry is adjacent) and this crescent of sand with soft machair and a turquoise sea is still a special place. 1km from township heading south; approach from township not by the new ferry road. 2238/MAGICAL ISLANDS.

1923
7/H20
ATMOS
L
Loch Nan Uamh, The Prince's Cairn near Arisaig 7km from Lochailort on A830 (1629/SCENIC ROUTES), 48km Fort William. Signed from the road (100m layby), a path leads down to the left. This is the traditional spot (pronounced Loch Na Nuan) where Charlie embarked for France in September 1746, having lost the

battle and the cause. The rocky headland also overlooks the bay and skerries where he'd landed in July the year before to begin the campaign. This place was the beginning and the end and it has all the romance necessary to be utterly convincing. Is that a French ship out there in the mist? The movie awaits.

1924 **Glenfinnan** www.glenfinnan.org Here he raised his standard to rally the clans
9/J20 to the Jacobite cause. For a while on that day in August 1745 it looked as if few
NTS were coming. Then pipes were heard and 600 Camerons came marching from the
LL valley (where the viaduct now spans). That must have been one helluva moment. It's thought that he actually stood on the higher ground but there is a powerful sense of place and history here. The visitor centre has an excellent map of Charlie's path through Scotland – somehow he touched all the most alluring places! Climb the tower or take the long view from Loch Shiel (1628/ROUTES). Nice church 1km (1885/CHURCHES) and a great hotel and bar (1180/VERY SCOTTISH HOTELS).

Culloden near Inverness 1910/BATTLEGROUNDS.

ROBERT I, THE BRUCE (1274–1329)

1925 **Bruce's Stone** Glen Trool near Newton Stewart 26km north by A714 via
11/L29 Bargrennan (8km to head of glen) on the Southern Upland Way (1989/LONG WALKS). The fair Glen Trool is a celebrated spot in Galloway Forest Park (1585/GLENS). The stone is signed (200m walk) and marks the area where Bruce's guerrilla band rained boulders onto the pursuing English in 1307 after routing the main army at Solway Moss. Good walks, including to Merrick which starts here (1959/HILLS).

1926 **Bannockburn** near Stirling The climactic battle in 1314, when Bruce decisively
10/N24 whipped the English and secured the kingdom (though Scotland was not legally recognised as independent until 1329). The scale of the skirmish can be visualised at the soon-to-be-rebuilt heritage centre but not so readily in the field. 1916/BATTLEGROUNDS.

1927 **Arbroath Abbey** www.historic-scotland.gov.uk Not much of the Bruce trail
10/R22 here, but this is where the famous Declaration was signed that was the attempt of
HS the Scots nobility united behind him to gain international recognition of the independence they had won on the battlefield. What it says is stirring stuff; the original is in Edinburgh. Great interpretation centre. 9.30-5.30pm.

1928 **Dunfermline Abbey Church** www.historic-scotland.gov.uk Here, some
10/P25 tangible evidence: his tomb. Buried in 1329, his remains were discovered wrapped
HS in gold cloth when the site was being cleared for the new church in 1818. Many of the other great kings, the Alexanders I and III, were not so readily identifiable (Bruce's ribcage had been cut to remove his heart). With great national emotion he was reinterred under the pulpit. The church (as opposed to the ruins and Norman nave adjacent) is open Easter-Oct, winter for services. Great café in Abbot House through graveyard (2145/MUSEUMS). Look up and see Robert carved on the skyline.

1929 **Melrose Abbey** www.historic-scotland.gov.uk On his deathbed Bruce asked
10/R27 that his heart be buried here after it was taken to the Crusades to aid the army in
HS their battles. A likely lead casket thought to contain it was excavated from the chapter house and it did date from the period. It was reburied here and is marked with a stone. Let's believe in this!

The Important Literary Places

1930 **Robert Burns (1759-96)** www.robertburns.org · Alloway, Ayr & Dumfries ·
9/L28 www.burnsmuseum.org.uk A well-marked heritage trail through his life and
haunts in Ayrshire and Dumfriesshire. **Alloway** Now with the (NTS) restoration of
Burns Cottage and 1km away, the new, state-of-the-art **Museum**, the bard has a
legacy and interpretive centre worthy of his international stature and appeal. 2137/
MUSEUMS. Both open 7 days 10am-5pm, 5.30pm Apr-Sep. Also in Alloway, the Auld
Brig o' Doon and the Auld Kirk where Tam o' Shanter saw the witches dance are
evocative, and the Monument and surrounding gardens are lovely. Elsewhere:
Ayr The Auld Kirk off main street by river; graveyard with diagram of where his
friends are buried; open at all times. **Dumfries** The house where he spent his
last years and mausoleum 250m away at back of a kirkyard stuffed with extravagant masonry. His howff in Dumfries, the **Globe Inn**, is very atmospheric – established in 1610 and still going strong (774/DUMFRIES). 10km north of Dumfries on
A76 at **Ellisland Farm** (home 1788-91) is the most interesting of the sites. The
farmhouse with genuine memorabilia, eg his mirror, fishing rod, a poem scratched
on glass, original manuscripts. There's his favourite walk by the river where he
composed *Tam o' Shanter* and a strong atmosphere about the place. Open 7 days
summer, closed Sun/Mon in winter. **Poosie Nansie's**, the pub he frequented in
Mauchline, is a must (1260/PUBS). **Brow Well near Ruthwell** on the B725
20km south of Dumfries and near Caerlaverock (1706/BIRDS), is a quieter place, a
well with curative properties where he went in the latter stages of his illness.

1931 **Lewis Grassic Gibbon (1901-35)** www.grassicgibbon.com · Arbuthnott,
10/S21 **near Stonehaven** Although James Leslie Mitchell left the area in 1917, this is
where he was born and spent his formative years. Visitor centre (01561 361668;
Mar-Oct 7 days 10am-4.30pm) at the end of the village (via B967, 16km south of
Stonehaven off main A92) has details of his life and can point you in the direction
of the places he writes about in his trilogy, *A Scots Quair*. The first part, *Sunset
Song*, is generally considered to be one of the great Scots novels and this area, the
Howe of the Mearns, is the place he so effectively evokes. Arbuthnott is
reminiscent of 'Kinraddie' and the churchyard 1km away on the other side of road
still has the atmosphere of that time of innocence before the war which pervades
the book. His ashes are here in a grave in a corner; the inscription: 'the kindness of
friends/the warmth of toil/the peace of rest'. From 1928 to when he died 7 years
later at the age of only 34, he wrote an incredible 17 books.

1932 **Neil Gunn (1891-1973)** www.neilgunn.org.uk · Dunbeath near Wick
6/P14 Scotland's foremost writer on Highland life, perhaps still not receiving the recognition he deserves, was brought up in this North East fishing village and based 3 of
his greatest yarns here, particularly *Highland River*, which must stand in any literature as a brilliant evocation of place. The **Strath** in which it is set is below the
house (a nondescript terraced house next to the shop) and makes for a great walk
(2011/GLEN & RIVER WALKS). There's a commemorative statue by the harbour, not
quite the harbour you imagine from the books. The excellent heritage centre
(www.dunbeath-heritage.org.uk) depicts the Strath on its floor and has a leaflet for
you to follow. Gunn also lived for many years near **Dingwall** and there is a
memorial on the back road to Strathpeffer and a wonderful view in a place he
often walked (on A834, 4km from Dingwall).

1933 **James Hogg (1770-1835)** St Mary's Loch, Ettrick The Ettrick Shepherd who
10/P27 wrote one of the great works of Scottish literature, *Confessions of a Justified Sinner*,
was born, lived and died in the valleys of the **Yarrow** and the **Ettrick**, some of
the most starkly beautiful landscapes in Scotland. **St Mary's Loch** on the A708,

28km west of Selkirk: there's a commemorative statue looking over the loch and the adjacent and supernatural seeming Loch of the Lowes. On the strip of land between is **Tibbie Shiels** pub (and hotel), once a gathering place for the writer and his friends (e.g. Sir Walter Scott) though currently not so recommendable. Across the valley divide (11km on foot, part of the Southern Upland Way. 1989/ LONG WALKS), or 25km by road past the Gordon Inn, Yarrow is the remote village of **Ettrick**, another monument and his grave (and Tibbie Shiels') in the churchyard. The James Hogg exhibition is at Bowhill House Visitor Centre (01750 22204).

1934
10/R27
Sir Walter Scott (1771-1832) Abbotsford, Melrose No other place in Scotland (and few anywhere) contains so much of a writer's life and work. This was the house he rebuilt from the farmhouse he moved to in 1812 in the countryside he did so much to popularise. The house, until recently lived in by his descendants, is run by trustees on a mission to raise millions for its upkeep. The library and study are pretty much as he left them with 9,000 rare books, antiquarian even in his day. Pleasant grounds and topiary and a walk by the Tweed which the house overlooks. His grave is at **Dryburgh Abbey** (1906/ABBEYS). There are monuments to Walt famously in Edinburgh (452/EDINBURGH VIEWS) and in George Square, Glasgow. House open Mar-Sep 9.30am-5pm; Sun 9.30am-5pm (in winter 11am-4pm).

1935
1
Robert Louis Stevenson (1850-94) Edinburgh Though Stevenson travelled widely – lived in France, emigrated to America and died and was buried in Samoa – he spent his first 30 years in Edinburgh. He was born and brought up in the New Town, living at **17 Heriot Row** from 1857-80 which is still lived in (not open to the public). Most of his youth was spent in this newly built and expanding part of the city in an area bounded then by parkland and farms. Both the **Botanics** (410/OTHER ATTRACTIONS) and **Warriston Cemetery** are part of the landscape of his childhood. However, his fondest recollections were of the **Pentland Hills** and, virtually unchanged as they are, it's here that one is following most poignantly in his footsteps. The cottage at **Swanston** (a delightful village with some remarkable thatched cottages reached via the city bypass/Colinton turnoff or from Oxgangs Rd and a bridge over the bypass; the village nestles in a grove of trees below the hills and is a good place to walk from), the ruins of **Glencorse Church** (ruins even then and where he later asked that a prayer be said for him) and **Colinton Manse** can all be seen, but not visited. Edinburgh has no dedicated Stevenson Museum, but **The Writers' Museum** at Makars' Court has exhibits (and of many other writers). The **Hawes Inn** in South Queensferry where he wrote *Kidnapped* has had its history obliterated in a brewery makeover.

1936
1
J.K. Rowling (we don't give a lady's birthdate) www.jkrowling.com · Edinburgh Scotland's most successful writer ever as the creator of Harry Potter, rich beyond dreams, was famously an impecunious single mother scribbling away in Edinburgh coffee shops. The most-mentioned is opposite the Festival Theatre and is now Spoon (143/BISTROS); the **Elephant House** (286/EDINBURGH COFFEE SHOPS) was another and gives you the idea. Harry Potter country as interpreted by Hollywood can be found at **Glenfinnan** (1924/MARY, CHARLIE & BOB) and **Glencoe** especially around the **Clachaig Inn** (1157/INNS). JK lives in 'writers' block' in Merchiston in Edinburgh (as do Ian Rankin and Alexander McCall Smith).

1937
1
Irvine Welsh (b.1958) www.irvinewelsh.net · Edinburgh Literary immortality awaits confirmation. There are *Trainspotting* tours but **Robbie's Bar** might suffice (351/EDINBURGH UNSPOILT PUBS); you will hear the voices.

The Most Enchanting Places

1938   **The Lost Valley** Glencoe The secret glen where the ill-fated Macdonalds hid
9/J21   the cattle they'd stolen from the Lowlands and which became (with politics and
2-B-2   power struggles) their undoing. A narrow wooded cleft takes you between the
ATMOS   imposing and gnarled 3 Sisters hills and over the threshold (God knows how the
LLL   cattle got there) and into the huge bowl of Coire Gabhail. The place envelops you
in its tragic history, more redolent perhaps than any of the massacre sites. Park on
the A82 6.5km from the visitor centre 300m west of the white bungalow by the
road (always cars parked here). Follow clear path down to and across the River Coe.
Ascend keeping burn to left; 1.5km further up, it's best to ford it. Allow 3 hours.
(1912/BATTLEGROUNDS.)

1939   **The Whaligoe Steps** Ulbster 10km south of Wick. 100m to car park by an
3/Q13   unsigned road off the A99 at the (modern) telephone box near sign for the Cairn of
LL   Get. Short walk from the car park at the end of cottage row to this remarkable
structure hewn into sheer cliffs, 365 steps down to a grassy platform – the Bink –
and an old fishing station. From 1792, creels of cod, haddock and ling were hauled
up these steps for the merchants of Wick and Lybster. Consider these labours as
you follow their footsteps in this wild and enchanting place. No rails and can be
slippy. Take great care!

1940   **Under Edinburgh Old Town** www.edinburgholdtown.org.uk Mary King's
1/D4   Close, a medieval street under the Royal Mile closed in 1753 (**The Real Mary
King's Close** 0845 070 6244); and the Vaults under South Bridge – built in the
18th century and sealed up around the time of the Napoleonic Wars (**Mercat
Tours** 0131 225 5445). History underfoot for unsuspecting tourists and locals alike.
Glimpses of a rather smelly subterranean life way back then. It's dark during the
day, and you wouldn't want to get locked in.

1941   **The Yesnaby Stacks** www.visitorkney.com · Orkney Mainland A cliff top
3/P10   viewpoint that's so wild, so dramatic and, if you walk near the edge, so precarious
LL   that its supernaturalism verges on the uneasy. Shells of lookout posts from the
war echo the melancholy spirit of the place. ('The bloody town's a bloody cuss/No
bloody trains, no bloody bus/And no one cares for bloody us/In bloody Orkney' –
first lines of a poem written then, a soldier's lament.) Near Skara Brae, it's about
30km from Kirkwall and way out west. Follow directions from Marwick Head
(1716/1718/BIRDS).

1942   **The Fairy Glen** Skye A place so strange, it's hard to believe that it's merely a
7/F17   geological phenomenon. Entering Uig on the A855 (becomes A87) from Portree,
ATMOS   there's a turret on the left (Macrae's Folly) by the Uig Hotel. Take road on right
LLL   marked Balnaknock for 2km and you enter an area of extraordinary conical hills
which, in certain conditions of light and weather, seems to entirely justify its legendary provenance. Your mood may determine whether you believe they were
good or bad fairies, but there's supposed to be an incredible 365 of these grassy
hillocks, some 35m high – well, how else could they be here?

1943   **Clava Cairns** near Culloden, Inverness Near Culloden (1910/BATTLEGROUNDS)
7/M18   these curious chambered cairns in a grove of trees near a river in the middle of
21st-century nowhere. This spot can make you feel a glow or goosepimples (1815/
PREHISTORIC SITES).

1944
7/M17
ATMOS
The Clootie Well www.blackisle.org · between Tore on the A9 & Avoch
Spooky place on the road towards Avoch and Cromarty 4km from the roundabout at Tore north of Inverness. Easily missed, though there is a marked car park on the right side of the road going east. What you see is hundreds of rags or clouts: pieces of clothing hanging on the branches of trees around the spout of an ancient well where the wearer might be healed. They go way back up the hill behind and though some may have been here a long time, this place seems to have been commodified like everywhere else so there's plenty of new socks and t-shirts with messages. It is all fairly weird.

1945
8/Q20
L
Burn o' Vat www.visitdeeside.org.uk · near Ballater This impressive and rather spooky glacial curiosity on Royal Deeside is a popular spot and well worth the short walk. 8km from Ballater towards Aberdeen on main A93, take B9119 for Huntly for 2km to the car park at the Muir of Dinnet nature reserve – driving through forests of strange spindly birch. Some scrambling to reach the huge 'pot' from which the burn flows to Loch Kinord. SNH visitor centre. Forest walks, 1.1km circular walk to vat, 7km to loch. Can be busy on fine weekends, supernatch when you find it deserted.

1946
11/N29
ATMOS
Crichope Linn near Thornhill A supernatural sliver of glen inhabited by water spirits of various temperaments (and midges). Take road for Cample on A76 Dumfries to Kilmarnock road just south of Thornhill; at village (2km) there's a wooden sign so take left for 2km. Discreet sign and gate in bank on right is easy to miss, but park in quarry 100m further on. Take care – can be very wet and very slippy. Gorge is a 10-minute schlep from the gate. We saw red squirrels! Durisdeer Church nearby is also enchanting (1868/CHURCHES).

1947
8/S17
LL
Hell's Lum Cave near Gardenstown, Moray Firth Coast Locally popular but still secret beach picnic and combing spot east of Gardenstown off the B9031 signed for Cullykhan Bay. From car park (200m from main road), you walk down to bay and can see on left a scar on the hill which marks the lum, approached along the shoreline possibly via a defile known as the Devil's Dining Room. Lots of local mythology surrounds this wild and beautiful spot. In the cave itself you hear what sounds like children crying.

The Necropolis Glasgow 1887/GRAVEYARDS.
Loanhead of Daviot near Oldmeldrum 1832/PREHISTORIC SITES.

Section 9
Strolls, Walks
& Hikes

Favourite Hills

Popular and notable hills in the various regions of Scotland but not including Munros or difficult climbs. Always best to remember that the weather can change very quickly. Take an OS map on higher tops. See p. 12 for walk codes.

1948
6/K14
2-C-3
✓✓ **Suilven** Lochinver From close or far away, this is one of Scotland's most awe-inspiring mountains. The 'sugar loaf' can seem almost insurmountable, but in good weather it's not so difficult. Route from Inverkirkaig 5km south of Lochinver on road to Achiltibuie, turns up track by Achin's Bookshop (2203/SHOPPING) on the path for the Kirkaig Falls; once at the loch, you head for the Bealach, the central waistline through an unexpected dyke and follow track to the top. The slightly quicker route from the north (Glencanisp) following a stalkers' track that eventually leads to Elphin, also heads for the central breach in the mountain's defences. Either way it's a long walk in; 8km before the climb. Allow 8 hours return. At the top, the most enjoyable 100m in the land and below – amazing Assynt. 731m. Take OS map.

1949
6/J15
2-B-3
✓✓ **Stac Pollaidh/Polly** near Ullapool This hill described variously as 'perfect', 'preposterous' and 'great fun'; it certainly has character and, rising out of the Sutherland moors on the road to Achiltibuie off the A835 north from Ullapool, demands to be climbed. Route everyone takes is from the car park by Loch Lurgainn 8km from main road. New path takes you (either way) round the hill and up from the north side. The path to the pinnacles is exposed and can be off-putting. Best half day hill climb in the North. 613m. Allow 3-4 hours return.

1950
6/J14
✓✓ **Quinag** near Lochinver Like Stac Polly (above), this Corbett (pronounced Koonyag) has amazing presence and seems more formidable than it actually is. Park off the A894 to Kylesku where great seafood awaits (1296/GASTROPUBS). An up-and-down route can take in 6 or 7 tops in your 5-hour expedition (or curtail). Once again, awesome Assynt!

1951
9/J27
2-B-2
NTS
✓ **Goat Fell** Arran Starting from the car park at Cladach before Brodick Castle grounds 3km from town, or from Corrieburn Bridge south of Corrie further up the coast (12km). A worn path, a steady climb, rarely much of a scramble but a rewarding afternoon's exertion. Some scree and some view! 874m. Usually not circular. Wineport on road to Brodick for refreshments; 2303/ARRAN. Allow 4 hours.

1952
9/K24
2-B-3
✓ **The Cobbler (aka Ben Arthur)** Arrochar Perennial favourite of Glasgow hillwalkers and, for sheer exhilaration, the most popular of the Arrochar Alps. A motorway path ascends from the A83 on the other side of Loch Long from Arrochar (park in laybys near Succoth road end, there are always loads of cars) and takes 2.5-3 hours to traverse the up 'n' down route to the top. Just short of a Munro at 881m, it has 3 tops of which the north peak is the simplest scramble (central and south peaks for climbers). Where the way is not marked, consult.

• •

5 MAGNIFICENT HILLS IN THE TROSSACHS

1953
10/L24
2-B-3
✓ **Ben Venue & Ben A'An** 2 celebrated tops in the Highland microcosm of the Trossachs around Loch Achray, 15km west of Callander; strenuous but not difficult and with superb views. Ben Venue (727m) is more serious; allow 4-5 hours return. Start from Kinlochard side at Ledard or more usually from Loch Katrine corner before Loch Achray Hotel. It's waymarked from the car park. Ben A'an (pronounced An) (415m) starts with a steep climb from the main A821 near the same

corner along from the Tigh Mor apartments (just before the corner). Scramble at top. Allow 2-3 hours. Very busy on fine days. The Byre at Brig o' Turk is decent.

1954
10/M23
2-B-3

Benn Shian Strathyre Another Trossachs favourite and not taxing. From village main road (the A74 to Lochearnhead), cross bridge opposite Munro Inn, turn left after 200m then path to right at 50m a steep start through woods. Overlooking village and views to Crianlarich and Ben Vorlich (see below). 600m. 3 hours return.

1955
10/L24
1-B-1

Doon Hill The Faerie Knowe, Aberfoyle Legendary hillock in Aberfoyle, only 1 hour up and back, so a gentle elevation into faerie land. The tree at the top is the home of the People of Quietness; one local minister had the temerity to tell their secrets (in 1692) and paid the price thereafter. Go round it 7 times and your wish will be granted, go round backwards at your peril (you wouldn't, would you?). From main street take Manse Rd by garden centre. 1km past cemetery, then signed.

1956
10/M24
2-B-3

Ben Ledi near Callander Another Corbett looking higher than it is with the Trossachs spread before you as you climb. West from town on A84 through Pass of Leny. First left over bridge to car park. Well trod path, ridge at top. Return via Stank Glen then follow river. Allow 4 hours. **Lade Inn** for a beer, anyone (1270/REAL ALE)?

• •

1957
10/H24
2-B-2
HS

✓ **Dunadd** Kilmartin, north of Lochgilphead Halfway from Kilmartin on A816. Less of a hill, more of a lump, but it's where they crowned the kings of Dalriada for half a millennium. Rocky staircases and soft, grassy top. Stand there when the Atlantic rain is sheeting in and... you get wet, presumably like the kings did. Or when the light is good you can see the glen and distant coast. Kilmartin House Museum nearby for info and great food (2154/HISTORY, 1394/TEAROOMS).

1958
11/N30
2-A-2

Criffel New Abbey near Dumfries 12km south by A710 to New Abbey, which Criffel dominates. It's only 569m, but seems higher. Exceptional views from top as far as English lakes and across to Borders. Granite lump with brilliant outcrops of quartzite. The annual race gets up and back to the Abbey Arms in under an hour; you can take it easier. Start 3km south of village, turnoff A710 100m from one of the curious painted bus shelters signed for Ardwell Mains Farm.

1959
11/L29
2-B-3

Merrick near Newton Stewart Go from bonnie Glen Trool via Bargrennan 14km north on the A714. Bruce's Stone is there at the start (1925/MARY, CHARLIE & BOB). The highest peak in Southern Scotland (843m), it's a strenuous though straightforward climb, a grassy ridge to the summit and glorious scenery. 4 hours.

1960
10/R25
BOTH 1-A-1

North Berwick Law The conical volcanic hill, a beacon in the East Lothian landscape. **Traprain Law** nearby (signed from A1), is higher, easy and celebrated by rock climbers, but has major prehistoric significance as a hill fort citadel of the Goddodin and a definite aura. NBL is also simple and rewarding – leave town by Law Rd, path marked beyond houses. Car park and picnic site. Views 'to the Cairngorms' (!) and along the Forth. Famous whalebone at the top.

1961
10/R28
2-A-2

Ruberslaw Denholm near Hawick This smooth hummock above the Teviot valley affords views of 7 counties, including Northumberland. Millennium plaque on top. At 424m, it's a gentle climb taking about 1 hour from the usual start at Denholm Hill Farm (private land, be aware of livestock). Leave Denholm at corner of green by post office and go past war memorial. Take left after 2km to farm.

1962 **Tinto Hill** near Biggar & Lanark A favourite climb in South/Central Scotland
10/N27   with easy access to start from Fallburn on the A73 near Symington, 10km south of
2-A-2   Lanark. Park 100m behind Tinto Hills farm shop. Good, simple track there and back
         though it has its ups and downs before you get there. Braw views, 707m. Allow 2
         hours though the annual racers do it in less than 30 minutes.

1963 **Conic Hill** Balmaha, Loch Lomond An easier climb than the Ben up the road
9/L24   and a good place to view it from, Conic, on the Highland fault line, is one of the
2-A-2   first Highland hills you reach from Glasgow. Stunning views also of Loch Lomond
         from its 358m peak. Ascend through woodland from the corner of Balmaha (the
         visitor centre) car park. Watch for buzzards and your footing on the final crumbly
         bits. Easy walks also on the nearby island, Inchcailloch (2026/WOODLAND WALKS).
         1.5 hours up.

1964 **Ben Vrackie** Pitlochry Small mountain, magnificent views. **Moulin Inn** to
10/N21   return to for pub grub (1266/REAL ALE). Woods, moorland, a loch and a bit of a
2-A-2   steep finish (at 841m, it's a Corbett). For the start, take A924 from Moulin (1.5km
         uphill from Pitlochry), going straight ahead when the road turns left to the car park
         300m further on. Track well signed and obvious. 4 hours.

1965 **Kinnoull Hill** www.forestry.gov.uk · Perth Various starts from town and A85,
10/P23   eg Manse Rd (the path from beyond Branklyn Garden on the Dundee Rd is less fre-
1-A-1   quented) to the wooded ridge above the Tay with its tower and incredible views to
         south from the precipitous cliffs. Surprisingly extensive area of hill side common
         and it's not difficult to get lost. The leaflet/map from Perth tourist information
         centre helps. Local lurv spot after dark (that Quarry car park).

1966 **Bennachie** www.forestry.gov.uk · near Aberdeen The pilgrimage hill, an
8/R19   easy 528m often busy at weekends but never disappoints. Various trails take you
2-B-2   to 'the Taps' from 3 main car parks. (1) From the new Bennachie Centre: 3km
         north of Inverurie on the A96, take left to chapel of Garioch (pronounced Geery),
         then left (it's signed). Centre closed Mon. (2) 16km north of Inverurie on the A96,
         take the B9002 through Oyne, then signed on left – picnic here among the pines.
         (3) The Donview car park 5km north of Monymusk towards Blairdaff – the longer,
         gentler walk in. All car parks have trail-finders. From the fortified top you see what
         Aberdeenshire is about. 2 hours. Bennachie's soulmate, **Tap o' Noth**, is 20km
         west. Easy approach via Rhynie on A97 (then 3km). Eat at Gadies (926/NORTHEAST
         RESTAURANTS)

1967 **Heaval** Barra The mini-Matterhorn that rises above Castlebay is an easy and
5/C20   rewarding climb. At 1250ft, it's steep in places but never over-taxing. You see 'the
         road to Mingulay'. Start up hill through Castlebay, park behind the new-build
         house and find path via Our Lady, Star of the Sea. 1.5 hours return.

Hill Walks

The following ranges of hills offer walks in various directions and more than one summit. They are all accessible and fairly easy. See p. 12 for walk codes.

1968
5

Walks on Skye www.skyewalk.co.uk Obviously many serious walks in and around the Cuillin (1985/MUNROS, 1994/SERIOUS WALKS), but almost infinite variety of others. Can do no better than read a great book, *50 Best Routes on Skye and Raasay* by Ralph Storer (available locally), which describes and grades many of the must-dos. And other pocket guides from the tourist information centre.

1969
10/P24
3-10KM
CIRC
XBIKES
2-A-2

Lomond Hills near Falkland The conservation village lies below a prominent ridge easily reached from the main street especially via Back Wynd (off which there's a car park). More usual approach to both East and West Lomond, the main tops, is from Craigmead car park 3km from village towards Leslie trail-finder board. The celebrated Lomonds (aka the Paps of Fife), aren't that high (West is 522m), but they can see and be seen for miles. Also: easy start from radio masts 3km up road from A912 east of Falkland. 1372/TEAROOM and pubs in the village.
An easy rewarding single climb is **Bishop Hill**. Start 100m from the church in Scotlandwell. A steep path veers left and then there are several ways up. Allow 2 hours. Great view of Loch Leven, Fife and a good swathe of Central Scotland. Gliders glide over from the old airstrip below.

1970
10/R27
3KM
CIRC
XBIKES
1-A-2

The Eildons Melrose The 3 much-loved hills or paps visible from most of the central Borders and easily climbed from the town of Melrose which nestles at their foot. Leave main square by road to station (the Dingleton road); after 100m a path begins between 2 pebble-dash houses on the left. You climb the smaller first, then the highest central one (422m). You can make a circular route of it by returning to the golf course. Allow 2 hours. Good pub-grub options in Melrose; p. 152-3.

1971
10/N24
2-40KM
SOME CIRC
XBIKES
1/2-B-2

The Ochils www.friendsoftheochils.org.uk Usual approach from the 'hillfoot towns' at the foot of the glens that cut into their south-facing slopes, along the A91 Stirling-St Andrews road. Alva, Tillicoultry and Dollar all have impressive glen walks easily found from the main streets where tracks are marked (2003/GLEN & RIVER WALKS). Good start near Stirling from the Sheriffmuir road uphill from Bridge of Allan about 3km, look for pylons and a lay-by on the right (a reservoir just visible on the left). There are usually other cars here. A stile leads to the hills which stretch away to the east for 40km and afford great views for little effort from Dumyat (800 feet, 3 hour return) though the highest point is Ben Cleugh, 721m. Swimming place nearby is 'Paradise' (1673/WILD SWIMMING).

1972
10/R26
5-155KM
SOME CIRC
MTBIKES
1/2-B-2

The Lammermuirs www.lammermuirhills.com The hills southeast of Edinburgh that divide East Lothian's rich farmlands from the Borders' Tweed valley. Mostly high moorland but there's wooded gentle hill country in the watersheds of the southern rivers and spectacular coastal scenery between Cockburnspath and St Abbs Head (1760/WILDLIFE; 2054/COASTAL WALKS). Eastern part of the Southern Upland Way, this follows the Lammermuirs to the coast (1993/LONG WALKS). Many moorland walks begin at Whiteadder Reservoir car park (A1 to Haddington, the B6355 through Gifford), then 10km to a mysterious loch in the bowl of the hills. Excellent walks also around Abbey St Bathans; head off A1 at Cockburnspath. Through village to Toot Corner (signed 1km) and off to left, follow path above valley of Whiteadder to Edinshall Broch (2km). Further on, along river (1km), is a swing bridge and a fine place to swim. Circular walks possible; ask in village. The Yester estate near Gifford is nearer Edinburgh and a good foothill option (437/EDINBURGH WOODLAND WALKS), though it is now a shooting estate.

1973   **Knockfarrel**   Dingwall to Strathpeffer   A walk (around 8km) between the two
7/L17   towns north of Inverness along the ridge between the A834 and A835 that includes
3KM   Knockfarrel, an Iron Age fort site on a raised plateau with views of the valleys, Loch
CIRC   Ussie and the Cromarty Firth. Non-taxing, hugely rewarding and damned pleasant.
XBIKES   Find starts in either town or drive to Knockfarrel from the A835 Dingwall-Contin
1-A-2   road off the A9, turning at the sign for the red kites. Go past kite turnoff to the t-
junction, turn left and 500m further, finish on a rough track to the car park.

1974   **The Cheviots**   www.cheviot-hills.co.uk   Not strictly in Scotland but they strad-
10/S27   dle the border and Border history. Many fine walks start from Kirk Yetholm (such
as the Pennine Way stretching 400km south to the Peak district and St Cuthbert's
Way; 1993/LONG WALKS) including an 8km circular route of typical Cheviot foothill
terrain. See *Walking in the Scottish Borders*, one of many fine guides available at
Border tourist centres. Most forays start at Wooler 20km from Coldstream. Cheviot
itself (2676ft) is a boggy plateau; Hedgehope via the Harthope Burn more fun.

The Campsie Fells   near Glasgow   694/WALKS OUTSIDE GLASGOW.
The Pentland Hills   near Edinburgh   429/WALKS OUTSIDE EDINBURGH.

■■■ Some Great Easy Munros

✓ ✓ *There are almost 300 hills in Scotland over 3,000ft as tabled by Sir
Hugh Munro in 1891. Those selected here have been chosen for their
relative ease of access both to the bottom and thence to the top. Tackle only
what is within your range of experience and ability. All these offer rewarding
climbs. None should be attempted without proper clothing (especially boots)
and sustenance. You may also need an OS map or GPS thing. Never underes-
timate how fast weather conditions can change in the Scottish mountains.*

1975   **Ben Lomond**   Rowardennan, Loch Lomond   Many folk's first Munro, given
9/L24   proximity to Glasgow (soul and city). It's not too taxing a climb and has rewarding
views (in good weather). 2 main ascents: the tourist route is easier, from toilet
block at Rowardennan car park (end of road from Drymen), well-trodden all the
way; or 500m up past Youth Hostel, a path follows burn – the Ptarmigan Route.
Steeper but quieter, more interesting. Circular walk possible. 974m. 3 hours up.

1976   **Schiehallion**   near Kinloch Rannoch   Fairy Hill of the Caledonians and a bit of
10/M22   a must (though very busy). New path c/o John Muir Trust over east flank. Start
Braes of Foss car park 10k from KR. 10km walk, ascent 750m. 5 hours. 1083m.

1977   **Carn Aosda**   Glenshee   Very accessible, starting from Glenshee ski car park; fol-
10/M21   low ski tow up. Ascent only 270m of 917m, so bag a Munro in an hour. Easier still,
take chairlift to Cairnwell, take in peak behind and then Carn Aosda – and you're
doing three Munros in a morning (cheating, but hey). The Grampian Highlands
unfold. Another easy (500m to climb) Munro nearby is **Cam an Tuirc** from the A93.

1978   **Meall Chuaich**   Dalwhinnie   Starting from verge of the A9 south of Cuaich at
7/M20   Cuaich cottages. Ascent only 623m, though the total walk is 14km. Follow aqueduct to power station then Loch Cuaich. An easily bagged 951m.

1979   **An Teallach**   Torridon   Sea-level start from Dundonnell on the A832 south of
7/J16   Ullapool. One of the most awesome Scots peaks but not the ordeal it looks. Path
well trod; great scrambling opportunities for the nimble. Peering over the pinnacle

of Lord Berkeley's Seat into the void is a jaw-drop. Take a day. Nice coffee shop called Maggie's near start/finish (1402/TEAROOMS). 1,062m.

1980 **Beinn Alligin** Torridon The other great Torridon trek. Consult regarding start at
7/J17 NTS Countryside Centre on corner of Glen Torridon-Diabeg road. Car park by bridge on road to Inveralligin and Diabeg, walk through woods over moor by river. Steep-ish pull up onto the Horns of Alligin. You can cover 2 Munros in a circular route that takes you across the top of the world. 985m. Then you could tackle **Liathach**. (trickier; **Ben Eighe**, also from a start on Glen Torridon road, probably easiest).

1981 **Ben More** Mull The cool, high ben sits in isolated splendour, the only Munro
9/G23 bar the Cuillin not on the mainland. Sea-level start from layby on the coast road B8073 that skirts the southern coast of Loch Na Keal at Dhiseig House, then a fairly clear path through the bleak landscape. Tricky near the top but there are fabulous views across the islands. 966m.

1982 **Ben Hope** near Tongue The most northerly Munro and many a bagger's last;
6/L13 also a good one to start with. Steep and craggy with splendid views, the approach from the south is relatively easy and takes about 4 hours there and back. Go south from Hope (on the A38) on the unclassified road. 927m.

1983 **Ben Wyvis** near Garve Standing apart from its northern neighbours, you can
7/L17 feel the presence of this mountain from a long way off. North of main A835 road Inverness-Ullapool and very accessible from it, park 6km north of Garve (48km from Inverness) and follow marked path by stream and through the shattered remnants of what was once a forest (replanting in progress). Leave the dereliction behind; the summit approach is by a soft, mossy ridge. Magnificent 1,046m.

1984 **Lochnagar** near Ballater Described as a fine, complex mountain, its nobility
10/Q20 and mystique apparent from afar, not least Balmoral Castle. Approach via Glen Muick (pronounced Mick) road from Ballater to car park at Loch Muick (1608/LOCHS). Path to mountain well signed and well trodden. 18km return, allow 6-8 hours. Steep at top; the loch supernatural. Apparently on a clear day you can see the Forth Bridge. 1,155m. (Guess who's not been up these – yet.)

1985 **Bla Bheinn** Skye The magnificent massif, isolated from the other Cuillin, has a
7/G19 sea-level start and seems higher than it is. The *Munro Guide* describes it as 'exceptionally accessible'. It has an eerie jagged beauty and – though some scrambling is involved and it helps to have a head for exposed situations – there are no serious dangers. Take B8083 from Broadford to Elgol through Torrin, park 1km south of the head of Loch Slapin, walking west at Allt na Dunaiche along north bank of stream. Bla Bheinn (pronounced Blahven) is an enormously reward-ing climb. Rapid descent for scree runners, but allow 8 hours. 928m.

1986 **Ben Lawers** Killin & Aberfeldy The massif of 7 summits including 6 Munros
10/M22 that dominate the north side of Loch Tay are linked by a 12km twisting ridge that
NTS only once falls below 800m. If you're very fit, you can do the lot in a day starting from the north or Glen Lyon side. Have an easier day of it knocking off Beinn Ghlas then Ben Lawers from the visitor centre (now closed) 5km off the A827. 4/5 hours. **Ben Lawers Inn** on north Loch Tay/Killin road for sustenance (food 12noon-9pm).

1987 **Meall Nan Tarmachan** The part of the ridge west of Lawers (above), which
10/M22 takes in a Munro and several tops, is one of the easiest Munro climbs and is immensely impressive. Start 1km further on from NTS visitor centre down 100m track and through gate. Slog to start. 12km walk, climb 800m, allow 6 hours.

Long Walks

✓✓ *These walks require preparation, maps, good boots etc. Don't carry too much. Sections are always possible. See p. 12 for walk codes.*

1988
9/K22
2-B-3
The West Highland Way www.west-highland-way.co.uk The 150km walk which starts at Milngavie 12km outside Glasgow and goes via some of Scotland's most celebrated scenery to emerge in Glen Nevis before the Ben. The route goes like this: Mugdock Moor-Drymen-Loch Lomond-Rowardennan-Inversnaid-Inverarnan-Crianlarich-Tyndrum-Bridge of Orchy-Rannoch Moor-Kingshouse Hotel-Glencoe-The Devil's Staircase-Kinlochleven. The latter part from Bridge of Orchy is the most dramatic. **The Bridge of Orchy Hotel** (01838 400208; 1144/ROADSIDE INNS. Best; not cheap!) and **Kings House** (01855 851259) are both historic staging posts, as is the **Drover's Inn, Inverarnan** (784/CENTRAL HOTELS). When booking accommodation allow time for muscle fatigue and don't carry too much. Info leaflet/pack from shops or National Park Office (01389 722600). **START** Officially at Milngavie (pronounced Mull-guy) Railway Station (regular service from Glasgow Central, also buses from Buchanan St Bus Station), but actually from Milngavie shopping precinct 500m away. However, the countryside is close. From other end on Glen Nevis road from roundabout on A82 north from Fort William. The Way is well marked and there's a good *Official Pocket Companion*.

1989
11/J30
2-B-3
The Southern Upland Way www.southernuplandway.gov.uk 350km walk from Portpatrick across the Rhinns of Galloway, much moorland, the Galloway Forest Park, the wild heartland of Southern Scotland, then through James Hogg country (1933/LITERARY PLACES) to the gentler east Borders and the sea at Pease Bay (official end, Cockburnspath). Route is Portpatrick-Stranraer-New Luce-Dalry-Sanquhar-Wanlockhead-Beattock-St Mary's Loch-Melrose-Lauder-Abbey St Bathans. The first and latter sections are the most obviously picturesque but highlights include Loch Trool, the Lowther Hills, St Mary's Loch, Traquair, Melrose and the River Tweed. Usually walked west to east, the Southern Upland Way is a formidable undertaking... Info from **Ranger Service** (01835 825060). **START** Portpatrick by the harbour and up along the cliffs past the lighthouse. Or Cockburnspath. Map is on side of shop at the Cross.

1990
8/Q17
1-A-3
The Speyside Way www.moray.gov.uk A long distance route which generally follows the valley of the River Spey from Buckie on the Moray Firth coast to Aviemore in the foothills of the Cairngorms and thence to Newtonmore, with side spurs to Dufftown up Glen Fiddich (7km) and to Tomintoul over the hill between the River Avon (pronounced A'rn) and the River Livet (24km). The main stem of the route largely follows the valley bottom, criss-crossing the Spey several times – a distance of around 100km, and is less strenuous than Southern Upland or West Highland Ways. The Tomintoul spur has more hill-walking character and rises to a great viewpoint at 600m. Throughout the walk you are in whisky country with opportunities to visit Cardhu, Glenlivet and other distilleries nearby (1490/1483/WHISKY). Info from **Ranger Service** (01340 881266). **START** Usual start is from Spey Bay 8km north of Fochabers (from Buckie adds another 8km); the first marker is by the banks of shingle at the river mouth.

1991
7/K18
2-C-3
Glen Affric www.glenaffric.org In enchanting Glen Affric and Loch Affric beyond (2001/GLEN & RIVER WALKS; 1577/GLENS; 1664/WILD SWIMMING), some serious walking begins on the 32km Kintail trail. Done either west-east starting at the Morvich Outdoor Centre 2km from A87 near Shiel Bridge, or east-west starting at the Affric Lodge 15km west of Cannich. Route can include one of the approaches to the Falls of Glomach (1588/WATERFALLS).

1992 **The Cateran Trail** www.pkct.org Named after the Caterans who were marau-
10/P22 ding cattle thieves, this 100k hike crosses their old stamping ground, the splendid
2-B-3 hills and glens of Angus and Perthshire. Circular (100km) from a start at Blairgowrie
and 4/5 days to complete; there are also 5 sections: Blairgowrie-Bridge of Cally-
Glenshee-Glen Isla-Alyth. Good inn options on the way (1153/1156/ROADSIDE INNS).
All in splendid country, this is a well thought-out route.

1993 **St Cuthbert's Way** www.stcuthbertsway.fsnet.co.uk From Melrose in the
10/R27 Borders (where St Cuthbert started his ministry) to Lindisfarne on Holy Island off
2-A-3 Northumberland (where he died) via St Boswells-Kirk Yetholm-Wooler. 100km but
many sections easy. Bowden–Maxton and a stroll by the Tweed especially fine.
Check local tourist centres. Causeway to Holy Island a treat at the end.

Serious Walks

✓ ✓ *None of these should be attempted without OS maps, equipment
and preparation. Hill or ridge walking experience may be essential.*

1994 **The Cuillin Mountains** www.isleofskye.com · Skye Much scrambling and, if
7/G19 you want it, serious climbing over these famously unforgiving peaks. The Red ones
3-C-3 are easier and many walks start at the **Sligachan Hotel** on the main Portree-
Broadford road. Every July there's a hill race up Glamaig; the conical one which
overlooks the hotel. Most of the Black Cuillin including the highest, Sgurr Alasdair
(993m), and Sgurr Dearg, 'the Inaccessible Pinnacle' (978m), can be attacked from
the campsite or the youth hostel in Glen Brittle. Good guides are *Introductory
Scrambles from Glen Brittle* by Charles Rhodes, or *50 Best Routes in Skye and Raasay*
by Ralph Storer, both available locally, but you will need a map. (2/BIG ATTRAC-
TIONS; 1136/HOSTELS; 1593/WATERFALLS; 1985/MUNROS; 1656/WILD SWIMMING.)

1995 **Aonach Eagach** Glencoe One of several possible major expeditions in the
9/J21 Glencoe area and one of the world's classic ridge walks. Not for the faint-hearted
3-C-3 or the ill-prepared. It's the ridge on your right for almost the whole length of the
glen from Altnafeadh to the road to the **Clachaig Inn** (rewarding refreshment).
Start from the main road. Car park opposite the one for the Lost Valley
(1938/ENCHANTING PLACES). Stiff pull up then the switchback path across. There is
no turning back. Scary pinnacles two-thirds over, then one more Munro and the
knee-trembling, scree-running descent. On your way, you'll have come close to
heaven, seen Lochaber in its immense glory and reconnoitred some fairly exposed
edges and pinnacles. Go with somebody good as I once did. (1614/SCENIC ROUTES;
1256/ BLOODY GOOD PUBS; 1133/HOSTELS; 1912/BATTLEGROUNDS.)

1996 **Buachaille Etive Mor** Glencoe In same area as above and another of the UK's
9/J21 best high-level hauls. Not as difficult or precarious as the Eagach and long loved by
3-C-3 climbers and walkers, with stunning views from its several false summits to the
actual top with its severe drops. Start on main Glencoe road. 5km past King's
House Hotel. Well-worn path. Allow 6/7 hours return.

1997 **Ben Nevis** Start on Glen Nevis road, 5km Fort William town centre (by bridge
9/K21 opposite youth hostel or from visitor centre) or signed from A82 after Glen Nevis
2-B-3 roundabout. Both lead to start at Achintee Farm and the **Ben Nevis Inn** (handy
afterwards; 1057/FORT WILLIAM). This is the most popular and safest route. Allow
the best part of a day (and I do mean the best – the weather can turn quickly
here). For the more interesting arete route, consult locally. Many people are killed

every year, even experienced climbers. It is the biggest, though not the best; you can see 100 Munros on a clear day (ie about once a year). You climb it because... you have to. 1,352m. 7-9 hours return.

1998
7/J19
3-C-3

The Five Sisters of Kintail & The Cluanie Ridge Both generally started from A87 along from Cluanie Inn (1259/BLOODY GOOD PUBS) and they will keep you right; usually walked east to west. Sisters is an uncomplicated but inspiring ridge walk, taking in 3 Munros and 2 tops. It's a hard pull up and you descend to a point 8km further up the road (so arrange transport). Many side spurs to vantage-points and wild views. The Cluanie or south ridge is a classic which covers 7 Munros. Starts at inn; 2 ways off back onto A876. Both can be walked in a single day (Cluanie allow 9 hours). (1134/HOSTELS.)

From the Kintail Centre at Morvich off A87 near Shiel Bridge another long distance walk starts to Glen Affric (1991/LONG WALKS).

1999
7/N19
3-C-3

Glen More Forest Park www.forestry.gov.uk From Coylumbridge and Loch Morlich; 32km through the Rothiemurchus Forest (2023/WOODLAND WALKS) and the famous **Lairig Ghru**, the ancient right of way through the Cairngorms which passes between Ben Macdui and Braeriach. Ascent is over 700m and going can be rough. This is one of the great Scottish trails. At end of June the Lairig Ghru Race completes this course east-west in 3.5 hours, but generally this is a full-day trip. The famous shelter, Corrour Bothy between Devil's Point and Carn A Mhaim, can be a halfway house. Near Linn of Dee, routes converge and pass through the ancient Caledonian Forest of Mar. Going east-west is less gruelling and there's Aviemore to look forward to!

Glen & River Walks

See also Great Glens, p. 277-8. Walk codes are on p. 12.

2000
10/N21
UP TO 17KM
CIRC
XBIKES
1-B-2

✓ **Glen Tilt Blair Atholl** A walk of variable length in this classic Highland glen, easily accessible from the old Blair Rd off main Blair Atholl road near Bridge of Tilt Hotel, car park by the (very) old bridge. Trail leaflet from park office and local tourist information centres. Fine walking and unspoiled scenery begins only a short distance into the deeply wooded gorge of the River Tilt, but to cover the circular route you have to walk to Gilbert's Bridge (9km return) or the longer trail to Gow's Bridge (17km return). Begin here also the great route into the Cairngorms leading to the Linn of Dee and Braemar, joining the track from Speyside which starts at Feshiebridge or Glenmore Forest (1999/LONG WALKS).

2001
7/K18
5/8 KM
CIRC
BIKES
1-B-2

✓ **Glen Affric** www.glenaffric.org · **Cannich near Drumnadrochit** Easy short walks are marked and hugely rewarding in this magnificent glen well known as the first stretch in the great east-west route to Kintail (1991/LONG WALKS) and the Falls of Glomach (1588/WATERFALLS). Starting point of this track into the wilds is at the end of the road at Loch Affric; there are many short and circular trails indicated here. Car park is beyond metal road 2km along forest track towards Affric Lodge (cars not allowed to lodge itself). Track closed in stalking season. Easier walks in famous Affric forest from car park at Dog Falls. 7km from Cannich (1664/WILD SWIMMING). Waterfalls and spooky tame birds. Good idea to hire bikes at Drumnadrochit or Cannich (01456 415364). See also 1577/GLENS.

2002
10/L23
18KM · XCIRC
XBIKES
2-B-2

✓**Balquhidder to Brig o' Turk** Easy amble through the heart of Scotland via Glenfinglas (1607/LOCHS) with a handy pub (1307/GASTROPUBS) and tearooms (1378/TEAROOMS) at either end. Not circular so best to arrange transport. Usually walked starting at Rob Roy graveyard (1897/GRAVEYARDS), then Ballimore and past Ben Vane to the reservoir and Brig o' Turk. B o' T start offers some great walk options.

2003
10/N24
3KM + TOPS
CIRC
XBIKES
1-A-2

✓**Dollar Glen** Dollar The classic fairy glen in central Scotland, positively hoaching with water spirits, reeking of ozone and euphoric after rain. 20km by A91 from Stirling or 18km from M90 at Kinross junction 6. You walk by the Burn of Care and the Burn of Sorrow. Start at side of the volunteer-run museum or golf club, or further up road (signed Castle Campbell) where there are 2 car parks, the top one 5 minutes from castle. The castle at head of glen is open 7 days last entry 5.30pm (Oct-Mar till 4pm) and has boggling views. There's a circular walk back or take off for the Ochil Tops, the hills surrounding the glen. There are also first-class walks up the glens of the other hillfoot towns, Alva and Tillicoultry which also lead to the hills (1971/HILL WALKS).

2004
10/N24
3KM
CIRC
XBIKES
1-A-1

✓**Rumbling Bridge** near Dollar Formed by another burn off the Ochils, an easier short walk in a glen with something of the chasmic experience and added delight of the unique double bridge (built 1713). At the end of one of the walkways under the bridge you are looking into a Scottish jungle landscape as the Romantics imagined. Near Powmill on A977 from Kinross (junction 6, M90) then 2km. Up the road is The Powmill Milkbar (1385/TEAROOMS) serving traditional and tasty home-made food for nigh on 40 years. It's 5km west on the A977. Open 7 days till 5pm (6pm weekends). Go after your walk!

2005
10/P22
16KM
CIRC
BIKES
1-A-2

✓**Loch Ordie** near Dunkeld Not a walk through a specific glen or riverside but one which follows many burns past lochs and ponds, skirts some impressive hills and is all in all a splendid and simple hike through glorious country almost Highland in nature but close to the Central Belt. Loch Ordie is halfway on a loop that starts at a bend on the A923 Blairgowrie road on left about 6km from Dunkeld after the turnoff for Loch of the Lowes. Deuchary Hill, the highest here at 509m, can be climbed on a non-circular path from the main circuit. This is one of the best, most scenic walks in Perthshire. 16km; allow 4/5 hours, mostly level.

2006
10/Q21

✓**Glen Clova** www.clova.com Most walked of the Angus glens. Many start from end at Acharn especially west to Glen Doll (new ranger centre for orientation, etc). Also enquire at Glen Clova Hotel (1167/GET-AWAY HOTELS) – 2-hour Loops of (Loch) Brandy walk starts here – and repair there afterwards (great walkers' pub). Easy, rewarding walks!

2007
10/R23
1-A-1

✓**The Lade Braes** St Andrews Unlike most walks on these pages, this cuts through the town itself following the Kinness Burn. But you are removed from all that! Start at Westport at the traffic lights just after the garage on Bridge St or (marked) opposite 139 South St. Trailboard and signs. Through Coldshaugh Park (sidespur to Botanics on opposite bank) and the leafy glen and green sward at the edge of this beautiful town. Ends in a duck pond. You pass the back gardens of some very comfortable lives.

2008
7/M17
1-A-1

✓**The Fairy Glen** Rosemarkie On the Black Isle. On the main A832, the road to Cromarty, 150 metres after the Plough Inn on the right, a car park and information board. Beautiful, easy 3km walk with gorge, 2 waterfalls and some great birdlife. Can finish on Rosemarkie beach to picnic and look for dolphins. Some superb trees. Comfort food in main street for that picnic (1447/DELIS).

2009 **Falkland** Fife If you're in Falkland for the palace (1774/CASTLES) or the tearoom
10/Q24 (1385/TEAROOMS), add this amble up an enchanting glen to your day. Go through
3KM village then signed Cricket Club for Falkland Estate and School (an activity centre) –
CIRC car park just inside gate (with map) – and gardens are behind it. Glen and refur-
XBIKES bished path up the macadam road are obvious. Gushing burn, waterfalls – you can
1-A-2 even walk behind one! Couple of ok pubs.

2010 **The Big Burn Walk** Golspie A non-taxing, perfect glen walk through lush
6/N15 diverse woodland. 3 different entrances including car park marked from A9 near
6KM Dunrobin Castle gates but most complete starts beyond Sutherland Arms and
CIRC Sutherland Stonework at the end of the village. Go past derelict mill and under
XBIKES aqueduct following river. A supernature trail unfolds with ancient tangled trees,
1-B-1 meadows, waterfalls, cliffs and much wildlife. 3km to falls, return via route to castle woods for best all-round intoxication.

2011 **The Strath at Dunbeath** www.dunbeath-heritage.org.uk The glen or
6/P14 strath so eloquently evoked in Neil Gunn's *Highland River* (1932/LITERARY PLACES),
XCIRC a book which is as much about the geography as the history of his childhood.
XBIKES Starting below the row of cottages on your left after the flyover going north near
1-B-1 the much older Telford Bridge. A path follows the river for many miles. A leaflet
from the Dunbeath Heritage Centre points out places on the way as well as map
on its entire floor. It's a spate river and in summer becomes a trickle; hard to
imagine Gunn's salmon odyssey. It's only 500m to the broch, but it's worth going
into the hinterland where it becomes quite mystical (1899/GRAVEYARDS).

2012 **Tweedside** Peebles The riverside trail that follows the Tweed from town (Hay
10/Q27 Lodge Park) past Neidpath Castle (1662/WILD SWIMMING) and on through classic
5/12KM Border wooded countryside crossing river 2.5km out (5km round trip), or at
CIRC Manor Bridge 6km out (Lyne Footbridge, 12km). Pick up *Walking in the Scottish*
XBIKES *Borders* and other Tweedside trail guides at local tourist information centres.
1-A-1 Other good Tweedside walks between Dryburgh Abbey and Bemersyde House
grounds (1623/SCENIC ROUTES) and at Newton St Boswells by the golf course.

2013 **Failford Gorge** near Mauchline Woody gorge of the River Ayr. Start from
10/L27 bridge at Ayr end of village on B743 Ayr-Mauchline road (4km Mauchline). Easy,
3/5KM · CIRC marked trail. Pub in village great for ale (they brew their own: Windie Goat!) and
XBIKES local craic and particularly notable for food is the Sorn Inn east of Mauchline
1-A-1 (1276/GASTROPUBS). This is bucolic Ayrshire at its best.

2014 **Glen Lednock** near Comrie Walk from Comrie or take the car further up to
10/M23 monument or drive further into glen to reservoir (9km) for more open walks. From
3/5KM town take right off main A85 (to Lochearnhead) at the excellent **Deil's Cauldron**
CIRC bar/restaurant. Walk and Deil's Cauldron (waterfall and gorge) are signed after
XBIKES 250m. Walk takes less than 1hr and emerges on road near Lord Melville's monu-
1-A-1 ment (climb for great views back towards Crieff, about 25 minutes). Other walks up
slopes to left after you emerge from the tree-lined gorge road. There's also the
start of a hike up Ben Chonzie, 6km up glen at Coishavachan. This is one of the
easiest Munros (931m) with a good path and great views, especially to northwest.

2015 **Bridge of Alvah** Banff Details: 2033/WOODLAND WALKS, mentioned here
8/R17 because the best bit is by the river and the bridge itself. The single-span crossing
was built in 1772 and stands high above the river in a sheer-sided gorge. The river
below is deep and slow. In the right light it's almost Amazonian. Walk takes 1.5
hours from Duff House (2172/PUBLIC GALLERIES). There's a picture of Alvah upstairs
in the collection.

2016
10/R21
2KM · XCIRC
XBIKES
1-A-1

The Gannochy Bridge & The Rocks of Solitude near Edzell 2km north of village on B966 to Fettercairn. There's a lay-by after bridge and a wooden door on left (you're in the grounds of the Burn House). Through it is another world and a path above the rocky gorge of the River North Esk (1km). Huge stone ledges over dark pools. You don't have to be alone (or maybe you do).

2017 9/J23
10KM
CIRC
BIKES
1-A-1

Near Taynuilt A walk (recommended by readers) combining education with recreation. Start behind Bonawe Ironworks (2161/HISTORY) and go along the river side to a suspension bridge and thence to Inverawe Smokehouse (open to the public; café). Walk back less interesting but all very nice. Best not to park in Bonawe car park (for HS visitors, and it closes at 6pm).

2018
11/L30

Glen Trool near Newton Stewart A simple non-clambering, well marked route round Loch Trool. A circular 8km but with many options. And a caff at the visitor centre. 1585/GREAT GLENS.

▰▰▰▰ Woodland Walks

2019
9/G21

✓ ✓ **Ardnamurchan** www.ardnamurchan.com For anyone who loves trees (or hills, great coastal scenery and raw nature), this far-flung - peninsula is a revelation. Approach from south via Corran ferry on A82 south of Fort William or north from Lochailort on A830 Mallaig–Fort William road (1628/SCENIC ROUTES) or from Mull. Many marked and unmarked trails (see Ariundle below) but consult internet or locally. To visit Ardnamurchan is to fall in love with Scotland again and again. Woods especially around Loch Sunart (www.sunartoakwoods.org.uk). Good family campsite at Resipole (1203/CAMPING WITH KIDS) and lovely food at Lochaline (1015/BEST HIGHLAND RESTAURANTS).

2020
8/N17
1-4KM
CIRC
XBIKES
1-A-2

✓ **Randolph's Leap** near Forres Spectacular gorge of the plucky little Findhorn lined with beautiful beech woods and a great place to swim or picnic (1663/WILD SWIMMING), so listen up. Go either: 10km south of Forres on the A940 for Grantown, then the B9007 for Ferness and Carrbridge. 1km from the sign for **Logie Steading** (2178/SHOPPING) and 300m from the narrow stone bridge, there's a pull-over place on the bend. The woods are on the other side of the road. Or: take the A939 south from Nairn or north from Grantown and at Ferness take the B9007 for Forres. Approaching from this direction, it's about 6km along the road; the pull-over is on your right. This is one of the sylvan secrets of the North. Trailboard at site and at Logie Steading from which it's a 3.5km walk return, so you could simply head for here; there's a great café.

2021
9/J24
2-8KM
CIRC
XBIKES
2-A-2

✓ **Lochaweside** Unclassified road on north side of loch between Kilchrenan and Ford, centred on Dalavich. Illustrated brochure available from local hotels around Kilchrenan and Dalavich post office, describes 6 walks in the mixed, mature forest all starting from car parking places on the road. 3 starting from the Barnaline car park are trail-marked and could easily be followed without a guide. Avich Falls route crosses River Avich after 2km with falls on return route. Inverinan Glen is always good. The timber trail from the Big Tree/Cruachan car park 2km south of Dalavich takes in the loch, a waterfall and it's easy on the eye and foot (4km). The track from the car park north of Kilchrenan on the B845 back to Taynuilt is less travelled but also fine. Good pub at Kilchrenan. Also see 70/DIS-COVER.

2022 9/K25
3KM
CIRC
XBIKES
1-A-1

✓ **Puck's Glen** www.forestry.gov.uk · near Dunoon Close to the gates of the Younger Botanic Garden at Benmore (1493/GARDENS) on the other side of the A815 to Strachur 12km north of Dunoon. A short, exhilarating woodland walk from a convenient car park. Ascend through trees then down into a fairy glen follow the burn back to the road. Some pools to be swum.

2023
7/N19
1-A-2

✓ **Rothiemurchus Forest** www.rothiemurchus.net · near Aviemore The place to experience the magic and the majesty of the great Caledonian Forest and the beauty of Scots Pine. Approach from B970, the road that parallels the A9 from Coylumbridge to Kincraig/Kingussie. 2km from Inverdruie near Coylumbridge follow sign for Loch an Eilean; one of the most perfect lochans in these or any woods. Loch circuit 5km (1604/LOCHS). Info, sustenance and shopping at the Rothiemurchus visitor centre at Inverdruie (**Druie**, their café daytime only).

2024
7/N20

✓ **Uath Lochans** Rothiemurcus A less frequented place and a very fine walk in the same neck of the woods as one of several around Glen Feshie. Off the B970 road between Kincraig and Coylumbridge/Aviemore signed Glen Feshie, 2km to car park on the right. 3 walks marked around the lochans, all a dawdle. Best take you around Farleitter Crag with views over the treetops (red route is not as long as it says, maybe 1.5 hours).

2025
9/H21
5KM
CIRC
MTBIKES
1-A-2

✓ **Ariundle Oakwoods** Strontian 35km Fort William via Corran Ferry. Walk guide brochure at Strontian tourist information centre. Many walks around Loch Sunart and Ariundle (www.sunartoakwoods.org.uk): rare oak and other native species. You see how very different Scotland's landscape was before industrialisation. Start over town bridge, turning right for Polloch. Go on past Ariundle Centre, with good home-baking café and park. 2 walks; well marked.

2026 9/L25
3KM
CIRC
1-A-2

✓ **Inchcailloch Island** Loch Lomond Surprisingly large island near Balmaha, criss-crossed with easy, interesting woodland walks with the loch always there through the trees. A pleasant afternoon option is to row there from Balmaha Boatyard (£10 a boat at TGP). They also run a regular ferry; 01360 870214.

2027
10/N22
3-3KM
CIRC
XBIKES
1-A-2

The Birks o' Aberfeldy Circular walk through oak, beech and the birch (or birk) woods of the title, easily reached and signed from town main street (1km). Steep-sided wooded glen of the Moness Burn with attractive falls especially the higher one spanned by bridge where the 2 marked walks converge. This is where Burns 'spread the lightsome days' in his eponymous poem. Excellent tearoom and all-round life enhancer, the **Watermill**, back in town (1379/TEAROOMS). Allow 2 hours.

2028
10/P22
3-2KM
CIRC
XBIKES
1-A-1

The Hermitage, Dunkeld www.visitdunkeld.com On A9 2km north of Dunkeld. Popular, easy, accessible walks along glen and gorge of River Braan with pavilion overlooking the falls and, further on, Ossian's Cave. Also uphill Craig Vinean walks starts here to good viewpoint (2km). Several woody walks around Dunkeld/Birnam – there's a good leaflet from the tourist information centre. 2km along river is **Rumbling Bridge**, a deep gorge, and beyond it great spots for swimming (1659/WILD SWIMMING).

2029
7/N19

Glenmore Forest Park www.forestry.gov.uk · near Aviemore Along from Coylumbridge (and adjacent Rothiemurchus) on road to ski resort, the forest trail area centred on Loch Morlich (sandy beaches, good swimming, water sports). Visitor centre has maps of walk and bike trails and an activity programme. Glenmore Lodge (01479 861256) is Scotland's Outdoor Training Centre and well worth a visit. They know a lot about walking!

2030 **Above the Pass of Leny** Callander A walk through mixed forest (beech, oak,
10/M24 birch, pine) with great Trossachs views. Start from main car park on A84 4km
2 OR 4KM north of Callander (Falls of Leny are on opposite side of road, 100m away). Various
CIRC options marked and boarded where marshy. Another short but glorious walk is to
XBIKES the **Bracklinn Falls** – signed off east end of Callander Main St; start by the golf
1-A-1 course (1km; see also 1670/WILD SWIMMING). Also loop to the Craggs (adding
another 2km).

2031 **Loch Tummel Walks** near Pitlochry Mixed woodland north of Loch Tummel,
10/N22 reached by the B8019 from Pitlochry to Rannoch. Visitor centre at Queen's View
2 -15KM (1647/VIEWS), 01796 473123; and walks in the Allean Forest which take in some
CIRC historical sites (a restored farmstead, standing stones) start nearby (2-4km). There
BIKES are many other walks in area: the Forestry Commission brochure is worth following
1-B-2 (available from visitor centre and local tourist information centres). (1613/LOCHS.)

2032 **The New Galloway Forest** www.forestry.gov.uk Huge area of forest and
11/L30 hill country with every type of trail including part of Southern Upland Way from
Bargrennan to Dalry (1989/LONG WALKS). Visitor centres at Kirroughtree (5km
Newton Stewart) and Clatteringshaws Loch on the Queen's Way (9km New
Galloway). Glen and Loch Trool are very fine (1585/GLENS); the Retreat Oakwood
near Laurieston has 5km trails. Kitty's in New Galloway has great cakes and tea
(1373/TEAROOMS). There's a river pool on the raiders' road (1671/WILD SWIMMING).
One could ramble on...

2033 8/R17 **Duff House** www.duffhouse.org.uk · Banff Duff House is the major
7KM attraction around here (2172/PUBLIC GALLERIES), but if you've time it would be a
CIRC pity to miss the wooded policies and the meadows and riverscape of the Deveron.
XBIKES To the Bridge of Alvah where you should be bound is about 7km return; 1.5 hours
1-A-2 return. See also 2015/GLEN & RIVER WALKS.

2034 7/L17 **Torrachilty Forest & Rogie Falls** www.forestry.gov.uk · near Contin &
1-4KM **Strathpeffer** Enter by old bridge just outside Contin on main A835 west to
CIRC Ullapool or further along (4km) at Rogie Falls car park. Shame to miss the falls
XBIKES (1601/WATERFALLS), but the woods and gorge are pleasant enough if it's merely a
1-A-2 stroll you need. Ben Wyvis further up the road is the big challenge (1983/MUNROS).

2035 **Abernethy Forest** near Boat of Garten 3km from village off B970, but hard
8/N19 to miss because the famous ospreys are signposted from all over (1711/BIRDS).
Nevertheless this woodland reserve is a tranquil place among native pinewoods
around Loch Mallachie with dells and trails. Many other birdies twittering around
your picnic. They don't dispose of the midges.

2036 **Fochabers** www.fochabers-heritage.org.uk On main A96 about 3km east of
8/Q17 town are some excellent woody and winding walks around the glen and Whiteash
Hill (2-5km). Further west on the **Moray Coast Culbin Forest**: head for Cloddy-
moss or Kentessack off A96 at Brodie Castle 12km east of Nairn (1772/CASTLES).
Acres of Sitka in a sandy coastal forest.

2037 **Templeton Woods** www.camperdownpark.com · Dundee Extensive and
10/Q23 atmospheric woodlands on the edge of Dundee just beyond the Kingsway dual
carriageway, turning 3km on Coupar Angus road. Many trails to walk or bike; visitor
centre. Red squirrels and roe deer may scamper. Relatively new Birkhill Cemetery
on the way in is a joy (1900/GRAVEYARDS).

Where To Find Scots Pine

Scots Pine, with oak and birch etc, formed the great Caledonian Forest which once covered most of Scotland. Native Scots Pine is very different from the regimented rows of pine trees we associate with the forestry plantations which now drape much of the countryside. It is more like a deciduous tree with reddish bark and irregular foliage; no two ever look the same. The remnants of the great stands of pine are beautiful to see, mystical and majestic, a joy to walk among and no less worthy of conservation perhaps than a castle or a bird of prey. Below are some places you will find them.

2038
8/Q20
Glentanar www.glentanar.co.uk · Royal Deeside Near Ballater, 10-15km southwest of Aboyne.

2039
10/P20
Around **Linn of Dee** (1624/SCENIC ROUTES), especially the back road to Mar Lodge (1238/HOUSE PARTIES).

2040
10/M24
Strathyre near Callander South of village on right of main road after Loch Lubnaig.

2041
10/L24
Achray Forest www.forestry.gov.uk · near Aberfoyle Some pine near the Duke's Pass road, the A821 to Loch Katrine, and amongst the mixed woodland in the 'forest drive' to Loch Achray.

2042
10/L22
Blackwood of Rannoch www.rannoch.net South of Loch Rannoch, 30km west of Pitlochry via Kinloch Rannoch. Start from Carie, fair walk in. 250-year-old pines; an important site.

2043
9/L25
Rowardennan Loch Lomond End of the road along east side of loch near Ben Lomond. Easily accessible pines near the lochside, picnic sites, etc.

2044
7/H17
Shieldaig Notably the island in the loch opposite the pub/hotel (998/ HIGHLANDS) but to wander among on the approach from the south, especially on the coast road from Applecross. .

2045
7/J17
Shores of **Loch Maree, Loch Torridon** and around **Loch Clair, Glen Torridon**. Both near the **Beinn Eighe National Nature Reserve** (1762/GREAT WILDLIFE RESERVES). Visitor centre on A832 north of Kinlochewe.

2046
7/L18
Glen Affric near Drumnadrochit 1577/GLENS. Biggest remnant of the Caledonian Forest in classic glen. Many strolls and hikes possible. Try Dog Falls (on main road) for Affric introduction.

Rothiemurchus Forest 2023/WOODLAND WALKS.

Native pinewoods aren't found south of Perthshire but there are fine plantation examples in southern Scotland at:

2047
10/Q27
Glentress near Peebles 7km on A72 to Innerleithen. Mature forest up the burn side, though surrounded by commercial forest.

2048
11/N29
Shambellie Estate near Dumfries 1km from New Abbey beside A710 at the Shambellie House, 100yds sign. Ancient stands of pine over the wall amongst other glorious trees; this is like virgin woodland. Planted 1775–80. Magnificent (and great new garden nearby: 1520/GARDENS in the trees).

Coastal Walks

2049
9/F26
XCIRC
XBIKES
2-B-2

✓✓ **Kintra** Islay On Bowmore-Port Ellen road take Oa turnoff: then Kintra signed 7km. Park in old farmyard by campsite (1190/WILD CAMPING). A fabulous beach (1560/BEACHES) runs in opposite direction and a notable golf course behind it (2086/GOLF IN GREAT PLACES). This walk leads along north coast of the Mull of Oa, an area of diverse beauty with a wonderful shoreline. The walk to the American Monument is spectacular (1.5km or 6km circular; 1846/MONUMENTS).

2050
8/T18

✓✓ **The Bullers of Buchan** near Peterhead 8km south of Peterhead on A975 Cruden Bay road. Park and walk 100m to cottages. To the north is the walk to Boddam and Longhaven Nature Reserve along dramatic cliffs and south past Slains Castle (1810/RUINS). The Bullers is at start of walk, a sheer-sided hole 75m deep with outlet to the sea through a natural arch. Walk round the edge, looking down on layers of birds (who may try to dive-bomb you away); it's a wonder of nature on an awesome coast. Take great care (and a head for heights).

2051
6/K12

✓✓ **Cape Wrath & The Cliffs of Clo Mor** www.capewrath.org.uk Britain's most northwesterly point reached by ferry from 1km off A838 4km south of Durness; a 10-minute crossing then 40-minute minibus ride to Cape. Ferry holds 12 and runs May-Sep (call for times: 01971 511246) or ferryman direct (07719 678729): John Morrison on his boat for 30 years. At 280m Clo Mor are high though not the UK's highest. For cliffs, ask to be put off the bus (which goes to the Stevenson lighthouse) and reduce the walk to 3km. The caff here **Iozone**, is always open (I've never been). Around 8 trips a day, weather and MoD range permitting. Bikes are ok. Easter-Sep. In other direction, the 28km to Kinlochbervie is one of Britain's most wild and wonderful coastal walks. Beaches include Sandwood (1558/BEACHES). While in this area: **Smoo Cave** 2km east of Durness is worth a visit.

2052
6/J14
1-B-2

✓ **Old Man of Stoer** near Lochinver Easy, exhilarating walk to the dramatic 70m sandstone sea stack. Start at lighthouse off unclassified road 14km north Lochinver. Park and follow sheep tracks; cliffs are high and steep. 7km round trip; 2/3 hours. Then find the Secret Beach (1566/BEACHES).

2053
11/N30
1-A-2

✓ **Rockcliffe to Kippford** An easy and can be circular stroll along the Scottish Riviera through woodland near the shore (2km) past the Mote of Mark, a Dark Age hill fort with views to Rough Island. The better cliff top walk is in the other direction to Castlehillpoint. Good teashop in Rockcliffe (1407/TEAROOMS) and famed waterside pub, the Anchor, in Kippford (1309/GASTROPUBS).

2054
10/S25
5-10KM
CIRC · XBIKES
1-B-2

✓ **St Abbs Head** Among the most dramatic coastal scenery in southern Scotland, scary in a wind, rhapsodic on a summer's day. Extensive wildlife reserve and trails through coastal hills and vales to cliffs. Best to park at visitor centre on St Abbs village road 3km from A1107 to Eyemouth and follow route (1760/WILDLIFE). Nice caff, interpretation centre, gallery. Good pub grub at **New Inn**, Coldingham.

2055
7/H18

Applecross This far peninsula is marvellous for many reasons (1616/SCENIC ROUTES) and there are fine walks in and around Applecross Bay foreshore including river and woodland strolls. See *Walks on the Applecross Peninsula*, available locally.

2056 9/H21
10KM RET
XCIRC
BIKES
1-B-1

Singing Sands Ardnamurchan 2km north of Acharacle, signed for Arevegaig. 3km to Arevegaig and park before wooden bridge (gate may be locked). Cross wooden bridge, following track round side of Kentra Bay. Follow signs for Gorteneorn, and walk through forest track and woodland to beach. As you pound the sands they should sing to you whilst you bathe in the beautiful views of Rum,

Eigg, Muck and Skye (and just possibly the sea). Check at tourist information centre for directions and other walks booklet. 'Beware unexploded mines', it says.

East from Cullen Moray Coast This is the same walk mentioned with reference to Sunnyside (1556/BEACHES), a golden beach with a fabulous ruined castle (Findlater) that might be your destination. There's a track east along from harbour. 2 hours return. A superb coastline.

8KM · XCIRC
XBIKES
1-A-1

2058 Crovie-Troup Head Moray Coast Another Moray Coast classic that takes in the extraordinary cliff-clinging village of Crovie and the bird-stacked cliffs of the headland. Start at car park and viewpoint above Crovie 15km east of Banff off B9031. Park and walk to end of village, then follow path to Troup Head. 5km return. Shorter walk (1.5km) from RSPB car park 2km off B9031 east of Crovie/Gardenstown, signed for Northfield. Big sky and sea and birdlife.

8/S17

2059 The South Sutor Cromarty The walk, known locally as The 100 Steps though there are a few more than that, from Cromarty village (1545/COASTAL VILLAGES, 1411/TEAROOMS, 1017/HIGHLAND RESTAURANTS) round the tip of the south promontory at the narrow entrance to the Cromarty Firth. East of village past bowling green then up through woods to headland. Good bench! Go further to top car park and viewpoint panel. Perhaps return by road. You may see dolphins in that sea!

7/M17
5KM
CIRC
XBIKES
1-A-1

2060 St John's Point & Scotland's Haven East Mey near Thurso A short, secret walk between Thurso and John o' Groats on this northernmost headland. Brilliant views to Dunnet Head and south Orkney. Follow signs then pass the Castle of Mey (1775/CASTLES). After 2km turn left, signed **The Tea Cosy** (for snacks and cake before or after; 1403/TEAROOM). Park there and go through long gate at the bend of the road, finding a path to right of the gorse heading for the sea. You don't see the stacks, the Men of Mey where the 5 tides meet, till you're almost there. Following track to right mostly carved out of heather you arrive at a narrow, steeply banked cove called Scotland's Haven. A perfect shelter! Then back. 1 hour.

6/Q12
2KM
CIRC
XBIKES
1-B-2

2061 Ceannabeinne Township Trail near Durness I like this walk as it's near my favourite beach (1554/BEACHES), 7km east of Durness. There's a layby; 3 marker boards direct you on the path and relating the story of the township abandoned in 1842. A short, life-enhancing stroll through history and splendid coastal scenery.

6/L12
1KM CIRC
XBIKES
1-B-2

2062 The Chain Walk Elie Adventurous headland scramble at the west end of Elie (and Earlsferry). Britain's only Via Ferrata? Go to end of the road then by path skirting golf course towards headland. Hand- and footholds carved into rock with chains to haul yourself up. Emerge by Shell Bay Caravan Park. Watch tide; don't go alone.

10/R24
2-B-2

2063 Cock of Arran Lochranza This round trip usually starts at Lochranza castle, a breathtaking coastal trail round the north end of the island (see 2249/FANTASTIC ISLAND WALKS). Great for twitchers, ramblers and fossil hunters. Strong boots advisable. Approximately 4 hours, around 12km.

9/J26
2-B-2

2064 Island Coasts See also Fantastic Walks in the Islands, p. 379–81, but 3 spectacular walks from the last edition, recommended by reader John Dera (of Bermuda): **Duirinish** coast on **Skye**, a long (8-12 hours) route with some of the best coastal architecture in the UK: sea arches, waterfalls, stacks. For starts, consult. **Minginish** coast, also on **Skye**, with views to the small isles, Hebrides and the Cuillin with fantastic geology and sea eagles above. 6-8 hours. **The Westray Way** on **Orkney** with splendid cliffs, huge numbers of birds, Old Man of Hoy and other breathtaking views. Takes about 4 hours.

3/P11
7/F19
7/F18

Outdoor Activities

Scotland's Great Golf Courses

Those listed open to non-members and available to visitors (including women!) at most times unless stated. Handicap certificates may be required

AYRSHIRE

2065
9/K28
LLL
✓ ✓ ✓ **Turnberry** www.turnberry.co.uk · 01655 334032 Ailsa (championship), Kintyre and Arran courses. Possible by application, cheaper if you're at the hotel (745/AYRSHIRE HOTELS). Among the UK's top 3 courses: superb. Golf academy a great place to learn.

2066
9/K27
✓ ✓ **Royal Old Course** www.royaltroon.com · 01292 311555 · Troon Very difficult to get on. No wimmen. Staying at Marine Highland Hotel (01292 314444) helps. Easier is **The Portland Course** (also 01292 311555) across the road from Royal (shorter, more sheltered). And 751/AYRSHIRE HOTELS for the adjacent Piersland House Hotel.

2067
9/K27
✓ **Glasgow Gailes/Western Gailes** www.glasgowgolfclub.com · 0141 942 2011/01294 311649 Superb championship links courses next to one another. Near Troon and Prestwick above and below, 5km south of Irvine off A78.

2068
9/L27
Old Prestwick www.prestwickgc.co.uk · 01292 671020 Original home of the Open and 'every challenge you'd wish to meet'. Hotels opposite cost less than a round. Unlikely to get on weekends (Sat members only).

EAST LOTHIAN

2069
9/R25
✓ ✓ **Gullane No.1** www.gullanegolfclub.com · 01620 842255 One of 3 varied courses surrounding charming village on links and within driving distance (35km) of Edinburgh. **Muirfield** is nearby, but you need an introduction. Gullane is okay most days except Sat/Sun. (Handicap required for no.1 only – under 24 men, 30 ladies.) No.3 best for beginners. Visitor centre acts as clubhouse for non-members on nos.2/3. Clubhouse for members/no.1 players only.

2070
9/R25
LL
✓ ✓ **North Berwick East & West** www.northberwick.org.uk · 01620 892726/892135 East (officially the Glen Golf Club) has stunning views. A superb cliff-top course and not too long. West is the third-oldest course in the world and more taxing (especially the classic Redan), used for Open qualifying. In UK top 30 and world top 100 courses, this is a very fine links.

2071
9/Q25
Musselburgh Links www.musselburgholdlinks.co.uk · 0131 665 5438 The original home of golf (recorded here in 1672), but this local-authority-run 9-hole links is not exactly top turf and is enclosed by Musselburgh Racecourse. Nostalgia still appeals though. **Royal Musselburgh** (01875 810260) nearby for the serious game. Dates to 1774, fifth-oldest in Scotland. On both you play through history.

NORTH EAST

2072
10/R23
✓ ✓ **Carnoustie** www.carnoustiegolflinks.co.uk · 01241 802270 3 good links courses; even possible (with handicap cert) to get on the championship course (though weekends difficult). Every hole has character. **Buddon Links** is cheaper and relatively quiet. Combination tickets available. A well-managed and accessible course, increasingly a golfing must.

2073
8/T19

✓ **Murcar Links** www.murcarlinks.com · 01224 704354 · Aberdeen
Getting on **Royal Aberdeen** Course is difficult, but Murcar is a testing alternative, a seaside course 6km north of centre off Peterhead road signed at roundabout after Exhibition Centre. Handicap certificate needed. Other municipal courses include charming 9-hole at Hazelhead (in an excellent 3-course complex).

2074
8/T18
LL

✓ **Cruden Bay** www.crudenbaygolfclub.co.uk · 01779 812285 · near
Peterhead On A975 40km north of Aberdeen. Designed by Tom Simpson and ranked in UK top 50, a spectacular links course with the intangible aura of bygone days. Quirky holes epitomise old-fashioned style. Weekends difficult to get on.

2075
7/N17
L

✓ **Nairn** www.nairngolfclub.co.uk · 01667 453208 Traditional seaside links, one of the easiest championship courses to get on. Good clubhouse, friendly folk. Nairn Dunbar across town also has good links. Handicap certificate required.

2076
6/N16
LL

✓ **Royal Dornoch** www.royaldornoch.com · 01862 810219 Sutherland championship course laid out by Tom Morris in 1877. Recently declared 5th-best course in the world outside the US, but not busy or incessantly pounded. No poor holes. Stimulating sequences. Probably the most northerly great golf course in the world – and not impossible to get on. Sister course the **Struie** also a treat.

2077
8/T19

The Trump Golf Course www.trumpgolfscotland.com Surrounded by controversy as well as a uniquely special sand-dune system, Donald Trump's 'best golf course in the world' opens 2012 (the rest of the £750 million hotel and villa resort later). We'd expect this ego-extravagant championship course to be rather good.

FIFE

2078
10/R23
L

✓ ✓ ✓ **St Andrews** www.standrews.org.uk · 01334 466666 The
home and Mecca of golf and the largest golf complex in Europe. Old Course most central and celebrated. Application by ballot the day or year before (handicap certificate needed) or buy an 'Old Course Experience'. For Jubilee (1897, upgraded 1989) and Eden (1914, laid out by Harry S. Colt paying homage to the Old with large, sloping greens), apply the day before or in advance (01334 466718). Similar arrangements for the New Course (1895, some rate the best); probably has easiest access. Less demanding are new Strathtyrum and Balgove (upgraded 9-hole for beginners, not advance bookable) courses. All 6 courses contiguous and in town. The new Castle Course is a 320-acre clifftop course for all abilities (no handicap needed, open Mar-Nov) and the Dukes Course (part of Old Course Hotel) 3km away is a great alternative to the links. Reservations (and ballot). There's a whole lot of golf to be had – get your money out!

2079
10/R24
L

✓ ✓ **Kingsbarns** www.kingsbarns.com · 01334 460860 Between Crail
and St Andrews, one of Fife's newest and Scotland's best courses. In all top rankings. Challenging and a beautiful location on a secret coast. Not cheap.

2080
10/Q24

✓ **Ladybank** www.ladybankgolf.co.uk · 01337 830814 Best inland course
in Fife; Tom Morris-designed again. Very well kept and organised. Good facilities. Tree-lined and picturesque. Hosts Open qualifying rounds.

2081
10/R24

Elie www.golfhouseclub.co.uk · 01333 330301 Splendid open links kept in top
condition; can be windswept. The starter has his famous periscope and may be watching you. Adjacent 9-hole course, often busy with kids, is fun (01333 330955).

2082 **Crail** www.crailgolfingsociety.co.uk · 01333 450686 **Balcomie Links** origi-
10/R24 nally designed by that legendary Tom Morris (again), or **Craighead Links** new
sweeping course. All holes in sight of sea. Not expensive; easy to get on.

2083 **Lundin Links** www.lundingolfclub.co.uk · 01333 320202 Challenging seaside
10/Q24 course used as Open qualifier. Some devious contourings. In the village there is
also a separate 9-hole course, Lundin Ladies, open to all (01333 320832).

ELSEWHERE

2084 ✓ ✓ ✓ **Gleneagles** www.gleneagles.com · 0800 389 3737 Legendary
10/N24 golf the mainstay of Perthshire resort complex (1092/COUNTRY-
LL HOUSE HOTELS). 4 courses include PGA centenary which will host 2014 Ryder Cup.

2085 ✓ ✓ **Roxburghe Hotel Golf Course** www.roxburghe.net 01573 450333 ·
10/S27 near Kelso Only championship course in the Borders. Designed by Dave
Thomas along banks of River Teviot. Part of the Floors Castle estate. Open to non-
residents. Fairways bar/brasserie clubhouse. (See also 795/BORDER HOTELS).

Good Golf Courses In Great Places

2086 ✓ **Machrie** www.machrie.com · 01496 302310 · Islay 7km Port Ellen. Worth
9/F26 going to Islay (2304/ISLANDS) just for the golf. Machrie (Golf) Hotel is sparse
LL but convenient. Old-fashioned course to be played by feel and instinct. Splendid,
often windy isolation. Some problems with course and hotel mean changes at TGP,
so check. The notorious 17th, Iffrin (it means Hell), vortex shaped from the dune
system of marram and close-cropped grass, is one of many great holes. 18 holes.

2087 ✓ **Macrihanish** www.machgolf.com · 01586 810213 · &
9/G28 **Macrihanish Dunes** www.macrihanishdunes.com · by Campbeltown
LL Amongst the dunes and links of the glorious 8km stretch of the Machrihanish
Beach (1557/BEACHES). The Atlantic provides thunderous applause.

2088 ✓ **Southerness** www.southernessgolfclub.com · 01387 880677 · Solway
11/N30 Firth 25km south of Dumfries by A710. A championship course on links on
L the silt flats of the firth. Despite its prestige, visitors do get on. Start times available
10am-12noon and 2-4pm. There are few courses as good as this at these prices.
Under the wide Solway sky, it's pure – southerness.

2089 ✓ **Rosemount** www.theblairgowrlegolfclub.co.uk · 01250 872622 ·
10/P22 Blairgowrie Off A93, south of Blairgowrie. An excellent, pampered and well-
managed course in the middle of green Perthshire, an alternative perhaps to
Gleneagles, usually easier to get on and rather cheaper.

2090 ✓ **Boat of Garten** www.boatgolf.com · 01479 831282 Challenging,
8/N19 picturesque course in town where ospreys have been known to wheel
overhead. Has been called the Gleneagles of the North; certainly the best around,
though not for novices. 18 holes.

2091 ✓ **Tain & Brora** www.tain-golfclub.co.uk · 01862 892314 &
6/M16 www.broragolf.co.uk · 01408 621911 2 northern courses that are a delight
L to play on. Tain designed by Tom Morris in 1890. Brora stunning with good clubhouse, hotel (980/HIGHLAND HOTELS) and coos on the course. With Royal Dornoch
(above), they're a roving-golfer must.

2092 **Glencruitten** www.obangolf.com · 01631 562868 · Oban Picturesque course
9/H23 by the renowned James Braid on the edge of town. Head south (A816) from Argyll
Sq, bearing left at church. Course is signed. Quite tricky with many blind holes. Can
get busy, so phone first. 18 holes.

2093 **Gairloch** www.gairlochgolfclub.com · 01445 712407 As you enter town from
7/H16 south on A832, it overlooks the bay and a perfect, pink, sandy beach (1567/
L BEACHES). Small clubhouse with honesty box out of hours. Not the most agonising
course; and on a clear day with views to Skye, you can forget agonising over anything. 9 holes.

2094 **Harris Golf Club** www.harrisgolf.com · 01859 550226 · Scarista, Isle of
5/E16 Harris Phone number is for the secretary but no need to ring: just turn up on the
LLL road between Tarbert and Rodel and leave £20 in the box. First tee commands one
of the great views in golf and throughout this basic but testing course, you are
looking out to sea over Scarista beach (1561/BEACHES) and bay. The sunset may put
you off your swing. 9 holes.

2095 **New Galloway** www.nggc.co.uk · 01644 420737 Local course on south edge
11/M29 of this fine wee toon. Almost all on a slope but affording great views of Loch Ken
and the Galloway Forest behind. No bunkers and only 9 short holes, some well
steep but exhilarating play. Easy on, except Sun. Just turn up.

2096 **Minto** www.mintogolf.co.uk · 01450 870220 · Denholm 9km east of Hawick.
10/R28 Spacious parkland in Teviot valley. Best holes 3rd, 12th and 16th.
Vertish Hill www.hawickgolfclub.com · 01450 372293 · Hawick A more
challenging hill course. Both among the best in Borders. 18. Best holes 2nd and
18th. An excellent guide to all the courses in the Borders is available from tourist
information centres: *Freedom of the Fairways*.

2097 **Gifford** www.giffordgolfclub.com · 01620 810591 Dinky 9-hole inland course
10/R26 on the edge of a charming village, by-passed by the queue for the big East Lothian
courses and a guarded secret among regulars. Generally ok, but phone starter
(above) for availability. I was touched when they wrote to thank me for this entry a
few editions back. *Golf World* called it 'the best 9 holes in Scotland'.

2098 **Strathpeffer** www.strathpeffergolf.co.uk · 01997 421219 Very hilly (we do
7/L17 mean hilly) course full of character and with exhilarating Highland views. Small-
town friendliness. You play up there with the gods and other old codgers. 18 holes.

2099 **Elgin** www.elgingolfclub.com · 01343 542338 1km from town on A941 Perth
8/P17 road. Many memorable holes on moorland/parkland course in an area where links
may lure you to the coast (**Nairn**, **Lossiemouth**). 18 holes.

2100 **Durness** www.durnessgolfclub.org · 01971 511364 The most northerly golf
6/L12 course on mainland UK, on the wild headland by Balnakeil Bay, looking over to
LL Faraid Head. The last hole is over the sea. Only open since 1988, it's already got
cult status. 2km west of Durness. 9 holes.

2101 **Traigh** www.traighgolf.co.uk · 01687 450337 · Arisaig A830 Fort William-
7/H20 Mallaig road, 2km north Arisaig. Pronounced Try - and you should. The islands are
LL set out like stones in the sea around you and there are 9 hilly holes of fun. Has
been called 'the most beautiful 9 holes in the world'.

The Best Cycling

EASY CYCLING

2102
10/S27

✓ **The Borders** The Borders with its gentle hills, river tracks and low urbanisation seems to be paving the cycleway both for mountain biking (see below) and for more leisurely and family pursuits. Good linkage and signage and many routes, eg the 4 Abbeys, the Tweed Cycleway, the Borderloop and individual trails. Guides available from tourist information centres for almost all the Border towns. There's ample choice for all abilities and ages. See also 7 Stanes (below).

2103
8/Q18
20KM
CAN BE CIRC

✓ **Speyside Way Craigellachie-Ballindalloch** The cycling part of the Way (1990/LONG WALKS), with great views; flat and no cars. Goes past distilleries. Circular by return on minor roads.
START Craigellachie by rangers' office.

2104
10/M25
55KM

Forth & Clyde Canal Glasgow-Falkirk Wheel East out of the city, urban at first then nice in the Kelvin Valley; Kilsyth Hills to the north. Falkirk Wheel should be seen (4/ATTRACTIONS).
START The Maryhill Locks, Maryhill Rd.

2105
11/L29
15KM
CAN BE CIRC

Glentrool near Newton Stewart Two routes from visitor centre (1610/LOCHS, 1925/MARY, CHARLIE & BOB). Deep in the forest and well signed. Briefly joins public road. The 7 Stanes sections can be difficult (see below).
START Glentrool visitor centre off A714. Bike hire at **Kirroughtree** and network of trails listed from here (see below).

2106 1
12KM/
VARIOUS
CIRC

Edinburgh Trails Edinburgh streets can be a nightmare for cyclists and there's lots of uphill graft. But there is a vast network of cycle and towpaths especially north of the New Town. Another good run is to Balerno from Union Canal towpath in Lower Gilmore Place. End at Balerno High School.

2107
10/L24
11KM
CAN BE CIRC

The Trossachs www.lochlomond-trossachs.org · near Aberfoyle & Callander Many low-level lochside trails. Consult tourist information centres. Nice run is Loch Ard Circle from Aberfoyle going west (signed Inversnaid Scenic Route) or Loch Katrine to Callander. Bike hire Loch Katrine, Callander, Aberfoyle.

2108
8/N19
20KM
CIRC

Loch an Eilean near Aviemore Lots of bike tracks here in the Rothiemurchus Forest. This one goes past one of Scotland's most beautiful lochs (1604/LOCHS) and you can go further to Loch Insh via Feshiebridge and around Glen Feshie. Probably best to get a route leaflet at Rothiemurchus Centre or Aviemore Visitor Centre.
START Signed from B970 at Coylumbridge.

2109
9/K26

Cumbrae Take ferry from Largs (every 15 minutes, 30 minutes in winter) to beautiful Cumbrae (and visit the classic Ritz and fab Cumbrae Bistro; 1363/CAFÉS). 4 or 5 routes around the island. One a stiff pull to a great viewpoint. Others stick to sea level. Consult leaflet from tourist information centre. All these roads are quiet.

MOUNTAIN BIKING

2110
10, 11

✓✓ **7 Stanes** www.7stanes.gov.uk · Borders & South West Ambitious and hugely popular network of bike trails in south of Scotland, different lengths and abilities in each place. Include **Glentress/The Tweed Valley** (see below), **Newcastleton, Forest of Ae, Dalbeattie, Mabie, Glentrool** (see above), and **Kirroughtree** (see above). Routes at all levels. Many challenges. Good signage throughout.

2111
10/Q27

✓ ✓ **Glentress Forest** www.thehubintheforest.co.uk · **near Peebles** Specially constructed mountain-bike trails. Well signed and well used in this hugely popular national cycling centre. New complex of facilities and café in 2011. Trails for all levels, plenty of flowing descents and drops. The serious downhill stuff is nearby at **Traquair** where the **7 Stanes** cross-country route also starts (see above).

2112
11/M29
25KM · CIRC

Clatteringshaws Near Glentrool (see above). Various routes around Clatteringshaws Loch in the Galloway Forest and Hills. Most are easy, but some serious climbs and descents. Visitor centre has tearoom.

2113 8/Q20
25KM
CIRC

Glen Tanner www.royal-deeside.org.uk · Deeside Good way to encounter this beautiful glen in the shadow of Mount Keen. Quite difficult in places. **START** Tombae on the B976 opposite junction of A97 and A93.

2114
7
XCIRC

Great Glen, Fort William-Loch Lochy Easy at first on the Caledonian Canal towpath. Later it gets hilly with long climbs. Great views. **START** Neptune's Staircase at Banavie near Fort William.

2115
10
25KM
CIRC

Perthshire & Angus, Glenfernate-Blair Atholl Beautiful Highland trail that takes in forests, lochs and Glen Tilt (2000/GLEN WALKS). Mainly rough track. Follow directions from tourist information centre leaflets. **START** On the A924 14km east of Pitlochrie, 500m east of school.

The Only Open-Air Swimming Pools

2116
10/S20

✓ **Stonehaven Outdoor Pool** www.stonehavenopenairpool.co.uk · 01569 762134 · **Stonehaven** The Friends of Stonehaven Outdoor Pool won the day (eat your hearts out North Berwick) and saved a great pool that goes from length to strength. Fabulous 1930s Olympic-sized heated salt-water pool (85ft). Midnight swims from 10pm Jul/Aug on Wednesdays (is that cool, or what?). Jun-Sep only: 10am-7.30pm (10am-6pm weekends). Heated salt-water heaven.

2117
9/K25

✓ **Gourock Bathing Pool** 01475 631561 · **Gourock** The only other open-air (proper) pool in Scotland that's still open – or will be again in 2012 after a major facelift. On coast road south of town 45km from Glasgow. 1950s-style leisure. Heated (to 88°), so it doesn't need to be a scorcher (brilliant, but choc-a-block when it is). Expect it to be open May-early Sep weekdays until 8pm.

2118
6/Q13

✓ **The Trinkie** Wick On south side of town, follow cliff walk up from harbour or by car through housing estate. 2km. Not an organised set-up but a pool sluiced and filled by the sea within a natural formation of rocks. A bracing stroll, never mind immersion. Needs TLC. Wickers also go to the North Baths near the harbour (Wick side) and opposite the wee lighthouse. 2 rare open-air swim spots in the far north: midnight midsummer swimming, anyone? (Well, not in wet 2011.)

2119
9/G22

The Bathing Pool Glengorm Estate, Mull A pool sluiced and filled by the sea by an Iron Age fort on the headland of this beautiful estate 7km north of Tobermory off the Dervaig road. Some seaweed fringing but once it was filled with white sand and they say one day it may be restored. In the meantime, for swimming baggers and the like. 45 minutes from the best coffeeshop on Mull (1377/COFFEE SHOPS) and you can stay and lord it up in the castle (2306/MULL).

2120
10/R23
The Step Rock Pool St Andrews Shallow bathing pool between West Sands and East Sands beaches below the Aquarium and the Seafood Restaurant (1319/SEAFOOD). Since 1903 when the gentlemen used to swim here naked, a shallow alternative to the colder sea and more recently the East Sands Leisure Centre. Costumes advised these days.

■■■■ Especially Good Watersports Centres

2121
10/R24
✓ **Elie Watersports** www.eliewatersports.com · 01333 330962 · Elie Great beach location in totally charming wee town where there's enough going on to occupy non-watersporters. Easy lagoon for first timers and open season for inexperienced users. Wind-surfers, kayaks, water-ski. Also mountain bikes and inflatable 'biscuits'. 1283/GASTROPUBS, 2081/GREAT GOLF.

2122
9/K26
✓ **Scottish National Watersports Centre** 01475 530757 · Cumbrae · www.nationalcentrecumbrae.org.uk Frequent ferry from Largs (centre near ferry terminal so 5km Millport) then learn how to pilot things that float. Scotland's premier instructor facility. You need to book – call them, then bob about doon the watter. Great range of courses. 2-bunkroom accommodation available.

2123
10/P25
✓ **Port Edgar** www.edinburghleisure.org.uk · 0131 331 3330 · South Queensferry End of village, under and beyond the Forth Road Bridge. Major marina, water sports centre. Berth your boat, hire dinghies (big range). Big tuition programme for kids and adults including canoes. Home to Port Edgar Yacht Club.

2124
10/M26
✓ **Strathclyde Park** www.northlan.gov.uk · 01698 266155 Major water sports centre 15km southeast of Glasgow and easily reached from Central Scotland via M8 or M74 (junction 5 or 6). 200-acre loch and centre with instruction on sailing, canoeing, windsurfing, rowing, water-skiing. Hire canoes, Lasers and Wayfarers, windsurfers and trimarans. Call booking office for sessions/times.

2125
7/N19
✓ **Loch Insh Watersports** www.lochinsh.com · 01540 651272 · Kincraig On B970, 2km from Kincraig towards Kingussie and the A9. Marvellous loch site launching from gently sloping dinky beach into the shallow forgiving waters of Loch Inch. Hire of canoes, dinghies and windsurfers as well as rowing boats; river trips. Archery and mountain biking. An idyllic place to learn anything. Watch the others and the sunset from the balcony restaurant (1027/BEST HIGHLAND RESTAURANTS). Chalets and apartments. Sports Apr-Oct 9.30am-5.30pm.

2126
7/N19
✓ **Loch Morlich Watersports** www.lochmorlich.com · 01479 861221 · near Aviemore By Glenmore Forest Park, part of the plethora of outdoor activities hereabouts (skiing, walking, etc). This is the loch you see from Cairngorm and just as picturesque from the woody shore. Surprising coral-pink beach! Canoes, kayaks, rowing boats and dinghies with instruction in everything. Evening hire possible. Coffee shop up top. Good campsite adjacent (1198/CAMPING WITH KIDS).

2127
11/M30
✓ **Galloway Activity Centre** www.lochken.co.uk · 01644 420626 · Loch Ken near Castle Douglas 15km north on A713 to Ayr. Dinghies, windsurfers, canoes, kayaks, tuition, biking. Also the Climbing Tower (so you zip-wire and take that leap of faith). Mountain biking, Laserquest and archery. All this by a serene and forgiving loch by the Galloway Forest (1611/LOCHS). Phone for times and courses. Open Mar-Nov.

The Best Surfing Beaches

A surprise for the sceptical: Scotland has some of the best surfing beaches in Europe.

WEST COAST

2128
5/F13
✓✓ **Isle of Lewis** Probably the best of the lot. Go north of Stornoway, north of Barvas, north of just about anywhere. Leave the A857 and your day job behind. Not the most scenic of sites, but the waves have come a long way, even further than you have. Derek at Hebridean Surf Holidays (07881 435915) will tell you when and where to go.

2129
9/D22
✓ **Isle of Tiree** Exposed to all the Atlantic swells, gorgeous little Tiree ain't just great for windsurfing. Stay at Millhouse, self-catering hostel (01879 220435); good facilities.

2130
9/G28
✓ **Macrihanish** Near Campbeltown at the foot of the Mull of Kintyre. Long strand to choose from (1557/BEACHES). Clan Skates in Glasgow (0141 339 6523) usually has an up-to-date satellite map and an idea of both the west and (nearest to central belt) Pease Bay (see below).

NORTH COAST

2131
6/P12
✓✓ **Thurso** Surf City: well not quite, but it's a good base to find your own waves. Especially to the east of town at Dunnet Bay – a 5km-long beach with excellent reefs at the north end. They say it has to be the best right-hand breaking wave on the planet! When it ain't breaking, go west to...

2132
6/N12
✓ **Melvich & Strathy Bay** Near Bettyhill on the North Coast halfway between Tongue and Thurso on the A836. From here to Cape Wrath the power and quality of the waves detonating on the shore have justified comparisons with Hawaii. And then there's **Brims Ness** and many others on this north coast (consult your usual surfy websites).

2133
6/Q13
Wick On the Thurso road at Ackergill to the south of Sinclair's Bay (1250/HOUSE PARTIES). Find the ruined castle and taking care, clamber down the gully to the beach. A monumental reef break, you are working against the backdrop of the decaying ruin drenched in history, spume and romance.

EAST COAST

2134
10/S25
✓ **Pease Bay** South of Dunbar near Cockburnspath on the A1. The nearest surfie heaven to the capital. The not-very-nice caravan site has parking and toilets. Very consistent surf here and popular. Info and surf school from **Momentum**; 07796 561615. Many other beaches here on East Lothian/Berwickshire coast.

2135
8/T17
Rattray Head between Peterhead & Fraserburgh 5km off A90. Fab faraway eco hostel/B&B 300m from brilliant secret 15km beach with cool surf. (B&B 01346 532236; www.rattrayhead.net)

2136
8/T19
Nigg Bay Just south of Aberdeen (not to be confused with Nigg across from Cromarty) and off the vast beach at Lunan Bay (1565/BEACHES) between Arbroath and Montrose. There's 4 spots around **Fraserburgh** (the broch).

Consuming Passions

For Edinburgh museums, see p. 77–80; Glasgow museums, see p. 122–4.
☕ *signifies notable café.*

2137
9/K28
☕

✓✓ **Robert Burns Birthplace Museum** www.burnsmuseum.org.uk · 0844 493 2601 · Alloway, Ayr After years of neglect and make-do, the restored cottage where Burns was born and the brilliant contemporary museum/gallery/coffee shop 1km into the village are an appropriate paean to his memory, an evocation of his times and works and interesting and fun places to visit. Cottage is a row of rooms with set pieces and slightly unnerving voiceovers, the museum has state-of-the-art and technology exhibits exploring not just the well-kent and comic aspects (*Tam o' Shanter, Auld Lang Syne*, the Kilmarnock Edition) but the wider implications of his national significance and a modern translation of his influence: the Fame Game, the Trysting Tree. Enough from me: quite simply the new must-go-see. Open AYR 10am-5pm, 5.30pm Apr-Sep. Caff much better than before.

2138
10/R25
☕

✓✓ **National Museum of Flight** www.nms.ac.uk · 0131 247 4238 · near Haddington 3km from A1 south of town. In the old complex of hangars and Nissen huts by East Fortune, an airfield dating to World War I with a large collection of planes from gliders to jets and especially wartime memorabilia respectfully restored and preserved. Inspired and inspiring displays; not just boys' stuff. Marvel at the bravery and sense the unremitting passage of time. From East Fortune the airship R34 made its historic Atlantic crossings. More recent Concorde is an experience: hugely impressive outside, claustrophobic in (especially queueing to leave). But did David Frost and Joan Collins ever join the Mile-High Club? Annual air show mid July. 7 days; 10am-5pm. Weekends only in winter.

2139
10/R24
ATMOS

✓✓ **The Secret Bunker** www.secretbunker.co.uk · 01333 310301 · near Crail & Anstruther The nuclear bunker and regional seat of government in the event of nuclear war: a twilight labyrinth beneath a hill in rural Fife so vast, well documented and complete, it's both fascinating and chilling. Few museums are as authentic or as resonant, even down to the claustrophobic canteen with bad food. Makes you wonder what 300 people would have made of it, incarcerated there, what the Cold War was all about and what secrets the MoD is brewing these days for the wars yet to come. Mar-Oct 10am-5pm.

2140
10/Q23
☕

✓✓ **Verdant Works** www.rrdiscovery.com · 01382 309060 · Dundee West Henderson's Wynd near Westport. Award-winning heritage museum that for once justifies the accolades. The story of jute and the city it made. Immensely effective high-tech and designer presentation of industrial and social history. Excellent for kids. Almost continuous guided tour. Café. 7 days 10am-6pm; winter Wed-Sat till 4.30pm and closed Mon/Tue. Every Sun from 11am.

2141
5/E13
☕
ATMOS
L

✓✓ **The Blackhouse Village** www.gerrannan.com · 01851 643416 · Gearrannan, Lewis At the road end (3km) from A858, the west coast of Lewis, an extraordinary reconstruction of several blackhouses, the traditional thatched dwelling of the Hebrides. One is working Black House Museum (set 1955) with café. Another is a hostel (closed 2011) and 3 are self-catering accommodation (1122/HOSTELS). Great walk starts here. Apr-Sep 9.30am-5.30pm. Closed Sun.

2142
6/Q13

✓✓ **Wick Heritage Centre** www.caithness.org · 01955 605393 · Bank Row, Wick Amazing volunteer-run civic museum, jam-packed with items about the sea, town and that hard land. Upstairs and downstairs, stretching halfway along the street. Few places have so much meticulously gathered that lovingly portrays and evokes the spirit of a place. The much-used words 'secret gem' are entirely appropriate here. They got a Queen's Award but somebody should give these ladies MBEs or something. Easter-Oct 10am-last entry 3.45pm. Closed Sun.

2143
5/F13
HS
ATMOS

The Blackhouse at Arnol www.historic-scotland.gov.uk · 01851 710395 · Lewis A857 Barvas road from Stornoway, left at junction for 7km, then right through township for 2km. A blackhouse with earth floor, bed boxes and central peat fire (no chimney hole), occupied by the family and their animals. Remarkably, this house was lived in until the 1960s. Smokists may reflect on that peaty fug. Open all year 9.30am-5.30pm (4.30pm in winter, Oct-Feb). Closed Sun.

2144
6/P15

Timespan www.timespan.org.uk · Helmsdale Far-northern town where a historic strath comes down to the sea was a special place (presumably) then and now. This museum and arts centre records and cleverly presents this, well, span of time. Makes you think! Great wee café by the bridge in its geology garden. While you're here, don't miss the hotel (999/HIGHLAND HOTELS), the **Mirage** café (1019/HIGHLAND RESTAURANTS), **Gilbert's** bistro and in keeping with the time thing, the fascinating **20th Century Collectibles** (2206/VERY SPECIAL SHOPS). Centre open Mar-Oct 10am 5pm, Nov-Feb Sat/Sun 11am-4pm and Tue 2-4pm.

2145
10/P25

The Abbot House www.abbothouse.co.uk · Dunfermline Maygate in town centre historic area. Very fine conversion of ancient house showing the importance of this town as a religious and trading centre from this millennium to medieval times. Encapsulates history from Margaret and Bruce to the Beatles. One of the few tourist attractions where 'award-winning' is a reliable indicator of worth. Café, tranquil garden; gate to graveyard and abbey. 7 days 9.30am-4.30pm. Excellent coffee shop by ladies who can cook and bake and an excellent mac cheese.

2146
9/H23
ATMOS
LL

Easdale Island Folk Museum www.easdalemuseum.org On Easdale, an island/township reached by a 5-minute (continuous) boat service from Seil 'island' at the end of the B844 (off the A816, 18km south of Oban). Something special about this grassy hamlet of whitewashed houses on a rocky outcrop which has a pub, a tearoom and a craft shop, and this museum across the green. The history of the place (a thriving slate industry erased one stormy night in 1881, when the sea drowned the quarry; 1668/SWIMMING HOLES) is brought to life in displays from local contributions. Easter-Sep 11am-5pm.

2147
4/V5
ATMOS
L

Shetland Museum & Archives www.shetland-museum.org.uk · 01595 695057 · Lerwick Impressive, landmark, purpose-built contemporary space developed from what remained of the Lerwick waterfront. 60,000 images bringing the story of these fascinating islands to life. Also the Up-Helly-Aa story (22/FESTIVALS)! Hays Dock Café/Restaurant worth a visit in its own right. 2284/SHETLAND. 7 days 10am-5pm (Sun from 12noon).

2148
6/M13
L

Strathnaver Museum www.strathnavermuseum.org.uk · 01641 521418 · Bettyhill On north coast 60km west of Thurso in a converted church which is very much part of the whole appalling saga, a graphic account of the Highland Clearances told through the history of this fishing village and the strath that lies behind it whence its dispossessed population came; 2,500 folk were driven from their homes – it's worth going up the valley (from 2km west along the main A836) to see (especially at Achenlochy) the beautiful land they had to leave in 1812 to make way for sheep. Detailed leaflet of Strath to follow by car and foot. Find the poignant and beautiful **Rosal Clearance Township** about 6km from A836 via B871, 45 minutes' walk from the car park. Café on roadside by museum for sustenance. Museum Apr-Oct Mon-Sat 10am-5pm.

2149
7/H18
L

✓Applecross Heritage Centre www.applecrossheritage.org.uk · Applecross Along the strand from the Potting Shed (1012/RESTAURANTS) and Applecross Inn (1169/GET-AWAY HOTELS) adjacent the lovely church built on an ancient monastery, a well-designed building and lay-out of the story of this remarkable, end-of-the-world community. Reading room with comfy chairs! May-Oct 12noon-5pm.

2150
8/T17
L

✓The Museum of Scottish Lighthouses Fraserburgh · 01346 511022 · www.lighthousemuseum.org.uk At Kinnaird Head near the harbour. A top attraction, so signed from all over. Purpose-built and very well done. Something which may appear of marginal interest made vital. In praise of the prism and the engineering innovation and skill that allowed Britain once to rule the seas (and the world). A great ambition (to light the coastline) spectacularly realised. *At Scotland's Edge* by Allardyce and Hood is well worth taking home, as is Bella Bathhurst's *The Lighthouse Stevensons*. 10am-5pm (Sun from 12noon); till 4pm in winter.

2151
7/H18
LL

✓Bright Water Visitor Centre & Gavin Maxwell House 01599 530040 · www.eileanban.org · Eilean Ban, Skye You don't have to be a Maxwell fan, *Ring of Bright Water* reader or otter-watcher to appreciate the remarkable restoration of this fascinating man's last house on the island under the Skye Bridge. Skye is a natural haven and the Stevenson Lighthouse superb. Contact centre for guided tours of the cottage, the lighthouse and the hide (otters not guaranteed but quite likely). Book and meet at Otter Gate on the bridge. Apr-Sep, Mon-Fri 2pm.

2152
9/K21

West Highland Museum www.westhighlandmuseum.org.uk · Cameron Square, Fort William Off main street in listed building. Good refurbishment yet retains mood; the setting doesn't overshadow the contents. 7 rooms of Jacobite memorabilia, archaeology, wildlife, clans, tartans, arms, etc all effectively evoke the local history. Great oil paintings line the walls, including a drawn battle plan of Culloden. The anamorphic painting of Charlie isn't so bonny, but a still fascinating snapshot. 10am-5pm (4pm in winter). Closed Sun except Jul/Aug.

2153
6/P12

Mary-Ann's Cottage www.caithness.org · Dunnet On north coast off A836 from Thurso to John o' Groats, signed at Dunnet; take the road for Dunnet Head. Lived in till 1990 by Mary-Ann Calder, 3 generations of crofters are in these stones. But not nostalgic or heritage-heavy, just an old lady's house, the near present and past and still the geraniums! Compare to that other old lady's house 10 minutes up the road (Castle of Mey; 1775/CASTLES). Open summer 2-4.30pm.

2154
9/H24
☕

Kilmartin House www.kilmartin.org · 01546 510278 · near Lochgilphead North of Lochgilphead on A816. Centre for landscape and archaeology interpretation – so much to know of the early peoples and Kilmartin Glen is littered with historic sites. Intelligent, interesting, run by a small independent trust. Excellent organic-ish café (1394/TEAROOMS) and bookshop without the usual tat. Some nice Celtic carvings. Mar-Oct 10am-5pm daily; 11am-4pm Nov/Dec. Closed Jan/Feb.

2155
10/R21

Pictavia www.pictavia.org.uk · 01356 626241 · Brechin South of Brechin on the Forfar road at Brechin Castle. Centre opened summer '99 to give a multimedia interpretation of our Dark Age ancestors. Sparse on detail, high on kid-orientated interactivity. Listen to some music, pluck a harp and argue about the Battle of Dunnichen – was it that important? Gentle parkland beyond, nice for kids. Usual crap shopping. All year 7 days 9am-5pm (from 10am Sun).

2156
7/M17

Cromarty Courthouse Museum www.cromarty-courthouse.org.uk · 01381 600418 · Church Street, Cromarty Housed in an 18th-century courthouse, this award-winning museum uses moving, talking models to bring to life a court-room scene and famous Cromarty figures to paint the varied history of this quite special little town. 12noon-4pm. Closed Fri/Sat. **Hugh Miller's Birthplace** is next door. Born in 1802 and best known as the father of geology he was remarkable in many ways and this tells his singular story. Apr-Sep 12noon-5pm. Oct Tue, Thu/Fri.

2157 **Skye Museum of Island Life** www.skyemuseum.co.uk · Kilmuir On A855
7/F17   Uig-Staffin road 32km north of Portree. The most authentic of several converted cottages on Skye where the crofter's life is recreated for the enrichment of ours. The small thatched township includes agricultural implements and domestic artefacts, many illustrating an improbable fascination with the royal family. Flora Macdonald's grave nearby (1848/MONUMENTS). Apr-Oct 9.30am-5pm. Closed Sun.

2158 **Auchendrain** Inveraray 8km west of town on A83. A whole township recon-
9/J24   structed to give a very fair impression of both the historical and spatial relationship
⌨   between the cottages and their various occupants. Longhouses and byre dwellings; their furniture and their ghosts. Tearoom. 7 days. Apr-Sep 10am-5pm.

2159 **Inveraray Jail** www.inveraryjail.co.uk · Inveraray The story of Scottish
9/J24   crime and punishment told in award-winning reconstruction of courtroom with cells, where waxwork miscreants and their taped voices bring local history to life. Guided Peterhead tours can't be far off. All year, 9.30am-6pm (winter 10am-5pm).

2160 **Arctic Penguin aka Maritime Heritage Centre** www.inveraraypier.com ·
9/J24   Inveraray One of the world's last iron sailing ships moored so you can't miss it at the lochside. More to it than would first appear: displays on the history of Clydeside (the *Queens Mary* and *Elizabeth* memorabilia, etc), Highland Clearances, the *Vital Spark*. Lots for kids to get a handle (or hands) on. 7 days 10am-6pm; 5pm winter.

2161 **Bonawe Ironworks Museum** www.historic-scotland.gov.uk · Taynuilt At
9/J23   its zenith (late 18th-early 19th century), this ironworks was a dark, brutal, fire-
HS   breathing monster. But now, all is calm as the gently sloping grassy sward carries you around from warehouse to foundry and down onto the shores of Loch Etive to the pier, where the finished product was loaded on to ships to be taken away for the purpose of empire-building (with cannonballs). Apr-Sep daily until 5.30pm.

2162 **Scottish Fisheries Museum** www.scotfishmuseum.org · 01333 310628 ·
10/R24 Anstruther In and around a cobbled courtyard overlooking the old fishing harbour in this busy East Neuk town. Excellent evocation of traditional industry still alive (if not kicking). Impressive collection of models and actual vessels including those moored at adjacent quay. Crail and Pittenweem harbours nearby for the full picture (and fresh crab/lobster). Open all year 10am-5.30pm, Sun 11am-5pm (closed 4.30pm in winter). 1353/FISH & CHIPS a must!

2163 **National Museum of Costume** www.nms.ac.uk · New Abbey near
11/N30 Dumfries Another obsession that became a (national) museum. On 2 floors of Shambellie House set among spectacular woodlands. Fab frocks etc. from every period. Apr-Oct 10am-5pm. Lovely new gardens nearby; 1520/GARDENS.

2164 **The Scottish Maritime Museum** www.scottishmaritimemuseum.org
10/L25 Over 2 sites: Irvine (01294 278283) and Dumbarton (01389 763444). Dumbarton has the ship model experiment tank while Irvine boasts a massive Victorian engine shed full of the bits that non-engineers never usually see; and there's the hulk of an old clipper at Irvine harbour. Completely fascinating. Irvine Easter-Oct, Dumbarton all year Mon-Sat. 10am-4pm.

The Most Interesting Public Galleries

For Edinburgh, see p. 78-81; Glasgow, p. 122-3 and p. 129. ☕ *: notable café.*

2165
10/P25
☕
ADMISSION

✔ ✔ **Jupiter Artland** www.jupiterartland.org · 0131 257 4170 · **Wilkieston** West of Edinburgh. Not a public gallery as such but an open-air artland assembled by Robert and Nicky Wilson in the groves and gardens of their home, Bonnington House. In an unfolding story, some of the UK's leading artists have been commissioned to produce site-specific work there for you to discover: Andy Goldsworthy, Anthony Gormley, Anish Kapoor and an enormous landform by Charles Jencks which you pass through when you arrive; and many others. This is art exposure and extraordinary patronage on a grand scale. Best get directions from the website. Allow 1.5 hours on site. Book online. May-Sep, Thu-Sun. Lovely courtyard caravan caff.

2166
10/Q23
☕

✔ ✔ **Dundee Contemporary Arts** www.dca.org.uk · 01382 432000 · **Nethergate, Dundee** State-of-contemporary-art gallery (by award-winning architect Richard Murphy) with great café (887/DUNDEE RESTAURANTS), cinema facilities, etc. which transformed the cultural face of Dundee. Well used, well loved!

2167
8/T19

✔ ✔ **Aberdeen Art Gallery** www.aagm.co.uk · **Schoolhill, Aberdeen** Major gallery with temporary exhibits and eclectic and significant permanent collection from Impressionists to Bellany but especially 19th and 20th century British and Scottish. Large bequest from local granite merchant Alex Macdonald in 1900 contributes fascinating collection of his contemporaries: Bloomsburys, Scottish, Pre-Raphaelites. Excellent watercolour room. An easy and rewarding gallery to visit. 10am-5pm (Sun 2-5pm). Closed Mon.

2168
10/P23

✔ **The Fergusson Gallery** www.scottishmuseums.org.uk · **Marshall Place, Tay Street, Perth** In distinctive round tower (a former waterworks). The assembled works on two floors of J.D. Fergusson (1874-1961) and his partner Margaret Morris. Though he spent much of his life in France, he had an influence on Scottish art and was pre-eminent amongst The Colourists. It's a long way from Perth to Antibes 1913 but these pictures are a draught of the warm south. Mon-Sat 10am-5pm.

2169
10/Q24

✔ **Kirkcaldy Museum & Art Gallery** www.scottishmuseums.org.uk Near railway station, but ask for directions (it's easy to get lost). One of the best galleries in central Scotland. Splendid introduction to the history of 19th/20th-century Scottish art. Lots of Colourists/McTaggart/Glasgow Boys. And Sickert to Redpath. And famously the only public collection in Scotland showing Scotland's best-selling artist: one Jack Vettriano who was a Fife lad. Kirkcaldy doesn't get much good press but this and the parks (1533/PARKS) are worth the journey (plus Valente's: 1349/FISH & CHIPS). 7 days till 5pm.

2170
11/M31
NTS

✔ **Hornel Gallery** www.nts.org.uk · **Kirkcudbright** Hornel's (Broughton) house is a fabulous evocation with a collection of his work and atelier as was. 'Even the Queen was amazed'. Beautiful, atmospheric garden stretches to the river. Apr-Oct 12noon-5pm. Garden all year round. Tearoom only on occasion. The **Jessie M. King House** is 100m down the same road towards the Tolbooth.

2171
8/P17

✔ **Moray Art Centre** www.morayartcentre.org · 01309 692426 · **Findhorn** Part of the Findhorn Community/Foundation/park and eco village. Another very good reason for visiting this life-affirming place. Fascinating building in keeping with the creative and ingenious architecture all around you with an interesting programme of exhibitions and workshops. Tue-Sat; check online for details.

2172
8/R17
☕

✓ **Duff House** www.duffhouse.org.uk · 01261 818181 · Banff Nice walk and easy to find from town (it's a major attraction). Important outstation of the National Galleries of Scotland in meticulously restored Adam house with interesting history and spacious grounds. Ramsays, Raeburns, portraiture of mixed appeal and an El Greco. Go further up the Deveron for a pleasant stroll (2033/WOODLAND WALKS). Nice tearoom. Opening times online or ring to check.

2173
11/N29

✓ **Sculpture at Glenkiln Reservoir** near Dumfries Take A75 to Castle Douglas and right to Shawshead; into village, right at T-junction, left to Dunscore, immediate left, signed for reservoir. Follow road along lochside and park Not a gallery at all but greening bronze sculpture, the 20th-century collection of Sir William Keswick, scattered in the Galloway Hills 16km southeast of Dumfries. 4 you can see from the road, others you find near the reservoir (but allow 2 hours). Epstein, Moore, Rodin in the great outdoors!

2174
3/Q10

✓ **The Pier Arts Centre** www.pierartscentre.com · 01856 850209 · Stromness, Orkney On main street (1544/COASTAL VILLAGES), a gallery on a pier which could have come lock, stock and canvases from Cornwall. Permanent St Ives-style collection assembled by one Margaret Gardiner: Barbara Hepworth, Ben Nicholson, Paolozzi and others shown in a sympatico environment with the sea outside. Important early-20th-century pictures complemented by work of recent contemporaries. Partners with the Tate. A rare treat! Mon-Sat 10.30am-5pm.

2175
10/L26

Paisley Museum & Art Gallery www.museumsgalleriesscotland.org · 0141 889 3151 · High Street, Paisley Collection of world-famous Paisley shawls and history of weaving. Other exhibitions usually have a local connection and interactive element. Notable Greek Ionic-style building. 11am-4pm, Sun 2-5pm. Closed Mon.

2176
9/F22
☕

Calgary Art In Nature Calgary, Isle of Mull Contemporary artwork and sculpture to be found on a trail through the woods adjacent to the wonderful beach at Calgary Bay on the far west coast of Mull and an exhibition gallery space. The project of Matthew Reade who ran the Calgary Farmhouse Hotel (the tearoom remains), the 1km trail is fun rather than thought provoking, but it's a great idea, nice for kids in one of the best of places.

2177
9/L28

Rozelle House www.south-ayrshire.gov.uk · Ayr In Rozelle Park, the only art in these parts. Monthly exhibitions including local artists' work. 4 galleries and additional 5 rooms featuring the Alexander Goudie collection in Rozelle House; craft shop. All year Mon-Sat 10am-5pm, Apr-Oct also Sun 2-5pm. Closed Tue.

☕ signifies notable café.

2178
8/N17
☕

Logie Steading www.logie.co.uk · near Forres In beautiful countryside 10km south of Forres signed from A940 Forres-Grantown road. Near pleasant woodlands and brilliant picnic spot (directions: 2020/WOODLAND WALKS), with lovely walled garden around the big house nearby (Apr-Dec). Much better than your usual crafty courtyard to visit and browse. Includes Giles Pearson's Country Furniture, Helen Trussell's beautiful second-hand bookshop (2205/VERY SPECIAL SHOPS), a farm shop and the **Olive Tree Café**, a home-baking tearoom with integrity. Seems fitting as the estate was built with the fortune of the guy who invented the digestive biscuit! 1396/TEAROOMS. Mar-Dec, 7 days 10.30am-5pm.

2179
7/N16
☕

Anta Factory Shop www.anta.co.uk · 01862 832477 · Fearn Off B9175 from Tain to Nigg ferry, 8km through Hill of Fearn, at disused airfield. Shop with adjacent pottery. Also in Edinburgh: Anta is a classy brand. Tartan curtain fabric; rugs, throws and pots. You can commission furniture to be covered in their material. Pottery tour by arrangement. Shop. All year daily 9.30am-5.30pm (Sun 10am-5pm, ring for winter hours). Pottery Mon-Fri only. Nice café shuts 4pm.

2180
7/M16

Tain Pottery www.tainpottery.co.uk Off the A9 just south of Tain (opposite side of A9 to road signed for Anta at Fearn; see above). Big working pottery, big stuff and often big, perhaps OTT design, hand-painted and very popular (they do the National Trust for Scotland and are stocked all over the UK). Daily in summer, 9am-6pm (Sat/Sun 10am-5pm). Closed Sun in winter.

2181
6/L12

Balnakeil Durness From Durness and the A836 road, take Balnakeil and Faraid Head road for 2km west. Founded in the 1960s in what one imagines was a haze of hash, this craft village is still home to downshifters and creatives, ie talented people. Paintings, pottery, weaving, silk, glass, wood and jewellery in pre-fab huts where community members work and hang out (the site was an early-warning station). **Cocoa Mountain** (01971 511233) make here their heavenly thin chocolate you get all over the north and in Auchterarder and have a chocolate bar open all year round (9am-6pm; 11am-4pm in winter). **Loch Croispol Bookshop** (01971 511777) where 2 blokes, Kevin and Simon, have established a browserie par excellence: the shelves surrounding café tables (home-made changing menu) with often notable art on show. It's open all year too (closed Mon/Tue in winter). The **Balnakeil Bistro** is also a daytime café and gallery, so various snack options. Some businesses seasonal. All open in summer, daily 10am-6 pm (mostly).

2182
6/J14

Highland Stoneware www.highlandstoneware.com · Lochinver & Mill Street, Ullapool On road to Baddidarach as you enter Lochinver on A837; and on way north beyond Ullapool centre. A large-scale pottery business including a shop/warehouse and open studios that you can walk round (Lochinver is more *engagé*). Similar to the ceramica places you find in the Med, but less terracotta: rather, painted, heavy-glazed stoneware in set styles. Many broken plates adorn your arrivals. Great selection, pricey, but you may have luck in the Lochinver discount section. Mail-order service. 9am-6pm weekdays, and Sat in summer.

2183
10/R24

Crail Pottery www.crailpottery.com · Crail At the foot of Rose Wynd, signposted from main street (best to walk). In a tree-shaded Mediterranean courtyard and upstairs attic, a cornucopia of brilliant and useful things. Open 9am-5pm (weekends from 10am). Don't miss the harbour nearby, one of the most romantic neuks in the Neuk. Good tearoom on way to harbour (1406/TEAROOMS).

2184
10/N21

✓ **MacNaughton's** www.macnaughtonsofpitlochry.com · Station Road, Pitlochry On main street corner, this the best of many. A vast, old-fashioned family-owned outfitter (no longer the MacNaughtons) with acres of tartan attire including obligatory tartan pyjamas and dressing gowns! Make their own cloth; 9m kilts made in 6-8 weeks. This is the real McCoy. 7 days till 5.30pm (4pm Sun).

2185
1/XE1

✓ **Kinloch Anderson** www.kinlochanderson.com · Dock Street, Leith, Edinburgh A trek from uptown but firmly on the tourist trail and so much better than the High St, ie the tartan-tainted Royal Mile. Independent, family-run company since 1868, they are experts in Highland dress and all things tartan; they've supplied *everybody*. They design and manufacture their own tartans, have a good range of men's tweed jackets; even rugs. Mon-Sat 9am-5.30pm.

2186
11/K28

✓ **House of Burns** Kirkoswald A major new visitor development in South Ayrshire on A77 in this strip of village made famous by its Burns characters and graveyard (1894/GRAVEYARDS). The Costley family have set up shop opposite and it is some shop. It includes a tearoom, pâtisserie, ice-cream factory, farm and general Scottish-produce emporium stocking selected good stuff and well-known brands including, of course, their own. Souter Johnnie's pub adjacent is a great pub-grub destination (1291/GASTROPUBS). 7 days 9am-5pm, pub till 9pm.

2187
10/R27

✓ **Harestanes Countryside Centres** near Jedburgh Off A68 at Ancrum, the B6400 to Nisbet. Farm steading complex on Monteviot Estate (1504/GARDENS) with café/exhibition/superior crafts including the excellent **Buy Design** showing furniture, ceramics and glass. Easter-Oct 10am-5pm. Event programme. Best tearoom 1km down the road at Woodside (1383/TEAROOMS).

2188
9/K26

Octopus Crafts near Fairlie On A78 Largs-Ardrossan south of Fairlie. Crafts, wines, cookshop, excellent restaurant (1328/SEAFOOD RESTAURANTS) and a seafood deli. An all-round roadside food-to-love experience; the sign says Fencebay Seafood & Crafts. All hand-made and/or hand-picked; even wines are well chosen. Good pots. Glass and wood. Choice utensils. Farmers' market last Sunday of month.

2189
8/N17
☕

Brodie Country Fare www.brodiecountryfare.com · between Nairn & Forres By A96 near Brodie Castle (1772/CASTLES). One of those drive-in one-stop consumer experiences full of brands, full of people. Deli food, a fairly up-market womenswear boutique and every crafty tartanalia of note. Self-serve restaurant gets as busy as a motorway café; naturally you have to walk through everything else to get there. 7 days till 5.30pm (5pm in winter).

2190
7/L17
☕

Falls of Shin Visitor Centre www.fallsofshin.co.uk · near Lairg Self-serve café/restaurant is notable (1033/BEST HIGHLAND RESTAURANTS) in the visitor centre and shop across the road from the Falls of Shin on Achany Glen road 8km south of Lairg (1602/WATERFALLS). Unlikely emporium perhaps in far-flung Sutherland though no longer quite Harrods of the North (ex-proprietor Mohammed al Fayed's estate is here). Lots of Highland produce and the café. 9.30am-6pm all year.

2191
7/F17

Edinbane Pottery www.edinbane-pottery.co.uk · Skye 500m off A850 Portree (22km) to Dunvegan road. A great working pottery where the various processes are often in progress. Wood-fired and salt-glazed pots of all shapes and for every purpose. Mon-Fri 9am-6pm; 7 days Easter-Oct.

2192
7/F18

Skye Silver www.skyesilver.com · Colbost 10km Dunvegan on B884 to Glendale. Long established and reputable jewellery made and sold in an old Skye schoolhouse in a distant corner; Three Chimneys restaurant and Red Roof coffee shop nearby (2291/2299/SKYE RESTAURANTS). Well-made, Celtic designs, good gifts. Mar-Oct 7 days, 10am-6pm.

2193
8/P17

Findhorn Pottery www.findhornpottery.com · **Findhorn** Deep in both the Findhorn Community (since 1971) and the spreading park, it's more than interesting to wander through the eco-village to this long-standing pottery and shop. 3 potters work away here (including Brian Nobbs who helped to build it) and their ware is for sale. It's the real deal! Apr-Dec 10.30am-5.30pm (Thu from 11.30am, Sun 12 noon). From 1pm Jan-Mar. They never stop.

2194
9/F23
HS

Iona Abbey Shop www.iona.org.uk/abbey · **Iona** Via CalMac ferry from Fionnphort on Mull. Crafts and souvenirs across the way in separate building. Proceeds support a worthy, committed organisation. Christian literature, tapes, etc. but mostly artefacts from nearby and around Scotland. Celtic crosses much in evidence, but then this is where they came from! Also on the way to and from the abbey, **Aosdana** gallery (jewellers) and **Oran Creative Crafts** in restored steadings are well worth a browse.

2195
5/F13

Borgh Pottery Borve **Lewis** On northwest coast of island a wee way from Stornoway (25km north on A857) but no great detour from the road to Callanish where you are probably going. Alex and Sue Blair's pleasant gallery of hand-thrown pots with different glazes; domestic and garden wear. Knits. Open all year 9.30pm-6pm. Closed Sun.

2196
11/M30
☕

Galloway Lodge Preserves www.gallowaylodge.co.uk · **Gatehouse of Fleet** Main street, same building as the PO. Packed with local jams, marmalades, chutneys and pickles. Scottish pottery by Scotia Ceramics, Highland Stoneware and Dunoon. Good presents and jam for you. 10am-5pm. Self-service coffee shop best in the village, home-made and old-style – good for mum, gran and bairns!

2197
9/J21
☕

Crafts & Things **near Glencoe Village** On A82 between Glencoe village and Ballachulish, overlooking Loch Leven. Eclectic mix, perhaps more things than crafts. Mind, body and mountain books (and this one) and reasonably priced knit/outerwear. Good coffee shop doing salads, sandwiches, Luca's ice cream and home baking, with local artists' work on walls. All year, daily until 5.30pm.

The Very Special Shops

2198
8/T19
☕

✓✓ **Hammerton Stores** www.hammertonstore.co.uk · 01224 324449 · 336 Great Western Road, Aberdeen On road west to Deeside somewhere in a suburb. Susan Watson's love affair with Aberdeen and life. Not only a deli, more a superior provisioner where essentials include art and cool pottery and books including mine. Wines, beers, cheeses, proper French pâtisserie and brands are all carefully selected. Tables outside where you can snack and reflect how nice it would be to have a place like this in your neighbourhood. My Broughton St Edinburgh awaits. 7 days 7.30am-6.30pm, Sat/Sun 8am-5.30pm.

2199
10/N21
☕
LL

✓✓ **House of Bruar** www.houseofbruar.com · **Pitlochry** Extraordinarily successful countryside mall, a courtyard emporia if not euphoria. The shopaholic honey pot on A9 north of Blair Atholl. In the various floors and chambers they sell an enormous range of clothes, textiles and anything you might need for the home, garden or body. Not just any old brand either but top end and selective. It really can claim to be the Harrods of the North. The vast food section sells the best of Scottish everything and there's always a queue at the self-service café with tables in and out. There often seems more folk here than in Pitlochry. Strategically placed where you want to stop on the A9, Bruar is the very best of the roadside retail explosion. Falls nearby for non-retail therapy (1600/WATER FALLS). 7 days 9am-5pm.

2200
10/N22
☕

The Highland Chocolatier www.highlandchocolatier.com · Grand-tully Part of Legends coffee shop (1308/TEAROOMS), Iain Burnett's chocolateria is a Perthshire destination in itself. A splurge of artisan chocolate-makers in recent years but Iain's meticulously crafted and beautifully presented individual and boxed chocs are in a class of their own. Indulge. 10am-5pm. 7 days.

2201
6/K14
L

Drumbeg Village Stores www.drumbegstores.co.uk · 01571 833235 On the single-track road that runs from Kylesku to Lochinver, halfway along amidst some of the most spectacular scenery in Scotland (1618/SCENIC ROUTES), an exceptional store in tiny Drumbeg township. Over 700 items in stock, a great deli selection, local produce, fruit 'n' veg in the adjacent shack. Bringing a whole new dimension to the 'shop local' mantra, at least they're unlikely to ever get Tescoed. Teahouse also in village and brilliant guest house (977/HIGHLAND).

2202
7/H16
☕

Hillbillies and the Mountain Coffee Co. 01445 712316 · Gairloch In the middle of the straggly town amidst great coastal (and mountain) scenery, a bookshop/coffee shop totally at one with its location and the people who appreciate it. Inspired selection of outdoor, thought-provoking and just good books. Maps, great stuff for presents and the caff with bagels, soup and unfeasibly big scones. Been here a while, this place, but gets better. 9am-6pm. Closed Dec-Feb.

2203
6/J14
☕

Achin's Bookshop www.scotbooks.freeuk.com · Lochinver At Inver-kirkaig 5km from Lochinver on the 'wee mad road' to Achiltibuie (1619/SCENIC ROUTES). Enduring, unexpected haven of books in the back of beyond providing something to read when you've climbed everything or are unlikely to climb anything except the mount of knowledge. Outdoor wear too and hats. Path to Kirkaig Falls and Suilven begins at the gate (1861/MONUMENTS). Easter-Oct 7 days; 9.30am-6pm (winter Mon-Sat 10am-5pm). Café 10am-5pm, summer only.

2204
7/H19
LL

Floraidh 01471 833347 · by the Isle Ornsay Hotel, Skye Sleat peninsula adjacent the landmark Eilean Iarmain Hotel (2261/SKYE), more or less on the quayside of this mystic cove. Hand-made, stylish clothes in tweed and wool mainly but also silk and linen; a bespoke boutique in the best of taste. Easter-Oct.

2205
8/N17
☕

Helen Trussell's Books 01309 611373 · Logie Steading near Forres Logie Steading 10km south of Forres is worth visiting for many reasons (2178/SHOPPING, 2020/WOODLAND WALKS) but Helen Trussell's extensive second-hand bookshop is a real find in a place perfectly sympatico with browsing. Bargains and a great hardback section, antiquarian and specialist Scottish, travel, natural history. Folk come from far and wide. Coffee shop over-by. 7 days Mar-Dec 11am-5pm.

2206
6/P15

20th Century Collectibles www.Helmsdale.org · Helmsdale Main street near Mirage (1019/HIGHLAND RESTAURANTS) and Bridge Hotel (999/HIGHLAND HOTELS) and also Timespan, the interesting trip-through-time heritage centre (2144/HERITAGE). Whereas here you rummage and browse through 20th-century memorabilia, bric-à-brac, clothes, jewellery, ornaments and yes, collectibles. *StB* doesn't do antique or vintage shops but Euan Gibson's eye and enthusiasm make this shop off the northern road to nowhere remarkable. Who would expect a bit of camp this far from Brighton? Admirably avoids tartanalia. Happen by!

Where To Buy Good Scottish Woollies

2207
8/P17
✓✓ **Johnston's Cashmere Centre** Elgin Johnston's is, as they say, one of the last of the Mohicans actually making textiles in Scotland. They are 'the only British mill to transform fibre to garment' (yarns spun at their factory in Elgin and made into garments in the Borders). They stock their own ranges including couture cashmere, many of which are sold internationally as well as other quality brands. This extensive mill shop, the high-quality and classy 'home' section, heritage centre and café is a serious visitor attraction hereabouts. The jumpers, bunnets and cardies are more classic than cool but they won't fall apart and they ain't made in China. Lovely garden adjacent the pulsating mill with free tours Mon-Fri (30 minutes) from the woolstore through dyeing, pearling, spinning and weaving into their cloth and scarves. You will want to buy something! Mon-Sat 9am-5.30pm, Sun 11am-5pm. Near the cathedral (1794/RUINS).

2208
3/Q10
7/M18
✓ **Judith Glue** www.judithglue.com · 01856 874225 · Kirkwall, Orkney · Bridge Street, Inverness · 01463 248529 Opposite the cathedral in Kirkwall. Distinctive hand-made jumpers, the runic designs are signature. Also the individual Highland and Orkney ceramics and jewellery, condiments and preserves. Landscape prints of Orkney are by twin sister, Jane. Great new café in Orkney shop (2307/ORKNEY). Mon-Sat 9am-6pm (later in summer), Sun from 10am.

2209
1/A4
✓ **Belinda Robertson** www.belindarobertson.com · 0131 557 8118 · 13a Dundas Street, Edinburgh Queen of commissioned cashmere not so much couture as once was but more accessible in her Edinburgh showroom. Part of the collection is still made in Hawick. Closed Sun.

2210
7/G19
Ragamuffin www.ragamuffinonline.co.uk · Armadale Pier, Skye On the pier, so one of the first or last things you can do on Skye is rummage through the Ragamuffin store and get a nice knit. Every kind of jumper and some crafts in this Aladdin's cave within a new-build shed; including tweedy things and mad hats. 7 days 9am-6pm (Sun 10am-5pm). Also in Edinburgh's Royal Mile.

2211
10/R27
Lochcarron Visitor Centre www.lochcarron.com · Selkirk If you're in Galashiels (or Hawick) which grew up around woollen mills, you might expect to find a good selection of woollens you can't get everywhere else; and bargains. Well, no. Loch Carron used to be in Gala but here is a big attraction with award-winning mill tours, exhibits, an okay mill shop and a coffee shop. 9am-5pm. Closed Sun. No mill tours Fri/Sat.

2212
10/R28
Hawick Cashmere www.hawickcashmere.com · Hawick Factory in Hawick since 1874, with visitor centre beside the river on Duke St. Also shops in Kelso and Edinburgh. 'State-of-the-art colours and designs'. Not only, but mostly cashmere. Mon-Sat 9.30am-5pm; Sun 11am-4pm (in season).

Harris Tweed

2213
5
Tweeds & Knitwear www.harristweedandknitwear.co.uk · 01859 502040 · Tarbert & Drinishadder Catherine Campbell's warehouse/garage and shop in Tarbert and croft/shop at 4 Plockropool, Drinishadder 6km south of Tarbert, also on the Golden Road (1621/SCENIC ROUTES). Bales of tweed in Tarbert with knitwear and clothing at the adjacent shop and in the croft. Closed Sun.

2214 **Luskentyre Harris Tweed** www.luskentyreharristweed.co.uk · 01859
5/E15   550308 · No 6, Luskentyre 2km off west coast on main road south to Rodel.
Donald and Maureen Mackay's place is notable for their bolder-coloured tartan
tweed. 9.30am-6pm Closed Sun.

2215 **Lewis Loom Centre** 01851 704500 · Stornoway Main street, far from Harris
5/F14   but near the tourists. Cloth and clothes. Demos and displays. Closed Sun.

2216 **Harris Tweed Shop** Tarbert Main street small emporium with range of
9/G25   Harris Tweed products. It's near the ferry. Mon-Sat 9.30am-5.30pm.

Not Just Garden Centres, More A Way Of Life

⌣ *signifies notable café. Others may have cafés that have not been
recommended.*

2217   √√ **Dougal Philip's New Hopetoun Gardens** near South
10/P25   Queensferry · 01506 834433 · www.newhopetoungardens.co.uk
⌣   The meticulously nurtured and always growing prize bloom of all (Scottish) garden
centres sprawling aesthetically among trees with 21 different zones and
demonstration gardens (including Oriental and Scottish). Everything you could
ever grow or put in a Scottish garden. Acres of accessories; big pots. Orangery
tearoom has verdant views and tasty home-made stuff. All year 10am-5.30pm.
Tearoom closes 4.30pm. New adjacent farm shop is not related.

2218   √√ **Floors Castle** www.roxburghe.net · Kelso 3km outside town off
10/S27   B6397 St Boswells road (garden centre has separate entrance to main
⌣   visitors' gate in town). Set amongst lovely old greenhouses within walled gardens
some distance from house, it has a showpiece herbaceous border, plant centre
and a first-class coffee shop, The Terrace (1368/TEAROOMS) and patio. 'Very good
roses'. Lovely kids' lawn. Centre is open all year. 10am-5pm. (1841/COUNTRY
HOUSES.)

2219   √√ **Glendoick** www.glendoick.com · 01738 860205 · Glencarse near
10/P23   Perth Take slip road off the A85, 10km from Perth, in the fertile Carse
⌣   of the Tay. A large family-owned garden centre long a destination, now with new
extension more than ever an absorbing visit. Well laid out, friendly and informed
staff. Lovely pagoda garden. The (Cox) family gardens 2km up the road open for
snowdrops (Feb) and rhodies and azaleas (Apr-mid June, Mon-Fri and Sun in May)
and is remarkable. Nice coffee shop with some home baking, hot meals; big on
soups. Good bookshop their 'Food Library' including Kenneth's own splendid book
(see Best Gardens, p. 265–9) and mine. You could spend hours here! 7 days till
5.30pm, 5pm winter.

2220   √ **Cally Gardens** www.callygardens.co.uk · Gatehouse of Fleet An
11/M30   extraordinary assemblage of herbaceous perennials in a gorgeous walled garden. Comprehensive sales online but a must to visit; see 1508/GARDENS.

2221   √ **Kinlochlaich Gardens** www.kinlochlaichgardencentre.co.uk · Appin
9/J22   On main A28 Oban-Fort William road just north of Port Appin turnoff, the

West Highlands' largest nursery/garden centre. Set in a large walled garden filled with plants and veg soaking up the climes of the warm Gulf Stream. The Hutchisons nurture these acres enabling you to reap what they sow. With a huge array of plants on offer it's like visiting a friend's garden and being able to take home your fave bits. Charming cottages and apartments. For the treehouse, book well ahead (01631 730342). 7 days 9.30am-5.30pm (dusk in winter).

2222
7/N19
☕

Inshraich www.kincraig.com · 01540 651287 · **near Kincraig, near Aviemore** On B970 between Kincraig and Inverdruie (which is on the Coylumbridge ski road out of Aviemore), a nursery that puts others in the shade. John and Gunn Borrowman carrying on (and developing) the horticulture of Jack Drake (from 1930s) and John Lawson (1949). Specialising in alpines and bog plants but with neat beds of all sorts in the grounds (and a wild garden) of the house by the Spey and frames full of perfect specimens, this is a potterer's paradise. **Potting Shed Tearoom** with famously good cakes and superb bird-viewing gallery (1725/BIRDS). Mar-Oct 7 days 10am-5pm.

2223
9/J26
☕

Mount Stuart Bute Gem of a garden centre at entrance car park adjacent visitor centre of magnificent Mount Stuart (1833/COUNTRY HOUSES). Plants, robust and usually good-looking, are from the glorious gardens over by. Great restaurant (741/ARGYLL) and farm shop, 10am-6pm. May vary; call 01700 503877.

2224
10/R27
☕

Woodside near Ancrum On B6400 off A68 opposite Ancrum turnoff just past Harestanes (2187/SHOPPING) and before Monteviot (1504/GARDENS), this is the walled garden of the big hoose that overlooks the Teviot. Beautiful, quiet place with displays, events and organic agenda. They really care about their plants and yours. Best tearoom around in a wooden cabin in corner (1383/TEAROOMS). 7 days 10am-5pm. Walk starts here to Peniel Heugh and the view (1850/MONU-MENTS).

2225
8/R20
☕

Raemoir Garden Centre www.raemoirgardencentre.co.uk · **Banchory** On A980 off main street 3km north of town. A garden centre that grew into a massive roadside emporium à la House of Bruar except that this is a side road in Deeside. Still it's packed with people and the stuff they browse and buy. Café and restaurant are excellent (1376/TEAROOMS). Somewhere there are plants! 7 days 9am-6pm. Tearoom till 5.30pm, restaurant till 4pm.

2226
10/N22
☕

Allium Garden Company 01796 482822 · **Ballinluig near Pitlochry** This, the project of Douglas Miller whose family (and he) used to have Jenners in Edinburgh, is on the A9 though you have to come off at Ballinluig and double back following the signs. Developing as a conscientious and connoisseurs' garden centre – products all selected for taste as well as suitability (plants have a money-back guarantee). Suppliers a key factor. Decent caff doing soup, salads and home baking. 7 days 9.30am-5.30pm. Sun 10am-5pm, caff earlier.

2227
10/R25
☕

Smeaton Nursery & Gardens 01620 860501 · **East Linton** 2km from village on North Berwick road (signed Smeaton). Up a drive in an old estate is this walled garden going back to early 19th century. Wide range; good for fruit (and other) trees, herbaceous, etc. Nice to wander round, an additional pleasure is the Lake Walk halfway down the drive through a small gate in the woods. 1km stroll round a secret finger lake in magnificent mature woodland (10am-dusk; 440/WOODLAND WALKS). Mon-Sat 9.30am-4.30pm; Sun 10.30am-4.30pm. Laid-back tearoom.

The Islands

The Magical Islands

2228
7/G18
✓ ✓ **Raasay** A small car ferry (car useful, but bikes best) from Sconser (between Portree and Broadford) on Skye takes you to this, the best of places. The distinctive flat top of Dun Caan presides over an island whose history and natural history is Highland Scotland in microcosm. The village with rows of mining-type cottages is 1km from the new jetty which is by the 'big house', home to the excellent Outdoor Centre. Sadly it went up in flames '09 though it has been rebuilt and will re-open with a full activity programme, accommodation and café in 2013. The views from the lawn, or the viewpoint above the house, or better still from Dun Caan with the Cuillin on one side and Torridon on the other, are exceptional (2244/ISLAND WALKS). The island hotel (15 rooms) and bar has been taken over by Raasay House meantime. There's a ruined castle, a secret rhododendron-lined loch for swimming, seals, otters and eagles. Find 'Calum's Road' and read the book. Much to explore but go quietly here.
Regular CalMac ferry from Sconser on Skye. Raasay House & Hotel 01478 660266 (www.raasay-house.co.uk).

2229
9/G25
✓ ✓ **Jura** www.theisleofjura.co.uk Small regular car ferry from Port Askaig on Islay or from Tayvallich takes you to a different world. Jura is remote, scarcely populated and has an ineffable grandeur indifferent to the demands of tourism. Ideal for wild camping and there's a (much improved of late) hotel and pub (2250/ISLAND HOTELS) in the only village (Craighouse) 12km from ferry at Feolin. Walking guides available at the hotel and essential especially for the Paps, the hills that maintain such a powerful hold over the island. Easiest climb is from Three Arch Bridge; allow 6 hours. In May they run up all of them and back to the distillery in 3 hours. The distillery where The Jura comes from is not as beautiful as the drink it produces: tours 01496 820385. **Jura House**'s walled garden, a hidden jewel set above the south coastline (1500/GARDENS) is closed at TGP. Corryvreckan whirlpool (2257/ISLAND WALKS) is another lure but you may need a 4WD to get close and its impressiveness depends upon tides. Barnhill, Orwell's house where he wrote *1984*, isn't open but there are many fascinating side tracks: the wild west coast; around Loch Tarbert; and the long littoral between Craighouse and Lagg. (Also 1568/BEACHES; 1889/GRAVEYARDS.) With one road, no street lamps and over 5,000 deer, the sound of silence is everything.
CalMac (01880 730253) 7 days, 5-minute service from Port Askaig. Passenger-only ferry from Tayvallich to Craighouse twice daily Easter to Sep (07768 450000). Bike hire in Craighouse (07092 180747).

2230
9/F23
✓ ✓ **Iona** 150,000 visitors a year, but Iona still enchants (as it did the Colourists and centuries of pilgrims), especially if you can get away to the **Bay at the Back of the Ocean** (1574/BEACHES) or sit in one of the many gardens. Or stay: **Argyll Hotel** best (01681 700334; 1163/GET-AWAY HOTELS); **St Columba Hotel** near the abbey has more rooms and its own lovely garden (01681 700304; 2306/MULL); or B&B. Abbey shop and nearby galleries (2179/SHOPPING). Pilgrimage walks on Tuesday (10am from St John's Cross). Bike hire from Finlay Ross shop (01681 700357) and Seaview Guest House at Fionnphort (01681 700235) if you're staying in the village. Everything about Iona is benign; even the sun shines here when it's raining on Mull and corncrakes thrive while elsewhere they disappear.
Regular 15-minute CalMac service from Fionnphort till 6pm, earlier in winter (01681 700512).

2231
9/F24
✓ ✓ **Colonsay** www.colonsay.org.uk Accessible to daytrippers but time ashore is short so you need to arrange accommodation. The island is a haven of wildlife, flowers and beaches (1555/BEACHES) and a serene and popular

stopover. 250m from the ferry, the refurbished hotel is congenial, convenient and way better than you might expect (2281/ISLAND HOTELS). Great bar; self-catering units nearby. Some holiday cottages and many B&Bs (check Colonsay website); camping not encouraged. Bar meals and supper at the hotel and Pantry at the pier. A wild 18-hole golf course and bookshop (sic) adjacent. Semi-botanical gardens at Colonsay House and fine walks, especially to Oronsay (2251/ISLAND WALKS). Don't miss the house at Shell Beach which sells oysters and honey.
CalMac from Oban (or Islay). Crossing takes just over 2 hours. Times vary.

2232
7/G20

✓ ✓ **Eigg** www.isleofeigg.net Run by a community (heritage) trust, this small, perfectly formed island seems in robust health, won a UK sustainable-energy award (it is almost self-sufficient) and has a growing, proactive population that many other islands would (and possibly will) die for. A wildlife haven for birds and sealife; otters, eagles and seal colonies. There's a friendly tearoom at the pier: home baking, licensed (boat hours only in winter); evening meals on request. The irrepressible Sue Kirk runs the shop and does B&B, self-catering (near Laig Bay and singing sands beach) and has a wee restaurant in her house (01687 482405). Check website for other B&Bs. **Glebe Barn** is a brill wee hostel (01687 482417); 1125/HOSTELS. Great walk to **Sgurr an Eigg**, an awesome perch on a summer's day (2258/ISLAND WALKS). Great events programme. You can camp.
CalMac (from Mallaig) (01687 462403) or better, from Arisaig. Arisaig Marine (01687 450224) every day except Thu in summer. Phone for other timings. No car ferry. Day trips to Rum and Muck. Bike hire 01687 462137.

2233
7/F20

✓ ✓ **Rum** www.islandofrum.com The large island in the group south of Skye, off the coast at Mallaig. The CalMac ferry plies between Canna, Eigg, Muck and Rum but not too conveniently and it's not easy to island-hop and make a decent visit (but see below). Rum, the most wild and dramatic, has an extraordinary time-warp mansion in Kinloch Castle which is mainly a museum (guided tours tie in with boat trips) though at TGP the long-running question mark over its future grows more acute. It currently houses a hostel (45 beds) and bistro (01687 462037), a contrast to the antique opulence above and below. Rum is run by Scottish Natural Heritage and there are fine trails, climbs, bird-watching spots. 2 simple walks are marked for the 3-hour visitors, but the island reveals its mysteries more slowly. The Doric temple mausoleum to George Bullough, the industrialist whose Highland fantasy the castle was, is a 9km (3-hour) walk across the island to Harris Bay. Sighting the sea eagles (the first to be re-introduced into the UK) may be one of the best things that ever happens to you.
CalMac ferry from Mallaig direct (twice a week) or via Eigg (2 hours 15 minutes). Better from Arisaig (Murdo Grant 01687 450224), summer only (can get 3 hours ashore). If you have the cash there are fast rides from Elgol, Skye (www.aquaxplore.co.uk) and from Inverie on Knoydart (www.seaknoydart.co.uk). Both will come for you at Mallaig.

2234
5/A15
NTS

✓ ✓ **St Kilda** www.kilda.org.uk There's nothing quite like St Kilda, anywhere. By far the most remote and removed of the islands here, it is an expedition to reach and one of a physical, cultural and spiritual nature. A World Heritage site and run by NTS, it occupies a special place in the Scottish heart and soul. NTS ranger's office on St Kilda is at 0844 493 2237. Sadly I have never been.
To visit: Kilda Cruises (www.kildacruises.co.uk) 01859 502060 from Leverburgh, Harris and see p. 300-1, Sealife Cruises.

2235
9/E22

✓ **Isle of Tiree** www.isleoftiree.com It is an isle, not just an island - flat, with lovely sand and grass and the weather's usually better than the mainland. A bit of wind does keep away the midges. Lots of outdoor activities: famously, windsurfing, but kayaking, birdwatching and other gentle pursuits. **The Scarinish**

Hotel (01879 220308) is friendly, local and loved, there are 3 guest houses, a wee hostel (01879 220435) and a campsite. Tiree has a unique character different to the islands on this page. But you may long for trees.
Daily flights from Glasgow (0871 700 2000) and Stornoway & CalMac ferries from Oban (daily in summer, about 4 hours).

2236 ✓ **Gigha** www.gigha.org.uk Romantic small island off Kintyre coast with
9/G26   classic views of its island neighbours. Easy mainland access (20-minute ferry) contributes to an island atmosphere without a feeling of isolation. Like Eigg, Gigha was bought by the islanders so its fragile economy is dependent on your visit. The island is run by a heritage trust. Gardens at **Achamore House** (1509/GARDENS) are a big attraction and the **Gigha Hotel** (2290/ISLAND HOTELS) provides comfortable surroundings. All very relaxed and friendly. **Boathouse** café-bar by the ferry for lunch and dinner (Apr-Sep; 01583 505123). 5 B&Bs including exceptional rooms at the big house (01583 505400) and golf (9 holes). Many trails and tracks; ask locally for leaflet. Double Beach where the Queen once swam off the royal yacht; two crescents of sand either side of the north end of Eilean Garbh isthmus.
CalMac ferry from Tayinloan on A83, 27km south of Tarbert (Glasgow 165km). One an hour in summer, fewer in winter.

2237 ✓ **Ulva** Off west coast of Mull; boat leaves Ulva Ferry on B8073 26km south of
9/F22   Dervaig. Idyllic wee island with 5 well-marked walks including to the curious basalt columns similar to Staffa, or by causeway to the smaller island of Gometra; plan routes at the Boathouse interpretive centre and tearoom (with Ulva oysters, home-cooked food 9am-4.30pm in summer). Sheila's (thatched) Cottage faithfully restored tells the Ulva story. No accommodation though camping can be arranged (01688 500264). A charming Telford church has services 4 times a year. Ulva is a perfect day away from the rat race of downtown Tobermory (and everywhere else)!
All-day 5-minute service (not Sat; Sun summer only) till 5pm. Ferryman (01688 500226).

2238 ✓ **Eriskay** www.cne-siar.gov.uk/eriskay Made famous by the sinking
5/D19   nearby of the SS *Politician* in 1941 and the salvaging of its whisky cargo, later immortalised by Compton Mackenzie in *Whisky Galore*, this Hebridean gem has all the idyllic island ingredients: perfect beaches (1922/MARY, CHARLIE & BOB), a lovely church, St Michael's (1871/CHURCHES), a hill to climb, a pub (called The Politician and telling the story round its walls; it sells decent pub food all day in summer), and the causeway to South Uist (the road cuts a swathe across the island). Limited B&B and no hotel, but camping is ok if you're discreet. Eriskay and Barra together – the pure island experience. (Also 2305/OUTER HEBRIDES).
CalMac ferry from Barra (Airdmhor) 40 minutes: 5 a day in summer, winter hours vary.

2239 **Mingulay** Deserted mystical island near the southern tip of the Outer Hebrides,
5/C20   the subject of one of the definitive island books, *The Road to Mingulay*. Now easily
NTS   reached in summer by daily trip from Castlebay on Barra with 1.5-hour journey and 3 hours ashore (ask at tourist information centre or Castlebay Hotel). Last inhabitants left 1912. Ruined village has the poignant air of St Kilda; similar spectacular cliffs on west side with fantastic rock formations, stacks and a huge natural arch, best viewed from boat. Only birds and sheep live here now.

2240 **Tanera Mór** www.summerisles.com Only recently been introduced to this,
6/J15   the largest and only inhabited of (around 20) Summer Isles by the Wilders who own and look after it. Summer Isles Sea Tours (07927 920592) will take you there 3 times a day in summer (not Sun). You can refresh at Rich and Lizzie's café (buffet supper on Wed). 6 self-catering cottages (01854 622252) and they do tutored art

and activity courses. They also have their own Summer Isles stamps (yes, they do!). Climb their hill, Meall Mór, or just chill. Theirs is truly an island life!

2241 **The Shiants** www.shiantisles.net 3 magical, uninhabited tiny islands off east
5/F15 coast of Harris. Read about them in one of the most detailed accounts (a love letter) to any small island ever written: *Sea Room* by Adam Nicolson, the guy who owns them. There's a bothy and it's possible to visit by visiting first his website or by Heridean Whale Cruises out of Gairloch; 1738/SEALIFE CRUISES.

2242 **Lismore** www.isleoflismore.com Sail from Oban (car ferry) or better from Port
9/H22 Appin 5km off the main A828 Oban-Fort William road, 32km north of Oban; there's a seafood bar/restaurant/hotel (1335/SEAFOOD RESTAURANTS) to sit and wait. A road runs down the centre of the island (heritage centre and a rather good café halfway, till 4pm in season; 01631 760020) but there are many hill and coastal walks; even the near end round Port Ramsay feels away from it all. History, natural history and air. Island bike hire from Mary McDougal (01631 760213) who will deliver to ferry, or Port Appin (01631 730391).
CalMac service from Oban, 4 or 5 times a day (2 on Sun). From Port Appin (32km north of Oban) several per day, 5mins. Last back 8.15pm; 9.45pm Fri & Sat; 6.35pm winter, but check (01631 562125).

2243 **Staffa** For many, a must, especially if you're on Mull. The geological phenome-
9/F22 non of Fingal's Cave and Mendelssohn's homage are well known. But it's still impressive. Several boat-trip options, many including the Treshnish Islands. *Trips from Mull (08000 858786). Trips from Iona/Fionnphort (01681 700338 or 01681 700358). Trips from Oban (01631 730686).*

CalMac www.calmac.co.uk · 08705 650000

▌▌▌ Fantastic Walks In The Islands

For walk codes, see p. 12.

2244 7/G18 **Dun Caan** Raasay Still one of my favourite island walks – to the flat top of a
10KM · XCIRC magic hill (2244/VIEWS), the one you see from most of the east coast of Skye. Take
XBIKES ferry (2228/MAGICAL ISLANDS), ask for route from Inverarish. Go via old iron mine;
2-B-2 looks steep when you get over the ridge, but it's a dawdle. And amazing.

2245 **The Lost Glen** Harris Not visited recently – hope the directions are still ok.
5/E15 Take B887 west from north of Tarbert almost to the end (where at Hushinish
12KM RET there's a good beach, maybe a sunset), but go right (was signed Chliostair Power
XCIRC Station) before the big house (1244/HOUSE PARTIES). Park here or further in and
XBIKES walk to dam (3km from road). Take right track round reservoir and left around the
2-B-2 upper loch. Over the brim you arrive in a wide, wild glen; an overhang 2km ahead is said to have the steepest angle in Europe. Go quietly; if you don't see deer and eagles here, you're making too much noise on the grass.

2246 **Walks on Lewis** 2 coastal walks in the north of Lewis. **Tolsta Head** via B895
5/G14 northeast of Stornoway and its continuation to the car park of **Traigh Mhor**;
3-11KM 1562/BEACHES. Head for the cliffs of the Head; walk combines magnificent sands,
CIRC · XBIKES big cliffs and impressive sea stacks. **The Butt of Lewis** from Port Nis
2-B-2 (2305/HEBRIDES) going north as far as you can get in the Hebrides. Start at the cemetery by Eoropaidh Beach. A fine, airy walk on mainly grassy paths, heading first for the Stevenson lighthouse. Can shorten to 3km or do fuller circuit.

2247 **Carsaig** Mull In south of island, 7km from A849 Fionnphort-Craignure road near
9/G23 Pennyghael. 2 walks start at pier: going left towards Lochbuie for a spectacular
15/20KM coastal/woodland walk past Adnunan Stack (8km); or right towards the imposing
XCIRC headland where, under the cliffs, the Nuns' Cave was a shelter for nuns evicted
XBIKES from Iona during the Reformation. Nearby is a quarry whose stone was used to
2-B-2 build Iona Abbey and much further on (12km Carsaig), at Malcolm's Point, the
extraordinary Carsaig Arches carved by wind and sea (take great care!).

2248 **Glengorm Estate** Mull Old, accessible estate 7km north of Tobermory off Der-
9/G22 vaig road with 3 easy-to-find and -follow routes. Good map in coffee shop (1377/
3KM COFFEE SHOPS), one of the best in the land for sustenance before and after (it can
CIRC get windy on the headlands). Walks vary from less than 30 minutes (the Flat Rock),
XBIKES through 1 hour (the Fort and bathing pool; 2119/OPEN-AIR POOLS) to 1.5 hours (to
2-B-2 Mingary Point). If you stay in the castle (2306/MULL) you can do the lot at your ease.

2249 **Cock of Arran** Lochranza Start and finish at Lochranza Castle following the
9/J26 signs to the magnificent shoreline. Divers and ducks share the littoral with seals.
11KM About 1km from where you meet the shore, look for Giant Centipede fossil trail.
CIRC Further on at opening of wall pace 350 steps and turn left up to Ossian's Cave.
XBIKES Path crosses Fairy Dell Burn and eventually comes out at Lochranza Bay. Allow 4/5
hours and stout boots.

2250 **Holy Island** The small island that sits so greenly and serenely in Lamlash Bay is
9/F24 1km away by hourly ferry (less frequently in winter; 07970 771960). Holy Isle is
6KM known as the spiritual sanctuary and World Peace Centre project of Samye Ling
CIRC Monastery (1224/1218/retreats) but you can freely walk around the littoral and
XBIKES easily to the top of the presiding single hill (Mullach Mòr). It's natural, beautiful
2-B-2 and spiritual; a walk to cherish.

2251 **Colonsay** 2231/MAGICAL ISLANDS. From hotel or the quay, walk to Colonsay House
9/F24 and its lush, overgrown intermingling of native plants and exotics (8km round trip);
12 + 6KM or to the priory on Oronsay, the smaller island. 6km to the Strand (you might get a
XCIRC lift with the postman) then cross at low tide, with enough time (at least 2 hours) to
BIKES walk to the ruins. Allow longer if you want to climb the easy peak of Ben Oronsay.
1-A-2 Tide tables at hotel. Nice walk also from Kiloran Beach (1555/BEACHES) to
Balnahard Beach – farm track 12km return.

2252 7/F18 **The Trotternish Ridge** The 30km Highland walk which takes in The Quirang
30KM and The Old Man of Storr (see below for both) offers many shorter walks without
XCIRC XBIKES climbing or scrambling as well as the whole monty.

2253 **The Old Man of Storr** Skye The enigmatic basalt finger visible from the
7/G17 Portree-Staffin road (A855). Start from car park on left, 12km from Portree. There's
9KM a well-defined path through woodland and then towards the cliffs and a steep
CIRC climb up the grassy slope to the pinnacle which towers 165ft tall. Great views over
XBIKES Raasay to the mainland. Lots of space and rabbits and birds who make the most of
2-B-2 it but an increasingly popular pilgrimage so expect human company, too.

2254 7/G17 **The Quirang** Skye See 1647/VIEWS for directions to start point. The strange
6KM formations have names (eg The Table, The Needle, The Prison) and it's possible to
CIRC walk round all of them. Start of the path from the car park is easy. At the first
XBIKES saddle, take the second scree slope to The Table, rather than the first. When you
2-B-2 get to The Needle, the path to the right between two giant pinnacles is the easiest
of the 3 options. From the top you can see the Hebrides. This place is
supernatural; anything could happen. So be careful.

2255 **Scorrybreac** Skye A much simpler prospect than the above and more quietly
7/F18   spectacular but mentioned here because anyone can do it; it's only 3km and it's
3KM   more or less in Portree. Head for Cuillin Hills Hotel off Staffin Rd out of town
BIKE   (2278/SKYE HOTELS). Shoreline path signed just below hotel. Passes Black Rock
XBIKES   where once Bonnie Prince Charlie left for Raasay, and continues round hill. Nice
1-A-1   views back to the bright lights and pink houses of Portree.

2256 **Hoy** Orkney There are innumerable walks on the scattered Orkney Islands; on a
3/Q11   good day, head to the north of Hoy for some of the most dramatic coastal scenery
20/25KM anywhere. Ferries from Houton. Stromness on the small MV *Graemsay* to Moaness
CIRC   and a car ferry more frequent from Houton east of Stromness with 20km drive to
MT BIKES start of walk. Make tracks north or south from junction near Moaness pier and
2-B-2   don't miss the landmarks, the bird sanctuaries and of course the Old Man himself
         if you've got the time. See 2064/COASTAL WALKS.

2257 **Corryvreckan** Jura The whirlpool in the Gulf of Corryvreckan is notorious.
9/H24   Between Jura and Scarba; to see it go to far north of Jura. From end of the road at
6/24KM Ardlussa (25km Craighouse, the village), there's a rough track to Lealt then a walk
XCIRC   (a local may drive you) of 12km to Kinuachdrach, then a further walk of 3km.
XBIKES   Phenomenon best seen at certain states of tide. There are boat trips from Crinan
2-C-2   and Oban – consult tourist information centres on Jura or at the hotel (2287/
         ISLAND HOTELS). 2229/MAGICAL ISLANDS.

2258 **Sgurr An** Eigg Unmissable treat on Eigg. Take to the big ridge. Not a hard pull;
7/G20   extraordinary views and island perspective from the top. 2232/MAGICAL ISLANDS.

███████ # The Best Skye Hotels

*Skye is large and has so many good places that it merits its own hotel and
restaurant sections among the islands. See The Best Skye Restaurants,
p. 386–7 and The Best of Skye, p. 388.*

2259   ✓ ✓ **The House Over-By at The Three Chimneys** 01470 511258 ·
7/F18   www.threechimneys.co.uk At Colbost 7km west of Dunvegan by the
6 ROOMS B884 to Glendale. When Eddie and Shirley Spear transformed their house over by
TEL · TV into the House Over-By, it was the first boutique-style accommodation in the
LOTS   Highlands. Refurbished and more than 10 years later it's still a model of under-
         stated luxury in a wild and woolly place. Adjacent or just over-by from their acco-
         lade-laden restaurant (in world's top lists) (2291/SKYE RESTAURANTS). Separate
         dining room for a healthy breakfast transforms into a light conservatory lounge in
         the evening. Outside the sheep, the sea and the sky.
         EAT After the long hike across the courtyard you deserve a treat!

2260   ✓ ✓ **Kinloch Lodge** www.kinloch-lodge.co.uk · 01471 833333 · Sleat
7/H19   Peninsula Just south of Broadford, 55km Portree. The ancestral but not
15 ROOMS overly imposing home of Lord and Lady Macdonald with newer build house adja-
TEL · TV cent adding 8 well-appointed rooms. Spacious, country drawing room. It's a family
NO PETS affair with Isabella and Tom in charge but Lady Mac is Claire Macdonald of cookery
LOTS   fame; her many books (and jam range) are for sale in the shop and there are cook-
         ery courses spring and autumn. Claire has handed over the kitchen to Michelin-
         starred Marcello Tully and you can bet that dinner in the perfect Highland lodge
         dining room is a mouth-watering treat from cute canapés to cheese flight finish.
         EAT At Lady Claire's and Marcello's elegant table. 2292/SKYE RESTAURANTS.

2261
7/H19
12 ROOMS
+ 4 SUITES
TEL · TV
NO PETS
LL
ATMOS
MED.EX

✓ **Eilean Iarmain** www.eileaniarmain.co.uk · 01471 833332 · Isleornsay, **Sleat** 60km south of Portree. Tucked into the bay this Gaelic inn with its great pub and good dining provides sympatico, comfortable base in south of the island. Their famously Gaelic, some find uncompromising approach to hospitality has evolved (no TVs except in the suites but there is WiFi), but this place has the indefinable 'it', hasn't changed much and really doesn't have to. Bar is local craic central. 6 rooms in main hotel best value (garden rooms are in the house over-by). Also 4 suites in steading – expensive but your Hielan' hame. Shop and gallery adjacent. You wander down to the quay; you don't want to wander anywhere else.
EAT Bar for atmosphere and grub; dining room for atmosphere and fine dinner.

2262
7/F18
6 ROOMS
TEL · TV
NO PETS
MED.EX

✓ **Ullinish Country Lodge** www.theisleofskye.co.uk · 01470 572214 · **near Struan** On west coast 2km from Sligachan-Dunvegan road. Fairly traditional throughout though the bedrooms with big, carved beds, have 'won design awards'. But dinner is the thing here: candlelit, contemporary dining well-sourced and beautifully presented (3 AA rosettes). Spectacular location rather than setting, there are views to the Black Cuillin and MacLeod's Tables and walks to die for all around. Johnson and Boswell once stayed at Ullinish. Brian and Pam Howard have put it back on the map. You must eat to stay, first night.
EAT A fair way to drive for dinner, but one of Skye's top tables.

2263
7/G19
9 ROOMS
TV · TEL
NO PETS
MED.EX

✓ **Toravaig House Hotel** www.skyehotel.co.uk · 01471 833231 · Sleat Main road south from Broadford to Armadale. Ken Gunn and Anne Gracie's personally run hotel along with Duisdale below; two brilliantly positioned places to eat and stay on Skye. Small and charming with contemporary refurbished rooms and pleasing Iona Restaurant with fine understated dining in an elegant setting: 5 courses, all the bits. As·below, you can get on the yacht and picnic over the sea.

2264
7/G19
17 ROOMS
TEL · TV
MED.EX

✓ **Duisdale House** www.duisdale.com · 01471 833202 · Sleat Only 4km up the road from Toravaig (above) nearer to Broadford, Ken and Anne's bigger hotel, refurbished boutique-style to a high standard (big wallpapers, luxe bathrooms). Hot tub on the garden deck, the gardens themselves quite gorgeous. The larger restaurant of the two; a little more casual. K&A love to sail and will take you out on the *Solus* most days 10.30am-4.30pm to see the seals, whales and Skye from a different perspective. Then back to a very congenial dry land and excellent staff who look after you.
EAT Either Toravaig or Duisdale – both excellent eats in the south.

2265
7/G18
11 ROOMS
APR-OCT
TEL
MED.INX

✓ **Viewfield House** www.viewfieldhouse.com · 01478 612217 · Portree One of the first hotels you come to in Portree on the road from south (driveway opposite gas station); you need look no further. Individual, grand but comfortable, full of antiques and memorabilia, though not at all stuffy (purposefully, no TV); this historic and comfortable, rambling house is also one of the best-value hotels on the island. Log fires; supper available if you want but you don't have to eat in. Croquet and at TGP plans to revive the grass tennis court. Track through the woods to town (15 minutes). Hugh Macdonald is your congenial host.

2266
7/G17
5 ROOMS
TEL
MED.INX

✓ **The Glenview** www.glenviewskye.co.uk · 01470 562248 · by Staffin 25km north of Portree on the A855 Staffin road just north of the Lealt Falls (1593/WATERFALLS). Kirsty and Simon's freshly made (rooms, dinner and their young family) in this new/old cosy roadhouse in the north. Simple, nice style and decor. No TV or phones (there is WiFi). You can really stop here!
EAT Simon from Australia in the kitchen. Straightforward, 2-choice menu; conscientious modern cookery. Great local reputation.

✓ **Greshornish Country House** www.greshornishhouse.com · 01470 582266 · Edinbane Report: 1166/GET-AWAY HOTELS.

2267
7/G18
14 ROOMS
TEL · TV
MED.EX

Skeabost Country House Hotel www.oxfordhotelsandinns.com · 01470 532202 · near Portree 11km west of Portree on the A850, the Dunvegan road. Venerable Skye chateau with fab interior restored and efficiently managed by Oxford Hotels. Conservatory, panelled dining room, original billiard room (and table), loads of public space and some sumptuous bedrooms. Exquisite grounds including the babbling River Snizort (hotel has salmon rights for 8 miles and own ghillie) and a sweet little 9-hole (though can do 18) golf course.

2268 7/G18
19 ROOMS
TEL · TV
MED.EX

Bosville Hotel 01478 612846 · Portree Refurbished rooms and thinks of itself as *the* place to eat in this hotel at the top of the brae heading north from centre on the road to Staffin. Chandlery Restaurant and Bistro (see below); urban standard of comfort and you are at the very heart of Portree.

2269
7/G18
7 ROOMS
MED.INX

Marmalade www.marmaladehotels.com · 01478 611711 · Home Farm Road, Portree Leave from corner of main square up hill away from sea and keep going 1.5km. Unlikely, almost suburban location until you see the view (from gardens and 4 of the 7 rooms). Portree's boutique hotel: rooms above the busy bar/restaurant popular with locals. Perhaps could do with a freshener but friendly staff (and friendly midges if you're out on the lawn in summer). Where to go on Skye for a pizza (though L'Incontro opposite the tourist office does 'em, too).

2270
7/G18
28 ROOMS
TV · TEL
MED.INX

Cuillin Hills Hotel www.cuillinhills-hotel-skye.co.uk · 01478 612003 · Portree On the edge of Portree (off road north to Staffin) near water's edge. Secluded mansion house hotel with nice conservatory. Decor a matter of taste but much tarting up recently and great views from most rooms. Nice walk from garden (2255/ISLAND WALKS). Somewhat atmosphereless; view of the Cuillin is the thing. **EAT** Dining room with a view in brasserie or dining room – the View: seafood, see art (with local art in exhibition).

2271
7/H19
84 ROOMS
CHP

Sabhal Mór Ostaig www.smo.uhi.ac.uk · 01471 888000 · Sleat Pronounced Sawal More Ostag. Part of the Gaelic College off A851 north of Armadale. Excellent inexpensive rooms in modern build overlooking Sound of Sleat. The penthouse is spectacular. Breakfast in bright café. Best deal on the island; you could learn Gaelic.

2272 7/G19
11 ROOMS
TEL · TV
MED.EX

Broadford Hotel www.broadfordhotel.co.uk · 01471 822414 · Broadford On left heading north out of Broadford. Long-established Skye hotel contemporarised by the people who also own the Bosville and Marmalade (above). Decent, not overdone look to new rooms. Busy bar (Gabbo) and bistro.

3 EXCELLENT B&Bs ON SKYE

2273
7/F18
3 ROOMS
MED.EX

✓ **The Spoons** www.thespoonsonskye.com · 01470 532217 · Skeabost Bridge 15km from Portree off Dunvegan road, 1km at Aird Bernisdale, a purpose-built luxury B&B overlooking Loch Snizort. Marie and Ian Lewis love their house and what they do and you will, too. Small but all done beautifully. Egyptian cotton, lotsa neat touches, splendid breakfasts with crêpes, home-made bread, fresh-laid eggs. You'll be lucky to get in here of course, so book ahead.

2274 7/G19
3 ROOMS
MED.INX

✓ **Tigh An Dochais** 01471 820022 · Broadford Signed and on road coming into Broadford from the south (the bridge and ferries). Stunning contemporary building by award-winning architects Dualchas, this long, light house makes the most of its location. Bedrooms open out to and practically merge with the (appropriately monochrome) littoral. Breakfast in upstairs lounge; bread home made, etc. A superb introduction to Skye.

2275 7/G18 · 4 ROOMS · +2 COTTAGES · APR-OCT · TV · MED.EX

✓ **Peinmore House** www.peinmorehouse.co.uk · 01478 612574 · **Portree** Traditional manor house built round courtyard just outside Portree (250m off B883 Braes road, 3km south on Broadford road). Traditional cf purpose-built above but spacious, light, tasteful with Margaret Greer's sure touches: family pics, wonderful flower baskets round courtyard, big rooms, choice DVDs. Another Skye plus.

■ The Best Island Hotels

This section excludes Skye which has its own hotels listings, p. 381-4.

2276 5/E16 · 6 ROOMS · MAR-DEC · DF · LL · EXP

✓✓ **Scarista House** South Harris · www.scaristahouse.com · 01859 550238 21km Tarbert, 78km Stornoway. On the west coast famous for its beaches and overlooking one of the best (1561/BEACHES). Tim and Patricia Martin's civilised retreat and home from home. Fixed menu meals in dining rooms overlooking sea. No phones or other intrusions (though TV in the kitchen and WiFi); many books. The golf course over the road is exquisite. Good family hotel but delightfully laid back. Great suites.
EAT A fixed menu but the place to eat in these Hebrides. 4 courses; good value for this quality. Notify fads and diets. Open to non-residents.

2277 9/G22 · 6 ROOMS · MAR-OCT · TEL · TV · NO PETS · £60-85

✓✓ **Highland Cottage** Mull · www.highlandcottage.co.uk · 01688 302030 Breadalbane St opposite Tobermory fire station. Street above harbour (from roundabout on road from Craignure). Small, comfy rooms named after islands (all themed). This is a well-run cottage-boutique; both cosy and chic. Small maybe but perfectly formed: relax into Jo Currie's simply delicious, easygoing fine dining.
EAT Where to eat on Mull. Fine without fuss in perfect parlour. 2306/MULL.

2278 9/J27 · 8 ROOMS · +5 COTTS · EASTER-OCT · TEL · TV · NO KIDS · MED.EX

✓ **Kilmichael House** Arran · www.kilmichael.com · 01770 302219 On road to Brodick Castle/Corrie, take left at bend by golf course. 3km down track to this bucolic haven far (but only minutes) from bustling Brodick. Various hens, peacocks and geese may attend your arrival. Unapologetically old-style country-house refined, so not great for kids. Rooms in house or garden courtyard – painstaking detail in food, service and surroundings. Also 5 cottages. All delightful.
EAT Competition for food on Arran but not finer dining.

2279 9/J27 · 20 ROOMS · TEL · TV · MED.INX

✓ **Douglas Hotel** Arran · www.douglashotel.co.uk · 01770 302968 The new esplanade: where the Ardrossan ferry comes in. Redefining Brodick for visitors. Haven't stayed at TGP but seems set to up the ante for all other hotels on the island while remaining (owner is local) very much part of its affairs. So you're plugged in and comfortably so. Design in everything; bistro, bar. The new Arran it.

2280 9/J27 · 13 ROOMS · TEL · MED.INX

✓ **Glenisle Hotel** Arran · www.glenislehotel.com · 01770 600559 As if suddenly there's too much choice on Arran, the Glenisle is a serious contender and well up with others as a contemporary, convivial small hotel. Advantage also of being in Lamlash (5km Brodick), so quieter. Overlooks bay, Holy Island (2251/WALKS). Nice bar and restaurant and other good eating options nearby. See 2303/ARRAN.

2281
9/F24
9 ROOMS
MAR-DEC
L
MED.EX

✓ **Colonsay Hotel** Colonsay · www.colonsayestate.co.uk · 01951 200316
Long established, well run and generally a superb island hotel 100m from the ferry on this island perfectly proportioned for short stays (2231/ISLANDS). The laird (and the wife) and their partners determined to turn this into a contemporary destination hotel. Cool public rooms and buzzy bar (especially Thu quiz nights). Mobiles only work in the garden. Stunning beach 5km. On your bike.

2282
9/G26
12 ROOMS
L
MED.INX

✓ **Achamore House** Gigha · www.achamorehouse.com · 01583 505400
The main house on this small-is-beautiful island (2236/MAGICAL ISLANDS) that's easy to reach from Kintyre. This was the house of James Horlicks (of Horlicks) who made the surrounding fabulous gardens one of Gigha's many attractions (1509/GARDENS). The inimitable Don Dennis runs his mail-order alternative-remedies biz from here but everything about the house, from the large, individual rooms with big, comfy beds to the lawn out front has a soothing, relaxing quality. Not all en-suite but all great value. Snooker room, library, big TV room.

2283
9/F26
10 ROOMS
TEL · TV
L
MED.EX

✓ **Port Charlotte Hotel** Islay · www.portcharlottehotel.co.uk · 01496 850360 Epitome perhaps of the comfy island inn. Modern, discreet approach to guests, sea swishing below, very much at the heart of this fine whitewashed village (1548/COASTAL VILLAGES). Good whisky choice and good, bistro-style food in dining room; and bar meals. Tourists in summer, hardcore twitchers in winter. Hotel supports local and Scottish artists and music. Jovial owner Grahame Allison is in the Gaelic choir.

2284 9/F26
7 ROOMS
+ 2 APTS
TEL · TV
MED.EX

✓ **Harbour Inn** Islay · www.harbour-inn.com · 01496 810330 Neil and Carol Scott's island restaurant with rooms is 2 doors up from the harbour in the centre of the main town on lovely, quite lively Islay. Rooms contemporary and comfy, lounge with views and notable restaurant, especially seafood. Bar with malts and bar meals (LO 8.30pm). 2 apartments across the street.

2285 9/F26
11 ROOMS
TEL · TV · DF
MED.INX

✓ **Bridgend Inn** Islay · www.bridgend-hotel.com · 01496 810212
Bridgend near Bowmore on the Port Askaig road. Comfortable roadside hostelry, long a fixture on the island by the A846/A847 crossroads and a gathering place for locals and visitors. Bar and dining room, same menu.

2286 9/F26
5 ROOMS
FEB-OCT, DEC
NO PETS/KIDS
MED.INX

✓ **An Taigh Osda** Islay · www.antaighosda.co.uk · 01496 850587
Bruichladdich on the road between Bridgend (Bowmore) and Port Charlotte. Probably the most purposefully boutiqueish on the island. Few but relaxing, quite stylish rooms and good dining room (residents only); 2-choice menu. Paul and Joan Graham your amenable hosts. They're working on the art!

2287
9/G25
17 ROOMS
L
MED.INX

✓ **Jura Hotel** Jura · www.jurahotel.co.uk · 01496 820243 Craighouse, 12km from Islay ferry at Feolin. The island hub given a new lease of life by Andy and Cath McCallum and young obliging team. Bedrooms being upgraded are simple and serviceable though not large. Bar for all local craic; they make visitors welcome. Grub here and all else you'll need (including WiFi). Camping on their grassy field to the sea is free.

2288
9/F22
6 ROOMS
£90 FULL
BOARD

✓ **Coll Hotel** Coll · www.collhotel.com · 01879 230334 Julie and Kevin Oliphant continue to win accolades for their brilliant island hotel and restaurant on Coll which to my shame and frustration I have never visited. All attempts have been thwarted though my time will come. Meanwhile I rely on reports, all of which are positive; some raves. It's got a nice garden, a deck and the Gannet Restaurant. 4 rooms have the islands view. I imagine it's rather perfect! Coll is 2.5/3 hours from Oban. Ferries sail all year round.

2289 **Castlebay Hotel** Barra · www.castlebayhotel.com · 01871 810223
5/C20 Prominent position overlooking bay and ferry dock. You see where you're staying
15 ROOMS long before you arrive. Old-style holiday hotel at the centre of Barra life. Perhaps
TEL · TV upgrading would spoil its charm though the bedrooms have improved a tad. Good
LL restaurant and bar meals (2305/OUTER HEBRIDES). Adjacent bar, famed for craic
MED.INX and car culture, has more than a dash of the Irish (1258/BLOODY GOOD PUBS) and a
busy pool table. Sea view superior rooms worth the premium.

2290 **The Gigha Hotel** Gigha · www.gigha.org.uk · 01583 505254 A short walk
9/G26 from the ferry on an island perfectly proportioned for a short visit; easy walking
12 ROOMS and cycling. Residents' lounge peaceful with dreamy views to Kintyre. Menu with
TEL · TV local produce, eg Gigha prawns and scallops and especially Laura's halibut (in bar
MED.INX or dining room). Island life without the remoteness. Also self-catering cottages.
2236/ISLANDS.

✓ **Argyll Hotel** Iona · 01681 700334 · **St Columba Hotel** Iona · 01681
700304 1142/SEASIDE INNS, 2306/MULL.

Kildonan Hotel Arran · 01770 820207 2279/ARRAN.

The Best Skye Restaurants

2291 ✓✓ **The Three Chimneys** www.threechimneys.co.uk · 01470 511258 ·
7/F18 Colbost 7km west of Dunvegan on B884 to Glendale. Shirley and Eddie
>£35 Spear's classic restaurant in a converted cottage on the edge of the best kind of
nowhere. This was the first restaurant in Scotland to prove that it didn't matter
where you were – if the food and atmosphere were right, people would find you.
Many followed in their footsteps. Shirley's put her feet up (well, a bit); Michael
Smith now making his own big reputation in the tiny kitchen out back. They shop
local for everything (Skye supplies have hugely improved following their example)
from Glendale leaves to local langoustines. Fastidious, smart service with a strong
kitchen team (Kevin Maclean, Issy Tomlin). It's a long road to Colbost but by the
start of your starter you know why you came. They can recommend some B&Bs
when their own rooms are (as usual) full. Closed Sun lunch. 2259/SKYE HOTELS.

2292 ✓✓ **Kinloch Lodge** www.kinloch-lodge.co.uk · 01471 833333 · **Sleat**
7/H19 Peninsula In south on Sleat Peninsula, 55km south of Portree signed
>£35 off the main Sleat road along a characterful track. The MacDonald family home
and hotel offers a taste of the high life without hauteur; their pics and portraits
surround you as you start with drinks in the drawing rooms and move to the elegant dining room. Lady Claire herself no longer in the kitchen (with her luxury
comestibles brand rolling out round the country). It all makes you want to stay for
one of her cookery courses. It's Michelin-starred chef Marcello Tully whose food
you come to adore. 6 courses (fixed menu so flag up fads/diets) including his 'special'. Great Ecossais/ Français cheeseboard with flight option. It's an 'experience
Skye through food' thing!

2293 ✓ **The Chandlery at The Bosville Hotel** 01478 612846 · **Portree** Chef
7/G18 John Kelly's fine dining in Portree wins awards and local approval (though they
>£35/ think it's expensive). A la carte and daily menu well thought-out, sourced and pre-
£15-25 sented. But you might do as well to stick with the out-front **Bistro**, Portree's
good-deal, good-food, drop-in option. Must book for the Chandlery. LO 8.30pm.
Bistro 9/9.30pm.

2294
7/F17
£15-25

✓ **Lochbay Seafood** www.lochbay-seafood-restaurant.co.uk · 01470 592235 · **Stein** 12km north of Dunvegan off A850. Small; simple fresh seafood in loch-side setting, David and Alison keep it simple and divine as they say. Apr-Oct lunch and dinner Tue-Sat. Report. 1326/SEAFOOD RESTAURANTS.

2295
7/G18
£15-25

✓ **Harbour View** 01478 612069 · **Bosville Terrace, Portree** On road to Staffin and north Skye with harbour view at least from the door. Local seafood in intimate bistro dining room which doesn't seem to have changed since it was somebody's front room in their cottage. Richard and Clare Smith have built a good local reputation. In summer you may have to put your name down and wait. Easter-Oct lunch and dinner. LO 9.30pm. Closed Mon.

2296
7/G18
£15-25

✓ **Sea Breezes** 01478 612016 · **Portree** On the harbour. And this is the other place for seafood (some say Sea Breezes, some say Harbour View above). Neil Macneil has seafaring connections and the seafood here can be as good and as fresh as it gets. Good (and usually packed) atmosphere in an authentic caff on the quay. Easter-Oct. Lunch and LO 9/9.30pm.

2297
7/G18
<£15

Café Arriba 01478 611830 · **Portree** Upstairs at the top of the road down to the harbour. A funky, bright, kinda boho caff on Skye with a view of the bay. Good bread/Green Mountain coffee/vegetarian. Day and evening menus (when it goes very eclectic: dishes from Asia/Africa-ish). Cosmo cuisine and atmosphere. Does the trick. 7 days. LO 9pm.

2298
7/G18
<£15

Caledonian Café **Wentworth Street, Portree** On the main street. Simple, serviceable caff open long hours in summer for hungry tourists who don't want to cough up loadsa dosh to eat. Hot specials and usual caff fare. Home baking and busy with their home-made ice cream. 7 days 9am-9pm.

3 GREAT NEW TEAROOMS ON SKYE

2299
7/E17

✓ **Red Roof Café Gallery** www.redroofskye.co.uk · 01470 511766 · **Glendale** Way out northwest at Glendale (beyond the 3 Chimneys, above). Craig and Elly's labour of love, the white bothy with the red roof, a gallery for Elly's work and a top wee tearoom with home-made everything using the nearby seafood and the Glendale leaves. Locally loved; so will you. Easter-Oct, 10am-5pm.

2300
7/F18

✓ **Jann's Cakes** **Dunvegan** Main road out of village, A863 to Broadford. A wee shack really but where Jann (and Lewis) Dove turn out an amazing array of brilliant home-made cakes, bread, chocolates, soup and yes, curries, tagines and other scrumptious and unlikely world food. This is a great wee find! Mar-Oct 10am-5pm, Nov/Dec/Feb 11am-3pm. Closed Sun.

2301
7/G17

✓ **The Small & Cosy Teahouse** www.smallandcosyteahouse.co.uk · 01470 562471 · **Digg** In the north, main road to Staffin; the well, small and cosy, very happy teahouse. Bread and soup, cakes and a big variety of tea. An excellent prospect after a walk on the (Trotternish) ridge, Old Man of Storr, Quirang, etc. 12noon-6pm. Closed Mon.

The Best of Skye

2302
7/H19

The Bridge Unromantic but easy and free; from Kyle. The **Ferries** Mallaig-Armadale, 30 minutes. Tarbert (Harris)-Uig, 1 hour 35 minutes (CalMac, as Mallaig). **The Best Way to Skye** Glenelg-Kylerhea www.skyeferry.co.uk 5-minute sailing. Continuous Easter-Oct. Winter sailings – check tourist information centre. Community run. See 7/SCOTTISH JOURNEYS.

WHERE TO STAY & EAT
See Skye Hotels p. 381-4 and Skye Restaurants, p. 386-7.

WHAT TO SEE
The Cuillin (2/BIG ATTRACTIONS); **Raasay** (2228/MAGICAL ISLANDS), (2244/ISLAND WALKS); **The Quirang** (1634/VIEWS), (2254/ISLAND WALKS); **Old Man Of Storr** (2253/ISLAND WALKS); **Dunvegan** (1781/CASTLES); **Eas Mor** (1592/WATERFALLS); **Elgol** (1641/VIEWS); **Skye Museum Of Island Life** (2157/MUSEUMS); **Flora Macdonald's Grave** (1848/MONUMENTS); **Skye Silver**, **Edinbane Pottery** and **Carbost Craft** (2191/2192/SHOPPING); **Fairy Pools** (1656/WILD SWIMMING); **Duirinish** and **Minginish** (2064/COASTAL WALKS).

Tourist Info 01478 612137 **CalMac** www.calmac.co.uk · 08705 650000

The Best of Arran

2303
9/J29

Ferry Ardrossan-Brodick, 55 minutes. 6 per day Mon-Sat, 4 on Sun.
Ardrossan-Glasgow, train or road via A77/A71 1.5 hours.
Claonaig-Lochranza, 30 minutes. 9 per day (summer only).
The best way to see Arran is on a bike. Hire: 01770 302244 or 01770 302377.

WHERE TO STAY

8 ROOMS
+5 COTTAGES
TEL · TV
NO KIDS/PETS
EXP

✓ **Kilmichael House** 01770 302219 · **Brodick** Individual and discreet mansion 3km from the main road and into the glen. Elegant interior and furnishings in house and courtyard rooms and a more refined world away from the bland, grey conformities of the world even here. Still *the* place to eat on Arran, but book (2278/ISLAND HOTELS). Also has self-catering cottages.

20 ROOMS
TEL · TV
MED.EX

✓ **Douglas Hotel** www.douglashotel.com · 01770 302968 · **Brodick** On the front where the ferry comes in, you can't miss it even at night, lit large. High quality and complete renovation of local eyesore by local lad who made good (in Russia), this has raised the game in Arran immeasurably. Contemporary design and fixtures throughout. Whisky Bar and Bistro, the new place to go on this or any other island.

13 ROOMS
MED.INX

✓ **Glenisle Hotel** www.glenislehotel.com · 01770 600559 · **Lamlash** A carefully refurbished and rethought hotel in Lamlash looking out to Holy Isle. Local stone, colour and texture in evidence in well-appointed bedrooms, bar and restaurant. Calm, efficient and friendly: a perfect stay in lovely Lamlash – you put in distance from downtown Brodick.

28 ROOMS
+36 IN SPA
TEL · TV
MED.INX

Auchrannie House www.auchrannie.co.uk · 01770 302234 · **Brodick** Once an old mansion now expanded into a holiday complex. House has best rooms, eats (Eighteen69 Restaurant) and small pool. But the Spa Resort, like a Holiday Inn in the country, is perfect for families: good modern rooms, bigger pool and leisure facilities. Juice Bar here means Scottish 'juice'. Upstairs restaurant a bit Glasgow Airport but fits all sizes! There's also Brambles bistro. Plenty indoors for Arran weather but also out: Arran Adventure Centre on hand. Burgeoning timeshares.

13 ROOMS
TV
MED.INX

The Lagg Hotel www.lagghotel.com · 01770 870250 · Kilmory South of Arran 25km Brodick and ferry. In a rare sylvan setting with serene river terraces, an old coaching inn with an almost olde English ambience. Log fires, local reputation for food, great lounge bar, whisky and wine. This is a fine retreat. 500m to Kilmory Beach, the largest on the island.

17 ROOMS
TV
L
MED.INX

Kildonan Hotel www.kildonanhotel.com · 01770 820207 · Kildonan In the south of the island (Brodick 16km) on a beautiful strand overlooking Pladda Island and lighthouse; Ailsa Craig spectral beyond. Great outside terrace (with big stones) for gazing out to sea. Some rooms so-so. Happy, popular bar with grub and conservatory dining room. It's somehow special.

9 ROOMS
EASTER-DEC
TEL · TV · CHP

Lochranza Hotel www.lochranza.co.uk · 01770 830223 · Lochranza Small hotel with tranquil views over bay and 13th-century castle. Basic accommodation but home-spun hospitality. Beer garden with food all day in season. Good malts.

S.Y. Hostel www.hostellingscotland.com · 0845 293 7373 · Lochranza 30km from Brodick. Recently refurbished. 1132/HOSTELS.

WHERE TO EAT

>£35

✓ **Kilmichael House** www.kilmichael.com · 01770 302219 · Brodick The finest dining on Arran. Fixed menu. See above.

<£15

Brodick Bar & Brasserie Brodick Best bistro food in Brodick by common consensus but what of the Douglas (see below). Goes like a fair and can feel like a canteen on summer evenings. Long blackboard menu. Pizzas. Food until 10pm. Off north end of main street by Royal Mail. Lunch and LO 9pm. Bar till 12midnight.

£15-25

Douglas Hotel Bistro www.douglashotel.com · 01770 302968 · Brodick Hadn't tried at TGP but with the exceptional attention to detail in this enterprise, expect the new top-notch informal diner on the island (see above).

£15-25

The Wineport 01770 302101 · Brodick On the A841 north of Brodick (5 km) at Cladach just before Brodick Castle beside Arran Brewery and where you come off Goat Fell (1951/HILLS). Newer venture by the family who have the Brodick Bar (above). Lunch and lighter menu during the day, bistro at night in season. Accessible food in light surroundings. Apr-Sep. Dinner Wed-Sat.

£25-35

Creelers www.creelers.co.uk · 01770 302810 · Brodick Long-established and most credible seafood on the island. Small so depends as always on the team, but great when we were there. Owned by the same folk who have Creelers in Edinburgh (212/EDINBURGH SEAFOOD). This is where they have the smokery and you can order lobsters and langoustine. Here you really do eat local and seasonal. Wild garlic soup one night in our spring! See 1329/SEAFOOD RESTAURANTS.

<£15

The Pierhead Tavern 01770 600418 · Lamlash Main road. Very serviceable, good-value pub grub with long menu and specials. Home-made chips, even with chicken tikka masala (and rice). Big helpings. The PHT is the people's choice. Lunch and LO 9pm.

£25-35 **Trafalgar** 01770 700396 · **Whiting Bay** On the Shore Rd among many hotels, the Trafalgar for a very long time has been where on Arran you go for your tea, ie dinner. Nothing too fancy, mind, just the Knoners cooking up what we like. An institution, their old-style dining room. The best steaks! Evenings only. You'd better book. LO 8.30pm. Fri/Sat only in winter.

<£15 **Fairways** 01770 600296 · **Lamlash Golf Course Clubhouse** The word 'unprepossessing' doesn't do justice to this clubhouse bar and dining room looking out across... the fairways. Smart city types will love its unreconstructed sixties simplicity. And here, simply, the best fish 'n' chips and other homespun favourites on Arran. 7 days in season. Buy drinks at the bar. LO 8.30pm.

£15-25 **Coast** www.coastarran.co.uk · 01770 700308 · **Whiting Bay** Main road and on the strand with conservatory overlooking the sea. Pleasant, light café with home-made bistro fare: burger/TexMex/pasta by day, more interesting at night. 10am-4pm, supper LO 9pm. Closed Mon. Shorter winter hours, closed Jan/Feb.

WHAT TO SEE

NTS **Brodick Castle** 5km walk or cycle from Brodick. Impressive museum and gardens. Tearoom. Flagship NTS property (1779/CASTLES).

2-A-2 **Goat Fell** 6km/5hr great hill walk starting from the car park at Cladach near castle and Brodick or sea start at Corrie. Free route leaflet at tourist information centre. 1951/HILLS.

1-B-1 **Glenashdale Falls** 4km, but 2-hour forest walk from Glenashdale Bridge at Whiting Bay. Steady, easy climb, sylvan setting. 1591/WATERFALLS.

Corrie The best village 9km north of Brodick. Go by bike. 1553/COASTAL VILLAGES.

Arran Distillery In Lochranza. Not the most evocative but visitor centre, tour and tasting of the Arran Single Malt. 10am-6pm (Sun from 11am). Winter hours vary (01770 830264).

Machrie Moor Standing Stones Off main coast road 7km north of Blackwater Foot. Various assemblies of Stones, all part of an ancient landscape. We lay down there.

1-B-2 **Glen Rosa, Glen Sannox** Fine glens: Rosa near Brodick, Sannox 11km north.

2-B-2 **Holy Island** Walk. 2251/ISLAND WALKS.

Tourist Info 01770 303774 **CalMac** 08705 650000 · www.calmac.co.uk

The Best of Islay & Jura

2304
9/G24

Ferry Kennacraig-Port Askaig: 2 hours; Kennacraig-Port Ellen: 2 hours 10 minutes. Port Askaig-Feolin, Jura: (01880 730253) 5 minutes, frequent daily. Passenger ferry from Tayvallich near Crinan May-Sep; 077684 50000.
By Air Flybe (0871 7002000) Glasgow to Port Ellen Airport in south of Islay.

WHERE TO STAY

7 ROOMS
TEL · TV
MED.EX

✓**Harbour Inn** www.harbour-inn.com · 01496 810330 · Bowmore, Islay Harbourside inn with conservatory lounge, Schooner bar for seafood lunch and less formal supper, and dining room with Modern British menu. Bedrooms vary but all mod and con. 2284/ISLAND HOTELS.

10 ROOMS
TEL · TV
L
MED.INX

✓**Port Charlotte Hotel** www.portcharlottehotel.co.uk · 01496 850360 · Port Charlotte, Islay Restored Victorian inn and gardens overlooking sea in conservation village. Restful place and views. Good bistro-style menu. Eat in bar/conservatory or dining room. 2283/ISLAND HOTELS.

4 ROOMS
NO PETS
MED.EX

✓**Inns Over-By** www.theinnsoverby.co.uk · 01496 810330 · Bowmore, Islay On the square, foot of main street. Same folk as the Harbour Inn (above). 4 contemporary, quiet rooms, 3 with views over the loch. Haven't stayed.

5 ROOMS
FEB-OCT, DEC
MED.INX

✓**An Taigh Osda** www.antaighosda.co.uk · 01496 850587 · Bruichladdich, Islay Stylish, contemporary mansion over the road from the sea. The distillery is next door. (Taigh is pronounced Tie.) 2286/ISLAND HOTELS.

11 ROOMS
TEL · TV
MED.INX

✓**Bridgend Inn** www.bridgend-hotel.com · 01496 810212 · Bridgend, Islay Middle of island on road from Port Askaig, 4km Bowmore. Roadside inn with good pub meals and surprising number of rooms. 2285/ISLAND HOTELS.

17 ROOMS
L
MED.INX

✓**Jura Hotel** www.jurahotel.co.uk · 01496 820243 · Craighouse, Jura The island hotel and all-round social centre does all you want it to (including free camping and use of their facilities). Good bar, decent grub. Upgrading in progress will make this one of the friendliest and quietly contemporary hotels in the islands. Situated in front of the distillery by the bay. See 2287/ISLAND HOTELS.

7 ROOMS
DF
L
MED.INX

✓**Ardlussa House** Jura · www.ardlussaestate.com · 01496 820323 · Jura Hard to be more far-flung than this: the Ardlussa Estate occupies the north of Jura and this lived-in family house is a welcome destination after a single-track journey (20km from Craignure). The Fletchers share their splendid wild backyard with you. George Orwell's house is on their land. B&B; dinner served. Kids run free.

5 ROOMS
TV
NO KIDS/PETS
MED.INX

Kilmeny Farm www.kilmeny.co.uk · 01496 840668 · near Ballygrant, Islay Margaret and Blair Rozga's top-class guest house just off the road south of Port Askaig (the ferry). Huge attention to detail, great home-made food (dinner available Tue and Thu), house-party atmosphere and shared tables. Though small.

5 ROOMS
TV
NO C/CARDS
MED.INX

Glenmachrie 01496 300400 · near Port Ellen, Islay On A846 between Bowmore and Port Ellen near airport. Same family of Kilmeny owners (above). Here it's Rachel's award-winning farmhouse with everything just so (fluffy bathrobes, toiletries supplied, fruit bowl and a sweet on the pillow). Meals in sister guest house up the road (see below).

6 ROOMS
TV
NO KIDS/PETS
NO C/CARDS
MED.INX

Glenegedale House www.glenegedalehouse.co.uk · 01496 300400 · **near Port Ellen, Islay** The newer venture by Rachel Whyte near Glenmachrie and opposite the airport. It would be hard to find a homelier airport hotel... anywhere! This the more deluxe option, Rachel flits between the two but most likely here: her 5-star B&B. Dinner on request.

Camping, Caravan Site www.kintrafarm.co.uk · 01496 302051 · **Kintra Farm, Islay** Off main road to Port Ellen; take Oa road, follow Kintra signs 7km. Jul-Aug. Grassy strand, coastal walks. 1190/WILD CAMPING.

Islay Youth Hostel www.syha.org.uk · 01496 850385 · **Port Charlotte, Islay**

WHERE TO EAT

✓ **Harbour Inn** Bowmore, Islay, **Port Charlotte Hotel** Port Charlotte, Islay. See *Where to Stay*. Most consistent best bets for dinner.

£15-25 ✓ **Ardbeg Distillery Café** www.ardbeg.com · Islay 5km east of Port Ellen on the whisky road. Great local reputation for food. Beautiful room. Food home-made as are those Ardbegs. Most vintages and Ardbeg clothes to boot. All year Mon-Fri (7 days Jun-Aug) 10am-LO 4pm.

£15-25 ✓ **The Antlers** www.theantlers.co.uk · 01496 820123 · Craighouse, Jura Middle of the ribbon of village, an alternative to the hotel; Grahame and Stephen's (not a gay thing; one is married to the GP, one to the headmistress, so well woven into the Jura life) bistro popular with locals and visitors. Daytime and evening (till 9pm); must book. Local seafood and what you want though not all home-made. Closed Mon. Check winter hours. May be for sale at TGP.

Bridgend Inn Bridgend, Islay. Consistently good for food. See *Where to Stay*.

<£15 **Kilchoman Distillery Café** www.kilchomandistillery.com · 01496 850011 · **Rockside Farm, Islay** The new distillery in the northwest off the A847 from Bridgend (12km). This caff has much to like, especially the secret-recipe Cullen Skink. Mon-Sat 10am-5pm (not Sat in winter).

WHAT TO SEE

Islay: The Distilleries especially Ardbeg (good café), Laphroaig and Lagavulin (classic settings), all by Port Ellen; Bowmore perhaps more convenient (1475/WHISKY); **Wildlife Info & Field Centre** at Port Charlotte; **American Monument** (1846/MONUMENTS); **Oa & Loch Gruinart** (1715/BIRDS); **Port Charlotte** (1548/COASTAL VILLAGES); **Kintra** (2049/COASTAL WALKS); **Finlaggan** The romantic, sparse ruin on island in Loch Finlaggan: last home of the Lords of the Isles. Off A846 5km south of Port Askaig, check tourist information centre for opening.

Jura (2229/MAGICAL ISLANDS): **The Paps of Jura; Corryvreckan, Barnhill** (2257/ISLAND WALKS); **Killchianaig, Keils** (1889/GRAVEYARDS); **Lowlandman's Bay, Corran Sands** (1568/BEACHES); **Jura House Walled Garden** utterly magical (1500/GARDENS).

Tourist Info 01496 810254 **CalMac** 08705 650000

The Best of The Outer Hebrides

2305 **Ferries** Ullapool-Stornoway, 2 hours 40 minutes (not Sun).
Oban/Mallaig Lochboisdale, South Uist and Castlebay, Barra up to 6.5 hours.
Uig on Skye-Tarbert, Harris (not Sun) or Lochmaddy, North Uist 1 hour 40 minutes.
Also Leverburgh, Harris-Berneray (not Sun) 1 hour.
By Air Flybe (0871 7002000) from Inverness/Glasgow/Edinburgh. Otter to Barra/
Benbecula from Glasgow (1/2 a day).

WHERE TO STAY

6 ROOMS MAR-DEC DF · LL EXP	✓✓ **Scarista House** South Harris · www.scaristahouse.com · 01859 550238 20km south of Tarbert. Cosy haven near famous but often deserted beach; this celebrated retreat offers the real R&R and a lovely dinner. Also self-catering accommodation. Report: 2276/ISLAND HOTELS.

4 ROOMS
TEL · L
MED.EX
✓ **Broad Bay House** Lewis · www.broadbayhouse.co.uk · 01851 820990
11km north of Stornoway on east of island on the sea via B895 to Back. Purpose-built with big, light dining and lounge area and outside deck. Spacious, contemporary rooms with big TV, iPod docks, etc. Ian and Marion solicitous but discreet. Ian knows everywhere you might want to go and you'll want to stay a while in this chilled-out back of beyond. Top grub (with choice) and a decent wine list.

5 ROOMS
TEL · TV
LL
MED.EX
✓ **Auberge** Carnish, Lewis · www.aubergecarnish.co.uk · 01851 672459
45 minutes and way out west from Stornoway by A8011 parts of which have been upgraded. New-build, all-mod-con hotel and what is undoubtedly the farthest-flung French restaurant in the UK (though food not only French). Richard and Jo-Ann Leparoux have settled here and who wouldn't: that view, that beach!
EAT Informal and proper bistro; toujours la plage.

21 ROOMS
MED.INX
✓ **Hotel Hebrides** Tarbert, Harris · www.hotel-hebrides.com · 01859 502364 Very contemporary new-build hotel right by the pier where the boat comes in so convenient and probably just what you want (but the Harris Hotel nearby is cosier; see below). Rooms, restaurant and bar are light, uncluttered kinda modern. I'd say a good base for Harris trails.

9 ROOMS
+4 CHALETS
TEL · TV
MED.INX
✓ **Borve Hotel** Borve, North Lewis · www.borvehousehotel.co.uk ·
01851 850223 32km north of Stornoway on a mainly long, straight road to Port of Ness. Surprisingly contemporary though perhaps a little soulless hotel with boutique-style rooms (not sure about the art), bar and restaurant which are busy at weekends. Probably the smartest stay Stornoway way.

7 ROOMS
MAY-SEP
LLL
MED.INX
✓ **Baile-Na-Cille** Timsgarry, West Lewis · 01851 672241 Near Uig 60km west of Stornoway. This is about as far away as it gets but guests return again and again to the Collins' house overlooking that incredible beach. Hospitable hosts allow you the run of their place – the books, the games room, the tennis court and perhaps others of the many beaches near here in their boat. All home-made grub (bread, ice cream, etc) in communal dining room with amusing RAF overtones. Great value and especially good for families. 1099/HOTELS KIDS.
EAT Beautiful beach view and a unique dining experience open to non-residents.

8 ROOMS
TEL · TV
DF
MED.INX
✓ **Tigh Dearg (Red House) Hotel** Lochmaddy, North Uist · 01876 500700 www.tighdearghotel.co.uk Iain Macleod's personally run, contemporary new-build hotel: being red, it stands out for miles and stands out also for the level of style and efficiency in these far-flung islands where the beaches and the sky are immense. Leisure Club includes sauna/steam. Good disabled access; family suite.

5 ROOMS
TV · DF
L
CHP

Gallan Head Aird Uig, Lewis · www.gallanheadhotel.co.uk · 01851 672474 Long way west (by A8011, turning right before Uig stores, signed from road) in a former RAF outpost, a surprisingly modern kind of motel in a great spot and with good food. Rooms simple and very inexpensive (not all ensuite). **EAT** Haven't tried but the word is very good about Dave's food.

LL

Castlebay Hotel Castlebay, Barra · www.castlebay-hotel.co.uk · 01871 810223 Overlooks ferry terminal in the village so superb views. Decent dining, atmospheric bar. Report: 2289/ISLAND HOTELS, 1258/BLOODY GOOD PUBS.

26 ROOMS
TEL · TV
MED.INX-EX

Royal Hotel Stornoway, Lewis · www.royalstornoway.co.uk · 01851 702109 The most central of the 3 main hotels in town, all owned by the same family. HS-1 bistro and Boatshed (probably best hotel dining). The **Cabarfeidh** (01851 702604) is the upmarket ie most expensive option – probably the best bedrooms. These hotels are about the only places open in Lewis on Sun. The **Caladh Inn** (pronounced Cala) and its caff 11, are possibly best value. 11 has self-service buffet. Best all-round is the Royal.

22 ROOMS
TEL · TV
NO PETS
MED.INX

Harris Hotel Tarbert, Harris · www.harrishotel.com · 01859 502154 In the township near the ferry terminal so good base for travels in North/South Harris. Variety of public rooms and diverse range of bedrooms (view/non-view, refurbished/non-refurbished, standard/superior), some of which are large and very nice. Friendly and well run. Food not a strong point, but adequate in the hotel-like dining room. Both bar and conservatory have better atmosphere. Well tidy garden.

11 ROOMS
TEL · TV
NO PETS · LL
MED.INX

Pollachar Inn South Uist · 01878 700215 South of Lochboisdale near Eriskay causeway (and ferry for Barra; 2216/ISLANDS). An inn at the rocky end of the Uists. Excellent value, good craic and the view/sunset across the sea to Barra. Rooms refurbished to an ok standard. The pub-grub menu uses local produce. LO 8.45pm.

Hostels Simple hostels within hiking distance. 2 in Lewis, 3 in Harris, 1 each in North and South Uist. Am Bothan at Leverburgh is independent and funky. The Blackhouse village in North Lewis is exceptional (1123/HOSTELS).

WHERE TO EAT

<£15

✓ **Loch Croistean** near Uig and Timsgarry, Lewis · 01851 672772 About 30 minutes from Stornoway on the road into the sunset, Marianne Campbell's schoolhouse converted into a tasteful, laid-back tearoom and restaurant. Simple good food; soup, sandwich and cake all home-made of course and buffet suppers Fri/Sat in season. 12noon-8pm Mon-Sat (Wed-Sat in winter). Closed Sun.

LL
<£15

✓ **Skoon Art Café** South Harris · www.skoon.com · 01859 530268 Near the golden Golden Road (1621/SCENIC ROUTES) 12km south of Tarbert or follow the sign off A859 then 4km to Geocrab (pronounced Jocrab). Andrew and Emma Craig's café in a gallery (his work on the walls). All done well – interesting soups, great home-baking. Apr-Sep Tue-Sat daytime only; weekends in winter (or check).

£25-35

Digby Chick James Street, Stornoway, Lewis · 01851 700026 Over 10 years ago, DC set a new contemporary dining standard in Lewis, and still does. Seafood a speciality; a solid reputation. Can't go wrong here. Mon-Sat, lunch and LO 8.30pm.

£15-25

The Thai Café Church Street, Stornoway. Lewis · 01851 701811 Opposite police station. Though there are palms out in the rainswept street, you couldn't be further from Phuket. Mrs Panida Macdonald's restaurant an institution here; you may have to book. Great atmosphere and excellent real Thai cuisine. Some recent grumpy reviews but the majority say, 'yeah'. Lunch and LO 11pm. Closed Sun.

<£15 **Coffee Shops: An Lanntair Gallery** Stornoway, Lewis · www.lanntair.com **& Callanish Visitor Centre** Lewis · www.callananishvisitorcentre.co.uk An Lanntair, an all-embracing arts and cultural centre, is a great rendezvous spot and has a good view of the ferry terminal. Lunch and evening menu. The Callanish caff is far better than most visitor centres. Daytime only but till 8pm summer (1814/PREHISTORIC SITES).

>£35 **Scarista House** Harris · www.scaristahouse.com Dinner possible for non-residents. A 20-minutes Tarbert, 45-minutes Stornoway drive for best meal in the Hebrides. Fixed menu. Book. See *Where to Stay*.

L **Beach House** Port of Ness, Lewis · 01851 810000 You drive and drive £15-25 (though it's mainly a long straight road) north from Stornoway until you come to the end – there's a harbour, a beach (1562/BEACHES) and this welcome café/restaurant where Hamish and Norma Robb will look after you and feed you well. Good vibe. Open all year, am-pm but like everywhere else on Lewis, closed Sun.

<£15 **First Fruits Tearoom** Tarbert, Harris · 01859 502439 Near tourist information centre and ferry to Uig, Skye. Home cooking that hits the ferry-waiting spot. Good atmosphere. Snacky menu includes all-day breakfast, OJ. 10am-4pm Apr-Sep.

DA **Orasay Inn** Lochcarnan, South Uist · www.orasayinn.com · 01870 610298 £15-25 You don't get remoter than this but it's always packed. In summer you may have to book days ahead (or weeks for accommodation) so that says it all. Midway between Lochmaddy and Lochboisdale signed off the spinal A885, go 3km then left at the shrine. Then 500m. No, it ain't easy to find. Conservatory and bar serving good, home-cooked comfort food and fresh seafood: cod, shellfish and 'witches'. Also 5 inexpensive rooms. Open all year, lunch and LO 9pm.

<£15 **The Anchorage** Leverburgh, South Harris · 01859 520225 All-round family restaurant/café/bar at the pierhead where the boat leaves for Berneray and the Uists. But better than your average terminal caff with most stuff home-made and cooked to order. Friendly! Mar-Sep (weekends in winter) 12noon-9pm. Closed Sun.

<£15 **Stepping Stones** Balvanich, Benbecula · 01870 603377 8 km from main A855. Nondescript building in ex- (though sometimes operational) military air base. Serving the forces and the tourists – it aims to please. 7 days, lunch and LO 9pm (winter hours may vary). Menu changes through day.

The Boatshed at The Royal Hotel Stornoway & '11' at The Caladh Inn (see above). Best hotel options and maybe your **only Sunday option on Lewis**.

Tourist Info 01851 703088 **CalMac** www.calmac.co.uk · 08705 650000

WHAT TO SEE
Eriskay & Mingulay (2238/2239/ISLANDS); **Golden Road** (1621/SCENIC ROUTES); **Beaches** At Lewis, South Harris and South Uist (1562/1561/1559/BEACHES); **Dolphins** (1734/DOLPHINS); **Balranald Reserve** (1768/NATURE RESERVES). **Scarista Golf** (2094/GOOD GOLF); **Surfing** (2128/2129/SURFING BEACHES). **St Clement's Church & St Michael's Church** (1870/1871/CHURCHES); **Blackhouse of Arnol** (2143/HERITAGE); **Barpa Lanyass & Callanish Stones** (1829/1814/PREHISTORIC); **Harris Tweed** (p. 372-3).

2306
9/G23 **Ferry** Oban-Craignure, 45 minutes. Main route; 6 a day. Lochaline-Fishnish, 15 minutes. 9-15 a day. Kilchoan-Tobermory, 35 minutes. 7 a day (Sun in summer only). Winter sailings – call tourist information centre.

WHERE TO STAY

✔✔ **Highland Cottage** www.highlandcottage.co.uk · 01688 302030 · **Breadalbane Street, Tobermory** Opposite fire station a street above the harbour. Like a country house, well... a country cottage in town. Top spot for grub. Report: 2277/ISLAND HOTELS.

✔ **Tiroran House** 01681 705232 · **Mull** A treat and a retreat way down in the southwest of Mull near Iona. Light, comfy house in glorious gardens with excellent food and flowers. Sea eagles fly over. Report: 1162/GET-AWAY HOTELS.

✔ **Argyll Hotel** www.argylhoteliona.co.uk · 01681 700334 · **Iona** Near ferry and on seashore overlooking Mull on road to abbey. Laid-back, cosy accommodation, home cooking, good vegetarian. Report: 1142/SEASIDE INNS.

5 ROOMS
EXP ✔ **Glengorm Castle** www.glengormcastle.co.uk · 01688 302321 · **near Tobermory** Minor road on right going north outside town takes you to this fine castle on a promontory set in an extensive estate which is yours to wander (excellent walks; 2248/WALKS IN THE ISLANDS). Fab views over to Ardnamurchan, little peaks to climb and a natural bathing pool (2119/OUTDOOR POOLS). Spacious bedrooms (old-style comfy) in family home (the Nelsons) – use the library, complementary bar and grand public spaces. Loads of art, lawn and gardens. Excellent self-catering cottages on estate. B&B only. Excellent coffee shop/restaurant over by (1377/COFFEE SHOPS).

3 ROOMS
MED.INX ✔ **Achnadrish House** www.achnadrish.co.uk · 01688 400388 · **Dervaig** Off road (3km) to Dervaig, 15 minutes from Tobermory, a family-run boutique B&B with friendly, knowledgeable hosts and tasteful furnishings. Some of Mike Story's story is made out east so Asian twist to breakfast. A comfortable haven.

26 ROOMS
TEL · TV
GF · DF
MED.INX **Western Isles Hotel** www.westernisleshotel.co.uk · 01688 302012 · **Tobermory** At the end of the bay high above the harbour, this Tobermory landmark has one of the most commanding positions of any hotel in Scotland with spectacular views from (some) rooms, conservatory brasserie, dining room and especially the terrace. For congenial owners Richard Nealan and Esplin Chapman, this is a work in progress and in this old edifice there is much to do. But they're getting there and we and Tobermory are with them on that!

81 ROOMS
TEL · TV
MED.EX **Isle of Mull Hotel** www.crerarhotels.com · 0870 9506267 · **Craignure** Strung-out, low-rise hotel round Craignure Bay near the ferry from Oban (hotel can pick you up); possibly the best of the bigger, proper hotels on Mull. Decent rooms, spa and pool. Bit of a drive to an alternative restaurant (which you will want to find).

16 ROOMS
TV · DF
MED.INX **Tobermory Hotel** www.thetobermoryhotel.com · 01688 302091 · **Tobermory** On the waterfront. Creature comforts, great outlook in the middle of the bay. 10 rooms to front. Very well regarded chef Helen Swinbanks good in the kitchen though the dining room is low on atmosphere. Very much downtown Tobermory, this is an excellent place to locate for all Mull wanderings.

St Columba Hotel www.stcolumba-hotel.co.uk · 01681 700304 · Iona
Shares some ownership and ideals of the Argyll (above) and very close on the road
and adjacent to the abbey. Larger and more purpose-built than the Argyll, so some
uniformity in rooms. Nice views; extensive lawn and market garden. Relaxing and
just a little religious. Menu has good vegetarian options. Rooms include 9 singles.

S.Y. Hostel In Tobermory main street on bay. Report: 1131/HOSTELS.

Caravan Parks At Fishnish (all facilities, near ferry) Craignure and Fionnphort.

Camping Tobermory on the Dervaig Rd, Craignure (1201/CAMPING WITH KIDS).
Calgary Beach and at Loch Na Keal shore (1187/WILD CAMPING).

WHERE TO EAT

£25-35   ✓✓ **Highland Cottage** 01688 302030 Only real fine dining on Mull and
the local night out so must book. All the niceties. See 2277/ISLAND
HOTELS.

£25-35   ✓✓ **Ninth Wave** www.ninthwaverestaurant.co.uk · 01681 700757 ·
near Fionnphort In the south of Mull near the ferry for Iona. Is this the
furthest (2 hours to Tobermory) you can go in the UK for a good dinner? Well,
probably and lots of people do. Carla Lamont in the kitchen and the garden, John
out front (in a kilt) and on the boat. The terroir supplies your table in this surprisingly contemporary conversion in the quiet deep south. Simple choice, fixed-price
menu fine-dining style. Easter-Oct. Closed Mon. Dinner only. Book!

LL
£15-25   ✓ **Café Fish** 01688 301253 · Tobermory Macdonald sisters' brilliant caff
doing what it says on the tin in the white building at the pier on corner of the
bay. Bright, bustling upstairs room and terrace on the dock – Johnny's boat at the
quayside supplies the shellfish, the rest is properly sourced (mussels from
Inverlussa). Home cooking, sensible wine list, nice puds. Lunch and 6-9pm. Mar-
Dec. New diner/coffee shop with home baking, **The Pier**, opening downstairs at
TGP. They will be doing the real fish 'n' chips.

   ✓ **Glengorm Farm Coffeeshop** Excellent daytime eats outside Tobermory.
The best casual daytime dining. Report: 1377/TEAROOMS.

The Waterfront 01688 302365 · Tobermory Above Macgochan's pub (the
next best thing to the Mishnish), a smart and very credible seafood restaurant, sister of the big-reputation place at the pier in Oban (765/OBAN). Still settling in at
TGP but good things expected. 7 days in summer. Lunch and LO 9pm.

Mull Pottery www.mullpottery.com · 01688 302592 · Tobermory
Mezzanine café above working pottery just outside Tobermory on road south to
Craignure. Outside deck. Evening meals (best atmosphere) and daytime menu.
Cecilia Rapsoso makes everything; sometimes with a homespun Portuguese twist.
All year. LO 9pm. Closed Mon.

The Bellachroy www.thebellachroy.co.uk · 01688 400314 · Dervaig Some
might say The Bellachroy *is* Dervaig. The oldest inn on Mull; the Hansons have
upped the game. The rooms are fine, the food in pub or lounge is fresh and local
with big helpings. Lunch and dinner.

£25-35 **Mishdish** www.mishdish.co.uk · 01688 302662 · Tobermory On the front next to and part of the legendary Mishnish (1254/BLOODY GOOD PUBS), run by the latest Macleods. A good-looking seafront, mainly seafood restaurant where I haven't eaten so I can't say but this family clearly knows what they're doing. However, they have competition. You choose! Lunch and dinner. All year round.

<£15 **Island Bakery** www.islandbakery.co.uk · 01688 302225 · Tobermory Tom and Marjorie Nelson's Main St bakery-deli with quiches, salads and old-fashioned fancies. And increasingly well known (Scotland-wide) for their packaged crumbly biscuits. 7 days 8am-5pm; Sun 10am-4pm.

<£15 **The Chip Van aka The Fisherman's Pier** 01688 302390 · Tobermory Tobermory's famous meals-on-wheels under the clock tower on the bay. Fresh, al fresco: usually a queue. However, they don't actually make those chips! All year, 12.30pm-9pm. Closed Sun in winter. 1347/FISH & CHIPS.

WHAT TO SEE

Duart Castle 5km Craignure. Seat of Clan Maclean. Impressive from a distance, homely inside. Good view of clan history and from battlements. Teashop (1780/CASTLES). **Eas Fors** Waterfall on Dervaig to Fionnphort road. Very accessible series of cataracts tumbling into the sea (1592/WATERFALLS). **The Mishnish** No mission to Mull complete without a night at the Mish (1254/BLOODY GOOD PUBS). **Ulva & Iona** (many references). **The Treshnish Isles** (Ulva Ferry or Fionnphort). Marvellous trips in summer (1707/BIRDS); walks from **Carsaig Pier** and on **Glengorm** estate (2247/2248/ISLAND WALKS); or up **Ben More** (1981/MUNROS); **Croig** and **Quinish** in north, by **Dervaig** and **Lochbuie** off the A849 at Strathcoil 9km south of Craignure: these are all serene shorelines to explore. **Aros Park** forest walk, from Tobermory, about 7km round trip.

Tourist Info Craignure · 01680 812377 All year. **Tobermory** · 01688 302182 **CalMac** www.calmac.co.uk · 08705 650000

The Best of Orkney

2307 **Ferry** Northlink (0845 6000449). Stromness: from Aberdeen – Tue, Thu, Sat, Sun,
3 takes 6 hours; from Scrabster – 2/3 per day, takes 1.5 hours.
John o' Groats to Burwick (01955 611353), 40 minutes, up to 4 a day (May-Sep
only). Pentland Ferries from Gills Bay (near John o' Groats) to St Margaret's Hope
(01856 831226) – 3 a day, takes 1 hour.
By Air Flybe (0871 7002000). To Kirkwall: from Aberdeen – 3 daily;
from Edinburgh – 2 daily; from Glasgow – 1 daily; from Inverness – 2 daily;
from Wick – 1 daily (not weekends).

WHERE TO STAY

✓ ✓ **Balfour Castle** www.balfourcastle.co.uk · 01856 711282 ·
Shapinsay On Isle of Shapinsay, a fabulously appointed castle, grounds
and top chef mainly for exclusive use. Arrive by helicopter or launch. Dream on,
those of ordinary means! Report: 1239/HOUSE PARTIES.

10 ROOMS **The Lynnfield** www.lynnfieldhotel.co.uk · 01856 872505 · **Kirkwall** Holm
TEL · TV Rd adjacent to Highland Park (1482/WHISKY) and overlooking the town. Kirkwall's
MED.INX most comfy (though rooms old-style), sporting 4 stars and with good local reputa-
tion for food. And congenial.

18 ROOMS **West End Hotel** www.westendkirkwall.co.uk · 01856 872505 · **Kirkwall**
TEL Central, comfortable and conscientious hosts (Gifford and Robert); that's what folk
MED.INX say though I've never been so no tick yet; reports please.

8 ROOMS **Foveran Hotel** www.foveranhotel.co.uk · 01856 872389 · **St Ola** A964
TEL · TV Orphir road; 5km from Kirkwall. Scandinavian-style, low-rise hotel is a friendly,
NO PETS informal place serving traditional food using local ingredients; separate vegetarian
MED.INX menu. Great value. Small but comfy and light rooms; garden overlooks Scapa Flow.

16 ROOMS **Merkister Hotel** 01856 771366 · **Harray** Overlooking loch, north but midway
TEL · TV between Kirkwall and Stromness. A fave with fishers and twitchers; handy for
MED.INX archaeological sites and possibly the Orkney hotel of choice. Rooms small and
B&B-ish; good bar meals.

42 ROOMS **Stromness Hotel** www.stromnesshotel.com · 01856 850298 · **Stromness**
TEL · TV Orkney's biggest hotel at the heart of the Orkney matter and overlooking the har-
CHP bour. Rooms so-so but very good value. Even has lifts. Central and picturesque
Flattie Bar a wee gem.

3 ROOMS **The Creel** www.thecreel.co.uk · 01856 831311 · **St Margaret's Hope** Not
MED.INX many and not fancy rooms but great location; food very much the thing. Breakfast
and dinner. See next page.

S.Y. Hostels www.syha.org.uk · 01856 850589 · **Stromness** Excellent
location. **Kirkwall** · 01856 872243 The largest.
Other hostels at Hoy, North and South Ronaldsay, Birsay, Sanday.

✓ **Bis Geos Hostel** www.bisgeos.co.uk · 01857 677420 · **Westray** Hostel
with 2 self-catering cottages. Traditional features and some luxuries.

✓ **The Barn** www.thebarnwestray.co.uk · 01857 677214 · **Westray** Near
Pierowall. 4-star self-catering hostel in renovated stone barn. Great views.

Peedie Hostel 01856 875477 · **Ayre Road, Kirkwall** On the front. Private bedroom (3), sleep 2 or 4, own keys.

Camping/Caravan **Kirkwall** · 01856 879900 & **Stromness** · 01856 873535

WHERE TO EAT

£25-35 ✓ **The Creel Inn & Restaurant With Rooms** www.thecreelinn.co.uk · 01856 831311 · **St Margaret's Hope** On South Ronaldsay, 20km south of Kirkwall and a great drive. An accolade-laden restaurant and long Orkney's finest. Excellent value for this standard; the Craigies excelling here since 1985.

£25-35 ✓ **Judith Glue Café Restaurant** www.judithglue.com · 01856 874225 · **Kirkwall** Can't miss it opposite St Magnus Cathedral. At last an eating-out place that serves and champions Orkney produce: the ale, the seafood, the cheese. JG long known for the knits and quality souvenirs (and puffin stuff), now (opened summer '11) effortlessly the place to eat in town. Home-made, black-board menu. 9am-6pm (8pm Jun, 10pm Jul/Aug).

>£35 ✓ **Balfour Castle** www.balfourcastle.co.uk · 01856 711282 · **Shapinsay** You can pop over to Shapinsay outwith their exclusive-use periods. Chef Jean Baptiste Bady cooking up the best meal in the far North; they'll collect you from Kirkwall Pier. Phone/email for details.

£25-35 **Foveran Hotel** 01856 872389 · **St Ola** 4km Kirkwall. Excellent views and ok, locally sourced food. See *Where to Stay*.

£25-35 **The Lynnfield** 01856 872505 · **Kirkwall** Best hotel meal in Kirkwall. See *Where to Stay*.

£15-25 **The Hamnavoe Restaurant** 01856 850606 · **35 Graham Place, Stromness** Off main street. Seafood is their speciality, especially lobster. Apr-Oct; lunch week-ends only, dinner Tue-Sun 6.30pm-9pm. Nov-Mar open weekends only.

<£15 **Julia's Café & Bistro** 01856 850904 · **Stromness** Home baking, blackboard and vegetarian specials. A favourite with the locals. Gets busy – fill yourself up before the ferry journey! Open all year, 7 days 9am-5pm (from 10am Sun). Phone for winter opening hours.

The Van **Brough of Birsay** Bere bannocks (a speciality), home-made soups, Orkney cheese from a van in the car park at the Brough with spectacular views. 7 days from 11am.

WHAT TO SEE

Skara Brae 25km west of Kirkwall. Amazingly well-preserved underground labyrinth, a 5,000-year-old village. Report: 1812/PREHISTORIC SITES.

The Old Man of Hoy On Hoy; 30-minute ferry 2 or 3 times a day from Stromness. 3-hour walk along spectacular coast. See 2256/ISLAND WALKS.

Standing Stones of Stenness, The Ring of Brodgar, Maes Howe Around 18km west of Kirkwall on A965. Strong vibrations. Report: 1813/PREHISTORIC SITES.

Yesnaby Sea Stacks 24km west of Kirkwall. A precarious cliff top at the end of the world. Report: 1941/ENCHANTING PLACES.

Italian Chapel 8km south of Kirkwall at first causeway. A special act of faith. Inspirational and moving. Report: 1866/CHURCHES.

Skaill House 01856 841501 · **Skara Brae** 17th-century mansion built on Pictish cemetery. Set up as it was in the 1950s; with Captain Cook's crockery in the dining room looking remarkably unused. Apr-Sep; 7 days 9.30am-6pm (or by appointment). Tearoom and visitor centre and HS link with Skara are adjacent.

St Magnus Cathedral (1866/CHURCHES); **Stromness** (1544/COASTAL VILLAGES); **The Pier Arts Centre** (2147/INTERESTING GALLERIES); **Tomb of the Eagles** (1819/PREHISTORIC SITES); **Marwick Head** and many of the smaller islands (1716/BIRDS); **Scapa Flow** (1913/BATTLEGROUNDS); **Highland Park Distillery** (1482/WHISKY); **Puffins** (1718/BIRDS).

Craft Trail & Artists' Studio Trail Take in some traditional arts and crafts. Lots of souvenir potential but generally high-quality stuff. The tourist information centre has details and maps.

Many walks. Download walking guides: **www.walkorkney.com**
Tourist Info 01856 872856

The Best of Shetland

2308
4

Ferry Northlink (0845 600 0449). Aberdeen-Lerwick: Mon, Wed, Fri – departs 7pm, 12 hours. Tue, Thu, Sat, Sun – departs 5pm (via Orkney, arrives 11.45pm), 14 hours.
By air Flybe www.flybe.com (0871 700 0535). To Sumburgh: from Aberdeen (5 a day, 3 Sat, 3 Sun). From Inverness (2 a day). From Glasgow (1 a day). From Edinburgh (3 a day, 2 a day at weekends). May vary.

WHERE TO STAY

6 ROOMS
MAR-OCT
TV · LL
MED.INX

✓**Burrastow House** 01595 809307 · **Walls** 40 minutes from Lerwick. Most guides and locals agree this is the place to stay on Shetland. Peaceful Georgian house with views to island of Vaila. Wonderful home made/produced food. Full of character with food (set menu; order day before), service and rooms the best on the island.

22 ROOMS
TEL · TV
MED.INX

✓**Busta House Hotel** www.bustahouse.com · 01806 522506 · **Brae** Historic country house at Brae just over 30 minutes from Lerwick. Elegant and tranquil. High standards: the Rocks family are hospitable hosts. Excellent food; famously great malt selection. Pronounced Boosta.

30 ROOMS

St Magnus Bay Hotel www.stmagnusbayhotel.co.uk · 01806 503372 · Far, far away in the northwest of the mainland 50km from Lerwick on the Hillswick coast, a distinctive, wooden-built (in 1900) hotel (renovation ongoing). Have to admit I still haven't been here but all reports are good.

Kveldsro Hotel www.shetlandhotels.com · 01595 692195 · **Lerwick**
Pronounced Kel-ro. Probably best proposition in Lerwick; overlooking harbour.
Reasonable standard at a price. Locals do eat here.

Westings, The Inn On The Hill www.westings.shetland.co.uk · 01595
840242 · **Whiteness** 12 km from Lerwick. Breathtaking views down Whiteness
Voe. Excellent base for exploring. Large selection of real ales. Campsite alongside.

S.Y. Hostel: Islesburgh House www.islesburgh.org.uk · 01595 692114 ·
Lerwick Beautifully refurbished and central. A 5-star hostel. Apr-Sep.

Camping Bods (fisherman's barns). Cheap sleep in wonderful sea-shore settings. **The Sail Loft** at Voe; **Grieve House** at Whalsay; **Windhouse Lodge** at
Mid Yell; **Voe House** at Walls; **Betty Mouat's Cottage** at Dunrossness;
Johnnie Notions at Eshaness. Remember to take sleeping mats. Check tourist
information centre for details: 01595 693434.

WHERE TO EAT

£25-35   ✓ **Burrastow House** Walls & **Busta House Hotel** Brae See *Where to
Stay, previous page. The best meals in the islands. My Shetland reporters do
go to Busta.

<£15   ✓ **Hays Dock Café Restaurant** www.haysdock.co.uk · 01595 741596 ·
Lerwick Part of the Shetland Museum & Archive. Contemporary, beautiful
space with great views of Lerwick Harbour. Excellent, all-day café, dinner Tue-Sat.

<£15   ✓ **Frankie's** www.frankiesfishandchips.com · 01806 522700 · **Brae**
Busta Voe and the marina great new addition to Shetland eating out (or in).
Takeaway and caff. Local seafood, homebaking, sustainable fish policy. 9.30am-
8pm. Sun from 1pm (closed Sun in winter).

<£15   **The Spiggie Hotel** www.thespiggiehotel.co.uk · 01950 460409 ·
Dunrossness 8km Sumburgh Airport, 32km Lerwick. Small, personally run country hotel that is especially good for bar meals.

<£15   **Scalloway Hotel Restaurant** www.scallowayhotel.com · 01595 880444 ·
Scalloway 12km west of Lerwick in a picturesque place. Building a reputation for
quality food. 7 days; restaurant evening only and Sun lunch.

£25-35   **Monty's Bistro** 01595 696555 · **Mounthooly Street, Lerwick** Up the road
from tourist office. Renovated building in light Med décor. Best bet in town. Good
service; imaginative menu using Shetland seasonal ingredients. Bar weekends
only. Bistro closed Sun/Mon (open Mon evening in season). Lunch and LO 9pm.

<£15   **The Olive Tree** 01595 697222 · **Lerwick** Nice deli/café/takeaway in the Toll
Clock Shopping Centre. Home-made stuff. Daytime only.

£15-25/
£25-35   **The Maryfield Hotel** 01595 820207 · **Bressay** 5-minute ferry ride from
Lerwick to Bressay. Better known for its seafood rather than accommodation, both
bar and dining room menus worth a look. LO are for those off the 8pm ferry but
book ahead. Don't miss the return ferry.

<£15 **The Peerie Shop Café** www.peerieshopcafe.com · 01595 692816 · The Esplanade, Lerwick A local delicacy! 9am-6pm. Closed Sun. *Pub food also recommended at the following:*

<£15 **The Mid Brae Inn** 01806 522634 · Brae 32km north of Lerwick. Lunch and supper till 8.45pm (9.30pm weekends), 7 days. Big portions of filling pub grub.

The Pierhead 01806 588332 · Lower Voe

WHAT TO SEE

Mousa Broch & Jarlshof See 1816/PREHISTORIC SITES. Also **Clickimin** broch.

Shetland Museum & Archives See 2147/HISTORY & HERITAGE.

Old Scatness 01595 694688 A fascinating, award-winning excavation – site of one of the world's best-preserved Iron Age villages. Ongoing and accessible; climb the tower and witness the unearthing first-hand. Tours, demonstrations and exhibitions. 5 minutes from airport. Open summer only.

St Ninian's Isle Bigton 8km north of Sumburgh on West Coast. An island linked by exquisite shell-sand. Hoard of Pictish silver found in 1958 (now in Edinburgh). Beautiful, serene spot.

Scalloway 12km west of Lerwick, a township once the ancient capital of Shetland, dominated by the atmospheric ruins of Scalloway Castle.

Noup of Noss Isle of Noss off Bressay 8km west of Lerwick by frequent ferry to Bressay and then wee boat (also by boat trip direct from Lerwick; check tourist information centre); limited in winter. National Nature Reserve with spectacular array of wildlife.

Up-Helly-Aa www.up-helly-aa.org.uk Festival in Lerwick on the last Tuesday in January. Ritual with hundreds of torchbearers and much fire and firewater. Norse, northern and pagan. A wild time can be had.

Sea Races The Boat Race every midsummer from Norway. Part of the largest North Sea international annual yacht race.

Bonhoga Gallery & Weisdale Mill 01595 830400 Former grain mill housing Shetland's first purpose-built gallery. Good café.

Island Trails Historic tours of Lerwick and the islands. Book through tourist information centre (or 01950 422408). Day trips, evening runs or short tours.

Tourist Info 01595 693434

Index

The numbers listed against index entries refer to the page on which the entry appears and not the entry's item number.